CONTENTS

Chapter 1 Introduction	1
Why conduct a drugs prevention survey?	2
Previous assessments of drug usage	2
The importance of public perceptions of drug usage and drugs control	3
The structure of the survey	3
Questionnaire structure and administration	4
Sample selection methods	5
The structure of the report	6
Chapter 2 How many people use drugs?	7
The prevalence of drug usage	8
Patterns of drug usage	9
Polydrug usage	11
Frequent and injecting usage	13
Availability of drugs	16
Comparisons with other drug usage surveys	18
Chapter 3 What kinds of people use drugs?	21
Age and drug usage	21
Gender and drug usage	24
Socioeconomic status and drug usage	26
Ethnicity and drug usage	28
Employment and drug usage	31
Demographic variation in drug usage: multivariate analyses	34
Booster versus main sample variation	37
Contact with drug users or drug usage and personal drug usage	38
Lifestyle and drug usage: choice of leisure activities	42
Comparisons between licit and illicit drug usage	44
Association across drug types	48
Drug usage in four towns: Summary of Chapters 2 and 3	49
Chapter 4 Locational variation in illicit drug usage	51
Broad geographic variation between cities	52
Intra-urban locational clustering of drug users	53
The demographic profile of 'drug areas'	55
Urban deprivation and drug usage	57
Intra-urban locational variation in drug distribution	58
Public perceptions of locational variation in drug usage	59
Summary of Chapter 4	65
Chapter 5 Public perceptions of local crime rates and other problems	67
Integration into the local community	67
Satisfaction with the local area	69
Problems highlighted in the local area	69
Worry about crime and fear of crime in the local area	71
Comparison between national and local pictures of crime and problems	73
Comparison between drug related and other crimes or problems	75
Comparing the views of drug users and non-drug users	77
Changing patterns of crime and drug-related problems	79
The possible effects of perceived crime and drug usage on behaviour patterns	80
Crime, drugs and fear - a multivariate analysis	83
Summary of Chapter 5	88
Chapter 6 Public perceptions of drugs and drug misuse	91
Awareness of drugs	91
Public assumptions regarding drug usage	96
Comparing licit with illicit drugs	104
Perceptions of cause in drug usage	106
Perceptions of the transition from 'soft' to 'hard' drugs	109
Perceptions of personal knowledge regarding drug usage	110
Summary of Chapter 6	111
Chapter 7 Options for controlling or reducing the misuse of drugs	113
Primary prevention: controlling demand	113
The likely effectiveness of drugs education	114
Appropriate targets for drugs education	116
Parents' views on drugs education	117
Parents' views on the likelihood of their children taking drugs	118
Organisations which should be responsible for education	120
Secondary prevention: controlling demand and supply	122

Contents

Police control of demand	122
Customs control of supply	128
Tertiary prevention: harm reduction	131
Improvement of treatment and rehabilitation	132
Summary of Chapter 7	134

Chapter 8 The public profile of drugs related agencies	137
Awareness of specialist agencies	137
Patterns of awareness	139
Implications for the targeting of drugs related information	143
Comparing specialist with non-specialist agencies as a first recourse	145
Personal contact with users of advice agencies	148
How satisfied are people with the help and advice agencies give them?	149
Agencies which should provide a recourse	151
Co-ordination between agencies	153
Summary of Chapter 8	153

Chapter 9 Drugs control policies and the public's views on legalisation	155
Models of drug usage	155
Developing drugs prevention	157
Controlling supply	158
Controlling distribution	161
Controlling supply and demand	164
Controlling medically supplied drugs	165
The elasticity of the drugs market	166
Controlling demand	168
Alternatives to control	173
Public views regarding legalisation and decriminalisation	177
Altering social or economic structures	181

Summary of Chapter 9	183
Chapter 10 The views and habits of the general public: messages from the household survey	185
References	191

Appendix 1	197
Data tables for Chapter 2	197
Data tables for Chapter 3	204
Data tables for Chapter 4	222
Data tables for Chapter 5	237
Data tables for Chapter 6	245
Data tables for Chapter 7	258
Data tables for Chapter 8	269
Data tables for Chapter 9	278
Appendix 2 Sample questionnaire	283
Appendix 3 Sampling methods and sample structure	315
Main sample 'random' selection of respondents	315
Booster sample 'quota' selection of respondents	316
Response rates	317
Refusal rates in the main sample	317
Geographic structure of the sample	318
Demographic structure of the sample	318
Age structure of the sample	319
Gender structure of the sample	320
Socioeconomic structure of the sample	320
Ethnic structure of the sample	321
Employment structure of the sample	321
Are our samples representative of the towns?	322

Chapter 1 INTRODUCTION

Drug usage is a phenomenon which has existed for rather longer than most civilisations. Yet the study of drugs prevention is a subject still in its infancy. We have, for a long time, been treating those who are already using drugs and we have also put a great deal of effort into minimising the distribution of unprescribed drugs. Such activities have, at least in part, preventive aims. Nevertheless, the full scope of prevention remains a matter of considerable debate, as does the nature of its ultimate goal.

To illustrate the complexity of the issue, we can describe the number of potential 'targets' for drugs prevention. Prevention can be directed at those already using or dealing in drugs. It can be designed to deter people from ever trying drugs, or to persuade them not to experiment further. Alternatively it can aim to minimise the 'collateral damage' associated with drug usage by turning people away from drug related crime and persuading them to adopt the least harmful methods of drug usage. Similarly prevention can be aimed at either small, localised user groups, or large varied sectors of the population. The options for both policy and practice are extensive. So where should one start in developing a drugs prevention strategy?

One crucial start point lies in establishing the views of those most likely to be affected by any form of drugs prevention. In line with the broad nature of drugs prevention, this means looking at the views both of the general population, who are all in some respects *potential* drug users, and the smaller group of those with a personal history of drug usage. A second and equally crucial start point in the study of drugs prevention relates directly to this last group of individuals. Just how small a group *are* those with a personal history of drug usage? We would argue that without taking these two basic factors into account, one cannot adequately formulate a coherent drugs prevention policy. In fact, one cannot even determine whether drugs prevention is in itself a suitable goal.

Although substantial and important research has been carried out on drug usage and drugs prevention over a long period of time, the research described in this report presents the first purpose-designed survey of the general population to look in *detail* at *both* these issues. The provision of essential funding by the Central Drugs Prevention Unit of the Home Office, enabling this type of survey to be carried out, perhaps serves as an indicator of how important the drugs prevention issue has lately become. We would like to emphasise here that the survey was very much a joint venture between ourselves and the CDPU and benefited from the fieldwork support provided by Public Attitude Surveys Limited.

To describe the survey in more detail, it deals with a broad range of issues relating to drug usage and to the public's perceptions of and attitudes towards such usage. In particular, it provides an estimate of self-report drug use from both a general population sample and a booster sample of young individuals thought to be 'at risk' of drug usage. It also provides data from these two samples regarding their views on the causes of drug use, the extent to which such usage poses a problem for the individual or for society and the viability and desirability of a range of methods for controlling drug usage. To give context to the data obtained, the survey also addresses other related aspects of lifestyle such as alcohol and tobacco usage and at the broader level, allows a comparison to be drawn between the impact drug usage has on an area and the impact of other potentially problematic activities, both licit and illicit. The survey took place in four distinct locations, chosen to give as broad and as diverse a picture of British drug usage and attitudes towards drug usage as possible. Consequently, not all of its results can readily be generalised to Britain as a whole. The present survey was only carried out on urban populations but we are currently conducting a second survey which, when the results are available, will allow comparisons to be made between urban and rural areas. We look forward therefore to the results of the 1992 British Crime Survey and also, hopefully, to other future national surveys relating to the issues we discuss here.

Since it is the first survey of this type in Britain, we must add the caveat that it necessarily cannot provide all the answers on the very wide range of topics covered by drugs prevention. It has concentrated on patterns of usage, on the perceived extent of problems in local areas, and on the possibilities for drugs prevention education. There are many other questions we would have liked to ask on other kinds of prevention initiatives. Inevitably there are some questions which, if we were doing the survey again now, we would have worded differently and issues which we would have discussed in greater detail if we had had the time. What we hope is that in presenting these initial results on drug usage and on people's views regarding both usage and prevention, the survey will whet people's appetite to explore the issues and in particular, the more unexpected findings further.

Why conduct a drugs prevention survey?

In 1989, the Home Office set up a national Drugs Prevention Initiative, targeted primarily at discouraging members of the public from an initial trial of illicit drugs. This large scale Drugs Prevention Initiative came as a response to the widespread belief that illicit drug usage and drug related illness and crime might be on the increase within the United Kingdom. The main focus of the initiative is on intervention at the level of local communities. To this end, the Central Drugs Prevention Unit, which is co-ordinating the initiative, has to date set up twenty Drugs Prevention Teams located in a range of cities across the United Kingdom. The approach taken by the Drugs Prevention Teams varies across teams, as a consequence of the deliberate decision to encourage approaches relevant to that locality, and the different skills and approaches available within each team. However, their central brief remains the same, with a primary aim being to reduce drug usage within their area of operation and a secondary aim being harm minimisation, the latter being defined in terms of such drugs related risks as HIV infection.

Although the Drugs Prevention Initiative was established as a response to the belief that drug usage and its associated problems were on the increase, very little data were actually available regarding the validity of this assumption at the time the initiative began. There was a similar paucity of data regarding the attitudes of the general public towards drugs related issues. Given the aims of the Drugs Prevention Teams and their brief to work within local communities, the lack of both types of data represented a serious gap in available information. As a response to this problem, the present drug usage survey was commissioned by the Central Drugs Prevention Unit (CDPU), with the aim of providing data which would inform the Drugs Prevention Initiative.

Given the amount of research work which has to date been devoted to drugs related issues, the statement that little data were available prior to this survey regarding drug usage and attitudes to drug usage within the general population requires some justification. To this end we have outlined below the types of drugs data available prior to this survey.

Previous assessments of drug usage

Previous estimates of drug *usage* within the population relied on data provided by:
- statutory notification of users of certain kinds of drugs by GPs to the Home Office
- statistics of the amounts and values of drugs seized by the police and Customs and Excise
- registers and statistics of drug crimes known to the police and those convicted of drugs offences
- estimates of the price and purity of street drugs
- studies and the views of experts on changing patterns of usage amongst addicts, which may indicate broader general drug usage
- research studies in specific areas using direct contact with known drug users

None of the above methods are capable of providing accurate data regarding the nature of drug usage in the *general* population. Using estimates based on these methods to gauge *absolute numbers* of such users will result in an underestimate of usage, since each of the methods is subject to quite significant under-reporting. Not all drug users, for example, contact their GP, seek treatment at clinics, or fall foul of the law, and only a small percentage of drugs is seized by customs or police. The price and purity of a street drug *may* be an accurate reflection of levels of supply and demand but does not provide any quantitative data.

In contrast, using the estimates to assess general population *patterns* of usage may result in an exaggeration of the problems associated with drug usage. The presence of easily acquired cheap drugs in a pure form could be interpreted as indicating a worrying increase in general levels of usage. However, it could equally well be interpreted as indicating a form of usage with fewer negative side effects. For example, low prices can result in decreases in drug related crime and greater purity can lead to fewer medical problems. More direct estimates based on research relating to known drug users is subject to similarly ambiguous interpretation. Such studies are inevitably based either on 'high risk' users who have come to the attention of GPs, clinics or other drug related services or on the selection of drug users from the general population by 'snowballing' (see below) or similar methods of contact.

Unell (1991) argues that the relationship between problematic and general patterns of usage can be assumed valid to the extent that *trends* in the former give an indication of trends in the latter. This statement involves the assumption that the composition of the targeted or 'problematic' populations is similar to that of the general population as a whole. Where this assumption fails, even an analysis of trends would not in practice be useful. The nature of the research methods used to date prevents the required assumption from being met. Certain sections of the population are more likely to come to the attention of clinics than others. Female users with children may for example be less willing to attend a statutory clinic than other users since they may believe they face a risk of losing their children. Black users may be reluctant to attend a clinic staffed by white workers. Injecting users are more likely to be in contact with hospital services as a consequence of the greater health risks associated with this type of usage.

Selective general population estimates are likely to be similarly flawed. A popular method of sampling drug users is to 'snowball': that is, to establish contact with one drug user and then contact others via this target person. Naturally, the data gathered are dependent on certain features of the person initially targeted. If the user is white he or she is more likely to have white friends than if he or she is black. This point applies equally to all other demographic variables. Since the individuals are not selected in any controlled way, other hidden biases are also likely to creep into the data. Consequently, the population targeted is unlikely to be representative of the general population. Targeting a *particular* group of individuals such as children, or members of a particular socio-economic group, allows any bias to be made explicit, but again does not allow the transferral of conclusions drawn from the target group data to the general population.

In short, although previous estimates of drug usage can be of value in certain other contexts, they are not of substantial value in the present context where a primary aim is to assess patterns of usage within the general population in order to inform preventive action.

The importance of public perceptions of drug usage and drugs control

Policy regarding drug usage is unlikely to prove successful if it fails to satisfy the requirements of the public to whom the policy makers are chiefly responsible. Two forms of information regarding public opinion on drug usage and drug control policies are of value in this context: the level and accuracy of the public's *knowledge* regarding the issues surrounding drug usage and, secondly, public *opinion* on these issues. The two forms of information are inter-related in policy terms. If the public's perception of drug usage is inaccurate, then policies addressing the real nature of any problem may seem oblique or potentially harmful in the eyes of the public. Knowing the structure of the public's knowledge base allows this situation to be reconciled by the provision of more accurate information.

On the other hand, there are points at which public opinion within a democracy must be held to circumscribe the nature of an issue. For example if, following the provision of accurate information, majority opinion considered drug usage as a *crime* rather than a *leisure pursuit*, it would be ineffective to dispute with this opinion at the political level, although it might still be valid to dispute it at the intellectual or ethical level. An assessment of public perceptions of drug usage is, therefore, required to determine both the *nature* and the *direction* of policy decisions.

The structure of the survey

The initial methodological decisions on the survey comprised *where* to undertake it and *what method* to use to obtain the most reliable data. Given the connection with the Drugs Prevention Initiative, it was obviously sensible to select locations also being used by DPI teams. We ruled out the possibility of a national survey early on, mainly because we were aware that there might be significant locational effects in both patterns of drug usage and attitudes towards drugs. A national survey would provide too few people in any one place to look at locational issues in drug usage. We were also aware that the British Crime Survey would contain some comparable questions, which could, later, be used to judge how our results compared with a national sample.

Restricting the survey to four towns and to the boundaries of the Drugs Prevention Team initiatives within those towns still meant that the geographical area surveyed in each place was relatively large. The four locations chosen were intended to reflect a range of possible patterns of drug usage and different parts of the United Kingdom. They were Bradford, Glasgow, the London Borough of Lewisham, and Nottingham. For Bradford, Glasgow and Lewisham, the remit of the Drugs Prevention Teams followed the local authority boundaries and hence so did we. In Nottingham, the area was defined by the Drugs Prevention Team and consequently also by us as the health authority boundary.

Since we were starting from almost no knowledge as to the pattern and level of drug usage we would find, nor the degree of resistance there would be to talking about drugs - and since we suspected that the views and knowledge of drug users might be different from those of non-drug users - the first stage of the survey was to carry out a qualitative discussion group exercise with small numbers of people from different social and age groupings in each town. This was done for the Central Drugs Prevention Unit by Cragg Ross Dawson. Detailed methods are given in the technical report (PAS 1992). Results indicated a surprising willingness to talk about drugs problems and possible solutions, but also confirmed our suspicion that drug users might have different views from non-drug users - and that young people might differ substantially from older people. We also obtained an idea of which names were used in each area for different drugs - crucial for the self-report element of the survey on drugs usage.

Covering such large geographic areas in a relatively short time meant using a survey company to administer the questionnaires. We rejected the idea of entirely self-completion postal questionnaires, because we considered we would obtain a very low response rate given people's (quite natural) suspicions as to why we might be doing such an exercise and whether the drug usage part would really be confidential. Face-to-face contact with someone who could explain the purpose of the questionnaire was essential.

Yet face-to-face contact minimises anonymity and may itself bias self-report responses relating to what are, after all, illegal acts. Since we also wished to produce a sample as close as possible to a random sample of the general population in each area, we had to interview people in their own homes. This obviously further reduces anonymity. For these reasons, and to create comparability with the British Crime Survey, we decided to mix face-to-face interviewing on attitudes and views with self-completion for the drug usage part of the survey.

The qualitative part of the study had shown differences in views between age groups. To increase the numbers of young people taking part in the study, the Central Drugs Prevention Unit decided to add a booster sample of young people for each of the four towns, the aim being to increase the number of young people and also to increase the number of drug users sampled. After very considerable discussion, the Unit decided to concentrate this booster sample in more deprived areas of the towns, in the hope that there would be enough drug users in the sample to be able to look at their views properly. The financial resources available permitted a main sample size of around 1,000 people and an additional booster sample of around 250 young people in each town (making a total survey sample size of 5,000).

A summary of the survey methods is given in Appendix 3 and a more detailed discussion can be found in the technical report available from Public Attitude Surveys Ltd. (PAS 1992). For present purposes we will outline only the main features of the method and the structure of the samples obtained. These aspects of the survey should be borne in mind when assessing the data referred to in this report, as they necessarily have an effect on the nature of the data obtained. They will also be of paramount importance should a replication of the survey be carried out, whether for validation or follow-up purposes.

The allocation of responsibility for different aspects of the survey was as follows. The survey was based on a questionnaire designed primarily by the Central Drugs Prevention Unit (CDPU) in consultation with PAS. The Sheffield research team provided suggestions for the structure of the questionnaire and was responsible for data analysis, but did not take any decisions regarding the final *content* of the questionnaire. The questionnaire was administered by interviewers working for PAS between 25th February and 25th May 1992. PAS were responsible for the final sample structure, although they were responding to a brief given jointly by CDPU and the Sheffield team. Sample collection methods were determined by agreement between all three groups.

Questionnaire structure and administration

A copy of the final questionnaire is provided in Appendix 2. From this it can be seen that for analysis purposes, the questionnaire divides roughly into ten sections, dealing respectively with:

1. views of the local area, including the prevalence of crime and other problems
2. perceived levels of local drug usage and awareness of areas in which drug usage is concentrated
3. comparison of local and national prevalence of drug usage, crime and other problems
4. views regarding the causal influences on drug usage
5. general and specific knowledge regarding particular drugs
6. personal drug usage
7. knowledge of and opinions regarding drug related agencies
8. general and specific views on drugs education
9. views regarding control and legalisation
10. demographics and lifestyle

The first section of the questionnaire, as described above, was based on similar items derived from the British Crime Survey 1992. This will enable some comparisons to be drawn between our samples and the much larger sample obtained via the latest British Crime

Survey, once this becomes generally available. The final section of the questionnaire also provides some level of standardisation with other surveys, for example by defining socioeconomic status along the lines recommended by OPCS (OPCS 1980). All other sections of the questionnaire are specific to this survey and have direct relevance to the questions addressed by the survey.

Following a dynamic pilot of the questionnaire it was decided that the self report usage section should be administered on the basis of a confidential self-completion questionnaire given to respondents (a similar method to that used in the 1992 British Crime Survey). This section was given to respondents who were asked to complete it in private and hand it back to the interviewer in a sealed envelope. The remainder of the questionnaire took the form of a face-to-face interview carried out where possible with only the respondent and the interviewer present in the room. Both sections of the questionnaire were completed in the respondent's home on the same date. Where relevant, attempts were made to match the ethnicity of interviewer and respondent and to provide translations of the questionnaire items.

The decision to administer the questionnaire via interviewers rather than in some more anonymous fashion is of importance in that it may be argued that the consequent lack of anonymity had some effect on response rates or response style. Although the section of the questionnaire dealing directly with *personal* drug usage was administered as a self-completion booklet rather than as part of the face-to-face interview, the presence of an interviewer at a respondent's home may still reasonably be held to have influenced responses. With regard to this aspect of the survey it should however be noted that it is possible to obtain weightings for the anonymity effect which could be applied to the data at some later stage. To this end, we have outlined suggestions for a possible validation study relating to the importance of anonymity in self-report drug usage (Leitner et al. 1992).

Sample selection methods

Diverse methods are available for obtaining data from the general population. In the present context, the major decisions to be made regarding data collection were whether the sample(s) should be collected following a random or a quota selection of individuals and whether such selection should be structured or unstructured. Broadly speaking, the advantage of random sampling is that it allows the responses obtained to be regarded as representative of those of the general population. In contrast, quota sampling allows for the inclusion of respondents who provide some form of focus for the research - drug users being one example in the present context. The advantage of structuring a sample - for example by ensuring that the number of respondents in each demographic category matches that noted in the general population - is that it allows a greater degree of statistical control over the results obtained.

The methodological decisions outlined above were complicated by two constraints on the survey. The first of these was the time constraint noted above, since data collection could occupy only a relatively short period of time, given that it began in February 1992 and a requirement made of the survey was that interim results should be available by October 1992. The second inherent constraint was the need to provide substantial data derived from drug *users* whilst at the same time maintaining the sample as a *general* population sample.

To optimise the survey results whilst operating within these constraints, it was decided that data should be obtained from two distinct types of sample. The first type of sample was to be selected on a random basis and is referred to in this report as the '*main sample*'. The second sample, selected on a quota basis, is referred to as the '*booster sample*'.

The rationale for selecting the *main* sample on a random basis was, as suggested above, to ensure that any results obtained could be regarded, in the broadest sense, as representative of the general population. PAS selected 1,000 individuals for this sample from each town, obtaining the interviews by selecting individuals via a fixed decision hierarchy. The first layer of this hierarchy involved a selection of specific enumeration districts, the enumeration districts being selected in such a way as to maximise the socio-economic spread of respondents in the sample. The second layer of the decision hierarchy involved a selection of addresses from *within* each ED on the basis of the Postcode Address File.

The PAF was used in preference to the Electoral Roll, since the introduction of the community charge tax has made the latter rather unreliable for research purposes. The final layer of the decision hierarchy involved the selection of an individual within each household using a Kish Grid technique. This technique comprises listing the names of all relevant individuals in the household and matching this list against the last digit of the address serial number in order to select the person to be interviewed. This latter decision is the most truly 'random' decision made in the selection process.

The implications of the selection process for the

structure of the main sample are outlined in greater detail below. All interviews were obtained from individuals aged over 16. Although obtaining data from younger individuals might have been of interest, the ethical and practical constraints involved, including, for example, obtaining parental consent, were held to militate against this course of action.

The rationale for selecting a *booster* sample obtained by quota sampling was twofold. First, it provided a sample of individuals within the population thought to be at high 'risk' of drug usage - namely young individuals (ie those in the 16-25 age bracket) of low socioeconomic status living in deprived urban areas. Second, assuming the validity of the previous point, it provided a means of increasing the number of actual drug users sampled within the survey. PAS selected 250 individuals for this sample from each town. They first selected only those enumeration districts which fell into ACORN categories D, G, H and I (that is, from areas comprised of older terraced housing, council estates, inner metropolitan areas, or non-family areas). Then from each of these enumeration districts they set an age and sex quota to be met by interviewers, which itself was based on CACI data (see PAS Technical Report 1992) relating to the actual demographic composition of the ED.

Two points should be noted from the above discussion of selection methods. First, no attempt was made to structure the main sample. This means that we have relatively little statistical control over the data we can produce from this sample. It also means that the sample, although in one sense representative of the general population, is also subject to demographic biases, which, in another sense, make it unrepresentative of this same population. This difficulty is discussed in greater detail below. The second point of importance to note is that since the basis on which the two samples were collected varied - one being a random and one a quota sample - the data obtained from each of them *cannot* be pooled. Note finally that as already pointed out both samples were from urban rather than rural populations.

Although in the case of the main samples we have endeavoured to obtain a technically 'random' population sample, it is important to realise that for research purposes there is no such thing as a *true* random sample. By way of illustration, a research population will never match the actual population in terms of the number of mentally ill people it contains. Similarly, although a random sample of individuals can be *selected* they cannot necessarily all be contacted or constrained to take part in the survey. Consequently there will always be some element of statistical bias in a survey, however well constructed. It is essential to make such biases explicit. With this in mind, the demographic and geographic structure of our sample is discussed in some detail in Appendix 3. Note that although, where relevant, we have mentioned the structure of the booster sample, any demographic biases observed in this sample are not, strictly speaking, of particular importance, since this sample makes no claims to be representative of the general population.

The structure of the report

Having described the sample and questionnaire, and having addressed the likelihood of sampling bias, we can now turn to the main findings from the research. We start by presenting the patterns of drug usage for the main and booster samples (Chapters 2 and 3), since, in looking at people's attitudes towards drug problems and drug prevention, it is important to be aware of the extent of knowledge about drugs and contact with drugs in the general population and among different age groups and social groupings. Variation in drug usage may not only be by demographic variables, however, but may also reflect geographical patterns, whether influenced by cultural patterns or factors determining distribution and availability. We address these points in Chapter 4.

In looking at whether people think that drugs pose a problem for them in their local area (Chapter 5), we have chosen to set this in the context of what they think about their area in general and whether they find drugs related problems as more or less significant than problems of crime and disorder. We also look in this chapter at whether either crime or drugs related problems affect their views of their area and their fear of crime. In Chapter 6 we look at people's perceptions of and knowledge concerning the drugs problem seen more generally.

The methods which could be used for drugs prevention vary widely, from education in schools to the work of the police and Customs and Excise. People's views about these are addressed in Chapter 7, whilst Chapter 8 deals more specifically with people's views on the role and likely effectiveness of local drugs agencies. Chapter 9 deals with the controversial and complicated topic of people's views on the legalisation of presently illegal drugs. It also addresses the equally controversial and complex issue of the effectiveness of present drugs prevention methods. A brief summary and conclusion form Chapter 10.

Chapter 2
HOW MANY PEOPLE USE DRUGS?

Asking people whether they have used drugs, particularly illegal drugs, is obviously a very sensitive matter. As discussed in the last chapter, we felt that the most appropriate way of dealing with this problem was to collect information on personal drug habits using a self-completion questionnaire which people completed anonymously. Everyone taking part in the survey had initially been assured of complete confidentiality and this reassurance was reiterated in the case of the self-report drug usage questionnaire. Respondents were asked to complete this questionnaire in private and return it to the interviewer in a sealed envelope. Of course, there were several variables which were not under our control. Some respondents may have believed - erroneously - that interviewers might open the envelopes. Other respondents may have felt constrained by the presence of members of their household, even given that they were completing the questionnaire in private. Clearly, we cannot guarantee that all respondents felt there was absolute confidentiality and that everyone gave an honest response as a consequence. Nevertheless, we felt that, in both respects, the self-completion questionnaire gave the best methodological protection which could be devised in the context of a Household Survey.

So, how reliable is the method we used? Do people tend to hide their drug usage or do they boast about it? Whilst no methodological assessment of this method of measuring drug usage has as yet been attempted in Britain, research in the United States suggests that it is a reliable means of obtaining *baseline* prevalence data (cf. Rouse, Kozel and Richards 1985). The emphasis here on the term 'baseline' is of some importance, since the US experience is that *under*-reporting of personal drug usage constitutes a significantly greater problem than over-reporting. Data on the one 'fake' drug included in the present research, namely 'semeron', supports the conclusion that this is likely to be the trend in Britain also - people in our survey did *not* tend to claim that they had used semeron. It is also important to note in this context the tendency of 'random' population surveys to under-represent homeless individuals and individuals in institutional settings (cf. Eysenck 1975). This is of particular relevance to drugs research since it entails the loss of a specific sub-group of individuals known to show high levels of drug usage. Bearing these points in mind, the data presented in this chapter - and in particular our main sample data - is best regarded as a *lower* level estimate of likely drug usage within the locations assessed.

Each self completion item asked respondents to consider their usage of the following named drugs: cannabis, heroin, amphetamines, LSD, cocaine, ecstasy, crack, psilocybin, methadone, diconal, amyl nitrite, temazepam, temgesic, semeron, barbiturates, DF118s, triazelam, 'pills', tranquillisers, and solvents. In addition, respondents were encouraged to add relevant details concerning any drug they had used which did *not* appear on the named list of drugs. The instructions for completion of the items emphasised that only *non-medical* usage should be reported and implied that all the named drugs were controlled drugs. In fact, amyl nitrite is technically a legal drug and semeron, as noted above, is a non-existent drug included in the list as a control on the accuracy of self report. The self completion questionnaire asked respondents to provide information on the following:

1. whether they had *ever* used any of the drugs

   if they had used a drug:

2. whether they had used the drug within the last year

   if they had used a drug recently:

3. how regularly they used the drug
4. whether they had *ever* injected it
5. whether the drug was readily available in their city/borough

The number and percentage of respondents answering positively to each of these items is outlined separately for each sample and location in Tables 2.1 to 2.5 in Appendix 1. Tables 2.6 and 2.7 respectively - also in Appendix 1 - give summary data for drug usage and summary statistics for variations between locations and sample types. For the sake of brevity, the figures for frequency of drug usage presented in these tables relate only to those respondents claiming to have used a named drug at least *once per month*. A more detailed profile of the full frequency range of drug usage for specific sub-groups of drugs is given below. Since there were statistically significant differences in drug usage across location and since there is also a conceptual difficulty in amalgamating across locations which were, after all, specifically selected to represent four *distinct* areas in Britain, any summary data presented either in the text or in Appendix 1 refers to an *average* of the relevant percentages for each location.

The prevalence of drug usage

Two distinct prevalence measures were used within the survey. The first (whether a respondent had *ever* used a drug) can be regarded as a measure of the 'lifetime' prevalence of drug usage, that is, the likelihood that any given individual or group will use a drug within their *lifetime*. The second (whether the respondent had used a drug *within the last year*) can be regarded as a measure of the prevalence of drug usage within the population at a *given moment in time*. The use of both measures in the present context is of value since they can be used to address different issues. For example, if we wish to know the likely immediate demand on resources such as specialist drugs units it would be most appropriate to use estimates relating to *recent* rather than to lifetime usage. On the other hand if we wish to consider the risk of any particular sub-group in the population using drugs, estimates relating to *lifetime* drug usage would be more appropriate. Whilst data for both measures are presented here, this type of distinction should be borne in mind when considering the practical implications of the data.

Figure 2.1
Lifetime drug usage and drug usage within the last year: Main sample

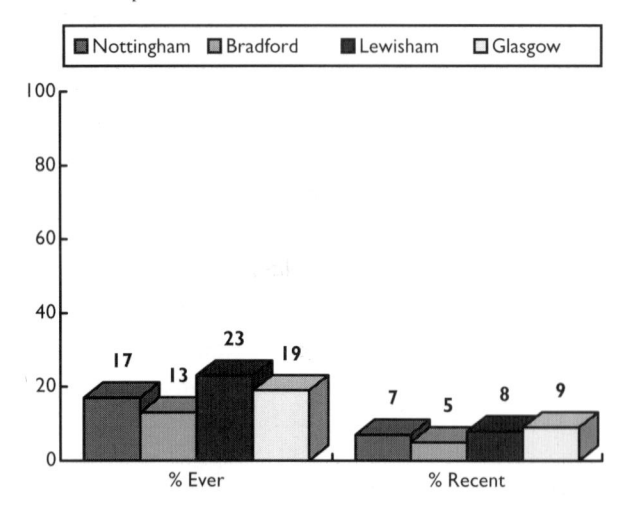

Percentage of respondents who had **ever** taken an illicit drug (% Ever)/Percentage of respondents who had taken an illicit drug **within the last year** (% Recent).

As can be seen from Figure 2.1 the majority of respondents in all main samples had not used *any* drug either within the last year or, indeed, at all. Having said which, the levels of usage reported were certainly not negligible. Between 14% and 24% of respondents had used an unprescribed drug at some point in their lives. Looking at recent usage this figure reduces to between 5% and 9%, dependent on location. Locational variation was statistically significant for both measures of prevalence, with Glasgow and Lewisham showing the greatest prevalence, Bradford the least and Nottingham ranging somewhere in between.

Figure 2.2
Lifetime drug usage and drug usage within the last year: Booster sample

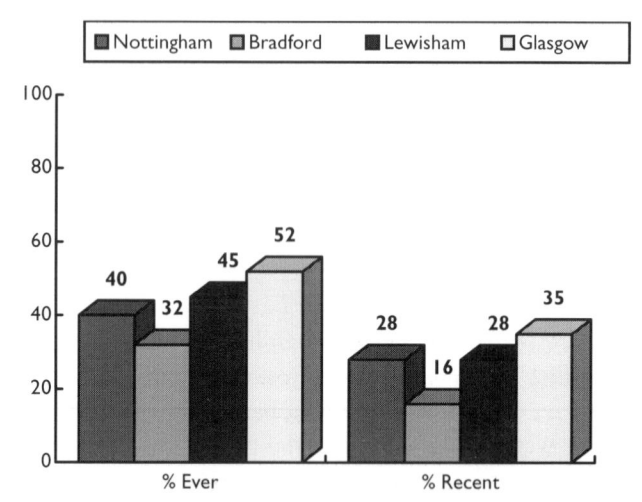

Percentage of respondents who had **ever** taken an illicit drug (% Ever)/Percentage of respondents who had taken an illicit drug **within the last year** (% Recent)

As predicted, the distinction between main and booster samples was also statistically significant, with the booster sample showing higher levels of drug usage on both prevalence measures. Lifetime usage for this sample ranged between 33% and 52%, dependent on location, and usage within the last year lay between 17% and 35%. Nevertheless it was still the case that in all locations *except* for Glasgow the majority of respondents claimed never to have used an unprescribed drug. Locational variation was again significant and followed a broadly similar pattern to that for the main sample with Glasgow > Lewisham = Nottingham > Bradford.

To put these estimates into perspective, they equate, if assumed to represent the actual habits of the British population, to around 1 in 15 people in the general population having *recently* used a drug and around 1 in 4 people in 'high risk' groups having done so. In terms of *lifetime* drug usage these figures rise to up to 1 in 5 people in the general population and up to 1 in 2 people in 'high risk' groups. Whilst such figures may seem quite high in *absolute* terms, for what is, after all, an illicit practice, it should be noted that we do not have any equivalent general population self-report estimates for other illicit practices (even at the level of committing such offences as fiddling one's tax or speeding). Consequently we simply cannot know whether the estimates are also high in *relative* terms.

One aspect of the data which is clear however, is that both lifetime usage and recent usage varied significantly across sample *type* and sample *location*. The distinction between main and booster samples outlined above reached an extremely high level of statistical significance for both recent usage and usage *per se*, indicating as anticipated that the booster samples had a much greater level of personal experience with drug usage than the main samples. With regard to location, respondents in Glasgow and Lewisham showed the highest levels of personal experience of drug usage and respondents in Bradford the lowest. Since this finding was consistent across both sample type and prevalence measure this probably represents a real distinction between the locations.

In summary, a brief overview of the responses to our self-completion items suggests that drug usage, at least at the level of experimental or 'one off' usage, is a fairly common behaviour in the general population and a very common behaviour in sub-groups selected to be 'at risk' of drug usage. In the absence of self-report data relating to other forms of illicit behaviour we cannot draw any conclusions here about whether rates of drug usage in the population are high in relative as well as absolute terms. We can however discuss whether the *patterns* of drug usage suggested by our data are problematic or not. This issue is addressed below.

Patterns of drug usage

Prevalence alone cannot be taken to indicate whether drug usage in the population is *problematic* or not. Having said which, the term 'problematic' in this context needs to be defined quite carefully. Some will argue, for example, that *any* level of drug usage in the population is problematic and that the higher the prevalence rate, the greater the problem. Used in this sense the term 'problematic' is, we feel, of more conceptual than practical value. Our ability to gauge how commonly the law is broken in this instance does *not* help in determining such factors as the need for drug rehabilitation clinics. Unlike the case for many other illicit activities drug usage as such has no *necessary* practical consequences for society. Many drug users carry out precisely the same range of activities as non-drug users and their behaviour does not impinge

either on the well being of any other individuals or on the resources of society as a whole. With this in mind, we tie our use of the term 'problematic' to those patterns of usage which *do* have practical implications either in terms of resources or in terms of more direct risks such as viral transmission. In particular, we consider the *types* of drugs which are most commonly being used, the *frequency* of usage, the *mode* of usage and the precise demographic patterns which describe drug usage within the population.

Prevalence by drug type

As suggested above, estimates relating to the *differential* prevalence of a range of drug types can be useful in assessing whether drug usage is problematic. In practical terms this relates to the way in which resources need to be structured. How we interpret such information depends, however, on how we ascribe levels of harm to the different drug types. In the drugs literature, problematic patterns of drug usage tend in this context to be tied to the *absolute* levels of harm associated with particular drugs. Unfortunately, the harmfulness of any given drug is itself a matter of considerable debate amongst the drugs related professions. To avoid the confusion this generates, we tie our discussion here to the *relative* levels of harm ascribed to distinct drug types. There is a general consensus, for example, that certain drugs, such as cannabis, are *relatively* low risk drugs in health terms, in comparison to certain other drugs, such as heroin, cocaine or tranquillisers. Using this consensus, we compare prevalence rates across drug types to provide some indication of whether the drugs used by the general population suggest a problematic pattern of usage.

Figure 2.3
Lifetime usage by drug type: Main sample

1% or less	2–5%	6–10%	10+%
heroin	amphetamines	(none)	cannabis
cocaine	LSD		
crack	psilocybin		
ecstasy	amyl nitrite		
methadone			
diconal			
temgesic			
barbiturates			
DF 118s			
triazelam			
tamazepam			
tranquillizers			
pills			
solvents			

Percentage of respondents who have **ever** used a named drug (based on percentages averaged across the four locations)

In all four main samples, the percentage of respondents who claimed to have used any drug *other* than cannabis *within the last year* was negligible. However, the percentage of respondents who claimed they had used a particular drug at least once in their life was not insignificant for a broad range of drugs, as can be seen from Figure 2.3. Amphetamines, LSD, ecstasy, psilocybin, amyl nitrite and 'pills' (unspecified sleeping pills etc.) had all been used at least once by between 1% and 5% of respondents, depending on location.

Figure 2.4
Lifetime usage by drug type: Booster sample

1% or less	2–5%	6–10%	10+%
crack	heroin	amphetamines	cannabis
methadone	cocaine	LSD	
diconal	temazepam	ecstasy	
temgesic	pills	psilocybin	
barbiturates	tranquillizers	amyl nitrite	
DF 118s	solvents		
triazelam			

*Percentage of respondents who have **ever** used a named drug (based on percentages averaged across the four locations)*

Preferences in the main samples were matched in the booster samples by the rank ordering of different drug types, cannabis still being easily the most popular drug. However, in the booster samples the number of respondents who had used drugs *other* than cannabis at least once in their lives was much higher than in the main samples, as can be seen from Figure 2.4. *Recent* usage of a wide range of drugs was also more common for this sample than for the main sample. Between 1% and 10% of respondents in the booster samples had recent personal experience of taking a drug *other* than cannabis - the most popular drugs again being amphetamines, LSD, ecstasy, psilocybin and amyl nitrite. To complete the picture, it is worth noting that the *absolute* prevalence of cannabis in terms of *recent* usage was also rather higher for this sample than for the main sample, ranging between 16% and 33%. Whilst we have summarised the findings here without regard to location, it should be borne in mind that some locational variation was apparent and for the interested reader the full picture is given in Tables 2.1 and 2.2 in Appendix 1.

In summary, the patterns of usage outlined here suggest that in the general population, any widespread and consistent usage of drugs is likely to be restricted to cannabis, a *relatively* low risk substance in drug terms. However, limited usage of a *range* of drugs, including the most stringently controlled drugs, clearly occurs amongst a small but not insignificant proportion of the population. In our target sample of young people living in areas of relative urban deprivation, levels of drug usage were significantly higher and general usage of a broader range of drugs was more common. In *absolute* terms the sample was therefore also more likely to use drugs generally regarded as being very harmful in health terms. Nevertheless, it should be noted that the *relative* prominence of cannabis as opposed to drugs such as ecstasy, tranquillisers or crack was maintained in the booster samples. This suggests that, although drug usage *per se* has a greater incidence in this targeted group, *patterns* of usage are not necessarily more problematic from the point of view of drug *type* than in the general population.

In addition to overall patterns of differential prevalence, the prevalence of *individual* drugs is of interest for its own sake. It is clear, for example, from Tables 2.1 and 2.2 in Appendix 1 that whilst the emphasis in the literature on cannabis is justified from a prevalence viewpoint, the rather more substantive emphasis on 'opiates' is not. As an illustration, 1% of respondents in all main sample locations and 3% or less of respondents in all booster sample locations had taken heroin. In terms of absolute numbers of users these figures are very small for a drug which still features prominently not only in the drugs literature but also in prevention and harm reduction policies. Again, it is worth remembering here that prevalence is only one relevant measure and the issue of whether the emphasis on opiates is justified in terms of absolute levels of medically or socially defined 'harm' is still open to debate.

In certain sections in the remainder of this chapter we have pooled the data from three distinct groups of drug type, in order both to avoid tedious repetition of data applying only to drugs used by an insignificant proportion of respondents and because certain statistical analyses can only sensibly be carried out using a fairly large number of respondents. The three groups of drugs used are defined by their apparent prevalence in the general population, based on the data outlined above. That is, we have separated drugs into ones which 10% or more of respondents have used (i.e. cannabis); drugs which more than 1% but less than 10% of respondents had used (i.e. amphetamines, LSD, psilocybin, pills and amyl nitrite); and drugs which only around 1% of the population had used (i.e. heroin, crack and cocaine). Any drugs with lower than 1% prevalence across both samples and all locations were excluded from the analyses using these drug groupings. The three groups are referred to respectively as 'cannabis', 'non-opiates' and 'opiates', the latter two labels relating to the chemical base from which the *majority* of drugs within each category derive.

Polydrug usage

As with the issue of drug type and relative harm, we find also some consensus in the literature and amongst drugs professionals that *eclectic* usage of a range of drugs, whether by an individual or by the population in general, is indicative of a problematic profile of usage. Whether such eclectic usage actually occurs is, however, one of the most heavily debated issues in the drugs field. Do people who use one drug also use others or do drug users tend to stick to a single drug of choice or at least a small range of *similar* drug types? From a drugs prevention viewpoint, the relevance of this issue is that polydrug usage is a rather more dangerous strategy in health terms than other more restricted forms of drug usage.

Figure 2.5
Lifetime polydrug usage by sample

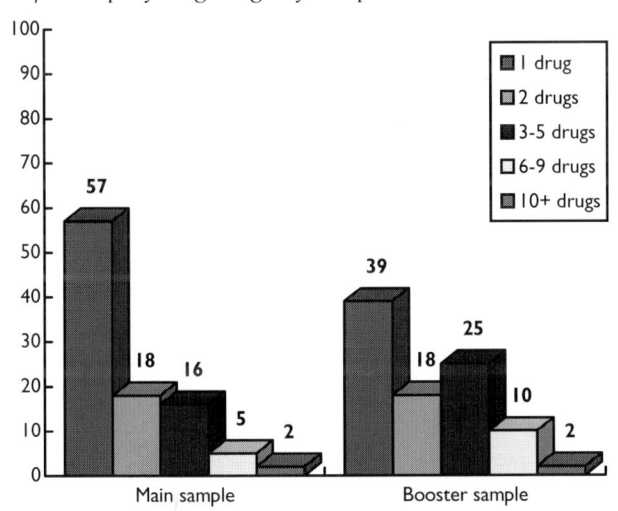

Percentage of drug users who had used one or more than one type of drug in their lifetime, averaged across location.

As with the term 'problematic' usage, the precise meaning of 'polydrug' usage in this context is open to varying interpretations. As a consequence of both the low absolute numbers of drug users in our samples and the structure of the self-completion questionnaire, we cannot look at polydrug usage in terms of the *simultaneous* usage of different drugs. Partly for pragmatic reasons, therefore, 'polydrug usage' will here be taken to refer to an *overlap* between different drugs in our respondents' drug using histories. From the patterns observed we assess whether using one kind of drug is associated with using another kind of drug, both across the lifetime of each respondent and within the year prior to the interview. We also address the issue of whether particular groups of drugs are connected together in usage patterns, or whether little consistency is shown across individuals in the more eclectic patterns of drug use. Summaries of polydrug usage by drug type, sample and location are given in Tables 2.8-2.11 in Appendix 1.

Figure 2.5 refers *only* to those who had used a drug at least once in their lifetime. It shows that lifetime drug usage in our main sample is largely restricted to a single drug of choice. However, a sizeable proportion of drug users - around 34% depending on location - have tried up to five different drugs. In the booster sample, this pattern is reversed, with the percentage of drug users who have taken only *one* drug forming a minority. Around 53% of these respondents - again depending on location - had used somewhere between two and nine different types of drugs over their lifetime. Whilst the difference between locations is not as sharp as that between sample type, main sample usage of a moderate to large number of different drugs was around 6% greater in Glasgow and Lewisham than in Nottingham or Bradford. In the booster sample the disparity between locations is rather more distinct, with Glasgow and Bradford showing around 15% more respondents using a moderate to large range of drugs than Lewisham, and Nottingham showing values somewhere in between the two.

The distinction between sample types and to a lesser extent between locations is maintained for polydrug usage measured within the last year. Around 50% of booster sample respondents in each location had *recently* tried more than one type of drug, whilst around 37% of main sample respondents had done so. The most prominent location for polydrug usage in the main sample was Glasgow, which had around 5% more respondents using a moderate to large range of drugs than the other three locations. The rank ordering of location in the booster sample for recent polydrug usage was also similar to that for lifetime usage with Glasgow = Bradford > Nottingham > Lewisham. Whilst it is clear from Figure 2.6 that the majority of respondents had *not* used a wide range of drugs within the last year, the number who *had* done so is not - in the main sample at least - substantially lower than that noted for lifetime polydrug usage. This suggests that even where experimentation with a range of drugs is sequential rather than simultaneous, it is nonetheless quite likely to be conducted over a *relatively* short period of time.

To establish more firmly the nature of this pattern

of polydrug usage, we carried out a qualitative comparison of recent polydrug usage for seven specific drug types, taking the number of cases across location in which a recent user of one drug had also taken another type of drug. We limited our comparison to those drugs which showed at least some non-negligible proportion of users in the main sample and ensured that the three types of drug group considered earlier were all represented. These two criteria gave us the following drugs to consider: pills or tranquillisers (taken as a composite since they tended to be used by the same groups of individuals), cannabis, heroin, cocaine, LSD, ecstasy and amphetamines.

Figure 2.6
Polydrug usage within the last year by sample

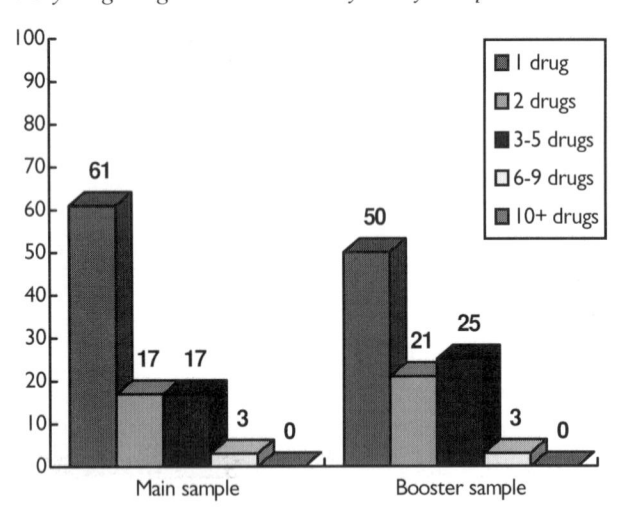

[Bar chart showing Main sample: 61, 17, 17, 3, 0; Booster sample: 50, 21, 25, 3, 0. Legend: 1 drug, 2 drugs, 3-5 drugs, 6-9 drugs, 10+ drugs]

Percentage of drug users who had used one or more than one type of drug within the last year, averaged across location.

The data presented in Tables 2.8 and 2.9 in Appendix 1 outline the profile of polydrug usage for these drug types. Although numbers of users are very small for certain drugs, the general pattern observed in both main and booster samples suggests that users of drugs belonging to our 'opiate' drug category - in this instance heroin and cocaine - appeared to be more likely to follow polydrug usage patterns than users of 'non-opiates'. With regard to particular drug types, users of cannabis and pills or tranquillisers were the drug users *least* likely to engage in polydrug usage, the number of cases in which cannabis users had taken other drugs being particularly low. In short, cannabis *users* were most likely just to stick to cannabis. However, if people were using several drugs, cannabis was very likely to be one of them. In this it was followed by amphetamines and LSD. So, there appear to be some drugs which, whilst *in themselves* most likely to be used in isolation, are prone to being added to a more eclectic pattern of usage by those adopting a 'polydrug' usage pattern. As a further dimension of polydrug usage, it seems that some drugs tend to form a group of 'mutually used' drugs. Ecstasy, LSD and amphetamines being a good case in point. Where any of these drugs were being used, individuals showed a fairly strong likelihood of also using one or both of the other drugs.

Figure 2.7
Association between the usage of different drug types: Main sample

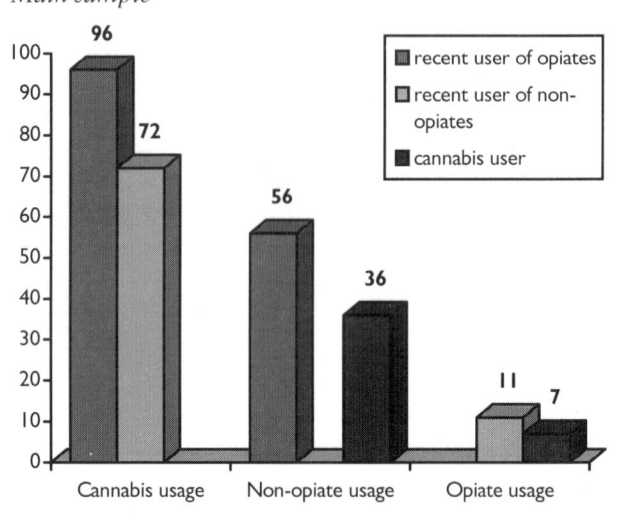

[Bar chart showing Cannabis usage: 96, 72; Non-opiate usage: 56, 36; Opiate usage: 11, 7. Legend: recent user of opiates, recent user of non-opiates, cannabis user]

Percentage of recent drug users in each drug usage category also using a drug from one or both other categories, averaged across location.

Whilst numbers of users are too small to make any more definitive statements on the basis of the above qualitative analysis, the data outlined in Tables 2.12 and 2.13 in Appendix 1 provide quantitative support for the broad conclusions drawn. Figures 2.7 and 2.8 summarise this data for the main and booster samples, showing the percentage of recent users in each drug group (cannabis, 'non-opiates' and 'opiates') who claimed also to have recently taken a drug from one or both of the other drug groups. From these data it can be seen that the pattern of polydrug usage across the three drug types is not symmetrical. Users of 'opiate' drugs were more likely to use either 'non-opiates' or cannabis than vice versa and similarly, 'non-opiate' drug users were more likely to use cannabis than vice versa.

Little locational variation was noted in this pattern of polydrug usage, although some differences between the two types of sample did emerge. The association between 'opiates' and 'non-opiates' and equally between 'non-opiates' and cannabis was slightly stronger in the booster sample than the main sample. Conversely, the association between 'opiates' and cannabis was slightly *weaker* in the booster sample as compared to the main sample.

Figure 2.8
Association between the usage of different drug types: Booster sample

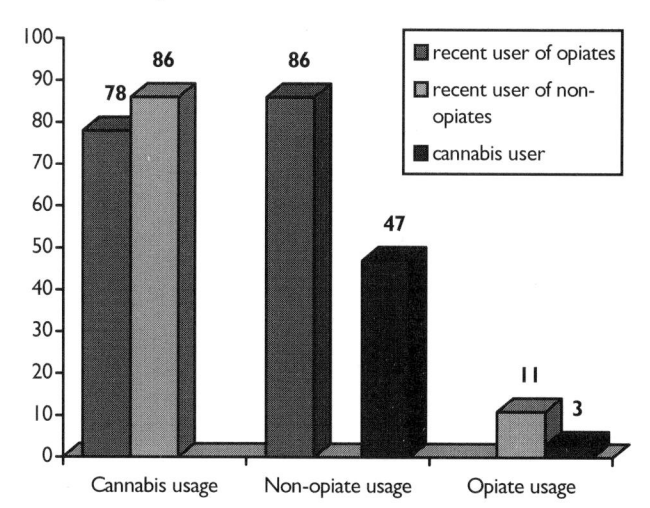

[Bar chart showing:
- Cannabis usage: recent user of opiates 78, recent user of non-opiates 86
- Non-opiate usage: cannabis user 86, recent user of opiates 47
- Opiate usage: recent user of non-opiates 11, cannabis user 3]

Percentage of recent drug users in each drug usage category also using a drug from one or both other categories, averaged across location.

It is important to note that the asymmetrical link between drug groups is *not* simply a function of their relative prevalence. Prevalence cannot in itself predispose towards polydrug usage, although where determined by availability it *may* decide which individual drugs are the most popular ingredients in an already eclectic pattern of usage. This data, together with the qualitative data summarised earlier, whilst suggesting little about the direction of causal association linking the drug types, *does* suggest therefore that eclectic patterns of drug usage follow the pattern 'opiates' > 'non-opiates' > cannabis, with 'opiate' drug users stepping outside their own category of drug in a majority of cases.

Frequent and injecting usage

Alongside polydrug usage and the usage of particularly harmful types of drugs, the potential for 'problematic' patterns of usage in the population can be gauged from the incidence of frequent and injecting drug usage. We need to distinguish here between what may be seen as 'problematic' for the individual and what is 'problematic' for society. Whilst both frequent and injecting usage may be controlled in the individual case and consequently unproblematic in a *clinical* sense for the individual, they can be of considerable importance at the population level. Conversely, whilst individuals may be placing their own health at considerable risk by a particular mode of drug usage, this will not become a problem for society as a whole until the prevalence of such behaviour reaches a relevant threshold. This threshold being represented by, for example, the point at which frequent usage implies a likely strain on resources or injecting usage significantly increases the likelihood of secondary infection and viral transmission (HIV etc.). In the present discussion we are concerned with establishing whether levels of frequent and injecting usage present any threat to the population as a whole, rather than in establishing whether any given individuals are putting themselves at risk.

Figure 2.9
Frequent drug usage and injecting drug usage: Main sample

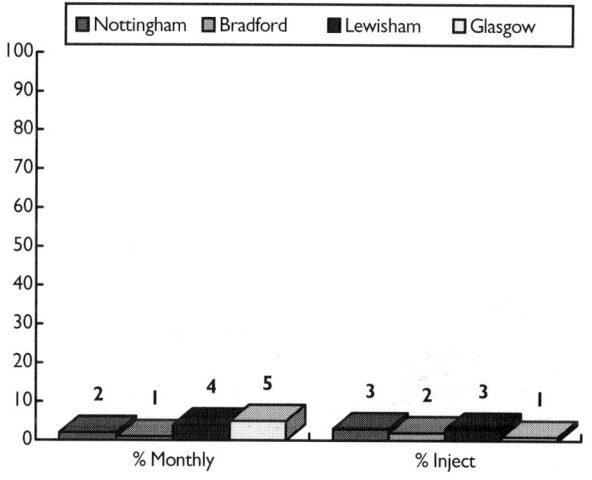

[Bar chart with legend: Nottingham, Bradford, Lewisham, Glasgow
- % Monthly: 2, 1, 4, 5
- % Inject: 3, 2, 3, 1]

Percentage of **recent** users of a drug who used the drug at least **once per month**/Percentage of **recent** users of a drug who had **injected** the drug.

As demonstrated by Figure 2.9, both frequent and injecting usage were, in absolute terms, very low within our main sample. No more than 3% of respondents in any location claimed to have injected an unprescribed drug and only 5% or less across locations claimed to be using a drug with a frequency greater than or equal to monthly. However the extent of frequent usage was dependent on location, with statistically significant levels of variation following the pattern noted earlier for prevalence *per se*, with Glasgow = Lewisham > Nottingham > Bradford. No such locational dependence was shown for injecting usage, although here it should again be borne in mind that our figures for injecting usage were very low.

In the booster sample also, there was a very low absolute level of injecting usage. However, *frequent* drug usage was rather more common. In all locations the incidence of frequent usage in the booster sample was statistically greater than that in the corresponding main sample. This is a pattern worth noting, since it suggests that whilst in the general population drug usage appears to be largely sporadic or experimental, usage within sub-groups of the population at greater risk of drug usage is also likely to be more consistent or intense. This notwithstanding, it is still the case that only a minority of users appear to take their drug of choice with any great regularity. With regard to locational effects, both injecting usage and frequency of usage in the booster sample followed the by now familiar trend with Glasgow > Lewisham > Nottingham > Bradford, although this location effect was only statistically significant for frequency of usage.

Figure 2.10
Frequent drug usage and injecting drug usage: Booster sample

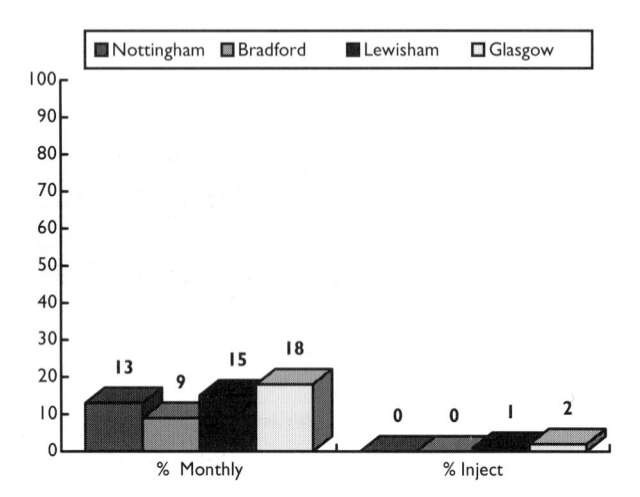

Percentage of **recent** users of a drug who used the drug at least **once per month**. Percentage of **recent** users of a drug who had **injected** the drug.

The fact that absolute levels of injecting usage are low in both booster and main samples is a particularly important finding given the place this method of drug usage holds both in the literature and, more particularly, in prevention work. It is also a fact which at face value contrasts quite sharply with the implications drawn from previous research findings. To illustrate this we can take as an example the work of Unell (1991) in Nottingham, which is fairly representative of a range of local area studies. Unell's research suggested that between 30% and 40% of drug users are likely to inject. Clearly the absolute values which our estimates imply are rather lower than this and certainly the implications drawn for levels of injecting usage in the general population are much less frightening.

The disparity between our figures and those cited above is probably best explained by the survey methodologies used in each case. Unell's work, like that of the broad range of local service oriented studies, was based on data collected solely from individuals volunteering for or referred to a drugs agency. Whilst this type of data is valuable for the purposes for which it was collected, it is perhaps not the best type of data on which to base estimates of *general population* drug usage. It is entirely plausible that individuals attending a drugs agency *would* be more likely to show problematic patterns of usage, such as injecting usage, than drug users drawn from the general population. Consequently estimates based solely on agency data will tend to over-estimate absolute levels of problematic usage.

In support of this interpretation, it should be noted that our data are much closer to the estimates derived from a recent study of injecting usage in Glasgow (Frischer 1992). Frischer's study is one of the few recent studies to have used a range of data sets *other* than agency data. Using unnamed identifier information, obtained from police and health service sources, Frischer estimated a general population level of injecting drug usage of around 1-2% with 'at risk' groups (in this case males aged 20-24) showing an incidence of injecting usage of around 4-5%. Whilst the latter figure is still substantially higher - even holding age and gender constant - than our 'at risk' estimates for injecting usage, it is nevertheless significantly closer to these than to the estimates obtained by Unell and by similar agency based studies.

Our discussions with drugs professionals in the four locations suggest that our estimates of injecting usage are at least representative of observations of drug usage 'on the ground'. This is more particularly the case for Bradford and Nottingham however, since in Glasgow and Lewisham it was suggested that true estimates might be closer to those of Frischer's 'at risk' group. Nonetheless, even accepting the possibility that our estimates are as much as 50% out in some cases, we are left with the conclusion that within the general population even individuals 'at risk' of drug usage are highly unlikely to engage in injecting drug usage. Hence *general* prevention tactics and general health provisions for drug users need not focus on injecting users. On the other hand, injecting users, although a small group in terms of absolute numbers are potentially at greater risk of harm than the general run of users. So directing specialist resources at the small potential group of injecting users may show substantial returns in terms of a reduction of certain specific risks to the health of the general population such as viral transmission. Equally, it would clearly be of benefit to the injecting users themselves.

Frequency of use and injecting usage are attributes which can be applied to drug *types*, as well as to drug *users*. Tables 2.3 and 2.4 in Appendix 1 outline the tendency of each drug type considered to be used for injecting purposes or with a frequency greater than once per month. Comparing across only those drug types for which the prevalence of usage was not negligible, the most frequently used drugs across all four main sample locations were cannabis, amphetamines and ecstasy. In the booster samples, although cannabis, amphetamines and ecstasy retained the most *consistent* pattern of frequent usage across the four locations, there was a greater degree of locational variation. Whilst the low numbers of users across a range of drugs precluded us from carrying out statistical analyses for most individual drugs, we were able to pool data using the three drug groups outlined earlier and these analyses are discussed below.

Not surprisingly, given the general profile of drug usage within our main sample, frequent usage was significantly greater for cannabis than for either 'non-opiates' or 'opiates' in all four locations. It is worth noting, however, that 'opiate' drug usage was more polarised than 'non-opiate' drug usage. Around 6% of users taking 'opiates' took them daily whilst virtually all other users had only taken them once, or tended to take them less than monthly. On the other hand, the spread of 'non-opiate' drug usage was much broader with a proportion of users falling into each frequency category. Again, the majority had only taken these drugs once or at least less than monthly. This implies that whilst cannabis and 'opiate' drug users show a range of usage patterns, 'opiate' drug users in the general population are split into two distinct categories definable as 'experimental' users and 'potentially problematic users', the former being the largest single category.

Neither the prominence of cannabis nor the polarity of 'opiates' was maintained in the booster sample frequency patterns for the three drug types. As shown in Figure 2.12 'opiates' and to a lesser extent 'non-opiates' were almost as likely to be used *frequently* as cannabis. Users of both 'opiates' and 'non-opiates' were also equally likely to be spread across a range of frequency categories. Another disparity between main and booster samples was that 'non-opiates' rather than 'opiates' were the most likely type of drug to be taken either only once or on a very sporadic basis by their users. Whilst it should be borne in mind that numbers of users within the 'opiate' drug group are fairly small, the disparity observed here between the patterns of main and booster samples suggests that frequent usage of higher risk substances is likely to be more of a problem in sub-groups of the population at generally greater risk of drug usage *per se*. Having said this, it is important to note that the majority of users of any drug type were not using their drug of choice regularly.

Patterns of injecting usage by drug type also showed some disparity between main and booster samples. As is demonstrated by Figure 2.13 'opiates' and 'non-opiates' were equally likely to be injected by main sample drug users, but within the booster sample, 'opiates' were significantly *more* likely to be injected than

Figure 2.11
Frequency of usage by drug group: Main sample

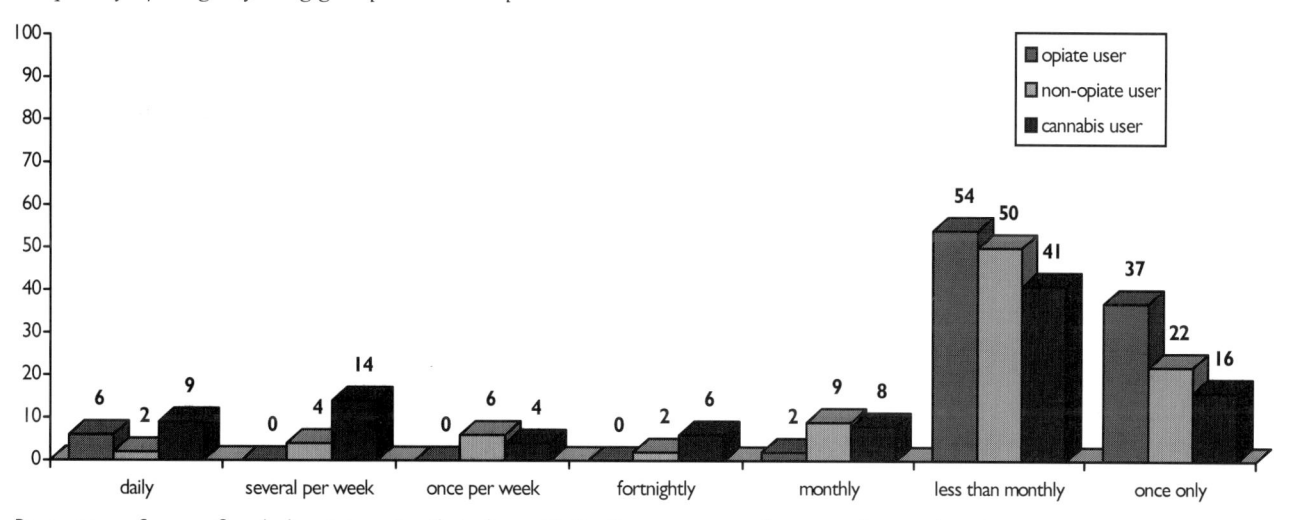

Percentage of users of each drug type using their drug with the frequency stated, averaged across location.

Figure 2.12
Frequency of usage by drug group: Booster sample

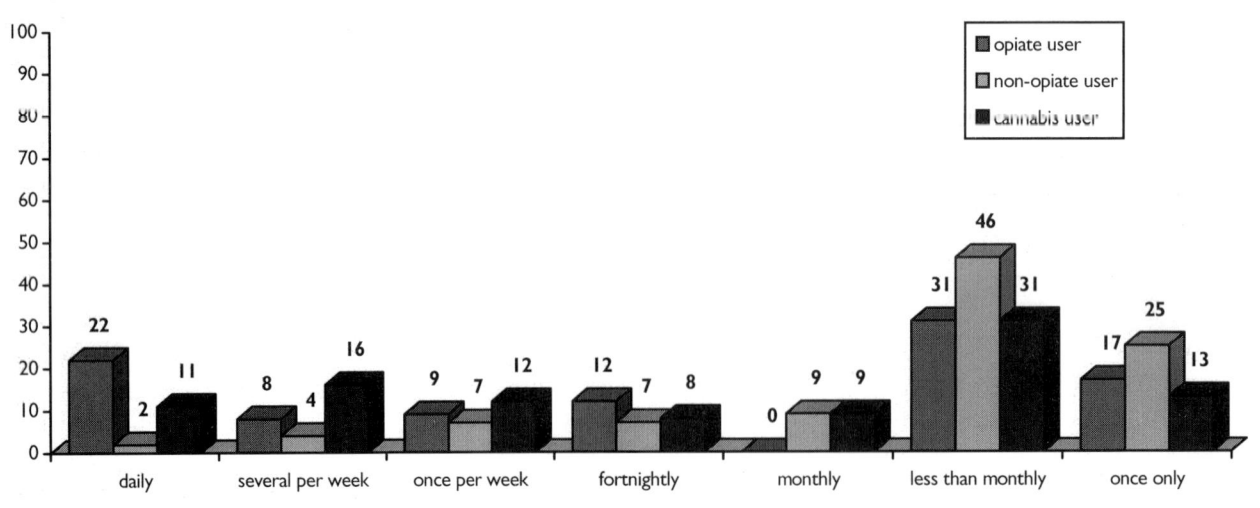

Percentage of users of each drug type using their drug with the frequency stated, averaged across location.

'non-opiates'. Again, it should be borne in mind that absolute numbers of 'opiate' drug users were quite low, so this pattern may not be representative of this type of drug user in general. The most notable and perhaps also most predictable finding for injecting usage and drug type was the very marked distinction between cannabis and the other two drug groups. Only one individual in the entire sample claimed to have injected cannabis!

Figure 2.13
Injecting usage by drug type

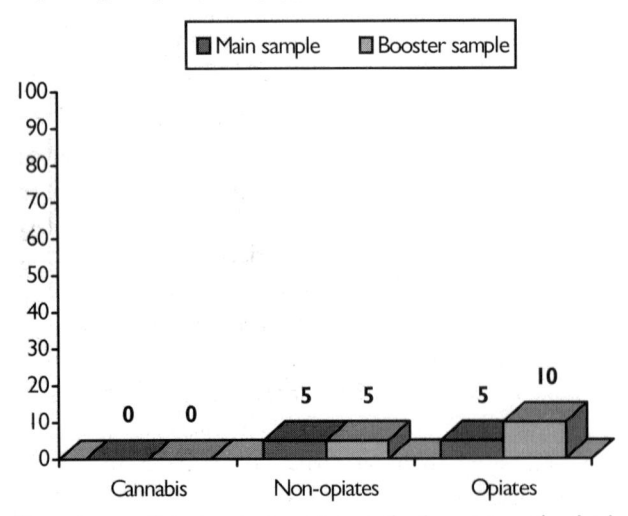

Percentage of respondents using each drug type who had **injected**, averaged across location.

Since there are clear distinctions in injecting usage both between drug types and between individual drugs, it is worth noting that estimates of locational variation in injecting usage are likely to depend to an extent on the prevalence of particular drugs within a population at the time any survey is carried out. For example, a not insignificant number of drug using respondents in Glasgow stated that they would have some difficulty in obtaining particular 'opiate' type drugs. This could account for our present estimates of injecting usage in that location being rather lower than those of Frischer. This is important in methodological terms since, generally speaking, studies of injecting usage tend not to control for the prevalence of different drugs within the location being assessed.

Availability of drugs

Whilst some drug users in Glasgow may have experienced difficulty in obtaining their drug of choice, very few other respondents appeared to have had any problem at all in obtaining whichever drug they preferred. The data outlined in Table 2.5 in Appendix 1 indicate that across the whole range of drugs, the percentage of users stating that a drug was readily available in their city or borough rarely fell below 70%. The consistently high levels of ready availability cited across all locations and for all drug types demonstrate clearly that drug usage, problematic or otherwise, is unlikely at the present time to be curtailed by patterns of availability. The only drug which showed a consistently *lower* level of respondents claiming its ready availability was psilocybin, which is a drug naturally restricted by the seasonality of its growing cycle!

Availability was, to an extent, dependent on drug type. Cannabis and 'non-opiates' were less readily obtainable than 'opiates'. This may be a function of the greater *difficulties* reported by Customs and Excise in

Figure 2.14
Availability by drug type: Main sample

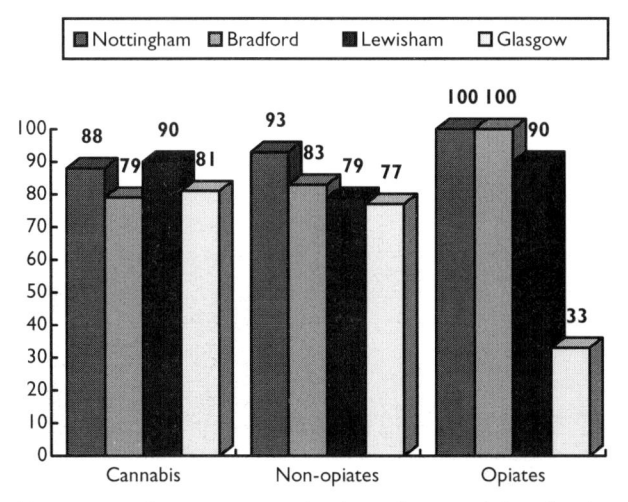

[Bar chart: Nottingham, Bradford, Lewisham, Glasgow
- Cannabis: 88, 79, 90, 81
- Non-opiates: 93, 83, 79, 77
- Opiates: 100, 100, 90, 33]

Percentage of **recent** users of a drug who stated that the drug was **readily available** in their city or borough.

controlling the entry of opiates into the country. It might equally be taken simply to reflect the greater popularity of cannabis and non-opiates. Whatever the reason for differential availability, it seems that availability as such is also determined in part by locational factors, perhaps consequent on the operation of distribution networks. By way of illustration, we can compare across Figures 2.14 and 2.15. These Figures show that both main sample and booster sample respondents

Figure 2.15
Availability by drug type: Booster sample

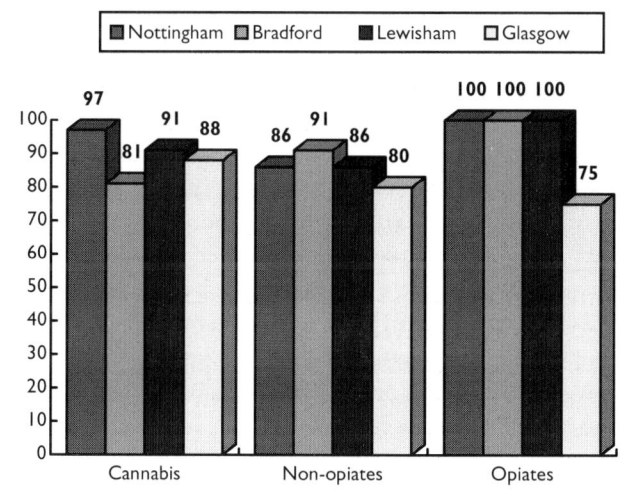

[Bar chart: Nottingham, Bradford, Lewisham, Glasgow
- Cannabis: 97, 81, 91, 88
- Non-opiates: 86, 91, 86, 80
- Opiates: 100, 100, 100, 75]

Percentage of **recent** users of a drug who stated that the drug was **readily available** in their city or borough.

in Glasgow were significantly more likely than their counterparts in the other three locations to state that they had difficulty in obtaining their drugs of choice, particularly the 'opiate' drugs. Whilst this information may be useful in the short term, for example in adding to other data on supply control or distribution networks, previous research suggests that such local pockets of reduced availability tend not to be stable over time. This locational variation is therefore best interpreted as a phenomenon restricted to the particular time at which the survey was carried out.

Availability was also one of the few drug 'usage' measures which showed little disparity between the main and booster samples. However, the booster sample were still on the whole slightly *more* confident in their ability to obtain drugs locally. The implications of these high figures for availability are quite major, notably for drugs prevention policies. They suggest that for the population in general and perhaps more specifically for potential high risk groups (such as the young people in our booster sample areas), it is choice, rather than availability, which determines drug usage. Consequently, it becomes of considerable importance that the choice of potential drug users be properly informed - and that young people, in particular, are given sufficient help to respond to the likelihood of drugs being around in their locality.

In summary, the prevalence of drug usage within our sample, measured both by lifetime usage and by usage within the last year varied very considerably across types of drugs. Quite a high proportion of people, especially in the booster sample, had used cannabis at least once in their lifetime. A significant number had used amphetamines, LSD, psilocybin, amyl nitrite and, in the booster sample, ecstasy, but very few in any sample had used or tried heroin, cocaine, crack, methadone, diconal, temgesic, barbiturates, DF118s, triazelam, temazepam, solvents, tranquillisers or other forms of unprescribed pills. Whether the prevalence levels are regarded as high or not, our data suggest that, in the main, *modes* of drug usage are *not* particularly problematic. Injecting usage and frequent drug usage would seem to be at rather lower levels than has previously been thought to be the case and the *types* of drug in general circulation are those least threatening in health terms. On a rather more depressing note, it was apparent that few drug users felt that their tendency to use drugs had been in the least restricted by the *availability* of any drug. This suggests that the onus in drugs prevention needs particularly to be on educating demand.

Comparisons with other drug usage surveys

Comparing across a range of studies to establish the likely objective validity of baseline estimates is valuable in any form of prevalence research. It is of particular importance in the case of research relating to illicit behaviours, where any tendency of respondents to misrepresent their behaviour can reasonably be taken to be at a premium. Whilst there is an abundance of drugs-related data with which we could have compared our survey findings, we have chosen to restrict our comparisons to those surveys with relevantly similar methodologies. Specifically, we looked only at self-report data gathered using similar methodologies and question structures to our own and relating to the particular drug types we had included within our survey. Although this necessarily restricted the data available to us, any other approach would have confounded the effects of any real differences in prevalence estimates with the effects of methodological constraints.

British general population surveys

Sadly, relevant British data relating to drugs prevalence are rather sparse. We managed to track down only three general population data sets. The first, carried out by OPCS in 1969 on behalf of the Home Office and cited in an unpublished Home Office report by Marks et al (1973) surveyed around two thousand 16-65 year olds regarding their lifetime drug usage. (We are grateful to Joy Mott for bringing this report to our attention). The second, carried out by NOP in 1982 and cited in the Daily Mail comprised a survey of lifetime drug usage for around one thousand 15-21 year olds in England and Wales, with an additional very small Scottish sample of 57 individuals. The final survey we traced was carried out by MORI in 1991 on behalf of the Health Education Authority and was a health and lifestyle survey in the context of which around seven thousand 16-19 year olds from England and Wales were asked about their lifetime drug using habits. The lifetime prevalence estimates which can be derived from these sources for a range of drug types are summarised in Figure 2.16.

The first point to note from the survey data outlined in Figure 2.16 is that the two most recent surveys for England and Wales - which were carried out using similar age ranges of respondent - broadly concurred in their estimates of prevalence despite being conducted around ten years apart from one another. Comparing their estimates with our own main sample lifetime prevalence estimates for under 24 year olds shows that we also concur with the ballpark figures they suggest, although MORI's estimates for the usage of psilocybin and amyl nitrite are slightly higher than our own.

Figure 2.16
Previous estimates of general population drug usage in Britain

Source	Cannabis	Amphet-amines	LSD	Heroin	Cocaine	Solvents	Amyl Nitrite	Psilocybin
OPCS (1969) N=1968 Age group 16-65 England and Wales	2		<1	<1	<1			
NOP (1982) N=1268 Age group 15-21 England and Wales	13-28	3-10	2-4	0-1	1-3			
NOP (1982) N=57 Age group 15-21 Scotland	21	8	8	7	9	2		
MORI (1991) N=7711 Age group 16-19 England and Wales	25	5	6	1	1		10	6

Estimated percentages of drug users based on self-report lifetime usage

The estimates of the only recent population survey for Scotland did not match our own figures in the case of either heroin or cocaine usage, being substantially higher than our estimates for Glasgow in both cases. Since the sample size in this instance was around half that of our own sample for the age group considered and also failed to match the figures for England and Wales by a very considerable margin, we are tempted to put this particular disparity down to sampling error in the NOP survey. The Scottish figures cited for cannabis, amphetamines, LSD and solvents on the other hand were rather lower than our own estimates for Glasgow. This disparity may be a consequence of locational variation in Scotland, since it is not clear which areas NOP used for their survey.

Perhaps the most interesting comparison to be made is that between our survey and the 1969 OPCS survey. Our estimates of lifetime heroin and cocaine usage broadly concur with the OPCS estimates, despite the more than twenty year gap between the surveys. Our estimates for usage of LSD are slightly higher than those of OPCS and our figures for cannabis usage very substantially so. Whilst it is obviously impossible to say whether the match between the 1969 survey and our own relates to any real trends in drug usage over time, the disparities noted do support suggestions in the drugs literature and by the drugs professionals we talked to that whilst opiate usage has remained fairly stable over time, the use of non-opiates and cannabis has tended to increase.

Although demographic analysis in the surveys outlined above was rather limited, all three surveys did, not surprisingly, concur with our finding that drug usage was more prevalent amongst males than amongst females. More interestingly they were all also in agreement with the idea that drug usage is higher in London and in the North than in other locations. This would also be in line with our findings from the present survey.

We look forward to the publication of the 1992 British Crime Survey data on self-report drug usage. This will provide us with further and more up to date population estimates of drugs prevalence in Britain based on a sampling methodology similar to our own, but carried out on a much larger sample size. However, we would like to note here our concern that the context of a crime survey may depress people's willingness to talk about usage.

Local area surveys

Whilst the number of local area prevalence studies, including studies within the four locations we sampled, is quite large, we were unable to find any studies using a similar methodology to our own for Glasgow, Bradford or Nottingham. We are, however, able to compare our own data for Lewisham with a survey carried out on a sample of around three hundred 15-24 year olds for the Home Office by RSGB (1992) as part of a project to evaluate the Drugs Information Line in that area. The prevalence estimates which can be derived from this survey for those drugs which we also looked at are presented in Figure 2.17

Figure 2.17
Summary of Lewisham Drugs Information Line data for drugs prevalence (RSGB 1992)

Drug Type	Lifetime usage	Usage within last year
Alcohol	81	73
Tobacco	60	48
Cannabis	38	27
Ecstasy	15	8
LSD	14	7
Amphetamines	11	7

Estimated percentages of drugs users based on self-report lifetime usage

RSGB's figures for both lifetime and recent usage of unprescribed drugs within Lewisham were also very close to our own, although their estimates for LSD and ecstasy were slightly higher than ours. It is not possible directly to compare their figures with our own for lifetime and recent alcohol and tobacco usage, since the structure of the questions relating to these drugs were substantially different in the two surveys, but it is worth noting that again our figures, discussed in greater detail later, would suggest a similar range of estimates.

It should be noted that although sample sizes for the relevant age groups are fairly small in both our survey and that of RSGB, the similarity between the two sets of figures is of particular importance since they were conducted within roughly the same geographic area.

European general population surveys

Household surveys of population drug usage are a rather more common phenomenon in areas of Europe other than Britain. Nevertheless, we came across only one relevant similar survey carried out within recent years. This was carried out by Sandwijk, Cohen and Musterd (1991) in Amsterdam on a sample of 5,900 individuals aged 12 years and older. The sample compared here with ours forms part of a longitudinal analysis of trends in drug usage. Relevant data derived from this survey are presented in Figure 2.18

Figure 2.18
Summary of Amsterdam Household Survey on drugs prevalence (Sandwijk et al. 1991)

Drug Type	Lifetime usage	Usage within last year
Alcohol	86	78
Tobacco	68	46
Cannabis	25	10
Ecstasy	1	1
Amphetamines	4	<1
Heroin	1	<1
Cocaine	5	1

Estimated percentages of drug users based on self-report lifetime usage

Interestingly, these figures for drug usage in Amsterdam very closely match our own for most of the drugs considered. Only three of the total of ten estimates for unprescribed drugs differed from our own by more than one percent. These were for lifetime and recent usage of cannabis and lifetime usage of cocaine. With regard to the disparities in cannabis usage it should be noted that as a consequence of the Dutch Opium Law of 1976, cannabis is legally distinct from a range of other drugs and as a consequence of the more lenient attitude adopted towards it by the relevant authorities, is very much more readily obtainable in Amsterdam than in any of our four locations. With regard to the disparity in cocaine usage it is similarly worth noting that although distinct from the patterns observed in three of our four locations, the Amsterdam pattern is within one percent of matching our own figures for Lewisham, which, within our sample, is perhaps the single best match for Amsterdam in terms of type of municipality.

The demographic profile of drug usage within the Amsterdam survey also matched our own findings (for further details of which see Chapter 3). Males, the unemployed, younger individuals and in particular the under 30s were all significantly more likely to use a range of unprescribed drugs and those ethnic minorities represented within the survey were less likely than the white majority ethnic population. A stronger link was found in the Amsterdam survey between choice of leisure activity and drug usage in general, although the particular patterns observed were similar, with alcohol showing a rather closer link to a range of leisure pursuits than any controlled drug and cannabis showing a closer link than other unprescribed drugs.

Figure 2.19
Summary of National Institute on Drug Abuse Household Survey on drugs prevalence (NIDA 1988)

Drug Type	Lifetime usage	Usage within last year
Alcohol	83	66
Tobacco	73	32
Cannabis	37	13
Solvents	5	1
Tranquillizers	4	1
Heroin	1	<1
Cocaine/crack	1	<1
Injecting usage	1-2	

Estimated percentages of drug users based on self-report lifetime usage

American general population surveys

The National Household Survey on Drug Abuse carried out by the National Institute on Drug Abuse is part of an ongoing programme to measure the prevalence and correlates of drug usage within the US general population aged 12 and older. To date nine similar surveys have been carried out. The data presented in Figure 2.19 are taken from the 1988 sweep of the survey, which had 8,243 respondents.

This survey was perhaps the most distinct from our own, although our estimates for opiate use and injecting usage were not vastly different. Our rough estimates for the use of alcohol and tobacco were also fairly similar. Nevertheless, six of the ten possible estimates for the prevalence of unprescribed drugs were substantially higher than our own. Given the accepted disparity between the prevalence of drug usage in the US and Britain this finding is not particularly surprising. The match between estimates of injecting usage within our sample and the NIDA sample is, however, of considerable interest, since this was the only similar sample to our own in which an estimate of this mode of usage had been made and it closely matches our own estimates, despite the evident differences in the prevalence of drug usage between the two samples.

The demographic profile of drug usage within the US also matches our own data and that of the other surveys considered above. Males and younger individuals, in particular the under 35s were more likely to have used drugs both recently and within their lifetime. Figures for ethnic minorities suggested that in most ethnic minority groups drug usage is *less* prevalent than amongst the majority white population. An exception being the black population for which the prevalence of drug usage is broadly similar to estimates for the white population.

In summary, the data we have been able to obtain for previous drugs prevalence surveys methodologically similar to our own suggest that the ballpark figures we have obtained for drug usage are likely to be a fairly accurate baseline estimate of drugs prevalence. The demographic profile of drug usage is also remarkably consistent not only across studies but also across countries, suggesting that the distinctions we have noted are likely to be extremely stable ones. Although we cannot draw any firm conclusions regarding changing trends in drug usage across time, a comparison of our own figures with those for the only readily available figures for Britain *pre* 1970 provides some limited support for a notion popular in the literature, namely that opiate usage has remained relatively stable across time whilst the prevalence of cannabis and other non-opiates has been increasing. A comparison of our data with findings from another location in Europe and with estimates for the United States suggests, as would be predicted, that Britain is closer to its European neighbours in terms of drug usage than it is to the US.

Chapter 3

WHAT KINDS OF PEOPLE USE DRUGS?

Knowing *how* people use drugs is not the only issue of importance in gauging whether drug usage in a population is problematic or not. Knowing *which* groups of people use drugs is of equal value in this context. A widespread pattern of usage has, for example, substantially different implications for society than a concentration of drug usage in any one group. By way of illustration, if one clearly defined group stands out as the most prominent drug using group it may be that important social controls on drug usage have for some reason failed within this section of society. In more immediate practical terms it is also of value to know which groups are most likely to use drugs. Such information can be used to suggest which groups are the most appropriate targets for drugs related information or services. Finally, at a broader level, developing a demographic profile of drug usage may provide us with some insight into the most likely causal pathways of relevance to this behaviour.

Since cannabis is the *only* drug for which we have a substantial proportion of users across both samples and all locations, any discussion relating to results pooled across the whole range of drug types will relate largely to the use of cannabis. However, it should be noted that the demographic variation shown by cannabis usage *was* matched to a greater or lesser extent by other drug types. To make these links between drug types more explicit we have again compared across the three drug groups outlined earlier and where usage levels were sufficiently high to provide information also on other *individual* drugs we have considered in greater detail the extent to which these mimic the demographic patterns shown by cannabis.

The particular aspects of demography considered here are age, gender, socioeconomic status (as defined by the Office of Population Censuses and Surveys: OPCS), ethnicity and both lifetime and present employment status. Summary values for drug usage within these demographic categories are given by sample type in Tables 3.1-3.7 in Appendix 1 and summary statistics for variation within these demographic groups are given by location in Tables 3.8-3.15 in Appendix 1.

Age and drug usage

The major factor which differentiates patterns of drug usage is age - young people are more likely to use drugs.

Statistically significant differences between different age groups were noted for four of the five self-report items in all four locations. Injecting usage was the only item *not* to show any significant differences across age groups and it is worth bearing in mind that the absolute numbers of injecting users in each location were very low. Since for obvious reasons the age groups comprising the booster sample were somewhat restricted, it is not surprising that for most drug usage items little significant variation was shown across age groups in this sample. Consequently, although there *were* some - albeit marginally - significant differences across

Figure 3.1
Lifetime drug usage by age group
Main sample

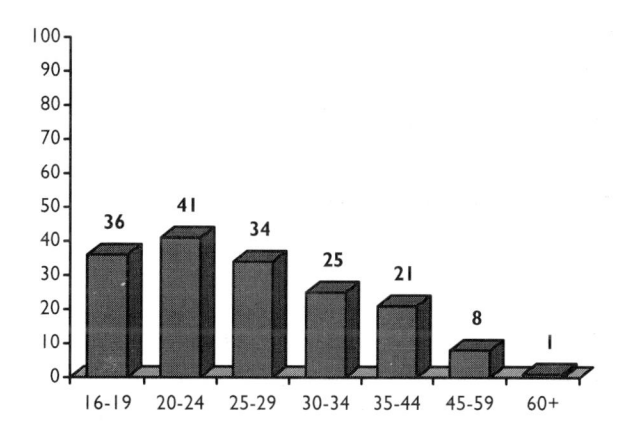

Age group	%
16-19	36
20-24	41
25-29	34
30-34	25
35-44	21
45-59	8
60+	1

Booster sample

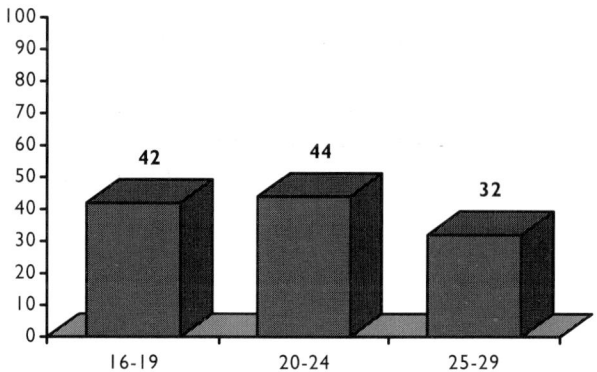

Age group	%
16-19	42
20-24	44
25-29	32

*Percentage of respondents in each age group who had **ever** used an unprescribed drug (based on percentages averaged across the four locations)*

age groups in two of the four booster sample locations, we have chosen not to discuss these here. For interested readers, these differences are outlined in the Tables cited above and the booster sample age profile for lifetime and recent drug prevalence is given in the text. Table 3.20 in Appendix 1 gives a summary of the significant differences between our main and booster samples for respondents aged under 29.

Looking at Figure 3.1, it can be seen that there are two clear splits in the *lifetime* prevalence of drug usage. These separate the under 30s from their *older* counterparts and the 45+ group from their *younger* counterparts. The single most prominent drug using group in the main samples being aged under 24. Since we unfortunately have no reliable baseline data from previous research, we cannot say whether the higher prevalence of drug usage in the younger age groups is indicative of any real shift in drug usage across time. Given that social mores regarding drug usage have altered substantially in recent history and recall across an expanse of time is in any case rarely completely accurate, it may simply be that the older individuals in our sample are misrepresenting their lifetime drug usage. On the other hand, it may be that there *was* a significant change in the profile of drug usage for those born after around 1948. This would certainly match popular assumptions regarding patterns of drug usage in the late 1960s and early 1970s when these individual would have been in their late teens or early 20s.

Assuming that people are accurately representing at least their *present* drug using behaviour we *can* conclude from the data that at any one point in time younger individuals are far more likely than older individuals to be using unprescribed drugs. As Figure 3.2 indicates, the decline in drug usage from younger to older respondents is a smooth progression from 16 to 60 for usage *within the last year*. Some locational variation in the *most* prominent drug using age group was noted, for both lifetime usage and recent drug usage. In Bradford and Glasgow, the 16-19 year olds were the single group most likely to report drug usage. In Nottingham, the 25-29 year olds were the most likely to report *lifetime* usage of a drug, but the 16-19 and 20-24 year olds were more likely to report using a drug *recently*. Lewisham displayed the *oldest* overall profile of drug users, with 20-24 and 30-34 year olds having an equivalently high level of usage for both the lifetime prevalence and recent prevalence items. These differences between the locations may be a function of external pressures such as the types of drug most readily obtained, or they may be the result of factors intrinsic to a location, for example cultural variations in drug usage. Assuming such

Figure 3.2
Drug usage within the last year by age group

Main sample

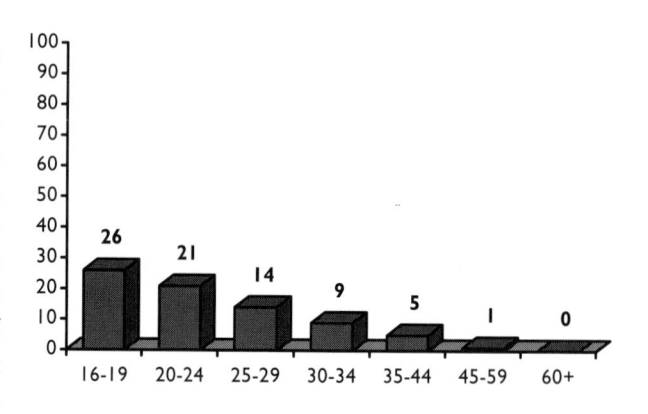

Age	%
16-19	26
20-24	21
25-29	14
30-34	9
35-44	5
45-59	1
60+	0

Booster sample

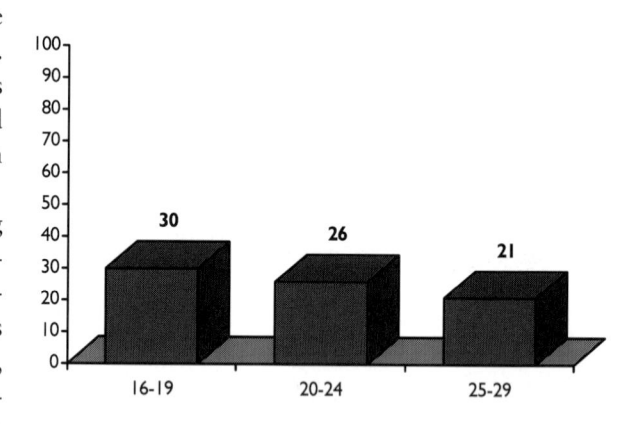

Age	%
16-19	30
20-24	26
25-29	21

Percentage of respondents in each age group who had used an unprescribed drug **within the last year** (based on percentages averaged across the four locations)

variation to hold across time it would be of interest to investigate further into the possible causal mechanisms operating here.

Frequency of usage also showed a clear decline from younger to older age groups, as Figure 3.3 demonstrates. In all four locations the 16-19 year olds were the single group most likely to use drugs with a frequency greater than or equal to monthly. It should be borne in mind here that the absolute numbers of recent drug users within at least the two oldest age groups were very low, so data on frequency of usage is more reliable for the younger and mid-range age categories.

Figure 3.3
Frequency of usage by age group: Main sample

Age group	%
%16-19	14
%20-24	8
%25-29	6
%30-34	4
%35-44	1
%45-59	0
%60+	0

Percentage of recent drug users in each age group using their drug with a frequency of greater than or equal to monthly, averaged across location

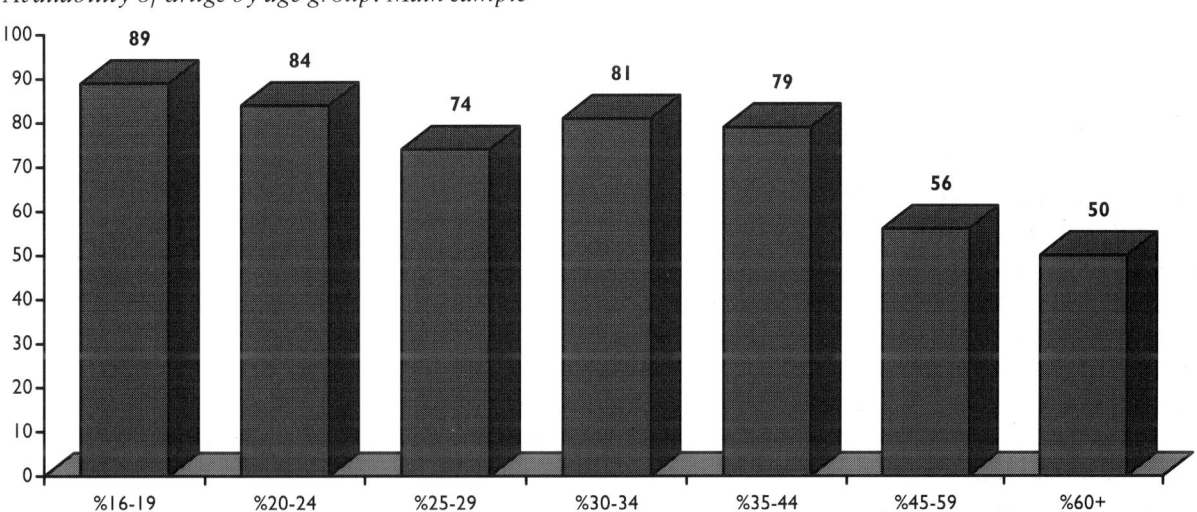

Figure 3.4
Availability of drugs by age group: Main sample

Age group	%
%16-19	89
%20-24	84
%25-29	74
%30-34	81
%35-44	79
%45-59	56
%60+	50

Percentage of recent drug users in each age group stating that they could readily obtain their drug(s) of choice in their city or borough, averaged across location

The tendency of the youngest age group in our sample to take drugs with a greater frequency than older drug users was apparently matched by their ability to obtain drugs. As Figure 3.4 indicates, there was a modest - but in all locations highly significant in statistical terms - tendency for 16-19 year olds to be the group *most* confident in their ability to obtain drugs locally. This point again emphasises the need at least to reinforce preventive activities on the supply side with demand oriented measures. Supply side restrictions alone do not seem to have created any impression amongst even the youngest groups that drugs are difficult to obtain.

The prominence of younger age groups in drug usage was not a trend restricted to cannabis. As Figure 3.5 demonstrates, they were also the most prominent users of both the 'opiate' and 'non-opiate' drug groups we looked at. The age variation shown for these two drug groups was statistically significant in the majority of locations, with the exception of Nottingham in the case of 'opiates' and Bradford in the case of 'non-opiates'. In the case of Nottingham at least, this is probably the consequence of low numbers of recent drug users in the relevant category rather than an indication of the true picture. Whilst under 30 year olds were the most prominent users of virtually *all* drug types, some variation was noted across drug type. The 16-19 age group were the most prominent users of both cannabis and 'non-opiates', but the most prominent user group for 'opiates' were the 25-29 year olds. Similar slight variations appeared for a number of individual drug types - for example, 'pills', tranquillizers and cocaine which were favoured by an older age group, but in the main the numbers of recent users precluded any statistical analysis of these differences.

Figure 3.5
Usage of different drug types by age group: Main sample

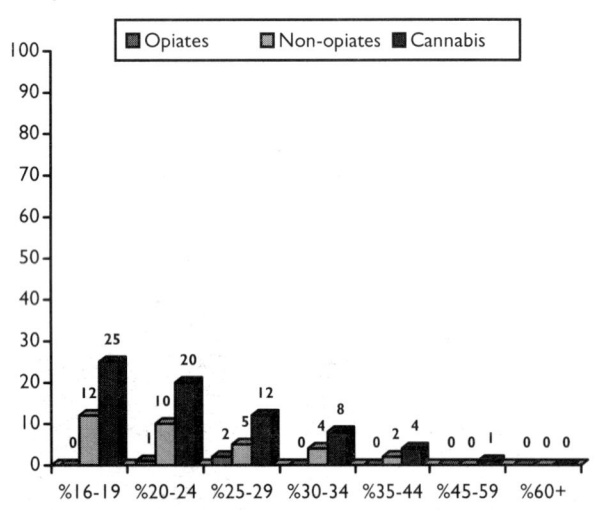

[Bar chart showing % of respondents by age group (16-19, 20-24, 25-29, 30-34, 35-44, 45-59, 60+) for Opiates, Non-opiates, and Cannabis. Values: 16-19: 0, 12, 25; 20-24: 1, 10, 20; 25-29: 2, 5, 12; 30-34: 0, 4, 8; 35-44: 0, 2, 4; 45-59: 0, 0, 1; 60+: 0, 0, 0]

*Percentage of respondents in each age category who had used each of the three drug types **within the last year**, averaged across location*

In summary, the clear finding for all four main sample locations is that age and drug usage are very much linked, with younger people showing higher levels of both recent and lifetime usage for a broad range of drugs. Unfortunately, since there is a paucity of previous general population surveys, we cannot comment directly on any *changing* trends in the age groups most likely to use drugs. We cannot say, for example, whether the lifetime figures cited are a function of people using drugs *only* whilst in their youth. Nor can we say whether drug usage amongst the young is now higher than in previous decades or whether young people are simply more likely to admit drug usage now or to have a greater chance of recalling it because is it is a more recent experience for them. Since there are clear disparities in drug usage across age groups even within a relatively small distribution - for example between 20 and 30 year olds - it would definitely be worth joining both the United States and other European countries in carrying out a general population drug usage survey every few years in an effort to answer such questions as these.

Gender and drug usage

Whilst gender differences in drug usage were also very much apparent in our survey, as would be expected on the basis of most previous research into risk-taking behaviours in general, they were for the most part less extreme than the equivalent differences between age groups. Gender differences were also dependent to a greater extent on location and drug type. That having

Figure 3.6
Lifetime drug usage by gender

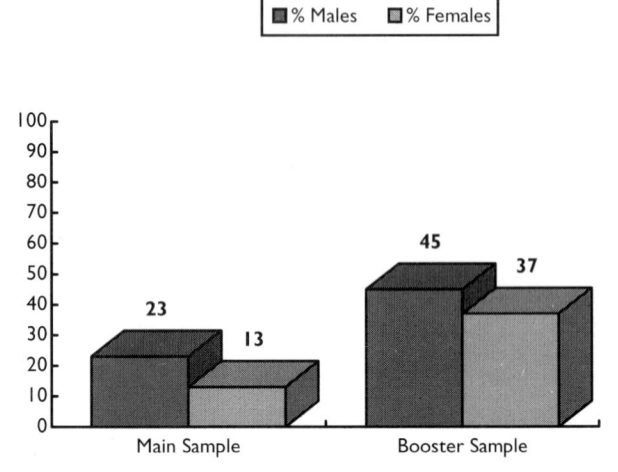

[Bar chart showing % Males and % Females for Main Sample (23, 13) and Booster Sample (45, 37)]

*Percentage of male and female respondents who had **ever** used an unprescribed drug (based on percentages averaged across the four locations)*

been said, males proved, with very few exceptions, to be most prone to drug usage, whether this was measured in terms of prevalence or mode of usage.

In all four main samples, a significantly higher proportion of males than females reported ever having used an unprescribed drug. As can be seen from Figure 3.6, this pattern was broadly matched by gender differences in the booster sample. Some locational variation was again noted, however, with the profile of main sample females being closer to that of males in Glasgow and Bradford than was the case in either Lewisham or Nottingham. Furthermore, the female profile in *all* booster sample locations was much closer to that of males than was the case in the main sample and in Bradford's booster sample no significant gender differences in lifetime usage were noted.

WHAT KINDS OF PEOPLE USE DRUGS?

Figure 3.7
Drug usage within the last year by gender

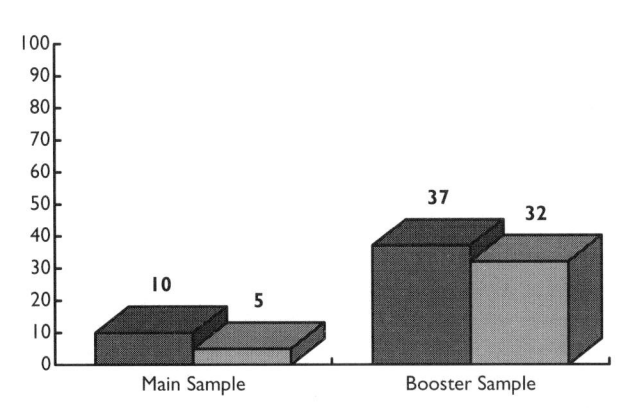

[Bar chart: % Males vs % Females. Main Sample: 10, 5. Booster Sample: 37, 32]

*Percentage of male and female respondents who had used an unprescribed drug **within the last year** (based on percentages averaged across the four locations)*

The pattern found for lifetime usage held also for recent drug usage in three of the four locations in both types of sample (Figure 3.7). The exceptions here being Glasgow in the main sample and Lewisham in the booster sample. As with lifetime usage, females in the booster sample were closer to their male counterparts than was the case in the main sample.

Figure 3.8
Frequency of drug usage by gender

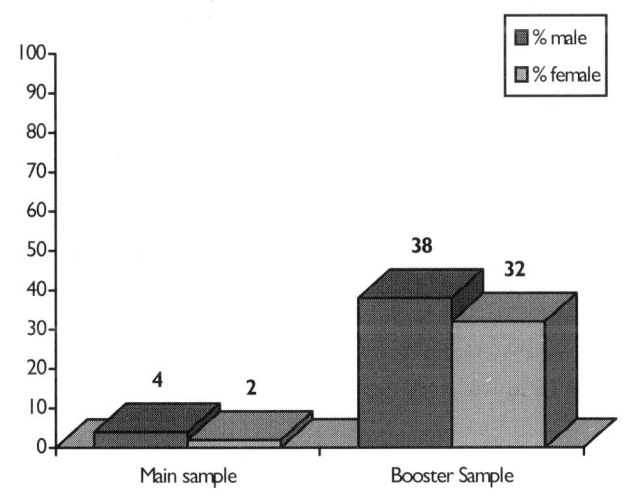

[Bar chart: % male vs % female. Main sample: 4, 2. Booster Sample: 38, 32]

Percentage of recent users of a drug using their drug with a frequency greater than or equal to monthly, split by sample and gender, averaged across locations

Whilst in general males were also the more frequent users of a drug, the pattern for frequency of drug usage was more equivocal and showed an even greater dependence on location than the previous two measures of drug usage. In the main sample, statistically significant gender differences were found in Nottingham and Lewisham, but Bradford and Glasgow showed no disparity between the genders. In the booster sample the - again slightly *less* extreme differences - between the genders were on the other hand *only* noted in Glasgow and Bradford. The percentage disparity found between the genders, averaged across location, is shown for both sample types in Figure 3.8

As with age trends in drug usage, the distinctions noted above between the genders did not stretch in most cases to injecting usage. The *only* significant difference in any location or sample was for the main sample in

Figure 3.9
Availability of drugs by gender

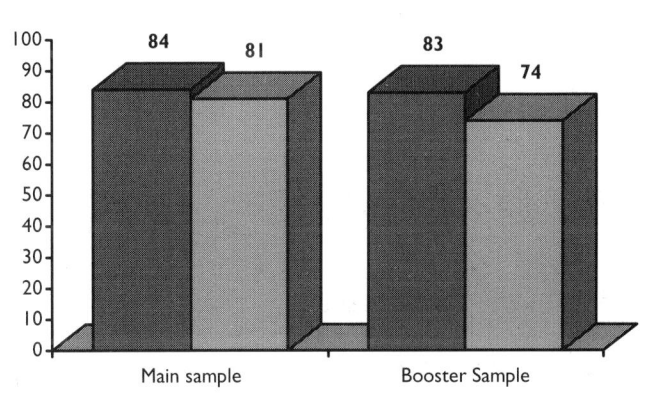

[Bar chart: % male vs % female. Main sample: 84, 81. Booster Sample: 83, 74]

Percentage of recent drug users stating that their drug of choice was readily available in their city or borough, split by sample and gender, averaged across location

Lewisham. Here, females were found to be less likely than males to exhibit this type of risk taking behaviour. It is important to remember here that the lack of any disparity in all other locations is almost certainly due to the low absolute numbers of injecting users within our sample.

Perhaps unexpectedly, gender differences in prevalence measures of drug usage were largely matched by differences in self-report *availability* of drugs. Percentage gender differences in the availability of drugs, averaged across location, are summarised in Figure 3.9. In all main sample locations, with the exception of Bradford, females were significantly *less* likely to state that drugs were readily available. The pattern was slightly more equivocal in the booster sample, but in Nottingham and Glasgow at least, females were still less likely to feel confident in their ability to obtain drugs. It is of course impossible to say whether these findings relate to

Figure 3.10
Usage of different drug types by gender

	% male	% female
Main sample: Cannabis	9	4
Booster Sample: Cannabis	31	19
Main sample: Non-opiates	5	1
Booster sample: Non-opiates	18	9

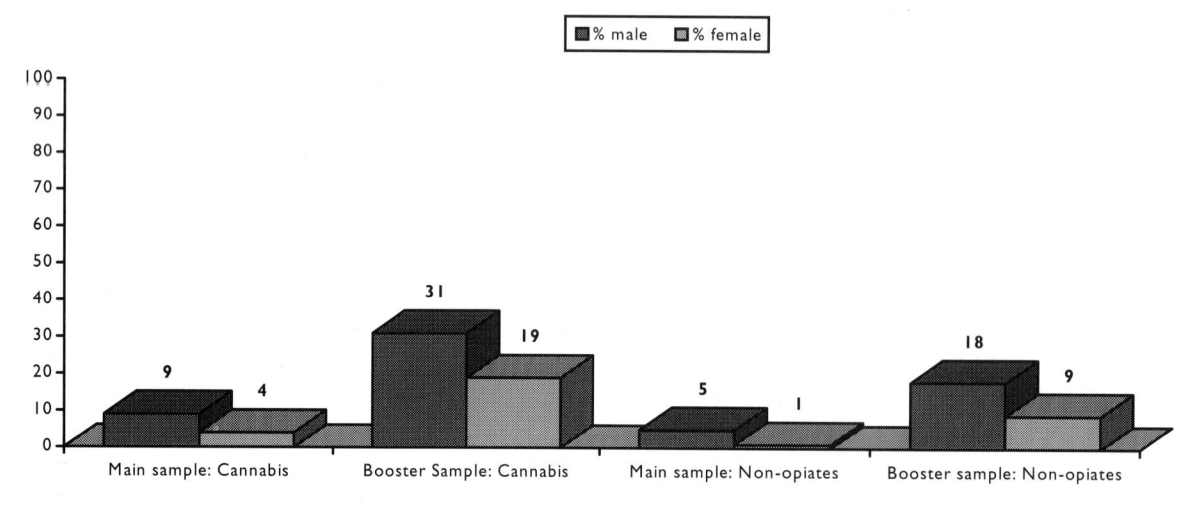

Percentage of respondents taking cannabis or non-opiates within the last year by sample and gender, averaged across location

actual differences in drugs supply or whether one gender is simply drawing a less accurate picture than the other. Availability is likely to be strongly linked with factors other than the distribution of drugs as such. It may, for example, be linked strongly with friendship networks. Whatever the cause of the distinction between the genders in our sample, much more detailed research into the demographics of drugs distribution would be worthwhile.

Whilst the gender differences in prevalence held for the vast majority of drugs considered individually, they did not hold for the combined sub-group of 'opiates'. Only Lewisham's main sample showed *any* statistically significant gender differences for this group of drugs, although it is worth pointing out that here the pattern followed was again for males to be more prevalent users than females. The absolute number of 'opiate' users was admittedly fairly small, but the general trend seemed to be for cannabis and 'non-opiate' usage (summarised in Figure 3.10) to match overall gender differences in prevalence more closely than 'opiate' usage. Having said which, even the more consistent patterns shown by cannabis and 'non-opiates' were dependent to a greater extent on location than were the comparable age differences discussed earlier. For example, no significant gender differences were noted for cannabis usage in Glasgow's main sample and no significant differences were noted for either cannabis or 'non-opiate' usage in Lewisham's booster sample.

In summary, whilst gender differences were not as extreme as age differences and seemed more susceptible to locational variation, they were still an important covariate of drug usage. Men were more likely to have used drugs and to be using drugs than women. They were also more likely to think of drugs as easily available. Whilst this effect may be the consequence of a lack of knowledge or certainty in one or other gender, it might be worth following through in greater detail in the event that it proves to be a 'real' phenomenon matched by similar age differences in availability.

Socioeconomic status and drug usage

Socioeconomic status is becoming increasingly controversial as a means of demographic labelling. Concern about its validity centres both around the political impact of such labels and around the rather amorphous nature of the concept itself, which, by definition, is based partly on economic and partly on social characteristics. This debate is of particular relevance to our booster sample, since socioeconomic status as presently defined is a very difficult concept to use in relation to young people. The traditional measure, which we followed, uses the socioeconomic status of the head of the household as a proxy for the socioeconomic status of young people. This is something of a problem given that, by the time young people have left education, their own status may vary considerably from that of the head of the household, even assuming that they are still living at home. Our justification for using standard socioeconomic classifications for the Household Survey is that, however inadequate the concept may seem, it remains for the present a prominent variable in most analyses of illicit behaviour and it is similarly important to the development of social policy. As a consequence we are tied to using it if we wish our data either to be compared to other data or to be used in directing policy.

In the event, the majority of the differences noted between standardly defined socioeconomic groups in our sample did *not* reach statistical significance. Patterns of variation in drug usage based on socioeconomic status were also less consistent than those noted for either age or gender, showing a greater dependence on drug type, location and on the measure of usage considered. Furthermore, the limited range of effects which *were* consistent across sample type and/or location were less marked than comparable gender or age effects. This

Figure 3.11
Lifetime drug usage by socioeconomic status

Main sample

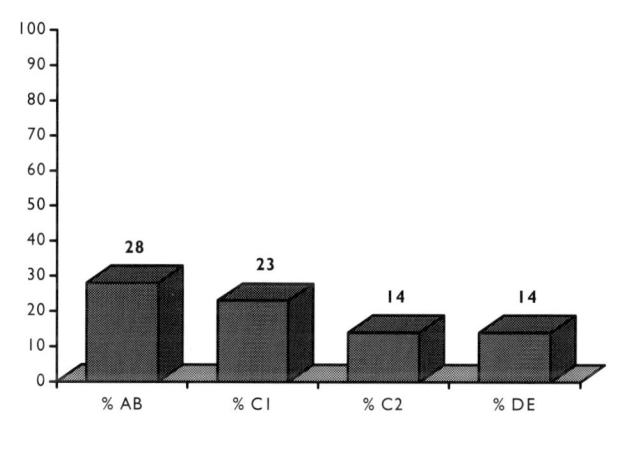

[Bar chart: % AB = 28, % C1 = 23, % C2 = 14, % DE = 14]

Booster sample

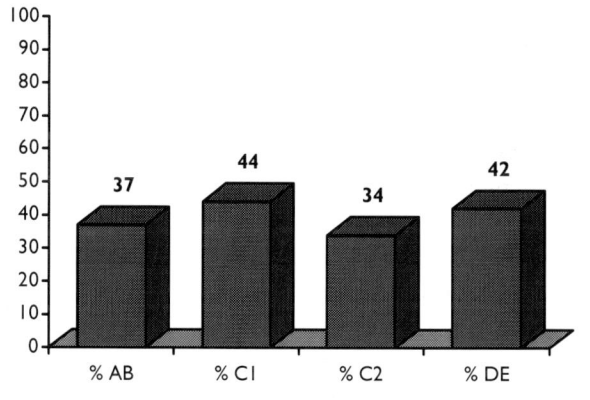

[Bar chart: % AB = 37, % C1 = 44, % C2 = 34, % DE = 42]

*Percentage of respondents in each socioeconomic group who had **ever** used an unprescribed drug (based on percentages averaged across the four locations)*

profile is predictable in the case of the booster sample, since here the majority of respondents stemmed from roughly the same socioeconomic groups, so we will restrict most of the present discussion to our main sample.

In the main sample, the socioeconomic pattern we observed was not entirely what the literature would predict. Previous studies, particularly those focusing on networks of known users, have emphasised drug usage amongst those in lower status socioeconomic groups, notably the DE group. Drugs prevention has also, to date, focused on these groups. Our prevalence data did not generally match this expected pattern. With regard to lifetime drug usage, summarised in Figure 3.11, respondents in the AB and C1 socioeconomic groups proved to be the most prominent users in three of the main sample locations, the exception being Bradford, where no significant differences were observed.

As demonstrated by Figure 3.12, this disparity between expectations based on the literature and the actual profile of our data was broadly maintained for drug usage within the last year. However, for this latter measure of prevalence the differences observed only reached statistical significance in two main sample locations, namely Nottingham and Lewisham. Since there has been such emphasis on the DE group in drugs related work, it is worth commenting on general trends as well as on those differences which actually reached statistically significance. Taking the data as a whole, the general trend observed across *all* main sample locations suggests that if our findings are accurate there will be at any given point in time a greater preponderance of *higher* socioeconomic status drug users in the population. One interesting aspect of this finding being that, although it did not match expectations from the drugs literature, it did appear from our discussions with drugs professionals to have a close match with experience 'on the ground'.

Whilst it is entirely possible that the bulk of the variance discussed above is accounted for by cannabis usage - which is now generally acknowledged to be prominent in higher socioeconomic status groups - it should be noted that a range of individual drugs other than cannabis showed the same pattern. In two locations - namely Lewisham and Nottingham - a *range* of 'non-opiate' drugs, including amphetamines, amyl nitrite and psilocybin, were also significantly more likely to be used by the AB and C1 groups. Furthermore, the general trend across this group of drugs in all four locations and both main and booster samples was for prevalence in most cases to be greatest amongst the AB and C1 groups. With regard to 'opiates', significant differences in this direction were also noted for cocaine, although *not* for either crack or heroin.

Figure 3.12
Drug usage within the last year by socioeconomic status

Main sample

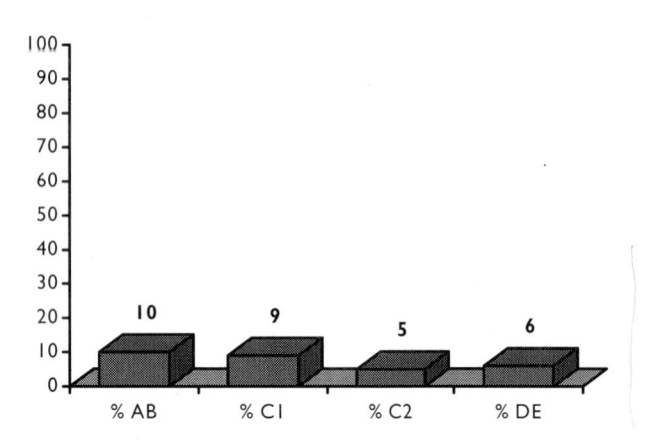

Group	%
% AB	10
% C1	9
% C2	5
% DE	6

Booster sample

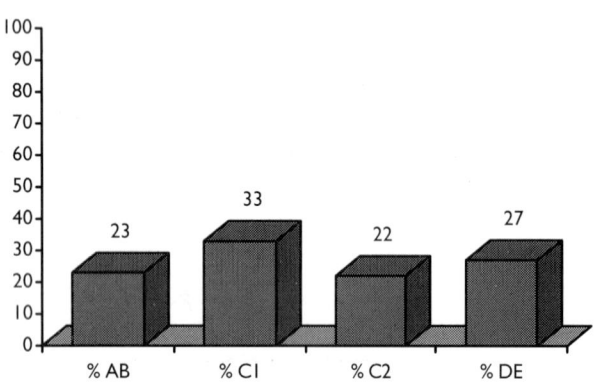

Group	%
% AB	23
% C1	33
% C2	22
% DE	27

*Percentage of respondents in each socioeconomic group who had used an unprescribed drug **within the last year** (based on percentages averaged across the four locations)*

We suspect that the apparent disparity between the above findings and much of the discussion regarding socioeconomic groups in the literature and in drugs prevention work stems from a general tendency to conflate *prevalence* with *mode of usage*. Much of the literature, perhaps not surprisingly in the absence of previous major prevalence studies in Britain, concentrates on frequent or injecting usage and on the use of 'opiates', in particular crack and heroin. Whilst we do not have sufficient numbers of 'problematic' users in the present survey to adequately discuss socioeconomic differences in these modes of usage, the general trends observed in our data *were* for very frequent and injecting usage to be more prominent in the C2 and DE groups. Similarly, heroin tended to be a more prominent drug amongst these socioeconomic groups. This distinction between the patterns observed for prevalence and mode of usage supports the notion that one needs to put any disparities between the socioeconomic groups in context, rather than assuming that drug usage is a unitary phenomenon.

Whilst for the most part any distinctions in availability noted between the socioeconomic groups were not statistically significant, two locations in the main sample did show significant disparity. In Nottingham and Lewisham, socioeconomic groups C2 and DE were rather more likely to state that they could readily obtain their drug of choice in the city or borough than were the AB and C1 groups. Broadly speaking, however, any distinctions between the socioeconomic groups tended to be very much dependent on the individual drug considered. Again, this suggests that more detailed work on the demography of drugs distribution might be of interest.

In summary, our data suggest that if *prevalence* is at issue, the higher status socioeconomic groups are the most prominent in drug usage. This finding is in contrast to previous work using different survey methods. Prior emphasis on the C2 and DE groups both in the literature and in drugs prevention work may be justified in terms of *modes* of usage rather than prevalence as such. Frequent or injecting usage may, for example, hold greater prominence in the lower status socioeconomic groups, although we cannot confirm this with the present data set. Nevertheless, our results suggest that drugs prevention work needs to place more emphasis on higher status socio-economic groups if we are to reduce the prevalence of drug usage. Perhaps the most important point to be drawn from this is that both research and policy must distinguish between usage as such and modes of usage if we are to obtain a realistic picture of drug using behaviour.

Ethnicity and drug usage

Ethnicity is a concept which is at least as controversial as socioeconomic classification. Since the vast majority of the drugs literature has interpreted ethnicity in the light of historical definitions based on the genetic concept of 'race' we have also followed this typology in order to make comparisons feasible, rather than following the more recent move towards cultural definitions of ethnicity. Having said which, it is important to note that, unlike the case for socioeconomic status, membership of a specified ethnic group was in our survey determined on the basis of *self-assignment* to given categories.

The distribution of ethnic minorities in our sample is outlined in Table A3.7 in Appendix 3. As this data readily demonstrates, the ethnic mix in our survey is such that meaningful statistical analyses can only be carried using the very broadly defined groups 'white', 'black' 'asian' and 'other'. Furthermore, for *location specific* analyses the spread of ethnic groups is such that only two locations (Lewisham and Bradford) are of any real value in comparing statistical differences between ethnic groups. Similarly, within these locations it is also only viable to compare between 'white' respondents and respondents from the single most prominent ethnic minority group, 'black' respondents in the case of Lewisham and 'Asian' respondents in the case of Bradford. This has meant that for our location based analyses we were unable to compare *across* ethnic minorities. Although in the multivariate analyses which we will discuss later we *were* able to do so, since in this context data from the four locations could be pooled, controlling for location identity. Whilst the absolute numbers of respondents from ethnic minorities were quite low within the sample as a whole, it is very important to note that for the analyses discussed here we had perfectly adequate numbers of respondents from ethnic minority groups to justify the conclusions reached. Indeed, we had rather larger numbers of ethnic minority respondents than the broad range of previous studies which have highlighted ethnicity as a covariate of drug usage. Although here we consider only those results which can be validated in statistical terms, the interested reader will find detailed figures for ethnicity and drug usage based on data for all four locations in Appendix 1.

Whilst we have in the foregoing discussions chosen to highlight only significant *differences*, we will in the case of ethnicity emphasise also any *failure* to find significant differences. We take this approach to the data because there is in the literature a marked emphasis on minority ethnic groups as the primary drug users. Any failure to find substantial differences between ethnic groups in this context is therefore of some importance. Particularly since the British emphasis on minority groups does not match with empirical findings relating to ethnicity and drug usage derived from other European countries.

From Figures 3.13 and 3.14 it can readily be seen that our data for lifetime drug usage matches more closely the broader European picture than that generally presented in the British literature. In Lewisham, no significant differences were observed for main sample lifetime drug usage, whilst in the booster sample a statistically significant finding was that *white* respondents were *more* likely to have used drugs than their black counterparts. This data is particularly interesting, in that the drugs professionals we talked to in Lewisham felt that it gave an accurate representation of drugs prevalence within their area.

Figure 3.14
Lifetime drug usage by ethnic group: Bradford

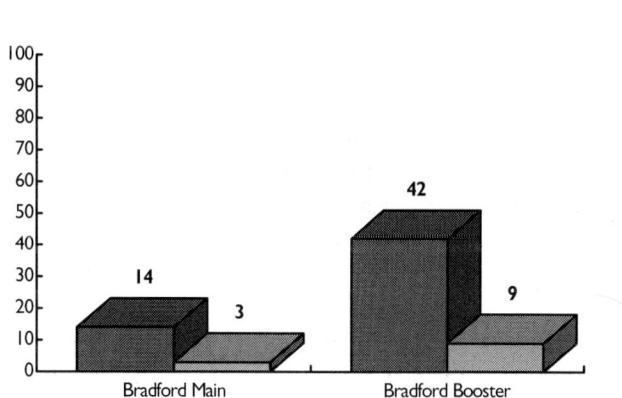

Figure 3.13
Lifetime drug usage by ethnic group: Lewisham

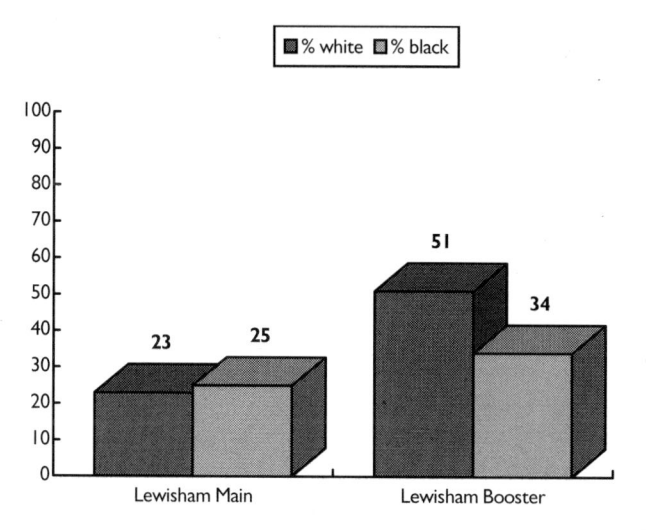

Percentage of respondents in each ethnic group who had **ever** used an unprescribed drug

Percentage of respondents in each ethnic group who had **ever** used an unprescribed drug

In Bradford, where the comparison drawn was between white and Asian rather than white and black, a strong disparity between ethnic groups was shown for lifetime drug usage in *both* main and booster samples.

In both samples a statistically significant finding was that white respondents were *more* likely than Asian respondents to have used an unprescribed drug. Again, the distinction was stronger within the booster sample than within the main sample. It should be noted here that drugs professionals working in Bradford were concerned that any problem of drug usage in the Asian community might be *under* estimated by these figures, since the primary users in this ethnic group were seen by them to be under-16 year olds, who of course were not represented in our survey. Having said which, any concomitant under-representation within the age groups which *were* included in our survey would have to be fairly extreme to render non-significant the white/Asian divide noted here.

Figure 3.15
Drug usage within the last year by ethnic group: Lewisham

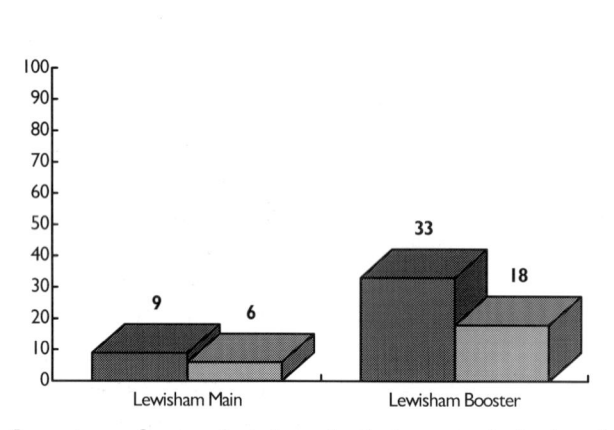

[Bar chart showing: Lewisham Main – % white: 9, % black: 6; Lewisham Booster – % white: 33, % black: 18]

Percentage of respondents in each ethnic group who had used an unprescribed drug **within the last year**

The patterns noted for recent drug usage were broadly similar to those noted for lifetime usage (cf. Figures 3.15 and 3.16). In Lewisham, no significant differences were noted between white and black respondents in the main sample, but in the booster sample the finding was that white respondents were significantly *more* likely than black respondents to have taken an unprescribed drug within the last year. This pattern was matched exactly in Bradford, where of course the comparison was between white respondents and Asian respondents.

Whilst the number of recent users of any drug who represented an ethnic minority were too small to make *location based* comparisons for mode of usage or preference for different drug types meaningful, it is worth noting the general trend *across* locations. This suggested, as will be discussed in more detail in the context

Figure 3.16
Drug usage within the last year by ethnic group: Bradford

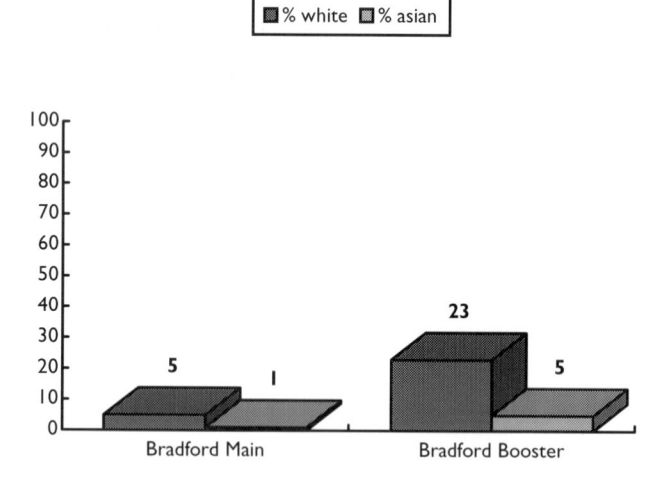

[Bar chart showing: Bradford Main – % white: 5, % asian: 1; Bradford Booster – % white: 23, % asian: 5]

Percentage of respondents in each ethnic group who had used an unprescribed drug **within the last year**

of our multivariate analyses, that white respondents were the primary user group in terms of frequency of usage for all drugs other than cannabis. They also appeared from their self-report estimates of availability to have more ready access to a range of drugs than respondents in ethnic minorities. Whilst the absolute numbers of injecting users are too low to make any meaningful assessment of the distribution of ethnic groups on this mode of usage variable, the general profile of usage suggests that the prevalence/mode of usage distinction outlined earlier for socioeconomic status is unlikely to be of relevance in explaining the disparity between our results and earlier studies in the context of ethnicity.

It is important to note that whilst there *were* some demographic differences between ethnic groups in the locations considered even these could not have accounted for the disparity found between white respondents and respondents from ethnic minorities. Most of the significant demographic differences between the two groups were such as to predispose the ethnic minority groups *towards* drug usage. That is, they were more likely to be young, male and unemployed than their white counterparts—all factors which in themselves appear to promote drug usage. Whilst they were also significantly more likely to be of lower status socioeconomic groups, the multivariate analyses we will discuss later in this chapter confirm that the distinctions noted here between white respondents and black respondents are *independent* even of this demographic distinction.

We would argue that what *has* made the difference is, again, the type of methodology used in our survey. In the majority of previous studies addressing differences between ethnic groups, sampling has not been made on a random population basis. Examples of the type of methodologies which have formed the standard methods of data collection for drug usage surveys are: snowballing from one or more contact drug users (cf. Bean and Pearson 1992), collection of agency data (e.g. Unell *op cit*.), police arrest and conviction data (cf. Edwards 1981) and health service statistics (e.g. Ghodse and Rawson 1978). Whilst providing valuable information for a range of purposes, none of these modes of data collection are ideal for establishing accurate demographic profiles of drug usage within the population.

The profile of demographic trends established by snowballing techniques is obviously highly dependent on the identity of the initial contacts used. Bean and Pearson (*op cit*) have, for example, suggested a concentration of crack usage amongst the Afro-Caribbean population of Nottingham. However, they based this assumption on snowballing data in which the identity of the contacts was not specified. If the contacts themselves were Afro-Caribbean it is perhaps not surprising that their associates should also stem from this ethnic group. Agency data, as noted earlier, is prone to over-represent 'problematic' drug users and, more importantly in the present context, it is also known to over-represent lower status socioeconomic groups, since a disproportionate number of agencies are sited in the poorer areas. Ethnic minority groups are of course in turn over-represented within the lower socioeconomic status groups. Similarly, they are over-represented, for whatever reason, in arrest, conviction and health service data.

Given the above, it is of particular interest that the findings from our survey on ethnicity and drug usage match those for other European studies (e.g. Sandwijk et al. 1991) which themselves used random population sampling techniques. Although the specific ethnic groups considered in our survey did not match exactly those sampled in the other European work, this does illustrate the need to take account of sampling methodology when interpreting and comparing results, notably where these have quite major implications for such issues as social policy. In the same vein it is worth adding that the *patterns* of drug usage suggested by surveys in the United States, where the type of minority ethnic groups looked at do match those in our sample quite closely, are also similar to the patterns shown by our data, with blacks having roughly equivalent prevalence rates to whites and other ethnic minorities showing rather lower levels of drug usage.

In summary, our findings for ethnicity and drug usage challenge the findings of previous research. Specifically, we found that ethnic minorities in general were not the primary users of unprescribed drugs. Even the black ethnic groups, which have previously been seen as prominent in drug usage matched rather than exceeded the majority white group in terms of the prevalence of drug usage. Whilst we do *not* claim that the present study should be regarded in any way as definitive on this issue, we would suggest that future work on demographic variance in general and ethnicity in particular use methodologies which are suited to interpretation at a general population level.

Employment and drug usage

An individual's experience of employment and his or her ability to find paid employment are aspects of demography which have been associated with drug usage in a variety of different ways within the literature. The association has been drawn both directly and indirectly, in the latter case using unemployment or inappropriate employment as a measure of economic, social or psychological deprivation. Specific empirical outcomes drawn from this work suggest that unemployment *per se* leads to the use of unprescribed drugs (Peck and Plant 1986), that 'employment' outside the accepted bounds of society leads to unprescribed drug usage (Auld et al. 1986) and that employment under stressful or tedious conditions also leads to drug usage (Mensch and Kandel 1988).

The two aspects of employment addressed in the present study are rather more basic than the broad range of previous studies on employment and drug use. We simply posed the question of whether either a respondent's *lifetime* experience of employment (ie. whether they had ever been employed in a paid full-time or part-time occupation) or their *present* experience of employment (whether they were in a paid full-time or part-time occupation at the time of the interview) appeared to have any effect on their likelihood of using unprescribed drugs. Again, the salient advantage of our survey in this context is simply that it *is* a general population survey.

Whilst in this context the main sample is the most appropriate sample to consider, since it has been selected to represent the general population, we have included values for the booster sample in the discussion below for comparative purposes. The booster sample was of some value here, since it was entirely possible that the experience of employment amongst a younger and relatively more 'deprived' group of individuals might have a different effect to that seen in the general population. Note that respondents stating that they were students or house-parents at the time of the interview were excluded from any analyses involving present employment, since it is not altogether clear how one would classify these individuals in employment terms.

Figure 3.17
Lifetime drug usage and present employment

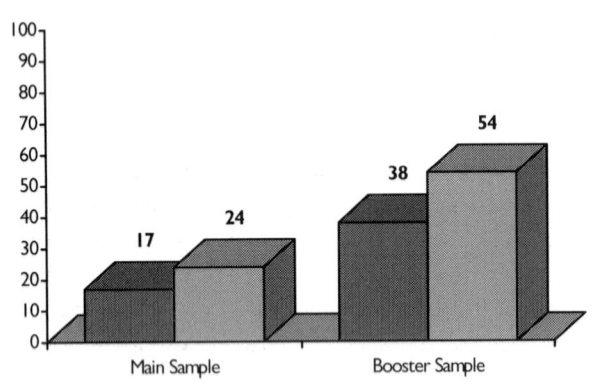

Percentage of respondents in each employment category who had **ever** taken an unprescribed drug, split by sample, averaged across location

Whilst for most drug usage items, a respondent's *lifetime* employment experience did *not* appear to influence their likelihood of drug usage, *present* employment status was a powerful predictor of likely drug usage. This will be the aspect of employment discussed in greatest detail below. As with socioeconomic status and, to a lesser extent, gender, the strength of any link between employment and drug usage was dependent on location.

As Figure 3.17 demonstrates, the overall disparity between employed and *un*employed respondents, notably in the booster sample, was quite marked. Presently unemployed respondents were more likely to state that they had during their *lifetime* used an unprescribed drug. Whilst the general trend was consistent across locations, the link between unemployment and lifetime drug usage only reached statistical significance for Glasgow's main sample and Lewisham and Bradford's booster samples.

Figure 3.18
Recent drug usage and present employment

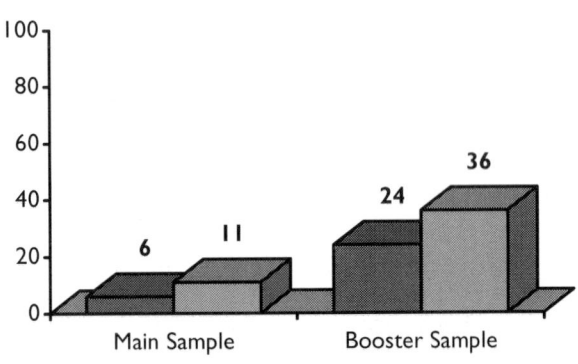

Percentage of respondents in each employment category who had taken an unprescribed drug **within the last year**, split by sample, averaged across location

A slightly less extreme, but nonetheless marked disparity between employed and unemployed respondents was noted for *recent* drug usage. Again, as Figure 3.18 indicates, *un*employed respondents were more likely to acknowledge drug usage than employed respondents. This trend reached statistical significance in a broader range of locations than had been the case for lifetime drug usage, within both main *and* booster samples. Specifically, the link between unemployment and recent drug usage reached significance for both main and booster samples in Lewisham and Bradford whilst in Nottingham it reached significance for the booster sample alone.

Turning to modes of drug usage, present employment proved to be one of the most interesting demographic variables. It was the only demographic variable to link with frequent drug usage across a *range* of booster sample locations and similarly the *only* variable to show a statistically significant link with injecting usage in main sample locations. Figure 3.19 summarises the data for frequency of usage and Figure 3.20 for injecting usage.

Although the general trend in the main samples was for presently unemployed respondents to show a greater likelihood of *frequent* drug usage than employed respondents, this link only reached statistical significance in Bradford's main sample. In the booster sample, the strength of the effect was less dependent on location, *failing* to reach significance only in Glasgow. The most striking disparity between employed and unemployed was in injecting usage. The general trend

Figure 3.19
Frequency of drug usage and present employment

[Bar chart showing % employed and % not employed. Main Sample: 3, 6. Booster Sample: 11, 22.]

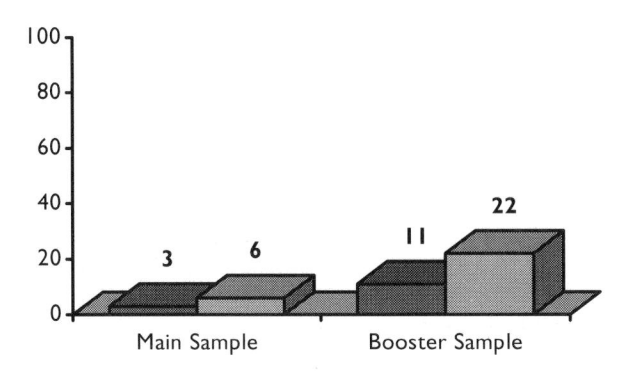

Percentages of respondents in each employment category who stated that they were taking their drug(s) of choice with a frequency greater then or equal to monthly, split by sample, averaged across location

Figure 3.20
Injecting drug usage and present employment: Main sample

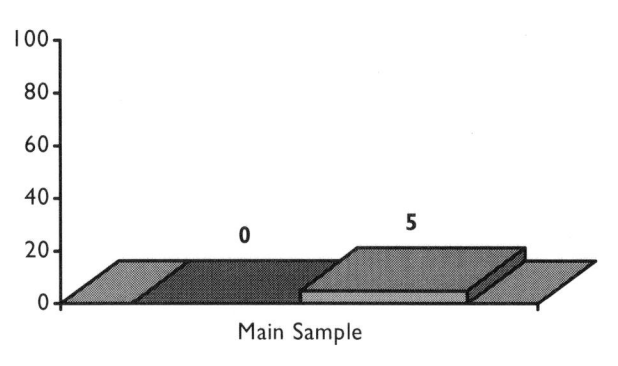

[Bar chart showing % employed and % not employed. Main Sample: 0, 5.]

Percentage of respondents in each employment category who stated that they had injected their drug(s) of choice, split by sample, averaged across location

was quite clearly for injecting drug users to be *un*employed, although this association only reached statistical significance in both Nottingham's and Glasgow's main sample.

It is important to realise here that the absolute number of presently unemployed respondents using drugs within the last year was in most locations quite small. We are consequently *not* assuming that the trends cited for either injecting or frequent usage represent definitive demographic differences. The importance of this data lies rather in the implications it has for future research. The *direction* of the trends noted was quite consistent across locations and in some locations at least reached statistical significance, despite the small numbers involved in the analyses. This indicates both that the links observed were in a number of cases closer than would be expected on the basis of chance alone and that this is an issue worth following up.

The only drug usage item which appeared to be associated with an individual's lifetime experience of employment was perceived availability of drugs. Ironically, this item was one which appeared to be largely *un*affected by *present* employment status. In both main and booster samples it was those individuals who had *never* been employed who were most likely to feel that drugs were readily available in their city or borough. The strength and nature of this link between 'chronic' unemployment and the perceived availability of drugs varied considerably between the sample types. In the main sample, the distinction between employed and unemployed was more extreme, but was also quite heavily dependent on location. Bradford being the only main sample location in which this general trend reached statistical significance. In the booster samples, on the other hand, the distinction between those with some experience of employment and those with *no* such experience was on average much smaller, but reached significance in all locations *except* for Glasgow.

Figure 3.21
Cannabis usage and present employment

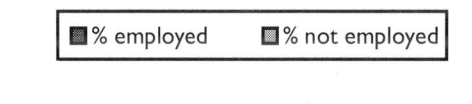

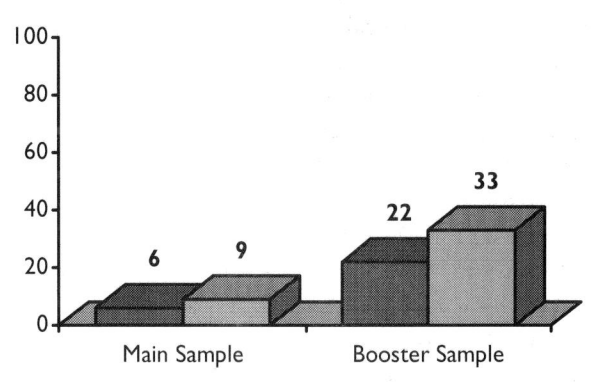

[Bar chart showing % employed and % not employed. Main Sample: 6, 9. Booster Sample: 22, 33.]

Percentage of respondents in each employment category who had taken cannabis within the last year, split by sample, averaged across location

Turning to the patterns noted for different types of

drugs, present rather than lifetime employment again becomes the salient variable. Using this as our measure of unemployment, the data suggest that any link between unemployment and the prevalence of drug usage is likely to hold for most if not all drug types. We did not have enough 'opiate' users in our sample to distinguish between the usage patterns of employed and unemployed respondents and similarly we did not have enough frequent or injecting users to separate employment data by drug type, but the general pattern was as would be expected from the above discussion. As can be seen from Figures 3.21 and 3.22, unemployed respondents in both the booster and main samples were more likely to have taken both cannabis and 'non-opiates' within the last year than employed respondents.

Figure 3.22
Non-opiate usage and present employment

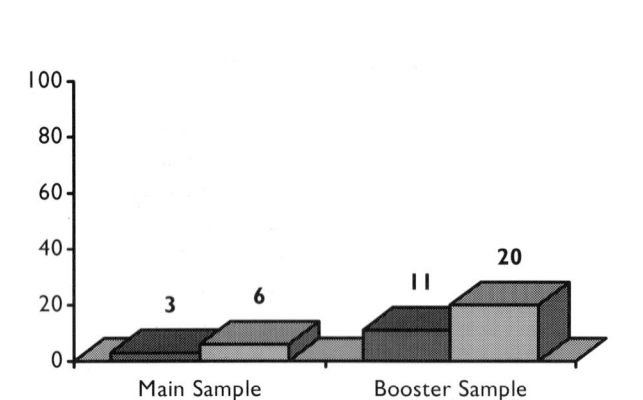

Percentage of respondents in each employment category who had taken non-opiates within the last year, split by sample, averaged across location

As a caveat, it should be noted again that although the general trend observed was fairly consistent, the strength of this effect was dependent on both location and sample type. In the main samples, the variance in cannabis usage between employed and unemployed was significant only for Bradford, whereas the variance in 'non-opiate' usage reached significance in both Bradford and Lewisham. In the booster sample, on the other hand, the variance in cannabis usage was significant for all locations *except* for Glasgow, whilst the variance in 'non-opiate' usage was only significant in Bradford.

The general profile of the data discussed above mimics the discussion of employment and drug usage in the literature. In short, it appears that whilst there *is* some link between the experience of being employed and one's likelihood of using drugs this depends both on how one measures 'being employed' *and* on what an individual's broader life circumstances are. To illustrate the kind of point at issue here, our data would be consistent with the idea that living in deprived economic circumstances tightens any link between unemployment and drug usage, whilst equally supporting the idea that other factors such as the geographic area one lives in might loosen it.

In summary, a respondent's present, although not, in the main, his or her lifetime experience of employment did seem to covary to an extent with the likelihood of drug usage. The general trend in our data was for presently *un*employed respondents to show both a greater prevalence of drug usage and a tendency to use less desirable modes of usage such as frequent and injecting usage. With regard to mode of usage, it is important to note here that the absolute number of recent drug users in our sample who were also unemployed was quite small. It is also important to note that in terms of statistical significance the link between employment and drug usage showed considerable dependence on both sample type and location. With these caveats in mind, the data can best be interpreted as a justification for carrying out further research on the link between employment and drug usage.

Demographic variation in drug usage: multivariate analyses

The patterns discussed above suggest that there *is* substantial variation in drug usage between distinct demographic groups. However, they say nothing about how *important* such variation is in accounting for drug usage. Similarly, they cannot be used to suggest that any one aspect of demography has an *independent* effect on drug usage. To assess these two aspects of the issue of demographic variation, we carried out a series of regression analyses for the main drug usage variables discussed above, taking main and booster samples separately. Since, obviously, a number of the demographic variables provided nominal data only, the regression analyses were carried out using 'dummy' variables for each demographic category. In the following discussion the results for these dummy variables are summarised and only the direction of effect and the amount of variance explained by each final model is presented. For the interested reader, a more detailed account of the regression analyses is given in Tables 3.16-3.19 in Appendix 1. A summary of the main findings is given in Figures 3.23-3.26.

In each case, the demographic variables included in our analysis were age, gender, socioeconomic status, ethnic origin, whether presently employed and whether ever employed. Since the ethnic origins of respondents in our 'other' category for ethnicity were rather varied, we excluded this group from the analyses, leaving the broad distinction 'white', 'black' and 'Asian' as the unit of analysis. As a practical point, it is also worth noting that the variables 'ever employed' and 'presently employed' were not sufficiently closely associated to result in the problem of multicollinearity which occasionally disrupts regression equations. We also included a variable for location to control for the statistical and conceptual differences between the four areas discussed earlier.

Figure 3.23
Summary of demographic regression models for usage of any drug: Main sample

Response	Variables in final model	Direction of effect	% of variance explained
lifetime usage	age	younger>older	14
	gender	males>females	
	ethnicity	white/black>asian	
	socioeconomic status	AB/C1>C2/DE	
usage within last year	age	younger>older	7
	gender	males>females	
	ethnicity	white/black>asian	
	socioeconomic status	AB/C1>C2/DE	
frequency of usage	age	younger>older	2
	gender	males>females	
	ethnicity	white/black>asian	
injecting usage	gender	males>females	<1
	age	younger>older	
drugs readily available	age	younger>older	9
	gender	males>females	
	ethnicity	white/black>asian	
	socioeconomic status	C2/DE>AB/C1	

variables in equation: location, age, gender, ethnicity (white, black, asian), socioeconomic status, presently employed, ever employed

The data summarised in Figure 3.23 confirm that within our main sample age, gender, ethnicity and socioeconomic status *did* operate independently from one another in their effect on both the prevalence of drug usage and the perceived availability of drugs. The direction of effect in each case was as outlined earlier. Working in concert, these demographic variables accounted for between 7% and 14% of the variance noted for these drug usage items. The patterns observed in our multivariate analyses for frequent and injecting usage were rather more equivocal. Socioeconomic status did not enter the final model for frequency of usage and neither socioeconomic status nor ethnicity entered the final model for injecting usage. These models were also the least successful in explaining drug usage. Only 2% of the variance in frequency of usage was accounted for by demographic variance and less than 1% of the variance in injecting usage was accounted for using this model. Given the relatively low numbers of both frequent and injecting users within our sample it is safest to conclude from this that our sample is not really an appropriate one from which to assess the effects of demography on these variable rather than to assume that demography does not in reality have a strong effect on these variables.

Figure 3.24
Summary of demographic regression models for each type of drug: Main sample

Response	Variables in final model	Direction of effect	% of variance explained
cannabis usage	age	younger>older	7
	gender	males>females	
	ethnicity	white/black>asian	
	ever employed	not employed>employed	
non-opiate usage	age	younger>older	3
	gender	males>females	
	ethnicity	white>black/asian	
opiate usage	no variables reached criterion		

variables in equation: location, age, gender, ethnicity (white, black, asian), socioeconomic status, presently employed, ever employed

To compare across drug types, we looked at the three drug groups defined earlier, using as a dependent variable a composite prevalence/frequency measure with a base point at 'never use' and an upper limit of 'use daily'. From Figure 3.24 it can be seen that the most successful model, predictably, was for cannabis usage, with demographic variance accounting for 7% of the variance observed in the tendency to use this drug. In the case of 'non-opiates' we only managed to account for 3% of observed variance using demographic variables and for 'opiate' usage none of the demographic variables reached significance. Again the more restricted success of these two models, particularly that for 'opiate' usage, is likely to be a function of the small numbers of drug users we had within these categories.

As with the models of drug usage in general, the

predominant factors in cannabis and 'non-opiate' usage were age, gender and ethnicity, all three operating independently and in this order of importance. However, once drugs were partitioned by type the effect of other demographic factors changed. Socioeconomic status was not significant in any model and, conversely, the effect of lifetime unemployment was significant in the case of cannabis usage. These distinctions between drug usage as a composite and drug usage as defined by drug type are of some importance, since they imply that causal pathways might also differ between drug types and similarly that drugs prevention may need to take account of differences between drug types.

Figure 3.25
Summary of demographic regression models for usage of any drug: Booster sample

Response	Variables in final model	Direction of effect	% of variance explained
lifetime usage	ethnicity	white/black>asian	6
	gender	males>females	
usage within last year	ethnicity	white/black>asian	5
	gender	males>females	
	age	younger>older	
frequency of usage	gender	males>females	2
	ethnicity	white/black>asian	
injecting usage	gender	males>females	<1
drugs readily available	gender	males>females	4
	ethnicity	black/asian>white	

variables in equation: *location, age, gender, ethnicity (white, black, asian), socioeconomic status, presently employed, ever employed*

As can be seen from Figures 3.25 and 3.26, our multivariate models were slightly less effective at explaining variance in the booster sample than in the main sample. Demographic variance accounted for between 5% and 6% of the variance in the two measures of general drugs prevalence, but accounted for only 4% or less of the variance across all other measures of drug usage, including prevalence partitioned by drug type. Comparing across the composition of the final models in each case suggests that the reduced success of the booster sample models is a consequence of the reduced significance of individual variables in each case.

That age and socioeconomic status were much less of a factor in the booster sample than in the main sample was, of course, predictable. However, it was interesting to note that, at least in the case of general drug prevalence, gender also seemed to be less of a factor, being rather less important than ethnicity which

Figure 3.26
Summary of demographic regression models by type of drug: Booster sample

Response	Variables in final model	Direction of effect	% of variance explained
cannabis usage	gender	males>females	4
	ethnicity	black>white/asian	
	presently employed	not employed >employed	
non-opiate usage	presently employed	not employed >employed	2
opiate usage	ever employed	not employed >employed	1
	presently employed	not employed >employed	

variables in equation: *location, age, gender, ethnicity (white, black, asian), socioeconomic status, presently employed, every employed*

had in turn been of less importance in the main samples. The distribution of the data for these two variables suggests that the best interpretation here is *not* that ethnicity is of any greater importance in the booster samples, but rather that, *independently of any age considerations*, males and females show a closer match for prevalence in the booster sample than in the main sample. A further interesting disparity between the booster and main samples lies in the importance of employment. Whilst not of any significance for overall drug usage, employment did become of substantial importance in the booster sample once we separated prevalence by drug type. Indeed it was the only demographic variable of any significance in accounting for variance in 'opiate' usage.

Returning briefly to our earlier discussions regarding ethnicity and drug use, the multivariate analyses of drug usage within the main sample show clearly that, *independently* of variance in other demographic factors, *white* respondents are the most prominent drug using group. Where black respondents are using drugs they matched the profile of white users rather than showing greater prevalence. The least prominent drug using group was represented by Asian respondents, who differed substantially from both whites and blacks in showing very much lower prevalence levels, again *independently* of any differences between the groups in terms of the other demographic variables. Whilst in the booster samples this pattern is matched for the majority of dependent variables, blacks were here the most prominent user group in terms of *cannabis* and black and Asian drug users were more likely than white drug users to report ready availability of drugs within their area. This disparity between the main and booster samples is of some interest, since those studies which have previously reported greater prevalence of drug usage amongst ethnic minorities have tended to be carried out in circumstances which produce a sample structure more similar to that of our booster sample than our main sample. We will discuss this point more fully later.

Taking the analyses for booster and main sample together, a number of important points can be made. The first, clearly, is that where numbers are adequate, demographic variance evidently can account for a reasonable proportion of the variance in drug usage. The second is that the locational variations discussed earlier appear to be a function *purely* of demographic variation, since such differences disappear once demographic variance is controlled for. This does not, however, make them irrelevant in practical terms, since they are nevertheless real differences. However, since the four locations were chosen to be as *distinct* as possible, this does suggest that the data for our samples can be broadly taken as indicative of likely patterns of drug usage in locations which match ours on the relevant demographic dimensions, fairly severe locational differences being readily subsumed by demographic variance.

The final point to note is the importance of taking multivariate measures of complex behaviours such as drug taking. Without a multivariate analysis, we could have determined *neither* the absolute importance of demographic variation, nor the relative importance of each individual demographic measure. Taking demographic variables as a composite model allows us to conclude that age, gender and ethnicity are all of direct and consistent importance across a range of drug usage measures and that they are likely to be more salient effects on drug usage *in the general population* than either socioeconomic status or employment status. Although clearly the latter are of some absolute importance. In the absence of multivariate measures, it would also have been difficult to draw any firm conclusions regarding the effects of variables such as ethnicity which are known to interact with other measures of demographic variation.

> **In summary,** although the prevalence levels outlined earlier indicate that cannabis is a drug with a fairly ubiquitous pattern of usage, we found substantial demographic variation in the extent to which even this drug was used. The patterns of demographic variation outlined earlier were in the main confirmed by our multivariate analyses, suggesting that statistically the most *prevalent* drug users in the general population are likely to be young, white

males in socioeconomic groups AB and C1. We were unable to account for substantial variation in frequent and injecting usage using only the demographic variables outlined above, although it is important to note here that the numbers of drug users within our sample were quite small.

Booster versus main sample variation

Given the evident importance of demographic variation in drug usage, it became rather a moot point whether the very strong distinction between our main and booster samples was a function of anything more than the obvious demographic disparity between them. Whilst clearly more 'at risk' of drug usage than our general population sample as a whole, the booster sample might well have been entirely representative of a sub-group of the main sample with a similar demographic profile.

The importance of this issue lies in the fact that in comparing the main sample with the booster sample on a range of measures, including attitudinal measures, we were interested in using them as a group of 'at risk' individuals with which to compare the low risk main sample. If the sole distinction between the two groups was on readily identifiable demographic variation, it would have been simpler and more justifiable from this point merely to use the main, general population, sample in each case and control for the effects of, in particular, age and socioeconomic group. These being the most salient distinctions between the main and booster samples.

Partitioning the effects of sample membership and demographic variation is not a straightforward procedure when the two samples being compared are drawn using different methodological techniques. As noted in Chapter 1, simply pooling the samples is *not* a valid option. To get around this difficulty, we set up a series of regression models which would partition out the effects of the salient methodological differences *before* assessing any residual effect of sample membership. From Chapter 1, it can be seen that the most relevant methodological distinction between the samples in the present instance lies in the deliberate bias introduced into the booster sample in terms of age and socioeconomic status. These variables were entered into the regression models - *prior* to assessing any other effects - both as individual and as interaction effects. The need to control for potential interaction effects stemming from the possibility that age and socioeconomic status operated in different ways within main and booster samples. The results of our final regression analyses are outlined in Figure 3.27 below and a more detailed account for the interested reader is given in Tables 3.21 and 3.22 in Appendix 1.

Figure 3.27
Summary of demographic regression models for drug usage: Full sample

Response	Variables in final model	Direction of effect	% of variance explained
lifetime usage	age	younger>older	15
	ethnicity	white/black>asian	
	gender	males>females	
	sample type	booster>main	
	presently in employment	not employed >employed	
	socioeconomic status	AB/C1>C2/DE	
usage within last year	age	younger>older	13
	gender	males>females	
	ethnicity	white/black>asian	
	sample type	booster>main	
	socioeconomic status	AB/C1>C2/DE	
	ever employed	not employed >employed	
frequency of usage	age	younger>older	6
	gender	males>females	
	sample type	booster>main	
	ethnicity	white/black>asian	
	ever employed	not employed >employed	
injecting usage	gender	males>females	<1
drugs readily available	age	younger>older	12
	gender	males>females	
	ethnicity	white/black>asian	
	sample type	booster>main	
	socioeconomic status	C2/DE>AB/C1	
cannabis usage	age	younger>older	11
	sample type	booster>main	
	ethnicity	white/black>asian	
	gender	males>females	
non-opiate usage	age	younger>older	6
	sample type	booster>main	
	gender	white/black>asian	
	ethnicity	males>females	
opiate stage	age	younger>older	<1

variables in equation: *location, whether booster or main sample, age, gender, ethnicity (white, black, asian), socioeconomic status, presently employed, ever employed, sample type*

In short, the analyses we carried out indicated that demographic variation between the samples did *not* fully account for the distinctions between them. Booster sample respondents were distinct from main sample respondents on all measures other than injecting usage and 'opiate' usage *independently* of their deliberately introduced biases in age and socioeconomic group. Moreover, the effect of sample membership was such that for all relevant measures booster sample respondents, as predicted, were at greater 'risk' of drug usage than their main sample counterparts. Knowledge of sample membership consequently increased the amount of variance in drug usage which could be explained by a multivariate model, notably for recent usage and frequent usage.

The possible causes of this distinction between main and booster sample are outlined in the next chapter, within which we consider the implications of local area profiles for drug usage. For the present it is important simply to note that our booster sample is at higher risk of drug usage than our main sample for reasons which cannot be entirely accounted for by demographic variance.

Contact with drug users or drug usage and personal drug usage

Although demography did account for a reasonable amount of the variance noted in drug usage within our sample, the majority of the variance was left unexplained. Clearly, there must be factors other than demographic identity operating in drug usage. One prominent candidate in the literature is the effect of *association* with drug usage. Since it seems reasonable to assume that individuals who have absolutely *no* exposure to drugs are unlikely themselves to become drug users, the issue here is not whether exposure *per se* increases the *likelihood* of drug usage, but rather whether association acts as a more *specific* determinant of drug usage.

To illustrate the point at issue here, we can consider the implications of different models of association. Some models consider that drug usage is stimulated by *specific and direct* social contact with drug use - for example peer-pressure from associates who are themselves drug users (cf. Smart and Adlef 1986). This type of model treats the effects of association with drug usage as a sort of viral transmission - drug using behaviour is passed from one individual to another in sequence. Other models view the link between personal drug usage and association with drug usage as less immediately causal. For example, drug usage is regarded as an endemic part of the 'culture' of particular population sub-groups. Membership of the sub-group entails drug usage not as a *direct function* of contact between individuals but because part of the ethos of group membership is to regard drug usage as a normal behaviour (cf. Forster and Salloway 1990). An individual who was not predisposed towards drug usage would therefore be unlikely to be a member of the group in the first place.

Whilst discussions concerning the nature of the link between association with drug usage and personal drug usage are a central feature of research in this area, it is important to realise that there may be no one single answer to the question being asked. It is entirely possible that different *forms* of association with drug usage stand in different relationships to personal drug usage. In the present survey, this aspect of the association issue was the one we chose to concentrate on, since for the purposes of drugs prevention it is important to specify as closely as possible the nature of any link with drug usage. To this end we asked our respondents to indicate, for the full range of drugs considered, the *type* of exposure they had had to drug usage. For each drug, they were asked to answer the following four questions:

— whether they knew someone who had been *offered* the drug
— whether they knew someone who had *taken* the drug
— whether they knew a *regular* user of the drug
— whether they had attended a *social event* where the drug had been used.

Whilst there will inevitably be some degree of overlap between these options, they are nevertheless logically distinct and provide some insight into both the extent and nature of a respondent's exposure to each drug. The degree of variance between sample types and locations and the demographic profile of these four types of association with drug usage are issues which we consider in detail in Chapter 6. Here, we will consider only the link between association with drug usage and personal drug usage. Summary values and statistics of relevance to this link are given by location and sample type in Tables 3.23-3.26 in Appendix 1.

As Figures 3.28 and 3.29 demonstrate, all four types of association with drug use showed a clear link with personal drug usage. Although the *significance* of this link varied across location and, to a lesser extent, sample type, the direction of the effect was very consistent. Exposure to drug usage at a variety of levels increased the likelihood that a respondent had personally used drugs both within their lifetime and within the last year. Note that the effect was substantially more marked in terms of *lifetime* drug usage than in terms of *recent* drug usage.

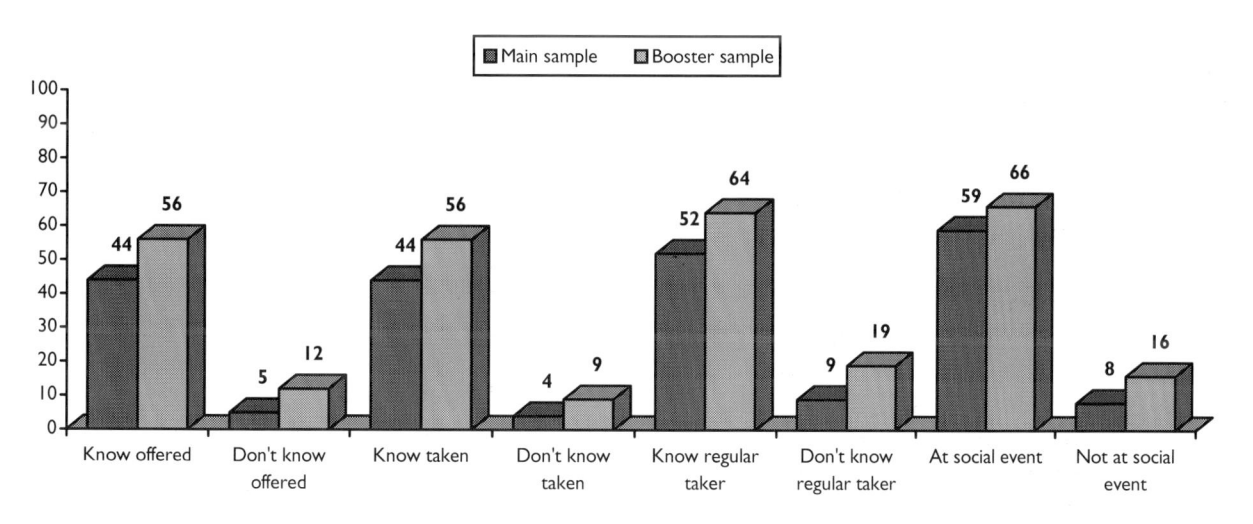

Figure 3.28
Association between exposure to drug usage and lifetime personal drug usage

	Main sample	Booster sample
Know offered	44	56
Don't know offered	5	12
Know taken	44	56
Don't know taken	4	9
Know regular taker	52	64
Don't know regular taker	9	19
At social event	59	66
Not at social event	8	16

*Percentage of those who knew someone who had been **offered** a drug who had themselves taken a drug/Percentage of those who did **not** know of anyone who had been offered a drug who had themselves taken a drug/Percentage of those who knew someone who had **taken** a drug who had themselves also taken a drug/Percentage of those who did **not** know anyone who had taken a drug who had themselves taken a drug/Percentage of those who knew a **regular** drug taker who had themselves also taken a drug/Percentage of those who did **not** know any regular drug takers who had themselves taken a drug/Percentage of those who had attended a **social event** where drugs had been taken who had themselves taken a drug/Percentage of those who had **never** attended a social event where drugs had been taken who had themselves taken a drug (all based on values averaged across location)*

Figure 3.29
Association between exposure to drug usage and personal drug usage within the last year

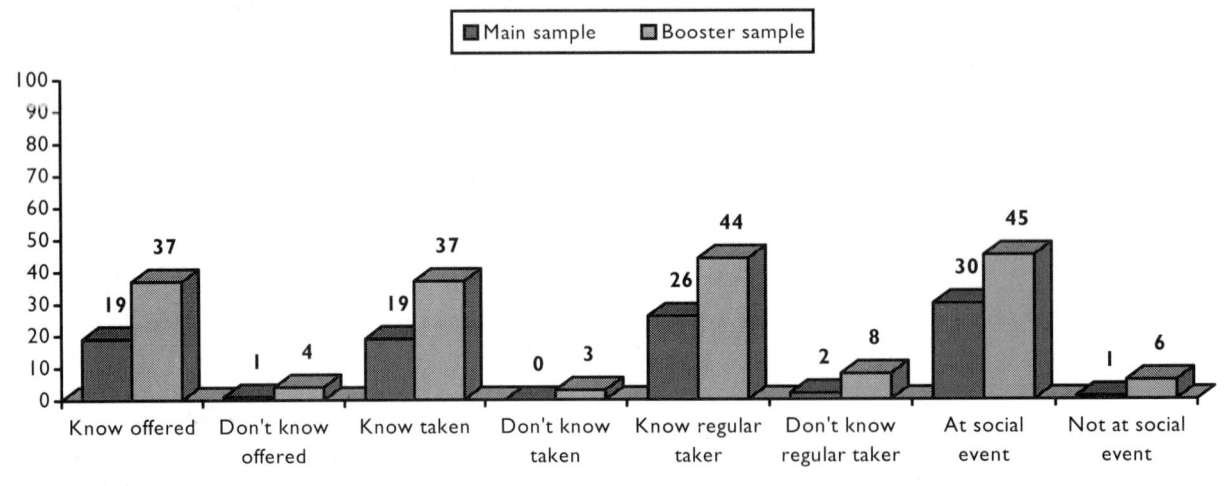

[Bar chart with Main sample and Booster sample values:
- Know offered: 19, 37
- Don't know offered: 1, 4
- Know taken: 19, 37
- Don't know taken: 0, 3
- Know regular taker: 26, 44
- Don't know regular taker: 2, 8
- At social event: 30, 45
- Not at social event: 1, 6]

*Percentage of those who knew someone who had been **offered** a drug who had themselves taken a drug/Percentage of those who did **not** know of anyone who had been offered a drug who had themselves taken a drug/Percentage of those who knew someone who had **taken** a drug who had themselves also taken a drug/Percentage of those who did **not** know anyone who had taken a drug who had themselves taken a drug/Percentage of those who knew a **regular** drug taker who had themselves also taken a drug/Percentage of those who did **not** know any regular drug takers who had themselves taken a drug/Percentage of those who had attended a **social event** where drugs had been taken who had themselves taken a drug/Percentage of those who had **never** attended a social event where drugs had been taken who had themselves taken a drug (all based on values averaged across location)*

Whilst any form of contact with drug usage increased the likelihood that a respondent had themselves used drugs, the 'intensity' of contact was also important. Knowing someone who had been offered drugs or who had taken them on a limited number of occasions was *less* likely to link with personal drug usage than acquaintance with a regular user or attendance at a social event where drugs were taken. However, it was noticeable that in the booster samples the intensity of the contact seemed to be of less importance than was the case in the main sample.

To determine the amount of variance in personal drug usage which could be explained by concomitant variation in exposure to drug usage, we carried out a series of regression analyses. The independent variables included in the analyses were the four measures of exposure to drug usage, plus a variable controlling for location. As we felt that this aspect of drug usage could not justify as detailed a treatment as we had given demographic variance, we chose in this instance to conflate prevalence and mode of usage, using as the dependent variable in each case a measure of frequency of usage with a base point at 'never use' and an end point of 'daily' usage.

Since the strength of the link between exposure to drug usage and personal drug usage appeared to be quite variable across drug types, we carried out the analyses separately for the three drug groups defined earlier. In each case exposure to drug usage was defined quite specifically as exposure to usage of the drug type being analysed. As with previous regression analyses 'dummy' variables were used to correct for the categorical nature of the explanatory variables entered into each model. A summary of the final models for main and booster samples respectively is given in Figures 3.30 and 3.31. A fuller description of each analysis is given in Tables 3.27 and 3.28 in Appendix 1.

As we had noted prior to the analysis, the effect of association with drug usage varied across drug types. The percentage of explained variance for cannabis was greater than that for 'non-opiates', with that for 'opiates' being the lowest in both main and booster samples. To an extent, this disparity between drug types will be a necessary function of their varying prevalence within the population. Cannabis users are relatively common within the population, 'opiate' users appear to be quite rare. In multiplying the probability of being an 'opiate' user with that of exposure to 'opiate' usage we are consequently multiplying the probabilities of two events which each have a low rate of occurrence, whilst in the case of cannabis users both events being multiplied are fairly common. This notwithstanding, the disparity between the explanatory value of association for cannabis usage as opposed to 'opiate' and 'non-opiate' drug types in these models is of importance in that it contrasts with previous ethnographic data (e.g. Burr

Figure 3.30
Summary of association with drug use models of drug usage: Main sample

Response	Variables in final model	Direction of effect	% of variance explained
frequency of taking cannabis	drugs at social event	positive	16
	know regular user	positive	
frequency of non-opiate usage	drugs at social event	positive	7
	know regular user	positive	
	know someone offered drugs	positive	
	know occasional taker	negative	
frequency of opiate usage	no variables reached criterion		

variables in equation: *whether know anyone who has been offered the named type of drug, whether know anyone who has taken the named type of drug, whether know anyone who is a regular taker of the named type of drug, whether have been at social event where the named type of drug has been taken, location*

1987) which has suggested that users of the rarer drugs tend to cluster together in mutually "supportive" sub-groups.

Figure 3.31
Summary of association with drug use models of drug usage: Booster sample

Response	Variables final model	Direction of effect	% of variance explained
frequency of taking cannabis	know regular user	positive	14
	drugs at social event	positive	
frequency of non-opiate usage	know regular user	positive	6
	drugs at social event	positive	
frequency of opiate usage	no variables reached criterion		

variables in equation: *whether know anyone who has been offered the named type of drug, whether know anyone who has taken the named type of drug, whether know anyone who is a regular taker of the named type of drug, whether have been at social event where the named type of drug has been taken, location*

The general profile of the successful models supports the conclusion that intensity of association is of some importance, in that knowing regular users or being at a social event where drugs were taken *was* associated with people themselves taking that drug. However, only one of the four successful models contained the *less* intense forms of association represented by acquaintance with someone who had been offered or who had once taken the relevant drug. In the other three models, such forms of association were of no independent significance. Within the one model in which they did appear as having an independent role - main sample usage of 'non-opiates' - the link shown was also rather equivocal. Knowing someone who had been offered 'non-opiates' slightly increased the chance that a respondent would themselves be a user of 'non-opiate' drugs, but knowing an occasional taker of these drugs showed a marginally significant tendency to *reduce* this likelihood.

It is worth noting with regard to the discussion followed earlier that the regression models outlined here cannot be used to indicate the *causal nature* of the link between personal drug usage and exposure to drug usage. Consequently, the above analyses could be used to support *either* the model of association as a specific mediator of drug usage, *or* the model which sees the interaction between association and personal drug usage as operating at the more general level of social interaction. Having said which, the fact that any links were stronger for lifetime usage than for recent usage slightly favours the broader form of model at least in the case of those having contact with a *regular* user of drugs. To fully determine the causal nature of the link we would need life history data indicating whether association was a precedent or an antecedent of personal drug usage. Given that in the case of cannabis usage at least the amount of variance explained by exposure to drug usage was quite considerable, this type of research might well be of value.

In summary, the extent of indirect exposure a respondent had to drug usage proved to be a fairly powerful indicator of whether they themselves were likely to have taken drugs. This finding was particularly strong in the case of cannabis usage and it linked more closely with an individual's lifetime experience of drug usage than with their recent experience of drug usage. The latter point implies that association operates at a broad 'cultural' level rather than being a specific or direct determinant of drug usage. This notwithstanding, the most important predictors of drug usage in this context were the more intense forms of exposure to drug usage, namely association with a regular user of a drug and attendance at a social event where drugs had been taken.

Lifestyle and drug usage: choice of leisure activities

Lifestyle analysis has been a recurrent theme in the American drugs literature for some time now and is increasingly becoming so in the British literature. Research has tended to address lifestyle both as a causal factor in drug usage and as a possible means of drugs *prevention*. Given the limited space available in our interview schedule, we clearly could not look at the full range of aspects of lifestyle which have been taken to be of importance in previous research. Consequently we chose to look at an aspect of lifestyle which we felt would tap into both the cause and prevention approaches to lifestyle analysis.

The particular aspect of lifestyle chosen was choice of leisure activity, respondents being given a list of common activities and asked both whether they took part in the activity at all and if they did with what frequency they engaged in it. Although this approach is not particularly sophisticated, similar variables to these *have* been found to relate to variations in victimisation and offending in studies from the United States, the Netherlands and the United Kingdom (Elliott 1993, Knol and Soetenhorst 1979).

With regard to the prevention aspect of drug usage, there is a general assumption in the literature that pro-

general public and drugs professionals, regarding the connection between very specific forms of leisure activity such as dances and parties and an increased propensity to use drugs. This link being particularly noticeable in the extent of recent concern regarding 'raves'.

The percentage of respondents engaging in particular forms of leisure activity is given by sample type and location in Table 3.29 in Appendix 1 and the association between drug usage and choice of leisure activity is summarised in Tables 3.30 and 3.31. A more detailed description of the regression analyses discussed in the text is given in Tables 3.32 and 3.33.

The general structure of the data suggested that in fact choice of leisure activity was *not* a particularly salient feature of drug usage within our sample, at least in the case of lifetime drug usage. A small number of links *were* shown to be significant for *recent* usage of particular drug types. These broad disparities between drug users and non-users are summarised in Figures 3.32 and 3.33.

The data presented in Figures 3.32 and 3.33, whilst in the main showing only the very flat distribution of drug users across most leisure activities, do point up certain patterns of association. For both drug type and sample type, these patterns mimic those discussed pre-

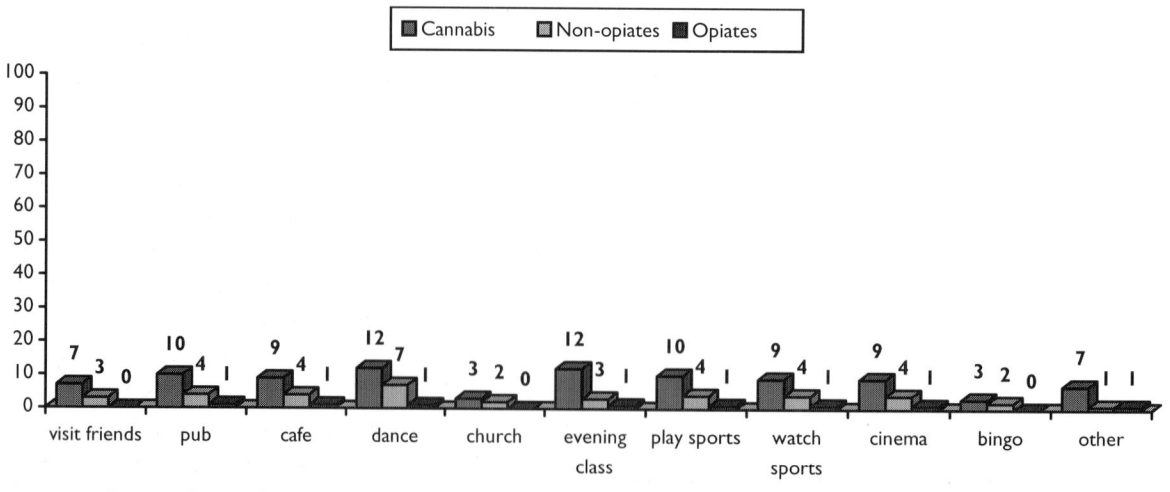

Figure 3.32
Drug usage and choice of leisure activity: Main sample

Percentage of respondents taking part in each form of leisure activity who had used drugs within the last year, averaged across location

viding drug users with alternative forms of leisure pursuit will either directly or indirectly help in reducing their tendency to use drugs (cf. Bell and Battjes 1985; Dorn and Murji 1992). As we will see in chapter 5, there is a similar general assumption, both on the part of the

viously for the effects of exposure to drug usage. Very little association appears between 'opiate' drug usage and choice of entertainment and the association which does appear for cannabis and 'non-opiates' is closer in the booster sample than in the main sample.

Figure 3.33
Drug usage and choice of leisure activity: Booster sample

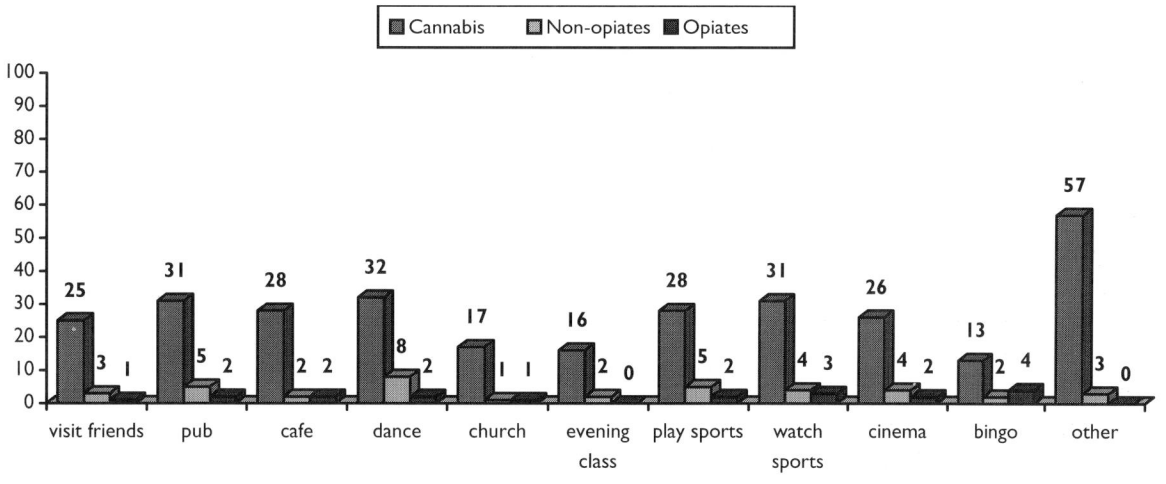

[Bar chart with legend: Cannabis, Non-opiates, Opiates. Values by activity:
- visit friends: 25, 3, 1
- pub: 31, 5, 2
- cafe: 28, 2, 2
- dance: 32, 8, 2
- church: 17, 1, 1
- evening class: 16, 2, 0
- play sports: 28, 5, 2
- watch sports: 31, 4, 3
- cinema: 26, 4, 2
- bingo: 13, 2, 4
- other: 57, 3, 0]

Percentage of respondents taking part in each form of leisure activity who had used drugs within the last year, averaged across location

The single closest association noted across locations and sample type was between both cannabis and 'non-opiate' drug usage and - in line with recent literature and indeed with the views of our own respondents - attendance at a dance or party. However, it should be noted that this association is certainly *not* a very close one and in any given location was not any more significant than that noted for a range of other activities in which young people could be expected to take part - for example going to the pub and watching or taking part in sports events. The activity which overall was *least* closely associated with all forms of drug usage in both main and booster samples was attendance at a church or other place of religious worship. Whilst this finding was quite robust across location and, more importantly, sample *type*, the actual preventive value to be found in substituting religion for opium is a matter open to debate!

Whilst in this instance the link between individual forms of leisure activity and drug usage proved rather minimal, it was entirely possible that a composite model of leisure activity might go rather further towards describing variations in drug usage. Consequently, we ran a series of regression models for both main and booster samples, using a combined measure of 'prevalence' and frequency for both the entertainment variables and the drug usage variables running from 'never used the drug/never take part in the form of leisure activity' to 'use the drug daily'/take part in the leisure activity daily'. As in previous regression analyses we controlled for the effect of location.

Comparing the success of the regression models outlined in Figures 3.34 and 3.35, it can be seen that although the amount of variance explained by choice of leisure activity was not particularly large in either main or booster sample, it was also not entirely trivial. Although in the main sample only cannabis usage really appeared to respond to a lifestyle analysis, in the booster sample around 6% of the variance in both cannabis and 'non-opiate' usage was accounted for by choice of leisure activity. Predictably, the profiles of the final models were very similar in all cases, with the tendency to cite dances or parties and going to the pub as

Figure 3.34
Summary of choice of leisure activity regression models for illicit drug usage: Main sample

Response	Variables in final model	Direction of effect	% of variance explained
frequency of using cannabis	dance	positive	4
	pub	positive	
	church	negative	
	cinema	positive	
	cafe	negative	
frequency of using non-opiates	dance	positive	1
	pub	positive	
	cafe	negative	
frequency of using opiates	sports	positive	<1%
	dance	positive	

variables in equation: *location, whether visit friends, whether go to pub, whether go to restaurant or cafe, whether go to dances or discos, whether go to church, whether go to evening classes, whether play sports, whether watch sports, whether go to cinema, whether go to bingo, whether choose other form of entertainment* favoured leisure activities being positively associated with drug usage and the tendency to cite going to a church or other place of worship being negatively associated with drug usage. Whilst either link could be interpreted as being a function of drugs distribution, either could equally well be interpreted as being a function of personality factors.

Figure 3.35
Summary of choice of leisure activity regression models for illicit drug usage: Booster sample

Response	Variables in final model	Direction of effect	% of variance explained
frequency of using cannabis	dance	positive	7
	pub	positive	
	bingo	negative	
frequency of using non-opiates	dance	positive	5
	church	negative	
	pub	positive	
frequency of using opiates	no variables reach criterion		

variables in equation: *location, whether visit friends, whether go to pub, whether go to restaurant or cafe, whether go to dances or discos, whether go to church, whether go to evening classes, whether play sports, whether watch sports, whether go to cinema, whether go to bingo, whether choose other form of entertainment*

In summary, our choice of leisure activities as an aspect of lifestyle which might link with drug usage proved to be a rather disappointing foray. Little variation in drug usage was shown between the majority of different forms of leisure activity. Furthermore, those activities which *did* link with drug usage - dances and parties on the positive side and church-going on the negative side - were such that any link could readily be accounted for on the basis of covarying demographic distinctions, or other coincidental variations in individual differences This is not to say that lifestyle is irrelevant to drug usage, but rather that we may need to develop more sophisticated models if we are to tap any relevant effects.

Comparisons between licit and illicit drug usage

Whilst clearly the main emphasis in this chapter is on the usage patterns observable for *controlled* drugs in our samples, it is of course the case that within Britain there is substantial usage of drugs which are not controlled by law. That the usage of *un*controlled drugs within our sample is quite extensive can readily be seen from Figure 3.36 which, it should be noted, takes into account only those respondents who used alcohol and tobacco on a *daily* or *weekly* basis. As we did not ask respondents to indicate the number of units of alcohol or the amount of cigarettes they used, we cannot gauge the exact nature of this form of drug usage. Nevertheless if we place these figures against those for the consumption of *unprescribed* drugs, alcohol and tobacco usage can clearly be seen to be very much more prevalent behaviours than the usage of controlled drugs. Between 29% and 52% of respondents across both samples and all locations used alcohol and tobacco several times a week or daily.

Sample type, location and drug usage

As with unprescribed drug usage, the extent of alcohol and tobacco usage also varied across sample and across location. Main sample respondents in Nottingham and Lewisham were significantly more likely to use alcohol on a frequent basis than their counterparts in either Glasgow or Bradford. Main sample respondents in Glasgow were, on the other hand, significantly more likely to use *tobacco* on a regular basis than respondents from the other three main sample locations.

The differences noted between booster sample respondents were not quite as extreme, although Nottingham booster respondents were more likely to use alcohol regularly than were respondents from the other three locations and again Glasgow's booster sample showed a higher prevalence of frequent tobacco use than the other samples. Comparing across samples, both Lewisham's and Bradford's main sample respondents were significantly *more* likely to use alcohol regularly than their booster sample counterparts. In contrast, Lewisham's, Bradford's and Nottingham's booster sample respondents were more likely to use *tobacco* than their main sample counterparts. An important point to note from this data is that the pattern for alcohol and tobacco usage does *not* fit neatly over the comparable divides noted earlier for the usage of controlled drugs across samples and locations. Those locations which show the greatest prevalence of unprescribed drug use are *not* identical with those which show the greatest prevalence of licit drug use and the distinction between main and booster samples is less extreme in the case of licit drugs.

Demography and legal drug usage

Tables 3.34-3.41 in Appendix 1 summarise the demographic split for alcohol and tobacco usage within our

Figure 3.36
Alcohol and tobacco usage by sample

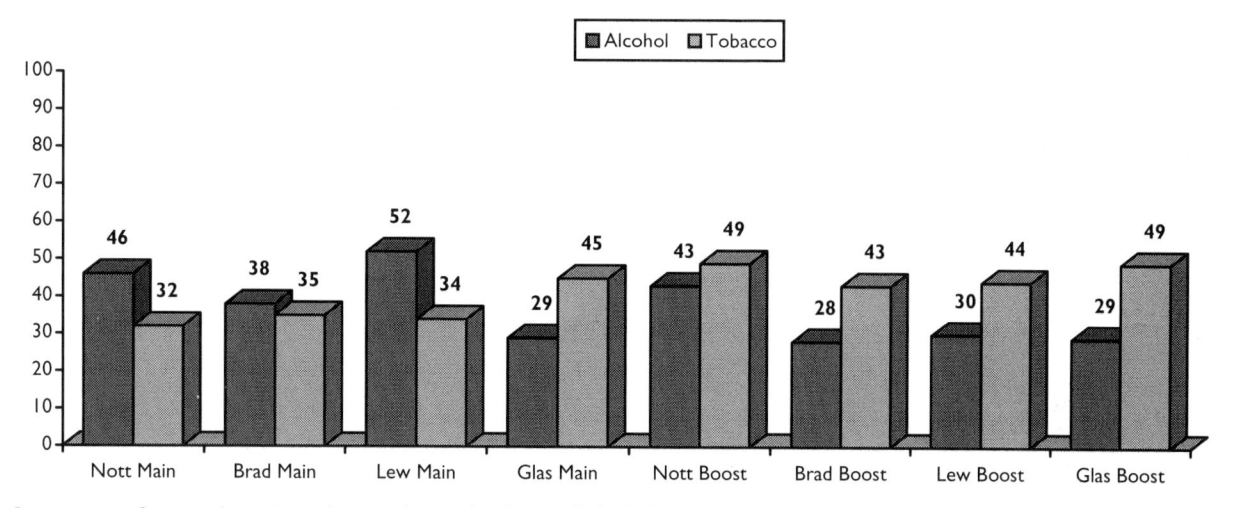

[Bar chart showing Alcohol and Tobacco usage percentages:
- Nott Main: Alcohol 46, Tobacco 32
- Brad Main: Alcohol 38, Tobacco 35
- Lew Main: Alcohol 52, Tobacco 34
- Glas Main: Alcohol 29, Tobacco 45
- Nott Boost: Alcohol 43, Tobacco 49
- Brad Boost: Alcohol 28, Tobacco 43
- Lew Boost: Alcohol 30, Tobacco 44
- Glas Boost: Alcohol 29, Tobacco 49]

*Percentage of respondents in each named sample who used alcohol or tobacco **daily** or at least **once per week***

two sample types. Table 3.42 summarises the statistical significance of any distinctions, by sample type and location. As a consequence of the very different prevalence levels, the comparisons we will be drawing between these two drug types will be made between those respondents using alcohol or tobacco on a *daily or weekly* basis and those who have used unprescribed drugs at all *within the last year*.

Whilst the location and sample type profile of licit drug usage does not match that for unprescribed drugs, the *demographic* profile of licit drug usage matches this quite closely. As with unprescribed drugs, young, white, males are the single group most likely to consume alcohol or tobacco on a regular basis. Also as is the case for unprescribed drugs a rather more mixed pattern emerges on socioeconomic status.

Males were significantly more likely than females to take alcohol regularly, to use tobacco regularly *and* to have used both cannabis and the group of 'non-opiate' drugs within the last year. Although age was also an important determinant of alcohol and tobacco usage, with younger individuals being more likely to use both substances regularly, the usage curve did not exactly match that followed by unprescribed drug use. The rapid tail-off of unprescribed drug usage towards the 45+ age groups was *not* noted in the case of licit drugs and the youngest age group (16-19 year olds) showed a comparatively *lower* level of alcohol and tobacco usage than their older counterparts, notably when they are matched against individuals in the 20-35 age range.

To summarise the rather mixed socioeconomic pattern of licit drug usage shown by our data: the pre-dominant users of tobacco were quite clearly those in socioeconomic groups C2 and DE, whilst the most prominent users of alcohol were in groups AB and C1. This finding is in contrast to a range of other studies (cf. Leek and Smith 1990) which indicate that *both* alcohol and tobacco usage are more problematic in lower socioeconomic status groups. This disparity is in all likelihood a consequence of the fact that neither different types of alcohol nor different modes of usage (heavy drinking versus light drinking) were separated out in this study. The heavy patterns of usage generally ascribed to lower status socioeconomic groups are usually restricted to certain types of alcohol and to use of an excessive number of units per session rather than representing the eclectic patterns of usage considered here. Taking the data as it stands, the broad pattern for alcohol usage across socioeconomic groups matches that shown by regular cannabis use, whilst the pattern for tobacco use matches more closely the comparable pattern for less prevalent drugs.

With regard to ethnicity, the main sample data showed that, as with unprescribed drugs, whites as the majority ethnic group were significantly more likely to use alcohol and tobacco than *either* the composite of minority ethnic groups or any minority group taken singly. Comparing across distinct minority ethnic groups similarly showed that respondents of Asian origin were less likely to use either alcohol or tobacco than black respondents. In the booster sample also, the pattern for alcohol usage matched that for unprescribed drug usage, with the greatest divide being between our Asian respondents who were *un*likely to use alcohol and both our black respondents and white respondents who showed broadly similar patterns of usage. In relation to tobacco usage, the pattern reverted to the more standard divide with white respondents showing higher prevalence rates than either black respondents or Asian respondents.

The patterns noted for lifetime and present employment also broadly matched those for unprescribed drugs in the case of tobacco usage, although *not* in the case of alcohol. It is worth adding here that the levels of statistical significance reached by any differences between groups were greater and more consistent across locations for both alcohol and tobacco than for unprescribed drugs. Summarising the patterns, those respondents *not* employed at the time of the survey were more likely to state that they used tobacco either daily or several times per week in both samples and most locations, but were in the main sample *less* likely to state that they used alcohol. Those individuals who had *never* worked were consistently less likely to have used either tobacco or alcohol than those who either were employed now or had been in the past.

As can be seen from the summary of our regression analyses outlined in detail in Tables 3.43 and 3.44 in Appendix 1 and summarised in Figures 3.37 and 3.38, the amount of variance accounted for by our demographic variables was also within the same range as that

Figure 3.37
Summary of demographic regression model for alcohol and tobacco usage: Main sample

Response	Variables in final model	Direction of effect	% of variance explained
alcohol usage	gender	male>female	20
	ethnicity	white>black>asian	
	socioeconomic status	AB/C1>C2/DE	
	ever employed	employed>not employed	
	age	older>younger	
	presently employed	employed>not employed	
tobacco usage	socioeconomic status	C2/DE>AB/C1	13
	ever employed	employed>not employed	
	presently employed	not employed>employed	
	ethnicity	white>black>asian	
	age	older>younger	

variables in equation: *location, age, gender, socioeconomic status, ethnicity (white, black, asian), presently employed, ever employed.*

accounted for in the case of unprescribed drug usage. As with unprescribed drug usage the amount of variance explained was also greater - although only very slightly so - in the main sample than in the booster sample. Finally, demographic variables were rather more succesful in accounting for variation in alcohol usage than for variation in tobacco usage.

Figure 3.38
Summary of demographic regression model for alcohol and tobacco usage: Booster sample

Response	Variables in final model	Direction of effect	% of variance explained
alcohol usage	ethnicity	black>white>asian	19
	gender	males>famales	
	socioeconomic status	AB/C1>C2/DE	
	age	younger>older	
	ever employed	employed>not employed	
tobacco usage	ethnicity	white>black>asian	13
	socioeconomic status	C2/DE>AB/C1	
	ever employed	employed>not employed	
	presently employed	not employed>employed	
	age	older>younger	

variables in equation: *location, age, gender, socioeconomic status, ethnicity (white, black, asian), presently employed, ever employed*

Lifestyle and legal drug usage

We did not attempt to measure the effect of association with alcohol or tobacco users on personal usage of these drugs, however, we did assess the effect of the other major variable examined in the case of unprescribed drugs, namely choice of leisure activity. Perhaps not surprisingly, given the general acceptance of alcohol into the fabric of social life, it was evident from the data that the association between alcohol usage and choice of leisure activity is much stronger than that between usage of any unprescribed drug type and leisure activity. This association was also closer for tobacco usage than for the usage of unprescribed drugs, although here the disparity was not as extreme, perhaps because tobacco is *not* accepted as part and parcel of social interaction in quite the same way as alcohol.

The strongest association noted in the main sample between alcohol usage and choice of leisure activity was, rather predictably, that between regular drinking and a preference for going to pubs. Around 51% of those respondents in each location who chose to spend their leisure time in pubs also drank alcohol regularly. Less predictably, playing or watching sports showed an equally close link with alcohol usage. Again, around

51% of respondents in each location who chose to play sports also drank alcohol regularly and around 52% of respondents who *watched* sports did so.

Tobacco usage was also linked with going to pubs, although to a lesser extent, with around 39% of respondents across locations who chose to go to pubs also smoking tobacco regularly. The single closest association in the case of tobacco was, however, with playing bingo! Around 58% of respondents who played bingo also smoked tobacco regularly.

The above main sample patterns were matched very closely in the booster sample for both alcohol and tobacco use. The link between church-going and *not* using drugs was substantially weaker in both main and booster sample for alcohol and tobacco usage than for unprescribed drugs. As with our discussion of choice of leisure activity and unprescribed drug usage, it should be noted here that variance in choice of leisure activity is fairly strongly dependent on demographic variation, so the links discussed here may be the function of demographic variation.

The major difference between the links shown by leisure activities with licit as opposed to unprescribed drugs (cf. Tables 3.45 and 3.46 in Appendix 1) was the amount of variance in alcohol - although not tobacco usage - accounted for by this aspect of lifestyle. As can

Figure 3.39
Summary of choice of leisure activity regression models for alcohol and tobacco usage: Main sample

Response	Variables in final model	Direction of effect	% of variance explained
uses alcohol daily or several times per week	pub	positive	26
	dance	positive	
	plays sports	positive	
	bingo	negative	
	church	negative	
	watches sports	positive	
	cafe	positive	
uses tobacco daily or several times per week	church	negative	7
	bingo	positive	
	cinema	negative	
	pub	positive	
	plays sports	negative	
	dance	positive	
	evening class	negative	
	other entertainment	positive	

variables in equation: *location, whether visit friends, whether go to pub, whether go to restaurant or cafe, whether go to dances or discos, whether go to church, whether go to evening classes, whether play sports, whether watch sports, whether go to cinema, whether go to bingo, whether choose other form of entertainment.*

Figure 3.40
Summary of choice of leisure activity regression models for alcohol and tobacco usage: Booster sample

Response	Variables in final model	Direction of effect	% of variance explained
uses alcohol daily or several times per week	pub	positive	39
	dance	positive	
	visit friends	negative	
uses tobacco daily or several times per week	pub	positive	8
	cinema	negative	
	plays sports	negative	

variables in equation: *location, whether visit friends, whether go to pub, whether go to restaurant or cafe, whether go to dances or discos, whether go to church, whether go to evening classes, whether play sports, whether watch sports, whether go to cinema, whether go to bingo, whether choose other form of entertainment.*

be seen from Figures 3.39 and 3.40, choice of leisure activity accounted for nearly 30% of main sample and nearly 40% of booster sample variation in alcohol usage. Since the success of the leisure activity models for alcohol is largely due to the greater number of different forms of leisure activity which appeared to be directly linked with alcohol consumption in one direction or the other we suggest that the distinction drawn by these regression models between alcohol and the other drugs considered is a function of the way in which alcohol usage pervades a vast array of the population's modes of relaxation. Neither tobacco nor unprescribed drugs appear to have the same strength of linkage with leisure, although tobacco shows a slightly stronger link than unprescribed drugs, or at least unprescribed drugs *other* than cannabis.

In summary, whilst not surprisingly the prevalence of alcohol and tobacco usage is significantly greater in our samples than that of unprescribed drugs, the demographic patterns noted for alcohol and tobacco match fairly closely those noted for the usage of unprescribed drugs. The only major disparity we observed between usage of licit and illicit drugs lay in the ability of a broad range of leisure activities to account for variation in alcohol usage, whilst largely failing to do so in the case of unprescribed drugs. Since the pattern noted for tobacco usage in this context was rather more similar to that for unprescribed drugs, at least in the case of cannabis, we attribute this finding to the pervasive presence of alcohol in the population's relaxation patterns.

Association across drug types - could taking cannabis or 'non-opiates' lead to taking 'opiates'?

A variant on both the association and polydrug usage issues discussed earlier is whether exposure to one type of drug usage *predisposes* an individual towards using other drugs. This issue is generally expressed in terms of the concern that using *relatively* less harmful drugs, but nonetheless illicit drugs, such as cannabis or certain non-opiates will inexorably lead people on to using more harmful and more heavily controlled drugs such as opiates. Whilst we cannot say anything about the *progression* of drug usage over time, since unfortunately we did not ask respondents when they started using each drug, we *can* address the related issue of the extent to which usage of one drug type is able to explain variance in usage of another drug type.

As noted in previous sections of this chapter there is some overlap between the tendency to use drugs in the 'non-opiate' drug group and the tendency to use drugs in the 'opiate' drug group. Similarly, there is an association between the use of 'non-opiates' and the use of cannabis. Moving down the accepted hierarchy, alcohol and tobacco usage are likely, given our figures for general drug usage, to overlap in certain instances with at least cannabis, if not with the rarer drug types. Since the potential for links between controlled and uncontrolled drugs has not been strongly emphasised in the literature we felt it was of particular importance to include this as a model of drug type association in our analyses.

Detailed information on the regression analyses we conducted to address this issue are given in Tables 3.47-3.52 in Appendix 1 and brief summaries are provided here in Figures 3.41 and 3.42. The main aim of the analyses presented was to establish whether in each case usage of the relevant drugs could account *independently* for any of the variance noted in the usage of drugs *above* them in the nominal hierarchy outlined above. That is, whether taking one drug is, by and of itself, associated with taking another drug, independently of other factors, such as one's demographic status. Since we were trying to establish whether any hierarchical pattern existed, we included every drug below the drug being analysed in the hierarchy in the model for that drug. So the variables in the regression equation for cannabis were alcohol and tobacco. For 'non-opiates' we included cannabis, alcohol and tobacco and for 'opiates' we included 'non-opiates', cannabis, alcohol and tobacco. In each case we included a dummy variable to control for the effects of location.

All the drug usage measures used were composite usage/frequency measures with a base point at 'never use' and an upper limit of 'use daily'.

Figure 3.41

Summary of drug usage regression models: Main sample

Response	Variables in final model	Direction of effect	% of variance explained
opiate usage	non-opiate usage	positive	6
	cannabis usage	positive	

variables in equation: *location, cannabis usage, usage of non-opiates (pills, tranquillisers, amphetamines, LSD, ecstasy, psilocybin, amyl nitrite), alcohol usage, tobacco usage.*

non-opiate usage	cannabis usage	positive	26

variables in equation: *location, cannabis usage, alcohol usage, tobacco usage.*

cannabis usage	tobacco usage	positive	3
	alcohol usage	positive	

variables in equation: *location, alcohol usage, tobacco usage.*

The models for both samples confirmed that usage of lower level drugs *could* account for a substantial proportion of variation in usage of higher level drugs in our nominal hierarchy. Comparing across the final models outlined in Figures 3.41 and 3.42 it can be seen that the significant variables were the same in each case for booster and main samples. However the percentage of variance accounted for was in each case *less* in the booster sample than the main sample.

Figure 3.42

Summary of drug usage regression models: Booster sample

Response	Variables in final model	Direction of effect	% of variance explained
opiate usage	non-opiate usage	positive	12
	cannabis usage	positive	

variables in equation: *location, cannabis usage, usage of non-opiates (pills, tranquillisers, amphetamines, LSD, ecstasy, psilocybin, amyl nitrite), alcohol usage, tobacco usage.*

non-opiate usage	cannabis usage	positive	37

variables in equation: *location, cannabis usage, alcohol usage, tobacco usage.*

cannabis usage	alcohol usage	positive	8
	tobacco usage	positive	

variables in equation: *location, alcohol usage, tobacco usage.*

The disparities noted between drug types suggested that the link between the use of cannabis and the use of 'non-opiates' was rather stronger than either the link between uncontrolled drugs and cannabis or 'opiates' and the full range of other drugs used. It was also of interest to note that both within and across models the hierarchy remained intact, with the use of 'non-opiates' being of greater explanatory value in accounting for opiate usage than cannabis, and the use of alcohol and tobacco failing to account for any variance in either 'opiate' or 'non-opiate' use.

Note that whilst the success of the models follows the prevalence of each behaviour, there is no necessary link here. It is also important to note that whilst usage of alcohol and tobacco do not account directly for usage of 'opiates' or 'non-opiates' they may do so indirectly via their association with cannabis. In both main and booster samples the use of alcohol and tobacco accounted for a similar proportion of variance in *cannabis* usage to that accounted for by non-opiate usage in the case of opiates. This suggests further that what we might be looking at here is some sort of generalised 'drug taking behaviour' with drug using respondents tending to take *both* controlled and uncontrolled drugs.

Although some respondents are clearly using both controlled and uncontrolled drugs, the overall profile of our data suggests that the link between uncontrolled and controlled drugs is weaker than that between different types of controlled drugs. This is of some interest given the similar demographic profiles shown by the usage of controlled and uncontrolled drugs. It suggests that if there is any real shift across time from one drug to another the move from one controlled drug to another will be more likely than the move from uncontrolled to controlled drugs. This may, of course, be due to the legal/illegal distinction or to cultural factors defining those substances which are seen as 'acceptable' drugs.

In summary, whilst the data from these regression models suggests that the frequently assumed hierarchy ranging from cannabis to 'non-opiates' and finally to 'opiates' has some basis in fact, it is important to note that we cannot confirm whether or not usage of a given drug type predisposes an individual towards using more harmful or more heavily controlled drugs. All we *can* say is that there is a clear and independent association between on the one hand cannabis and 'non-opiate' drug usage and on the other hand 'non-opiate' and 'opiate' drug usage. Interestingly the data suggest that there is a similar link between the use of uncontrolled drugs such as alcohol and tobacco and the use of cannabis. Since the demographic profile of controlled and uncontrolled drugs is similar, the most likely interpretation of this on the basis of the present data is that people are using cannabis for the same sorts of reasons they are using alcohol and tobacco. The same cannot be said for the use of 'opiates' and 'non-opiates' which showed no *independent* link with alcohol and tobacco usage. To answer the perennial question of whether 'soft' drug usage *leads* to 'hard' drug usage it would be necessary to have data relevant to the *timing* of usage of different drug types in the life histories of a range of respondents. Unfortunately these data were not collected in the present study, but the data outlined do provide some justification for a fuller analysis of this issue.

Drug usage in four towns: a summary of our findings on prevalence

Our self-report prevalence estimates of drug usage suggest that the majority of the general population have not used any form of unprescribed drug either recently or in their lifetime as a whole. However, the use of unprescribed drugs was certainly *not* a negligible phenomenon. A rough figure derivable from our estimates for drug prevalence in the general population would suggest that 1 in 15 have recently used an illicit drug and that 1 in 5 people have used an illicit drug within their lifetime. In sub-groups of the population selected to be 'at risk' of drug usage, comparable estimates would be up to 1 in 4 people for recent usage and up to 1 in 2 people for lifetime usage.

Whilst these figures seem quite high in absolute terms, we did not have access to comparable data for other self-reported illicit behaviours, so it is not possible to gauge whether they are also high figures in relative terms. It is equally important to note that whilst prevalence *per se* was fairly high, problematic patterns of drug usage were *not* particularly evident. Cannabis was a significantly more prominent drug than other 'non-opiate' drugs and 'non-opiates' were in turn substantially more popular than 'opiates', the latter form of unprescribed drug showing only negligible numbers of users in the population. Frequent usage, injecting usage and polydrug usage were also at low absolute levels, both in our general population sample and perhaps more importantly in our 'at risk' sample. On a more depressing note, it was evident that local availability of all drugs was extremely high - so high in fact that it must be concluded that any restriction on drug usage is governed by personal choice rather than by supply-side control.

The most important demographic covariates of

drug *prevalence* appeared from our data to be age, gender and ethnicity, taken in that order. The pattern observed for socioeconomic status being rather more equivocal. A profile of the group statistically most likely to use unprescribed drugs would describe them as young, white males in socioeconomic groups AB and C1. Although there was some indication that the pattern of problematic usage, for example frequent or injecting usage, might both differ in demographic terms from prevalence *per se* and be to an extent dependent on the type of drug being considered, we were unable to confirm this because of the low absolute numbers of 'problem' users within our samples. An individual's lifetime experience of employment and in particular their likelihood of being in employment at the time they were questioned about drug usage was also of some importance, since on a number of measures of usage unemployed individuals scored more highly than employed individuals. This particular distinction appeared to be at a premium in our target group of young individuals 'at risk' of drug usage.

Although substantial variation was found between the four areas studied, with Glasgow and Lewisham showing the greatest prevalence of drug usage and Bradford the least, the differences observed appeared to be a function of demographic variation between the locations. The fact that the distinctions between locations specifically chosen to represent very different types of area were so easily subsumed by demography suggests that our results are likely to be broadly representative of a range of locations matching these areas in demographic profile. As a cautionary note, it is worth bearing in mind here that very specific features of locations, such as the local drugs supply network, have the potential to affect quite strongly the drugs profile of a location at any given point in time. In the next chapter we discuss those locational effects operating *within* towns.

Whilst in the absence of suitable life history data we were *not* able to examine the *causal* pathways of drug usage, we were able to consider the *association* of unprescribed drug usage with a number of variables previously considered to be of importance in determining usage. In particular, we found that exposure to drug usage was strongly linked with *personal* drug usage, particularly in the case of fairly direct or intense contact such as acquaintance with regular drug users or participation in social events where drugs were used. Choice of leisure activity did *not* on the other hand link closely with the use of unprescribed drugs, although individuals taking part in the type of social events favoured by the younger members of society, for example dances, parties etc. were more likely to use drugs than those not doing so. It is very important to note here that neither of the observed patterns suggests in any way that drug taking is *stimulated* by the factors referred to.

Similarly, although we were able to show that the accepted hierarchy of drug usage leading from alcohol and tobacco to cannabis and from here to 'non-opiates' and then 'opiates' had some basis in fact, we could *not* establish whether this link was actually causal or whether it was a consequence of, for example, individual personality type or other predisposing factors.

Whilst the prevalence of alcohol and tobacco usage was, predictably, higher in our samples than equivalent estimates for the use of unprescribed drugs, the demographic profile of users of *licit* drugs broadly matched that of the users of unprescribed drugs. The most noticeable distinction between controlled and uncontrolled drugs lay in the ability of choice of leisure activity to account for variations in alcohol usage.

The fact that our figures for drug usage matched quite closely figures derived from other recent and methodologically similar studies suggests that our estimates of prevalence can at least be taken as a realistic baseline. Where data was available, the broad demographic variation shown by our survey was also supported by other studies. Comparing the data with prevalence estimates derived from other countries suggest that the British picture is likely still to be closer to the rest of Europe than to the substantially higher figures for drug prevalence in the United States.

Chapter 4
LOCATIONAL VARIATION IN ILLICIT DRUG USAGE

One recent interest in drug research has been whether different places show different levels of drug usage and of drug-related crime problems. If so, are high levels of drug usage associated with other kinds of social problems? The majority of studies have concluded, at least in America (cf. Haw 1985, Dembo et al 1986), that such variation *does* exist and that the form it takes is a concentration of both drug distribution *and* usage within areas of urban deprivation. This assumed pattern is a predictable one on the basis of studies dealing with other aspects of the alternative 'economy' of such areas (e.g. Nurco et al 1984). It has been established for some time now that areas high on a number of measures of urban deprivation are likely to suffer from high crime rates judged on a range of indices including theft, burglary and violent crime against individuals (Mayhew and Hough 1991 and Herbert 1982).

Although the accepted pattern of spatial variation in drug related behaviours is unsurprising, it is important to note that it is also less adequately substantiated than the area patterns for, say, property crime. Drug usage and, to a lesser extent, distribution, differ from other illicit activities in that they need not have a 'victim' - at least in the strict sense in which this label is defined by individuals who themselves feel that they have suffered in some way from the behaviour in question.

From a research viewpoint, crime which creates obvious victims has the advantage of being relatively transparent. Whilst under-reporting is significant and some victims - notably of violent crime - do *not* concur with the police view that they have been victims, the general tendency is for a significant proportion of individuals to report crimes against themselves or their property to some official body. Mayhew and Aye Maung (1992) estimate on the basis of British Crime Survey data that around one third of crimes against households or persons are reported to the police. This figure allows for a degree of confidence in at least base rate prevalence estimates for such crimes.

In contrast, the majority of drug users evidently do not and cannot be expected to report their own activities *or* those of their dealers. As outlined in our introductory chapter, this leaves us with significant problems in estimating usage and availability rates. The relevance of which in the present instance is that, almost without exception, the studies which have claimed to show locational variation in drug related behaviours have adopted methodologies which, whilst allowing them to access a large number of drug users, have the disadvantage that the users selected are likely to be unrepresentative of the general population. As a consequence, although the work is valuable as an *indicator* of whether spatial variation in drug patterns is a plausible concept, it cannot confirm the existence of such variation.

To illustrate this point more fully: Parker et al (1988) note that studies based on either snowballing or drug agency data - the methods most generally adopted in drugs research - tend to over-estimate the number of lower socioeconomic status drug users and conversely to under-estimate the number of high socioeconomic status users. The data we present in Chapter 2 would, of course, tend to support this observation. Since socioeconomic status is a strong determinant of area of residence, such inadvertent biases in a data set will inevitably skew the distribution of potential locations from which drug users can be assumed to derive. Similar problems exist with samples drawn via clinics and support groups, since together with drugs agencies *per se*, these tend to be sited in economically deprived areas and consequently will derive their clientele largely from these areas. Contacting drug users via non-area specific official agencies has not tended to resolve the problem, since the most common strategy used is to contact via either the police or the health services, both of which sources are similarly 'oversubscribed' by individuals from deprived areas (cf. Whitehead 1987).

Unfortunately, the potential biases noted above cannot be ironed out even by conducting geographic analyses within relatively small local areas. Deriving a sample via contact with any 'target' group of drug users, rather than via random sampling techniques, will exaggerate the importance of the particular drugs network in which those users or the contacts they provide are personally involved. In addition there is the self-evident problem that most studies dealing with locational variation in drug usage have had to rely on accurate reporting by a respondent of where they live. Since the activity which is being reported is illegal, this type of information is of dubious validity in the absence of external corroboration.

One of the advantages of the present survey is that the data from our main sample are not subject to the problems outlined above. The method of random sampling we used may have introduced slight demographic biases and conducting interviews at a respondent's home may have resulted in some under-reporting of drug usage. Nevertheless, we are at least secure in the knowledge that those of our respondents who reported personal drug usage *did* actually live in the areas to which they have been ascribed and had *not* been 'targeted' in any way likely to result in substantial statistical bias in the sample. In addition, we are able to tie the data to extremely *detailed* locational information relating to drug usage, since we are able to specify the identity of the particular enumeration district from which each individual respondent derived.

Broad geographic variation between cities

As noted in our introductory chapter, data from the present survey also have the advantage that they can be used to compare areas which are geographically distinct at the broad level of cross-country variation. Previous studies have considered locational variation at the level of intra-urban differences only. The distinctions in levels and modes of personal drug usage between the four areas sampled have been discussed in detail in the previous chapter. Here we will recap on the conclusions reached and their possible implications for locational variation.

It is important to realise that the four areas chosen for the survey were selected quite deliberately to represent four very different types of environment. Lewisham is a densely populated inner London borough with a broad ethnic mix. Nottingham is a middle-England city with a fairly young population, a large city centre and numerous satellite districts. Bradford is a northern English city with a considerable ethnic split, a concentration of residential areas around its inner city and a scattering of distinct smaller towns within its boundaries. Glasgow is a large Scottish city with a fairly limited ethnic mix, and an unusually large proportion of public housing distanced both from its city centre and from other privately owned residential districts. Although all four areas can be described in a variety of alternative ways, this basic profile provides some insight into the differences between them which may be helpful in the present context.

The salient differences noted in the last chapter between drug usage in the four locations suggested a division between Glasgow and Lewisham on the one hand and Nottingham and Bradford on the other. The former two areas showed a substantially greater prevalence of drug usage than the latter two, notably when the booster samples were taken into account. An equivalent split between the locations was also apparent for mode of usage, with drug users in Glasgow and Lewisham showing the greatest *frequency* of usage. Although the numbers of injecting users and users of individual drug types *other* than cannabis are fairly limited within our sample, a qualitative analysis of the data supports the patterns observed for these variables by previous studies in the locations considered. Glasgow, for example, accounted for the vast majority of cases of injecting usage in our sample, supporting Frischer's (1992) suggestion that the present prevalence of injecting drug usage in Glasgow distinguishes present populations both from earlier similar populations sampled in Glasgow and from similar sample populations in other cities. Respondents from Glasgow also showed a substantially greater likelihood of using amphetamines, temazepam and DF118s than respondents from the other three areas, supporting the work of Sokal et al. (1989) who have recorded an increase in the prevalence of amphetamine and temazepam usage within the location. Lewisham showed higher levels of cocaine and ecstasy usage than the other locations, which also confirms previous research (Strang et al. 1990, Mirza et al. 1991).

None of the above patterns are likely to be the sole consequence of differential availability of drugs. Over 70% of drug users in all four locations claimed ready access to their drug(s) of choice. Our analyses did indicate, however, that the majority of the variance discussed above *could* readily be accounted for by demographic variations between the locations. Multivariate analyses of all our measures of drug usage - lifetime and recent prevalence, frequency and injecting usage - suggested that any locational variation at the cross-city level could be subsumed by demographic variation. It should be noted that as a consequence of the relatively small numbers of recent drug users within our sample, these analyses were more robust for the *prevalence* measures than for the *mode* of usage measures. Whilst we cannot use our data to comment on statistical differences in the demography of usage for individual drug types, previous research suggests that such differences between locations are likely to be real, rather than an artefact of demography (e.g. Ditton and Speirits 1984). However, our data show that once drugs are partitioned into broader groups, in the present case cannabis, non-opiates and opiates, any locational variation between cities is again replaced by the effects of demography.

In summary, whilst our data support to some extent previous research in suggesting that for individual drugs there is locational variation at the cross-country level, we did not find any similar distinctions between cities in absolute prevalence levels which could not readily be accounted for by demographic variation. Nor did we find any distinctions in the broad *groups* of drugs likely to be used in any of the four locations sampled. With regard to modes of usage our data are more equivocal, being based on fairly small numbers of frequent and injecting drug users, however, we again found no statistical evidence of locational variation which could not be subsumed by demography. It is worth bearing in mind here that mode of usage is to an extent dependent on drug type and so local blips in particular modes of usage may reflect local variation in preferred drug type. This link, for example, would adequately explain our finding that Glasgow accounted for the majority of our injecting drug users.

Intra-urban locational clustering of drug users

In attempting to analyse lower level locational variation in drug usage, we were anxious to avoid creating artificial distinctions between areas by using very open-ended criteria of who is or is not a 'drug user'. On the other hand, we did not wish to exclude from analysis areas in which a substantial proportion of individuals had used drugs, but only on a 'one-off' or experimental basis, particularly since our prevalence data implied that the areas in which the predominant form of usage was experimental might differ from those areas in which drugs were used on a more frequent basis. To provide data on both aspects of usage we used two definitions of a 'drug user' and analysed them separately. Both our definitions were tied to recent drug usage, since we had to ensure that our respondents were talking about drug usage which had occurred whilst they were living at their present address. The first definition, which emphasised more persistent drug use, defined a 'drug user' as someone who used one or more drugs with a frequency of greater than or equal to once per month. The second definition took a 'drug user' to be someone who had used any drug within the last year. Since the prevalence of the three major drug groups on which we had data varied considerably, we also decided to analyse each drug group separately.

Figure 4.1
Distribution of drug users across postal districts: Main sample

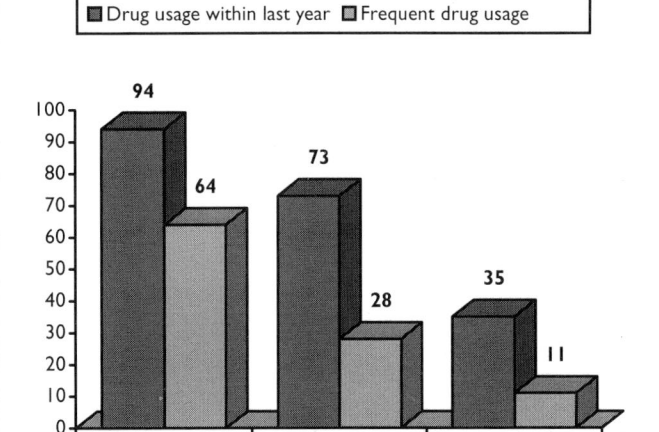

Percentage of postal districts sampled which contained drug users - based on usage within the last year and on frequent usage, averaged across location.

The sampling methods used in our survey meant that in each location we had a broad and representative spread of postal districts across the relevant town or borough and we also had a broad and representative spread of enumeration districts within each postal district. So, as a first stage in the analysis, we simply mapped the locations of those individuals using each of the three drug types - cannabis, non-opiates and opiates - onto the OS maps of the four areas. Using these data we discovered what proportion of postal districts contained drug users and within each postal district the proportion of enumeration districts which contained drug users. Proportions provided more useful information than any absolute values in this context because postal districts and, to a lesser extent, enumeration districts are highly variable in size. To give an illustration of this, a postal district can vary in size from between 2,000 to 10,000 households.

A summary of these data is given in Tables 4.1 to 4.4 in Appendix 1. Although we mapped the locations of both main and booster sample respondents, it should be borne in mind that as a function of the sampling techniques used our booster sample can only be representative of a limited subset of areas within each location, these being the relatively more deprived areas.

As Figures 4.1 and 4.2 demonstrate, some degree of clustering is occurring for all three drug types in both main and booster samples. Not all areas have drug users. Whilst the overall prevalence of drug use will determine to a degree the number of postal districts in which it is *possible* for drug users to be located, the absolute numbers of drug users in our sample were sufficient to determine in all cases whether the variance noted for cannabis and non-opiates was above chance and in a small number of cases we could assess this also for opiate usage.

Figure 4.2
Distribution of drug users across postal districts: Booster sample

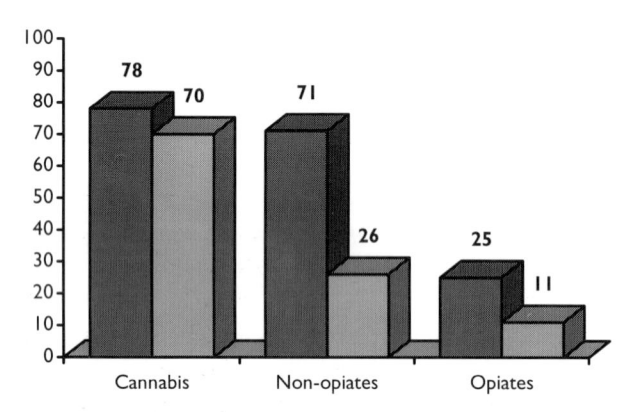

□ Drug usage within last year ■ Frequent drug usage

Cannabis: 78, 70
Non-opiates: 71, 26
Opiates: 25, 11

Percentage of postal districts sampled which contained drug users - based on usage within the last year and on frequent usage, averaged across location.

In the event, the question of whether any clustering was greater than would be expected on the basis of chance alone depended on a number of variables, notably the measure of drug usage used, the type of drug and the location in question. In all locations, the spread of cannabis users across postal districts was greater than that of non-opiate users and similarly the spread of non-opiate users was greater than that of opiate users, whichever measure of drug usage was taken into account. Predictably, our measure of frequent usage resulted in a greater degree of clustering than was the case for potentially experimental usage.

Whilst in about half of the cases considered, the distribution of both frequent and experimental drug users was *not* significantly different from chance, geographic variation was of importance in some towns and for certain drug types. Specifically, cannabis and non-opiate drug users - assessed on both a frequent and recent usage basis - were clustered in particular postal districts in Nottingham's main sample. This pattern was broadly matched in the comparable booster sample, although here the recent usage of non-opiates did not show significant clustering. Lewisham's main sample showed a significant level of clustering for cannabis usage on both measures of usage. Finally, Glasgow's booster sample - although not its main sample - showed significant clustering on both drug usage measures for cannabis and non-opiates.

Although the booster sample is of less value than the main sample for a geographic analysis, the fact that the booster sample *did* show a degree of clustering as well as the main sample implies that clustering can occur even within the equivalent types of postal district selected for that sample, namely comparatively deprived areas.

Figure 4.3
Distribution of drug users across enumeration districts: Main sample

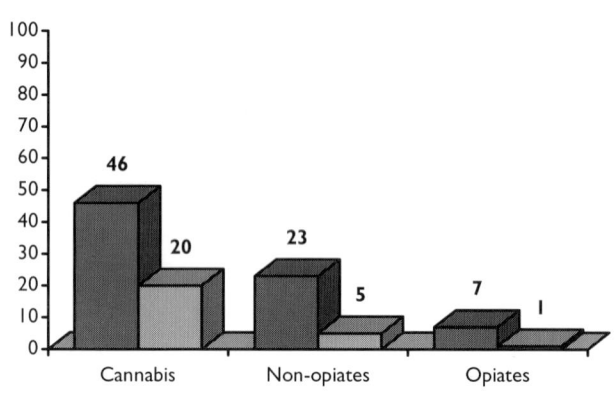

□ Drug usage within last year ■ Frequent drug usage

Cannabis: 46, 20
Non-opiates: 23, 5
Opiates: 7, 1

Percentage of enumeration districts sampled which contained drug users - based on usage within the last year and on frequent usage, averaged across location and across all postal districts in a location.

Turning to the distribution of drug users *within* a given postal district, it can be seen from Figures 4.3 and 4.4 that locational clustering of drug users is rather *more* apparent at this level. For example, although most postal districts contained cannabis users, these individuals were concentrated in particular parts of each postal district. Figures 4.3 and 4.4 show the percentage of enumeration districts which contained drug users, averaged across all relevant postal districts within an area. These figures suggest that the pattern of clustering observed for districts is maintained at the level of rather smaller local areas, with Glasgow's main sample showing less clustering than either Lewisham or Bradford and Nottingham showing the greatest degree of clustering.

Figure 4.4
Distribution of drug users across enumeration districts: Booster sample

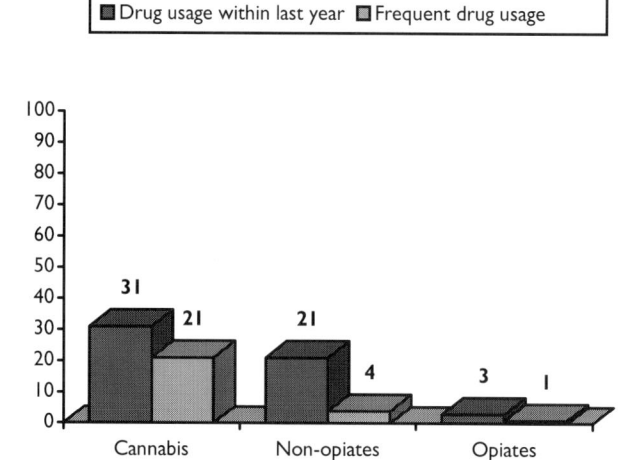

Percentage of enumeration districts sampled which contained drug users - based on usage within the last year and on frequent usage, averaged across location and across all postal districts in a location

Also as with locational variation at the broader level of postal districts, the clustering observed for enumeration districts was only statistically significant in a minority of cases. Again, it showed a dependence on factors such as the type of drug, the measure of drug usage and the identity of the town in question. To briefly summarise the patterns found: Nottingham's main and booster sample showed significant locational clustering for cannabis usage, based on both experimental and frequent usage and the main sample also showed a significant degree of clustering for experimental usage of non-opiates. Equally, both Glasgow's and Lewisham's main samples showed a clustering of non-opiate users, based on both measures of drug usage and Glasgow's booster sample showed a significant clustering of *regular* users of non-opiates. Bradford's main sample showed significant clustering for experimental usage of opiates and regular usage of non-opiates.

In summary, the distribution of drug users *does* show locational clustering in our data, both at the broad level of postal districts and at the level of the local communities likely to be represented by enumeration districts. The level of clustering observed varied both by location and by drug type. Cannabis users were geographically more widespread than users of non-opiate drugs and for both drug groups Nottingham showed the greatest degree of clustering whilst Glasgow showed the least. The limited number of opiate users in our sample prevented us from determining fully where these drugs would be placed in the pattern of clustering. Although we were not able to plot network maps of actual levels of *contact* between drug users, it was apparent that in a number of cases the enumeration districts with drug users - particularly opiate users - tended to abut one another, forming small pockets of drug users in the relevant postal districts. This may help to explain the fact that in previous research drug users have been shown to form acquaintanceship groups, a fact which has been interpreted as indicating that there are 'sub-cultures' of drug use.

The demographic profile of 'drug areas'

As discussed in the last chapter, the identity of the borough/city from which a respondent derives does not in itself explain a great deal of the variation in drug usage between respondents as measured by multivariate analyses. Yet there is significant variation between respondents from different areas in absolute terms, as a consequence it would seem of demographic variations. Consequently it is of some importance that we test whether similar demographic variation could also account for the distinctions noted above at the lower level of local geography.

To address this issue, we selected a number of districts from each of the four locations which had a *high* profile of drug usage and compared the population characteristics of these with districts which had a *low* profile of drug usage. As our initial analyses suggested that the identity of these districts did not vary substantially across the three drug groups we have amalgamated the data for cannabis, non-opiates and opiates in the following discussion. Again, we used two measures of drug usage, namely usage within the last year and frequent usage. As the booster sample had, of course, been selected with specific demographic biases built into it, analyses carried out on the main sample should be given greater credence, although we have included a number of booster sample analyses to establish likely demographic patterns in a subset of more 'deprived' areas.

The definition we used to label a district as 'high' or 'low' in drug users was based on the percentage of enumeration districts (EDs) within the boundaries of a given postal district which had frequent, or experimental users, respectively. Although to an extent arbitrary, this definition has certain advantages over other possible definitions in the present context. First, it avoids the issue of whether we have under-sampled drug users in any given postal district. A postal district from which we were able randomly to obtain drug using respondents in more than say 50% of its constituent enumeration districts is likely to be one with a high proportion of drug users, whether or not we have under-sampled the absolute number of users. Secondly, it allows the definition of a postal district as an area high or low in its number of drug users to depend on whether the neighbourhood *as a whole* has a high proportion of drug users, rather than on whether it contains a small pocket of drug users. Although we polarised 'drug districts' and 'non-drug districts' as much as possible, the exact definition of a 'drug area' in fact varied between locations as a function of the differential prevalence of drug usage. The profile of postal districts in each location as defined by the percentages of enumeration districts with drug users can be seen in Table 4.5 in Appendix 1. A description of the particular comparisons being drawn in the case of each location are outlined in Figure 4.5 above.

Given the above, it should be borne in mind that those locations for which we were able to compare between the greatest extremes - namely Glasgow and Lewisham - are the most likely to give a true picture of demographic variance between 'drug areas' and 'non-drug areas'. It should also be noted that given the nature of our data we are talking largely about cannabis usage and, to a lesser extent, usage of non-opiates.

Since the 1981 census data for our locations were likely to be quite inaccurate and we did not have access to the 1991 data, the demographic profile of each district had to be drawn from the picture presented by our main sample data for each district. Although this may include some inaccuracies, the main sample was, after all, specifically designed to be representative of the local-population in each area. The demographic profile of drug areas and non-drug areas is given in detail in Tables 4.6-4.15 in Appendix 1, here we will just summarise the main findings.

The comparisons made between our 'drug areas' and our 'non drug areas' suggested that the former were distinct from the latter on a number of demographic measures. Predictably, the most consistent of these in the main samples was age, with 'drug areas' tending to have a higher proportion of young people than non-drug areas. However, this distinction only reached statistical significance in Nottingham's main sample, for frequent drug usage, and in Lewisham's main sample for both recent and frequent usage. In the booster sample, not surprisingly, only one significant finding was noted for age and this suggests that based on recent usage only, Glasgow's 'drug areas' tended to have more residents in the 20-24 age band than its 'non-drug areas'.

Ethnicity also had a fairly consistent effect, although again this effect reached statistical significance in only about half of the cases considered. Nottingham's main sample drug areas, measured on the basis of both recent and frequent usage, had a significantly higher proportion of ethnic minorities than its non-drug areas. Lewisham's main sample followed this pattern, but only for drug usage measured on the basis of frequent usage. In Bradford's main sample, the pattern was reversed, with drug areas being significantly more likely to have a high proportion of white residents. The pattern for most booster sample locations matched that for the main samples, although the distinctions between drug areas and non-drug areas were less likely to reach statistical significance.

Bradford's 'drug areas' were also distinct from those of the other locations in terms of their employment profile. In Glasgow 'drug areas' defined by both

Figure 4.5
Comparisons drawn between 'drug areas' and 'non-drug areas'

	Usage within last year		Regular usage	
	'Drug areas'	'Non-drug areas'	'Drug areas'	'Non-drug areas'
Lewisham Main	70-100% of EDs	40-50% of EDs	50-70% of EDs	<40% of EDs
Bradford Main	50-70% of EDs	<40% of EDs	Too few regular users	
Glasgow Main	70-100% of EDs	<50% of EDs	>50% of EDs	<40% of EDs
Nottingham Main	>50% of EDs	<40% of EDs	>50% of EDs	<40% of EDs
Lewisham Booster	>50% of EDs	<40% of EDs	>40% of EDs	<40% of EDs
Bradford Booster	50-70% of EDs	<40% of EDs	40-50% of EDs	<40% of EDs
Glasgow Booster	70-100% of EDs	<40% of EDs	70-100% of EDs	<40% of EDs
Nottingham Booster	50-70% of EDs	<40% of EDs	40-50% of EDs	<40% of EDs

Definitions of 'drug areas' and 'non-drug areas' on the basis of the percentage of enumeration districts in a postal district which had recent or frequent drug users.

measures of drug usage were significantly more likely to have a high proportion of respondents presently unemployed. This was true also for Nottingham's main sample, which also showed a higher proportion of people who had never had paid employment in drug areas, although only for those drug areas defined by frequent usage. In Bradford, however, the only statistically significant difference between drug areas and non-drug areas on the basis of this criterion was for non-drug areas to have higher proportions of people who had never had paid employment. This finding presumably matches that noted for the ethnic split, with predominantly Asian areas, with lower levels of drug usage, tending to have higher levels of unemployment. Again, the pattern for the booster samples was similar to that for the main sample, although as previously, any distinctions were less likely to reach statistical significance.

The socioeconomic profile of our chosen areas was more equivocal, but also more consistently reached statistical significance. In Glasgow's main sample, drug areas, measured by both experimental and frequent usage, were significantly more likely to have a high proportion of C2 and DE socioeconomic groups than non-drug areas. This finding held also for Nottingham's main sample, if drug usage was measured on the basis of *frequent* usage, although if usage as such was at issue the situation was reversed, with drug areas having a significantly higher proportion of the AB socioeconomic groups. In Lewisham, the main sample drug areas appeared to be primarily represented by the C1 socioeconomic group. No statistically significant differences were noted for Bradford. The pattern was broadly similar for the booster sample, although the differences were not as clear cut. Finally, no significant gender differences between drug areas and non-drug areas were shown in any sample or location.

In summary, areas in which experimental or frequent drug usage were particularly prevalent tended to have a younger population, to have a greater proportion of ethnic minorities, a greater proportion of lower status socioeconomic groups and to have higher levels of unemployment. The direction of these findings was fairly consistent across both samples and most locations, although they only reached statistical significance in around half of the cases we considered. Perhaps the most interesting thing about these data is that they do not entirely match our findings for prevalence *per se*. Although the effects of age and experience of employment are consistent with our prevalence results, the pattern noted for socioeconomic status and ethnicity are in a direction counter to that noted for prevalence. Higher status socioeconomic groups and white respondents showed the *highest* prevalence rates for drug usage, but those areas which showed the greatest concentration of drug users were areas with high proportions of ethnic minorities and lower status socioeconomic groups. The distinction between prevalence rates and the clustering of drug usage does not suggest any inconsistencies in our data. What it *does* suggest is that the localisation of any 'drug problem' in a particular area may be due to factors other than those responsible for drug usage as such.

Urban deprivation and drug usage

Given the predominant profile of our 'drug areas' we felt that one obvious candidate to be considered as a factor in the clustering of drug usage was the level of 'deprivation' in an area. After all, three of the demographic variables considered above are in themselves standardly used as indices of the relative level of 'deprivation' attaching to an area. These variables are the proportion of lower status socioeconomic groups in an area, the proportion of ethnic minorities in an area and the proportion of people in long or short term unemployment. As noted above, our 'drug areas' therefore tended to be 'deprived' areas almost by definition. To confirm this pattern, we looked also at the predominant type of housing in the areas considered, this being a further reasonable guide to likely levels of deprivation.

For this analysis, we combined across ACORN ratings to give four major housing types: 'affluent housing', 'retirement housing', 'older housing' and 'council or inner city housing'. We then compared the proportion of respondents within our main sample living in each type of accommodation within our 'drug areas' and 'non-drug areas'. Again, we used our own data rather than the 1981 census data for each area as a whole, on the basis that it was more likely to be accurate. Since the booster sample had specifically been selected on the basis of local area ACORN ratings, we did not consider this sample for this particular analysis.

The ACORN profile of 'drug areas' and 'non-drug areas' is given in detail in Table 4.16 in Appendix 1 and summarised in Figures 4.6 and 4.7 in the text. As these figures demonstrate, this analysis gave us our strongest finding for the demographic profile of 'drug areas' versus 'non-drug areas'. In all four locations, for all potential measures of drug usage, drug areas were more likely to be predominantly represented in our sample by council or inner city housing. This finding reached very high levels of statistical significance indeed. Whilst the profile of drug areas in Glasgow is open to dispute, since it mirrors the higher level of public housing in Scotland as a whole and is therefore not, strictly speaking, a measure of relative deprivation, in the English cities we can take the 'drug areas' to be more deprived on this measure.

Figure 4.6
ACORN *profile of 'drug areas': Drug usage within the last year (Main sample)*

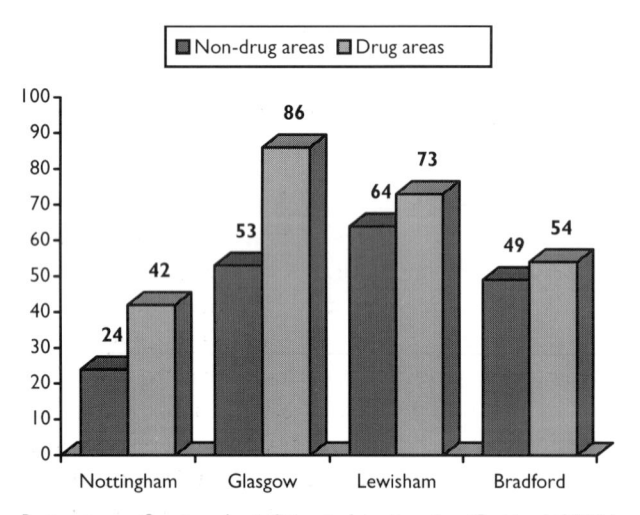

Percentage of respondents living in housing classified by ACORN as 'council or inner city housing' within postal districts classed either as 'drug areas' or as 'non-drug areas'

Interestingly, the pattern noted above was also matched at the city-wide level. The predominant differences between our four locations in terms of housing was that Lewisham and to a much greater extent, Glasgow had a greater proportion of council owned and inner city housing than either Nottingham or Bradford. They also clearly showed the greatest prevalence of drug usage. Again the distinction between the implications of ACORN type in Scotland and England should be borne in mind.

The profile of our 'drug areas' is not unexpected. Similar patterns have long been established for general offence and offender rates (Baldwin and Bottoms 1976). As far as *residential* areas are concerned higher crime rates *do* correlate with housing type, and especially tenure, and also with demographic indicators of social deprivation. It does not follow, however, that *all* deprived council estates have high crime rates nor is it to be expected that *all* areas with a high proportion of lower status socioeconomic groups will have a drug problem. The reasons why some areas do develop high crime rates whilst other, superficially identical areas do *not* has been the subject of general criminological interest and various explanations of why this occurs have been developed (Bottoms et al 1986, 1992a and 1992b, Wikström 1990, Wiles 1992). This type of analysis is likely to become of equal importance in drugs research.

Figure 4.7
ACORN *profile of 'drug areas': Frequent drug usage*

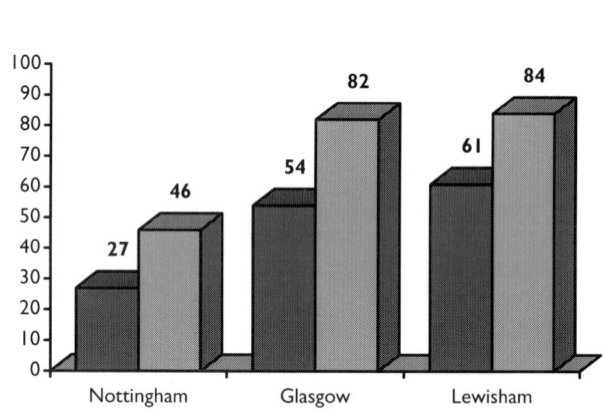

Percentage of respondents living in housing classified by ACORN as 'council or inner city housing' within postal districts classed either as 'drug areas' or 'non-drug areas'

In summary, our data clearly indicate that those areas in which drug usage clusters tend to be those areas which are predominantly composed of housing types suggestive of deprivation. Although we are not able from this data to discuss in detail other potential candidates likely to account for locational clustering, it should be noted that one of the most salient alternative candidates - namely drugs distribution networks - implies the same link with urban deprivation. Local areas with high levels of unemployment are likely to be particularly prone to the development of alternative economies. This aspect of potential locational clustering is considered briefly below.

Intra-urban locational variation in drug distribution

To provide a profile of the drug distribution side of the 'drug problem', we had asked respondents to indicate whether they felt that drugs could be obtained from any specific areas within their town/borough and to name these if they were able to. Although this does not provide any information on distribution networks it does allow us to assess whether the areas from which drugs are likely to be obtained match those within which they are most commonly used.

Since we felt that members of the general public and casual drug users were unlikely to have a very accurate view of where drug dealing occurred, we used only the views of frequent drug users for this analysis. As we hope to analyse the geographic data in greater depth at a later date we also decided not to carry out any very in-depth statistical analyses on the data at the present time. Consequently, we simply mapped out the areas named by users as drug dealing areas and compared these with the OS maps on which we had plotted our 'drug using areas'. Although a variety of areas *not* appearing as 'drug using' areas were labelled by regular drug users as dealing areas, there was a close overlap between our 'drug areas' and the areas most likely to be labelled by users as dealing areas. Since our 'drug areas' tended to be the more deprived areas sampled this goes some way towards confirming Lavelle et al's (1992) impression that people are more likely to go into than out of deprived areas to obtain drugs. Whilst not particularly surprising, this does highlight the fact that both aspects of the 'drugs problem' are tied quite closely to the problem of social and economic deprivation.

In summary, our data provides some, albeit limited, support for the view that areas of urban deprivation are not only likely to be areas in which drug usage clusters, but also areas in which drug dealing clusters. This has clear implications for drugs prevention, since it indicates that both aspects of the 'drugs problem' are tied quite closely to levels of social and economic deprivation.

Public perceptions of locational variation in drug usage

It is of interest to compare the *actual* geographic profile of drug usage within locations with the perceptions of residents in those locations regarding the distribution of drug usage. Similar comparisons drawn for property and personal crime suggest that residents in a city build up very strong and extremely long-lasting stereotypes of the districts within their cities, stereotypes which tend to last past the point at which they bear any relation to the actual profile of the districts in question (cf. Bottoms and Wiles 1986, Tonry and Morris 1988).

The data we obtained on perceptions of drug dealing allowed us to assess the extent of association between actual and perceived 'drug areas' and also allowed us to compare the views of drug users and non-drug users. Since the views of individuals regarding their own local area often tend to diverge from their views regarding other areas which are actually very similar, we also asked respondents to assess the scale of drug usage within their own local area, in comparison to the pattern of drug usage they perceived as applying to the rest of the borough/city. A detailed summary of these data is given in Tables 4.17 to 4.28 in Appendix 1.

Perceptions of a respondent's local area as a 'drug area'

The geographic area which individuals commonly see as being 'their area' tends to be highly specific - not extending, for example, past a radius of about 15 or 20 minutes walk from where they live. Consequently, we used enumeration districts as our unit of analysis for assessing our respondents' views of their own area. As the views of local residents regarding an area are also likely to differ quite substantially between individuals, depending on such factors as their age and whether they are transient or stable residents, we also used the *majority* view of an area to determine its profile as a 'drug area' in the eyes of local residents.

Figure 4.8 outlines the percentage of enumeration districts in each location in which a *majority* of respondents believed that their local area was comparatively *high* in drug users. Not surprisingly, the data suggest that most respondents are unwilling to state that there are more drug users in their own area than in other areas in the borough or city. This is similar to the results obtained if one asks about a range of other social problems, notably crime.

Interestingly, however, the pattern of responses observed in fact largely follows the actual pattern of drug use within our samples on a number of dimensions, suggesting that people are not *entirely* unrealistic in their views. Nottingham and Glasgow, for example, showed the highest proportion of EDs in which a majority of respondents stated that their local area was *comparatively* high in drug users and Bradford and Lewisham the lowest, for both main and booster samples. This matches the profile of the four locations in terms of the clustering of drug users, as outlined earlier, and therefore also matches the likelihood that a particular ED would be comparatively high in drug users.

In all main samples, the predominant response across EDs was for the local area to be seen as being comparatively low in drug users. The predominant response in all booster samples - with the exception of Nottingham - on the other hand was for respondents to state only that their area was about the *same* as other areas in the city. This disparity also matches the distinction in drug usage between the two types of sample. As such it could be the consequence either of greater levels of awareness or concern regarding drug usage, or of the greater visibility of drug usage within this sample as an 'at risk' group.

Figure 4.8
Respondents' views of their own local area as a drug area

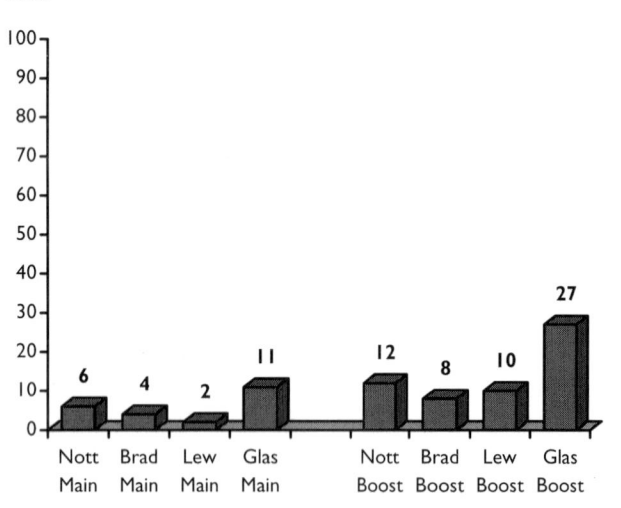

[Bar chart showing values: Nott Main 6, Brad Main 4, Lew Main 2, Glas Main 11, Nott Boost 12, Brad Boost 8, Lew Boost 10, Glas Boost 27]

Percentage of sampled enumeration districts in which a majority of respondents stated that their area is particularly high in drug users

Whilst the majority view of an area roughly matched the *risk profile* of the group of individuals making the assessment, it did *not* match very closely with the actual profile of an area in terms of our data on drug usage. Tables 4.18 and 4.19 in Appendix 1 summarise the correlations we ran to see whether the views of our respondents matched the actual drugs profile of an ED from our data. The latter is based both on the proportion of regular users of any drug in an ED and on the proportion of individuals who have used any drug within the last year. Although in Lewisham and Bradford the responses noted for the booster samples matched more closely the actual profile of an area than did those of their corresponding main samples, the reverse was the case in Glasgow and Nottingham. This pattern stemmed from an overestimation of the comparative standing of local areas as 'drug areas' by Nottingham's booster sample (they thought they were worse than they were) and a comparable *under*estimation of the local area by respondents from Glasgow's booster sample. More importantly it should be noted that for *all* samples the association between the perceived and actual profile of an area, although always in the correct direction, was in virtually all cases very low, with Nottingham's main sample being the only one in which *any* correlation reached even above 0.35. It is worth noting that the *best* estimate of a local area's profile was generally provided by those respondents who believed that the area was *high* in drug users, rather than by those who believed it to be low in drug usage. This is predictable, given that our respondents display a consistent tendency to *under*estimate the comparative standing of their local area as a 'drug area'. Similar informed underestimations of neighbourhood crime problems have been found for crime in general (Bottoms et al 1990).

The patterns outlined above suggest that when individuals are asked to make judgements about drug usage in their own local area, they use some form of general 'risk assessment' rather than relying on more specific knowledge, for example local knowledge about their area. This is implied by the fact that assessments of a respondent's local area match general trends for the *likelihood* that either they *or* their area are 'at risk' of drug usage, but do *not* match the *actual* profile of the area. If drug usage was well spread within the city and they themselves were in a high risk category, they were, for example, likely to say that their *area* was high in drug usage. These views can consequently be taken more as a measure of concern about drug usage than as anything more specific. Although we do not have the data to go into this more fully here, it might be interesting to pursue the idea of how and why people make particular judgements about their area of residence on this type of issue. This type of information could be of particular value in addressing such issues as the fear of crime.

In summary, the patterns observed suggest that respondents, even those within the more 'knowledgeable' booster samples, were not generally very good at estimating the relative standing of their own local area as an area in which drug users are to be found. This notwithstanding, the general profile of the city or borough in which a respondent lives *does* appear to affect in some way the perceptions of respondents regarding their *own* area. The broad pattern of actual drug use both between and within samples also matched quite closely the pattern shown by the proportion of respondents rating their own local area as relatively high in terms of the number of drug users. This suggests that our respondents may have been either expressing a generalised concern about drug usage or entering into some form of 'risk assessment' when asked to make estimates regarding their own area. There was also a strong tendency on the part of the majority of respondents to underestimate the actual profile of their area as a 'drug area'.

Perceptions of areas other than the local area as 'drug areas'

Although respondents are clearly not very good at judging the status of their own area in drug terms and for readily identifiable psychological reasons tend consistently to *under*estimate drug usage within their own area, it is conceivable that they might be rather better at judging the status of other areas, which they might tend to view more objectively. To address this, we asked respondents to say whether they thought there were any particular areas or places in their city or borough to which one would go if one wanted to *buy* drugs. We then asked those respondents who felt there were specific 'drug dealing' places to name the location(s) they had in mind and to explain how they had acquired this knowledge. Tables 4.20 to 4.28 in Appendix 1 outline the responses given, separating those respondents with and without personal knowledge of drugs *or* drug users. Figures 4.9 to 4.16 summarise this data.

As can be seen from Figure 4.9, the overall tendency across both samples and all four locations was for a clear majority of respondents both with and without experience of drugs or drug users to say that drug dealing *was* associated with particular areas. Some locational variation was noted, with respondents from Glasgow being rather more likely than respondents in the other locations to consider that drug dealing areas existed. This disparity matches the profile of responses outlined in Chapter 5 to the question of how big a problem drugs were in each of the locations and may simply be a consequence of the generally higher profile drug usage has in Glasgow as a consequence of research, policy and media attention.

The data above suggest that the prevailing view is overwhelmingly that drug dealing areas *do* exist and consequently that drug dealing is *not* an activity which is uniformly distributed within cities. This is also a view supported by the academic literature (cf. Dorn, Murji and South 1991). The only equivalent data available for other kinds of illegal activity in the UK is in relation to prostitution where similar local interpretations of 'red light' areas have been found (Bottoms et al 1990). In contrast, more general research on personal safety and violent crime suggests that 'danger areas' identified by the public in this context tend to be more amorphous locations, such as city centres or large parks (Shapland and Vagg 1988). It would be interesting to follow up this distinction using a range of other illicit activities.

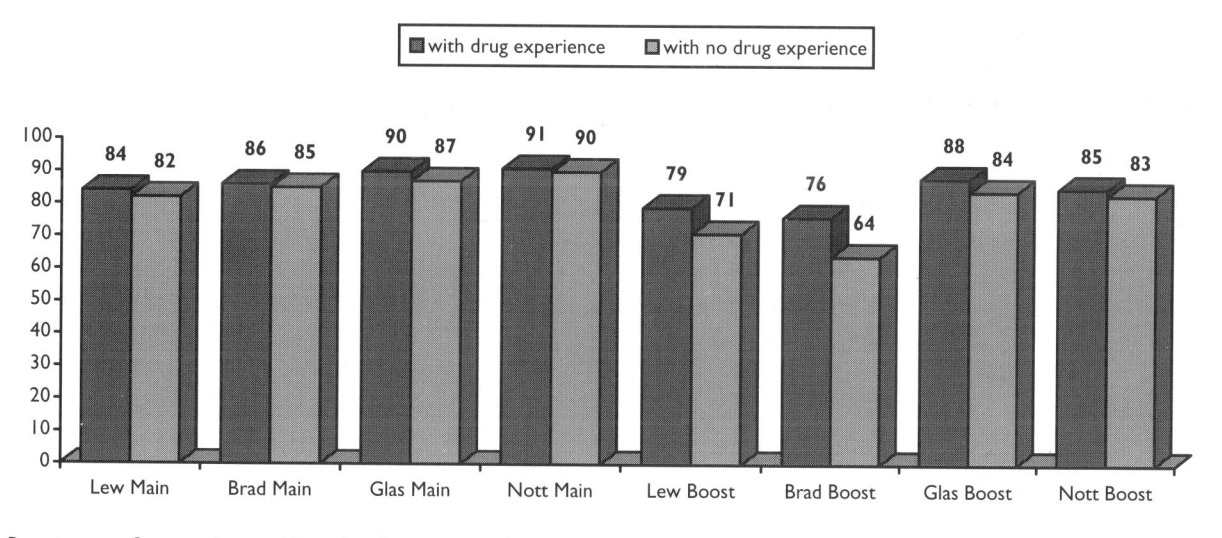

Figure 4.9
Views regarding the localisation of drug dealing

Percentage of respondents with and without personal experience of drug usage who felt that drug dealing was located in particular areas or places

Figure 4.10
Knowledge of drugs or drug users and the ability to name a place where drugs can be obtained

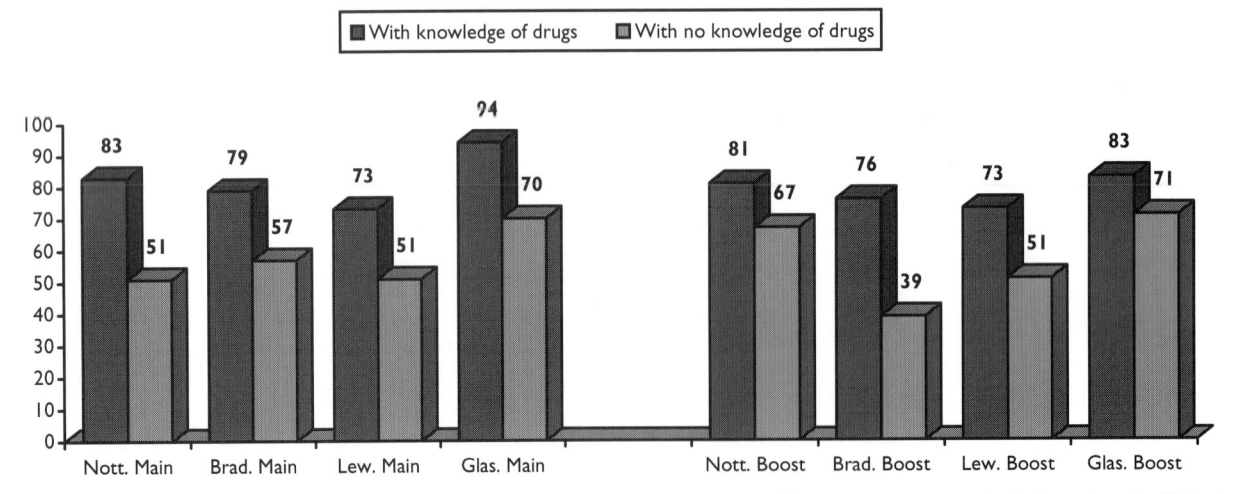

■ With knowledge of drugs   ■ With no knowledge of drugs

Location	With knowledge	With no knowledge
Nott. Main	83	51
Brad. Main	79	57
Lew. Main	73	51
Glas. Main	94	70
Nott. Boost	81	67
Brad. Boost	76	39
Lew. Boost	73	51
Glas. Boost	83	71

Percentage of respondents with and without knowledge of drug usage who could name an area in which they thought illicit drugs could be obtained.

Table 4.22 in Appendix 1 outlines the proportion of those respondents stating that drug dealing *was* localised who could also give a name to the types of places and areas they were thinking of. As can be seen from Figure 4.10 the majority of respondents who stated that there were particular areas went on to name at least one such area. Not surprisingly, direct personal knowledge of drug use significantly increased the ability of a respondent to name such a place. This finding held across all locations and both types of sample. Although the question was primarily intended to elicit the name of specific areas or districts, a number of respondents made rather more general statements regarding areas, such as labelling the 'inner city' or 'any deprived area' as an option. In the following summary of the data we will consider only the most *detailed* response given by any respondent, whether in itself this response named a specific area or not.

As can be seen from Figures 4.11 and 4.12, the distribution of responses to this item was distinctly polarised. Although a broad range of areas and types of places were named, the majority of respondents in all areas and both main and booster sample chose to name a particular residential area within their city or borough. A rather smaller proportion - between 1 and 16% depending on sample type and location - felt sufficiently confident in their knowledge to name a *very* specific location within a district, for example a pub or a particular road. No clear pattern emerged either for locational variation or variation across sample type. For example, Glasgow's main sample respondents were the *most* likely to name a particular place or neighbourhood, but Glasgow's booster sample respondents were the *least* likely to do so. As suggested earlier, the general tendency of respondents to name specific locations as drug dealing areas is quite different from people's practices with regard to certain other forms of illicit activity for which one tends to obtain much vaguer references which are practically the same for every town. It may be that this distinction relates to the structure of drug dealing which makes it a rather less opportunistic activity than many other crimes and which, equally, allow drug usage to mimic other licit consumer activities.

In contrast to the data outlined earlier, knowledge of drug use appeared in some cases to *restrict* the likelihood of a respondent naming *either* a neighbourhood or a specific place within the district. Possibly, more knowledgeable people were aware of the option of obtaining drugs in several locations, or of location being dependent on drug type. Equally possibly, very knowledgeable respondents felt more constrained in labelling areas because of perceived legal implications.

Whilst the percentage of respondents giving only very general labels to their perception of drug dealing areas was fairly low - between 1 and 7% - the types of places named were quite interesting. The same four general options were popular across both samples and all locations. These options were 'the city centre', 'pubs and clubs' 'council estates' and 'deprived areas'. Given that the vast majority of specific neighbourhoods named were also those comparatively high in levels of

Figure 4.11
Types of areas named as drug areas: Main sample

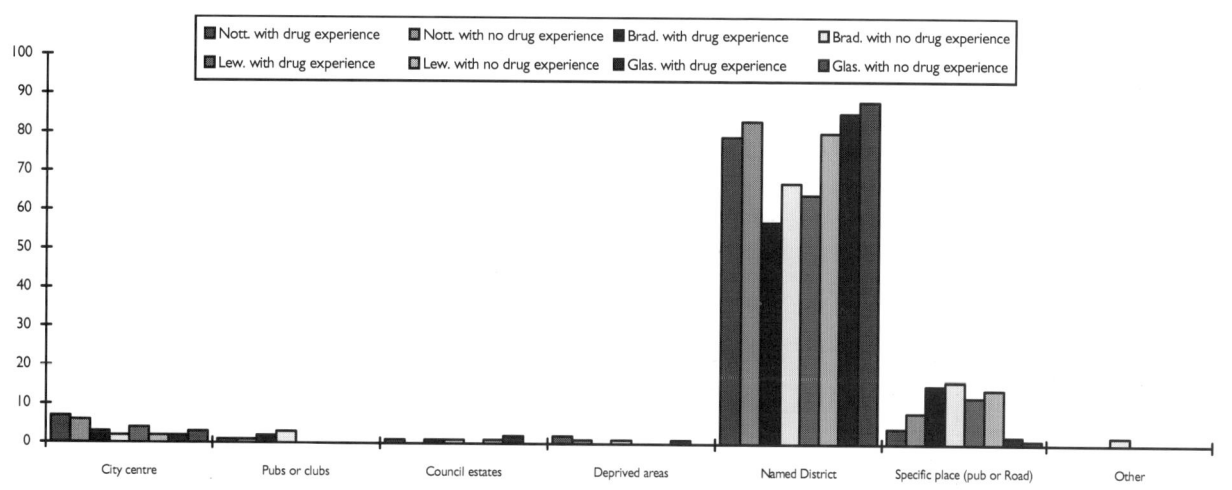

Percentage of respondents in each named sample who cited one of the listed places as an area where illicit drugs could be obtained.

Figure 4.12
Types of areas named as drug areas: Booster sample

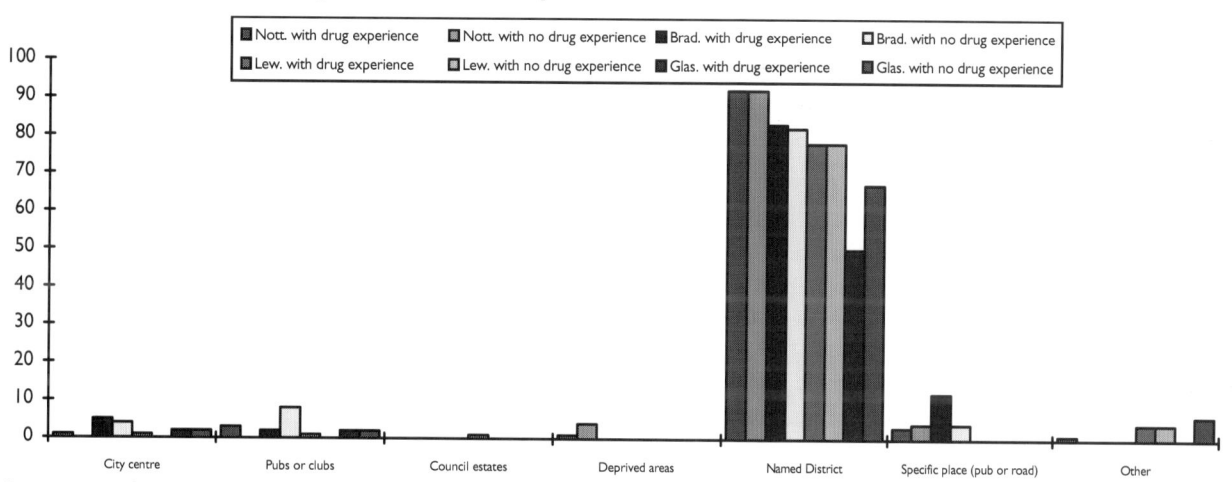

Percentage of respondents in each named sample who cited one of the listed places as an area where illicit drugs could be obtained

deprivation within the relevant city or borough, it would seem that the general public, whether knowledgeable regarding drug usage or not, concurs in its beliefs with our data and with the views of other researchers in regarding areas of deprivation as prime targets for drug dealing.

The number of separate neighbourhoods labelled by respondents as being associated with drug dealing of itself suggests, however, that not all areas named, whether deprived or not, actually *are* areas in which drug dealing occurs. As can be seen from Table 4.25 in Appendix 1, the number of neighbourhoods labelled as associated with drug dealing in Glasgow, for example, almost matches the total number of neighbourhoods within that city! Since our data set suggests that those areas high in their proportion of drug users are also labelled by knowledgeable individuals as the areas associated with drug dealing, we were able to compare the identity of the areas labelled earlier as 'drug areas' by virtue of the prevalence of drug usage within them with our respondents' views of the identity of 'drug areas' as defined by perceptions regarding drug dealing.

As indicated by Figures 4.13 and 4.14, the overall percentage of respondents naming any one of our 'drug

Figure 4.13
Comparison of perceived and actual 'drug areas': Main sample

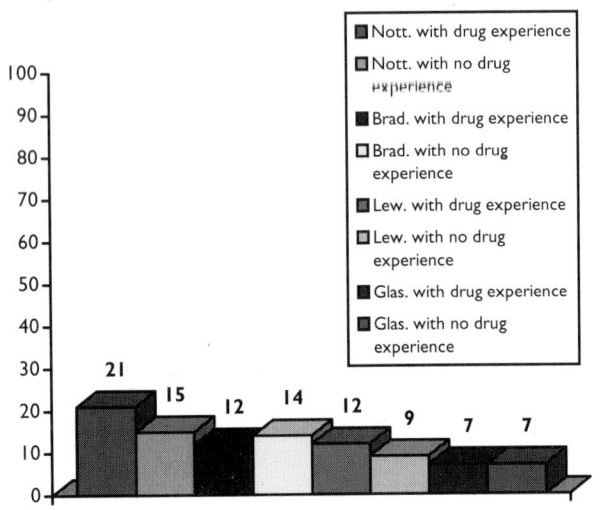

Percentage of respondents labelling as a 'drug area' an area which from our main sample data appeared to have a high proportion of drug users

Figure 4.14
Comparison of perceived and actual 'drug areas': Booster sample

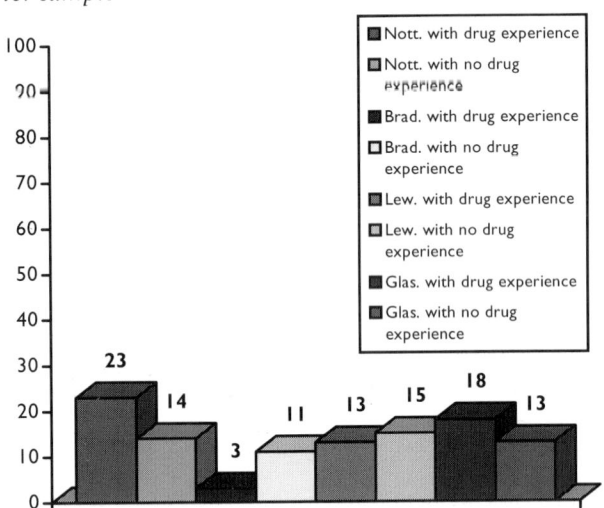

Percentage of respondents labelling as a 'drug area' an area which from our main sample data appeared to have a high proportion of drug users

areas' as a drug dealing area was quite low. Assuming our data to be correct, this disparity could stem either from a lack of accurate knowledge on the part of our respondents or from a shift in locations over time. Since public perceptions do tend to lag behind the actuality of a situation, we would expect to find people naming areas which have historically been 'drug areas', whether or not they are connected with drug usage or dealing at the present time. Not surprisingly, those with some form of direct knowledge of drug use were rather more likely to name areas which had a high proportion of drug users as drug dealing areas than were respondents *without* such knowledge. Similarly and correspondingly, booster sample respondents were more likely to name these areas than were main sample respondents.

The lack of accuracy in naming drug areas was at least partially explained by our respondents' explanations of how they had come by information regarding the identity of drug areas. As Figures 4.15 and 4.16 suggest, even the most knowledgeable samples - the booster samples and those samples defined by respondents who had direct knowledge of drugs - tended to derive their information via 'rumour'. Not unexpectedly, however, those with knowledge of drug use or drug users were significantly more likely to state that they had reached their conclusions via direct knowledge and correspondingly less likely to derive information from other more dubious sources, such as rumour or media infor-

mation. This finding held across both samples and all locations and was matched by a similar distinction between booster and main samples, with the former being, predictably, more likely to draw from personal experience. Whilst in the more experienced samples 'rumour' may be akin to a form of 'sub-cultural knowledge', any reliance on such external sources of knowledge may well account for both the very broad range of neighbourhoods labelled as drug dealing areas and the low association between areas with a high proportion of users and areas labelled as areas with dealers. Rumour even where based on fact tends to lag behind reality.

Aside from direct experience and rumour, the most popular source of information across all samples and locations was the local press. In all samples *except* Glasgow - where the 'national press' may well have been interpreted as the Scottish press - the national press lagged far behind the local press as a source of information. A similar pattern was noted for the use of local and national TV as a source of information. These findings are identical to those for other types of crime (Shapland and Vagg 1988). Whilst any form of 'media' information was used as a source of knowledge by significantly fewer respondents than were kept informed by their friends, relatives or neighbours, these findings nevertheless have obvious implications for prevention work involving the provision of information to the public.

Figure 4.15
Sources of knowledge regarding drug dealing areas: Main sample

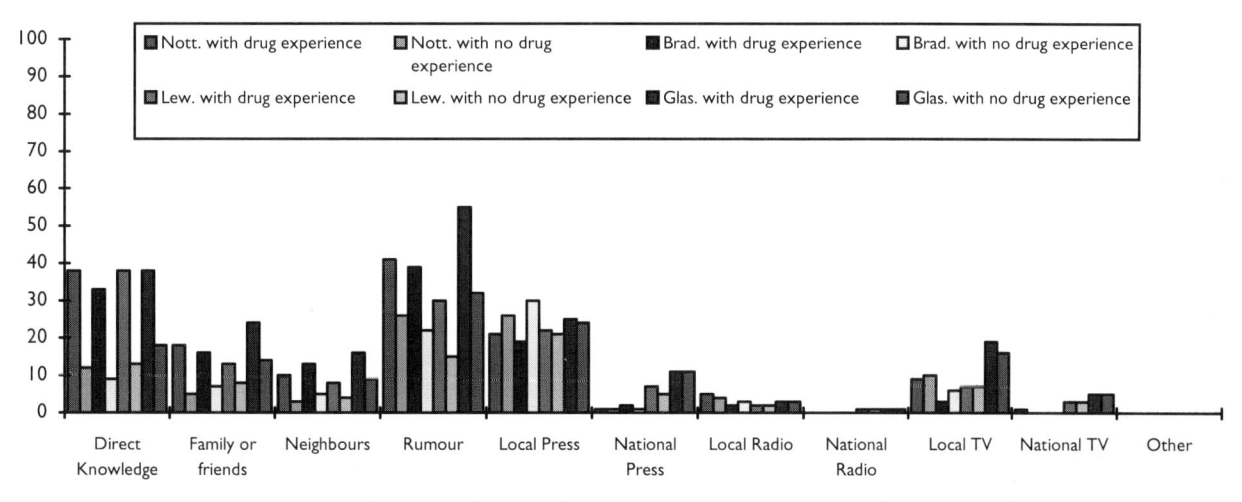

Percentage of respondents citing each source of knowledge listed as their main means of obtaining information regarding drug dealing

In summary, it appears that an awareness of 'drug areas' is built up via the same social networks which establish the reputation for areas on a broad range of other indices including perceived crime levels. As a consequence, public perceptions of the locations in which drug dealing or drug usage take place tend not to be very accurate. Nevertheless, the general view of the *types* of areas which can be labelled as 'drug areas' *does* seem to be fairly accurate, centring on specific residential locations and deprived areas in general.

Summary of Chapter 4

Whilst as we saw in Chapters 2 and 3, drug usage is fairly widespread, our data suggest that some locational clustering occurs both for drug usage and possibly also drug dealing. The profile of those areas within our sample which appeared to have a relatively high prevalence of drug usage and which also tended to be labelled by regular drug users as areas in which drugs could be obtained suggested that clustering of drug usage in particular local areas appears to be associated with levels of deprivation. This general profile, although admittedly not providing conclusive evidence, does tie

Figure 4.16
Sources of knowledge regarding drug dealing areas: Booster sample

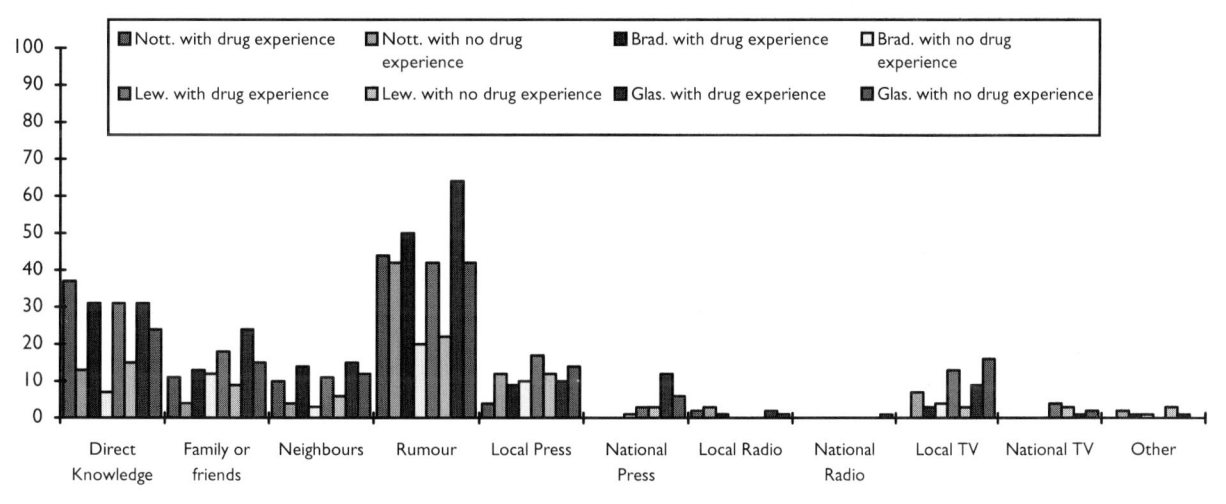

Percentage of respondents citing each source of knowledge listed as their main means of obtaining information regarding drug dealing

up quite well with the accepted, but largely unsupported, view of 'drug areas' as areas of urban deprivation in which the young have little else to do but take drugs. The over-representation of ethnic minorities in such areas is of interest in that it may partially account for previous research findings suggesting that ethnic minorities are the primary users and dealers of a range of drugs.

Without further, recent comparative social indicator data - such as that to come from the 1991 Census - it is impossible for us to take the analysis further at this stage - although this will be an exercise well worth doing. Further research also worth carrying out in this valuable area would be to determine whether the demographic correlates of drug usage are more or less important in absolute terms than other factors linking with local geography, such as 'drug cultures' and the networks formed for drug transport.

It is also clear from our analyses that the general public's attitude towards drug usage matches both our data and the accepted beliefs of previous researchers in suggesting that drug usage centres - to some extent at least - on 'deprived' areas. However, the view of the general public is also a somewhat extreme example of this view. This is perhaps not surprising, since the majority of people would appear, from our sample, to derive their knowledge of drug related locations largely from indirect, and possibly fallacious, sources of information such as local rumour and the media, rather than from direct experience.

We are not able in the present context to explore in any further detail intra-city variations in drug usage or drug supply. Nor can we deal in greater depth with the development of an area's reputation as a 'drug area'. Our results indicate, however, that finding out about locational effects in a general population survey is quite possible and that the results are of considerable relevance both to drugs prevention policy and to more general social policy. We would suggest that similar locational items are included in more local surveys on drugs usage or related issues and that they are extended in any replication of the current study.

Chapter 5

PUBLIC PERCEPTIONS OF LOCAL CRIME RATES AND OTHER PROBLEMS

Although the main focus of our questionnaire was on drugs related issues, we included a number of items not directly connected with drug usage. These items enabled us to put the views of our respondents in a broader context. In particular, we included questions concerned with our respondents' awareness of and attitudes towards local crime rates and other more general problems within their area. The format of several of these items will allow them to be compared with similar items within the British Crime Survey (Mayhew and Hough 1991). This has the advantage that we will be able to compare the views of our respondents regarding crime and other local problems with those of a much larger general population survey. It will also allow us to see whether respondents in our four locations were more or less concerned about crime than respondents in other areas of Britain. The value of such items in the present context lies in providing us with the opportunity to judge the relative importance our respondents place on drug related problems in comparison to other crimes and local problems.

Placing public concern about drugs related problems in the context of potentially similar concerns regarding other crimes and problems is particularly apposite in the present climate of crime prevention. Much has been made in recent years of the role of the community in policing itself (cf. Shapland and Vagg 1988, Skogan 1988/1989) and we have a great deal of information regarding the views of local residents on crimes occurring within their neighbourhood and their own personal experience of victimisation (Hough and Mayhew 1983, Kinsey 1984, Jones et al 1986). We also have a great deal of information about the controversial concept of 'fear of crime' which is now seen by many as almost as great a problem as crime itself (cf. Maxfield 1984, Hough and Mayhew 1985). In contrast, whilst increasing emphasis has been placed on the effects drug usage and drugs related crime may have on a community we in fact have very little information on the public's views regarding this issue. In the present chapter, we hope to go some way towards redressing this imbalance.

Integration into the local community

Research suggests that both an individual's perception of crime within their local area and their mode of response to any such problems depends on their level of integration into the local community. Those less well integrated into the community are more likely to see the level of crime and other problems within the area as quite high and conversely are *less* likely to engage in community directed activity to reduce the level of crimes and problems (Lavrakas 1985, Whitaker 1986). Whilst the direction of effect is not obvious here, it is apparent that integration is an important factor in public perceptions of crime at the community level. It is also, unfortunately, a difficult factor to measure, since the notion of 'community' is not unitary (cf. Williams 1976, Willmott 1987) and an individual's own causal attributions may affect their level of integration - or the extent to which they perceive their community as a whole to be an integrated one - as much or more than other more objective factors.

Since necessary constraints on the length of our questionnaire prohibited us from addressing the issue of integration in detail, we adopted a compromise position and included questions designed to provide both an objective and a subjective measure of our respondents' likely degree of integration into the community. The 'objective' item simply asked respondents to state how long they had lived in their local area. Local area again being defined as the community within about fifteen to twenty minutes walk of the respondent's home. The more 'subjective' item asked respondents to indicate whether they felt that their neighbourhood was one in which people tended to 'do things together' or 'help one another'. Table 5.1 in Appendix 1 provides a summary of the data obtained using these items.

From Figure 5.1 it can be seen that the majority of respondents in all four of our main sample locations had lived in their local area for at least five years. This suggests that their knowledge base regarding the area is likely to be quite extensive and similarly that the views they have regarding the area will be more than speculative. No significant differences were noted between locations in the length of time main sample respondents had lived in an area. As would be expected given the younger age range targeted for the booster sample, the length of time booster sample respondents had lived in their local area was slightly *less* than was the case for main sample respondents. There was also a greater degree of variation between locations. The most notable aspect of which was that booster sample

Figure 5.1
Respondents' length of time in their local area

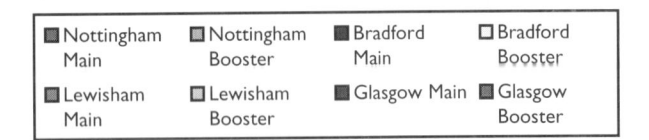

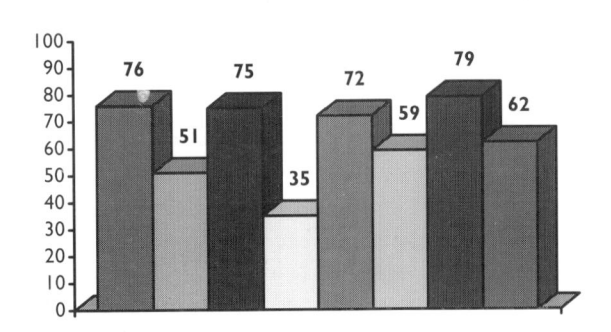

- Nottingham Main
- Nottingham Booster
- Bradford Main
- Bradford Booster
- Lewisham Main
- Lewisham Booster
- Glasgow Main
- Glasgow Booster

Values: 76, 51, 75, 35, 72, 59, 79, 62

Percentage of respondents who had lived in their local area for 5 years or more

Figure 5.2
Respondents' perception of their neighbourhood

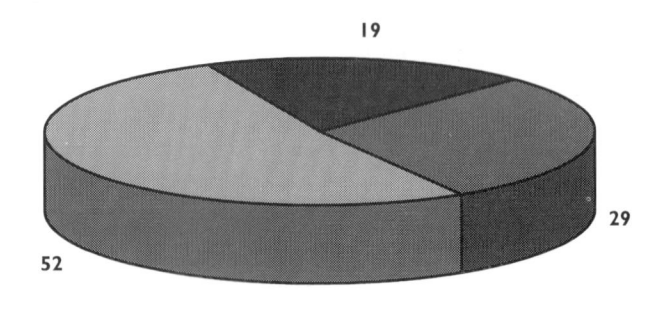

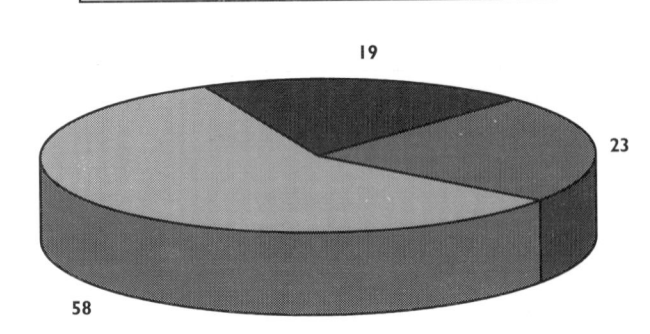

Main sample
- Help each other
- Go own way
- Mix

Values: 19, 29, 52

Booster sample
- Help each other
- Go own way
- Mix

Values: 19, 23, 58

Percentage of respondents viewing their neighbourhood as one in which people were likely to help each other, averaged across location

respondents in Bradford had lived in their local area for significantly *less* time than respondents from the other three locations. With the possible exception of Bradford, however, it is still possible to say that even our young booster sample respondents are representative of a group of individuals likely to have substantial local knowledge and from an objective viewpoint are likely to show a degree of integration into the local community.

In contrast, as Figure 5.2 suggests, the majority of respondents in all locations and across both samples did *not* feel that their neighbourhood stood out as one in which people tended to do things together or help one another. The prevailing view was rather that people tended to go their own way, with less than 30% of respondents in most locations feeling either that people did things together or that a mixture of strategies were followed. In the booster sample, the distinction between the number of respondents feeling that people tended to go their own way and the much smaller number of respondents feeling that people tended to do things together or to help one another was particularly marked. This statistically significant distinction between main and booster samples could be a consequence *either* of the age disparity between the samples, or of the type of urban districts from which the booster sample was selected, both the age structure of an area and its degree of urbanisation having been shown to link with its community structure (cf. Shapland and Vagg 1988).

Whatever the cause of the distinction between main and booster samples, it is apparent that a majority of respondents in *both* samples had a subjective impression of 'community spirit' that implied a lack of integration. As a caveat to this, we must obviously be wary of using one measure of 'doing things together' as a measure of 'community spirit' *per se*. Being part of a community is not just a matter of feeling that local people will help each other or do things together, it is also, for example, about knowing what is going on, and feeling that the local area conveys a coherent identity. We must be equally wary of assuming that a sense of 'community' is necessarily a good thing. Being part of a community can be about the experience of interrelationship and mutual responsibility, but it can also be about a lack of escape, social division and exclusion (Cohen 1982).

In summary, although our respondents are likely to be knowledgeable about their local area, the general pattern of responses suggests that in the main they did not feel strongly associated with their local community.

Satisfaction with the local area

In contrast to the above, the vast majority of respondents were apparently perfectly satisfied with the area in which they lived, as indicated by Figure 5.3. More than 80% of respondents in all *main* sample locations said that they were 'very' or 'fairly' satisfied with their area. The satisfaction of booster sample respondents was slightly less apparent, but their attitude was still very positive, with more than 70% of respondents in all booster sample locations stating that they were 'very' or 'fairly' satisfied with their area. Again, more detailed data on this item is given in Table 5.1 in Appendix 1.

Whilst the difference between main and booster sample respondents was a matter of degree rather than of direction of response, it was nevertheless statistically significant in all locations except Glasgow. The lower levels of satisfaction noted in most booster samples may again be attributed either to age differences between the samples or equally to distinctions between the levels of urbanisation across local areas.

Some locational variation in levels of satisfaction was also noted, with the main sample pattern suggesting that respondents in Nottingham and Bradford had more positive feelings about their local area than those in either Lewisham or Glasgow. Interestingly, this pattern was reversed in the case of the booster sample, where respondents from Glasgow and Lewisham were the *most* satisfied.

Since no specific attempt has been made to match the *main sample* locations in terms of area types, the responses from this sample cannot be taken to reflect any actual distinction between levels of satisfaction across location. In the case of the booster sample, however, respondents were taken from broadly comparable area types across location, so the distinctions between towns may be taken to reflect real differences, at least for this age group.

In summary, whatever the views of our respondents regarding community life in their local area, they were clearly in the main quite content to be living in their present locale. This is a common finding when people are asked about the areas in which they live and as such it may say more about cognitive dissonance than about any real satisfaction with particular areas.

Problems highlighted in the local area

Interestingly, satisfaction with an area does *not* necessarily reflect an absence of perceived problems within that area. It is commonplace for surveys to find that people feel that 'their area' is better than others, even though it may objectively have relatively *high* levels of social problems. Similarly, it is also possible for people to live happily in areas with stable criminal cultures and

Figure 5.3
Respondents' level of satisfaction with their local area

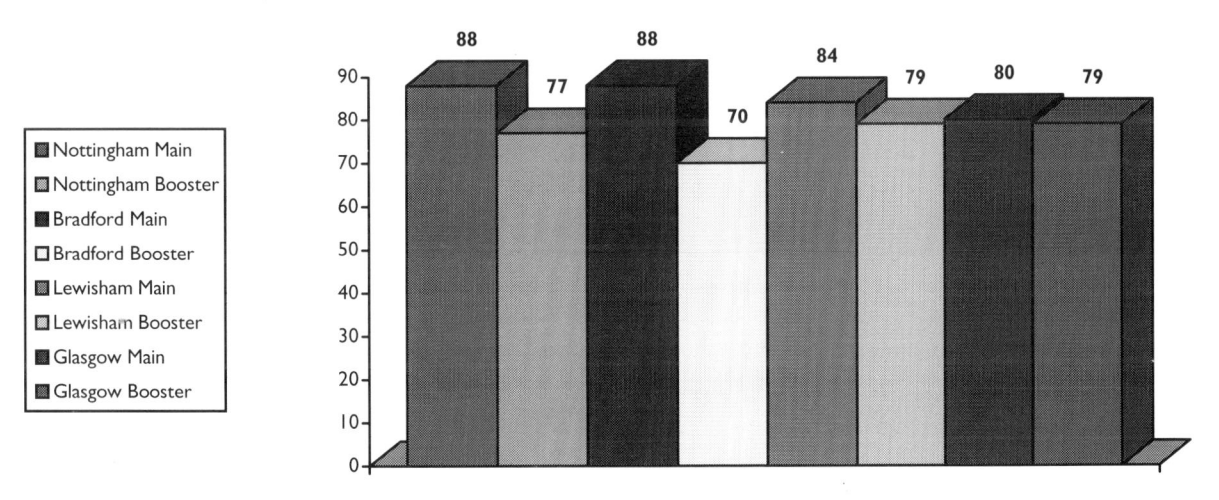

Location	Percentage
Nottingham Main	88
Nottingham Booster	77
Bradford Main	88
Bradford Booster	70
Lewisham Main	84
Lewisham Booster	79
Glasgow Main	80
Glasgow Booster	79

Percentage of respondents who stated that they were 'very satisfied' or 'fairly satisfied' with their local area resulting high victimisation rates (Bottoms et al. 1989). This dissociation between the level of crime or other problems in an area and residents' views of living within the area may stem from an inability of individuals to draw a comparison between their area and any other with which they are not so well acquainted. Or, it may be the case that residents regard the area in which they live as a reflection upon themselves and consequently exaggerate their expressed satisfaction with it. Whatever the cause, the only aspect of social disruption which has so far been shown to associate with decreasing levels of satisfaction are the extremes of spiralling crime rates and social decay which lead to almost complete social disorganisation (Skogan 1990).

area. The nature of those problems seen as most salient was the same in all locations. These were the amount of litter in an area and the effect of dogs running loose. Difficulties caused by teenagers and abandoned cars were also seen as relatively substantial problems. Not surprisingly given the small number of ethnic minorities within our sample, racially motivated attacks were not generally seen as a prominent problem.

Whilst the identity of those problems cited as most prominent by the booster sample was the same as for the main sample, booster sample respondents were more likely to consider that *all* the problems listed were 'very big' or 'fairly big' problems within their area. The most noticeable distinction was that between the two

Figure 5.4
Respondents' perception of the general problems in their local area: Main sample

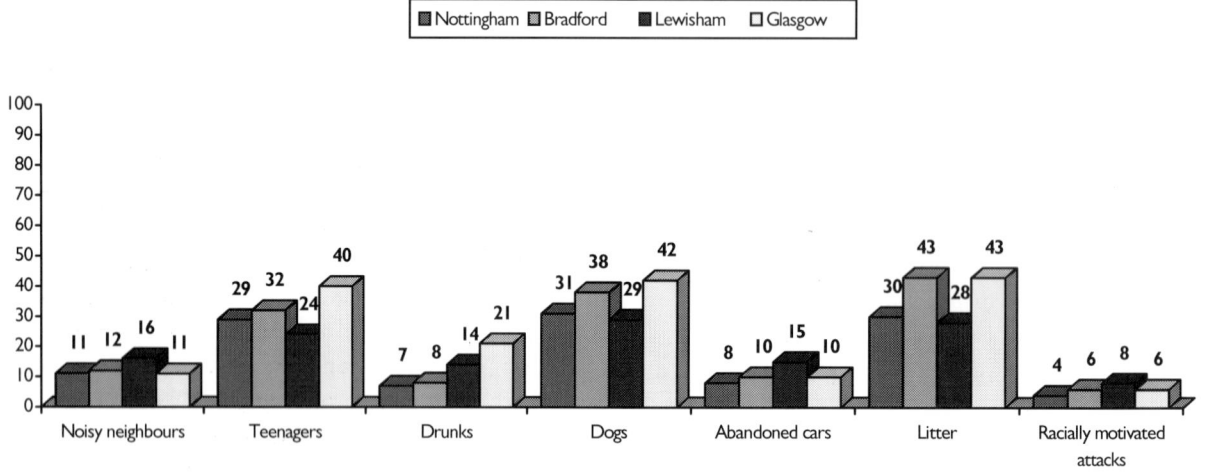

Percentage of respondents citing each problem listed as 'very big' or 'fairly big' problem in their area

Our respondents' perceptions of the extent of problems within their local area were unlikely to be at this extreme level, however we were interested in finding out their perceptions of problems more generally associated with disorder and crime. In particular, we were interested in assessing the levels of those problems which people tend to *feel* express the state of social order or disorder of the area in which they live (Shapland and Vagg 1988; Skogan 1990). A summary of responses to the items we included in our list of potential problems is given in Table 5.2 in Appendix 1. The range of problems suggested to respondents included: noisy neighbours, teenagers 'hanging around on the street', drunks, dogs, abandoned cars, litter and racist attacks.

From Figure 5.4 it can be seen that the majority of our main sample respondents *did* not feel that these things posed a very great problem within their local

samples' views on the problem of racially motivated attacks. The differences we found between main and booster samples were highly significant and are most likely to be a function of the greater urbanisation and 'deprivation' attached to the areas from which this sample was selected. They may also, however, reflect a greater level of concern in younger individuals over the nature and extent of social problems.

Although locational variation was limited, Glasgow appeared to be the one location in which respondents were most prone to report local problems. It stood out noticeably from the other three locations in both main and booster samples as being the location in which a substantial proportion of individuals reported a range of problems as being 'very big' or 'fairly big' problems in their area.

In general, the degree of perceived problems and

Figure 5.5
Respondents' perception of the general problems in their local area: Booster sample

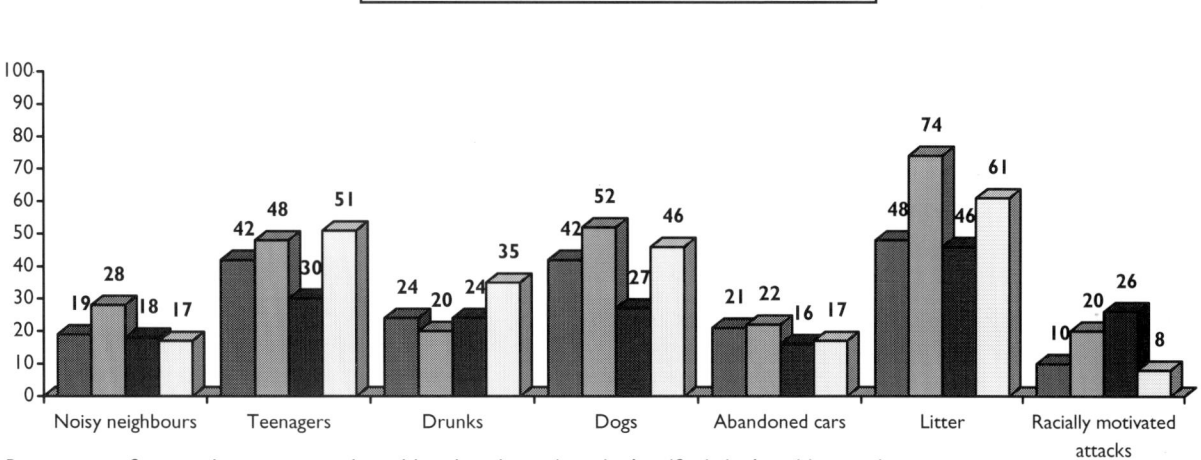

Legend: ■ Nottingham ■ Bradford ■ Lewisham □ Glasgow

Problem	Nottingham	Bradford	Lewisham	Glasgow
Noisy neighbours	19	28	18	17
Teenagers	42	48	30	51
Drunks	24	20	24	35
Dogs	42	52	27	46
Abandoned cars	21	22	16	17
Litter	48	74	46	61
Racially motivated attacks	10	20	26	8

Percentage of respondents citing each problem listed as a 'very big' or 'fairly big' problem in their area

therefore by implication of perceived social disorder was much higher in our locations than for comparable studies of other urban locations. The proportion regarding litter as a 'very big' or 'fairly big' problem was, for example, much higher than for samples of Sussex urban residents (Shapland et al. 1990). Similarly the 'dogs nuisance' was regarded as a substantially greater problem than in a comparable Midlands urban town surveyed by Shapland and Vagg (1988). This may be the function of real increases across time in the levels of social problems affecting urban life. Or it may be a function of increasing concern by members of the public over problems which have been with us consistently across time. Equally, it may be that our findings are specific to the areas we sampled. Again, we shall have to wait for the 1992 British Crime Survey findings to draw any firm conclusions.

> **In summary,** the majority of our respondents did not see any of a range of problems in their local area as being particularly salient. However, they were rather *more* concerned about the types of problems we suggested than respondents to previous similar studies. Perhaps more importantly, those respondents representing young people from relatively deprived areas showed very much higher levels of concern than the general population sample. This matches their similarly heightened concern about drug usage, an issue which we will consider further in later chapters. Whether such distinctions reflect any real increases in urban social disorder is a question we cannot answer in the absence of data relating to the profile of the country as a whole.

Worry about crime and fear of crime in the local area

Although the only problem in our 'social disorder' list which was very clearly a crime, namely racially motivated attacks, was *not* seen by the majority of our sample as being a significant problem in their local area, the same was not true of other forms of crime. Table 5.3 in Appendix 1 summarises responses to this item, which asked respondents to state how worried they were about becoming a victim of burglary, mugging, theft of or from a car and, in the case of female respondents only, a victim of rape. This elicited a fairly strong response, with between 40% and 70% of individuals in all samples stating that they were 'very worried' or 'fairly worried' about becoming the victim of burglary or mugging, and between 30% and 60% of women in all samples stating that they were equally worried about the possibility of becoming rape victims. As with previous surveys, such as those mentioned above, burglary proved to be the form of crime listed which worried the greatest proportion of individuals, with fear of mugging and rape being at a roughly equivalent and slightly lower level and theft of or from a car being in most cases the crime *least* likely to worry respondents. We know that there are high levels of fear of rape in England and Wales, but this level of fear of burglary in the four towns is very much greater than that found in previous studies, such as the British Crime Survey (cf. Hough and Mayhew 1985).

Levels of worry about crime differed quite widely both across and within samples for all crimes listed *except* burglary. In both main and booster samples,

Figure 5.6
Worries about becoming a victim of crime: Main sample

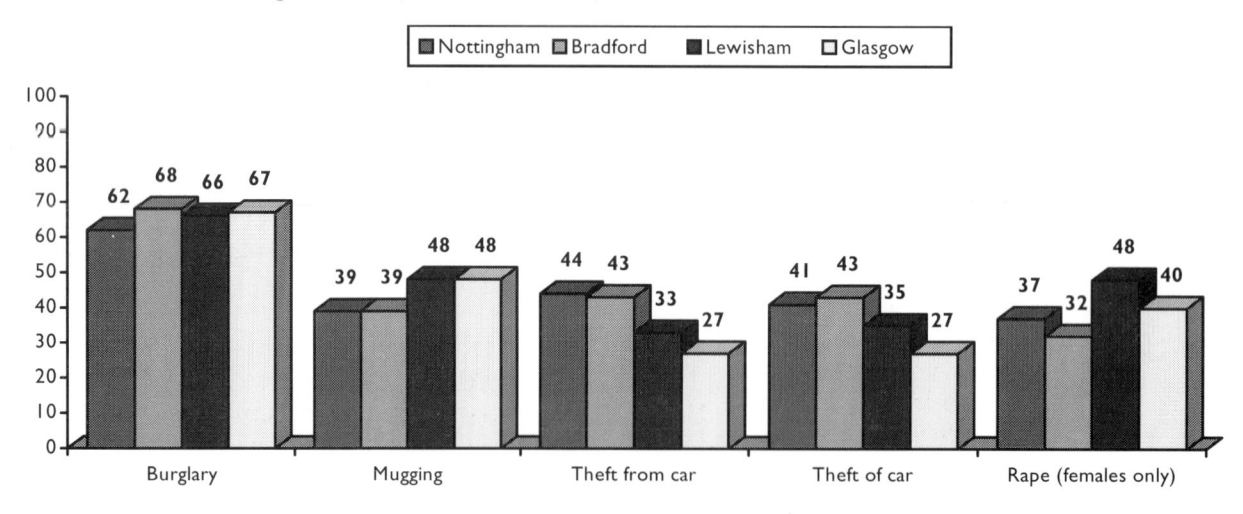

[Bar chart with legend: Nottingham, Bradford, Lewisham, Glasgow]

- Burglary: 62, 68, 66, 67
- Mugging: 39, 39, 48, 48
- Theft from car: 44, 43, 33, 27
- Theft of car: 41, 43, 35, 27
- Rape (females only): 37, 32, 48, 40

Percentage of respondents 'very' worried or 'fairly' worried about becoming a victim of particular types of crime

comparable levels of concern were shown for burglary in all four locations. However fears about being mugged were greater in Lewisham and Glasgow than they were in Nottingham or Bradford, again for both main and booster sample. This pattern was reversed for car related crimes, with Bradford and Nottingham showing the greatest levels of concern in both samples. The only distinction between the main and booster samples in relation to crime type and location was that whilst female respondents from Lewisham and Glasgow showed substantially greater fear of rape than their counterparts in Nottingham and Bradford, female respondents in all four booster sample locations showed equally high levels of fear of rape. This may be a consequence of the greater levels of demographic variation in the main as opposed to the booster samples, all females in the latter sample being drawn from young individuals primarily of lower socioeconomic status.

A more disturbing distinction between main and booster samples becomes apparent if one compares the profile of responses presented in Figure 5.6 with that in Figure 5.7. Fears regarding both mugging and rape were substantially higher in all booster samples than in the corresponding main samples, this being a finding which reached very high levels of statistical significance. This disparity is disturbing in that it matches more objective data on the risk profile of young individuals in deprived areas in relation to violent crime against the person (cf. Walmsley 1986).

In contrast to the pattern noted for fear of crime

Figure 5.7
Worries about becoming a victim of crime: Booster sample

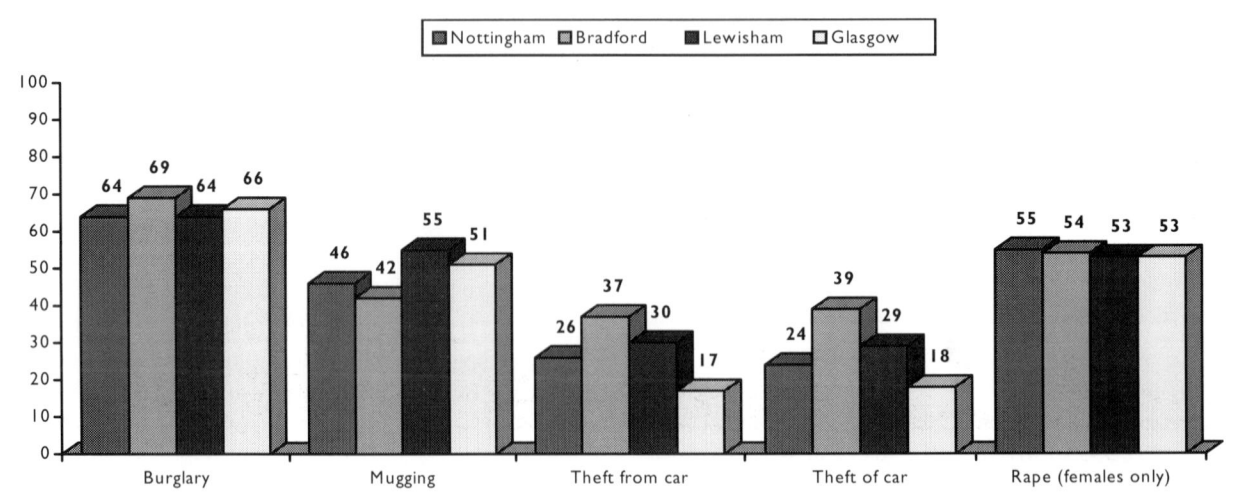

[Bar chart with legend: Nottingham, Bradford, Lewisham, Glasgow]

- Burglary: 64, 69, 64, 66
- Mugging: 46, 42, 55, 51
- Theft from car: 26, 37, 30, 17
- Theft of car: 24, 39, 29, 18
- Rape (females only): 55, 54, 53, 53

Percentage of respondents 'very' worried or 'fairly' worried about becoming a victim of particular types of crime against the person, worries about car related crimes were significantly *lower* in booster sample car owners than in main sample car owners. Without further data it is not possible to investigate the cause of this disparity but possible options are that differences in age affect attitudes towards the experience of property crime, or that the booster samples' greater concern regarding crimes against the person serves to reduce in comparison their fears regarding property crime.

Comparing our main sample figures for fears or worries about crime with those of other general population samples (e.g. Hough and Mayhew 1985, Mayhew et al 1989) suggests that unlike the case for 'social disorder' type problems, our data were very similar to that for previous surveys. It should be borne in mind, however, that concern about crime can be disproportionate to the actual likelihood that an individual will become a victim of the crime under consideration (van Dijk 1978). It is also worth noting here (cf. Shapland et al 1990) that one component of the 'fear or worry about crime' response allows it to be distinguished from more *objective* calculations which people may make concerning crime. This aspect is the judgement made regarding the *seriousness* of any consequences of the crime event should it materialise.

In summary, respondents in our sample did seem fairly concerned about the prospects of becoming the victim of a crime. The most salient of the crimes suggested appeared for most people to be burglary. The levels of concern shown in relation to this crime being rather higher than in previous studies. Perhaps more importantly, we found an important distinction between the attitudes of our main and booster samples to different types of crime. The booster sample were relatively more concerned about crimes against the person and less concerned about the type of property crime represented by theft of or from a car. This pattern matches the actual demographic distribution of crime and highlights the greater risk individuals living in relatively deprived areas face with regard to becoming the victims of very serious forms of crime.

Comparison between national and local pictures of crime and problems

Although, unfortunately, the list of problems and crimes used did not match exactly those discussed above, respondents *were* asked to draw a comparison between the extent of problems and crimes within their local area with the national picture for such things. Specifically, we asked respondents to consider whether burglary, drunks, car theft, litter, vandalism and racially motivated attacks were more of a problem locally, more of a problem nationally, or were roughly similar levels of problem. The responses obtained to this item are summarised in Tables 5.4 and 5.5 in Appendix 1.

As can be seen from a comparison of Figures 5.8 and 5.9, the responses to this item in the questionnaire followed the distinctions between the samples noted earlier. Booster sample respondents were in all cases *more* likely than main sample respondents to consider the problems listed as more of a problem *locally* than

Figure 5.8
Comparative views on the problem of crime: Main sample

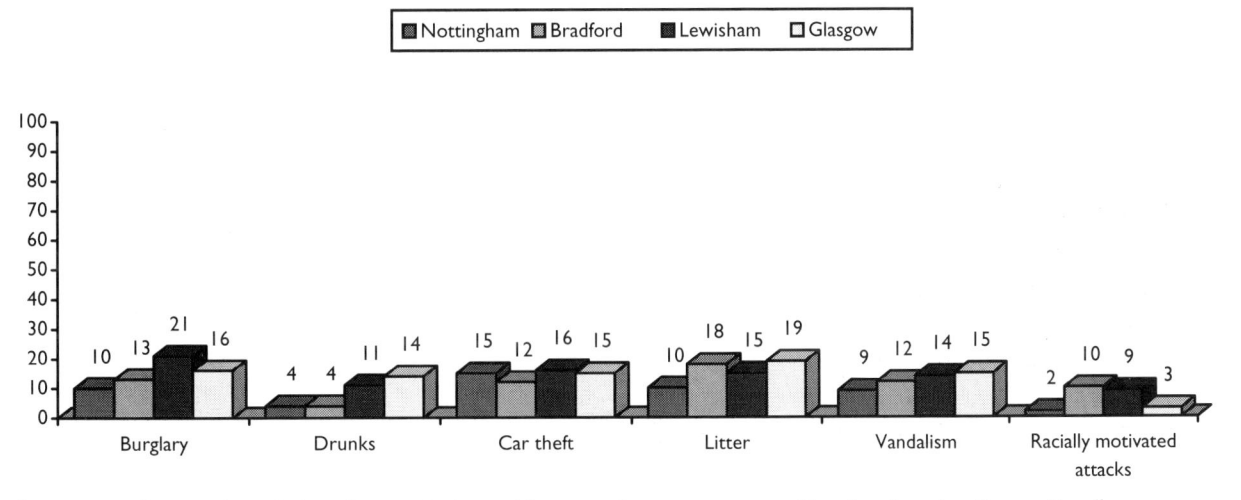

Percentage of respondents feeling that particular problems or crimes were more evident locally rather than nationally

nationally. Having said which, it is important to note that in most cases respondents from all locations and both samples felt that *all* of the listed problems were more of a problem nationally than locally, this being, as suggested earlier, a common response to questions regarding the local area.

The *relative* willingness of our booster sample respondents to state that problems were apparent at the local level is important. It suggests either that young people are more worried about crime than the general population or that individuals in deprived areas have a level of concern about crime which matches their greater degree of vulnerability. Whichever explanation is the most valid, we can certainly conclude from these data that young people in the areas we sampled *are* taking the problems of crime and disorder seriously. Main sample respondents were not only *relatively* more likely than booster sample respondents to state that a problem was national rather than local, they also showed a greater *absolute* likelihood of stating that problems were national rather than local.

A distinct disparity was also apparent between *types* of crime or problem. Across both samples and all locations, the problem most likely to be thought of as national rather than local was that of racially motivated attacks. This level of consistency was not however matched by other types of problem, which proved to be more location dependent. The data for both main and booster samples suggested that in general, litter was seen as more likely to be a local problem in Glasgow and Bradford, whilst burglary was salient in Lewisham and car related crime in Nottingham. The specificity of the main crime/disorder problem in a *local* area fits previous data on small geographical neighbourhoods (again see Shapland and Vagg 1988). It is interesting that similar differences are maintained at the much larger level of cities or boroughs. Note that the distinctions between types of problem noted here are *relative* only and it remains the case that all problems were thought by the majority of respondents to be greater nationally than locally.

In summary, our respondents showed a strong tendency to state that a broad range of potential crimes and problems were more salient at the national than at the local level. Locational differences in attitudes were however apparent, particularly in respect of the types of any problems perceived as local problems. Litter, for example, was more likely to be seen as a local problem in Glasgow and Bradford, whilst respondents in Lewisham were more concerned about burglary and respondents in Nottingham about car related crime. A strong disparity between the main and booster sample was also evident, with booster sample respondents being more likely to state that *all* types of problems were local rather than national. This distinction between the samples is consistent with the generally more troubled attitude of the booster sample to a range of issues and may reflect the problems of living in relatively deprived areas.

Figure 5.9
Comparative views on the problem of crime: Booster sample

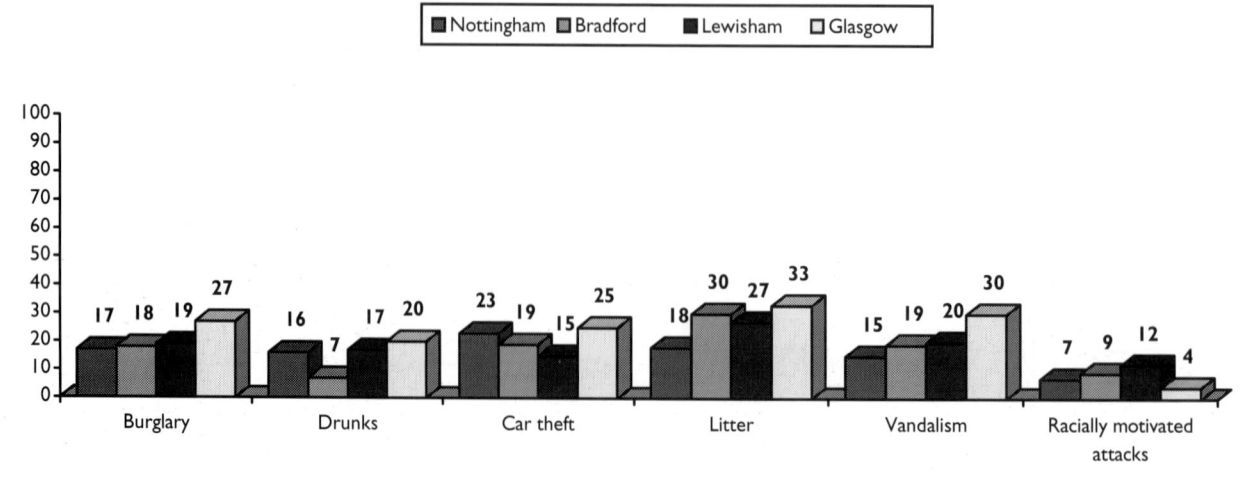

	Nottingham	Bradford	Lewisham	Glasgow
Burglary	17	18	19	27
Drunks	16	7	17	20
Car theft	23	19	15	25
Litter	18	30	27	33
Vandalism	15	19	20	30
Racially motivated attacks	7	9	12	4

Percentage of respondents feeling that particular problems or crimes were more evident locally rather than nationally

PUBLIC PERCEPTIONS OF LOCAL CRIME RATES AND OTHER PROBLEMS

Comparison between drug related and other crimes or problems

Having summarised above the views of our respondents on a variety of crimes and problems posing a potential threat to their local area, it is of interest to consider how these views compare with similar views regarding *drug related* crimes and problems. The list of problems in this category given to respondents to consider were: glue sniffing, 'drug users', drugs being offered for sale, drug related illness, theft for drugs and crime carried out under the influence of drugs. As with the 'social disorder' type of problem and the issue of crime, respondents were asked both to indicate the *absolute* level of any problem locally and to *compare* any local problems with their perception of the same problems nationally. Summary data for the views of our respondents on these issues are given in Tables 5.2, 5.4 and 5.5 in Appendix 1.

As Figure 5.10 suggests, drug related problems on the whole, appeared to feature as *less* of an absolute problem locally than some other non-drug related problems, such as litter, teenagers and dogs, in the eyes of our main sample respondents. A notable exception to this rule was provided by Glasgow. Here, the percentage of main sample respondents rating drug related problems as 'very big' or 'fairly big' in their local area was comparable to or greater than the percentage giving the same response for the 'social disorder' type of non-drug related problem.

Figure 5.10
Respondents' perceptions of drug related problems in their local area: Main sample

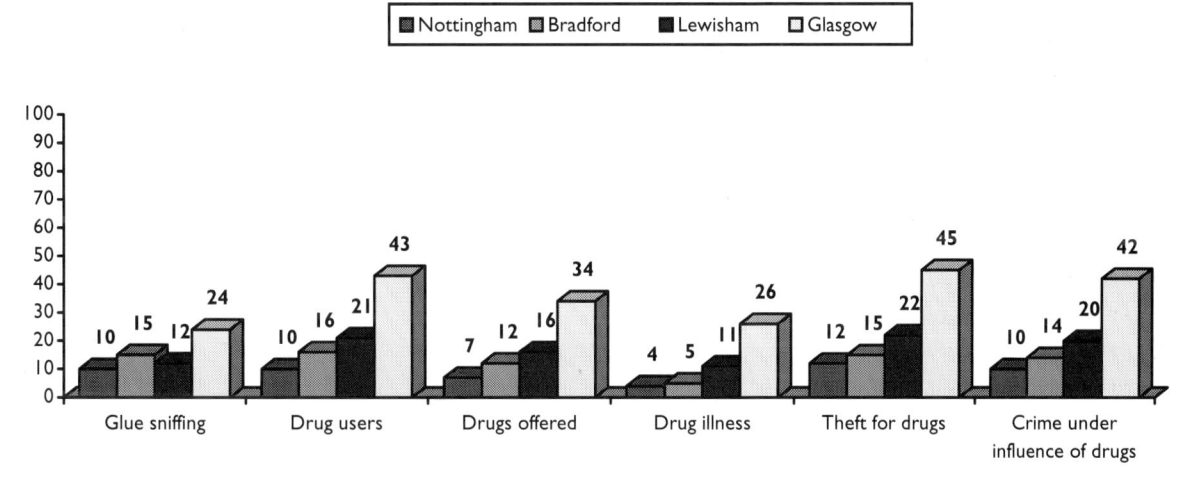

Problem	Nottingham	Bradford	Lewisham	Glasgow
Glue sniffing	10	15	12	24
Drug users	10	16	21	43
Drugs offered	7	12	16	34
Drug illness	4	5	11	26
Theft for drugs	12	15	22	45
Crime under influence of drugs	10	14	20	42

Percentage of respondents citing each problem listed as a 'very big' or 'fairly big' problem in their area

Figure 5.11
Respondents' perception of drug related problems in their local area: Booster sample

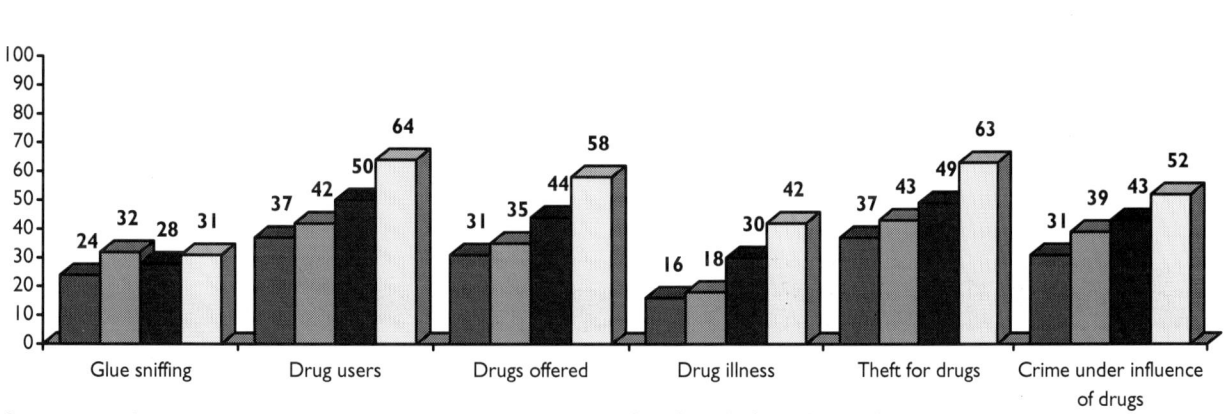

Problem	Nottingham	Bradford	Lewisham	Glasgow
Glue sniffing	24	32	28	31
Drug users	37	42	50	64
Drugs offered	31	35	44	58
Drug illness	16	18	30	42
Theft for drugs	37	43	49	63
Crime under influence of drugs	31	39	43	52

Percentage of respondents citing each problem listed as a 'very big' or 'fairly big' problem in their area

In the booster sample (Figure 5.11), respondents from *both* Glasgow and Lewisham rated drug related problems as, on average, *greater* than non-drug related problems. For all four booster sample locations, drugs were also seen as a greater problem in absolute terms than had been the case for the main sample. This not withstanding, the percentage of respondents seeing any drugs problem as significant in the local area remained a minority even in the booster sample, for all locations except Glasgow.

The distinctions noted above both between sample type and between locations were highly significant in statistical terms. However, the interpretation of these differences must be placed in context. It should be noted, for example, that the response patterns for levels of drugs related problems matched very closely the patterns for *awareness* of drugs related issues taken from our data. It is possible, therefore, that distinctions such as that noted between Glasgow and the other locations are the result of the greater salience of drugs in the public eye in this location, rather than relating to any actual distinction in the extent of local drug related problems. Having said which, both patterns of course also match our drug prevalence data.

Perhaps most importantly, it should be borne in mind that the non-drug related problems discussed above were mostly of a fairly trivial nature, whilst the drugs related problems were in fact mostly very serious. The fact that the majority of the main sample and around half the booster sample felt that drugs were *less* of a problem in their area than things such as litter or dogs running loose suggests that drugs are *not* a particularly salient problem in most local areas. Certainly, even in the booster sample, the percentage of respondents feeling that drugs were a problem locally was rather lower than the percentage showing concern about crime *per se*. Nevertheless, a significant minority of people in most locations and a *majority* of young individuals from Glasgow and Lewisham's more deprived areas *did* consider drugs to be a substantial problem in their area.

As with other problems, both main and booster sample respondents were in the majority of cases much more likely to state that drug-related problems were a bigger problem nationally than locally. A comparison between Figures 5.12 and 5.13 suggests that other patterns noted in the context of non-drug related problems were also matched in the case of drug related problems. In particular, main sample respondents were more likely than booster sample respondents to state that a problem was greater both in relative and absolute terms at the national than the local level.

Of greater note perhaps is the fact that the percentage of respondents in *both* samples and *all* locations rating drugs as a primarily local problem was much *lower* than the equivalent percentage rating non-drug related problems - whether serious or trivial - as greater locally. Either drugs really *are* much less of a problem at a local level than alternative measures of crime or social disorder, or people are more distanced from the problems of drug usage than they are from problems such as litter and abandoned cars or crimes such as burglary and mugging.

The particular *type* of drug-related problem featuring most prominently in public perceptions as a local

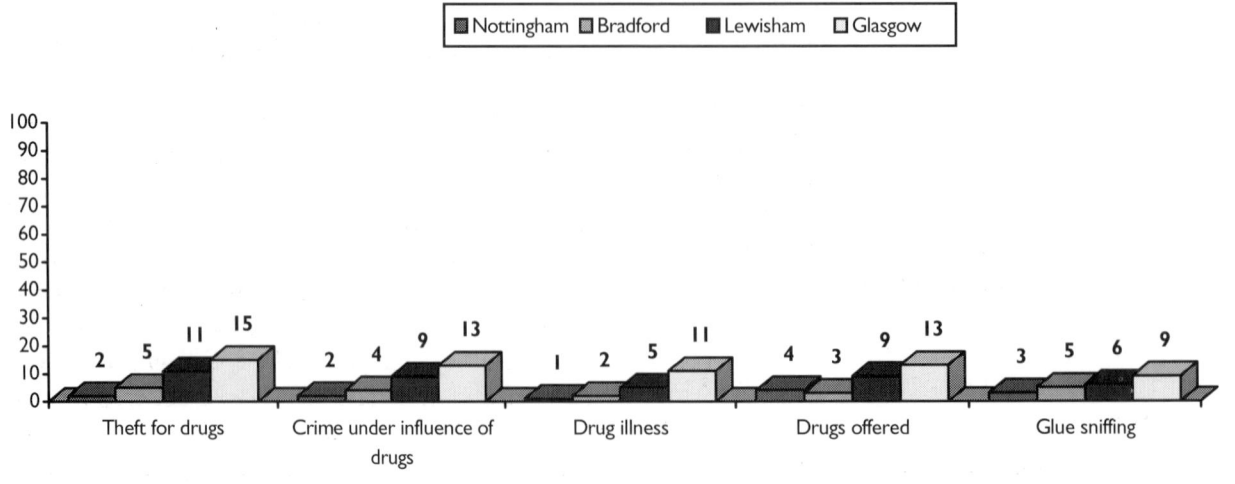

Figure 5.12
Comparative views on drug related problems: Main sample

Percentage of respondents feeling that particular problems or crimes were more evident locally rather than nationally

Figure 5.13
Comparative views on drug related problems: Booster sample

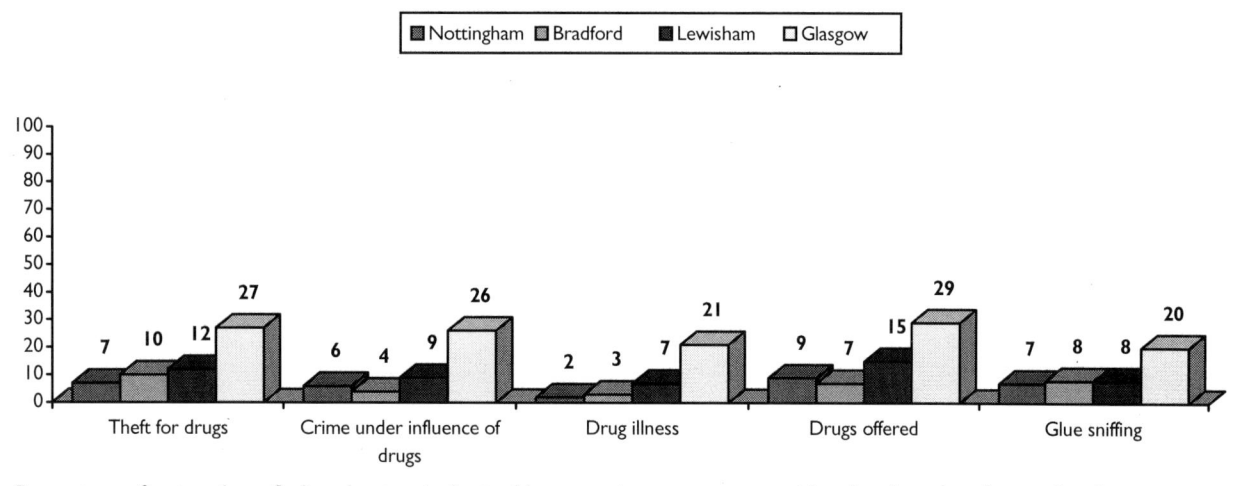

■ Nottingham ■ Bradford ■ Lewisham □ Glasgow

Theft for drugs	Crime under influence of drugs	Drug illness	Drugs offered	Glue sniffing
7, 10, 12, 27	6, 4, 9, 26	2, 3, 7, 21	9, 7, 15, 29	7, 8, 8, 20

Percentage of respondents feeling that particular problems or crimes were more evident locally rather than nationally

problem in both absolute and relative terms both across samples and across locations was theft carried out in order to provide the perpetrator with money to buy drugs. Other, slightly less prominent but nonetheless frequently labelled problems were the rather eclectic 'drug users' and the more specific 'drugs being offered for sale'. In all samples, the *least* problematic aspect of drug usage locally was held to be drug related illness and children and youths sniffing glue.

In summary, although a minority of our respondents felt that drugs were a salient problem in their local area, the vast majority were not concerned about drugs at this level. Respondents definitely felt that drugs were more of a problem at the national than at the local level. 'Social disorder' types of problems appeared to be rather more salient than drug related problems - and crimes, notably crimes against the person, were very much more salient in the eyes of our respondents. However, attitudes did vary across both sample type and location. Notably, booster sample respondents were much more likely than main sample respondents to rate drugs as a problem locally and respondents from Glasgow were more likely to see drugs as a problem than respondents from the other three locations.

Comparing the views of drug users and non-drug users

It is, of course, a moot point whether the views of our respondents are likely to reflect accurately the actual levels of any problems in their area. The prominence of certain problems in the minds of individuals *without* specialist knowledge may, for example, not reflect accurately the problems which are in fact of greatest import. It is interesting in this context to draw a comparison between those respondents with personal experience of using drugs and those with no such experience. Tables 5.6 and 5.7 in Appendix 1 summarise this data.

The data presented in Figure 5.14 suggest that in the main sample at least, people who have used drugs may have been sensitised to the issue of drugs related problems. Drug users in all four locations were significantly more likely than non-drug users to cite the whole range of drugs problems suggested here as being 'very big' or 'fairly big' problems in their local area. The type of drug related problem most likely to be seen as salient did not, however, vary substantially between drug users and non-drug users. Both groups were most likely to cite crime under the influence of drugs, theft for drugs and the eclectic 'drug users' as a problem.

Comparing Figures 5.14 and 5.15, it can be seen that the disparity between drug users and non-users on this issue was substantially less in the booster sample, only in fact reaching statistical significance in Lewisham and Bradford. Both users and non-users were more likely to cite any of the suggested drugs related problems as a problem in their local area than their main sample counterparts. These differences between main and booster samples may reflect real differences in their respective areas, but equally they are consistent with the idea that detailed knowledge of drug usage sensitises people to the existence of drugs related

Figure 5.14
Comparison of the views of drug users and non-drug users on drug related problems: Main samples

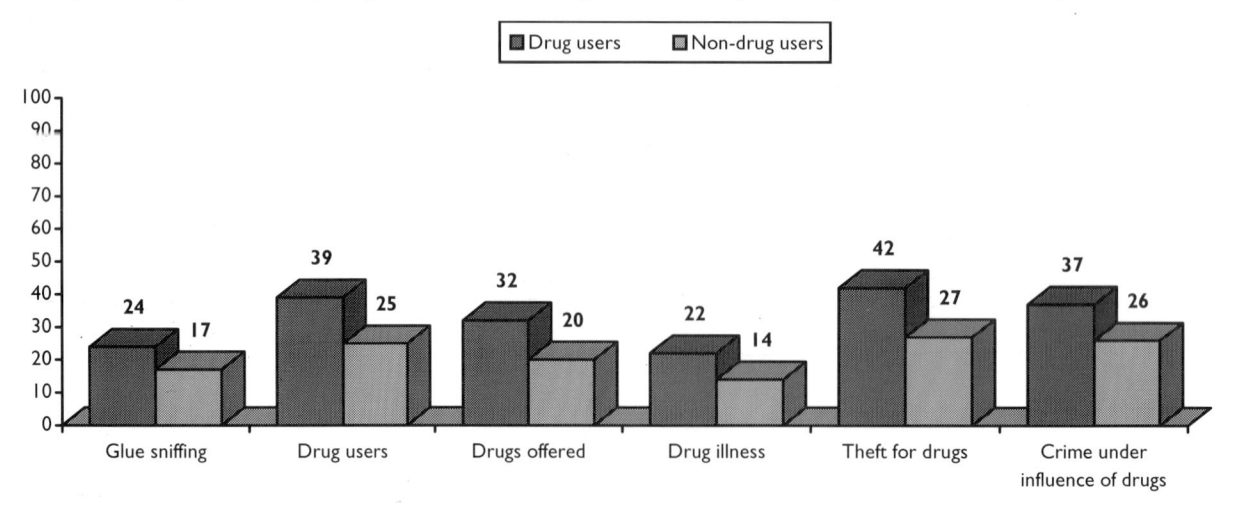

■ Drug users ■ Non-drug users

	Glue sniffing	Drug users	Drugs offered	Drug illness	Theft for drugs	Crime under influence of drugs
Drug users	24	39	32	22	42	37
Non-drug users	17	25	20	14	27	26

Percentage of drug users and non-drug users citing drug related problems as a 'very big' or 'fairly big' problem in their area, averaged across location

Figure 5.15
Comparison of the views of drug users and non-drug users on drug related problems: Booster sample

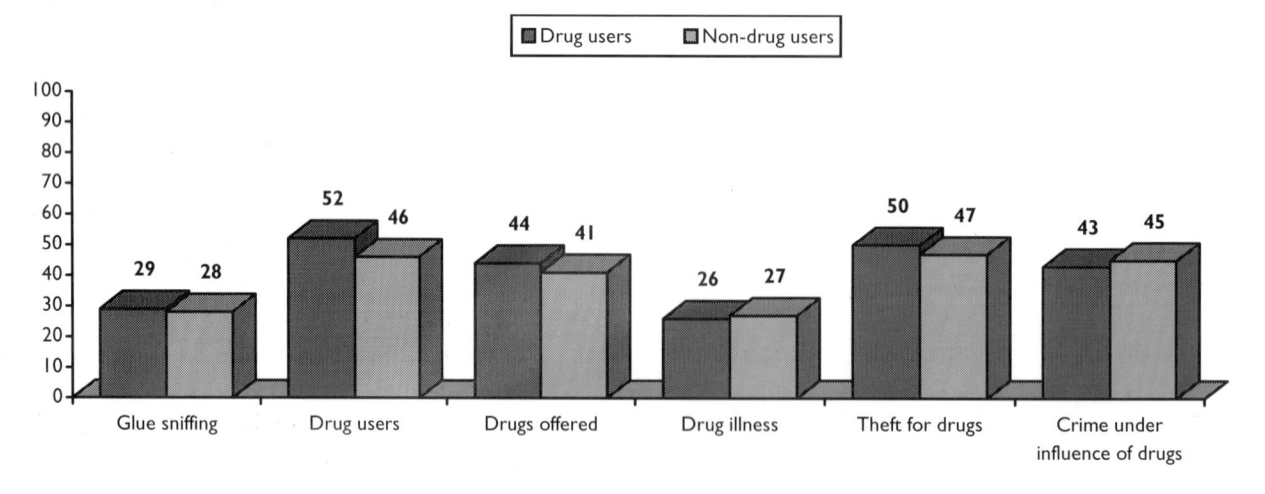

■ Drug users ■ Non-drug users

	Glue sniffing	Drug users	Drugs offered	Drug illness	Theft for drugs	Crime under influence of drugs
Drug users	29	52	44	26	50	43
Non-drug users	28	46	41	27	47	45

Percentage of drug users and non-drug users citing drug related problems as a 'very big' or 'fairly big' problem in their area, averaged across location

problems. As with the main sample, the type of problems most commonly cited are the same for drug users and non-drug users, with both suggesting that 'drug users' *per se* and 'theft for drugs' are problematic.

In summary, drug users appear to be substantially more concerned about local area problems associated with drug usage than non-drug users in the general population. Since in our generally more knowledgeable 'at risk' group this disparity was not particularly salient it would seem that even indirect exposure to drug usage increases either the awareness of or levels of concern about drugs related problems.

Changing patterns of crime and drug related problems

In addition to the more specific comparisons outlined above, the survey questionnaire also asked respondents to draw a broad comparison across time between the levels, with the majority feeling that levels of drug usage in their local area had increased over the last two years.

Comparing our respondents' views on crime levels and levels of drug usage indicated a disparity between samples which was consistent with that noted in earlier sections of this chapter. In all four booster samples, the

Figure 5.16
Respondents' views regarding the changing patterns of crime and drug abuse

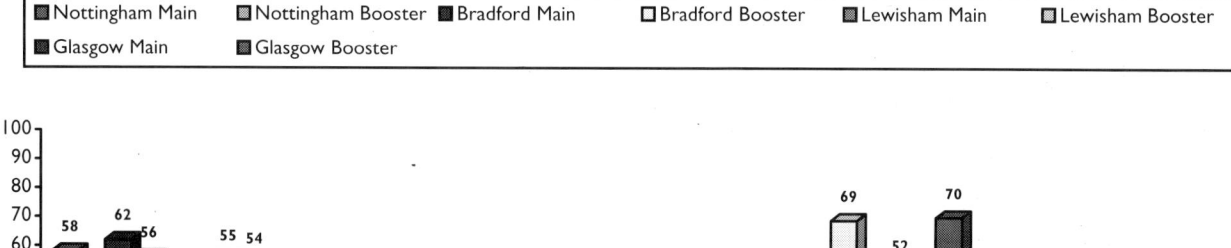

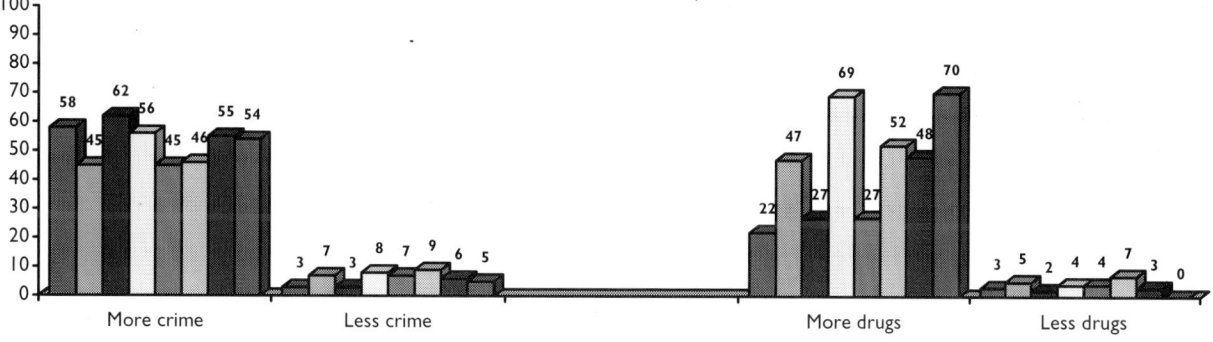

	Nottingham Main	Nottingham Booster	Bradford Main	Bradford Booster	Lewisham Main	Lewisham Booster
	Glasgow Main	Glasgow Booster				

More crime: 58, 45, 62, 56, 45, 46, 55, 54
Less crime: 3, 7, 3, 8, 7, 9, 6, 5
More drugs: 22, 47, 27, 69, 27, 70, 52, 48
Less drugs: 3, 5, 2, 4, 4, 7, 3, 0

Percentage of respondents feeling that there was either more or less crime/drug usage in their area now in comparison to two years previously

levels of crime and drug usage in their local area. Specifically, they were asked whether they thought crime and drug usage in their local area had increased, decreased or remained at about the same level in the two years prior to the interview. A summary of the responses obtained is given in Table 5.8 in Appendix 1.

As Figure 5.16 suggests, the views of our respondents matched closely those of a range of official bodies on the changing pattern of crime. The vast majority of respondents in both main and booster samples and across all four locations felt that crime had increased in their local area over the last two years. Only a negligible proportion of respondents felt that crime rates had actually gone *down* in their area over the two year period. These results are very similar to those of other comparable surveys, both nationally and locally.

The pattern for drug usage was more equivocal. Although very few people in either main or booster sample felt that levels of drug usage had gone down, the majority view of respondents in all main sample locations *except* for Glasgow was that the number of people using drugs had remained *constant* rather than increased. In Glasgow's main sample and in all four booster sample locations, the views of respondents on levels of drug usage matched their perceptions of crime

percentage of respondents feeling that rates of drug usage had increased was *greater* than those feeling that crime rates had increased. In all four main samples the converse was true. Again, this may be taken to reflect either the differential knowledge and experience of the two samples, or to reflect a greater level of concern regarding drug usage in our 'at risk' group.

In the absence of any relevant location specific data on crime, it is not possible to assess the accuracy of the views expressed by our respondents. However, the national pattern for changes in crime levels suggests that their perceptions are likely to be fairly accurate in the case of crime (van Dijk and Mayhew 1992; Mayhew and Aye Maung 1992). Since we do not have any detailed prevalence figures for drug usage in these locations over the two year period suggested, we can have no idea whether our main sample or our booster sample held the more accurate view regarding drug usage.

In summary, whilst the majority opinion of our sample was clearly that local crime rates had increased over the last two years, their views regarding recent changes in the levels of drug usage were more equivocal. Booster sample respondents tended to feel that drug usage was on the increase within their local areas, but main sample respondents felt rather that drug usage had remained stable. Some locational variation was also noted, with respondents in Glasgow being more likely than respondents in the other three locations to feel that drug usage had increased over the two year period. In the absence of more objective data it is not possible to say whether either distinction reflects actual variations in patterns of drug usage.

The possible effects of perceived crime and drug usage on behaviour patterns

In the foregoing discussion, we considered at length the perceptions held by our respondents regarding a range of crimes and problems and, in particular, their views regarding drug related problems. Since respondents clearly were concerned about crime and to a rather lesser extent about the problems associated with drug usage, it is of interest to see whether their views have in practice any effect on their behaviour.

Concerns about crime and drug-related problems could potentially operate at two levels in affecting an individual's behaviour. They could make them feel just generally dissatisfied or irritated or, they could engender a more extreme response by making individuals actually *afraid* of becoming a victim of criminal or drugs related activities. As a number of authors have pointed out, it is important to distinguish between these two types of response, because they have rather different meanings and rather different policy implications. If, for example, the most prominent response to perceived increases in levels of crime is fear as opposed to dissatisfaction, then if crime is increasing, policies directed at keeping the public well informed about crime may backfire by resulting simply in a more *fearful* public (Winkel 1987). On the other hand, if levels of worry are higher than actual risks, then the converse may be true.

We separated out the two possible effects of perceived levels of crime and drugs related problems by carrying out separate multivariate analyses for our respondents' level of satisfaction with their local area and for two measures of what we will call for the sake of brevity their 'fear of crime'. The general extent of satisfaction shown by our respondents for their area of residence has been discussed above. Before detailing the results of our multivariate analyses, we will outline below the 'fear of crime' profile for our sample.

'Fear of crime'

Fear of crime is, of course, a complex issue. It taps into a number of different aspects of psychology, relating not only to a person's ability to make some form of objective risk assessment, but also to such factors as their past experience and their susceptibility to suggestion. Given the limited length of our questionnaire, we obviously did not have the opportunity to address this issue in depth. With this in mind and also with a view to making our data as open to later comparison as possible, we chose to adopt a similar approach to the British Crime Survey in assessing our respondents' levels of fear for their personal safety.

The approach taken by the BCS is to use a single indicator variable as an, admittedly approximate, measure of 'fear of crime'. This variable is derived, very simply, by asking respondents 'how safe do you feel walking alone in this area after dark?'. In the case of individuals who for whatever reason do not normally go out alone at night, this question is phrased hypothetically 'how safe do you *think* you would feel ...etc.'. Although this question is necessarily rather narrow in scope, research suggests that in fact it correlates quite highly with a diverse range of more detailed assessments of fears for personal safety (cf. Skogan and Maxfield 1981). Since this item only deals with a very specific situation which may not be a relevant one for a number of people, we also included in the questionnaire an item which we felt would give a more absolute measure of 'fear of crime'. This item was phrased in broadly similar terms to the BCS item, but asked respondents how safe they actually or hypothetically felt about being alone at home after dark. One advantage of the way in which both these items are phrased is that it side-steps the rather heated debate about whether 'fear of crime' would more accurately be described as 'worry' or 'concern' or even 'annoyance' about crime. If a respondent is willing to state that they *do not feel safe* in a situation, they are clearly rather more than just concerned or worried about that situation. Summary data for the two 'fear of crime' items are given in Tables 5.9 and 5.10 in Appendix 1.

As Figure 5.17 suggests, the likelihood of our respondents being alone at night in either of the settings we considered depended very much on whether they were in the main or booster sample. Respondents in the main sample were *more* likely to be alone in their home at night but conversely less likely to be out walking alone than respondents in the booster sample. Whilst this pattern was fairly consistent across location, the disparity noted for the likelihood of walking alone at night

Figure 5.17
Respondents' likelihood of walking alone at night or staying at home alone at night

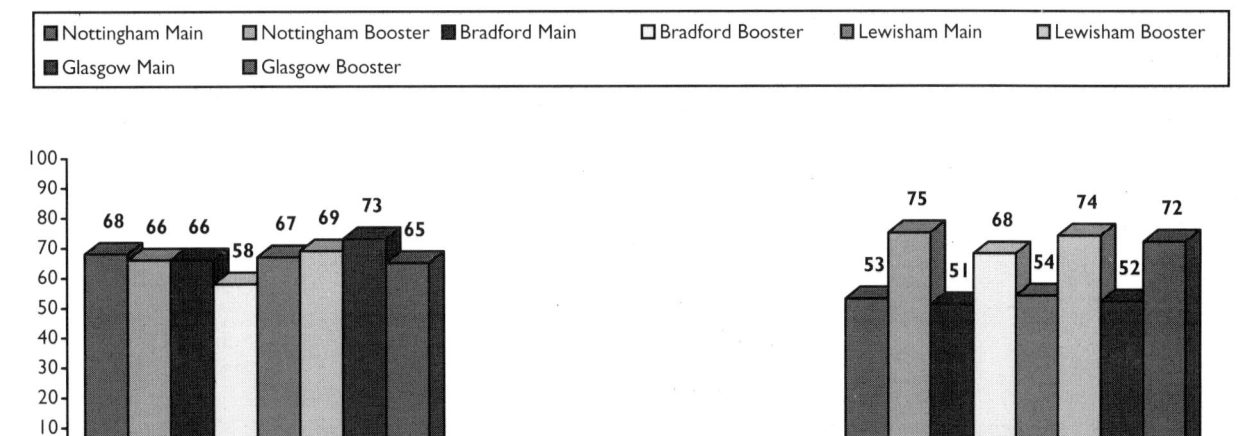

Legend: Nottingham Main, Nottingham Booster, Bradford Main, Bradford Booster, Lewisham Main, Lewisham Booster, Glasgow Main, Glasgow Booster

Stay at home alone: 68, 66, 66, 58, 67, 69, 73, 65
Walk alone: 53, 75, 51, 68, 54, 74, 52, 72

Percentage of respondents who sometimes stay alone at home at night/Percentage of respondents who sometimes walk alone at night

Figure 5.18
Respondents' level of fear of being alone after dark: Main sample

Legend: Nottingham Main, Bradford Main, Lewisham Main, Glasgow Main

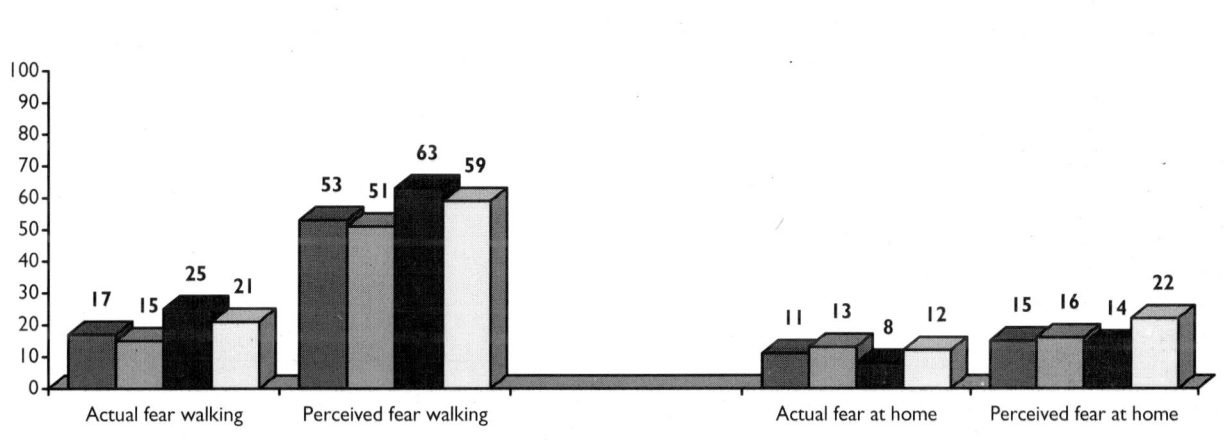

Actual fear walking: 17, 15, 25, 21
Perceived fear walking: 53, 51, 63, 59
Actual fear at home: 11, 13, 8, 12
Perceived fear at home: 15, 16, 14, 22

Percentage of respondents who actually walk alone at night who feel 'very unsafe' or 'a bit unsafe'/Percentage of respondents who do not walk alone at night but who think they would feel 'very unsafe' or 'a bit unsafe' doing so/Percentage of respondents who stay at home alone at night who feel 'very unsafe' or 'a bit unsafe' doing so/Percentage of respondents who do not stay at home alone at night but who think that they would feel 'very unsafe' or 'a bit unsafe' doing so

was much more distinct, reaching high levels of statistical significance in all four locations. This pattern is, of course, to be expected, given the age difference between the two samples.

The levels of actual or hypothetical fear in the two situations considered showed a less consistent pattern across locations (cf. Figures 5.18 and 5.19). Of those respondents who were accustomed to walking alone at night, the percentage reporting that they felt 'very unsafe' or 'a bit unsafe' doing so was greater in Nottingham, Bradford and Glasgow booster sample than in their corresponding main samples. However in the case of Lewisham, the reverse was true. An equivalent disparity between main and booster samples was shown by those respondents who were not accustomed to walking out alone at night in hypothesising about their likely levels of fear in this situation.

Perhaps not surprisingly, levels of fear amongst those individuals not accustomed to walking out alone at night were significantly greater in absolute terms

Figure 5.19
Respondents' level of fear of being alone after dark: Booster sample

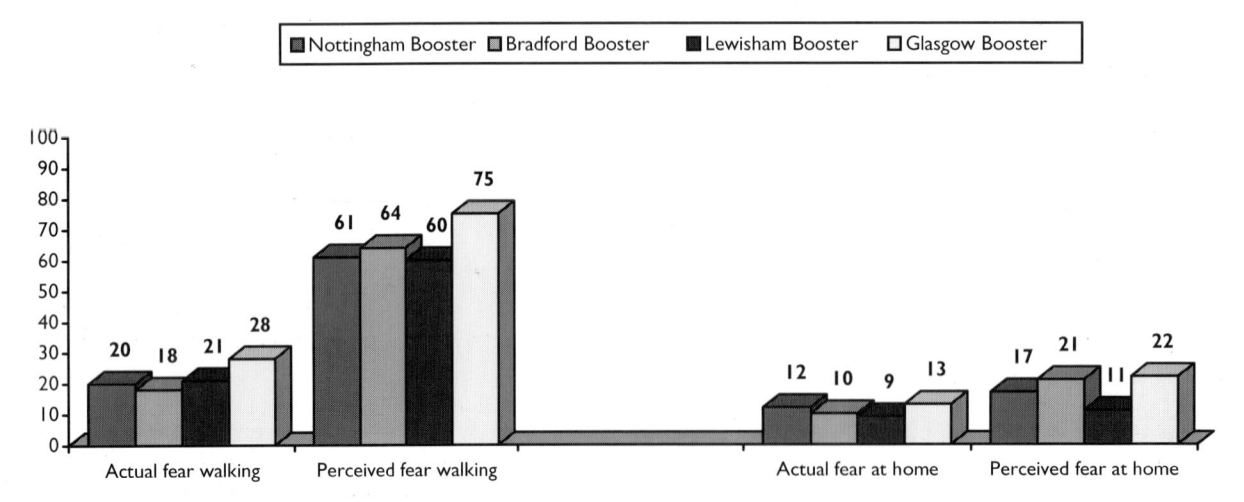

[Bar chart legend: Nottingham Booster, Bradford Booster, Lewisham Booster, Glasgow Booster]

Category	Nottingham	Bradford	Lewisham	Glasgow
Actual fear walking	20	18	21	28
Perceived fear walking	61	64	60	75
Actual fear at home	12	10	9	13
Perceived fear at home	17	21	11	22

Percentage of respondents who actually walk alone at night who feel 'very unsafe' or 'a bit unsafe'/Percentage of respondents who do not walk alone at night but who think they would feel 'very unsafe' or 'a bit unsafe' doing so/Percentage of respondents who stay at home alone at night who feel 'very unsafe' or 'a bit unsafe' doing so/Percentage of respondents who do not stay at home alone at night but who think that they would feel 'very unsafe' or 'a bit unsafe' doing so

than the levels of fear noted for those who *were* so accustomed. This distinction reached high levels of statistical significance and held true for all locations and across both samples. Of those used to walking alone at night, less than 30% in any location or sample showed any substantial level of fear. On the other hand, up to 75% of those *not* used to walking alone at night expressed fear at the idea of doing so. This latter figure is very high and suggests that people may, as has been suggested, be restricting their activities as a consequence of fear of going out alone after dark.

Using the item relating to fear of being at home alone at night as a more absolute measure of fear for personal safety, it appeared that only a minority of respondents had such fears regarding their personal safety. As with fear relating to walking outside after dark, it appeared that individuals with *no* experience of being alone at home after dark were the most afraid of this event. In the main sample, 12% or less of those individuals with some experience of staying at home alone felt 'very unsafe' or 'a bit unsafe' in doing so, whilst comparable figures for the respondents *without* the relevant experience ranged between 15% and 22%. A very similar pattern obtained in the booster sample. Again, these findings are highly statistically significant. No significant locational effects were noted.

Overall, the data suggest that respondents were more likely to be frightened of walking alone at night than of staying alone at home at night. This is not a surprising finding, although taken at face value it stands in contrast to the distinction between the percentages of respondents afraid of burglary and the *smaller* percentage afraid of being mugged. The data also suggest that the disparity in levels of fear between those acquainted with a situation and those not acquainted with a situation is rather greater than that between either locations or sample types.

In summary, although the majority of our respondents did have experience of being alone at night either at home or out walking, our data suggested that a substantial minority of individuals were accustomed to *never* being in either situation. The disparity between perceived levels of fear of being alone at night in either situation and the levels of fear experienced by individuals actually in the situation further suggested that people may be restricting their behaviour in such a way as to avoid a feared situation. In most locations, booster sample respondents showed a greater level of fear in walking alone after dark than their main sample counterparts. No substantial difference was noted between the two samples in terms of fear relating to being alone in one's home after dark. Given the age disparity between the main and booster samples, this pattern matches their actual likelihood of being victims of crimes against the person, which appears to be the type of crime a majority of individuals are generally concerned about.

Crime, drugs and fear - a multivariate analysis

Whilst a minority group of our respondents evidently are dissatisfied with their local area and/or show some level of fear at the prospect of being alone after dark, the analyses outlined above clearly cannot tell us whether their feelings are associated at all with their perceptions of crime and drugs related problems in their area. To answer this question, we ran a set of regression models. The dependent variables were:

- the likelihood that respondents who actually walk alone at night feel 'very unsafe' or 'a bit unsafe' (actual fear of walking alone at night)

- the likelihood that respondents who do not walk alone at night think they would feel 'very unsafe' or 'a bit unsafe' (perceived fear of walking alone at night)

- the likelihood that respondents would state that they were 'very satisfied' or 'fairly satisfied' with their local area (satisfaction with area)

We did not run any regression models for fears relating to being alone at home after dark, because comparatively few respondents had expressed such fears. For both the satisfaction and the fear of being alone after dark variables we ran one or more separate regression models using five different groups of potential problems in the area as the independent or explanatory variables. Location (town) and the length of time a respondent had been living in their local area were included as controls in every model. Each model was run separately for main and booster samples. The variables comprising each of the five 'problem' models are outlined below. The outcome of the regression models is summarised in Figures 5.20 to 5.29 and a more detailed account is given in Tables 5.11 to 5.20 in Appendix 1.

Explanatory model	Variables in model
'fear of crime'	worry about being the victim of burglary
	worry about being the victim of mugging
	worry about being the victim of theft of a car
	worry about being the victim of theft from a car
	extent to which racist attacks are seen as a problem in the local area
	location
	length of time in area
'drug related problems'	extent to which glue sniffing is seen as a problem in the local area
	extent to which 'drug users' are seen as a problem in the local area
	extent to which drug related illness is seen as a problem in the local area
	extent to which theft *for* drugs is seen as a problem in the local area
	extent to which crime under the influence of drugs is seen as a problem in the local area
	location
	length of time in area
'comparative crime'	the extent to which burglary is seen as a local rather than a national problem
	the extent to which car theft is seen as a local rather than a national problem
	the extent to which racist attacks are seen as a local rather than a national problem
	location
	length of time in area
'comparative drugs'	the extent to which drug users are seen as a local rather than a national problem
	the extent to which theft for drugs is seen as a local rather than a national problem
	the extent to which crime under the influence of drugs is seen as a local rather than a national problem
	the extent to which glue sniffers are seen as a local rather than a national problem
	the extent to which drug related illness is seen as a local rather than a national problem
	the extent to which drugs being offered for sale is seen as a local rather than a national problem
	location
	length of time in area
'general problems'	the extent to which noisy neighbours are seen as a problem in the area
	the extent to which teenagers are seen as a problem in the area
	the extent to which drunks are seen as a problem in the area
	the extent to which abandoned cars are seen as a problem in the area
	the extent to which litter is seen as a problem in the area
	location
	length of time in area

The range of variables available for inclusion in the above models is clearly not exhaustive. Given the list of potential crimes we could have considered, the available choice may seem particularly limited in the case of the 'fear of crime' and 'comparative crime' models. However, we feel that the composition of the models *does* allow us to provide a good approximation to the real picture of any link between fears for personal safety and satisfaction with an area on the one hand and a range of potential local problems including those associated with crime and drug usage.

Looking at the structure of the models in more detail, the variables included in the 'fear of crime' and 'comparative crime' models can be taken to represent four major forms of crime. Specifically, they represent a serious form of crime against property (burglary), a minor form of property crime (car theft), an undirected form of assault (mugging) and a targeted form of assault (racially motivated attacks). The two drugs models cover a fairly broad spectrum of drug related crimes and problems, including illness, drug related theft and the simple presence of drug dealers or users in an area.

It should be noted that we have chosen to analyse both perceptions of the *absolute* level of any given problem in an area and perceptions regarding the *relative* status of a problem in the local area as compared to the national picture for that problem. The rationale for analysing both types of response is that an individual's perception of his or her area may be influenced either by information assimilated *directly* from his or her experience of the area, or by information regarding the *relative* standing of the area in comparison to other areas. The two forms of information may of course operate in tandem as well as independently.

Figure 5.20
Summary of regression equations for comparative crime model: Main sample

Response	Variables in final model	Direction of effect	% of variance explained
actual fear of walking alone at night	burglary racist attacks	positive	1
perceived fear of walking alone at night	burglary	positive	2
satisfaction with area	burglary racist attacks car theft	negative negative negative	2

variables in equation: location, length of time in area, national versus local problem of burglary, national versus local problem of car theft, national versus local problem of racist attacks

Taking the main samples first, the regression models summarised in Figures 5.20 and 5.21 suggest that *relative* judgements regarding the level of crime or drug use in an area explain very little of the variance in either perceived or actual fear for personal safety in a given situation. The relative status of a problem in a local area as opposed to nationally also had very little association with a respondent's satisfaction with their local area. Having said which, it is worth noting that comparative views on the nature of *drug* related problems in an area appeared to be more closely associated with both fear of walking alone and satisfaction with the local area. The model including drugs related problems was able to account for between 3% and 7% of the variance in our dependent variables, whilst the crime model accounted for 2% or less of the variance in each case.

Figure 5.21
Summary of regression equations for comparative drugs model: Main sample

Response	Variables in final model	Direction of effect	% of variance explained
actual fear of walking alone at night	drug users drug illness	positive positive	3
perceived fear of walking alone at night	drug users	positive	5
satisfaction with area	drug users drug theft length of time in area location	positive positive positive Nottingham = Bradford > Lewisham = Glasgow	7

Variable in equation: location, length of time in area, drug users locally versus nationally, theft for drugs locally versus nationally, drug related crime locally versus nationally, glue sniffers locally versus nationally, drug related illness locally versus nationally, drugs offered for sale locally versus nationally

As a caveat to the above, it should be noted that the greater ability of the 'drugs' model to explain a respondent's satisfaction with their area, was at least partially accounted for by the presence of our control variables in the final model. Respondents who had lived in an area for a long time were, understandably, more likely to feel satisfied with the area than more recent residents and respondents in Nottingham and Bradford felt more satisfied with their local area than respondents in either Glasgow or Lewisham.

Figure 5.22
Summary of regression equations for crime model: Main sample

Response	Variables in final model	Direction of effect	% of variance explained
Actual fear of walking alone at night	mugging racist attacks	positive positive	17
perceived fear of walking alone at night	mugging theft of cars racist attacks	positive negative positive	15
satisfaction with area	burglary racist attacks theft of car mugging length of time in area	negative negative positive negative positive	5

variables in equation: location, length of time in area, worried about burglary, worried about mugging, worried about theft of car, worried about theft from car, worried about racist attacks

Those models which took into account a respondent's views on the *absolute* level of a problem in their local area (cf. Figure 5.22) were substantially more successful than those which took into account their relative judgements of the status of a problem locally as compared to nationally. Our 'fear of crime' model was able to account for 17% of the variance in actual fear for personal safety and 15% of the variance in perceived fear for personal safety. These are quite substantial amounts, particularly given the multi-faceted nature of fears for personal safety. The 'fear of crime' model also accounted for a greater proportion of the variance relating to satisfaction with the local area than did the 'comparative crime' model, although here it should be noted that *neither* absolute nor relative *crime* models explained any very large proportion of the variance overall.

An important point to note with regard to the 'fear of crime' model is that the manner in which it accounted for the variance explained differed in the case of fear of walking alone at night and satisfaction with the local area. A respondent's perceived or actual fear of walking alone at night was most closely associated with their impressions regarding the likelihood of assault, whilst their satisfaction with the local area was more directly affected by the perceived likelihood of burglary. This distinction was most apparent in the case of actual fear of walking alone at night, for which the only relevant variables were perceptions of the likelihood of assault. As might be expected, the fear of crime is context dependent.

A further difference between the explanations of satisfaction and fear of walking alone at night related to the direction of effect shown for perceptions regarding 'theft of cars'. Whilst, understandably, beliefs that car theft was quite a likely event in the local area reduced a respondents level of satisfaction with an area, it apparently accounted for a *decrease* in actual fears for personal safety. A reasonable interpretation to put on this rather odd finding is that some comparison between different types of crime was tacitly being drawn by respondents. That is, respondents were choosing which of the aspects of crime they felt most concerned about. So the negative association between fears for personal safety and theft of cars is actually a measure of the strength of concern shown by fearful respondents for the possibility of an assault. They show less concern about car theft because they are focusing their attention more closely than non-fearful respondents on violent crimes.

Figure 5.23
Summary of regression equations for drugs model: Main sample

Response	Variables in final model	Direction of effect	% of variance explained
actual fear of walking alone at night	drug users glue sniffing	positive positive	3
perceived fear of walking alone at night	drug users length of time in area	positive negative	3
satisfaction with area	drug related crime drug users length of time in area	positive positive positive	9

variables in equation: location, length of time in area, problem of glue sniffing, problem of drug users, problem of people being offered drugs, problem of drug related illness, problem of theft for drugs, problem of drug related crime

In contrast to the pattern noted for relative judgements of the level of a problem in a local area, the drugs model (Figure 5.23) which took into account perceptions of the absolute level of a problem in the local area was substantially *less* successful than its fellow crime model in accounting for either actual or perceived fears for personal safety. It was still, however, rather better at accounting for variance in a respondent's degree of satisfaction with his or her local area.

It is worth noting that in the context of these models, a respondent's length of time in their local area both increased levels of satisfaction and decreased fears for personal safety. Although the total amount of variance accounted for is fairly small, it is also of interest to note that of the fairly broad range of drug related problems considered, a belief that drug users were a problem in the area was linked with greater levels of fear for personal safety, whilst in terms of satisfaction with an area, the closest association was instead with drug related crime.

Figure 5.24
Summary of regression equation for general problems model: Main sample

Response	Variables in final model	Direction of effect	% of variance explained
satisfaction with area	litter	negative	15
	noisy neighbours	negative	
	teenagers	negative	
	drunks	negative	
	abandoned cars	negative	
	dogs	negative	

variables in equation: location, length of time in area, noisy neighbours, teenagers, drunks, dogs, abandoned cars, litter

The model we have labelled 'general problems' (Figure 5.24) was considered only in the context of a respondent's degree of satisfaction with their area. We did not consider it in the context of fears for personal safety because any results would have been too difficult to interpret unambiguously depending for example on the degree to which such problems are actually regarded by the general public as a measure of social decay or instability.

The association between a respondent's view that a range of general problems such as litter and abandoned cars are a salient problem within their local area and his or her level of satisfaction with that area is in contrast very straightforward. As Figure 5.24 shows, the presence of litter, noisy neighbours, teenagers 'hanging around on the street', drunks, abandoned cars and dogs running loose all served to decrease satisfaction with a local area. Of the variables listed, the presence of litter did most to decrease satisfaction, probably as a result of its greater degree of visibility in comparison to the other types of problem, whilst the presence of dogs did least to reduce satisfaction. Although all the variables comprising the 'general problems' model entered into the final equation in their own right, their combined presence only accounted for 14% of the variance. This suggests that individually they are of fairly low absolute importance in determining a person's satisfaction with their local area.

In summary, the results of our regression models for the main sample suggest that worries about violent crime against the person account for a very respectable proportion of the variance observed in both actual and perceived fears for personal safety, as measured by a respondent's fear of walking alone after dark. The fact that an even greater proportion of the variance is not accounted for by this evidently very salient concern is probably the result of the 'bogey' factor. In similar research, it has been noted that people consistently report that they are afraid of 'monsters' or 'things leaping out at them'. This type of rather non-specific fear is known to reflect individual variation in life stresses and attitudes as well as actual differences in vulnerability (cf. Stanko 1987).

Problems surrounding drug usage do not appear to impinge on considerations regarding personal safety to anywhere near the same extent as specifically crime related problems, although they *do* appear to be of some relevance to an individual's satisfaction with living in their local area. Also of note is the fact that the influence which both fear of crime and concern over drug usage have stems largely from an individual's direct assessment of such problems, rather than from the drawing of any comparative conclusions regarding the position of their local area in the larger scheme of things.

Interestingly, although significant differences *were* noted between locations for both fear for personal safety and satisfaction with an area, location entered into only one final regression model, this being the comparative drugs model for satisfaction with an area. Even here, location accounted for only a negligible proportion of the variance. What this tells us is that the location effects discussed in earlier sections of this chapter are probably not direct, but result instead from differences between the areas in other salient variables such as the amount of crime or the amount of litter.

Figure 5.25
Summary of regression equations for crime model: Booster sample

Response	Variables in final model	Direction of effect	% of variance explained
actual fear of walking alone at night	mugging	positive	12
perceived fear of walking alone at night	mugging burglary	positive positive	10
satisfaction with area	mugging racist attacks	negative negative	2

variables in equation: location, length of time in area; worried about burglary, worried about mugging, worried about theft of car, worried about theft from car, worried about racially motivated attacks

Turning to the regression models for the booster samples, the first point to note is that all five models were *less* successful in explaining variance within the booster sample than they were variance within the main sample. The composition of the final models also differed in most cases. As Figure 5.25 demonstrates, the 'fear of crime' model which had been the most successful in the main sample accounted for only 12% of the variance in actual fear for personal safety and 10% of the variance in perceived fear. In both cases a 5% reduction in the amount of variance explained compared to the main sample models. It was also less successful in accounting for the variance in satisfaction with the local area.

As with the main sample, the most important single variable in both the model for actual fear for personal safety and perceived fear for personal safety was worry about the prospect of being mugged. Rather unexpectedly, however, worry regarding the prospect of burglary proved to be almost as important in this context as worry over mugging. In distinct contrast to the pattern observed in the main sample, worry over the likelihood of mugging was also the variable of greatest importance in the case of *satisfaction* with an area. Again, this may reflect the problems of living in relatively deprived areas.

The reduction in the amount of variance explained by the crime model in the booster as opposed to the main sample is probably a consequence of the reduced importance of variables *other* than worry over the likelihood of being mugged in the booster sample, since this latter variable was the sole variable in the final model for actual fear for personal safety and the most important variable in the equations for both perceived fear for personal safety and for satisfaction with an area. If, as seems to be the case from the results discussed earlier, the prospect of being mugged is a more salient problem for our younger booster sample than for our older main sample respondents, this would also explain its outweighing less serious problems in terms of a respondent's satisfaction with their local area.

The comparative crime model (Figure 5.26) failed to account for *any* variance in the satisfaction of booster sample respondents with their local areas. It also accounted for less than 3% of the variance in both actual and perceived fear for personal safety. This lack of success mirrors that for the same model in the main sample. It is worth noting, however, that the particular variables included in the main and booster sample final models varied. In the booster sample, the *only* variable of importance was worry over the prospect of burglary. It would be of interest to discover whether the generally heightened profile of burglary as a worrying event in the booster sample stems from an enhanced perception in this sample that burglary is associated with some form of violence.

Figure 5.26
Summary of regression equations for comparative crime model: Booster sample

Response	Variables in final model	Direction of effect	% of variance explained
actual fear of walking alone at night	burglary	positive	1
perceived fear of walking alone at night	burglary	positive	3
satisfaction with area	no variables reached criterion		

variables in equation: *location, length of time in area, national versus local problem of burglary, national versus local problem of car theft, national versus local problem of racially motivated attacks*

Figure 5.27
Summary of regression equations for drugs model: Booster sample

Response	Variables in final model	Direction of effect	% of variance explained
actual fear of walking alone at night	theft for drugs	positive	2
perceived fear of walking alone at night	no variables reached criterion		
satisfaction with area	theft for drugs	negative	6

variables in equation: *location, length of time in area, glue sniffing, drug users, people being offered drugs, drug related illness, theft for drugs, drug related crime*

The drugs model (Figure 5.27) which looked at a respondent's absolute judgements concerning the levels of drug related problems in their area accounted for 6% of the variance in an individual's satisfaction with his or her area in the booster sample. This makes it slightly *less* successful than the same model in the case of the main sample. However, *all* of the variance accounted for was explained by the problem of thefts to fund drug usage. This variable was also the only directly associated drug related problem in terms of actual fears for personal safety. None of the drugs variables were successful in accounting for any variance in perceived fear for personal safety in the booster sample.

Figure 5.28
Summary of regression equations for comparative drug model: Booster sample

Response	Variables in final model	Direction of effect	% of variance explained
actual fear of walking alone at night	no variables reached criterion		
perceived fear of walking alone at night	drug related illness	positive	1
satisfaction with area	drug related crime	negative	1

variables in equation: *location, length of time in area, drug users locally versus nationally, theft for drugs locally versus nationally, drug related crime locally versus nationally, glue sniffers locally versus nationally, drug related illness locally versus nationally, drugs offered for sale locally versus nationally*

The comparative drugs model (Figure 5.28) was particularly unsuccessful in the booster sample. It explained only 1% of the variance in levels of satisfaction with an area and perceived fear for personal safety and accounted for *none* of the variance in actual fear for personal safety. This may, however, be an indirect consequence of the booster sample's generally more heightened levels of awareness of the drugs issue in their local area. Respondents in the booster samples were more similar to one another in their levels of knowledge regarding drugs than respondents in the main sample and were also consistently more likely to see drugs as a local rather than a national problem.

Figure 5.29
Summary of regression equation for general problems model: Booster sample

Response	Variables in final model	Direction of effect	% of variance explained
satisfaction with area	litter	negative	8
	teenagers	negative	

variables in equation: *location, noisy neighbours, teenagers, drunks, dogs, abandoned cars, litter*

Finally, the 'general problems' model (Figure 5.29) also proved in the booster sample's case to be of less value in explaining variance in a respondent's degree of satisfaction with his or her local area than had been the case in the main sample. Again, this appears to be a consequence of fewer of the variables in the model being of any particular salience in the eyes of the booster sample. Litter and 'teenagers hanging around' accounted on their own for a total of 8% of the variance in satisfaction with the local area, but none of the other 'problem' variables featured as being of any importance at all. The reduced success of this model in the booster as compared to the main sample provides a case in point for the generally lower success rate of our chosen regression models in this sample. Within the booster sample, our selection of variables appears to be less appropriate than is the case for the main sample and each individual variable also tends to account for a lower proportion of the variance where it *is* of relevance.

Although the distinction between main and booster samples with regard to the regression models discussed above is not great in absolute terms, it does provide some grounds for speculation on what the prime motivations for fear of personal safety and for satisfaction with an area are. While demographic factors such as age and gender may account for some of the disparity between main and booster sample, previous research, such as that by Shapland et al. (1990), suggests that demography is unlikely to account for all of the relevant variance. Since a further salient distinction between main and booster samples is the choice of local area in terms of measures of deprivation such as housing type, it would be of interest to pursue this aspect of the data further at some later point.

In summary, although our models accounted for up to 12% of the variance in actual and perceived fears for personal safety and up to 8% of the variance in satisfaction with an area in the booster sample, they were rather less successful in this sample than in our main sample. This appeared for the most part to be the consequence of the importance of a range of variables being substantially less in the booster than in the main sample. Indeed, almost the only variable of any significant importance in the booster sample appeared to be the prospect of being exposed to violence against the person. Since our booster sample derived from relatively more deprived areas than the main sample, it would be of interest to see whether this factor in addition to more obvious demographic differences could account for the varying success of our multivariate models in the two cases.

Summary of Chapter 5

A clear majority of the respondents in both our main and booster samples had lived within their local areas for some considerable time. This suggests that they would have adequate knowledge regarding their local environment to justify accepting their views as indicative of the actual state of affairs as they perceived it. This point is worth noting not only for the purposes of the present chapter, but also for other sections of the report which deal with aspects of relevance to particular local areas - for example the aspects of drug usage which we discussed in the last chapter regarding knowledge of the areas in which drugs are purchased or used. Although the majority of respondents were also very satisfied with the area in which they lived, only a minority of respondents suggested that their area represented a strong community in terms of doing things together and mutual support or help. This was notably the case in the booster sample.

A range of problems and crimes within the local area were considered and respondents were asked to make both *absolute* judgements regarding the prevalence of these difficulties in their neighbourhood and *comparative* judgements matching the local to the national picture for the relevant problem. The primary distinctions of note were that the perception of both crime and 'social disorder' type problems was heightened in the booster samples. Respondents from all locations and both samples appeared to consider that crimes and more general problems were greater at the national than the local level. In all locations *other* than Glasgow, drug related problems were also regarded by the majority of respondents in both types of sample as *less* of a problem than crimes and in particular as substantially less of a problem than violent crimes against the person. A similar degree of consistency was shown in our respondents' tendency to state that crime was on the increase in their local area. However, booster sample respondents were much more likely than main sample respondents to consider that drug usage was also on the increase.

Finally, it appears that we can account for a quite substantial proportion of the variance noted in fear for personal safety by taking into account an individual's concern regarding violent crime in their area. Not surprisingly, expressed satisfaction with the local area stems generally from more mundane considerations regarding such problems as the amount of litter in an area, although this was less true in the booster sample, where concern regarding violent crime was definitely higher than in the main sample.

On the whole, drug related problems do *not* feature as a major concern in the light of either fear for personal safety or satisfaction with an area, although they *do* account for a not negligible proportion of the variance noted in our main sample for these target variables. The disparity noted between main and booster samples in the ability of the crime and 'social disorder' problems included in this survey to explain the variance in fear for personal safety and also satisfaction with a local area, together with the enhanced degree of concern over violent crime, suggest that further research into the effects of levels of deprivation on these issues would be of value.

Chapter 6
PUBLIC PERCEPTIONS OF DRUGS AND DRUG MISUSE

The views of our main sample, outlined in the previous chapter, suggest that to the general public drugs are seen as rather *less* problematic than a range of other indices of crime and social disorder. Although the profile of drugs as a 'problem' is higher in our booster sample, suggesting that for potentially 'at risk' groups drug usage may be a more salient issue, even this group tended to focus their attention on crime rather than drug usage within their area and in particular on the potential for violent crime.

The fact that people seemed to be concerned with the effects of crime *rather* than drug usage, particularly within their local area, does not, of course, imply that drugs are not an important issue to people in absolute terms. Since we now have some insight into the *actual* patterns of drug usage within the locations sampled, it is of interest to compare these patterns with our samples' *perceptions* of drug usage. Do people have an accurate view of the likelihood that they, or someone like them, might become a drug user? Do they have any idea of the seriousness of the possible consequences should they do so? Such issues are not only of importance in allowing us to put the views of our respondents in context, they also have direct implications for drugs policy. If we wish to change the drug taking habits of a population, we must ensure first that any knowledge base on which we are attempting to build is an accurate one. Policy makers need to have some idea of the public's views and the public needs equally to have accurate information regarding drug usage.

In addition to addressing the question of whether the public, as represented by our sample, has an accurate picture of drug usage, we will also add here to our earlier discussions regarding the likely sources of any drugs related knowledge the public may have, whether accurate or not. This will provide some insight into the best routes to be taken in disseminating information about drugs and drug usage.

Awareness of drugs

One of the most basic questions regarding public perceptions of drug usage must concern the extent to which the public is actually *aware* of drug usage. This question is of some importance in the present context for two distinct but related reasons. A respondent's views on *any* of the issues surrounding drug usage will depend to some extent on the breadth of their drugs-related knowledge base. Consequently the extent of that knowledge base is of importance to us from a methodological viewpoint. As noted above, an assessment of the public's awareness of drugs is of *direct* relevance to policy decisions. The interests of methodology and policy are related by the need for both to be based on accurate and *specific* information.

Even having an answer to the very simple questions of whether a person has heard of illicitly used drugs and whether they have had any personal contact with drug usage will provide us with considerable information. Someone who has no personal experience of drug usage and who has also never obtained even indirect information by association with a drug user, will be restricted to opinions derived from sources *external* to drug usage.

Externally generated opinions may stem from media coverage, from the expressed views of the respondent's peer group or may in the present instance, even be stimulated by the tone of the questionnaire itself. Whatever the probable external influences, it is important to distinguish between those people who have some direct or indirect knowledge of drug usage and those who do not. As noted in Chapter 1, groups with different knowledge bases will also have different *values* in terms of the relevance of their comments on specific issues. In policy terms, it may be that different sub-sections of the population may require different sorts of information regarding drug usage. Summary data on our respondents' drugs related knowledge base is given in Tables 6.1 and 6.2 in Appendix 1 and in Figures 6.1 and 6.2 below. More detailed information by drug type is given in Tables 6.3-6.8 in Appendix 1.

General awareness of drugs: spontaneous and prompted

'Awareness' is a very general concept and consequently estimates of awareness can be based on a variety of factors. In this survey we decided to concentrate in the first instance on the spontaneous and prompted recall of the *names* of illicit drugs. This provides perhaps the most basic level of information regarding the prominence of drugs in a person's knowledge base. The list of drugs used for *prompting* awareness in those not able to spontaneously recall having heard of a drug has been outlined in Chapter 2. Although any list is necessarily restrictive, the list of drugs used here can be seen as fairly comprehensive for present purposes, since in the majority of samples fewer than 5% of respondents named drugs *other* than those on the list. Similarly, only a negligible proportion of respondents claimed personal knowledge of the usage of drugs not on the list.

Whilst assessing awareness by providing a prompt can be regarded as restrictive, assessing *spontaneous* awareness may be regarded as too broad a method. Spontaneous recall is subject to both intensity and recency effects. If a recent public press conference has discussed a particular drug it is very likely that more of our respondents will have been able to name that drug than would have been the case in the absence of such a conference. Similarly, any long term campaign concerned with a particular drug will have established that

recall alone. Prompted recall on its own may inflate estimates of awareness, but used together with spontaneous recall it can provide a more accurate picture. In short, the two measures of awareness need to be used in concert. In the following discussion we will use the aspect of recall which we feel is most appropriate to the issue being addressed in each case.

General awareness of 'drugs', however defined, was fairly high in our samples, with the majority of respondents in all locations and both samples being able to recall spontaneously at least *one* drug which they thought was used illicitly. The percentage of respondents *unable* spontaneously to recall *any* drug was predictably and significantly higher in the main than in the booster sample, although it still never reached beyond 15% of respondents.

Both main and booster sample showed significant

Figure 6.1
The extent of knowledge regarding drugs and drug users: Main sample

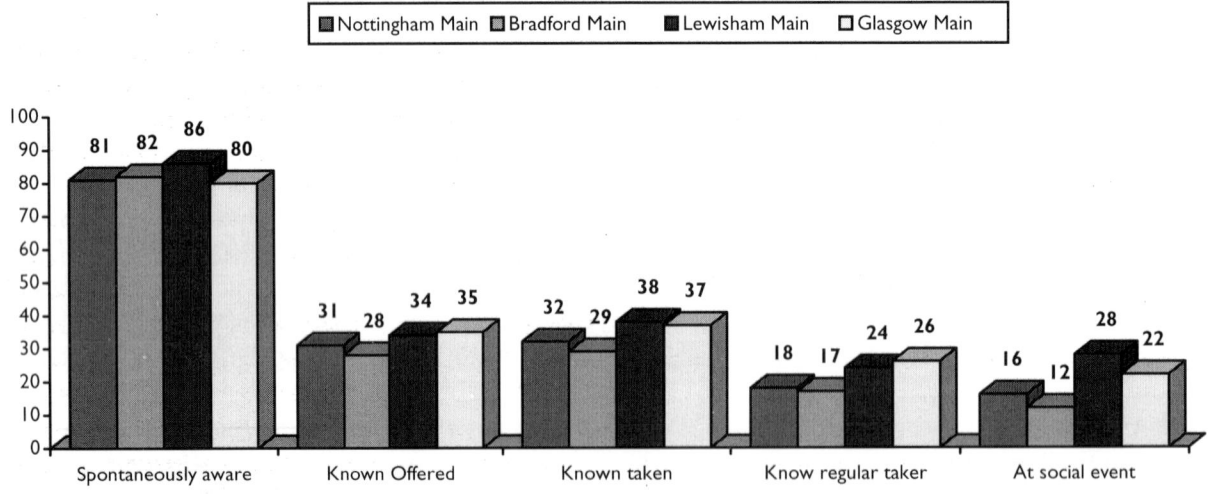

	Nottingham Main	Bradford Main	Lewisham Main	Glasgow Main
Spontaneously aware	81	82	86	80
Known Offered	31	28	34	35
Known taken	32	29	38	37
Know regular taker	18	17	24	26
At social event	16	12	28	22

Percentage of respondents spontaneously aware of one or more illicit drugs/Percentage of respondents who knew someone who had been offered an illicit drug/Percentage of respondents who knew someone who had taken an illicit drug/Percentage of respondents who knew someone who regularly took illicit drugs/Percentage of respondents who had attended a social event where drugs had been taken

drug in the memory of the public.

It is important to note, therefore, that these aspects of spontaneous awareness do not in all circumstances result in *mis*calculations. They will, for example, provide *accurate* estimates if the question we are asking is which drugs at the present moment in time have the highest public profile. For other purposes a more accurate estimate of awareness may be obtained by combining spontaneous and prompted awareness or, in certain cases, by *comparing* the increase in levels of awareness *following* prompting with that elicited by spontaneous

variance across location in their responses to the spontaneous recall item, but the effect was more extreme in the booster sample. Variance in the booster samples was largely accounted for by respondents in Bradford being around 10% less likely to be able to recall drug names than respondents from other locations. In the main sample, the variance was largely accounted for by the *greater* levels of spontaneous awareness in Lewisham, where respondents were about 5% more likely to spontaneously recall drug names than respondents in the other three locations.

Figure 6.2
The extent of knowledge regarding drugs and drug users: Booster sample

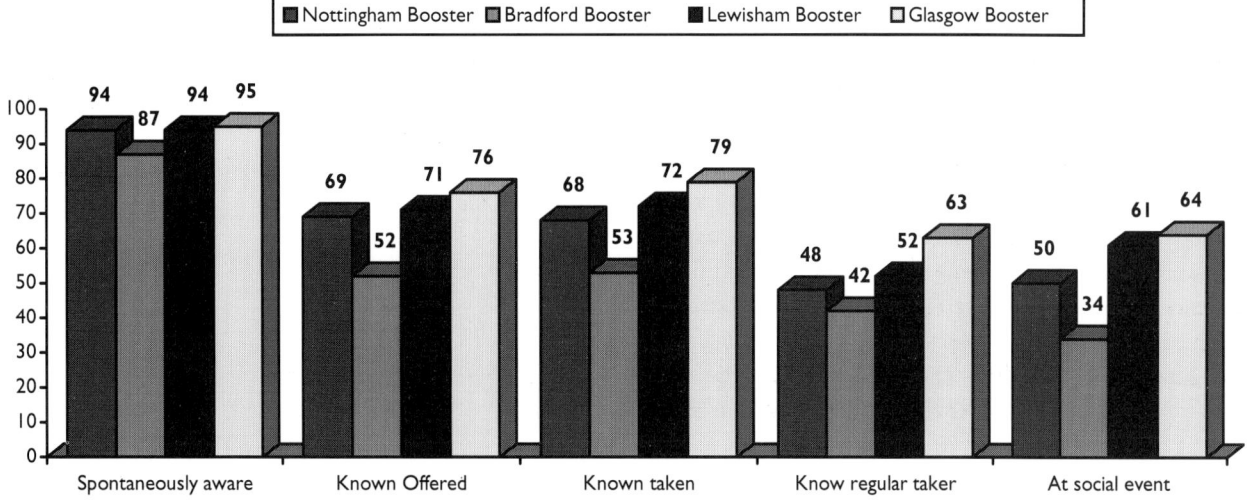

Legend: Nottingham Booster, Bradford Booster, Lewisham Booster, Glasgow Booster

Category	Nottingham	Bradford	Lewisham	Glasgow
Spontaneously aware	94	87	94	95
Known Offered	69	52	71	76
Known taken	68	53	72	79
Know regular taker	48	42	52	63
At social event	50	34	61	64

Percentage of respondents spontaneously aware of one or more illicit drugs/Percentage of respondents who knew someone who had been offered an illicit drug/Percentage of respondents who knew someone who had taken an illicit drug/Percentage of respondents who knew someone who regularly took illicit drugs/Percentage of respondents who had attended a social event where drugs had been taken

Following prompting, almost *all* respondents across both samples and all locations acknowledged at least one drug. This suggests two things. First, it implies that the public *does* have a strong, if basic, awareness of drugs being used illicitly. Second, the locational and sample type variations in *spontaneous* awareness, noted above, are likely to stem from differences *extrinsic* to the samples themselves, for example, the recency or intensity of any location's or group's exposure to information regarding drug usage. Had the differences been *intrinsic* to sample type *or* to location, providing prompts would not have substantially reduced the discrepancy between them.

The most stable and dramatic form of variance in recall applied to drug *types*. Cannabis, heroin and - dependent on sample - cocaine or ecstasy were the *most* likely drugs to be recalled spontaneously by a fairly wide margin. Between 30% and 60% of main sample respondents and between 40% and 80% of booster sample respondents named these drugs *spontaneously*. Amphetamines, LSD and 'crack' - a refined form of cocaine - formed a second group of drugs likely to be recalled by a sizeable minority. These were named by up to 40% of respondents in the main sample and up to 50% in the booster sample. Solvent abuse was cited by around 10% of respondents in all samples. Spontaneous recall of *any* other drug was either negligible *or* location specific. Temazepam followed the most strongly location-specific pattern, being named by more than 20% of respondents in both Glasgow's main and booster samples but by less than 2% of respondents in all other samples. This again supports the unusual prominence of this drug in Glasgow, an issue which may be deserving of further research.

From the foregoing discussion it can be seen that awareness of *specific* drug types follows the same pattern as awareness of drugs in general, with the booster sample showing greater overall levels of awareness than the main samples, but also a greater degree of variance. Differences between the main and booster samples reached high levels of statistical significance for all named drugs, with the exception of the created drug semeron and the actual drug diconal. Both of the latter were drugs of which virtually *no* respondents in either sample or any location claimed awareness.

Although we shall not deal in detail with differences between individual drugs, it should be noted that important differences in awareness emerged for different drug *groupings*. One such distinction is between drugs which have been focused on by media and government campaigns - for example, heroin and cocaine - and drugs which have had little such attention, such as triazelam and diconal. The former group of drugs is clearly distinct from the latter in terms of the public's awareness of its existence. This extreme distinction between the two groups does *not* appear from our prevalence estimates to be replicated in actual levels of usage. Consequently, the views of the public can be regarded at this most basic level as being out of line with the actual situation.

A second and perhaps more important distinction is between groups of drugs which have some accepted *medically relevant* function and groups of drugs which do not. In "Tackling drug misuse: a summary of the Government's strategy" (HMSO 1986) a dual definition is given for drug *misuse*. The first component of this definition refers to the "non-medical use of drugs which are intended for use only as part of a proper course of medical treatment". The second refers to the "illicit use of drugs which have no generally accepted medical purpose". Although questions of definition were not directly addressed in this study, the data for spontaneous awareness presented in Figures 6.1 and 6.2 suggests strongly that the *public's* use of the term 'drug' polarises around the second part of the definition.

To illustrate this more clearly, spontaneous awareness of the illicit use of pills and tranquillisers was displayed by 10% or less of all main sample respondents. Comparable figures for 'non-medical' drugs such as cannabis, heroin and cocaine were up to *six times* greater than this. Figures for the booster samples indicate that this distinction between medical and non-medical drugs holds even for people whom one might expect to have more specialist knowledge regarding drugs. If anything, the distinction was even greater in this sample with up to 80% of booster sample respondents being able to recall cannabis, heroin or cocaine whilst again only 10% or less could recall having heard of the illicit usage of 'medically relevant' drugs. Although prompting recall did much to redress this obvious imbalance, this apparent shift in pattern is likely to stem from the fact that individuals unable spontaneously to recall even such common drugs as cannabis are unlikely to admit to awareness of them following prompting. Furthermore, even with prompting, only 30% or less of respondents could recall hearing of the illicit use of in fact quite common non-medical drugs.

The failure to cite medically relevant substances as 'drugs' in the illicit sense also contrasts sharply with the actual levels of usage of these substances described in Chapter 2. Drugs such as heroin and cocaine, which were much more likely to be cited, show levels of self-report usage that are equivalent to or *less* than those for pills and tranquillisers across *all* samples. This disparity between the public's knowledge base and actual patterns of usage can be seen as problematic to the extent that it implies an equivalent disparity in the public's awareness of the likely effects of such substances. This flies in the face of an increasing emphasis by doctors and other medical practitioners on warning people of the consequences of misusing medical drugs.

In summary, general levels of awareness of drug usage were fairly high in all samples. However the levels of such awareness varied quite strongly as a function of sample type, sample location and, more importantly, drug *type*. The types of drug most commonly cited by both main *and* booster samples do not for the most part show a close association with *actual* patterns of usage. Instead, they focus on two axes, one of which appears to relate to the profile of a drug in terms of media or governmental campaigns, the other of which relates to whether or not a drug has a commonly accepted medical use. This pattern of awareness can be regarded as disturbing to the extent that it reflects a concomitant failure to recognise the relative levels of harm which can be inflicted by different drug types. Finally, it is worth noting that cannabis provided an exception to the disparity between awareness and prevalence, possibly as a consequence of its long-standing popularity as a leisure drug. In both samples and all locations it was the drug of which the majority of respondents were aware and *also* the drug which they were most likely to use.

Specific awareness: personal knowledge of drug users

The effects of indirect sources of information such as media or government campaigns would perhaps be expected to be modified by direct sources, such as personal contact with drug users. Referring back to Figures 6.1 and 6.2 we can see also the profile of our samples on direct sources of knowledge, measured by the percentage of individuals who:

- have known someone who has been *offered* a named drug
- have known someone who has *taken* a named drug
- who know someone who *regularly* takes a named drug
- have attended a *social* event where a named drug was taken

Predictably, this set of items shows an even greater disparity between main and booster samples than the more general awareness items. The majority of respondents in all main samples had *not* had any form of direct contact with drug use, whilst this pattern is inverted in the booster samples, where the majority of respondents *had* had such contact. Even for the booster samples, however, there is a clear distinction between such contact as knowing someone who has once been offered a drug or who has taken it on a limited number of occasions and knowing someone who takes a drug *regularly* or has *personally* attended a social event where drugs have been taken.

In the main samples around 35% of respondents knew someone who had been offered a drug or who had taken any drug on a limited number of occasions. Around 20% of respondents in this sample had either attended a social event where a drug was taken or knew a *regular* drug user. The pattern observed in the booster samples was similar, although the absolute numbers with both levels of knowledge were higher. Up to 80% of booster sample respondents knew someone who had been offered a drug or who had taken a drug on a restricted number of occasions and up to 60% knew a regular taker of some drug or had attended a social event where drugs were taken. These values are clearly quite high and suggest that the booster sample can validly be regarded as fairly knowledgeable about drugs at some level.

Within sample type, strong location effects were noted for all four direct knowledge items. As with spontaneous awareness, this effect was greatest in magnitude for the booster samples. In both booster and main samples respondents from Lewisham and Glasgow were significantly more likely to acknowledge all four forms of contact with drugs than respondents from either Bradford or Nottingham. Respondents in Bradford showed the lowest levels of contact in all cases. In the main samples, the discrepancy between locations was greatest for the closest forms of contact with drugs, namely attendance at a social event where drugs were taken and acquaintance with a regular drug user. In the booster samples, however, the strength of the locational effect was roughly equivalent across all four items.

Across both samples and all locations, the type of drugs with which respondents were *most* likely to have direct contact were: cannabis, amphetamines, LSD and ecstasy. The most prominent drug by quite a margin was cannabis. The precise ordering of the other three types was dependent on location. This pattern held for all four of our direct knowledge items. Levels of contact with other named drugs on our list varied much more widely with sample type and location. Note that the group of drugs about which respondents had most direct knowledge does *not* match closely the group about which levels of *general awareness* were highest. Heroin and cocaine featured quite strongly in public awareness, but were much less likely to be encountered directly, whereas the inverse was the case for amphetamines and LSD. Contact with drug usage, as would be expected, was closer to estimated prevalence levels than to the salience of a drug in the public eye.

In summary, levels of direct awareness of drug usage, measured by the degree of contact respondents had with named drugs, were fairly high in absolute terms across all locations and both samples. However there was the anticipated distinction between booster and main samples, with booster samples having a significantly higher level of contact with drug usage than the main samples. Location also had a strong effect on direct contact, with Lewisham and Glasgow generally showing the highest levels of such contact and Bradford the lowest. Although general levels of direct contact were high, there was also a distinction between contact involving regular users or the presence of drugs at a social event attended by the respondent, and contact which merely involves knowing someone who has been offered a drug or who has taken it on a restricted number of occasions. The latter was the more prominent form of direct knowledge in all cases. The prominence of different drug types also varied and here patterns of direct contact departed from those noted for general awareness of drugs. This suggests that effects external to drug usage, such as media or other information campaigns, are more likely to be informing spontaneous or prompted *awareness* of drugs, whilst predictably contact follows more closely the actual prevalence of drugs. Turning this last point on its head, the findings are quite encouraging from a methodological viewpoint, since they imply some level of accuracy in the self report data.

To summarise the information obtained from our 'awareness' items as a whole, it can be seen that awareness of drugs as being used illicitly was high in the general population and very high in target samples of young adults in areas of urban deprivation. Location appeared to have a strong effect on the levels of such knowledge, but this appeared to be a consequence of distinct patterns of public information, rather than of intrinsic differences across areas. With regard to drug types, *indirect* knowledge appeared to match the emphasis on drugs by media and government campaigns, with heroin and cocaine being very much to the fore. The prominence of cannabis in the public view cannot be explained in this way, however, and nor can the distinction apparently made between medical and non medical drugs, which departs from official definitions of illicit drug usage. Direct contact with drug usage was at a much lower level than general awareness of illicit drug use across both samples and all locations, but was certainly not insignificant. More than 10% of respondents in *all* main samples and more than 30% of respondents in *all* booster samples had some direct experience of drug usage. Patterns of contact were, as would be expected, closer to estimated prevalence levels than was the case for more general measures of awareness. Locational and sample type variance was noted in levels of direct contact and by definition these differences must be *intrinsic* to the samples. Overall, the booster samples had the greater level of experience and the locational pattern of contact followed the ordering Glasgow = Lewisham > Nottingham > Bradford.

Public assumptions regarding drug usage

Levels of awareness, direct or indirect, are not the only factor relevant to obtaining a picture of the public's perceptions of drug usage. The public might, for example, be *aware* of drug usage but not regard it as a problem, as was implied by the data we outlined in the previous chapter. It is consequently of importance to establish *how* drug usage is perceived by our respondents as well as *whether* it was perceived at all. Four aspects of this issue are addressed here:

- how *prevalent* respondents feel drug usage is
- how much of a *problem* they feel drug usage is in *absolute* terms
- how *harmful* they feel drug usage is
- what respondents see as the *cause* of drug usage.

The questionnaire items dealing with the first two of these aspects were phrased in fairly specific terms. Perceived prevalence was assessed by asking "How many people do you think take drugs nationally (in Great Britain)?" Perceptions regarding the extent of the drugs 'problem' were assessed by asking "How much of a problem would you say drug usage is *nationally*?" The harmfulness aspect was addressed by listing any drugs of which a respondent had claimed awareness and asking the respondent to indicate how beneficial or harmful they felt each drug was. Note that this last item caused some confusion amongst respondents who felt that a drug could not be considered in any way to be 'beneficial'. The fourth aspect, perceptions of causality, was investigated by listing a number of commonly cited causes of drug use, such as stress or the need for excitement, and asking respondents to rate each separately on the basis of how important an influence they felt it to be in drug usage. A detailed summary of responses to these items is given in Tables 6.9 to 6.20 in Appendix 1.

Views regarding the prevalence of drug usage

A very substantial majority - between 70% and 97% - of respondents across all samples felt that 'a lot' or 'quite a lot' of people in Britain were taking drugs. Not surprisingly, given the differential levels of both knowledge of and contact with drugs between the main and booster samples, the percentage of respondents feeling that drug usage is prevalent in Britain was rather higher in the latter sample for all locations (cf. Figure 6.4). Having said which, Figure 6.3 clearly shows that even the main sample were firmly convinced that drug usage is a prevalent behaviour in Britain. This being a view which is largely supported by our own prevalence data.

Figure 6.3
Respondents' perception of the prevalence of drug usage nationally: Main sample

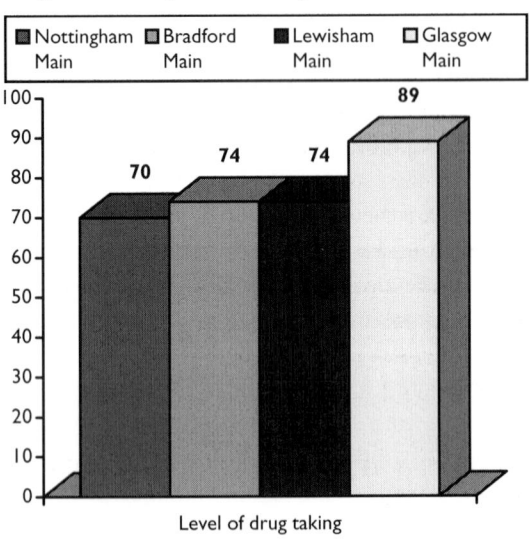

Percentage of respondents who felt that 'a lot' or 'quite a lot' of people take drugs nationally

In both main and booster samples, respondents from Glasgow were the most firmly convinced that drug usage was rife. The pattern of locational variation differed for main and booster samples, but only marginally. In the booster sample Nottingham, Bradford and Lewisham showed equivalent percentages of respondents feeling that drug usage was prevalent. In the main sample, respondents from Lewisham and Bradford were more likely than respondents from Nottingham to feel that drug usage was prevalent.

Figure 6.4
Respondents' perception of the prevalence of drug usage nationally: Booster sample

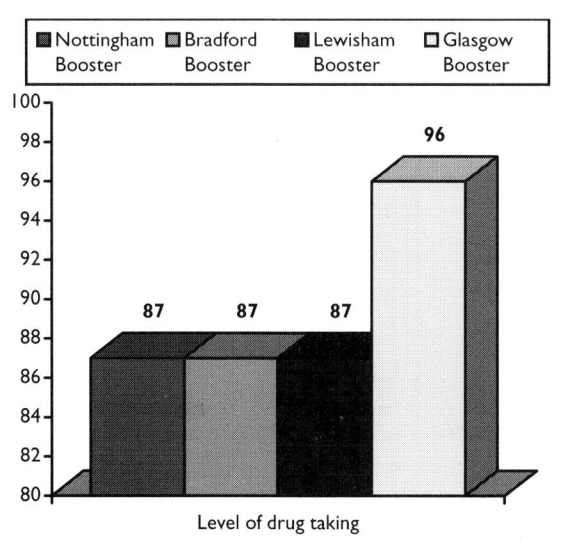

[Bar chart: Nottingham Booster 87, Bradford Booster 87, Lewisham Booster 87, Glasgow Booster 96 — Level of drug taking]

Percentage of respondents who felt that 'a lot' or 'quite a lot' of people take drugs nationally

Whilst the perceived prevalence of drug usage was uniformly high, it should be noted that the fact that respondents were, after all, being asked to respond to a fairly large questionnaire dealing with drug usage may have sensitised them to the issue. It is clear, though, that people are at least open to the idea that drug usage is in absolute terms a fairly common behaviour. For policy and more particularly drugs education purposes, it is of importance to know not only what the views of the public are regarding drug usage, but also whether these views vary across different sub-groups of the population. Any noticeable variation can be used to target those groups requiring further information. This issue is discussed below.

The demographic profile of beliefs in the prevalence of drug usage

Two possible dimensions along which views regarding the prevalence of drug usage might vary are an individual's personal experience of drug usage and their membership of particular demographic groups. To see whether either form of group membership had an effect on our respondents' views, we ran separate regression models for main and booster samples, using as a target variable the likelihood that a respondent felt that drug usage was prevalent in Britain. As explanatory variables we included the usual demographic measures, plus a measure of a respondent's personal experience with any of the three drug groups, cannabis, non-opiates and opiates. The latter measures were frequency of usage items taking as a base point 'never used' and as an upper limit 'use daily'. Since we knew that locational variation in perceptions of prevalence existed, we also included a dummy variable for location. The regression models are given in detail in Tables 6.10 and 6.11 in Appendix 1 and summarised in the text in Figures 6.5 and 6.6.

Figure 6.5
Summary of regression model for perceived prevalence of drug usage: Main sample

Response	Variables in final model	Direction of effect	% of variance explained
How many take drugs	socioeconomic status	AB/C1>C2/DE	6
	location	Glasgow>Bradford= Lewisham>Nottingham	
	gender	Females>males	
	frequency of taking cannabis	users>non-users	

variables in equation: *location, age group, gender, socioeconomic status, ethnicity (black, white, asian), frequency of taking cannabis, frequency of taking non-opiates, frequency of taking opiates*

Controlling for location, it can be seen that cannabis users, females and higher status socioeconomic groups were *more* likely than their counterparts in both main and booster samples to state that large numbers of individuals were using drugs in Britain. Whilst the amount of variation accounted for by these factors was not particularly great - 6% in the main sample and 4% in the booster sample - it nonetheless suggested that demography and to a lesser extent personal experience of drug usage are affecting people's perceptions of the prevalence of drug usage.

Figure 6.6
Summary of regression model for perceived prevalence: Booster sample

Response	Variables in final model	Direction of effect	% of variance explained
How many take drugs	socioeconomic status	AB/C1>C2/DE	4
	gender	Females>males	
	frequency of taking cannabis	users>non-users	
	location	Glasgow>Nottingham= Bradford>Lewisham	

variables in equation: *location, age group, gender, socioeconomic status, ethnicity (black, white, asian), frequency of taking cannabis, frequency of taking non-opiates, frequency of taking opiates*

The link between personal drug usage and the belief that drug usage is prevalent was an intuitive one, since users were more likely to feel that using drugs is a relatively common behaviour. The direction of effect for socioeconomic groups was also intuitive in both samples, since it followed actual prevalence levels, with the higher status groups being more likely to feel that drug usage was prevalent than the lower status groups. The gender effect was rather less intuitive in term of actual estimates of prevalence, since in both main and booster samples females were more likely than males to feel that drug usage was prevalent. The best explanation in this case is probably a heightened level of concern regarding usage in females than males. If so, this would match other gender differences in concerns regarding crime.

In summary, the vast majority of our respondents felt that drug usage was a prevalent behaviour in Britain. The public perception of prevalence levels seems also to be driven to an extent at least by actual estimates of prevalence. Respondents from the booster sample, from Glasgow, and from the higher status socioeconomic groups were all more likely to feel that drug usage is a relatively common behaviour, in line with their greater likelihood of using drugs in comparison to other groups of respondents. Not surprisingly, personal drug usage increased the likelihood that a respondent would feel that drug usage is common, although this finding is restricted to cannabis users rather than users of the, in fact, less prevalent drug groups we have labelled non-opiates and opiates. A less intuitive finding was that females showed a stronger tendency than males to believe that drug usage is common, suggesting that they may have a heightened degree of awareness or concern regarding drug prevalence, as they have for the prevalence or salience of other crimes.

Views regarding the extent of the drugs 'problem'

Public perceptions of the level of the 'drugs problem' in Britain matched those for levels of *usage*. Around 90% of respondents in both main and booster samples stated that drug usage was a 'very big' or 'fairly big' problem nationally. Again, it should be borne in mind that respondents were likely to be sensitised to the issue by virtue of taking part in our survey. This notwithstanding, the percentage of respondents viewing drugs as a problem nationally was extremely high. This supports our earlier interpretation of the greater salience of other illicit practices as potential problems.

Respondents, whilst feeling that, for example, violent crime is a relatively more problematic behaviour do feel that drug usage is a significant problem in absolute terms.

As with perceptions of prevalence, booster sample respondents were more likely to feel that drugs were a

Figure 6.7
Respondents' perception of the level of the national 'drugs problem': Main sample

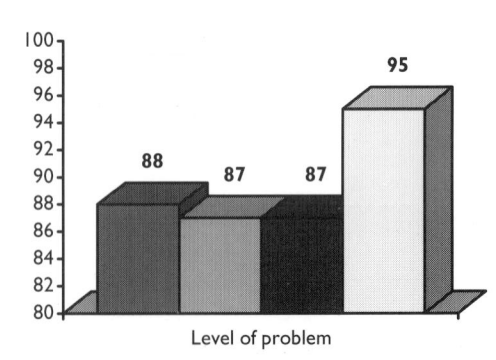

Nottingham Main: 88
Bradford Main: 87
Lewisham Main: 87
Glasgow Main: 95

Percentage of respondents who felt that drugs are a 'very big' or 'fairly big' problem nationally

problem than main sample respondents. A comparison of the data summarised in Figures 6.7 and 6.8 suggests that this pattern matches not only their generally greater level of concern for a variety of drugs related issues, but also their greater awareness of drugs and drug usage. Locational variation was also broadly similar to that noted for the perceived prevalence of drug usage. Both main and booster sample respondents in Glasgow were more likely to feel that drugs were a problem than respondents from the other three locations. Locational variation was less polarised in the booster sample than in the main sample, the distinction not being a direct split between Glasgow and the other locations but a more graded response pattern with Glasgow>Nottingham>Lewisham>Bradford.

Figure 6.8
Respondents' perception of the level of the national 'drugs problem': Booster sample

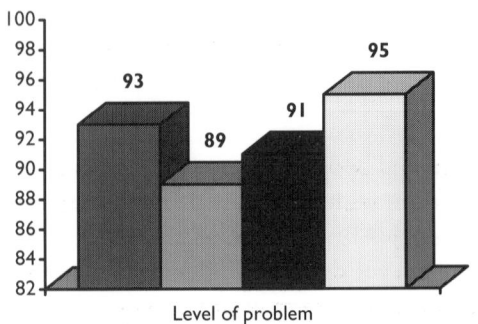

Nottingham Booster: 93
Bradford Booster: 89
Lewisham Booster: 91
Glasgow Booster: 95

Percentage of respondents who felt that drugs are a 'very big' or 'fairly big' problem nationally

The patterns of response shown suggest that at some level the public is very concerned about drug usage. Those members of the public who have the greatest degree of contact with drug usage and drug users were the most concerned about the potential problems arising from drug usage. Comparing the results presented here with those outlined in the previous chapter suggests, however, that people are in fact fairly distanced from drugs related problems in that they clearly view the problem as being a national one rather than one which pertains to their own local areas.

The demographic profile of beliefs in the 'problem' of drugs

As with our analysis of beliefs concerning the prevalence of usage, one of the factors we considered in relation to beliefs about the extent of a 'drugs problem' in Britain was the association of such beliefs with demographic variation. The explanatory variables used in the regression models we ran for this purpose exactly matched those used in the case of prevalence and again a more detailed account of the models can be seen in Tables 6.10 and 6.11 in Appendix 1.

Figure 6.9
Summary of regression model for the extent of the 'drugs problem'

Response	Variables in final model	Direction of effect	% of variance explained
Main sample			
How big a problem	socioeconomic status	AB/C1>C2/DE	6
	gender	Females>males	
	frequency of taking cannabis	Users> non-users	
Booster sample			
How big a problem	frequency of taking cannabis	Non-users> users	6
	socioeconomic status	AB/C1>C2/DE	
	gender	Females>males	

variables in equation: *location, age group, gender, socioeconomic status, ethnicity (black, white, asian), frequency of taking cannabis, frequency of taking non-opiates, frequency of taking opiates.*

Looking at the summary of this data, presented in Figure 6.9, it can be seen that variance in both general demography and personal experience of drug usage account for roughly the same proportion of the variance in beliefs regarding the extent of any drug problem in Britain as they did for beliefs regarding prevalence. With two notable differences, the final structure of the regression models was also the same for the two types of belief. One of the salient differences in the two sets of models was that in the case of beliefs regarding a British drug problem, location failed to have any effect independently of personal drug usage and demography. The other difference was that within the booster sample, although not the main sample, cannabis users were less likely to feel that drug usage was a problem than those who had not had experience of using cannabis.

In summary, the vast majority of our respondents felt that there was a big or fairly big drugs problem in Britain. This belief was particularly prominent in those groups most likely to be aware of and have contact with drug usage. Since all significant locational variation was accounted for on the basis of coincidental demographic variation between the locations sampled, we can take this as likely to be a fairly general finding. As a caveat to this, it should be noted that women, although *less* prominent as users themselves, were more likely to feel that there was a drugs problem than men. Perhaps more importantly, cannabis users - although not users of either non-opiates or opiates - within our 'at risk' booster sample, were significantly *less* likely to feel that there was a problem with drugs than their non-drug using counterparts.

Perceived levels of harm

Following in line with other perceptions regarding drug usage, the majority opinion of *almost all* drugs appears to be that they are distinctly harmful. The percentage of respondents assuming a named drug to be 'very harmful' rarely fell below 30% and was for the majority of drugs above 50% in both main and booster sample. In contrast, the familiar distinction between main and booster sample was reversed, with booster sample respondents generally being more likely to feel that drugs were *not* harmful.

Exceptions to the otherwise consistent view of drugs as being 'very harmful' lay along the two axes of drug type and location. Cannabis and psilocybin were generally regarded as *less* harmful than other drugs. From a medical viewpoint this matches the *actual* levels of harm that they can inflict. It also matches the popular view that 'natural' as opposed to chemically derived substances are less harmful. With regard to location, the profile for Lewisham and, notably, Lewisham's booster sample suggests that its population had a tendency to ascribe *lower* levels of harm to a *broader* range of drugs than was the case for other areas. Respondents from Glasgow's main and booster samples showed the opposite tendency, namely ascribing *higher* levels of harm to a broader range of substances.

Figure 6.10
Perceived harmfulness of drugs

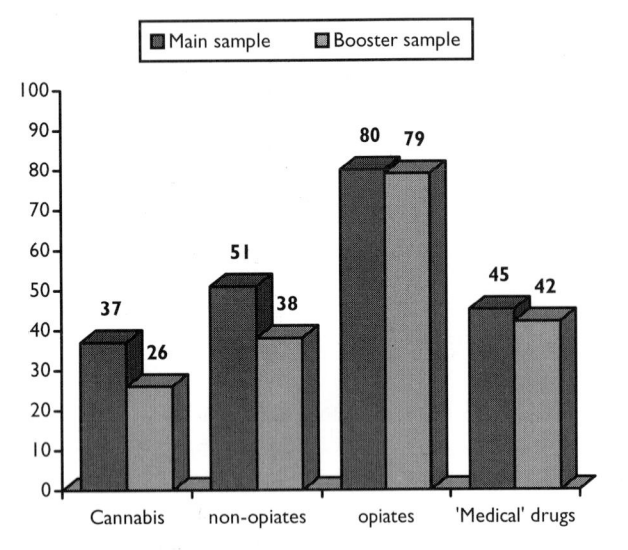

[Bar chart comparing Main sample and Booster sample perceptions across drug categories:
- Cannabis: 37 (Main), 26 (Booster)
- non-opiates: 51 (Main), 38 (Booster)
- opiates: 80 (Main), 79 (Booster)
- 'Medical' drugs: 45 (Main), 42 (Booster)]

Percentage of those respondents who had heard of a drug type saying it was 'very harmful', averaged across location. Note that 'medical' drugs here refer only to barbiturates, tranquillizers and 'pills'.

Since the public's spontaneously elicited use of the term 'drug' implies a distinction between medical and non-medical substances, it was possible that people would hold different views about the harmfulness of medically relevant substances, compared to non-medical drugs. The data summarised in Figure 6.10 suggest, however, that medically relevant substances - tranquillisers, pills etc. - were seen by both main and booster samples as equivalent to the non-opiates in harmfulness, and certainly as being more harmful than cannabis. The opiates, however, were perceived as far and away the *most* harmful drugs.

The medical viewpoint, as represented in major journals, maintains, for example, that tranquillisers are in fact *more* harmful than drugs such as heroin. They are seen as more readily addictive; as having a lower overdose threshold; and as requiring closer medical supervision to ensure a safe withdrawal. There appears hence to be a mismatch between actual and perceived levels of harm in relation to the opiates in terms of medical harm - but respondents may also have been thinking about social harm and cultural values put on different drugs. The findings are probably accounted for by the major negative publicity campaigns about heroin addicts etc. We can also see that the publicity about the harmful effects of tranquillisers and other pills taken not on prescription seems to have hit home, although clearly not to the same extent.

Our data for perceived levels of harm also followed the pattern noted earlier for more general awareness of the drugs. As can be seen from Figure 6.10, opiates were regarded by both booster and main samples as significantly more harmful than non-opiates and these in turn were regarded by both samples as less harmful than cannabis. Overall, therefore, the pattern adopted by our respondents views suggests that levels of harm may be attributed on the basis of the profile of a drug in the public's consciousness. Whilst a large number of individuals are likely to have experienced cannabis for themselves, this is not the case for other drugs about which people were happy to make judgements. Given the reliance of the public on second hand sources of information - and given that individuals are likely to pass on information whether correct or not - there is clearly a continuing need for accurate and specific information regarding the levels of harm - both medical and social - individual drugs can inflict to be disseminated.

The demographic profile of perceptions of harm

Since very few of our respondents will have had access to accurate measures of the actual degree of medical, psychological, or social harm a drug can inflict, it is of interest to consider which factors *other* than general awareness of the drugs named are influencing perceptions of harm. As with the previous analyses of beliefs regarding drug usage, the two most obvious candidates to spring to mind were demography and personal drug usage. We again carried out separate regression analyses for main and booster samples to determine what percentage of the variance in perceived levels of harm could be accounted for by either demography or drug usage.

The demographic variables we used were the same as for our other analyses of beliefs about drug usage. However, since public perceptions of harm are of particular importance to drugs policy, we decided to broaden our model slightly in the case of drug usage to include not just a measure of a respondent's own personal experience of drug usage, but also information on whether they had had any contact with a regular drug user. As levels of perceived harm had been shown to vary across drug types, we carried out separate regression analyses in each case for one drug from each of the drug groups outlined above. The drugs chosen were cannabis, heroin (as a representative of the group of opiate drugs), amphetamines (as a representative of the group of non-opiate drugs) and tranquillisers (as a representative of the group of medical drugs).

We also chose to analyse one drug in its own right rather than as a representative of a particular type of drug. This drug was ecstasy, which is becoming increasingly prominent as a potentially problematic drug. Although our data suggested that in fact both the public in general and 'at risk' groups *do* regard this drug as harmful, there has been some concern in the literature that people are in fact tempted to regard it as *less* harmful than it actually is (cf. Newcombe and Parker 1991). With this in mind we felt it worth considering *which* groups in society may be particularly likely to make this mistake. The regression analyses for this drug and for the four drugs listed previously are presented in detail in Tables 6.13 and 6.14 in Appendix 1. They are presented in summary form in Figures 6.11 and 6.12 below.

Variation in demography and both personal drug usage and more indirect forms of contact with drug usage was able to account for at least some of the differences observed in the perceived harmfulness of all

Figure 6.11
Summary of regression models for perceived harmfulness of a range of drugs: Main sample

Response	Variables in final model	Direction of effect	% of variance explained
harmfulness of cannabis	frequency of using cannabis	non user>user	7
	ethnicity	white> asian>black	
	location	Glasgow= Nottingham> Bradford> Lewisham	
	know regular user	without contact> with contact	
	age group	younger>older	
harmfulness of amphetamines	ethnicity	white> black=asian	11
	socioeconomic status	C2/DE>AB/C1	
	age group	older>younger	
	location	Glasgow> Nottingham> Lewisham= Bradford	
	know regular user	without contact >with contact	
	gender	females>males	

Response	Variables in final model	Direction of effect	% of variance explained
harmfulness of heroin	age group	younger>older	4
	ethnicity	white> black=asian	
	socioeconomic status	C2/DE>AB/C1	
	location	Glasgow= Nottingham> Lewisham= Bradford	
	know regular user	with contact >without contact	
harmfulness of tranquillizers	socioeconomic status	C2/DE>AB/C1	7
	ethnicity	white> black=asian	
	age group	younger>older	
	location	Glasgow> Lewisham= Bradford= Nottingham	
	know regular user	with contact >without contact	
harmfulness of ecstasy	age group	younger>older	11
	ethnicity	white> black=asian	
	socioeconomic status	C2/DE>AB/C1	
	location	Glasgow> Bradford= Lewisham= Nottingham	
	know regular user	with contact >without contact	
	gender	female>male	
	frequency of using ecstasy	non user>user	

variables in equation: *whether tried the relevant drug, whether know someone who is a regular user of the relevant drug, age group, gender, ethnicity (white, black, asian), location, socioeconomic status*

five of the drugs considered, the extent of the variation accounted for being largely dependent on the identity of the drug being considered. Interestingly, our models for main and booster samples showed very similar patterns and also accounted for equivalent proportions of the variation in both main and booster samples for all the drugs except for cannabis. In the case of cannabis the booster sample model was about twice as successful as that for the main sample. The similarity of the models of main and booster samples and the consistency of the direction of effect of the factors considered in each case suggests that demography and contact with drug usage are likely to be universal factors in accounting for perceptions of the harmfulness of drugs. This fact is likely to be of some importance for drugs education.

Figure 6.12
Summary of regression models for perceived harmfulness of a range of drugs: Booster sample

Response	Variables in final model	Direction of effect	% of variance explained
harmfulness of cannabis	frequency of using cannabis	non user>user	14
	know regular user	without contact >with contact	
	gender	males>females	
harmfulness of amphetamines	ethnicity	white> black=asian	11
	socioeconomic status	C2/DE>AB/C1	
	age group	younger>older	
	location	Glasgow> Nottingham= Lewisham= Bradford	
	know regular user	with contact >without contact	
	gender	females>males	
harmfulness of heroin	age group	younger>older	4
	ethnicity	white> black=asian	
	socioeconomic status	C2/DE>AB/C1	
	location	Glasgow= Nottingham> Lewisham= Bradford	
	know regular user	with contact >without contact	
harmfulness of tranquillizers	socioeconomic status	C2/DE>AB/C1	7
	ethnicity	white> black=asian	
	age group	younger>older	
	location	Glasgow> Lewisham= Bradford> Nottingham	
	know regular user	with contact >without contact	
harmfulness of ecstasy	age group	younger>older	11
	ethnicity	white> black=asian	
	socioeconomic status	C2/DE>AB/C1	
	location	Glasgow= Nottingham= Bradford> Lewisham	
	know regular user	with contact >without contact	
	gender	females>males	
	frequency of using ecstasy	non-user>user	

variables in equation: whether tried the relevant drug, whether know someone who is a regular user of the relevant drug, age group, gender, ethnicity (white, black, asian), location, socioeconomic status

The *least* successful model of the five was (in both the booster and the main sample) that for the harmfulness of heroin. Our demographic and drug usage variables accounted for only 4% of the variance in perceived levels of harmfulness for heroin. This is of interest since, of the drugs considered, it is the one which has received most media attention. It is also one of the drugs which the majority of our respondents were most likely to consider extremely harmful and the one which they were most likely to have heard of. The lack of demographic variance in views of harmfulness illustrated by our regression models implies that perhaps public campaigns have had a degree of success in encouraging a broad range of people to believe in the harmfulness of heroin.

For the four other types of drug, demographic variance and variance in the experience of drug usage explained a rather larger proportion of the variance in perceived harmfulness. The composition of the final models was broadly similar across both sample and drug type, although fewer demographic variables were of relevance in the booster sample, presumably as a consequence of the quota selection methods used in recruiting volunteers for this sample. The direction of effect for the demographic variables was the same in all models, suggesting as noted above that the nature of the demographic effect is a global one - membership of a particular group either increasing or decreasing the perceived harmfulness of drugs in general rather than affecting any one drug or group of drugs in particular.

For those models in which contact with drug usage was relevant this also operated in the same direction across most drug types. Cannabis, however, provided an exception to this otherwise consistent pattern. Both personal usage of cannabis and acquaintance with a regular user of cannabis were associated with *lower* estimates of its harmfulness. For all four of the other drugs, contact with regular users of the drug was associated with heightened levels of perceived harm. It is important to note also that the models for ecstasy and cannabis were the only ones for which *personal* drug usage was associated with perceived harmfulness and in these cases, having used the drug oneself was associated with *lower* perceptions of harmfulness. These findings held for both main and booster samples and are particularly important in the case of ecstasy, since they go some way towards confirming the dominant view in the drugs literature that users of this drug may be underestimating its harmfulness. The finding that contact with regular users of drugs other than cannabis is associated with heightened perceptions of the harmfulness of the drugs is a rather more encouraging finding.

A somewhat surprising finding was that in both samples and across all five drug types, *younger* respondents were *more* likely to view a drug as being harmful than older respondents. This seems paradoxical, since our prevalence data suggests that younger respondents are also the group most likely to *use* most of these drugs. Note that this contradiction is *not* explained by differences in personal drug usage since the regression models controlled for this. It may, however, be a function of the greater effort which health departments and the media have recently devoted to convincing younger age groups of the dangers of drug abuse. If so, such efforts have been effective at least at the perceptual level, if not yet at the behavioural level.

Other aspects of demography also failed to match the pattern which would be expected of them on the basis of our prevalence data. White respondents, who had been our most prevalent users, were *more* likely to perceive drugs as harmful than respondents from ethnic minorities. It would be interesting in this context to have compared the views of different ethnic groups also on the harmfulness of licit drugs such as alcohol or tobacco. Females, who showed much lower prevalence levels than males, were on the whole more likely to consider drugs harmful. A caveat to this last statement was the booster sample model for cannabis, where males were *more* likely than females to consider the drug as being harmful.

The only link between demographic variance and variance in the perceived harmfulness of drug usage which *did* follow a pattern predictable on the basis of our prevalence data was that shown by socioeconomic status. The lower status socioeconomic groups which were our *less* prevalent users, were *more* likely to perceive drugs as harmful than higher status groups. Although we obviously cannot make any definitive statements on the basis of the present data, the pattern noted in the foregoing discussion does suggest, as has been suspected for some time, that perceptions of harm do *not* undermine the tendency to use drugs. This is an issue which could certainly bear more detailed research.

Finally, it is worth noting with regard to the location effects discussed above that in both main and booster samples the effect of location on perceived harmfulness of drugs was shown by the regression models to be *independent* of any demographic or drug usage effects. In other words, the difference between towns for perceived harmfulness is a real effect which must find its explanation in some relevant distinction between the areas. Given that respondents in Glasgow appear to be most firmly convinced of the harmfulness of a range of drugs, one obvious candidate for this distinction is the public profile of drug usage.

In summary, the majority of respondents in both main and booster samples were convinced of the harmfulness of a broad range of drugs. However, some differences were noted in the levels of harm attributed to different drug types. Cannabis and psilocybin were considered as less harmful than either medically relevant drugs or 'non-opiates' which in turn were considered less harmful than opiates.

In contrast to the greater degree of concern consistently shown by the booster sample in relation to most aspects of drug usage, this sample was *less* likely than the main sample to consider drugs harmful. Given the quite extreme levels of support for the idea that all drugs are 'very harmful', this may simply be a consequence of the more knowledgeable sample having a less exaggerated view of likely levels of harm. Multivariate analyses of the demographic and drug usage profile of perceptions of harm conflict with the perceived disparity between main and booster samples, showing a general tendency for those groups *most* likely to use drugs to be the groups also *most* likely to consider drugs harmful. This has unfortunate implications for the idea that providing people with information relating to harmfulness will actually reduce drug usage. The only exception we found to this general rule was the tendency for respondents from lower socioeconomic status groups to be more likely to consider drugs harmful, although showing lower prevalence levels for usage than their higher status counterparts. On a more hopeful note, acquaintance with a regular user of a range of drug types *other* than cannabis linked significantly with a tendency to consider the relevant drug as more harmful.

Comparing licit with illicit drugs

As noted in Chapter 3, licit but harmful drugs such as alcohol and tobacco have very inflated prevalence rates in comparison to controlled drugs. Given which - and since our respondents clearly felt that controlled drugs *were* very harmful - it is worth comparing public perceptions of harm for these two legally defined types of drugs. Although, unfortunately, we did not ask respondents to rate alcohol and tobacco directly for harmfulness, we did ask one question which can get at this issue obliquely. Specifically, respondents were asked to indicate the extent to which they agreed with the comparative statement "there is little difference in health terms between smoking cannabis and smoking tobacco or drinking alcohol". Note that the responses obtained to this item are of relevance not only in the present context, but also to our discussion of the legalisation issue in Chapter 9. A detailed summary of responses to this comparative item can be found in Table 6.15 in Appendix 1.

Figure 6.13
Comparison between the use of cannabis and the use of either alcohol or tobacco

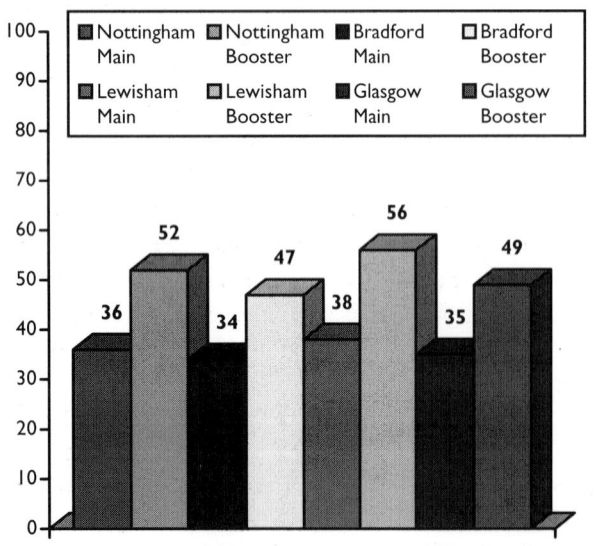

Percentage of respondents who 'agree strongly' or 'agree slightly' with the statement that "there is little difference in health terms between smoking cannabis and smoking tobacco or drinking alcohol"

As indicated by the data summarised in Figure 6.13, a substantial proportion of individuals in all locations and both samples *were* willing to concede that there was little difference in health terms between using cannabis and using either alcohol or tobacco. In the main samples this proportion represented a minority of respondents - although an admittedly large minority - with up to 38% of respondents in each location feeling that cannabis and alcohol or tobacco were equivalent. In the booster sample, up to 56% of respondents in the four locations were willing to endorse this view. Clearly in the more knowledgeable and 'at risk' groups, there is a strong feeling that at least *some* controlled drugs have inherently the same medical status as licit drugs, if not the same legal status.

Two further points can be made regarding the distribution of responses to this item. Firstly, the proportion of main sample respondents willing to support the comparative statement suggests that the general public is open to the idea of equating its own favoured leisure drugs with drugs which in absolute terms it is more likely to regard as taboo. Secondly, the perceived levels of harm associated with the two forms of drug - licit and illicit - are unlikely to provide the primary axis determining their usage. The majority of the main sample had used alcohol. The majority clearly had *not* used cannabis, yet around 35% of main sample respondents in *all* locations perceived the two as *equivalent* in terms of health risks.

As with our earlier analyses of people's beliefs regarding drug usage, we wanted to see whether the tendency to equate cannabis with alcohol and tobacco associated at all with variations in demography or personal experience of using drugs. Carrying out this type of analysis was of particular interest in the case of the main sample responses, since it might have been able to account for the surprisingly large minority of respondents in this sample who had supported the equation of cannabis with licit drugs. We carried out the same type of regression analyses as outlined previously, using age, gender, ethnicity and socioeconomic status as the explanatory demographic variables and including location as a control. Since personal experience of drug usage might have been particularly apposite in this context, we used a slightly broader set of drug usage items than previously, including whether a respondent had ever taken any kind of unprescribed drug and their frequency of using alcohol, tobacco, cannabis, non-opiates and opiates. All 'frequency' items as before had a base point at 'never' and an upper limit of 'use daily'. The results of our regression models are given in detail in Tables 6.16 and 6.17 in Appendix 1 and are given in summary form below.

Figure 6.14
Summary of regression models for comparisons between cannabis and licit drugs

Response	Variables in final model	Direction of effect	% of variance explained
Main sample			
there is little difference between alcohol or tobacco and cannabis	age group	older>younger	7
	frequency of cannabis usage	user>non-user	
	socioeconomic status	C2/DE>AB/C1	
	gender	males>females	
	ethnicity	blacks> asians>whites	
	frequency of alcohol usage	user>non-user	
Booster sample			
there is little difference between alcohol or tobacco and cannabis	frequency of cannabis usage	user>non-user	5
	socioeconomic status	C2/DE>AB/C1	

variables in equation: *location, age group, gender, socioeconomic status, ethnicity (white, black, asian), whether taken any illicit drug, frequency of taking cannabis, frequency of taking non-opiates, frequency of taking opiates*

Whilst, as Figure 6.14 demonstrates, both demography and drug usage clearly do associate with respondents' views on this item, the amount of variance accounted for by them is not particularly large, only 7% in the case of the main sample and 5% in the case of the booster sample, the final model for the main sample (which also accounted for a greater proportion of variance) containing rather more of our selected variables than that for the booster sample.

Not surprisingly, one of the primary explanatory variables in both final models was personal experience of drug usage. However, this effect was very specific in both models. Cannabis users, but not the users of other drugs, regardless of type, were more likely to equate cannabis with alcohol and tobacco than were non-cannabis users. Interestingly, main sample users of alcohol were also more likely to support the comparative statement than individuals who did not use alcohol or only used it infrequently. No similar effect was shown for tobacco usage. In both samples respondents of lower socioeconomic status were more likely than those of higher socioeconomic status to equate the licit drugs with the illicit.

Other demographic variables of some importance in the main sample, although not in the booster sample, were age and gender, with *older* age groups and males being more likely to equate the two drug types than younger respondents or females. Respondents from ethnic minorities were also more likely to equate the two drug types than white respondents. This latter finding provides some support for the suggestion given earlier that we should consider further the idea of cultural variation in 'acceptable' drugs.

One of the interesting aspects of the main sample regression model is that it indicates that demographic variation cannot be used to account for the large minority of respondents supporting the comparative statement. First of all, because the amount of variation either demography or personal drug usage can account for is fairly small. Perhaps more importantly, because the direction of effect of certain key variables in the final model is counter-intuitive. A long-standing view regarding the tendency to equate cannabis with licit drugs is that it is a view subscribed to largely by the young and by drug users themselves who do not realise the harmfulness of illicit drugs (cf. Smith and Gay 1971, Inciardi and McBride 1991). Had those respondents in the main sample who supported the comparison between cannabis and licit drugs been comprised only of individuals fitting this bill, the fact that they did so would consequently have been predictable on the basis of accepted forms of attitudinal variation.

In fact, whilst our data support the view that cannabis users are more likely to assume equivalence between cannabis and licit drugs than non-cannabis users, the broader implications of the above stereotype are *not* well supported in this context. It was our *older* rather than our younger respondents, and similarly respondents from lower rather than higher status socioeconomic groups, who were more likely to equate alcohol and tobacco in health terms. These two groups were our *least* prevalent drug users. More importantly, if we refer back to our harmfulness data, it is apparent that both the young and drug users appear to be *more* likely to consider drugs in general as harmful.

We have dealt with the above issue in some detail, because the size of the minority in our general population sample favouring the equation of cannabis with licit drugs was surprisingly large given accepted views regarding the public's perceptions of controlled drugs. It is important to remember, therefore, that the *majority* view of the main sample was that licit and unprescribed drugs could not be equated. It is also important to remember that because we did not ask respondents to rate alcohol and tobacco in terms of absolute levels of harm, we cannot determine whether the minority of the main sample and the majority of the booster sample were equating cannabis with alcohol and tobacco because they felt they were equally *harmless* or equally *harmful*.

> **In summary**, the majority of respondents in our main sample were *not* happy to equate cannabis with licit drugs in health terms, although the majority of our booster sample *were*. Whilst, predictably, individuals who used or had used cannabis themselves were more likely to equate licit with unprescribed drugs, so too were users of alcohol. The results of our multivariate analyses together with the profile outlined earlier for perceptions regarding the harmfulness of drugs pose a minor challenge to long-standing views regarding the nature of any equation made between licit and unprescribed drugs. This area of research might be worth further development.

Perceptions of cause in drug usage

A final aspect of the public's perceptions of drugs and drug misuse relates to the causal structures seen as inherent in drug usage. To address this issue, we simply asked respondents to indicate the level of their agreement with the statement that the following influences were important in drug usage: boredom, stress, the need for excitement, lack of parental guidance, presence at a club or party where drugs were available, unemployment, unhappiness at home, mental illness, the fun of taking drugs, fitting in with friends, declining moral standards and a method of coping with life. Whilst we could have used a much longer list of potential causes, or left respondents open to express their own specific perceptions of causality, we felt that our list was sufficiently comprehensive to provide an equitable balance between the constraints of time and the need to allow for a broad range of possible causes. A detailed outline of the responses to this item can be found in Tables 6.18-6.20 in Appendix 1. A summary of responses, partitioned by personal experience of drug usage is given in Figures 6.15-6.18 in the text.

As the general profile noted in Figures 6.15 to 6.18 shows, this item was one of the very few attitudinal items on which we found fairly close agreement between our main and booster samples. The only salient difference between the samples was, predictably, concerned with those items relating to 'moral decline' and 'lack of parental guidance', both items being significantly less likely to be endorsed by the booster sample as a potential cause of drug usage. Although this distinction between the samples is likely to be primarily a function of age, it may also stem from the greater personal knowledge of drug usage held by the booster sample, since drug users were also less likely to endorse these than non-drug users. Locational variation in

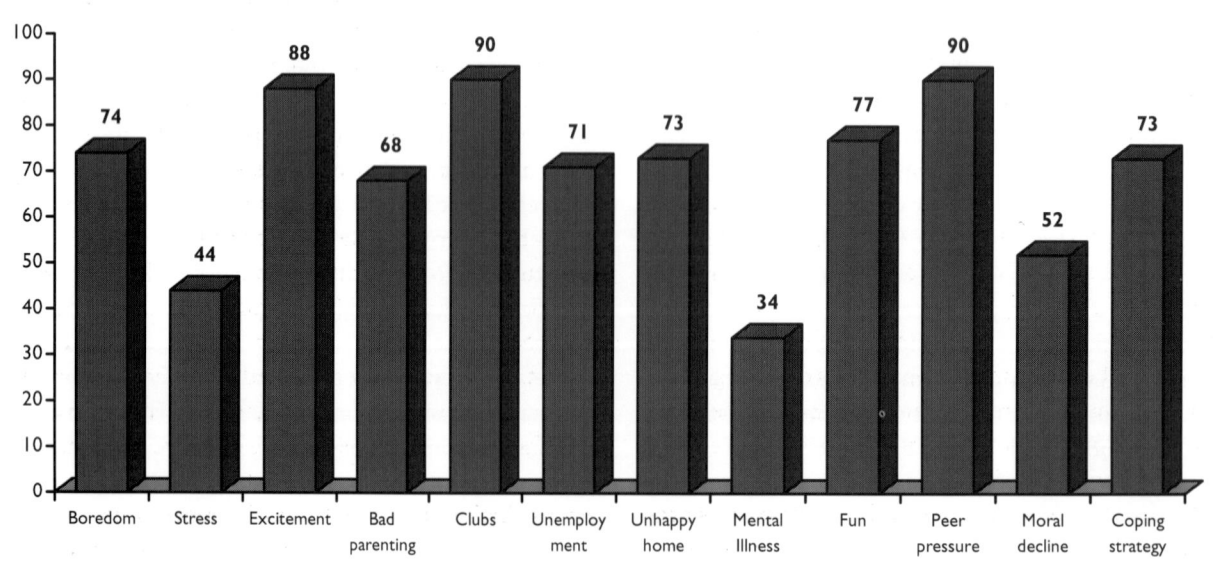

Figure 6.15
Perceived causes of illicit drug use: Main sample drug users

Category	%
Boredom	74
Stress	44
Excitement	88
Bad parenting	68
Clubs	90
Unemployment	71
Unhappy home	73
Mental Illness	34
Fun	77
Peer pressure	90
Moral decline	52
Coping strategy	73

Percentage of drug using respondents who cited each of the items listed as being a 'very important' or 'fairly important' cause of drug usage, averaged across location.

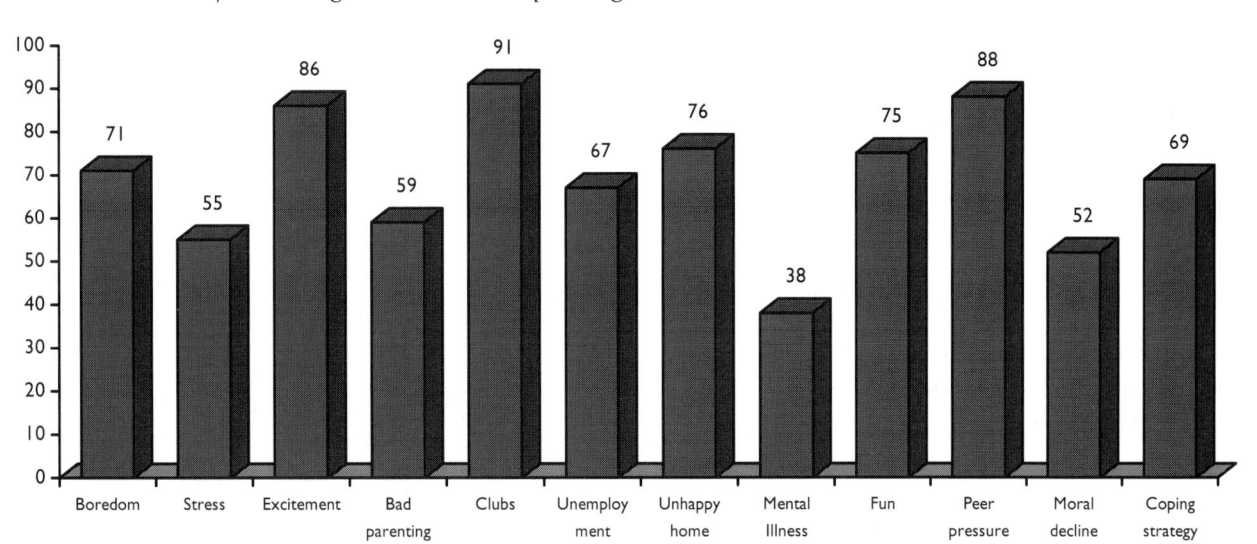

Figure 6.16
Perceived causes of illicit drug use: Booster sample drug users

Cause	%
Boredom	71
Stress	55
Excitement	86
Bad parenting	59
Clubs	91
Unemployment	67
Unhappy home	76
Mental Illness	38
Fun	75
Peer pressure	88
Moral decline	52
Coping strategy	69

Percentage of drug using respondents who cited each of the items listed as being a 'very important' or 'fairly important' cause of drug usage, averaged across location.

terms of the relative importance of different potential causes was also less apparent than had been the case for other attitudinal items, although the absolute importance attached to a small number of particular causes did vary between locations.

The general profile of response across both samples and all locations suggested that our respondents perceived virtually all the potential causes we had suggested to them as likely to be of importance in drug usage. In fact the only item for which a majority of respondents in one or both samples did *not* admit the possibility of providing an influence was that relating to 'mental illness'. This suggests that the general view of the public accords with the perception of drug usage as an activity carried out within the normal range of behaviour. Further support for this view is provided by the significant disparity between, on the one hand, 'stress' as a potential cause of drug usage and on the other hand, 'boredom' or 'the need for excitement' as potential causes. Between 70% and 90% of respondents favoured boredom and a need for excitement as potentially causative, whilst only around 45% of respondents thought that stress could be similarly causative. Whilst the public clearly feels that drug usage can be a response to a particular mood state, it therefore seems to lean away from those mood states more closely associated with 'illness'.

Other aspects of the distribution of responses suggest further that whilst drug usage is regarded as potentially stemming from reactions to an internal mood state, the public also believes that drug usage can be a consequence of a response to events outside the control of the individual. Around 70% of respondents felt that unemployment or an unhappy home life could result in individuals turning to drug usage and a similar proportion of our respondents endorsed drug usage as a 'coping strategy'.

The most popular causes in both types of sample - cited by around 90% of respondents in both cases - were 'going to clubs and parties' and 'fitting in with friends'. Since both these potential causes relate to an association or 'peer pressure' type of viewpoint, this suggests that the public have an 'infection' view of drug usage, in which if you know a drug user you are more likely to *become* a drug user. The fact that more than 60% of both main and booster sample respondents also endorse 'bad parenting" as a potential cause of drug usage suggests further that the public has a belief in people being 'made into' drug users.

The only significant locational differences in the main sample were for the 'bad parenting' and 'unemployment' options which respondents in Nottingham were more likely to cite than respondents from the other three locations. In the booster sample a range of locational differences was noted, mostly concerned with the mood state type of cause, for example the 'need for excitement' and 'boredom'. These were not consistent across location. The most salient and statistically the most highly significant disparity between locations in both samples was the tendency for respondents from Glasgow to be much more likely to cite 'unemployment' as a cause of drug usage than were respondents from the

Figure 6.17
Perceived causes of illicit drug use: Main sample non-drug users

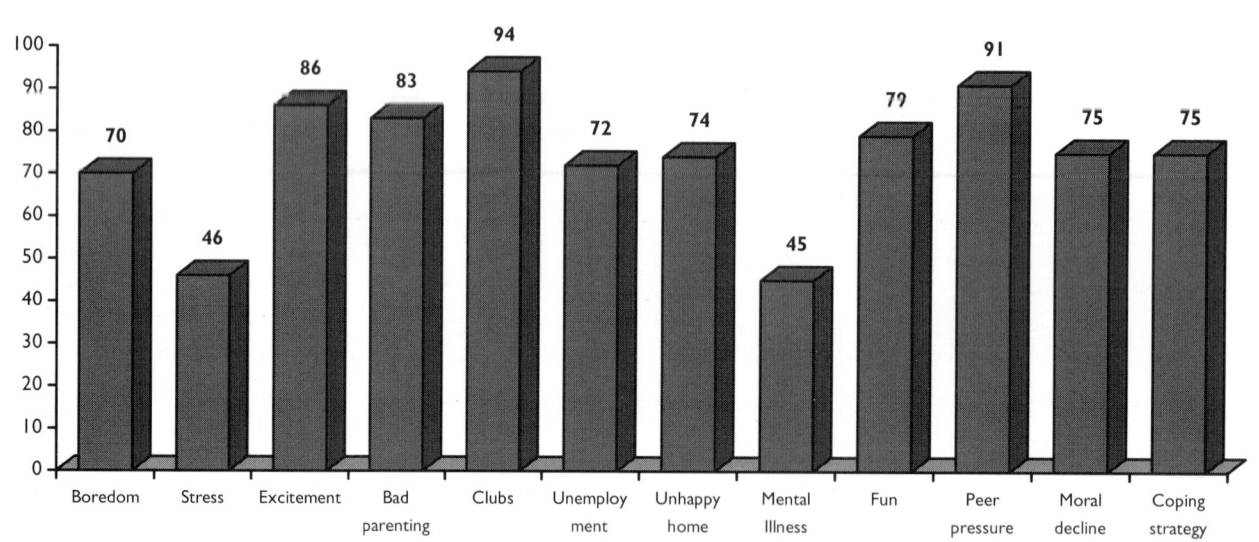

Category	%
Boredom	70
Stress	46
Excitement	86
Bad parenting	83
Clubs	94
Unemployment	72
Unhappy home	74
Mental Illness	45
Fun	79
Peer pressure	91
Moral decline	75
Coping strategy	75

Percentage of non-drug using respondents who cited each of the items listed as being a 'very important' or 'fairly important' cause of drug usage, averaged across location.

other three samples. It should be borne in mind here, that locational differences are particularly susceptible to the influence of external factors such as local media campaigns.

As with sample type and location, it was interesting to note that no very great disparity was observed in the views of drug users as opposed to non-drug users. The only broad divide observed between these two groups was in the main sample. Here, non-drug users were significantly *more* likely to cite 'bad parenting', 'mental illness' and 'moral decline' as causes of drug use. As suggested earlier, this implies that a more knowledgeable group are less likely to follow a 'traditionalist' line on drug usage. Although some differences were also noted between drug users and non-drug users in the booster sample, these were location dependent and also tended to be less extreme.

Figure 6.18
Perceived causes of illicit drug use: Booster sample non-drug users

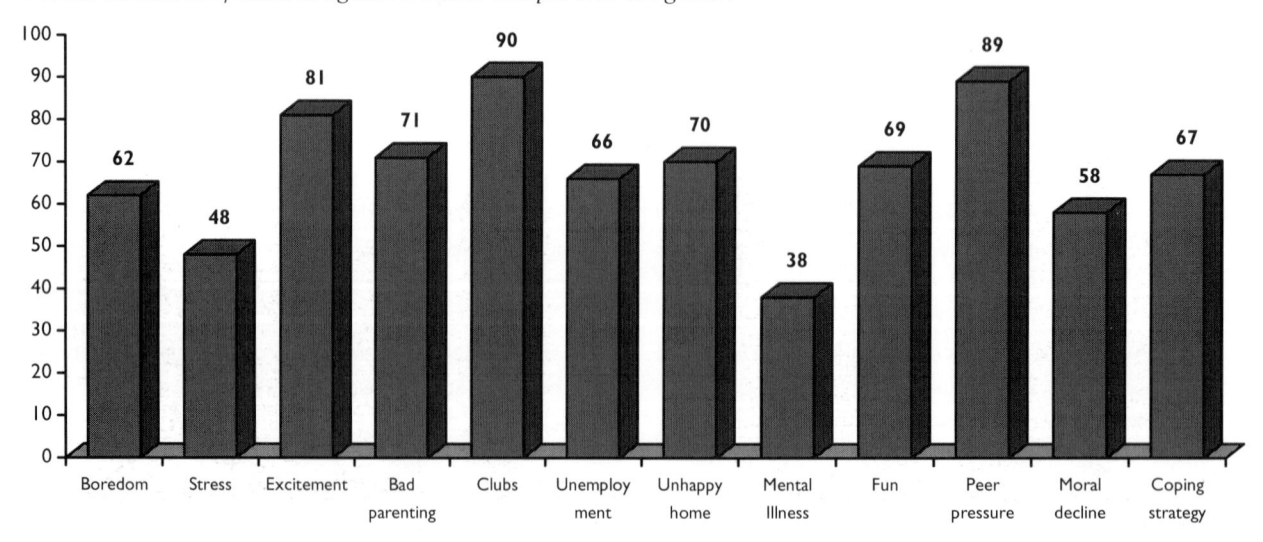

Category	%
Boredom	62
Stress	48
Excitement	81
Bad parenting	71
Clubs	90
Unemployment	66
Unhappy home	70
Mental Illness	38
Fun	69
Peer pressure	89
Moral decline	58
Coping strategy	67

Percentage of non-drug using respondents who cited each of the items listed as being a 'very important' or 'fairly important' cause of drug usage, averaged across location.

It is worth noting that the views of drug users and non-drug users are here of value for distinct purposes. Drug users will presumably be taking their own motivations into account in responding to this item and consequently their responses can be used to give us some insight into those potential causes which on the basis of subjective perceptions actually do influence people in their move towards drug usage. The views of non-drug users are important in that they provide an insight into how a non-specialist, general population audience views the motivations of drug users. The fact that the two sets of views are so close is particularly interesting in this context.

In summary, a wide variety of influences were seen by our respondents as potentially causative of drug usage, although external and to an extent random circumstances such as association with drug users or unemployment were seen as the major factors determining usage or non-usage. This not withstanding, the general view regarding personal control over usage seemed at the most basic level to be that the responsibility lies with the individuals themselves who are responding to environmental stressors by taking drugs. Whilst our respondents were willing to accept drug usage as a response to mood states, the favoured mood states were representative of the normal range of response rather than extremes such as stress or mental illness. Although some disparity was apparent between the views of drug users and non-drug users, personal experience of drug usage did *not* appear to have any overriding effect on judgements regarding the causal pathways of drug usage.

Perceptions of the transition from 'soft' to 'hard' drugs

In addition to asking our respondents to consider *external* influences on drug usage, we also asked them to consider causes of drug usage internal to the behaviour itself. Specifically, we asked them to rate the level of their agreement with the statement that "users of soft drugs progress onto hard drugs". This statement represents a view which has been consistently popular in the media and has also received tacit support from policy makers, whilst never having been well supported empirically (cf. Duster 1970).

In both samples and all locations, around half or more of our respondents showed their agreement with the media and policy makers in supporting the view that there is an inevitable progression from soft to hard drugs. Significant differences were observed in the tendency to support this view, with respondents from Lewisham being less likely to support it than respondents from the other three locations and booster sample respondents being less likely to support it than main sample respondents. Nevertheless, the broad spectrum of values suggest a high level of public support for an assumption relating to a topic about which we in fact have very little data.

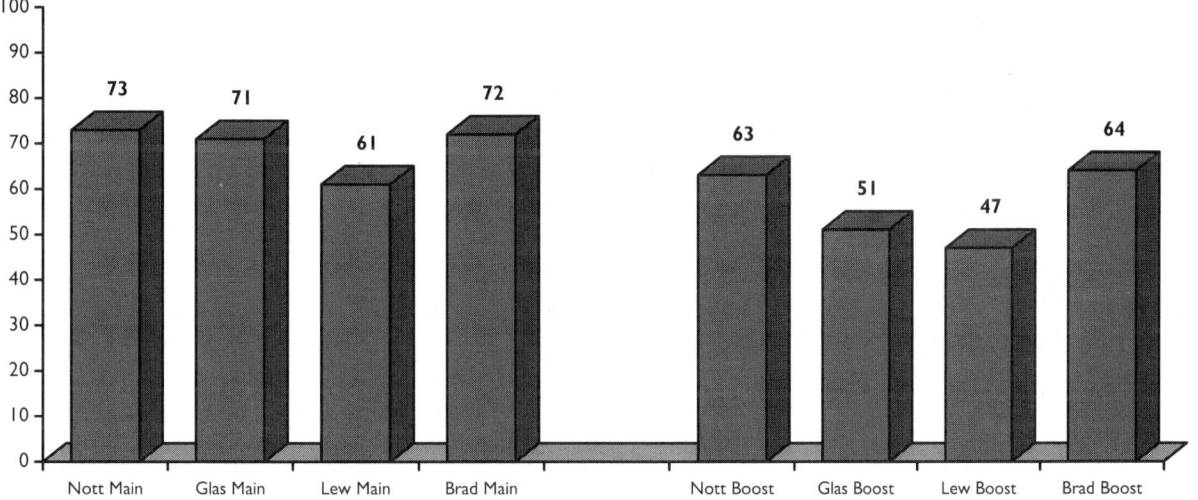

Figure 6.19
Respndents' views on the idea that 'soft' drug users progress on to using 'hard drugs'

Location	Percentage
Nott Main	73
Glas Main	71
Lew Main	61
Brad Main	72
Nott Boost	63
Glas Boost	51
Lew Boost	47
Brad Boost	64

Percentage of respondents stating that they 'agreed strongly' or 'agreed slightly' with the statement that "users of soft drugs progress onto hard drugs"

Figure 6.20
Summary of regression models for the progression from 'soft' to 'hard' drugs

Response	Variables in final model	Direction of effect	% of variance explained
Main sample			
soft drugs lead to hard drugs	ever used unprescribed drug	non-user>user	24
	frequency of using cannabis	non-user>user	
	age group	older>younger	
	socioeconomic status	C2/DE>AB/C1	
	ethnicity	white>black>asian	
Booster sample			
soft drugs lead to hard drugs	frequency of using cannabis	non-user>user	23
	ever used unprescribed drug	non-user>user	24
	age group	older>younger	
	socioeconomic status	C2/DE>AB/C1	
	ethnicity	black>asian->white	

variables in equation: *location, age group, gender, socioeconomic status, ethnicity, whether taken any unprescribed drug, frequency of taking cannabis, frequency of taking non-opiates, frequency of taking opiates*

To see whether any variance in the tendency to support the progression view stemmed from demographic variation or variation in the personal experience of drug usage we ran a similar type of regression model to those outlined earlier for other attitudinal variables. Our explanatory demographic variables were as before and our drug usage variables were the frequency of taking, respectively, cannabis, non-opiates and opiates, with frequency being measured as previously. A detailed account of the regression models is given in Tables 6.21 and 6.22 in Appendix 1.

As Figure 6.20 demonstrates, the view that 'soft' drug users progress onto 'hard' drugs was the one attitudinal variable which could most readily be accounted for on the basis of demography and personal drug usage. Variation in these items accounting for nearly a *quarter* of the total amount of variation in both main and booster samples.

From the composition of both final models it appears that drug users and higher socioeconomic groups were *less* likely to believe in the inevitable progression from 'soft' to 'hard' drugs than their appropriate counterparts. Interestingly, however, the direction of effect of both ethnicity and age group as explanatory variables differed between main and booster samples. In the main sample, younger age groups were more likely to believe that soft drugs lead to hard drugs, whilst in the booster sample younger age groups were *less* likely to believe this. Similarly, respondents from ethnic minorities were in the main sample *more* likely to believe in this progression, whilst in the booster sample they were less likely to do so. Although in the absence of further information this disparity cannot adequately be resolved, it is possible that it stems from the different levels of contact with drug usage the two groups have in the case of main and booster samples.

Since, unfortunately, we neither asked respondents to provide any details of *when* they started taking any drugs, nor asked them to give an account of why they felt they had taken a particular drug, we cannot unfortunately directly address the issue of whether 'soft' drugs in fact do lead to 'hard drugs'. Given that this is something of an important issue in drugs prevention and it is clear from the above data that the general public at least has very strong views on it, we feel that it is of the utmost importance that further research is carried out in this area, the most appropriate means being a form of life history analysis.

In summary, respondents from both our main and booster samples demonstrated considerable support for the view that there is an inevitable progression in drug usage from 'soft' to 'hard' drugs. Whilst this is a widely, if tacitly, held view both amongst policy makers and in the drugs prevention literature, very little data is actually available to confirm whether the public view is in practice a valid one. We would recommend further research into the progression issue as a matter of priority.

Perceptions of personal knowledge regarding drug usage

Having questioned our respondents extensively on their perceptions of drug usage, we decided to question them also on how well informed they themselves felt about the drugs issue. The purpose of this was twofold. Firstly, we wanted to see whether the public felt confident in the accuracy of their views. Secondly, we wanted to see whether their confidence matched the probable extent of their actual knowledge base.

PUBLIC PERCEPTIONS OF DRUGS AND DRUG MISUSE

Figure 6.21
Respondents' own perception of their level of knowledge regarding illicit drugs

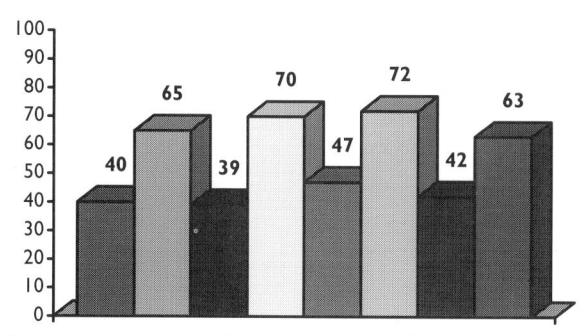

| ■ Nottingham Main | □ Nottingham Booster | ■ Bradford Main | □ Bradford Booster |
| ■ Lewisham Main | □ Lewisham Booster | ■ Glasgow Main | □ Glasgow Booster |

Nottingham Main: 40, Nottingham Booster: 65, Bradford Main: 39, Bradford Booster: 70, Lewisham Main: 47, Lewisham Booster: 72, Glasgow Main: 42, Glasgow Booster: 63

Percentage of respondents who regarded themselves as 'well informed' or 'fairly well informed' about drugs

As Figure 6.21 demonstrates, our samples *were* aware of the existence of likely gaps in their knowledge base and their levels of confidence also broadly matched their level of experience. When asked how well informed they felt themselves to be on the question of drug usage, less than half of our main sample respondents in all locations answered that they felt 'very well' or 'fairly well' informed. The booster samples were rather more confident in their level of information, with over 60% of the respondents in each of the four samples acknowledging that they felt 'very well' or 'fairly well' informed; again this was fairly consistent across location. The disparity between main and booster samples was highly statistically significant.

No such significant disparity was noted between locations. At first glance this seems rather surprising, since the locations differed very strongly in the extent to which their populations appeared to have direct experience of drug usage. However, given that levels of concern about drug usage did in the main match levels of experience in terms of location, the best interpretation is perhaps that more aware populations feel a greater need for information.

In summary, our respondents appeared to have a fairly realistic perception of their drugs related knowledge base. Since even the most knowledgeable groups were not, however, completely secure in their level of drugs information it is reasonable to assume that the public feels some need for further information on the drugs issue.

Summary of Chapter 6

The respondents in our samples were clearly aware of the usage of very prevalent, or heavily advertised, non-medical drugs and regarded such usage as a potentially dangerous - in health terms - response to particular social and emotional needs or pressures. They were also aware of the harmfulness of the inappropriate usage of medically relevant drugs, seeing them as approximately equivalent in harmfulness to the non-opiates, though much less harmful than the opiates (which is medically, though possibly not socially, incorrect). Note that there is unlikely to be a direct causal link between awareness and perceived harm, since other drugs which the majority of individuals had not heard of were nevertheless given very high ratings for harmfulness. There may, however be an indirect link, for example with the effects of media or educational campaigns. In broad terms, public perceptions of harm followed the pattern opiates>non-opiates=medical drugs>cannabis.

With regard to public perceptions of causality in drug usage, an individual's usage of drugs was seen, at the most basic level, as being a matter of free choice, although external events were believed strongly to influence the *likelihood* of such usage. Once an individual has experience of using some sort of drug, the public felt quite strongly that they were more susceptible to higher risk drug usage. Although differences are noted across locations and types of sample, this characterisation of drug usage was relevant at some level across the board, although the issue of progression from 'soft' to 'hard' drugs was heavily influenced by both demography and personal experience of drug usage.

Comparing the attitudes of main and booster samples, we found that the more knowledgeable booster sample tended to regard drug usage as both more prevalent and more of a 'problem' nationally. Yet the less knowledgeable main sample was more likely to regard drugs as harmful and addictive in the sense that 'soft' drug usage was felt to lead on to 'hard' drug usage. Neither match was exact and, particularly in the case of levels of harm, other factors must be accounting for a significant proportion of the variance. However, the patterns *do* suggest that the perception of drug usage is very much dependent on knowledge and experience of drug usage.

As implied above, the distribution of responses to the levels of harm item also provides an insight into the causal structure of our samples' knowledge base. Across all locations and both samples, those substances cited as *most* harmful were those which had received greatest political and media attention in recent years -

namely heroin, cocaine, crack and solvent abuse. This is perhaps ironic, since such emphases may arise as a matter of historical accident or acute pressures such as increased levels of supply, rather than deriving from more objective aspects of usage such as levels of medical or social harm. On a more hopeful note, respondents tended to feel that all drugs were harmful to some extent and there was also some evidence that they had a realistic view of the extent of their own knowledge regarding drug usage.

Chapter 7

OPTIONS FOR CONTROLLING OR REDUCING THE MISUSE OF DRUGS

The foregoing chapters outlined the level of self-report drug usage within the samples and established that many respondents felt that drugs are potentially, if not actually, a 'problem' at some level. This chapter considers a range of possible drugs control and prevention measures and outlines people's attitudes towards them. Although we included as broad a range of options as possible in the restricted framework of the questionnaire, the options discussed below necessarily represent a rather limited set of the full range of options available. We have, however gone to considerable effort to ensure that different *types* of measures have been addressed in recognition of the fact that drugs prevention and drugs control are *not* unitary phenomena.

Using van Dijk's (1990) typology for crime prevention, drugs control or prevention techniques can be categorised by the nature of their intended effect on the problems associated with drug usage. According to van Dijk, *primary* prevention methods are aimed at the general population (for example, education projects with school children); *secondary* prevention methods concentrate on groups at risk of drug usage; and *tertiary* prevention methods deal with those individuals who are already drug users and are essentially aimed at harm reduction.

To illustrate this typology in practical terms, primary and *secondary* prevention would include educational and informational responses, such as government and media campaigns; peer group education by reformed addicts; community-based health education centred on schools and classrooms and information and education programmes in prisons. Tertiary prevention would include such options as needle exchange schemes; the distribution of information regarding drugs related services; and various forms of medical intervention. Certain approaches could, of course, validly be placed in more than one category: for example outreach work in the community; supported living schemes; employment training; and employee assistance programmes.

In the present survey, very little information was gathered regarding the type of *tertiary* drugs prevention outlined above, since suitable methods for tertiary drugs prevention are highly dependent on the nature of the problem in a specific local area. The necessary brevity of the interview schedule also limited the extent of coverage of primary and secondary prevention methods which, as can be seen from the above list, are both numerous and diverse. Instead, the interviews concentrated on obtaining fairly detailed information regarding drugs education in general and in particular drugs education for children. Information was also gathered of relevance to more directly *control-related* aspects of primary and secondary prevention. Tertiary prevention was addressed *indirectly* by asking respondents to make judgements concerning the appropriate aims of such methods as drugs education. Although not conclusive in themselves, the latter sources of data are of particular value in suggesting suitable areas for further research. Detailed summaries of the data are given in Tables 7.1 to 7.25 in Appendix 1 and the broad profile of the data is shown within the text.

Primary prevention: controlling demand

The importance of drugs education

One item in the questionnaire schedule asked respondents to make an *absolute* judgement about the importance of education. This item was phrased as follows: "How important do you think it is to educate people about the effects and risks of taking drugs?". This turned out to be an issue on which our respondents appeared to hold very strong views. As indicated by Figure 7.1, there was almost total unity in the view that drugs education was either 'important' or 'very important'. The percentage of respondents agreeing to the importance of drugs education was above 95% in all eight samples. This indicates that agreement amongst respondents on this issue was substantially higher across both sample type and location than was the case for almost any other aspect of the drugs issue. It also clearly indicates that the public are, in the abstract at least, overwhelmingly in favour of such education.

We emphasise that the level of support outlined above refers to drugs education 'in the abstract' because, although our findings can be taken as indicating a high level of public support for drugs education, it *cannot* be taken as indicating a *preference* for education over all other measures of prevention. When respondents were to asked to make a *relative* judgement regarding the importance of drugs education by indicating their agreement with the statement "money would be better spent on education and TV campaigns rather than on trying to stop drugs being smuggled into the

Figure 7.1
Respondents' views regarding the importance of drugs education

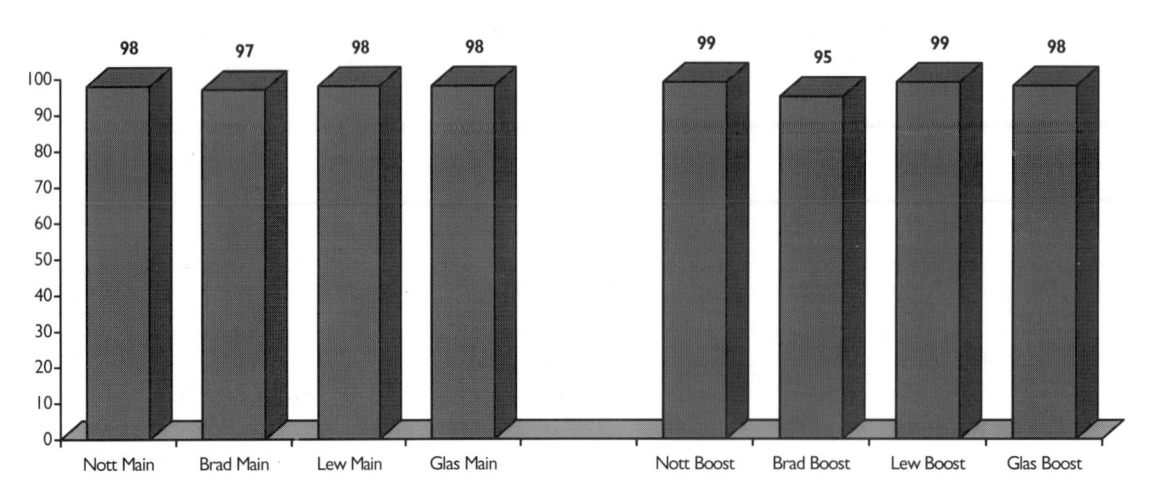

[Bar chart showing percentages: Nott Main 98, Brad Main 97, Lew Main 98, Glas Main 98, Nott Boost 99, Brad Boost 95, Lew Boost 99, Glas Boost 98]

Percentage of respondents stating that educating people about drugs is 'very important' or 'fairly important'

country", support for the option of drugs education fell to around 35% in the main samples and to around 50% in the booster samples (cf. Figure 7.25). It seems that whilst people are very concerned that drugs education should exist, they do not necessarily want it to entirely supplant other, perhaps more control-oriented approaches.

The likely effectiveness of drugs education

Two items in the survey schedule addressed the issue of how *effective* respondents felt drugs education was likely to be. The first item asked respondents to indicate the extent to which they agreed with the statement "If people were better educated about the risks of taking drugs many would not take them". The second item more baldly asked individuals to state how effective they thought drugs education would be. As can be seen from Figures 7.2 and 7.3, some slight discrepancy was noted between the public's perception that drugs education was important and their conviction that it would, in fact, deter people from taking drugs.

The lowest level of support was shown for the item suggesting that educating people would have some deterrent effect on their tendency to take drugs. Support for this item varied around 70% for all locations and both samples: the booster samples showing slightly, but not significantly *lower* levels of support. Responses to the more direct 'effectiveness of education' item were rather closer to the pattern observed for the 'importance of education' item, varying around 90% in all samples, with slightly *higher* levels of support being shown by three of the four booster samples.

Figure 7.2
Respondents' views regarding the likely effectiveness of drugs education: Main sample

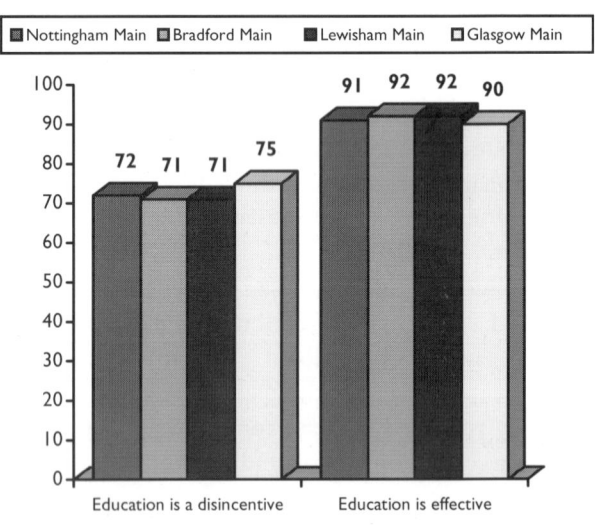

[Bar chart with legend: Nottingham Main, Bradford Main, Lewisham Main, Glasgow Main. Values — Education is a disincentive: 72, 71, 71, 75. Education is effective: 91, 92, 92, 90]

Percentage of respondents stating that they 'agree strongly' or 'agree slightly' with the statement "if people were better educated about the risks of taking drugs, many would not take them"/Percentage of respondents stating that drugs education would be 'very effective' or 'fairly effective'

As with any attitudinal response, both demographic variation and personal experience may be expected to affect how people view the impact of education on drug usage. Since any such variation is of some importance in drugs prevention, we assessed its impact by running a composite regression model for both booster and main samples. This model controlled for location and looked at the effect of gender, age group, ethnicity, socioeconomic status and the frequency of taking cannabis, non-opiates and opiates on a person's views regarding drugs education. Personal experience of drug usage was judged on the basis of frequency of usage with, as before, a base point at 'never used' and an end point at 'use daily'. Detailed results for the regression analyses are given in Tables 7.2 and 7.3 in Appendix 1.

Figure 7.3
Respondents' views regarding the likely effectiveness of drugs education: Booster sample

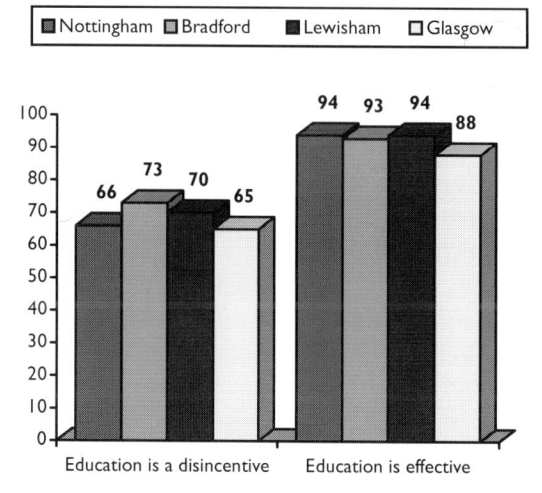

■ Nottingham ■ Bradford ■ Lewisham □ Glasgow

Education is a disincentive: 66, 73, 70, 65
Education is effective: 94, 93, 94, 88

Percentage of respondents stating that they 'agree strongly' or 'agree slightly' with the statement "if people were better educated about the risks of taking drugs, many would not take them"/Percentage of respondents stating that drugs education would be 'very effective' or 'fairly effective'

Although our model was unable to account for any of the, admittedly very small, degree of variation in views regarding the importance we *were* able to account for some of the variation noted in attitudes towards the *effectiveness* of drugs education using both demography and personal experience of drug usage. Whilst the amount of variation accounted for by our models remained quite low in absolute terms, the composition of the final models was quite consistent. A summary of the regression analyses is given in Figures 7.4.

In all four cases, the same factors were able to account for around 1-4% of the variation noted in beliefs regarding the likely effectiveness of drugs education. Specifically, white respondents were *less* likely to feel confident in the effectiveness of education, whether this was measured in terms of its deterrent effect or in broader terms, than were non-white respondents. Those respondents *with* experience of using cannabis, particularly on a frequent basis, were also less convinced by the likely effectiveness of drugs education than non-users or infrequent users. Finally, respondents from lower socioeconomic groups were less likely, in broad terms, to feel that education could be effective, although they were as confident as higher status groups in its more specific role as a *disincentive* to drug use.

Figure 7.4
Summary of regression models for respondents' views on education

Response	Variables in final model	Direction of effect	% of variance explained
Main sample			
Education a disincentive	socioeconomic status	AB/C1 > C2/DE	1
	age group	younger > older	
	ethnicity	black=asian > white	
	frequency of taking cannabis	non-users > users	
Education effective	socioeconomic status	AB/C1 > C2/DE	2
	ethnicity	black=asian > white	
	frequency of taking cannabis	non-users > users	
Booster sample			
Education a disincentive	ethnicity	black=asian > white	4
	frequency of taking cannabis	non-users > users	
Education effective	frequency of taking cannabis	non-users > users	3
	socioeconomic status	AB/C1 > C2/DE	
	ethnicity	black=asian > white	

variables in equation: *location, gender, age group, socioeconomic status, ethnicity, frequency of taking cannabis, frequency of taking non-opiates, frequency of taking opiates*

The patterns of response outlined above are most readily interpreted in the context of the set of education responses as a whole. In this context, it becomes clear that whilst respondents are uniformly in favour of drugs education there *are* quite distinct groups which feel less convinced of its viability *in practice*. That white ethnic groups and lower status socioeconomic groups should feel less convinced is of interest in terms of promoting education based drugs prevention measures. That certain types of *drug users* should also feel less convinced is of more direct practical concern, since drug using respondents may be considering the impact of drugs education on the basis of their own *personal* experience of its effect. In which case, it might be of value to enquire further as to the form of drugs education which they *would* consider likely to be effective. It should be noted here that no significant distinctions were noted between those using opiates and non-opiates and those without any experience of such drugs, the *only* type of drug usage which appeared to matter in this context was cannabis usage. Further data would be needed to establish the reasons behind this distinction.

In summary, the data outlined above show that an overwhelming majority of our respondents were in favour of drugs education, at least in the abstract. Having said which, they did not appear to regard it as of any greater importance than more control oriented measures and were also less convinced of its general viability in practice and more specifically of its viability as a deterrent. Interestingly, a prominent group of those individuals least likely to be convinced of the deterrent effect of drugs education were individuals within the highest prevalence categories for drug usage, namely white respondents and respondents with personal experience of cannabis usage. Although we cannot in this context confirm that they were considering their own likelihood of being deterred by drugs education, this suggests that

given such education. To establish our respondents' views on this aspect of the drugs education issue, we gave them the option of selecting the most appropriate targets for drugs education from a range of age groups and group identities. The options given were: children aged 9 to 11; children aged 12 to 18; young adults aged 19 to 25; parents; teachers; all adults; 'any other group'; and the rather catholic option of 'everyone'. The options were not taken as mutually exclusive. Percentages electing each particular group as an appropriate target for drugs education are given in Table 7.4 in Appendix 1.

As demonstrated by Figure 7.5, the most popular candidate group for drugs education across both samples and all locations was the 12 to 18 year olds, with percentage responses ranging between 54% and 64% dependent on sample type and location. The *least* popular option, again across all samples, was the eclectic option of educating all adults, with only between 14% and 30% of respondents, dependent on sample type and location, supporting this option. The percentage of respondents electing alternative options to the list given

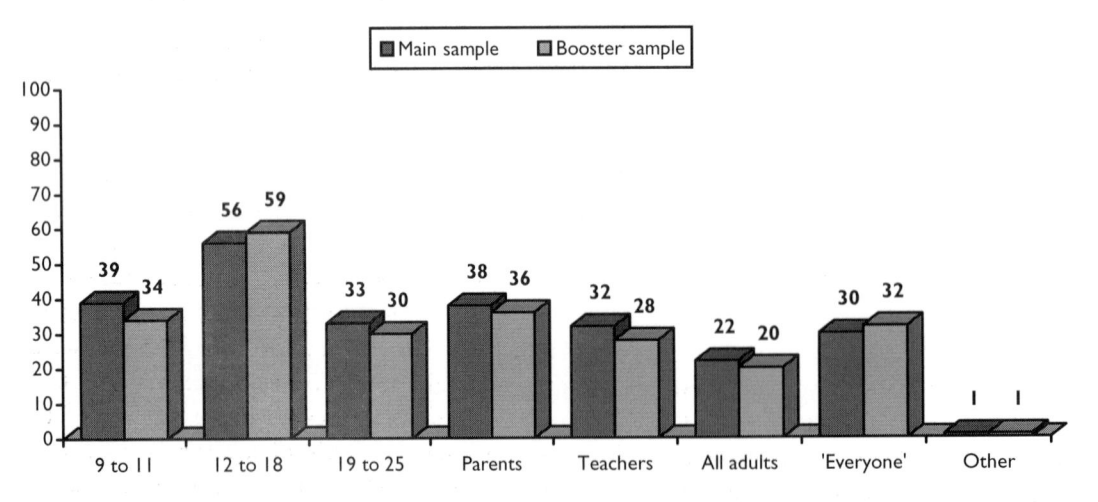

Figure 7.5
Groups perceived as suitable targets for drugs education

Percentage of respondents in favour of giving drugs education to particular named groups, averaged across location

further research on the opinions of groups likely to be targeted for drugs education, in particular focusing on the forms of education which they would feel likely to pose a deterrent effect, could be of value.

Appropriate targets for drugs education

Whilst the vast majority of respondents were clearly in favour of drugs education at some level, there remains the question of *which* individuals they feel should be

were negligible, indicating that the named options satisfied most respondents' views regarding possible targets. Note that this implies that very few people spontaneously brought 'drug users' to mind as a suitable category for drugs education.

Other response variations were fairly slight and largely a function of location, not following lines determined either by the type of sample of which the respondent was a member, or by the age group or category presented as a candidate for drugs education. One distinct exception to this generally flat distribution was given by Nottingham's booster sample, which showed consistently low levels of support for the education of any category of individual other than 12 to 18 year olds. Comparing across levels of support for the various options it is worth noting the unfortunate tension between the fairly high levels of support for drugs education for children and the comparatively low levels of support for drugs education for teachers. Since drugs education is likely to remain a school based phenomenon for the foreseeable future, it may be wise to disabuse people of their apparent confidence in the idea that teachers themselves are not in need of drugs education.

In summary, despite the extremely strong support shown by our respondents for drugs education in the abstract, it appears that a consideration of more concrete questions - such as who should receive such education and whether it could be effective - creates a rather diffuse response amongst our respondents. The exception to this rule in the present case is the view that 12-18 year olds are appropriately placed for drugs education which is favoured by the majority of respondents. One plausible interpretation of this distinction between education in the abstract and education as a concrete proposition is that people simply do not know which drugs education measures are likely to be effective and are uncertain of the groups to which drugs education is most appropriately applied. This would not be surprising given the paucity of public information on this subject.

Parents' views on drugs education

Parents in our sample who had children between the ages of 9 and 18 who were still in full time education were asked an additional set of questions relating to *actual* drugs education for their children. The three additional items they were given asked them to indicate whether they were *aware* of any of their children receiving drugs education at school or college; if they were, whether they *approved* of such education; and if they were *not* whether they would *like* any or all of their children to receive such education.

A summary of the responses obtained is given in Figures 7.6-7.8 below. Although the responses did vary to some extent with the age group of the children in question, this effect was not particularly significant, so the responses have been pooled across age groups. Since only a very small number of individuals in the booster samples had children in the appropriate age range, their responses are not considered here. It is, however, worth noting that all of these individuals were *aware* of their children receiving drugs education and all of them also approved of this education. Detailed percentage responses to the three items for the main sample locations are given in Table 7.5 in Appendix 1.

Figure 7.6
Parents' perception of whether their children presently receive drugs education: Main sample only

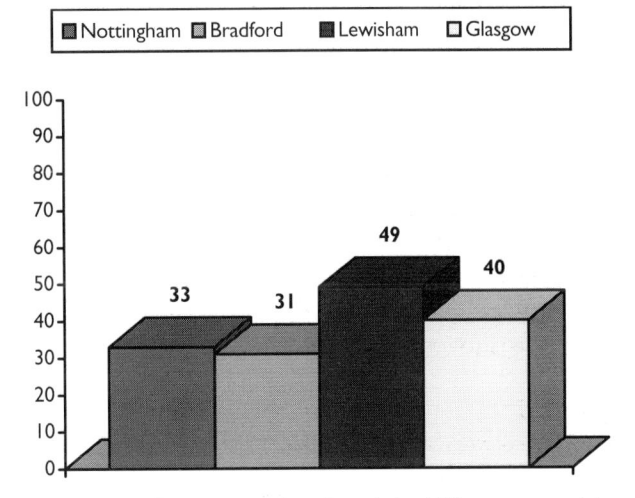

Percentage of parents stating that their children are receiving drugs education at school, averaged across different age groups of children

Whatever the actual state of affairs, it was clear from our data that the majority of our respondents were *not* aware of their children receiving drugs education. There were, however, significant locational effects with regard to this, with respondents in Lewisham and Glasgow being more likely to think that their children were receiving such education. These differences matched both our prevalence measures for drug usage in the four locations and general levels of awareness regarding drugs and drugs related issues. In all four locations the oldest child in the family was the most likely one to be seen as receiving drugs education. Since we do not have any sufficiently detailed information on the education policies in this regard within the local authorities considered, we unfortunately cannot match the perceptions of parents against the actuality of drugs education. What we can do, is to match parental perceptions against their feelings concerning drugs education

If we compare Figure 7.6 with Figures 7.7 and 7.8, it becomes clear that there is a distinct mismatch between the percentage of parents who are aware of their children actually receiving drugs education and the almost unanimous approval of drugs education shown by parents as a whole. Between 90% and 100% of parents in all locations who were aware of their children receiving drugs education also approved of such education. Similarly, between 80% and 100% of parents *not* aware of such education stated that they would *like* their children to receive drugs education. These are remarkably high figures in favour of a practice which is frequently regarded as controversial.

Figure 7.7
Parents' approval of the drugs education received by their children: Main sample only

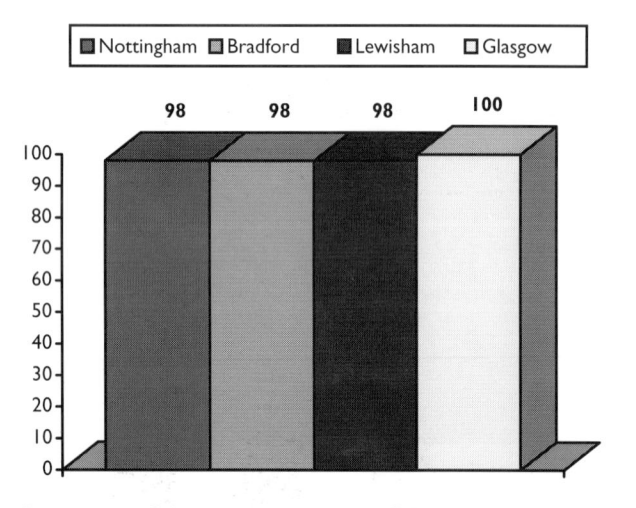

Percentage of those parents **aware** of their children receiving drugs education who also **approve** of them receiving this type of education, averaged across different age groups of children

Figure 7.8
Parents' views on potential drugs education for their children: Main sample only

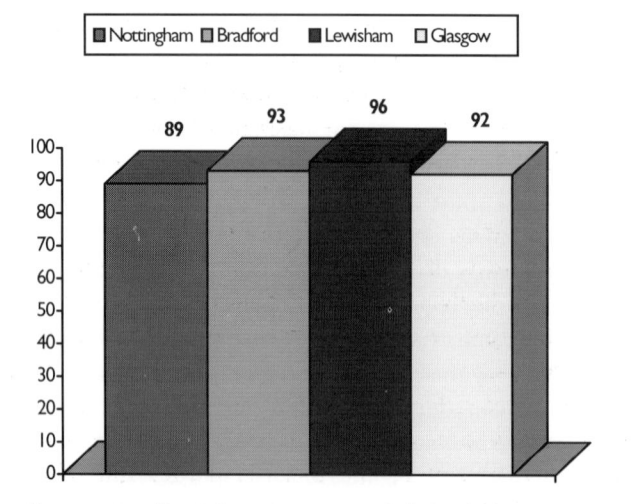

Percentage of parents **not** aware of their children receiving drugs education who would **like** them to have such education, averaged across different age groups of children

As might be predicted from the responses outlined earlier, there was a slight bias towards greater support for the education of the older children in the family. Levels of support for the youngest child in a family receiving drugs education being between 5% and 10% lower in a number of cases than levels of support for the oldest child receiving such education. This notwithstanding, it is clear from our data that the level of support given by respondents in general to the concept of drugs education is more than matched by the support provided by parents for this measure. This is a particularly important test of perceptions regarding drugs education since it addresses the views of those likely to be in close contact with the effects of such education.

In summary, parents showed a close to unanimous level of support for drugs education. This support extended not only to those parents who were already aware of their children receiving such education - and who therefore had had some opportunity to consider its merits - but also to those parents not yet aware of their children receiving drugs education. This is one sub-group of the population for whom there is clearly no separation between education as an abstract and as a concrete issue: parents *do* want drugs education for their children. Furthermore, a distinct mismatch is noticeable between the extremely high proportion of those in favour of drugs education and the rather moderate proportion of those actually aware of their children already receiving this education.

Parents' views on the likelihood of their children taking drugs

It would seem reasonable to assume that since parents are so strongly in favour of drugs education, they also feel that there is a distinct possibility that their children may be at risk of taking drugs in the future. In fact, this appears not to be the case. Or if it is the case, parents are quite reluctant to own up to the fact. Two items within our interview schedule allow us to address this issue. The first item asked parents to indicate whether any individuals in their children's peer group at school were taking drugs. The second item assessed parents' views on the likelihood that their *own* children might become involved in drug taking in the future. The item referring to a child's peer group asked parents to consider each of the drugs on our list separately, the item referring to their own children was rather more hypothetical and just used the term 'drugs' as a composite. Responses to the hypothetical item are given in detail in Tables 7.6

and 7.7 in Appendix 1. Positive responses to the 'peer group usage' item were so rare that these are discussed only in the text. Figures for drug usage within children's peer groups were in fact improbably low, given both the interest shown in drugs education *and* the actual levels of at least cannabis or non-opiate drug usage we know are likely to obtain in schools. The percentages of parents reporting children's peer group drug usage for *any* of the named drugs reached above one per cent in only *one* instance. This being in Bradford's main sample, where roughly 1% of parents felt that glue sniffing might be taking place. Given the likely extent of *actual* peer group usage for at least the most common range of drugs, this response shows either an extreme reluctance by parents to comment on drug usage amongst their children's peers *or* a worrying lack of awareness of this possibility. Since high levels of support were shown for drugs education being given to children, the former option may be the more plausible, particularly since this item was included in the face to face interview rather than in the confidential section of the interview schedule.

Figure 7.9
Parents' views on the likelihood of their children taking illicit drugs: Main sample only

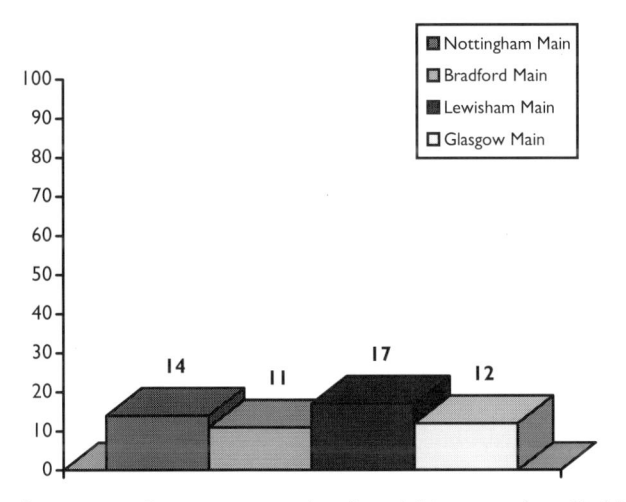

Percentage of parents stating that their children were 'very likely' or 'fairly likely' to take drugs in the future.

As indicated by Figure 7.9, the hypothetical item addressing the future likelihood of a person's own children becoming involved in drug usage drew out a *slightly* more realistic response. However, those parents willing to state that their children might take drugs still formed a quite small minority, representing only around 13% of the parents in our main samples. Although some locational variation was noted on this issue, the only significant distinction was between Lewisham and the other three locations. In drugs prevention terms the question of whether parents were actually convinced that their children were unlikely to take drugs, or whether they were simply reluctant to talk about the possibility is, to an extent, irrelevant. Whatever the cause of the low figures, it seems that parents need some encouragement to address the possibility that their children are at risk of taking drugs. This suggestion being in quite sharp contrast with our respondents' own views on drugs education for parents as opposed to children and, indeed, adults in general.

Figure 7.10
Comparison between drug users and non-drug users on the likelihood of their children taking drugs

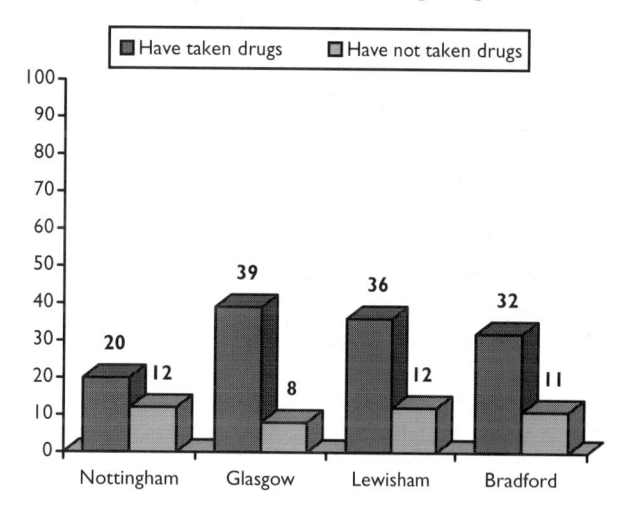

Percentage of respondents who had and who had not tried drugs feeling that their own children were 'very likely' or 'fairly likely' to take drugs in the future.

To establish whether personal experience of drug usage had any effect on a parent's views regarding the likelihood of their own children taking drugs, we partitioned the samples on the basis of whether respondents had ever used a drug themselves and ran our analyses again. As Figure 7.10 indicates, there were some significant differences between drug users and non-drug users, in a predictable direction. Drug users were more likely to support the idea that their own children might be at risk of taking drugs than were non-drug users.

Before concluding that drug users have a more realistic view of the situation, it is important to note that those parents stating that their children might take drugs in the future were still in the minority even for people who had used drugs themselves. Furthermore, the distinction between drug users and non-drug users was only significant for one end of the scale - drug users were more likely to state that their children *would* take drugs than were non-drug users, but they were equally likely to state they would not. Some variation was also noted across location and between drug types (cf. Tables 7.6 and 7.8 in Appendix 1) with drug using parents in Glasgow being more likely to support the notion that their own children were at risk of drug taking than drug using parents in the other locations. Also, recent cannabis users were on the whole more likely to suggest that their own children would use drugs than parents who were using either non-opiates or opiates. Again, it should be noted that the number of individuals in the latter category is quite small. Given an indication of some disparity between sub-groups within our sample it might be of interest in the future to assess whether parent's views on likely drug usage by their children match with the actual risk profile of the children, for example in terms of demography.

In summary, although parents are strongly in favour of drugs education, they seem to express rather unrealistic views in terms of the likelihood of their own children taking drugs. A very small percentage of our respondents stated that their children's peer group were taking drugs and the number of parents who felt that their own children were likely to take drugs at some point in the future formed a very small minority. Whether these findings relate to actual levels of knowledge or to a reluctance to discuss children's drug usage, it seems that the provision of some form of drugs education for parents might be a sensible course. It was also of note that whilst drug users were more likely to state that their children were at risk of taking drugs, the distinction between users and non-users was not as great as might be expected on this issue.

Organisations which should be responsible for education

Since there was very strong support for drugs education amongst at least one distinct group of respondents and moderate to high levels of support across the samples taken more generally, it is important to establish *who* our respondents feel should be providing such education. To address this issue, respondents were first asked to indicate the extent to which they agreed with the statement "It is the responsibility of the government to provide education about the risks of taking drugs", this being a fairly obvious option in the case of any form of public education. To provide a somewhat broader view of their feelings they were then given a range of options, which, whilst again including the government, also included local councils; schools or colleges; doctors or the medical profession; social services; the police; 'any other group' and the catholic 'everyone'. Respondents were asked to endorse one or more categories and the options were not regarded as mutually exclusive. A detailed summary of the responses given is provided in Tables 7.9 to 7.12 in Appendix 1.

Figure 7.11
Respondents' views regarding Government provision of drugs ecucation

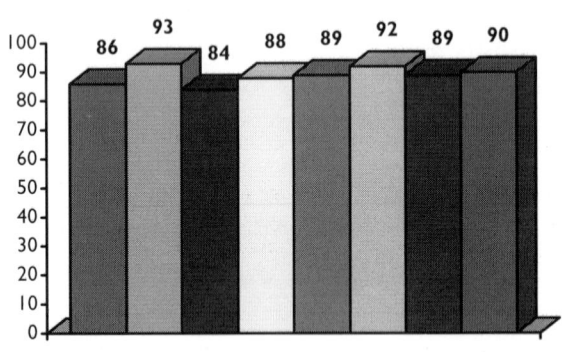

■ Nottingham Main   ■ Nottingham Booster   ■ Bradford Main   □ Bradford Booster
■ Lewisham Main   ■ Lewisham Booster   ■ Glasgow Main   ■ Glasgow Booster

86, 93, 84, 88, 89, 92, 89, 90

Percentage of respondents stating that they 'agree strongly' or 'agree slightly' with the statement that "it is the responsibility of the Government to provide education about the risks of taking drugs"

As is often found in surveys which deal with items suggesting government responsibility for social issues, the initial statement relating to government responsibility received support from more than 80% of our respondents in both samples and all locations (cf. Figure 7.11). Interestingly, support for government provision of drugs education was slightly *higher* in the younger, more 'at risk' booster samples. As with our previous analyses on drugs education, we ran a composite regression model to look at demographic variance and variance in personal experience of drug usage to see whether these factors differentiated between groups supporting and not supporting governmental provision of drugs education.

As Figure 7.12 indicates, there was in fact very little demographic variation or variation between users and non-users in the main sample. Our model accounted for less than 1% of the variation in support for government provision of education using these factors. The only real distinctions were amongst age groups and ethnic groups: older respondents and white respondents being more likely to support governmental provision of drugs education than their counterparts. This finding is not particularly surprising however and it is of greater importance to note that demographic groups across the board appeared to support government provision of drugs education and similarly to note that no distinctions were observed on the basis of personal drug usage.

Figure 7.12
Summary of regression models for respondents' perception that the government is responsible for providing drugs education

Response	Variables in final model	Direction of effect	% of variance explained
Main sample			
Government should educate	age group ethnicity	older>younger white>black=asian	1
Booster sample			
Government should educate	socioeconomic status	C2/DE>AB/C1	6

Variables in equation: *location, age group, gender, socioeconomic status, ethnicity, frequency of taking cannabis, frequency of taking non-opiates, frequency of taking opiates*

status socioeconomic groups. Although the number of individuals from higher status groups within our booster samples was necessarily low, this does suggest a degree of polarity across the groups on this variable. Note finally, that location had no independent affect on levels of support for government provision of drugs education in either main or booster sample.

Once other options were placed before our respondents, the general level of support for government provision of drugs education predictably fell. However, it remained above 50% in all but two cases. The two exceptions were Glasgow's and Bradford's booster samples. Furthermore, across all locations and both samples, the government remained at least the *second* most popular organisation to be responsible for education. Since a fairly eclectic range of other agencies was suggested to our respondents this does suggest quite strongly that people see the government as necessarily involved in the provision of drugs education at some level.

Looking at the data summarised in Figures 7.13 and 7.14, it can be seen that the most salient option in most people's minds was the provision of drugs education by schools and colleges. This is perhaps predictable, given the age group respondents were primarily

Figure 7.13
Respondents' views regarding the agencies responsible for drugs education: Main sample

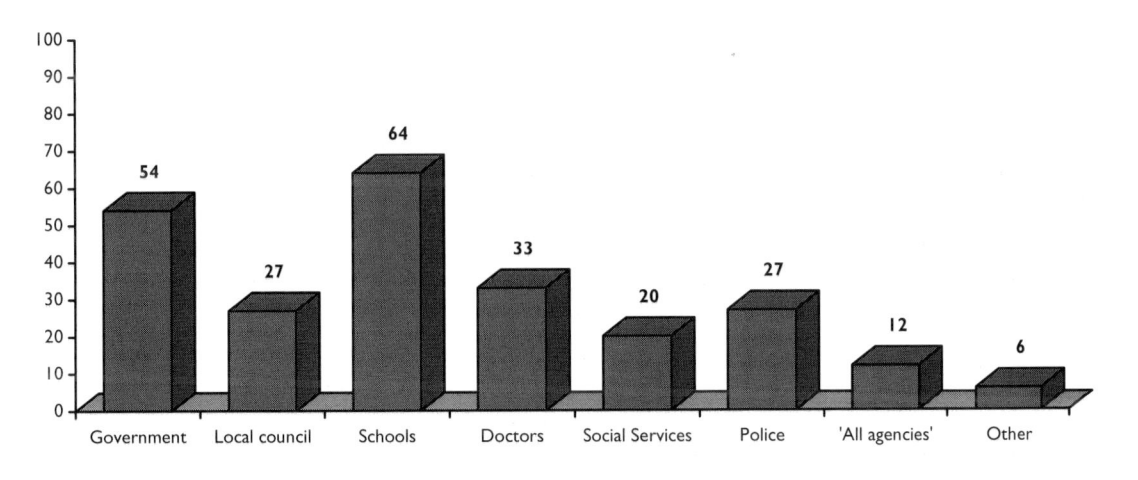

Agency	%
Government	54
Local council	27
Schools	64
Doctors	33
Social Services	20
Police	27
'All agencies'	12
Other	6

Percentage of respondents stating that each of the listed agencies has a responsibility for drugs ecucation, averaged across location

The demographic model of support for governmental intervention was slightly more successful in the booster sample, accounting for 6% of the variance observed. Interestingly, this variance was accounted for by the single factor of socioeconomic status: lower status socioeconomic groups being more likely to favour government provision of drugs education than higher

envisaging as receiving such education, but again, it sits uneasily with the apparent lack of support shown for the education of *teachers* in drugs related issues. As suggested earlier, this mismatch may stem from an unrealistic perception that teachers will necessarily be aware of the types of issue suitable for inclusion in such education.

Figure 7.14
Respondents' views regarding the agencies responsible for drugs education: Booster sample

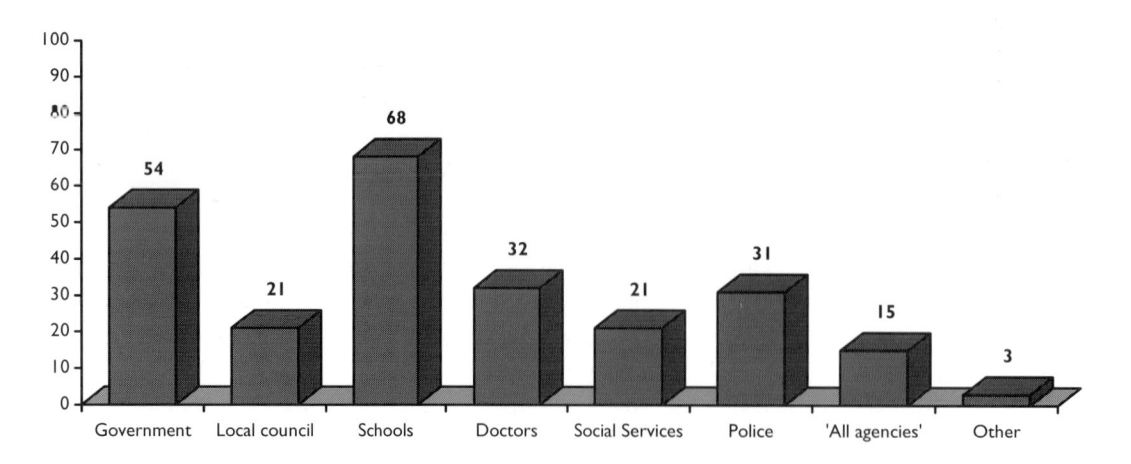

Percentage of respondents stating that each of the listed agencies has a responsibility for drugs education, averaged across location

Calls for the medical profession and the police to be responsible for drugs education showed roughly equal patterns of support, both being slightly *more* popular as appropriate agencies than either local councils or social services. To put this in perspective it must be borne in mind that in no case did the percentage support for any organisation *other* than schools or the government reach levels above 40%. Similarly, it is important to note that only a very small proportion of individuals suggested candidates for responsibility other than those on the list provided and less than 20% of respondents in any location or sample felt that responsibility should be equally shared between the list of candidates. Tables 7.13 and 7.14 in Appendix 1 detail the variations noted between locations and also between drug users and non-drug users. The data in these tables confirms that in fact the support for government and school based provision of drugs education is an across the board phenomenon showing little in the way of variation between sub-groups.

In summary, general levels of support for drugs education in our sample were high. In the sub-group of individuals who had children of school age, support was very high indeed. Drugs education was regarded as likely to be effective by the majority of respondents and although precise patterns varied across samples and age groups, the consensus view appeared to be that the 12 to 18 age group provides the most appropriate target for such education. Across all groups the organisations seen as most responsible for providing such education were the schools and central government. Since the former is under increasing control from the latter in terms of curriculum this suggests that the government is either directly, or indirectly, expected to be responsible for ensuring that such education is provided.

Secondary prevention: Controlling demand and supply

Police control of demand

Drugs education is clearly aimed principally at controlling *demand* for drugs rather than being concerned with any attempt to control supply. This distinction is less clear cut in the case of police action, which can be directed both at the control of supply and, either simultaneously or in parallel, at the control of demand. Those police control measures which are related to demand are predictably, at least in present times, based largely on interventionist forms of deterrence rather than on educational approaches. For example, police action is directed at deterring local drug users by stopping and searching, raiding suspected premises, arresting known users etc. All such measures may in practice have an effect on local supply chains. Whilst the survey could not cover the full range of police control measures, we did provide our respondents with the opportunity to give an opinion on both the desirability and likely effectiveness of a small subset of possible police action.

Specifically, we asked respondents to indicate how useful they felt "police stopping and searching people on suspicion in the street or in public places" would be as a method of reducing the number of people using drugs. Similarly, they were asked to consider how useful a measure "police warning or cautioning users about the risks but *not* prosecuting them" would be. In addition, respondents were asked to indicate the level of their support for measures targeted at users as opposed to suppliers and vice versa. Finally, we asked them the rather pertinent question of how well they felt their local police dealt with the drugs problem. Responses to all these items are given in detail in Table 7.15 in Appendix 1.

As previously, we ran a series of regression models to assess the effect of demographic variation and personal experience of drug usage on attitudes towards the range of drugs control and demand reduction measures considered here. The demographic factors included in the models were, as previously, gender, ethnicity, socioeconomic status and age group. The drug usage variables were slightly more extensive than in previous models, including not only present frequency of cannabis usage, and usage of opiates and non-opiates, but also whether a respondent had *ever* used any illicit drug. Detailed summaries of the responses to all police drugs control items are presented in Tables 7.16 and 7.17 in Appendix 1 and a brief account of each is given in the text.

Figure 7.15
Respondents' views regarding police searching on suspicion

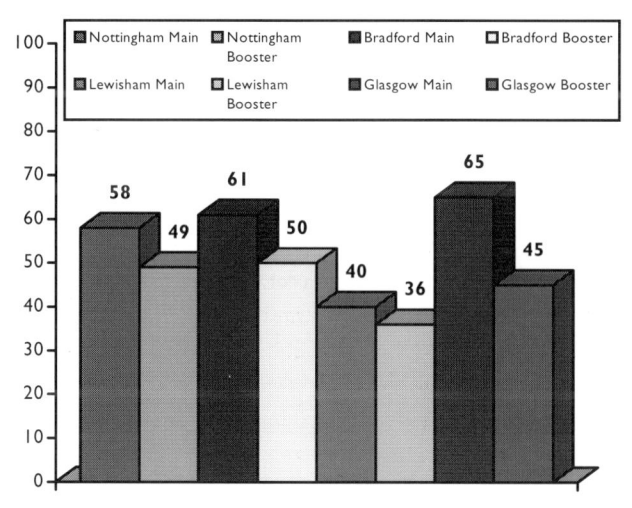

Percentage of respondents stating that searching on suspicion would be a 'very useful' or 'fairly useful' method of controlling drug usage

Given that searching on suspicion tends to be regarded as a rather controversial mode of policing, we found a surprisingly high level of support for this option amongst our respondents (Figure 7.15). However, the extent of such support varied considerably depending on sample type and location. In the main sample, between 50% and 60% of respondents were in favour of stopping and searching as a useful drugs control method, but the younger more 'at risk' booster sample showed consistently lower levels of support. The greatest disparity between samples was that between Lewisham and the other three locations with both Lewisham's main and booster samples showing significantly lower levels of support for stopping and searching than the other locations. In part this may be a consequence of the greater impact which this method of policing has had on the capital than on other areas. It is unlikely to be a function of the prevalence of drug usage in that location, since Glasgow, which had higher prevalence levels, showed considerable support for this technique, notably in the case of its main sample.

Figure 7.16
Summary of demographic and drug usage regression models for the perceived effectiveness of searching on suspicion

Response	Variables in final model	Direction of effect	% of variance explained
Main sample police should search on suspicion	ever taken illicit drugs	non-users>users	9
	ethnicity	white>black=asian	
	age group	older>younger	
	socioeconomic status	C2/DE>AB/C1	
	frequency of using cannabis	non-users>users	
	location	Bradford= Glasgow> Nottingham> Lewisham	
	frequency of using opiates	non-users>users	
Booster sample police should search on suspicion	ever taken illicit drug	non-users>users	5
	frequency of using non-opiates	non-users>users	
	age group	older>younger	

Variables in equation: *location, age group, gender, socioeconomic status, ethnicity, frequency of taking cannabis, frequency of taking non-opiates, frequency of taking opiates*

As can be seen from Figure 7.16, we were able to account for a reasonable proportion of the variance in attitudes towards stopping and searching, at least in our main sample, by dint of considering demographic identity and personal experience of drug usage. The majority of the distinctions noted between sub-groups were in a predictable direction. Drug users and respondents who had used drugs at some point in the past were significantly *less* supportive of stopping and searching techniques than non-drug users. Younger individuals were less in favour of such techniques than older individuals and, in the main sample at least, white respondents were more likely to be in favour of stopping and searching than black or Asian respondents. Less predictable distinctions were noted between socioeconomic groups, with lower status socioeconomic groups in the main sample being significantly *more* likely to favour stopping and searching than higher status groups. Also in the main sample, our location control variable proved to be of independent importance, with respondents in Bradford and Glasgow showing significantly greater support for stopping and searching than respondents in Nottingham and, more particularly, Lewisham. This confirms that our earlier finding regarding Lewisham is not simply the effect of demography but does reflect real locational variation.

Figure 7.17
Respondents' views regarding cautioning not prosecuting

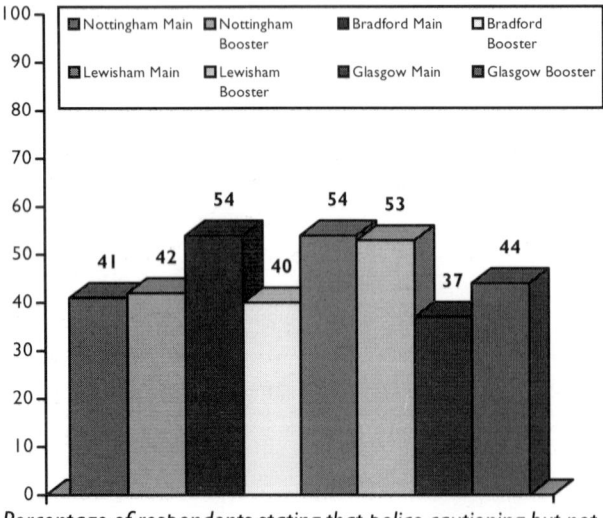

Percentage of respondents stating that police cautioning but not prosecuting drug users would be a 'very useful' or 'fairly useful' method of controlling drug usage

Whilst stopping and searching may be regarded as a controversial control technique from a liberal or individual civil rights perspective, cautioning drug users but *not* prosecuting them can be regarded as equally controversial from the standpoint of collective civil rights.

Nevertheless, this technique drew a not insubstantial level of support from our respondents (cf. Figure 7.17). Interestingly, those locations least in favour of stopping and searching were most likely to show support for cautioning but not prosecuting and vice versa. Specifically, Lewisham showed the strongest support for cautioning not prosecuting and Glasgow the least. No consistent differences were shown across locations between the main and booster samples. Bradford's booster sample showed lower levels of support than its main sample, Glasgow's booster sample showed a conversely higher level of support for cautioning than its main sample and in Nottingham and Lewisham levels of support were equivalent for the two sample types. Overall, support for cautioning rather than prosecuting was at a slightly lower level than support for the more interventionist option of stopping and searching, with between 40% and 50% of respondents being in favour of the former option. However, as can be seen from Figure 7.18, support for cautioning was rather more consistent across distinct sub-groups of the population than had been the case for the stopping and searching option, notably in the main sample.

Figure 7.18
Summary of demographic and drug usage regression models for the perceived effectiveness of cautioning rather than prosecuting

Response	Variables in final model	Direction of effect	% of variance explained
Main sample			
police should caution not prosecute	location	Bradford= Lewisham>Nottingham =Glasgow	1
	ever tried illicit drug	users>non-users	
	age group	older>younger	
	socioeconomic status	AB/C1>C2/DE	
	frequency of taking cannabis	users>non-users	
Booster sample			
police should caution not prosecute	ever taken illicit drug	users>non-users	3
	frequency of taking non-opiates	users>non-users	

variables in equation: *location, age group, gender, socioeconomic status, ethnicity, whether ever tried an illicit drug, frequency of taking cannabis, frequency of taking non-opiates, frequency of taking opiates*

In contrast with stopping and searching, but nevertheless predictably, the regression model showed that drug users were more likely to be in favour of cautioning than non-drug users. Indeed in the booster sample the distinction between users and non-users was the only one of the factors to be of any independent importance. Rather less predictably, older individuals in the main sample were *more* likely to favour cautioning than younger individuals. Again in contrast to the case for stopping and searching, higher status socioeconomic groups were significantly more likely to be in favour of

but main sample respondents showed a slightly higher level of support for the option of targeting users in the sense of 'busting' or raiding their houses. A detailed summary of the responses to these items is given in Table 7.18 in Appendix 1.

Two points are worth noting here. The first is the unanimity of support for measures relating to clamping down on drug suppliers. There was very little locational variation on this issue and the percentage of respondents favouring both raiding the houses of suppliers as an independent measure and concentrating on suppliers

Figure 7.19
Comparison between police efforts targeting users and targeting suppliers: Main sample

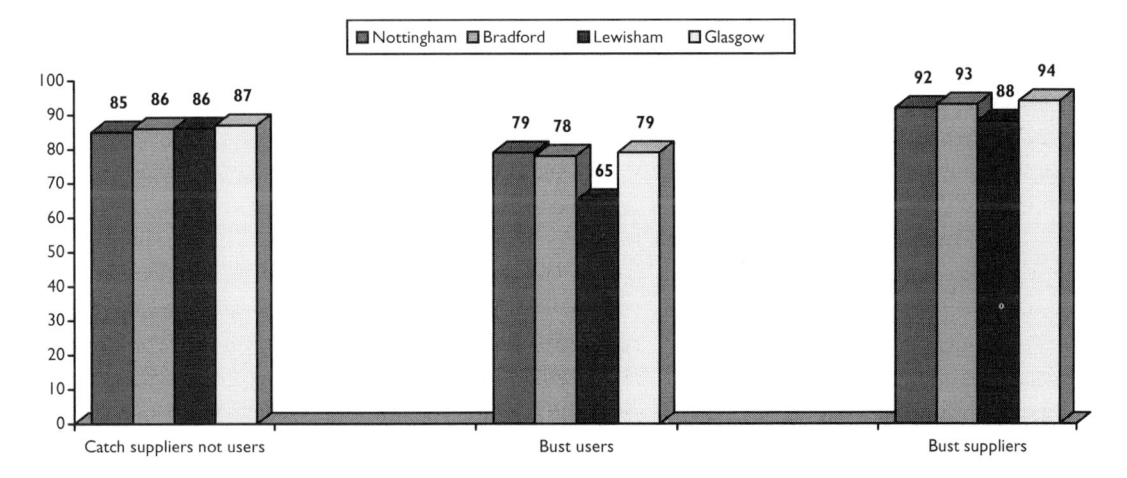

Percentage of respondents stating that they 'agree strongly' or 'agree slightly' with the statement "police time would be better spent catching drug suppliers rather than clamping down on users"/Percentage of respondents stating that police busting the houses of either users or suppliers would be 'very useful' or 'fairly useful' as a measure in reducing drug usage.

cautioning than lower status groups. Finally, a significant location effect was again found, independently of demographic variation. Respondents from Bradford and Lewisham being more likely to favour cautioning than those from either Nottingham or Glasgow. Although the absolute amount of variance accounted for by such distinctions is, as we have said, quite low, this type of locational distinction nevertheless has clear implications for policing, whether viewed from an operational perspective or from the more abstract viewpoint of research on policing.

Whatever the views of respondents on particular *methods* of policing, they had very distinct views on the appropriate *targets* of police efforts towards drugs control. As can be seen by comparing Figures 7.19 and 7.20, views were slightly more polarised on this issue in the booster sample than in the main sample. Both *types* of sample were substantially more in favour of responses targeted at drug suppliers rather than drug users,

as opposed to users was above 85% in all cases. The second point, which relates most notably also to efforts targeting drug users, is that a majority of respondents in both samples and all locations were in favour of methods of policing which are, from a civil rights standpoint, quite extreme: namely raiding a private domestic residence. This is perhaps indicative of the level of public concern that an agency they perceive as in some measure responsible for drugs control should succeed in that aim.

Notably, our regression models failed to account for any of the variation noted in responses to the comparative item asking respondents to gauge whether suppliers as opposed to users should be targeted. This is a strong indication that the view that *suppliers* should be the primary target rather than users has fairly universal support across a range of distinct sub-groups within the population. As Figure 7.21 shows, however, substantial variation was apparent between sub-groups in relation

Figure 7.20
Comparison between police efforts targeting users and targeting suppliers: Booster sample

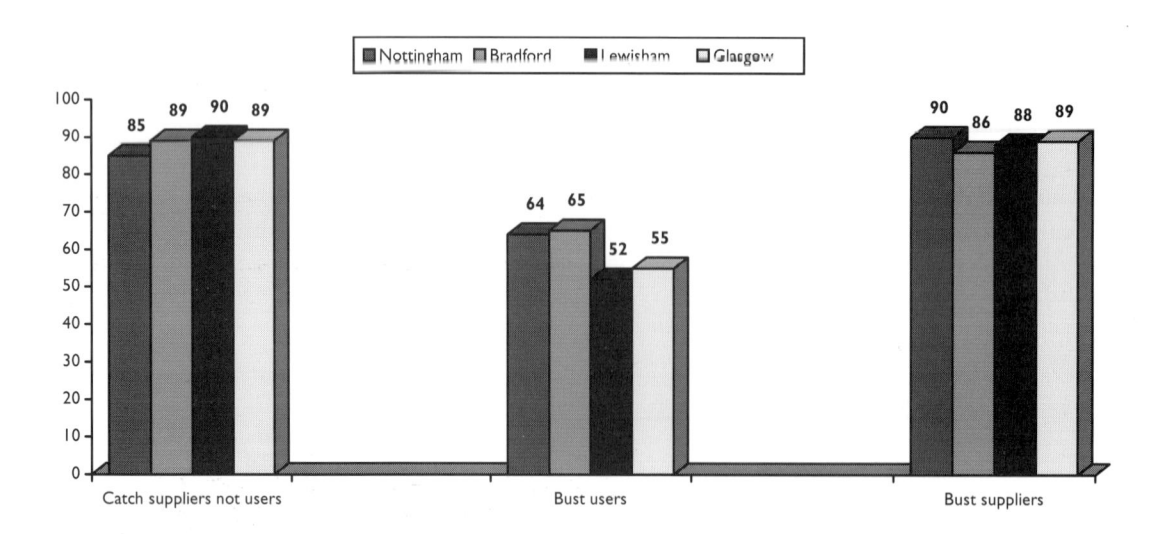

[Bar chart showing percentages for Nottingham, Bradford, Lewisham, Glasgow across three categories:
- Catch suppliers not users: 85, 89, 90, 89
- Bust users: 64, 65, 52, 55
- Bust suppliers: 90, 86, 88, 89]

Percentage of respondents stating that they 'agree strongly' or 'agree slightly' with the statement "police time would be better spent catching drug suppliers rather than clamping down on users"/Percentage of respondents stating that police busting the houses of either users or suppliers would be 'very useful' or 'fairly useful' as a measure in reducing drug usage.

to the viability of raiding domestic residences, notably in the case of such methods being used against users.

Although in the main, the pattern shown by our regression models was again fairly predictable with older rather than younger respondents favouring raids on both users and suppliers and non-drug users tending to favour these techniques to a greater extent than drug users, the direction of response was not always as consistent as one might have expected. A notable counter example, was the tendency of present users of non-opiate drugs within the main sample to show greater support for raiding suppliers than did respondents who were *not* using these drugs. This is in interesting contrast to the case for present cannabis users who showed less support for this measure than non-users. Not surprisingly, the pattern noted for users of non-opiates was *not* matched by any greater support on their part for raiding the houses of drug users. It could be accounted for either by reference to a greater dissatisfaction amongst users of non-opiates than amongst cannabis users for their own tendency to use drugs, or by reference to the greater likelihood that cannabis users will also be 'dealers' albeit at a fairly low level. Without further information we are unable to confirm which is the most likely form of explanation.

Other marked distinctions between sub-groups were that females in both main and booster samples were more likely to be in favour of raiding the houses of drug users than males. Similarly, white respondents in the main sample, although not the booster sample were more likely to favour raiding both the houses of users and suppliers than were black or Asian respondents. This pattern matches our earlier findings for another interventionist measure of policing, namely stopping and searching, and may reflect the apparently greater likelihood that ethnic minorities will be personally caught up in this kind of police action (Elliott *op cit.*).

Also as with the stopping and searching type of police response, we found that in the main sample, lower status socioeconomic groups were more likely to support raiding the houses of both users and suppliers than were higher status socioeoconomic groups. Unlike the case for ethnicity this is unlikely to be a reflection of any greater likelihood of higher status groups themselves being caught up in this type of action. Finally, at least in the case of the police raiding users, there was evidence of locational variation not attributable to demographic factors. Bradford's and Nottingham's main sample respondents being significantly more likely to favour raids than respondents in either Glasgow or Lewisham.

Figure 7.21
Summary of demographic and drug usage regression models for the perceived effectiveness of targeting suppliers as opposed to users

Response	Variables in final model	Direction of effect	% of variance explained
Main sample			
police should bust suppliers	frequency of using cannabis	non-users>users	5
	ethnicity	white>asian>black	
	ever used illicit drug	non-users>users	
	socioeconomic status	C2/DE>AB/C1	
	frequency of using non-opiates	users>non-users	
	age group	older>younger	
police should bust users	ever used illicit drug	non-users>users	15
	age group	older>younger	
	frequency of using cannabis	non-users>users	
	socioeconomic status	C2/DE>AB/C1	
	ethnicity	white>black=asian	
	gender	females>males	
	location	Bradford=Nottingham>Glasgow=Lewisham	
Booster sample			
police should bust suppliers	frequency of using cannabis	non-users>users	3
police should bust users	ever taken illicit drug	non-users>users	10
	frequency of taking cannabis	non-users>users	
	gender	females>males	
	age group	younger>older	

variables in equation: *location, age group, gender, socioeconomic status, ethnicity, whether ever tried an illicit drug, frequency of taking cannabis, frequency of taking non-opiates, frequency of taking opiates*

Having asked our respondents about a range of potential police approaches to controlling the demand for and supply of drugs, we then asked them to indicate how effectively they felt their local police actually dealt with the drugs issue. As indicated by Figure 7.22, responses to this item were somewhat equivocal. Less than half of our respondents in all samples, other than Nottingham's main sample, felt that their local police dealt 'very well' or 'fairly well' with drugs and even in the case of this one exception support only just reached the 50% mark. Perhaps predictably, support for the effectiveness of local police was lower in all booster samples than in their corresponding main samples, particularly in Glasgow.

Figure 7.22
Respondents' views regarding the effectiveness of their local police in dealing with drugs

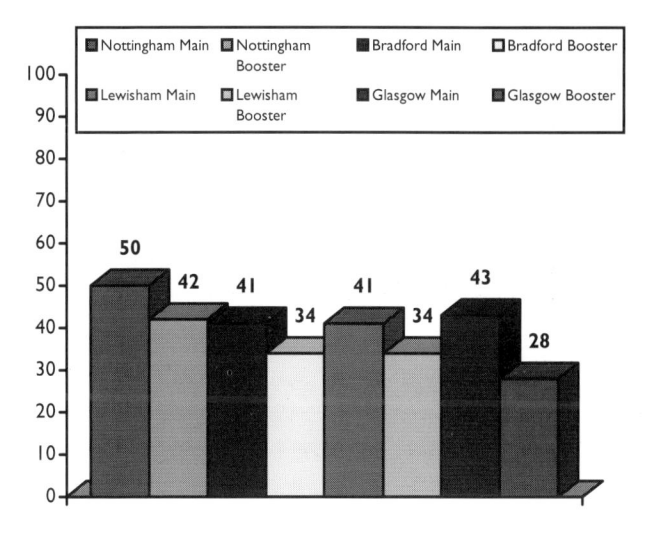

[Bar chart showing: Nottingham Main 50, Nottingham Booster 42, Bradford Main 41, Bradford Booster 34, Lewisham Main 41, Lewisham Booster 34, Glasgow Main 43, Glasgow Booster 28]

Percentage of respondents stating that their local police deal 'very well' or 'fairly well' with drugs

Although support for local police action was not encouragingly positive, it should be noted that the response did not imply any very great degree of *dissatisfaction* with local police. Since we did not ask our respondents to elaborate on the issue, we also cannot determine, unfortunately, whether any lack of support referred directly to police action or rather to factors outside the immediate control of the police. Respondents may, for example, have felt that the police were unable to act effectively because of a shortage of resources. Further research on this issue would clearly be of value in both policy and operational terms.

The only extra bit of information we can supply here on public attitudes towards local drugs policing is given by our demographic and drug usage regression models of these attitudes. As indicated by Figure 7.23 both demography and personal experience of drug usage appeared to be of some importance with regard to this issue, particularly in the case of our main sample. The composition of the final regression models was similar in both main and booster samples, with respondents who had not used illicit drugs feeling more confident in the effectiveness of the local police force than drug users and higher status socioeconomic groups showing stronger support for the local police than lower status socioeconomic groups.

Figure 7.23
Summary of regression models for respondents' views on the effectiveness of local policing

Response	Variables in final model	Direction of effect	% of variance explained
Main sample			
how well local police deal with drug usage	age group ever used illicit drug socioeconomic status	older>younger non-users>users AB/C1>C2/DE	9
Booster sample			
how well local police deal with drug usage	whether ever used illicit drug socioeconomic status	non-users>users AB/C1>C2/DE drug usage	3

variables in equation: *location, age group, gender, socioeconomic status, ethnicity, whether ever tried an illicit drug, frequency of taking cannabis, frequency of taking non-opiates, frequency of taking opiates*

Age group was also of considerable importance, in the main sample, if not the booster sample, with older respondents being more likely to state that their local police were effective than younger respondents. This latter factor being one which tends to be common to views on policing, however measured. Unfortunately, since we did not press respondents for an explanation of their attitudes, we cannot determine whether the effect of demography or personal drug usage on attitudes towards the local police's drugs control efforts stems from a respondent's views regarding the likely effect of such actions on their own lives, or whether it stems from a concern more nearly connected with the reduction of drug usage. Either way, this type of information is of value both operationally and in policy terms. A concrete example of its likely importance is given in the next chapter, where we consider the public's views on the interaction between the police and other drugs related agencies. Finally, it is worth noting that, in contrast to our regression models for specific forms of policing, we found no significant locational variation - independent of demography or personal drug usage - in attitudes towards the police. Insofar as police action in the four locales is distinct, this goes some way towards supporting the view that the public's low level of support for local police action is concerned with something other than, or in addition to, the nature of the action itself.

In summary, although support for a range of police demand reduction and drugs control options was significantly *lower* than for the option of education discussed earlier, it was still not trivial. Taken at face value, this is in fact somewhat surprising, since the particular options we asked our respondents to consider were fairly controversial. In particular, we found a surprising degree of support for both the prospect of cautioning rather than prosecuting drug users and for stopping and searching people suspected of being in possession of drugs. The level of support shown by the booster samples for the latter deterrence option is particularly unexpected given their acknowledged levels of drug usage. Support for these deterrence options notwithstanding, a very clear response from our samples was that police drugs action should be directed primarily at *suppliers* rather than users of illicit drugs. This view held firm across all four locations and across all the demographic groups we considered. Rather more demographic variation was accounted for in attitudes towards the more specific measures considered, although the direction of effect of this type of factor varied substantially across the options considered. Demographic variation and personal drug usage were also factors of some importance in determining our respondents' views towards the effectiveness of local police in reducing drug usage. However, support for the effectiveness of police action was quite low in both samples and across all locations. Note that this does not necessarily reflect directly on the action taken by local police, since a number of factors beyond their immediate control may be intervening here, a point which will be discussed at greater length in the next two chapters.

Customs control of supply

Unlike police responses to drug usage, customs control measures can be seen as more clearly associated with promoting a reduction in the *supply of* drugs rather than a reduction in the *demand for* drugs, although the two are linked at some level. As with police responses, however, the nature of potential customs efforts is quite diverse. Such efforts may, for example be directed at preventing drug supply at the point of entry, an instance of which would be baggage checking at airports, or they may be directed more nearly at the point of export, an instance of which might include the gathering of national and international information relating to the movement of drug consignments.

OPTIONS FOR CONTROLLING OR REDUCING THE MISUSE OF DRUGS

Since we could not, in the limited context of our interview schedule, present respondents with the full complexity of customs related responses to drugs, we settled for two items which we felt broadly spanned the point of entry/point of export distinction noted above. The first item asked respondents to indicate their support for the idea of "major efforts by police or customs targeting sources of supply" as a means of reducing drug usage. The second item asked respondents to indicate their support for the idea that "the way to decrease the number of people using drugs is to increase security

80% to 90% of respondents in both samples and all locations rated the control measures judged in *absolute* terms as very likely or fairly likely to be effective. Levels of support tended to be slightly lower in the younger booster samples, although this disparity was much less noticeable than had been the case for comparable items dealing with police control options. There was also a slight, but significant disparity in levels of support for the two forms of customs approach considered, with efforts targeting supply sources being favoured over efforts directed more specifically at stopping the entry

Figure 7.24
Respondents' views regarding customs control approaches to reducing drug usage: Main sample

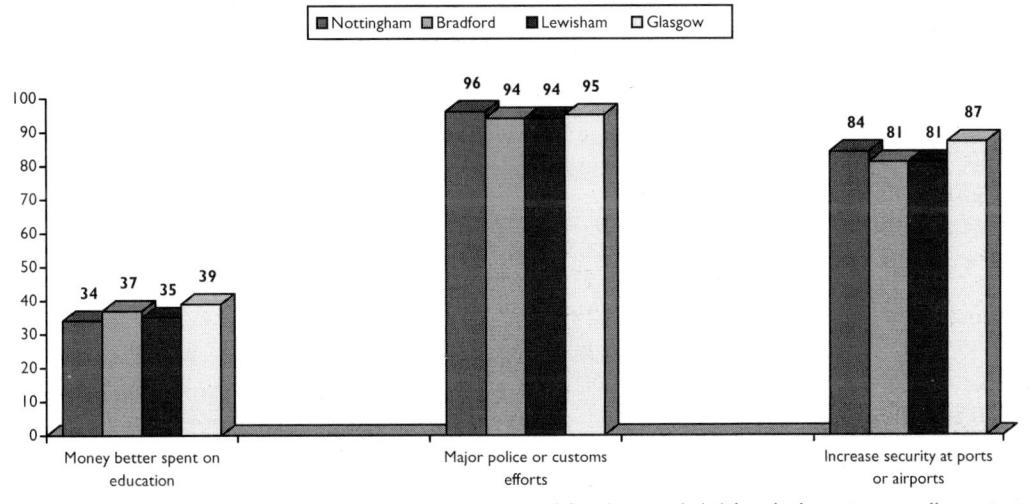

	Nottingham	Bradford	Lewisham	Glasgow
Money better spent on education	34	37	35	39
Major police or customs efforts	96	94	94	95
Increase security at ports or airports	84	81	81	87

Percentage of respondents stating that they 'agree strongly' or 'agree slightly' with the statement "money would be better spent on education and TV campaigns rather than on trying to stop drugs being brought into the country"/Percentage of respondents stating that major efforts by police or customs targeting sources of supply would be 'very useful' or 'fairly useful' in reducing drug usage/Percentage of respondents stating that they 'agree strongly' or 'agree slightly' with the statement that "the way to decrease the number of people using drugs is to increase security at ports and airports'".

at ports and airports". We also asked respondents to make a *relative* judgement on the likely effectiveness of customs control by indicating their support for the notion that "money would be better spent on education and TV campaigns rather than on trying to stop drugs being smuggled into the country". Given the evident popularity of education as a means of drugs control, this provides a quite powerful test of our respondents' attitudes towards customs control. A detailed summary of responses to all three items is given in Table 7.19 in Appendix 1.

As indicated by Figures 7.24 and 7.25 the public view of customs control measures, as represented by our respondents was extremely favourable. Around

of drugs into the country. This pattern of responses being consistent with the type of responses noted earlier for targeting suppliers rather than users of drugs.

As noted in previous discussions, the comparative item contrasting education campaigns with customs control indicated that only a minority of respondents felt that education could be a *more* successful drugs control technique than actually stopping drugs from coming into the country. This suggests that customs efforts find strong support in the public eye as a measure of drugs control whether they are viewed in absolute *or* relative terms. Again, it should be noted that the booster samples showed consistently *lower* levels of support for customs control than did the main samples.

Figure 7.25
Respondents' views regarding customs control approaches to reducing drug usage: Booster sample

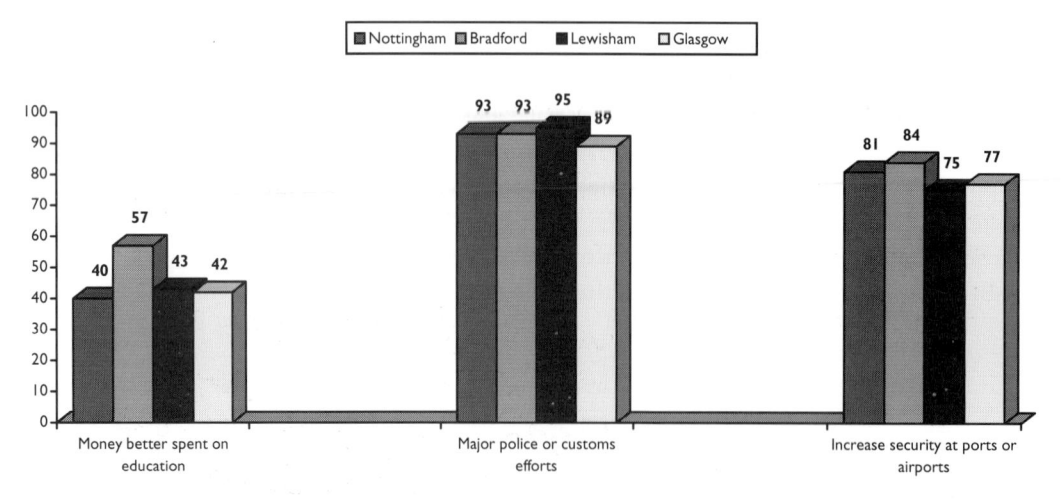

[Bar chart with legend: Nottingham, Bradford, Lewisham, Glasgow]

- Money better spent on education: 40, 57, 43, 42
- Major police or customs efforts: 93, 93, 95, 89
- Increase security at ports or airports: 81, 84, 75, 77

Percentage of respondents stating that they 'agree strongly' or 'agree slightly' with the statement "money would be better spent on education and TV campaigns rather than on trying to stop drugs being brought into the country"/Percentage of respondents stating that major efforts by police or customs targeting sources of supply would be 'very useful' or 'fairly useful' in reducing drug usage/Percentage of respondents stating that they 'agree strongly' or 'agree slightly' with the statement that "the way to decrease the number of people using drugs is to increase security at ports and airports".

Figure 7.26
Summary of demographic and drug usage regression models for the perceived effectiveness of major police and customs efforts targetting supply sources

Response	Variables in final model	Direction of effect	% of variance explained
Main sample			
major efforts to target supply sources	frequency of using cannabis	non-users>users	7
	ever used illicit drug	non-users>users	
	age group	older>younger	
Booster sample			
major efforts to target supply sources	frequency of using cannabis	non-users>users	4

variables in equation: *location, age group, gender, socioeconomic status, ethnicity, whether ever tried an illicit drug, frequency of taking cannabis, frequency of taking non-opiates, frequency of taking opiates*

To assess the effect of demography and personal drug usage on attitudes towards customs control, we again ran our composite regression model, using as a target variable the most popular customs control option, namely major police or customs efforts targeting sources of supply. The results are summarised in detail in Table 7.20 in Appendix 1. Although finding support from a majority of our respondents, even this item did show a substantial degree of demographic variation. As with previous models, Figure 7.26 indicates that our model accounted for a greater degree of variation in the main than in the booster sample, although both final models were similar. The variable of primary importance being personal experience of drug usage. Drug users and in particular respondents presently using cannabis being significantly less likely to support the likely effectiveness of customs control efforts in reducing the supply of drugs. In the main sample, this effect was mirrored by an age effect, with younger respondents also feeling less confident in the likely effectiveness of customs controls on drug supply than older respondents.

Unlike the case for policing actions, this particular example of attitudinal variation is unlikely to be connected with a respondent's perception that such actions will impinge directly on their own lives, consequently the disparity in support for customs control is likely to stem from real or perceived differences in the knowledge of customs control measures held by these distinct groups. Again, it is unfortunate that we were not able to consider responses in greater detail, as it would be of interest to know what particular aspects of customs control reduced the confidence of drug users and the young in its likely success.

In summary, our respondents showed considerable support for customs control efforts towards reducing drug usage, whether this was measured in relative or absolute terms. As with similar questions concerning police responses to drug usage, we found the highest level of support for those actions most likely to affect supply sources rather than, for example, users or couriers. Also as with police efforts, we found that the young in general and drug users in particular were less convinced of the likely effectiveness of customs efforts than other groups within our samples. As we will discuss in Chapter 9, they may have some grounds for their doubt.

Tertiary prevention: Harm reduction

As noted in the introduction to this chapter, we were unable to look closely at tertiary prevention - however, we did approach the issue obliquely, by looking both at what our respondents felt were the appropriate aims of drugs education and at the level of support they showed for medical models of drugs prevention. The former item dealt with the issue of tertiary prevention in the context of drugs education and asked respondents to state whether drugs education should aim to prevent people from *starting* to take drugs or should aim to help individuals *already* taking drugs. Respondents were given the option of endorsing one or other aspect of education or stating that *both* should be used. The item used to assess levels of support for medical models of harm reduction simply asked respondents to indicate the level of their support for the statement "More money should be spent on medical treatment and help for drug users". These data are summarised in detail in Table 7.21 in Appendix 1.

As is clearly demonstrated by Figure 7.27, a majority of our respondents favoured the prevention view of education over *either* of the other options. Although the booster sample showed greater support both for harm reduction measures and for the option of giving equal attention to both prevention and harm reduction, this was a matter of degree rather than any more notable distinction between the samples. What is notable is that for both samples, support for the *joint* use of both education measures was the second most popular option, being favoured by a substantially higher proportion of respondents than were willing to support solely harm reduction measures. This ordering of responses suggests that our respondents have a very decided preference for preventive education and do not feel that harm reduction *per se* is a particularly suitable goal for drugs education.

Figure 7.27
Respondents' views on the most appropriate aim of drugs education

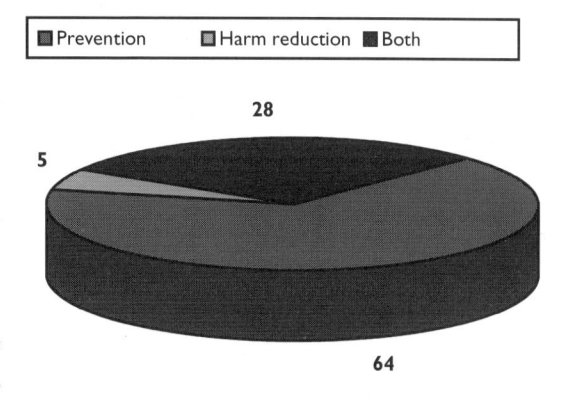

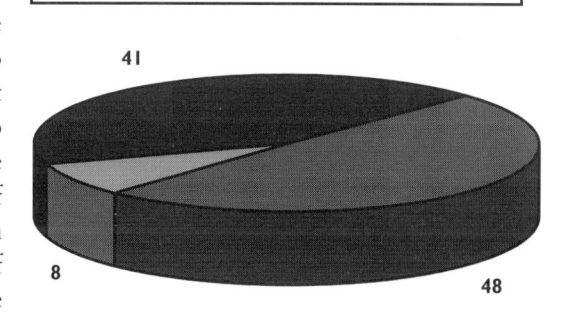

Main sample

Booster sample

Percentage of respondents feeling that either prevention, harm reduction, or a combination of aims was the most appropriate goal of drugs education.

It is important to add some caveats to the above interpretation of the results. In the first place, it should be noted that although the general profile of responses was similar across the four locations, the *level* of support for particular options varied considerably across locations. Nottingham, for example, showing the lowest level of support for the joint prevention/harm reduction option in both main and booster samples, whilst Lewisham and Bradford showed the highest level of support for this option in the main and booster samples respectively. A perhaps more important caveat is the extent to which respondents were actually aware of the nature of education measures directed at harm reduction. As the drug prevention teams we spoke to pointed out, the general public, in this country at least, has had very little exposure to any form of harm reduction measure. Consequently, the strength of their support for prevention types of education may stem from a lack of information, rather than from any more knowledgeable or committed viewpoint. Having said which it is worth bearing in mind that this was the only education item in our interview schedule which showed *any* significant tendency to divide our respondents and consequently it may be an issue which needs to be treated with some caution, at least up to the point where the public becomes better informed on drugs education measures as a whole.

Although the structure of this item was not amenable to multivariate analyses, we did split responses down to provide response profiles on the basis of both demographic categories and personal experiences of drug usage. These can be seen in Tables 7.22 to 7.24 in Appendix 1. The profiles suggest that, predictably, this issue was one on which the views of drug users and non-drug users were distinctly divided. Those respondents with personal experience of drug use were rather more likely than those who had never used an illicit drug to state that either harm reduction, or both prevention and reduction, were suitable aims for education. Whether this stems from any greater knowledge of the issue held by drug users, or simply from their view of how such measures could help their own position, we are not able to tell, but it would be of interest to compare the profiles of drug users and non-drug users once more information becomes available to the public.

Demography appeared overall to have less of an effect on attitudes than personal experience of drug usage. However, one clear demographic divide was apparent. Higher status socioeconomic groups were much more likely than their counterparts to state that *harm reduction* was an appropriate aim. No consistent ethnic or gender differences emerged for this issue in either main or booster samples. The expected age differences did emerge, with younger age groups in our main sample being more likely to favour harm reduction, but this distinction was not as great as previous divisions between the age groups noted for other items in the interview schedule.

In summary, although some locational and demographic variation was apparent, prevention rather than harm reduction was seen by our main sample respondents as clearly the most appropriate of the options for drugs education. Although, predictably, the booster sample showed a greater willingness to entertain harm reduction or mixed goals for education, even they appeared in the main to favour education directed at prevention. Without further information, we cannot tell whether the response patterns noted stem from genuine preferences or simply from a lack of knowledge. Given that the general public has received very little information relating to the option of harm reduction, the latter interpretation is, however, quite plausible. Certainly we found that drug users, taken as a group likely to be more knowledgeable on the subject, if not entirely objective, were much more likely to favour harm reduction goals for education. Whatever the cause of our respondents' views, it seems that this is one area of the drugs education issue which may spark controversy, at least if the public remain uninformed of the implications of available options.

Improvement of treatment and rehabilitation

The treatment and rehabilitation of drug users provides a common current through the otherwise diverse forms of drugs policy available. Whether or not drug users are arrested or educated, it is inevitable that at least some of their number will require some form of treatment or rehabilitation. Possible options for treatment and rehabilitation are themselves both numerous and diverse, ranging from crisis intervention to long term counselling and support, employment training etc. The needs which such options are required to meet also vary widely, from strictly medical needs, such as treatment for septicaemia, to more purely social needs, such as marriage guidance and employment training. The variety of these options reflect in turn the extensive degree of individual variation in both the physical and psychological correlates of drug usage and drug addiction.

Although treatment and rehabilitation are also major forms of tertiary prevention, it was not, strictly speaking, from this angle that they were addressed in the present survey. Instead, we considered the absolute level of importance ascribed by respondents to treatment and rehabilitation, as one of a possible range of drugs prevention measures. As noted above, the item used to address this issue asked respondents to indicate the level of their agreement with the statement "More money needs to be spent on helping drug users and giving them medical treatment". Two points are worth noting with regard to this item. Firstly, it considers only *one* potential form of treatment. Secondly, it differs from the other comparative or absolute judgements which respondents had been asked to make by providing a direct indication that support for the proposal has implications for resource allocation. It is important to bear both of these points in mind when interpreting the results now presented.

Figure 7.28
Respondents' views on the provision of medical treatment for drug users

| ■ Nottingham Main | □ Nottingham Booster | ■ Bradford Main | □ Bradford Booster |
| ■ Lewisham Main | □ Lewisham Booster | ■ Glasgow Main | ■ Glasgow Booster |

Nottingham Main: 67
Nottingham Booster: 67
Bradford Main: 66
Bradford Booster: 75
Lewisham Main: 74
Lewisham Booster: 81
Glasgow Main: 71
Glasgow Booster: 73

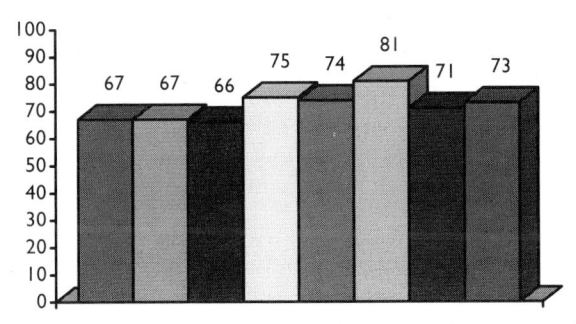

Percentage of respondents stating that they 'agree strongly' or 'agree slightly' with the statement that "more money should be spent on medical treatment and help for drug users"

Notwithstanding the implications for resource allocation, it can be seen from Figure 7.28 that support for the medical treatment of drug users was high across all samples, with between 60% and 80% of respondents in both samples and all locations supporting the statement outlined above. In all locations, except Glasgow, the booster samples were significantly more likely to support the goal of medical treatment than their main sample counterparts. There was some evidence also of limited locational variation, with Lewisham showing the strongest level of support in both booster and main samples. Although *absolute* values in favour of medical treatment for drug users were lower than those noted in support of educational measures, it is important to clarify that this does not necessarily imply a lesser degree of support in actuality, since as indicated above, respondents were being asked to make qualitatively different judgements in the two cases.

Whilst support for treatment and rehabilitation in general appeared to be strong, it is possible that the precise methods adopted in each case would have widely diverging levels of support. The form of approach outlined in the statement used here clearly follows a medical model. That is, it supports the view of a drug user as a passive receptor for paternalist care, or alternatively as a victim in need of interventionist treatment. Different forms of treatment or rehabilitation, perhaps not in alignment with this type of model, may meet with widely diverging levels of public support, particularly given the responses noted above for harm reduction forms of education.

Figure 7.29
Summary of demographic and drug usage regression models for the effectiveness of putting more money into medical treatment for drug usage

Response	Variables in final model	Direction of effect	% of variance explained
Main sample			
there should be more medical help for drug users	age group socioeconomic status frequency of cannabis usage ethnicity gender	younger>older AB/C1>C2/DE users>non-users black>asian>white females>males	2
Booster sample			
there should be more medical help for drug users	socioeconomic status	AB/C1>C2/DE	<1%

variables in equation: location, age group, gender, socioeconomic status, ethnicity, whether ever tried an illicit drug, frequency of taking cannabis, frequency of taking non-opiates, frequency of taking opiates

Although we again ran our demographic and drug usage regression model, it was apparent that in fact there existed little diversity of opinion on this issue (cf. Table 7.25 in Appendix 1). As Figure 7.29 shows, we found similar divides between sub-groups to those noted on the education issue, but they were able to explain only 2% or less of the variation noted, dependent on sample type. To summarise the distinctions briefly, we found that younger individuals and drug users were more likely to support the importance of medical treatment, as were ethnic minorities, females and members of higher status socioeconomic groups. In general however, the response profile suggests that medical treatment, like drugs education, is an issue which finds consistently high levels of support across a broad range of demographic groups.

In summary, our respondents showed strong support for the provision and improvement of medical treatment for drug users. This support appeared to be fairly consistent across a range of sub-groups within the population and although it did not rival the level of support shown for drugs education, it remained firm in the face of clear indications of financial cost. Unfortunately, given the necessarily limited attention paid to this issue within the scope of the survey, we are unable to determine whether all forms of treatment and rehabilitation would be equally acceptable to the public. Given previous responses to harm reduction questions, this seems at face value unlikely to be the case and hence it could prove an area of some importance for attitudinal research on the drugs issue.

Summary of Chapter 7

The main point to note from the foregoing discussion is that virtually *all* the measures suggested to respondents in the questionnaire for controlling drug usage or the effects of drug usage gained high or fairly high levels of support from respondents in both main and booster samples. This implies general support for some kind of positive action on drug usage.

The most favoured option of those presented to our respondents was education, with parents in particular showing an unusually high - almost unanimous - level of support for this method of drugs control. There is some indication that support for education centred around its function as a measure of primary prevention rather than harm reduction, though since many parents were not aware of their children receiving any drugs education, they may have found it difficult to comment on the relative likely effectiveness of each type.

Respondents were also very clear about which groups they felt held the responsibility for providing such education. Across all samples the organisations seen by most respondents as being responsible for the provision of drugs education were the schools and the government. Since the former is under increasing control from the latter in relation to the curriculum, this suggests that the government is expected either directly, or indirectly to be responsible for such education being provided.

Medical treatment of drug users, customs control measures and police control methods aimed at *suppliers* - not users - also found favour with both main and booster samples. Police methods aimed at *users* were significantly less popular. In short, all methods of drugs control were found likely to have some popularity. However, those directed towards the prevention of usage and the termination of supply sources seemed to be meeting with the greatest degree of approval across the broadest range of demographic groups.

Possibly the most interesting thing to come from the multivariate analyses run on demographic variation and variation between those with and without experience of drug usage, was that for the most part they failed to explain any very large degree of variation. This suggests that drugs control and drugs reduction methods are issues on which the public view is unusually consistent across demographic boundaries. The lack of variation between drug users and non-users on *most* issues was also surprising and may indicate that both groups are taking an objective stance on reduction and control issues. Having said which, those measures for which variation in the degree of support *was* apparent between users and non-users were the more 'interventionist' measures, such as searching on suspicion, or 'busting' suppliers and users, and similarly on potentially controversial measures such as education directed at harm reduction and increased levels of medical support for drug users.

The direction of effect of demographic variables and personal experience of drug usage was broadly similar in most instances, suggesting that the variance being tapped related to global differences in approach towards drugs control measures. Younger age groups, and those with personal experience of drug usage were more likely to favour a range of prevention and harm reduction measures, whilst older groups and non-drug users concentrated instead on interventionist and control oriented measures. Similarly, ethnic minorities were more likely to favour prevention and education measures rather than interventionist and in particular police oriented control measures, whilst respondents from the majority white ethnic group were willing also to support fairly extreme levels of police control, such as stopping and searching.

Finally, higher status socioeconomic groups, as tends to be found in attitudinal research, showed a predisposition to favour educational approaches to drugs prevention and similarly were willing to accept a broader range of non-interventionist/harm reduction types of approach than lower status socioeconomic groups. Although the absolute proportion of variance explained by these demographic distinctions was for the most part *relatively* small - around 10% or less of the variation being accounted for - it would be interesting to carry out further research into the distinctions noted. This could be of particular value if the public are to be given more comprehensive information on the drugs issue, since it would provide some not inconsiderable degree of insight into how such information might be targeted.

The extent to which the public attitudes discussed above are informed attitudes is something of a moot point. Levels of public information on drugs have been, until very recent times, rather limited and largely unidirectional. Since the drugs issue is a distinctly complex one, such a dearth of information will evidently have implications for the reliance even our respondents themselves may be able to place on their grasp of the issues. As noted in previous chapters, the public do seem to want more information about drugs and drugs control. One important area on which they may be lacking information is that dealing with the likely effectiveness of diverse drugs control measures. In Chapter 9, we will develop this point further, by considering available indicators to the success of some of the measures respondents were asked to comment on.

Chapter 8
THE PUBLIC PROFILE OF DRUGS RELATED AGENCIES

An issue pertinent to much of the discussion in previous chapters and in particular to that followed in the last chapter, is that of *who* should be responsible for drugs prevention and control and *how* they should go about it. The traditional response in Britain has been a diffuse one, whereby different styles of agency address, often at the local level and equally often on a voluntary basis, different aspects of the 'drugs problem' (cf. Tonry and Wilson 1990, Dorn and Murji 1992). Over this diffuse pattern of response is stretched the umbrella of necessarily more co-ordinated action by government controlled agencies. The primary aims of which agencies are determined jointly by ongoing changes in drugs policy and by emerging crises in various aspects of the drugs issue (cf. Pearson 1991).

If this picture of our response to drug usage sounds somewhat chaotic, it must be borne in mind that it can only be held to match the equally chaotic picture presented by the *nature* of drug usage. To take only one example, the *range* of agencies which a drug user could, quite appropriately, come into contact with in the course of his or her drug-using career is vast. Depending on the particular problem expressed by drug usage in any given instance, a user might come into either direct or indirect contact with both specialist statutory and voluntary drugs agencies, with non-specialist services such as the police, probation and social services, youth and community services, psychological and marriage guidance services, education departments and, particularly if drug usage presented a long term problem, with a range of health services including hospitals, specialist clinics and general practitioners.

The potential role of agencies in the reduction of drug usage and in particular drug misuse is clearly and necessarily a very broad one, spanning all forms of prevention, treatment and rehabilitation. If central government or government agencies are taken into consideration, the potential agency remit covers every aspect of the drugs issue, including very specific control measures. The public's view of this set of arrangements is important, especially since the role or roles which a given agency can appropriately adopt will tend to be determined in part at least by both public policy and public funding.

The range of potential questions caught up in this single issue of the role of drugs related agencies is too broad to be covered exhaustively by a survey of this nature. However, the survey was able to address a number of aspects of agency mediated responses which may prove useful in informing further work. In particular, we elected to address the role of agencies in providing *direct* help and information to drug users. Respondents were asked to provide information on their awareness of this form of service provision, on their views regarding the actual and potential effectiveness of a range of agencies and, perhaps most pertinently, to indicate who they felt *should* be responsible for providing this type of service. Since our work had been directed to some extent by a need to provide feedback to the Drugs Prevention Teams forming part of the present government's Drugs Prevention Initiative we highlighted the role of these teams in our interview schedule.

We also addressed, although only fleetingly, the prominent issue of whether co-operative work between statutory but non-specialist agencies, such as the police, and specialist agencies, such as the Drugs Prevention Teams, would be desirable from the public's standpoint. A detailed summary of our data on these topics is given in Tables 8.1 to 8.16 in Appendix 1.

Awareness of specialist agencies

General levels of awareness

An obvious starting point is the extent to which the public are actually aware of the existence of specialist drugs agencies. To address this, we simply asked respondents to indicate which organisations they were aware of *locally* "working to increase people's awareness about drugs, or to provide advice, information or help". Although responses to this item were spontaneous rather than prompted, we were anxious, for analysis purpose, to provide as comprehensive a code frame as possible. We were also anxious to consider specialist agencies since, in a sense, they exist to provide a front-line resource for drugs-related help and information. The list of agencies we used to code for awareness was consequently selected in consultation with the Central Drugs Prevention Unit, the market research company (PAS) and with the Drugs Prevention Teams in our four locations: our aim being to ensure adequate coverage of all prominent *local* specialist agencies. The emphasis on 'increasing people's awareness about drugs' appeared to centre our respondents' thoughts also on this type of specialist service, since very few respondents mentioned other non-specialist organisations.

In all four locations one of the options provided for in the code frame was the Drugs Prevention Team (DPT). In Lewisham the other options were: Brockley Drugline, the Dual Team and Phoenix House. In Nottingham the options were: Drugs Dependants Anonymous and the Health Shop. In Bradford the options were: the Bridge Project and Project 6. In Glasgow the only option we could come up with was the rather eclectic term 'local advice agency'. However, respondents in all locations were given the possibility of adding to the list *other* local agencies or organisations of which they were aware.

Since, as noted earlier, we were focusing to some extent on the Drugs Prevention Teams in our four locations, we gave respondents some additional prompting if they failed spontaneously to name a Drugs Prevention Team as providing local support for drug users. In fact, we asked interviewers to provide *two* additional prompts to stimulate awareness of the Drugs Prevention Teams. As an initial prompt, respondents were simply asked whether they had ever heard of the team working in their area. As a second, more detailed, prompt they were given a written and fairly lengthy description of the aims of the Drugs Prevention Teams. Since later items in this section of the questionnaire consequently refer to those spontaneously aware of agencies *other* than the Drugs Prevention Teams, but to those both aware spontaneously *and* as a consequence of prompting of the Drugs Prevention Teams, it should be borne in mind that we are not providing a level playing field for any comparison between the two types of agency. Responses for each agency and also for the single and dual prompt categories in the case of DPTs are given in detail in Table 8.1 in Appendix 1. In Figures 8.1 and 8.2 below, we present only levels of *spontaneous* awareness for all agencies and for the sake of brevity summate across all named agencies other than the DPTs in each location.

A quick glance at Figures 8.1 and 8.2 conveys immediately the very low levels of spontaneous awareness of drugs related agencies, whether included in our list or named by the respondents themselves. The highest percentage positive response across both samples and all locations was provided by Glasgow's main sample and here only 10% of our respondents were able to name a drugs related agency in their local area. Note that this is the largest percentage positive response *despite* the fact that responses for *different* named agencies are summated for each sample. The lack of spontaneous awareness in the main samples is not unexpected, since in broad terms these general population samples are composed of individuals with little experience of drug usage. However, the equally low levels of spontaneous awareness in the booster samples are a matter for greater concern, since the individuals within these samples represent a distinct target group for the services of the drugs related agencies.

Figure 8.1
Respondents' awareness of drugs related agencies: Main sample

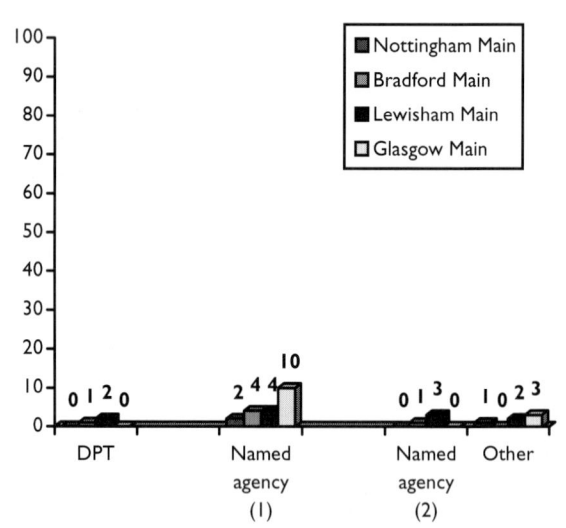

Percentage of respondents spontaneously aware of each type of drugs related agency

Figure 8.2
Respondents' awareness of drugs related agencies: Booster sample

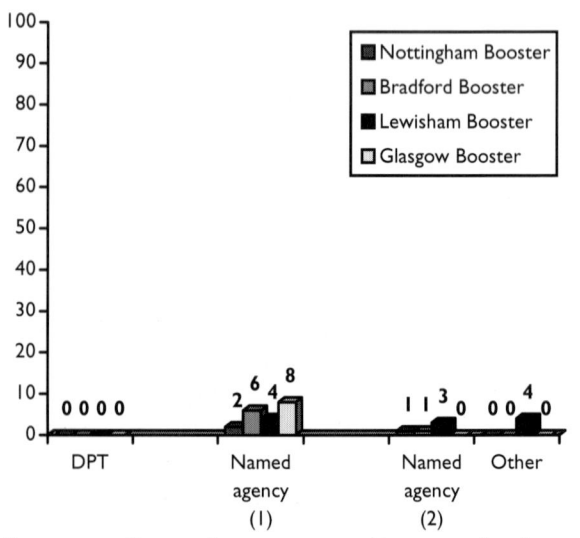

Percentage of respondents spontaneously aware of each type of drugs related agency

The lack of spontaneous awareness of the DPTs is in a sense not surprising, since they are of fairly recent standing. However, it should be noted that they are also in a fairly unique position amongst local drugs agencies in having the option of devoting a considerable proportion of their budget to advertising. Following the initial prompt, the percentage of respondents claiming awareness of the Drugs Prevention Teams rose significantly in both main and booster samples. Response levels following prompting were roughly equivalent in the two types of sample, with between 10% and 20% of respondents acknowledging the existence of their local Drugs Prevention Team. The additional, more detailed, prompt elicited at most only an additional 2%-3% of respondents claiming awareness of the DPTs.

Given the extensive nature of the prompting and the concomitant likelihood that some respondents were claiming an assumed rather than an actual awareness, these figures are still not high, but they *are* a great improvement over levels of spontaneous awareness. Since no prompts were given for agencies other than the DPTs it is, as we suggested earlier, unfortunately impossible to compare levels of awareness *across* these agency types. It is also of little value to compare levels of awareness of the different DPTs, since they have been established for different lengths of time and have used different levels and styles of advertising.

Whilst, given constraints on time, we were *not* able to discuss the public profile of drugs related agencies with all of the local agencies themselves, we were able to present the data, in the format outlined in the above Figures, to the Drugs Prevention Teams. Our discussions with them suggested that they were not unhappy with the outcome. One prominent view expressed by the Teams was that whilst they did have the *option* of using a fairly large advertising budget, they did not in practice feel this to be the most appropriate use of their resources. Quite rightly, they felt that the extent and nature of the other demands upon their services made the likely costs of advertising their existence to the general public something of a luxury.

In summary, general levels of public awareness of specialist local drugs agencies were very low. Less than 10% of respondents in any location were able to name spontaneously one or more agencies and the figures for those able to cite an agency were more commonly between zero and 3%. In both main and booster samples, spontaneous awareness of the Drugs Prevention Teams was at somewhat lower levels than comparable figures for other types of local agencies. Given that the Teams have not been in existence for any great length of time, this is not, however, very surprising. Providing additional prompts for the DPTs did stimulate greater levels of awareness. However, even with very extensive prompting less than a fifth of our sample in any given location claimed awareness of their local Teams.

Patterns of awareness

Although advertising the existence of a drugs related agency to the general public may be a luxury, ensuring that those individuals likely to be in need of its services are aware of its existence is something closer to a necessity. We consequently decided to address the issue of whether those respondents most likely to be in need of the services of our named local agencies were in fact in any degree more likely to be aware of their existence than respondents unlikely to need their services. Whilst the structure of our data was not amenable to any in-depth statistical analysis of this issue, we *were* able to draw broad comparisons across groups and the profiles we derived are presented in detail in Tables 8.2 to 8.9 in Appendix 1. For the sake of brevity, we have in the text summarised data across locations and drawn a distinction only between the composite 'named agencies' - representing an averaged response rate for all local agencies named - and the Drugs Prevention Teams. Since very few individuals showed spontaneous awareness of the DPTs, we used the responses to our initial prompt to draw the profiles outlined below. As noted earlier, this means that the absolute values noted for the DPTs should not be compared to those for the other named agencies.

As indicated by the data outlined in Chapters 2 and 3, certain demographic groups are significantly *more* likely than others both to use drugs and to use drugs in ways which may place them 'at risk' whether in health or social terms. The salience of drugs agencies in the eyes of those most likely to need their services can therefore be addressed in two ways. Firstly, we can compare levels of awareness in drug users as opposed to non-drug users. Secondly, we can draw similar comparisons between those groups in the population at greatest *potential* risk of drug usage and those whose profile suggests the least potential risk. Since the implications of each approach are in practice distinct, we decided to consider both comparisons for present purposes.

Personal drug usage and awareness of drugs related agencies

As noted in previous sections of this report, drug usage and hence drug users can be defined in a variety of different ways. One important distinction which could have been drawn in the present instance would have been between *forms* of drug usage, for example, frequent as opposed to occasional usage, or injecting usage as opposed to oral ingestion or inhalation. Given the likely prominence of drugs agencies for 'problem users' as opposed to users who are, or perceive themselves to be, in control of their drug usage, this *type* of distinction would have been of particular relevance in the present instance. Since our samples did not contain sufficient numbers of regular or injecting users we unfortunately could not address any distinctions in the awareness of agencies running along these lines. Instead, we looked at two rather more basic distinctions, namely that between users of different types of drugs and that between individuals who *had* used any form of unprescribed drug and those who had not.

Figure 8.3
Personal experience of drug usage and awareness of drugs related agencies: Main sample

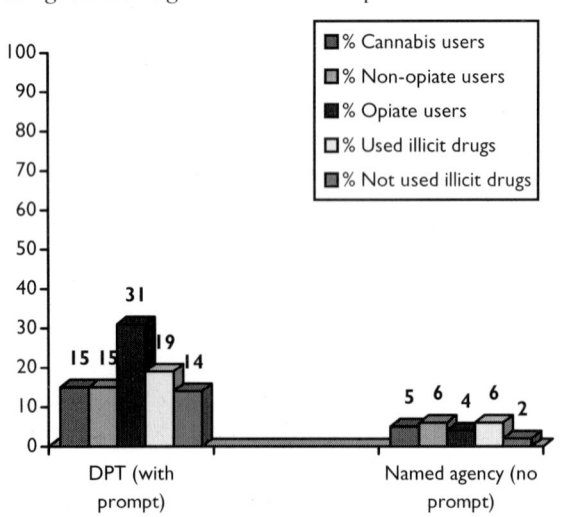

Percentage of respondents in each drug usage category aware of each type of drugs related agency, averaged across location

Considering the main sample first, it can be seen from Figure 8.3, that the drug usage profiles of those aware of Drugs Prevention Teams, following an initial prompt, were broadly similar to those of respondents who were aware of other types of named agency. However, with regard to drug type, main sample opiate users seemed more likely to be aware of the DPTs than did users of cannabis or non-opiates. For other types of named agency the levels of awareness of users of different drug types appeared to be more closely matched. Although we must be cautious in interpreting this distinction, since the absolute numbers of opiate users were fairly small in our samples and locational variation was apparent, the disparity is interesting in that it matches a concern expressed by the Drugs Prevention Teams we talked to. The Teams showed a fairly strong consensus in stating that opiate users had a conspicuously high profile for agencies given their in fact fairly low absolute prevalence levels. Since agencies can of course only concentrate their attentions on those users coming forward for help or advice it would be useful to establish whether this type of disparity between users of different drug types is a real phenomenon and also to examine the extent to which it affects a range of different agencies.

Although for both DPTs and other named agencies levels of awareness were slightly greater amongst those who had used drugs than amongst those who had not, the disparity between the two groups was rather less than one might have expected, particularly in the case of the DPTs. Given that drugs agencies exist to serve not only the needs of drug users themselves but also of those likely to be affected indirectly by drug usage - for example the families of drug users - the equivalence between users and non-users would not have been disturbing if general levels of awareness of agencies had been rather higher. In the present circumstances, this equivalence unfortunately indicates that the awareness of drugs related agencies is as *low* amongst drug users as it is in the general population. Absolute figures are necessarily higher for the DPTs, for the reasons stated earlier and yet we still found that only around one fifth of drug users were aware of the DPTs. This pattern has two implications. Firstly it suggests that there is some failure on the part of drugs agencies to reach an obvious target group of people in the general population likely to be in need of their services. Secondly, and ironically, this failure may be, in practical terms, a 'success', since the drugs professionals we talked to felt that they were already inundated with work. If a very much broader group of drug users was made aware of their services it seems reasonable to assume that these demands could only increase.

As indicated by Figure 8.4, the drug usage profiles drawn for the booster samples' awareness of drugs-related agencies proved to be very similar to that noted for the main samples. Drug users in general showed similar levels of awareness to non-drug users for both the DPTs and other local agencies. The small number of opiate users we had in our sample were also more likely to acknowledge awareness of both the DPTs and other

THE PUBLIC PROFILE OF DRUGS RELATED AGENCIES

Figure 8.4
Personal experience of drug usage and awareness of drugs related agencies: Booster sample

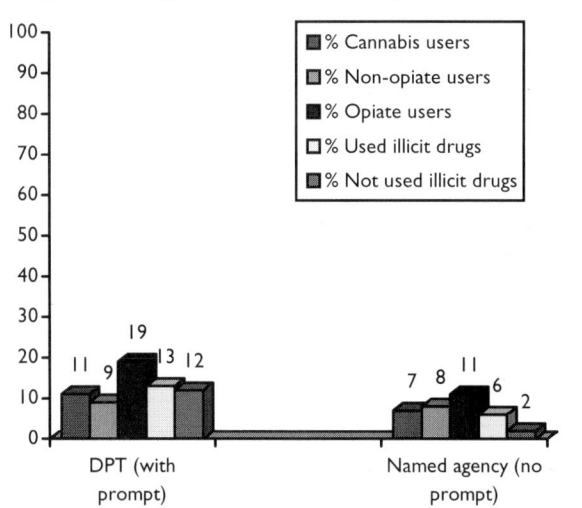

Percentage of respondents in each drug usage category aware of each type of drugs related agency, averaged across location

local agencies than were users of cannabis or non-opiate drugs. Although, of course, the samples are not directly comparable, this similarity between their profiles is of interest in that it implies that our results are not a function of the uneven geographic distribution of drugs agencies noted in previous chapters. Even in relatively deprived areas, where agencies tend to be sited, awareness of their existence is not substantially greater amongst drug users than amongst members of the public who have never used drugs.

In summary, the rather low general levels of awareness of specialist local drugs agencies noted above do not appear to be the function of any targeting of drug users. Levels of awareness amongst the drug users within our sample were as low as for the non-drug using population. This was the case both for the DPTs and for other types of named agency, although again the pattern was slightly stronger in the case of the DPTs. It appeared from our data that opiate users may be more likely to have some awareness of local agencies than users of other drug types, although we cannot confirm this distinction without further information. Whatever the distribution of awareness amongst users of different drug types, the fact that only around one fifth of drug users are presently likely to be aware of a prominent form of local advice service has clear resource implications in the event that such services are to become better advertised and consequently more widely known.

Demographic profile and awareness of drugs related agencies

From the data presented in Chapters 2 and 3 we have very clear ideas of the demographic profile of drug usage within our samples, at least in prevalence terms. As with the distinction between drug users and non-drug users discussed above, we would hope that, whatever general levels of awareness in the population were, those groups within the population most likely to need the services of a specialist drugs agency would have a heightened awareness of their existence. Note again that detailed demographic profiles for the spontaneous awareness of drug related agencies in each location and sample type are given in Tables 8.2 to 8.9 in Appendix 1. As with drug usage *per se* we have in the text averaged across locations for the sake of brevity.

Figure 8.5
Age group and awareness of Drugs Prevention Teams

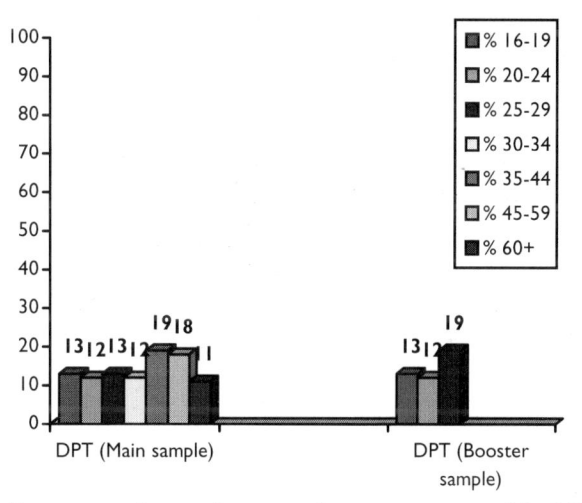

Percentage of respondents in each age group aware of the DPTs, average across location.

Taking the Drugs Prevention Teams first, we can compare Figure 8.5 with earlier figures relating to the prevalence of drug usage in different age groups. This comparison shows up two quite distinct differences between the profile followed by drug prevalence and the profile for *awareness* of the Drugs Prevention Teams. The first is that the distribution of awareness is much flatter than that for prevalence, at least in the main samples. Put more simply, drug *users* tend to be quite strongly clustered in the younger age groups, whilst levels of *awareness* of drugs agencies are broadly similar for all groups. The second and perhaps more important distinction is that the median, or most popular, ages for awareness of drugs agencies are, in both main and booster samples, substantially *older* than the ages which show the greatest prevalence of drug usage.

Individuals aged under 24 were the most prominent users of unprescribed drugs whether measured on the basis of lifetime prevalence or drug usage within the last year, in both our main and booster samples, but the groups most likely to be aware of specialist drugs agencies are in the case of our main sample within the age band 35-59 and in the booster sample the small group of 25-29 year olds. This indicates a distinct mismatch between the groups most likely to *have* relevant information and the groups most likely to *need* this information on a personal basis. Clearly, information can be passed across age groups, for example from knowledgeable parents to less knowledgeable children, but this does not alter the fact that a primary target for drugs advice and information show an even lower degree of awareness of a prominent source of such information than their less 'at risk' counterparts.

Figure 8.6
Age group and awareness of other named drugs prevention agencies

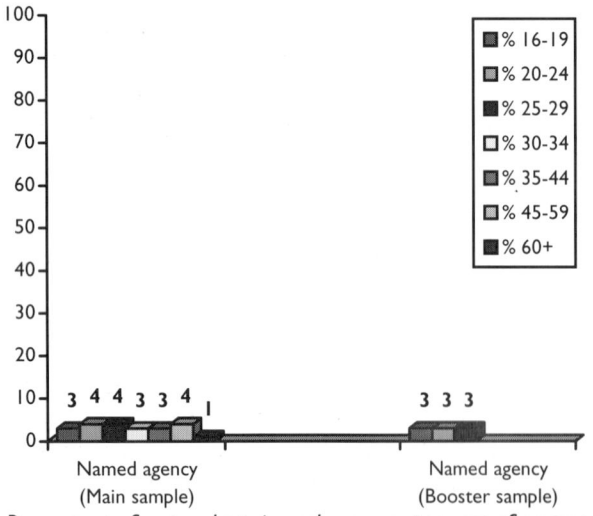

Percentage of respondents in each age group aware of a named drugs agency, averaged across location.

Turning to other local specialist agencies, it can be seen from Figure 8.6 that again the pattern noted for DPTs is largely matched by that for drugs agencies in general. The only salient difference is that there are *no* obvious peaks of awareness for any particular age groups. All age groups have equally little awareness of the existence of local drugs agencies. Again, it must be noted that drugs agencies have no shortage of clients and consequently may be well advised to turn their resources towards the clients they have rather than towards advertising their existence to potential clients. Nevertheless, it is in broader terms unfortunate that those age groups 'at risk' of drug usage are apparently no more, or possibly even less, aware of a potential source of help than is the general public.

Figure 8.7
Gender and awareness of drugs prevention agencies

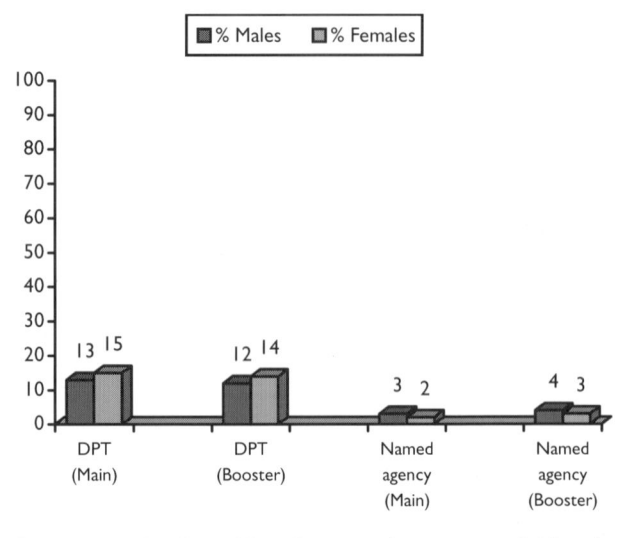

Percentage of male and female respondents aware of either the DPTs or other named drugs agencies, averaged across location.

Although, as Figure 8.7 indicates, any gender differences in awareness of the specialist local agencies are slight, the *pattern* noted for age groups is nevertheless matched for gender. As we saw in Chapters 2 and 3, males are very much the most prominent users of unprescribed drugs. They are *not*, however, substantially more likely to be aware of the existence of local specialist drugs agencies than are females. In fact, in the case of the Drugs Prevention Teams at least, they seem, albeit slightly, *less* likely to be aware of their existence. Again, this suggests a mismatch between levels of awareness of drugs agencies and the likely profile of need for these services, notably since general levels of awareness of specialist agencies are in any case rather low.

Measured in terms of drugs prevalence, the match between need and access to information appears to be rather better for socioeconomic status than for other demographic variables. As Figure 8.8 demonstrates, the AB and C1 groups, who were the most prominent drug using groups within our samples were also, in most cases the most likely groups to show an awareness of the existence of local specialist drugs agencies. The exception to this being awareness of the Drugs Prevention Teams within our booster sample, where individuals from the DE socioeoconomic groups were the group most likely to be aware of a DPT.

Figure 8.8
Socioeconomic status and awareness of drugs prevention agencies

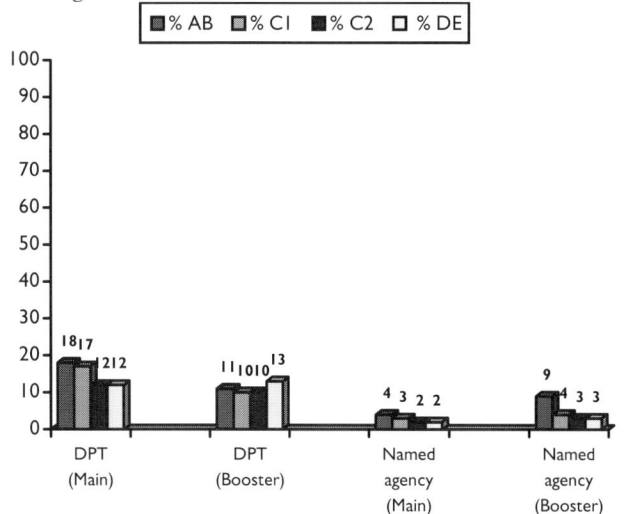

Percentage of respondents in each socioeconomic category aware of either the DPTs or other named drugs agencies, averaged across location.

Figure 8.9
Ethnicity and awareness of drugs prevention agencies

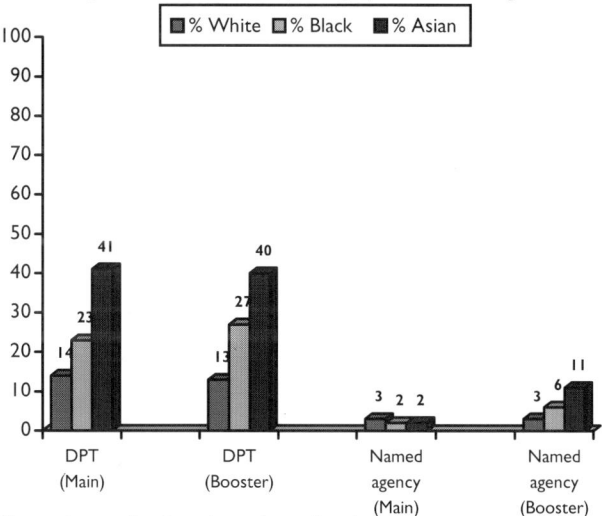

Percentage of respondents in each ethnic group aware of either the DPTs or other named drugs agencies, averaged across location.

In contrast to the above, the *greatest* mismatch we found between the demographic profile of drugs prevalence and the demographic profile of likely need for specialist resources was in terms of ethnicity. As Figure 8.9 readily demonstrates, respondents from ethnic minorities were much *more* likely to be aware of the existence of local specialist drugs agencies than respondents from the white majority ethnic group. Note here that a slightly different pattern was observed for named local agencies other than the DPTs. Specifically, ethnic minorities were more likely to be aware of DPTs than white respondents in *both* main and booster samples, but in the case of named agencies this disparity was restricted to the booster sample. Unfortunately, we cannot determine with the present data whether this represents any real differences between the distribution of information in relatively deprived as opposed to mid-range or more affluent areas by the two types of agency. Further work on this might be of interest, however, since it may be appropriate to target different groups in different locations.

In summary, there appeared to be something of a mismatch between those demographic groups showing the greatest 'risk' of drug usage - as measured by prevalence - and those groups most likely to be aware of the existence of specialist local agencies. This mismatch was most notable in the case of age group and ethnicity. Older respondents and respondents from ethnic minorities being the most likely to be aware of such agencies, whilst also being amongst the least prominent user groups for unprescribed drugs. Whilst this picture was broadly similar for both Drugs Prevention Teams and other forms of named local agencies, the patterns were more pronounced in the case of the DPTs.

Implications for the targeting of drugs related information

Interestingly, we found the whole issue of the targeting of drugs information - who should one target, how should one target, should one put resources into targeting or divert them to more immediate needs - to be a rather controversial one for the drugs professionals we spoke to. Whilst the major concern centred naturally around the lack of available resources, a prominent subsidiary concern was the likelihood of targeting, and perhaps consequently labelling groups *inappropriately*. Since we have no data of particular relevance to determining whether one *should* target information, we will have to beg this question, but we feel our data can be used to address the related issue of how one can target the most appropriate groups. The implications we wish to draw here being more nearly concerned with the *nature* of our data than with the patterns observed.

To address - using our data - the concept of targeting, it is important to recognise that in the foregoing discussion we were talking about groups 'at risk' of drug usage in terms of *prevalence* rather than in terms of their likelihood of problematic usage, however one wishes to measure this. We were also talking about a respondent's *awareness* of an agency rather than any measure of their likelihood of attending an agency in practice. As we suggested in Chapter 4, these two factors are likely to interact, since at least established specialist agencies have tended to attract a disproportionate amount of 'problematic' drug users, for obvious reasons.

To illustrate the above point more fully, it is worth noting that in fact certain of the trends in awareness of drugs-related agencies outlined above do *not* match recorded attendance at specialist agencies. For example, whilst awareness of both DPTs and local agencies was greater amongst higher socioeconomic groups, it is the lower status socioeconomic groups who are most likely to attend drug agencies or clinics (Smart 1985). Similarly, whilst respondents from minority ethnic groups were as likely or more likely to be aware of the agencies than respondents from the majority white ethnic group, there is in fact a great deal of concern, amongst academics and policy makers at least, that minority ethnic drug *users* are less likely than white users to approach an agency (cf. Awiah et al. 1990). Note here, that not all of the drugs professionals we spoke to agreed with the reasoning behind the latter concern, some feeling that any under-representation of ethnic minority users at drugs agencies was a consequence of their lower absolute levels of drug usage.

Two likely explanations of the distinction between our assessment of awareness and actual attendance at a drugs agency became apparent from our discussions with the Drugs Prevention Teams. The first, suggested above, is that agencies are more likely to attract problem users and less likely to attract those who are able to handle their drug usage on their own. The second possibility we picked up was a concern on the part of drugs-related agencies to bring their services to the attention of those demographic groups who are seen either as being under-represented at drugs agencies, or as being in greater need of drugs-related services. This brings us to a disparity between the DPTs and other specialist local agencies and also to something we see as a tension between two possible roles of specialist agencies.

Whilst the slight demographic distinctions in levels of awareness noted between the DPTs and other local agencies may have stemmed simply from the different lengths of time the two types of agency have been in operation, it is important to realise that they may equally have been due to the *different briefs* the agencies have with regard to drug usage. The remit of established local agencies has historically been very much in the domain of harm reduction and rehabilitation whilst the remit of the newly introduced DPTs is to a much greater extent concerned with drugs *prevention*. If these rather different briefs are maintained, the two types of service need to target information at rather different groups within the population. For example, it is less imperative that the DPTs, whose central aim is *primary* prevention, target drug users and in particular problem users than is the case with the harm reduction and rehabilitation oriented agencies. Conversely it is of *more* importance that they reach the mass of the general public who may have indirect contact with drug usage and who are themselves potential future drug users.

The tension between prevention and harm reduction at this level lies in the fact that the demographic groups most likely to be in need of preventive measures are unlikely to be the same groups for whom harm reduction measures are at the greatest premium. Prevention policies, at least as they have been formulated in the not too distant past (cf. Advisory Council on the Misuse of Drugs 1984), are primarily aimed at stopping the spread of drug usage and hence are most nearly concerned with drug *prevalence*. Harm reduction strategies on the other hand are more closely concerned with limiting the 'collateral damage' associated with drug usage and hence tend to centre around problematic usage, the recent concern with the effect of injecting usage on the spread of AIDS being a case in point. Although the area is still under-researched, there is sufficient data to provide one concrete example of this distinction. Those in greatest need of harm reduction measures appear quite strongly in the drugs literature as being those lacking in social or, more specifically, financial support (cf. Dembo and Burgos 1976, Collins et al 1985, McKegany et al 1990). Our data on socioeconomic groups suggests that this is *not* the group in greatest need of drugs prevention from a purely prevalence viewpoint.

The implications of any match or mismatch between awareness of drugs agencies and either attendance at these agencies or prominence as a group in need of drugs-related help and advice consequently depends very much on one's viewpoint. Looking at things from a purely *prevalence* viewpoint we found a strong indication that on the whole potential target groups were lacking in information. This data could, however present a rather different profile for someone looking at harm reduction. Our 'closest' match between need and awareness was shown by socioeconomic status, with the higher status groups having greater levels of awareness. From a harm reduction viewpoint, this finding could in fact could represent a *mis*match of information to need.

In short, the implications of any form of targeting are very closely tied with the *aims* of the particular agency doing the targeting. Inappropriate forms of targeting are likely to result from an unclear formulation of the goals of relevant agencies. In the present instance, for example, we would see our data as being primarily of value to agencies aiming at drugs prevention, since we have not been able to present any information on 'problem users'. Although this seems an obvious point, the type of distinction being made between the targeting needs of drugs prevention and those of harm reduction - both as traditionally defined - was not one which was readily apparent in either policy documents or publications for public consumption. It was, however, a distinction which drugs professionals were very much aware of.

> **In summary,** our data clearly suggest that levels of awareness of specialist drugs agencies are quite low and particularly low for 'at risk' groups within the population. However, the implications this has for the drugs agencies themselves depends very much on the roles they are seen as playing in drugs *prevention*. This point relates to a distinction between those groups within the population which are most likely to be the target of drugs prevention work and the groups which are most likely to be targets for *harm reduction*. To the extent that the identity of these two groups differs, we need to be very clear about the aims we are pursuing in targeting information and equally clear about determining what we mean by the 'drugs problem'.

Comparing specialist with non-specialist agencies as a first recourse

We chose to consider our respondents' awareness of *specialist* drugs agencies in some detail above. This was both because it is reasonable to see them as being in the 'front-line' of drugs prevention and because our respondents were unlikely to name other agencies as working locally to raise the profile of drug usage and provide help and advice. We did, however, also obtain a broader picture of the agencies seen by the public as providing a first recourse for drugs-related help and advice. Specifically, we asked respondents where they felt people in their area could go to if they needed "advice and help about drugs". We also asked parents where they would "turn to for help and advice" if they found their children taking drugs. A detailed summary of the responses to these items is given in Tables 8.10 and 8.11 in Appendix 1.

These items in our interview schedule differed from that discussed previously in not implying that the agencies mentioned should be ones *specifically concerned with* drug usage. By making this distinction it is possible to explore where people may initially tend to go to for drugs-related help and advice given that the majority are unaware of the specialist services which are available for this purpose. As with the discussion of specialist drugs services, it is important to bear in mind that the profile of the Drugs Prevention Teams in our respondents' awareness may be artificially high, since those initially unaware of their existence were given fairly detailed descriptions of their aims and function.

The first recourse for the general public

The data presented in Figure 8.10 imply quite strongly that for the general public the profile of *any* agencies likely to be of some help in providing drugs related advice or information is rather low. Even the most popular recourse for advice was named by only around a third of our main sample respondents. Comparing the popularity of specialist local agencies with that of *non-specialist* agencies suggests however, that whilst our respondents were not inclined to label the latter as working to raise the profile of drug usage in the local area, they were *more* likely to see them as an available first recourse for advice. Named specialist local agencies were in fact the *least* popular of all the options suggested by our respondents.

Figure 8.10
Agencies providing a first recourse: Main sample

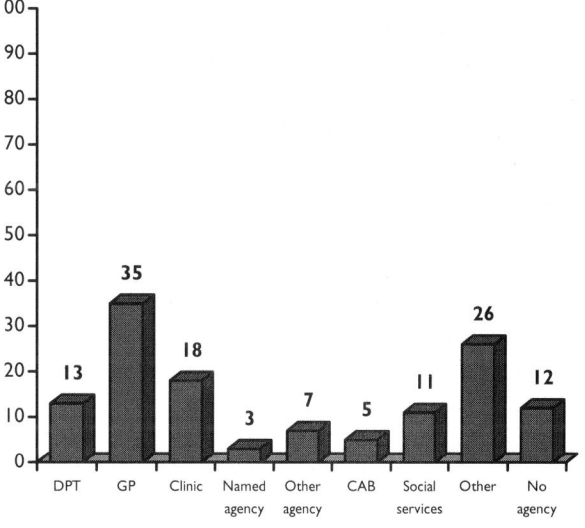

Agency	%
DPT	13
GP	35
Clinic	18
Named agency	3
Other agency	7
CAB	5
Social services	11
Other	26
No agency	12

Percentage of respondents stating that an agency was available to give advice in their city or borough, averaged across location

Of the suggestions made by our respondents, the *most* popular option was the local GP. This can be taken either as suggesting that our respondents held strongly to the medical model of drug usage, or more simply as suggesting that GPs provide an important community resource for help and advice in general. Whatever interpretation is given, it is important to note that in all locations respondents were significantly more likely to suggest seeking advice from a GP than from any other service. This has clear implications for the demands likely to be made on this service in relation to drugs usage and consequently also for the training of GPs in relation to this issue.

The second most popular *agency* named was also of a medical nature, being the rather broadly defined 'clinic'. This provides some further support for the view that the general public tends to default to a medical model of drug usage. Non-medical options such as Social Services, Citizens' Advice Bureaux and indeed our specialist drugs agencies gained only a minimal positive response from our respondents. Perhaps the most salient result from our main sample, however, was that respondents were more likely to name sources of advice such as friends or relatives, or to say that *no* sources of advice were available, than to cite any agency apart from GPs and clinics. Little variation was noted across either sample type or location in this ordering of available sources of advice.

Figure 8.11
Agencies providing a first recourse: Booster sample

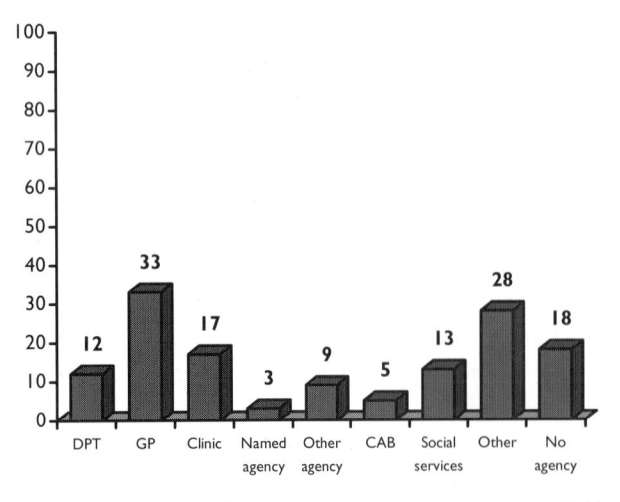

Agency	%
DPT	12
GP	33
Clinic	17
Named agency	3
Other agency	9
CAB	5
Social services	13
Other	28
No agency	18

Percentage of respondents stating that an agency was available to give advice in their city or borough, averaged across location

As indicated by Figure 8.11, responses from our booster sample broadly matched the pattern of responses from the main sample, with medical options being the most prominent recourse for drugs related advice in most people's minds. A number of important differences emerged between the samples however. The most notable difference was that a larger proportion of drug users stated that at least one agency - namely clinics - were available to give drugs related advice. This distinction between the main and booster samples can be interpreted in two ways. In the first place it can be taken as a positive sign that 'at risk' individuals such as the young and those in relatively deprived areas are more likely to be aware of a resource available to provide them with drugs related help and advice. Less positively, it can be taken as being a function of the greater likelihood of drugs clinics being sited in deprived areas. These options are not necessarily mutually exclusive.

A second distinction between the main and booster samples, and one which has no positive interpretation open to it, is the greater likelihood of booster sample respondents to state that *no* source of drugs related advice or help was available to them in their local area. To clarify this point, the majority of responses in our main sample's 'other' category referred to options such as friends or relatives. In the booster samples the predominant category in the 'other' option referred instead to 'no-one'.

In summary we found that in practice non-specialist agencies and in particular medical services were more popular with both our main and booster sample respondents as a first recourse for advice than the specialist agencies discussed earlier. The implication being that people will not naturally turn to any source of advice other than, for example, GPs and clinics. Consequently, any new agency seeking to offer a source of drugs prevention advice will need to establish a substantial public profile if it wishes to be seen as readily accessible. Given which, the delivery of new forms of drugs prevention services is likely to be as problematic in its establishment as has been the delivery of new forms of crime prevention services. We found very little meaningful locational variation with regard to this issue.

The first recourse for parents

We distinguish here between parents and the general public, because parents are in many senses a 'special' target for drugs prevention initiatives. This is largely because they are perceived as holding an almost unique position in terms of their potential for influencing drug usage in future populations. Whether they are able or willing to exercise such control and whether it is appropriate for them to attempt to do so are salient issues in themselves. Nevertheless, they do in practice form a common target for drugs prevention advice and it is consequently important to establish whether they feel themselves to have ready access to relevant sources of advice.

Since the agencies to which a parent might turn for advice are likely to differ slightly from those to which adults might turn for their own purposes, the list of agencies used for the purpose of coding this item differed slightly from that outlined above. It also proved to be rather less complete than the earlier list, since a majority of parents suggested an option other than those given in our list. Our list included GPs, teachers or schools, social workers, social services, friends or relatives and the police. Since the number of parents in the booster samples was minimal, the data discussed here are taken from the main samples only.

Figure 8.12
Agencies parents would turn to for advice if their children were using drugs: Main sample only

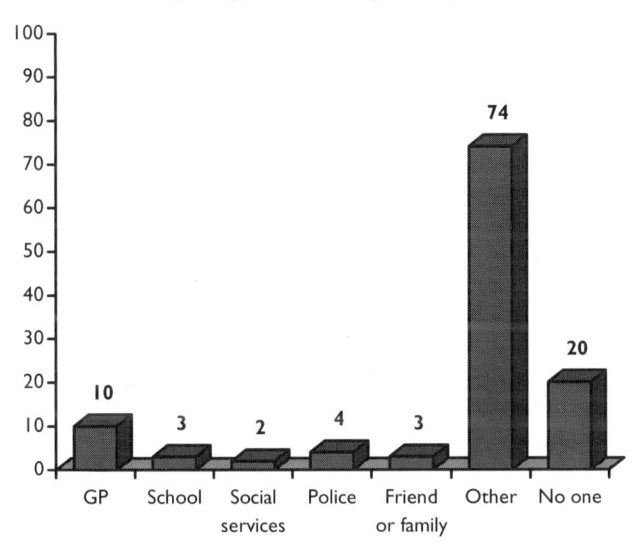

Percentage of parents who stated that they would turn to each of the agencies listed for advice if their children used illicit drugs, averaged across location

The level of confidence shown by the parents in our main sample in the availability of local agencies able to give drugs-related help and advice was lower even than that shown by our sample as a whole. In all locations only 10% or less of parents stated that they would go to one of our named agencies for advice if they became aware of their children taking drugs. Support for the named agencies was also quite polarised, with GPs again proving twice as popular as any other named agency. Police, teachers and schools were the second most popular *agencies* named and social workers or social services the least. In contrast to our findings for the sample as a whole, parents placed friends and relatives on a par with social workers or social services, with no more than 3% of parents in any location stating that they would turn to this group for help or advice.

Since up to 80% of parents in any given location named an option falling into the 'other' category, it is of some importance to describe this option more fully. In contrast to the picture noted for our samples in general, a substantial proportion of parents were spontaneously likely to mention specialist local advice agencies as their first recourse for drugs related advice. Combining the individual values for separate drugs advice centres named in the 'other' category shows that around 97% of those parents who named an advice option *not* on the list provided chose a specialist advice agency as the appropriate recourse. Of these, the single most popular option by a significant margin was the local Drugs Prevention Team. This being the case, we cannot justifiably conclude that parents are more likely than other members of the general public to have some *spontaneous* awareness of specialist agencies . We can justifiably conclude, however, that mention of the DPTs has set up a strong expectation in this particular target group that this resource should be able to provide drugs related help and information at need. Again little variation was noted between locations.

Whilst such parental interest in the role of specialist advice agencies is encouraging, it should be borne in mind that a substantial proportion of parents still felt that they had nowhere to turn to should they need advice in relation to the use of drugs by their children. To put a figure on this, we can combine the group of parents giving 'no-one' as the stated option for advice with those giving either 'no-one' or 'myself' as the relevant 'other' option. Although some locational variation was apparent, this suggests that between 15% and 25% of parents feel that there is no suitable agency in their local area to give them advice on their children's drug usage.

A number of important points can be drawn from the above discussion. Firstly, it can be seen that parents in our sample tended to feel that specialist local drugs agencies were a more accessible first recourse for advice regarding a child's drug taking than the statutory agencies which were seen as more accessible by the sample as a whole. The reluctance of parents to approach *either* one of the statutory agencies, *or* the usual unofficial social support networks such as friends or relatives, is in sharp contrast to the tendency of individuals to approach these sources of advice in relation to other problems they may have. It may stem from a defence reaction whereby individuals are reluctant to expose themselves and more particularly their children to official or social censure. This interpretation is supported by the fact that parents who were themselves drug users were significantly less likely to name a statutory agency than parents who were not drug users. If this is the correct interpretation, the data point up one potentially very useful role specialist agencies can play in providing a socially and legally 'neutral' source of information or advice.

Secondly, the data suggest that a substantial proportion of parents are either unaware of the options available or would feel reluctant to employ these options in the event that they realised that their children were taking drugs. This finding stands in rather sharp contrast with the overwhelming support shown by the parents in our sample for the desirability of drugs education for their children. This contrast suggests that whatever role we may be conceiving for parents to play in our drugs prevention initiatives, the present reality is that they themselves are likely to feel somewhat nonplussed by the issue and probably in need of somewhere to turn to for advice themselves.

In summary, parents were more likely than other members of our main, general population, sample to name specialist local agencies as a first recourse for drugs related advice. Conversely, they were less likely to name either statutory agencies such as GPs or Social Services and similarly less likely to name informal support networks such as friends or relatives as a first recourse. We suggest that this disparity might stem from the greater reluctance of parents to expose themselves and, more particularly their children to official or social forms of censure. If this is the case, then specialist advice agencies may serve a very useful function in providing a 'neutral' support and advice service for individuals unlikely to come forward for help under other circumstances. As with the more general responses discussed earlier, we found a disturbingly high proportion of parents - up to 25% in some locations - who felt that they would have *nowhere* to turn to for advice if their children started taking drugs.

Personal contact with users of advice agencies

For those respondents who had named a given *agency* as a first recourse for drugs related advice, we included an item in our interview schedule which asked them whether they actually knew of anyone who had approached the agency in question. We did not ask them to specify whether the 'person' referred to was themselves or a friend or acquaintance, although we assume the latter to have been the most popular option. Whilst the absolute numbers we are talking about here are fairly low, the distribution of responses was quite interesting. A detailed summary of this distribution is given separately for each location and both sample types in Table 8.12 in Appendix 1. A brief summary of the data, averaged across locations, is given in the text.

Figure 8.13
Contact with users of advice agencies: Main sample

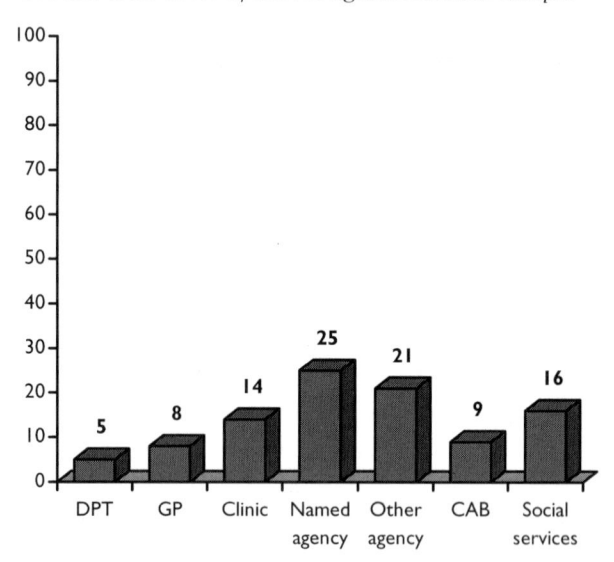

Percentage of those respondents aware of an advice agency who also knew someone who had attended an agency for drugs related advice, averaged across location

As can be seen from Figures 8.13 and 8.14 the proportion of respondents aware of someone who had attended a named advice agency was fairly small, less than 25% in most cases. Interestingly, the likelihood of knowing someone who has *attended* an agency for advice followed an inverse pattern to the likelihood that a respondent would name an agency as an available *recourse* for advice. Respondents who named a specialist local agency - although not the DPTs - as a recourse for advice were more likely to claim acquaintance with someone who had used this service than other respondents. Similarly, respondents naming Social Services - one of the least popular options - as a recourse for advice, were the second most likely to state that they knew of someone who had attended this agency for advice. Conversely, those respondents naming GPs or clinics as an available resource were much less likely to state that they knew of someone who had attended for advice.

THE PUBLIC PROFILE OF DRUGS RELATED AGENCIES

Figure 8.14
Contact with users of advice agencies: Booster sample

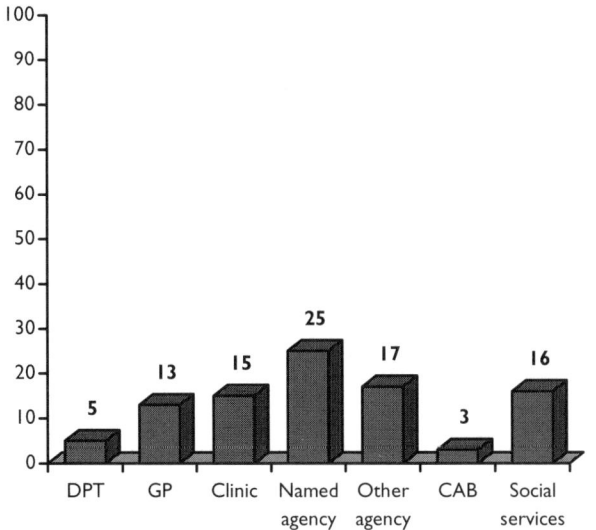

[Bar chart showing percentages: DPT 5, GP 13, Clinic 15, Named agency 25, Other agency 17, CAB 3, Social services 16]

Percentage of those respondents aware of an advice agency who also knew someone who had attended an agency for drugs related advice, averaged across location

Although numbers were small, this pattern was consistent across both samples and all locations and does not seem to be purely a function of our limited sample size, since the smaller booster samples generally showed a *higher* percentage positive response overall than their matching main samples. Unfortunately, since we did not ask all our respondents to indicate whether they knew someone who had attended a particular advice agency, we cannot judge whether the pattern noted is an indication that perceived sources of advice differ slightly from those resources which individuals *in practice* choose to go to when they feel a real need for advice. However, this would seem a plausible explanation for this finding. Note that the substantially lower values noted for association with a client of a DPT in comparison to selection of a DPT as an available source of advice suggests similarly that theory - informed by our descriptions of DPTs - exaggerates practice.

In summary, the small percentage of respondents able to name an agency available to give drugs-related advice was matched by an even smaller number of respondents who were also acquainted with someone who attended the relevant agency for advice. Since we did not ask all our respondents whether they knew someone who had attended an agency for advice we are unable to confirm which are in fact the most 'popular' agencies. However our data suggest that the agencies most likely to be *perceived* as an available resource may not be the same agencies as those most likely in practice to be *attended* for advice.

How satisfied are people with the help and advice agencies give them?

The actual effectiveness of agencies in general

People's awareness of drugs-related agencies and similarly their tendency to see these agencies as an approachable resource available to give help and advice are important factors in assessing the public profile of the agencies. It is of equal importance, however, to gauge whether those individuals who in the event attend a given agency are satisfied with the help and advice they receive. The number of respondents in our sample likely to have attended a drugs agency themselves was bound to be fairly small and so we addressed this issue obliquely by asking respondents who claimed acquaintance with the client of a drugs agency to state how satisfied they felt that their 'friend or acquaintance' had been with the advice or help they had received. Although not an ideal means of assessing levels of satisfaction, this approach did provide some useful insights into this aspect of our respondent's perceptions of drugs related agencies. Detailed summaries of the data are given for both sample types and each location in Table 8.13 in Appendix 1. Summary data, averaged across location, is provided in the text.

Figure 8.15
Respondents' perceptions of the actual effectiveness of agencies: Main sample

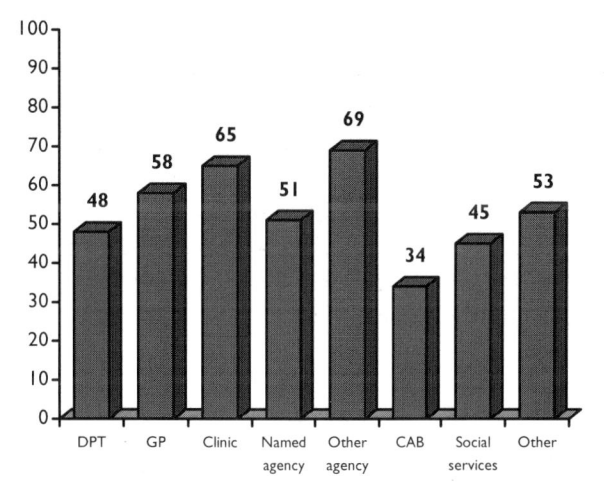

[Bar chart showing percentages: DPT 48, GP 58, Clinic 65, Named agency 51, Other agency 69, CAB 34, Social services 45, Other 53]

Percentage of respondents who knew someone who had attended an agency for drugs related advice and who also thought that this advice had been useful, averaged across location

149

As Figures 8.15 and 8.16 suggest, we found considerable variation in the levels of satisfaction attested to by those respondents acquainted with the client of any given drug agency. Significant distinctions were noted between different types of agency, between main and booster samples and between locations. Having said which, responses were in most cases fairly positive with more than 50% of respondents feeling that satisfactory help or advice had been received.

Specialist local agencies - although not the DPTs - and those options *not* on our original list, notably forms of informal social support such as friends, relatives, or the local religious minister held the most general consensus for having given useful advice. The named local agencies which *were* included in our list were regarded as the next most useful source of advice. Information regarding the actual effectiveness of the local Drugs Prevention Teams is somewhat limited. Only a small number of individuals were aware of someone who had attended a DPT for advice and amongst these individuals the response profile varied so widely across locations that no consensus view can be provided here. It is also worth noting that, as suggested earlier, the DPTs have adopted different aims and objectives, not all of which emphasise direct *individualised* help to members of the public.

Figure 8.16
Respondents' perceptions of the actual effectiveness of agencies: Booster sample

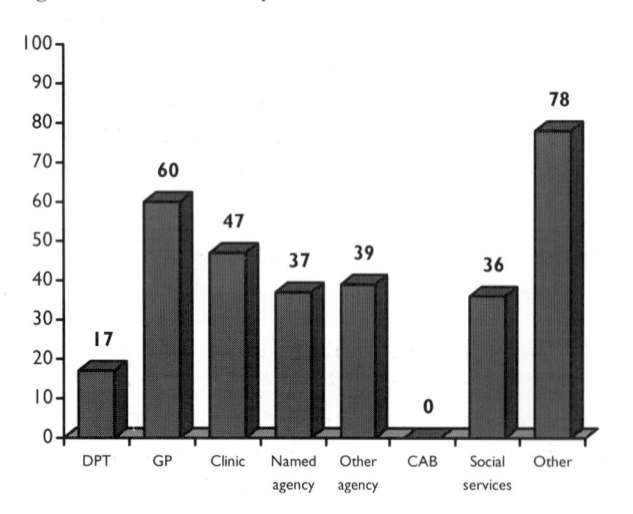

Agency	%
DPT	17
GP	60
Clinic	47
Named agency	37
Other agency	39
CAB	0
Social services	36
Other	78

Percentages of respondents who knew someone who had attended an agency for drugs related advice and who also thought that this advice had been useful, averaged across location

Responses for the high profile *national* agencies, represented here by Social Services and Citizens' Advice Bureaux, were also very variable and the consensus suggested that attitudes towards the advice they had been able to give were *not* as positive as was the case for the more specialised and locally based agencies. This is perhaps not surprising, since national agencies are not dedicated to dealing with drug usage in the same way as the local agencies discussed above. As with the DPTs, it should also be noted that responses for the Citizens' Advice Bureaux proved too limited numerically and too widely varying across location to provide any consensus view.

Satisfaction with medically oriented services, in the present case represented by drugs clinics and GPs, matched and in the main samples exceeded the levels of satisfaction noted for both specialist local agencies and more nationally known services. Some variation was again noted however, with the booster samples being generally less convinced of the usefulness of the advice given by clinics than the main samples and responses relating to GPs tending to be quite polarised across locations. Respondents in Lewisham and Bradford were significantly more satisfied with the service provided by GPs than either their main or booster sample counterparts in Nottingham and Glasgow.

Essentially, the patterns outlined above suggest that although *overall* levels of satisfaction with the advice given by agencies were fairly high, substantial variation in attitudes was apparent. Whether a response was favourable or unfavourable depended not only on the nature of the agency but also on its location and on the age and social circumstances of the respondents questioned. Since, within any given area, the provision of drug services is effectively controlled by centralised agencies which cover very large areas in population terms and employ a relatively small number of workers, the extreme levels of variation noted here may be partly a consequence of *individual* variation in service provision. To clarify this point it can be noted that in referring to a particular *agency*, a number of individual respondents may also have been referring to the same individual, or group of individuals, working at that agency. In the absence of more detailed information, the effects of such individual level variation are very hard to tease apart from broader effects such as locational variation.

The potential effectiveness of Drugs Prevention Teams

Since, as noted earlier, the DPTs are all of relatively recent standing and were also a particular concern of ours in the present context, we included an additional item in the interview schedule asking all respondents to

THE PUBLIC PROFILE OF DRUGS RELATED AGENCIES

indicate their views on the potential effectiveness of the Drugs Prevention Team in their local area. As can be seen from Figure 8.17, this rather hypothetical item drew considerable support for the DPTs from our respondents, with more than 70% of them in all locations and both samples feeling that the work of DPTs could be very or fairly effective in reducing drug usage within their local area.

Figure 8.17
Respondents' views on the potential effectiveness of DPTs

- Nottingham Main
- Nottingham Booster
- Bradford Main
- Bradford Booster
- Lewisham Main
- Lewisham Booster
- Glasgow Main
- Glasgow Booster

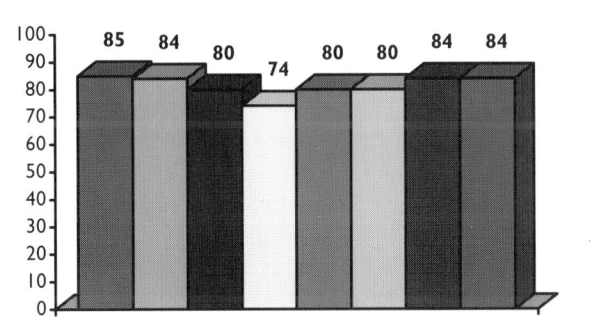

85, 84, 80, 74, 80, 80, 84, 84

Percentage of respondents stating that the drugs prevention teams could be 'very effective' or 'fairly effective'

Although all locations gave a very positive response to this item, respondents in Nottingham and Glasgow were slightly more supportive of the potential effectiveness of DPTs than both their main and booster sample counterparts in the other two locations. Given that the DPTs are a fairly recent concept and that our respondents had evidently not had much direct contact with their services, the overall levels of support for this type of service indicate that people are quite enthusiastic about the prospect of some sort of statutory drugs advice agencies operating within their local area.

In summary, although few respondents showed spontaneous awareness of the DPTs and even less had experienced any direct or indirect contact with these newly established agencies, there appeared to be a strong feeling that their work could be very useful in reducing drugs usage. In part, the level of support shown for the potential work of the agencies must have been inspired by our description of their goals and aims. This implies that people do feel that a gap in presently available drugs services exists to be filled.

Agencies which should provide a recourse

Following along the same vein as that begun above, we asked our respondents which agencies they felt *should* be providing drugs-related help and advice. This item in the interview schedule was of particular relevance since clearly our respondents did not feel very confident of being able to approach any of the listed agencies - as presently constituted - for drugs related advice. Since we used roughly the same list of options for coding purposes as we had used when asking respondents about services which they presently felt were available for providing advice, the two sets of data are in fact directly comparable. Detailed responses to the present item are given in Table 8.15 in Appendix 1. In the text, summary data is provided, again averaging across location.

Figure 8.18
Respondents' views regarding the agencies which should be responsible for giving drugs related advice: Main sample

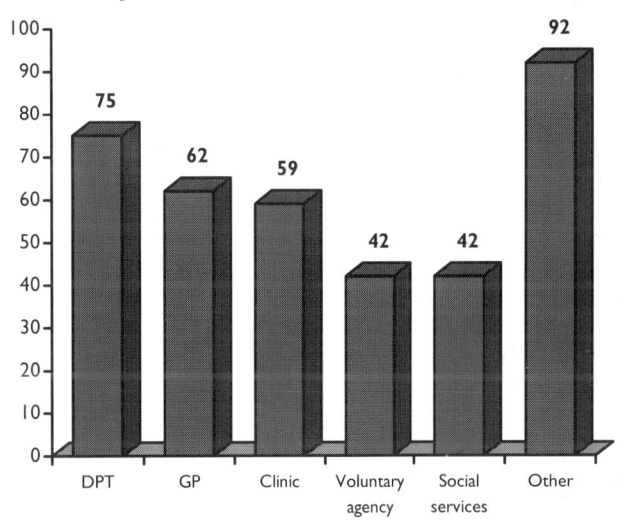

DPT 75, GP 62, Clinic 59, Voluntary agency 42, Social services 42, Other 92

Percentage of respondents who stated that each of the listed agencies should be responsible for giving drugs related help and advice, averaged across location

Considering first the responses of our main sample, summarised in Figure 8.18, it is apparent, as implied by our hypothetical item regarding the DPTs, that people feel the need for some form of specialist agency to provide local drugs help and advice. Although considerable variation was shown between locations in the precise patterns of response, specialist agencies, represented either by the DPTs or by named local agencies, proved in all cases to be the single most popular main sample option for the provision of drugs related help and advice. It is possible that the description of the DPTs given to most respondents may have set up an expectation that specialist units should be responsible

151

for providing drugs related help and advice. Nevertheless, this item did give respondents the option of rejecting this option. It is consequently apparent that our main - general population - sample were willing to give a mandate for the existence of specialist drugs prevention agencies as, at least, an initial contact for those in need of drugs related help and advice. Having said which, the medical options for advice, represented by GPs and clinics and in this instance also hospitals - mentioned by a sizeable minority of respondents in our 'other' category - were a close rival to specialist agencies, being favoured by a majority of respondents in all locations.

Social Services and other central agencies mentioned in the 'other' category found substantially less support as the appropriate service to provide drugs related help and advice in most locations, although, if we combine responses, a majority of respondents in Lewisham supported these, as did a majority of respondents in Bradford. In contrast to the rather low popularity of these national agencies as potential providers of drugs related advice and support, the most popular 'other' options for the main sample were all directly or indirectly linked to central government.

Figure 8.19
Respondents' views regarding the agencies which should be responsible for giving drugs related advice; Booster sample

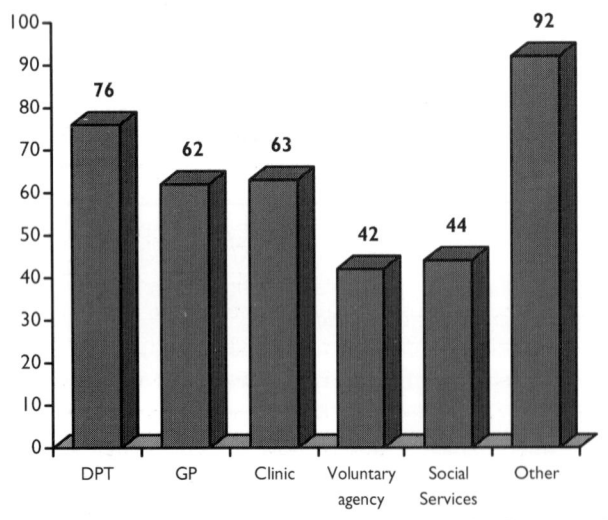

Bar chart showing: DPT 76, GP 62, Clinic 63, Voluntary agency 42, Social Services 44, Other 92.

Percentage of respondents who stated that each of the listed agencies should be responsible for giving drugs related help and advice, averaged across location

The pattern noted for our booster sample respondents was slightly different to that presented above for the main sample. In the first place, they showed a slightly higher level of support overall for the provision of drugs related help and advice by *any* named agency.

Secondly, they were less equivocal in their support for specialised drugs agencies. When we combined the list of agencies we had provided for respondents with those suggested by the respondents themselves, specialist units were the single most popular agency option in all booster locations.

Also in contrast to the main sample, the informal support networks provided by friends and relatives were the most popular *overall* option in all locations except Lewisham. Since our booster sample respondents did not show a comparable tendency to state that friends and relatives were *actually* available for support and advice, this response may simply be representative of a predictable lack of faith in 'official' agencies amongst young individuals in relatively deprived areas. Other patterns of response shown by the booster sample matched more closely those for the main sample, with GPs and clinics rivalling specialist agencies and Social Services and similar centralised agencies being rather less favoured.

In summary, although the pattern of responses we found when asking our respondents to state which services should be available as a first recourse for people seeking drugs-related help and advice broadly matched their responses when asked to state which drugs advice agencies were available locally, there was one notable exception. This exception is a particularly important one, since it suggests that a majority of the general population, as represented by our main sample, felt that there should be specialist drugs agencies. What format they feel these agencies should take is unclear, since we did not ask detailed questions about structure or funding. However from the general profile of main sample responses it seems likely that respondents would favour some form of statutory or at least centrally funded agency. More research into this issue would be desirable, since it is clearly of importance to match services both to the expectations and needs of the public. Our booster sample - representing younger adults in relatively deprived areas - although still favouring specialist agencies above a range of other agency options, were more likely than the main sample to feel that non-agency options were the most appropriate. Since they were generally more inclined to rely on informal forms of support over the whole set of available options, their views seem best interpreted as indicating a general lack of confidence in 'official' sources of support.

Co-ordination between agencies

Whilst issues surrounding the identity and effectiveness of agencies providing drugs related advice are of primary importance, there also remains the question of co-ordination. If a fairly diffuse range of services is required, as suggested in the introduction to this chapter, there must be some level of contact *between* agencies to ensure appropriate transfer or referral of clients from one agency to another. This is not an issue which was addressed in any great detail in the present survey, but one item was included which dealt with the specific issue of whether the *police* should work closely with other agencies to reduce levels of drug abuse. Specifically, respondents were asked to indicate how *useful* they felt it would be if the police were to work with other help and advice agencies with regard to drug usage. A summary of these data is given in Table 8.16 in Appendix 1.

Figure 8.20
Respondents' views regarding the usefulness of co-operation between the police and drugs related agencies

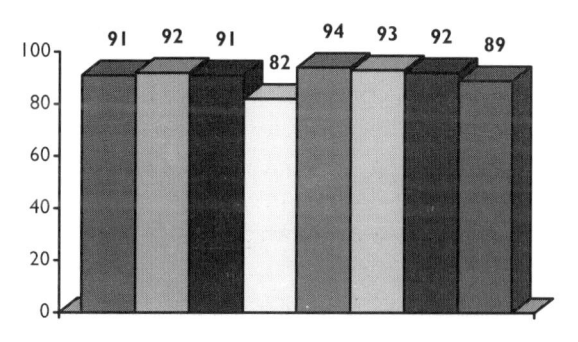

Percentage of respondents stating that it would be 'very useful' or 'fairly useful' for police to work with drugs related advice agencies

The responses outlined in Figure 8.20 above give a very clear indication of the public's support for police co-ordinating their actions with drugs related agencies. Over 80% of respondents in both samples and all locations thought that such co-ordination would be very or fairly useful. Little in the way of locational variation was noted, although Bradford's booster sample was significantly less convinced by the viability of such co-ordination. Although we cannot go into the issue in depth here, it is worth noting also that the drug users in both main and booster samples showed even *higher* levels of support for a co-ordination between the police and other drugs related agencies even than other respondents.

In summary, the idea that police should co-ordinate their actions with other drugs related agencies found almost unanimous favour with our respondents in both main and booster samples. This gives a very clear indication of the public's likely attitudes on this issue. It also blends well with their general attitude towards drug users, as outlined in the last chapter, in that whilst they clearly regard drug suppliers as appropriate targets for interventionist police action, they tend to be less convinced that this is an appropriate response to drug users.

Summary of Chapter 8

Levels of spontaneous awareness of drug-related agencies were rather low in both main and booster samples. Some prompting increased substantially the numbers of respondents in all samples recalling the existence of DPTs and might also have increased awareness of other agencies, had this option been available in the questionnaire. Nevertheless, it remained the case that only a *minority* of respondents were aware of *any* drugs related agency, including the DPTs. Also in a minority were the number of respondents in all samples who felt that any of the named statutory or voluntary agencies were available in their area to provide drugs related advice. Many people seemed to feel that they would have to rely on their own resources, or those of friends and neighbours, if they were to be confronted with any drug related problem.

Producing a network of agencies which different members of the public will be happy to approach and which have a sufficient public profile for parents and others to be aware of their existence will clearly be a considerable task. Generic statutory agencies such as Social Services have, of course, the advantage of considerable visibility, but because of their other duties, they may not be as appropriate for those most at risk of drug usage and certainly the public is inclined to view them as inappropriate in the case of drugs related help and advice. Conversely, medically oriented agencies which also have high visibility but which would be easily overloaded by any further claims on their services are strongly favoured by the public in this context.

Once respondents were made aware of the existence of DPTs they had fairly strong expectations concerning both their responsibility for helping individual drug users and their likely effectiveness in reducing drugs misuse. These expectations may not be consonant with the DPTs' actual aims and objectives, which may involve working with relevant professionals, rather than an individualised service to the general public. However, they do emphasise our respondents' preference for some form of statutory and specialised drugs agency. Consequently a suitable compromise solution to the provision of drugs related help and advice might be this type of agency, perhaps more closely oriented to the public's preference for individual support.

Certainly this *type* of agency found the greatest level of public support within our survey and with judicious advertising might also attain a suitable level of visibility. How such agencies might be structured and funded is a rather thorny issue. Presently, for example, the vast majority of specialist drugs agencies are voluntary agencies, yet our respondents in relation to a number of drugs related issues clearly expressed a preference for centrally funded forms of drugs help and advice. Considerable further research is therefore needed to untangle this issue and to specify exactly what kinds of advice and help people in different roles need and what mechanisms would be most effective for the delivery of drugs advice both in terms of prevention and harm reduction.

It is quite likely, from the discrepancies in the survey results between parents and those acting as friends to the clients of drugs agencies, that different mechanisms may be required for different groups in society. Parents, for example, felt much *less* happy than other members of the general public with the option of obtaining advice from both 'official' bodies and from informal social support networks such as friends and relatives. Similarly, our booster sample of young people from relatively deprived areas felt rather more disenchanted with a whole range of 'official' services than their main sample counterparts. To complicate the issue still further, it is clear that the aims and requirements of prevention and harm reduction are not necessarily always fully compatible, either at the individual level or at the level of the population as a whole. Whatever service provision is made in the future, it must take into account the full complexity of this issue.

Although the present range of drugs-related agencies was not highly visible, nor considered readily accessible, a substantial minority of respondents, notably in the booster samples, were aware of someone who had actually attended an agency in relation to drugs usage. The general consensus of these individuals appeared to be that reasonably good advice had been given to drug users by the agencies. This suggests that the difficulty people felt they would have in gaining drug-related advice lay in deciding which agency to approach and how to gain access to it, rather than in any lack of confidence in the type of advice an agency might provide. It is worth noting, however, that levels of satisfaction with any advice obtained varied greatly dependent on location, sample type and type of agency.

Finally, it seems that whichever agencies are available to provide drugs-related help and advice, people feel that it would be of value for external agencies such as the police to work in close co-ordination with them. This view reflects both our respondents' concern that some concerted effort is made to do something about the 'drugs problem' and their general receptiveness to non-punitive forms of control for drug usage such as drugs education.

Chapter 9

DRUGS CONTROL POLICIES AND THE PUBLIC'S VIEWS ON LEGALISATION

The preceding chapters considered the prevalence of drug usage and the public's perceptions of both drug usage and drugs prevention. The present chapter aims to provide some context for the foregoing discussion, by giving a broader overview of the actuality of drugs prevention and by considering the levels of support shown by our respondents for an as yet largely untried method of drugs prevention, namely legalisation. Our purpose in addressing these topics is not to provide any very detailed or definitive account of drugs prevention methods. Nor are we attempting to provide any solutions to the 'drugs problem'. What we *are* hoping to do is to provide some insight into the inherent complexity of the drugs issue.

Before considering any specific *methods* of drugs prevention, it is worth looking at the *aims* which lie behind this response to drug usage. As has been implied earlier, drugs prevention is by no means a unitary phenomenon. Its diverse nature is a function not only of the different aspects shown by the 'drugs problem', but also of the different *attitudes* adopted by those engaged in the business of prevention. The effect of attitudinal changes on the historical vagaries of British drugs policies is an issue which has been addressed in some detail by a number of authors (cf. Dorn and South 1987, Berridge 1990, Whynes and Bean 1991). In the following discussion we are concerned more immediately with outlining the basic conceptual models of drug usage which have been adopted and the implications each model has for the goals pursued in drugs prevention.

Models of drug usage

The conceptual models of drug usage which lie behind our attitudes towards drugs prevention are of considerable importance. Where models are logically distinct, they can imply both different end goals for drugs prevention and, more immediately, different methods of prevention. It is therefore worth ensuring that the structure of these models is made *explicit,* notably when they are acting as determinants of actual drugs policy. If our models of drug usage are *not* clearly delineated or if they act only as tacit motivators of policy we will be unable to determine either what constitutes a 'success' in drugs prevention or what tactics we should adopt in dealing with drug usage and drug users.

This is not to say that in practice a range of measures deriving from distinct views of drug usage cannot at any level be 'mixed and matched'. Many of the possible measures overlap between models and any given agency may find that its immediate purposes are best served by adopting a range of methods. What is implied, however, is that if our overall, long-term policy towards drug usage is to be a coherent one, we must determine *which* ultimate goal we are pursuing. There can be no completely objective solution to the 'drugs problem' since the goal of drugs prevention is determined by our conceptual start point. To illustrate this, we outline below three prominent and distinct conceptual models of drug usage and indicate their possible implications for drugs prevention.

Model 1: The drug user as 'victim'

The conception of the drug user as a 'victim' is a model which is predominantly European in origin. It has two aspects which are of relevance to drugs prevention. The first is that the user is seen largely as an 'innocent party' in need of help. The second, which stems logically from this, is that there must be an 'aggressor' to provide the victimisation. Two common versions of the 'aggressor' in this model are:

- the 'user/dealer'
- the 'drug baron' dealer.

The user/dealer model of the aggressor entails a localised, weak economic view of victimisation. For example, drug users are seen as the victims of their own peer groups or of local dealers who are themselves drug users. Both dealer and 'user' in this model are consequently a victim of human weakness - whether chemical or moral - and the profits of drug dealing are assumed to be retained within a local cycle of drug usage. In prevention terms, this model of victimisation implies a largely treatment-oriented approach towards the reduction of drug usage. Having said which, it should be noted that the model suffers from a degree of internal inconsistency on this issue. Users should be treated and dealers punished, but it is not always clear *what* should occur when the same person serves both roles. Treatment within the criminal justice system is not, for instance, always a coherent option. In terms of broader policy issues, the model implies that prevention is best organised by local organisations for local needs. Variants on this approach to drug usage provided support for the medical model of drugs prevention which was peculiar to Britain in period 1940s-60s.

The 'drug baron' view of the aggressor in this model is a more recent view of drug usage as a form of victimisation. Variants on this theme supported the 'war on drugs' form of policy extant in Britain from around the 1980s. This approach views drug dealing as operating from a broader international base. The emphasis is shifted away from local weak economic models of drug usage and drug dealing to models in which dealing operates at an international level, run by individuals or organisations who are not themselves drug users, but who make significant amounts of money out of exploiting human weakness. In prevention terms, the 'drug baron' type of model avoids, at least superficially, the tension created by labelling the same groups of individuals as both users and dealers.

Both of the 'victim' type views of drug usage support treatment and rehabilitation as a natural component of behaviour towards drug users. However, the 'drug baron' form of the model, in practice, emphasises penal aspects of control to a greater extent than the user/dealer model. It also necessarily supports a more active role for *central* government, since the drugs problem is seen as having national and international rather than local roots. This aspect of the model is, incidentally, more than a simple account of where drugs come from, since the 'drug baron' view also de-emphasises the role of demand and emphasises instead the *creation* of demand. To illustrate the practical implications of these features of the model, any emphasis on demand reduction may, on this view, take second place to preventing the external creation of demand. At the individual level there is also the possibility that low-level user/dealers may be caught up in the rhetoric of 'evil drug barons' and perhaps dealt with inappropriately.

Model 2: The drug user as 'criminal'

The concept that drug users are criminals is one which has historically dominated US thinking on drug usage to a greater extent than European, and in particular British thinking. Although it bears obvious similarities to the 'aggressor' aspects of the victim model outlined above, it is logically distinct in assuming for the drug *user* a greater proportion of the responsibility or 'blame' for their own drug usage.

Fundamentally, this model, as is apparent from the title we have given it, equates drug usage with any other illicit activity. Although in practice treatment and rehabilitation may form part of the approach taken towards drug usage - as is increasingly the case in the US - these aspects are under-emphasised in comparison to penal sanctions. In drugs prevention terms, the user is regarded as in control of their actions and hence likely to respond to punitive forms of deterrence. The most appropriate aims of drugs prevention are consequently seen as oriented towards this form of control.

Unlike the victim model, the criminal model does not suffer from any major tensions generated by the need to distinguish between user and dealer. What is appropriate for one is, broadly, appropriate for the other. As will be seen in later sections of the chapter this view of drug users, whilst theoretically coherent, may have similar practical disadvantages to the 'drug baron' model in terms of dealing with drug usage within the criminal justice system. It is also, in general terms, less likely to provide treatment-oriented approaches as a *necessary* backdrop to any sanctions. Although the victim and criminal models are distinct both in this latter respect and in terms of where they place the emphasis on responsibility for drug usage, it should be noted that, to date, penalties for illicit drug usage have formed the backdrop to any approach, however treatment oriented.

Model 3: The drug user as 'legitimate consumer'

Defining the drug user as a 'legitimate consumer' is a concept which differs markedly from the above models. Firstly, it has not been adopted by any nation state in recent history. Secondly, it implies a total lack of penal control in relation to drug users. The drug user is seen as expressing his or her right to free choice in terms of leisure activities and consequently is not viewed as an appropriate target of any sanctions.

Two basic variants of the model exist. The first regards the drug user as exercising the rights of a legitimate consumer and similarly sees the drug *dealer* as fulfilling a legitimate economic role. The second variant sees the drug user as exercising a legitimate right, but disbars the dealer from a legitimate role by defining dealing as an incitement to self-harm. The latter form of the model, incidentally, runs into the 'user/dealer' problem of delineating the single most appropriate goal for prevention when one person serves both functions. Punitive approaches to the 'dealer' may, for example, prove to be incompatible with treatment oriented approaches towards the person in their role as 'user'.

Whilst harm reduction and treatment oriented forms of prevention are the hallmark of the 'legitimate consumer' model, the extent to which these goals are seen as a policy requirement also varies in different formulations of this concept. In some formulations, drug users are seen not only as personally responsible for their own drug usage but *also* as personally responsible for coping with the effects of such usage. In other formulations, the state is seen as being in some respect responsible for harm reduction, either on humanitarian grounds or as a result of practical considerations relating to the likely effects of drug usage on the population as a whole. In contrast to both the 'victim' and 'criminal' models, drug usage is nevertheless seen as a pragmatic rather than as a strictly moral or legal problem.

In summary, three basic attitudes can be adopted towards drug usage and drug users, each of which implies a distinct mix of goals and measures for drugs prevention. The first model sees drug users as 'victims' and drug dealers as 'aggressors'. The ultimate goal of drugs prevention is seen as preventing both supply and usage. The appropriate measures to be taken are oriented towards treatment and rehabilitation in the case of users and towards penal sanctions in the case of *dealers*. The second model of drug usage views both dealer and user as 'criminal'. Whilst the primary goal of drugs prevention is also to prevent both supply and usage, penal forms of deterrence are seen as being the most appropriate measure to take in *both* cases. The third model of drug usage interprets drug users as being legitimate consumers of a leisure resource. In some formulations of this model drug dealers are also seen as legitimate. On the basis of this model drugs prevention is either regarded as completely oblique to the real issue of drug usage or is regarded as having harm reduction or some other pragmatic end as its primary goal.

Developing drugs prevention

The models outlined above are deliberately simplified to allow a clear separation of their possible implications for drugs prevention. Nevertheless, the choice between victim, criminal and legitimate consumer is a real one and forms the basis for heated debate in the drugs prevention literature. How one goes about determining *which* conceptual model to adopt and hence which goals to pursue is also a matter for debate. The 'best' model may be that which is seen to be most closely related to the actuality of drug usage. On the other hand, given that our political views are democratic, it could equally be argued that we should simply follow the model which best represents the majority view regarding drug usage, whether or not this view is an accurate one. A range of distinct views and compromise solutions can readily be developed by anyone considering how to conceptualise drug usage.

One factor complicating the theoretical debate is that whilst *a priori* assumptions regarding drug usage may be a matter of choice, the effectiveness of individual methods of prevention is not. This is not, of course, a problem unique to drugs prevention; pragmatic considerations and political, social or moral viewpoints are often uneasy companions. Assuming, however, that our main aim is tied in some degree to drugs prevention, it is of some importance that we balance the often diverse requirements of models and methods. Whilst in the absence of any overt attempt to do so the likely effectiveness of particular drugs prevention measures may still inform the conceptual model we adopt, the chosen model is equally likely to inform the measures we use, regardless of their effectiveness.

The following discussion will consider available data regarding the *likely* success of a variety of prevention methods in reducing both the supply of and the demand for drugs. For each method we will outline the agencies most likely to be involved, the methods used and the particular problems likely to be faced. Where relevant information is available we will also consider empirical data relevant to the *actual* success of particular prevention measures in decreasing drug usage or supply. Whilst no attempt will be made to tie the methods considered to one or more of the conceptual models of drug usage outlined above, it should be borne in mind that different models in practice support different methods of prevention. Equally, whatever the favoured model of drug usage, it is unlikely that any one method of prevention can effectively be adopted or discarded in isolation from policy decisions regarding the others. This is a part of the problem we face in balancing methods of drugs prevention with conceptual models of drug usage.

The data outlined in previous chapters is also of relevance to the following discussion. In particular, the views of both drug users and those members of the general public who are not themselves drug users are of interest. We will not, however, attempt to draw any very detailed links between the two sets of data. This is, in part, because we wish to avoid biasing the discussion towards any particular conceptual model. It is also because, although clear preferences did emerge, our survey suggested that the public in fact shows considerable support for *all* of the diverse measures outlined here.

Drugs control policies can be categorised according to whether their major emphasis is on the reduction of supply or on the reduction of demand. The ordering of the discussion below follows this distinction. We would emphasise, however, that policy options for supply and demand are in practice interlinked and the effectiveness of one policy may interact with the effectiveness of another, whatever the basic rationale behind the measure used. Finally, it should be noted that in the case of existing prevention measures our focus in this discussion tends to be on difficulties rather than successes. This is necessarily the case. Most, if not all, drugs prevention measures work to some extent, the question is how *well* they work and this is primarily a function of the extent and nature of any associated problems.

Controlling supply

Reducing supplies at the point of origin

A number of methods exist for reducing the supply of drugs at their point of export. These tend to involve an eclectic set of organisations including police, Customs and Excise and both national and international legal services. The most common methods adopted are:

- crop substitution
- crop eradication
- provision of support for international efforts to curb the production and trafficking of drugs.

Although promising in theory, all of the above options are in practice problematic. Crop eradication and substitution are expensive measures and need to be continued *ad infinitum* if they are to be effective. If crop *eradication* is used on a short term basis, the effects on supply will also be temporary, since new drug crops will inevitably replace those eradicated. If crop *substitution* is used on a limited basis, the same applies and there is the additional problem that the measure could prove counter-productive, for example by providing fertile ground for farmers who have been given new expectations of wealth.

The effectiveness of international efforts to curb drug trafficking depends on the degree of international consensus which can be achieved. A number of economic and political factors militate against such consensus being complete. Although their precise identity has changed over time, all the countries which have been major exporters of drugs in general and opiate based drugs in particular, have to date been distinguished by the weakness of their economies. Drug crops can be a major source of income not only to poor farmers, but also to poor governments. By way of illustration, the Bolivian Minister of the Interior interviewed by the Guardian newspaper in 1986 noted that for the previous year 50% of Bolivia's export earnings were derived from cocaine. Malyon (1985) observed that for the same year cannabis production contributed more to Jamaican foreign exchange earnings than all other exports combined. In the absence of expensive long term crop substitution programmes, countries in this position would be committing economic suicide in abiding by any international agreement to curb drug trafficking.

Even assuming international agreement regarding drugs control, political interests can run counter to an effective reduction in drug trafficking. Dorn and South (1987), for example, cite a number of instances in which state controlled organisations such as the CIA, involved in promoting their own country's political goals, coincidentally allowed those groups in other countries most closely tied to the drugs trade to rise to a position of power. More overtly *positive* political goals may also result in a failure to curb the drugs trade. The promotion of licit trade between countries can, for example, result in an incidental increase in *illicit* trade.

> **In summary**, although curbing drug supplies at their point of origin is an attractive proposition it is subject to a number of practical difficulties. The most salient of these are that it relies on a level of international consensus and support which is, as a function of the drugs trade itself, likely in practice to be lacking. Even where this difficulty can be overcome, the nature of reliable interventions is such that they are likely to prove extremely expensive.

Controlling supplies at the point of entry

Whilst a range of distinct agencies, including Customs and Excise, may be engaged in controlling the export of drugs from their point of origin, controlling drug supplies at their point of entry is explicitly a Customs control measure. A variety of methods exist to further this end, which are neither mutually exclusive nor centred on precisely the same aim. Amongst these, the most prominent methods are:

- monitoring the entry *into* the country of people and goods
- collecting information regarding drug trafficking
- monitoring the exit *out* of the country of profits derived from drug dealing

As with control measures aimed at the export of drugs, the above measures are impressive in terms of their *potential* effectiveness, but rather less impressive in terms of their *actual* likelihood of working. Monitoring the entry of goods or people into the country is problematic for a variety of reasons. At the most basic level, the influx of people and goods into the country takes place at a rate which makes it impractical to monitor *all* entries for possible importation of illicit drugs. Even were it possible to monitor a greater number of such entries, the advisability of this measure is questionable, since the resultant slowing of commercial and human traffic would be likely to prove unpopular. In recognition of this fact, Customs and Excise tend instead to target such types of surveillance on those people and goods which either detailed profiling or intelligence information suggest are the most likely candidates for the importation of drugs.

Whilst obviously representing a more realistic response to controlling importation by courier or goods transport, this form of directed response is not without its own problems. In the first case, exporters of drugs are as likely to be aware of the value of profiling and information gathering as Customs and Excise. Consequently, the profile of drugs couriers or goods used as a cover for drugs is likely to be fluid rather than static and a proportion at least of any information gathered is likely to be *mis*information. In a similar vein, exporters of drugs will actively be seeking to ensure that those seizures most likely to be effected are those targeting couriers or amounts of drugs which are expendable to them. Any low level seizure may even prove counter-productive, providing either a diversion from wider scale exports or a warning signal for the exporter. In addition, successful seizures may incur political difficulties such as those attendant on arresting the nationals of other countries.

Customs and Excise are of course also aware of the difficulties attached to low-level seizures and do not necessarily regard such seizures as an end in themselves. Instead, they may be used to promote the second response outlined above, namely gathering information on the broader picture of drug trafficking. Such intelligence measures have over the last twenty or so years become an increasingly prominent aspect of the methods used by Customs. However, even setting aside the problem of misinformation outlined above, a number of difficulties also apply to intelligence gathering as a response to the entry of drugs into a country.

Information relating to drug trafficking can be derived either indirectly, by observing patterns of drug dealing, or directly, from informants. Given the international nature of the type of patterns most relevant to customs control, *indirect* methods of intelligence gathering require a level of international support which, as noted earlier, may well not exist. Those countries best placed to provide information are likely also to be those countries benefiting most from the drugs trade. Even were this not the case, a successful diversion of drug traffic away from one country is likely to result in its transferral to a second country. Given which, some reluctance may be noted even on the part of *non*-drug producing nations in helping the customs inquiries of another nation.

Moving to the *direct* sources of information represented by individuals and groups with some involvement in the drugs trade, the difficulties centre not around gaining access to the information, but around its likely accuracy and what, in the event, can in fact be done with it. Those individuals most likely to impart information - for example individuals 'planted' within a supply chain or genuinely acting as low level couriers - are those *least* likely to have any information worth imparting. When accurate and important information *is* obtained from such individuals it is only of value if apprehending higher level dealers or seizing large quantities of drugs is a viable proposition. The viability of either end result is likely again to depend on the level of international co-operation which can be achieved.

Even assuming that different nations *are* willing to work in close concert on this issue, it is not clear what the long term effects of intelligence based methods will be. As with methods such as crop eradication and crop-substitution, we are ultimately faced with what is commonly called the "push down/pop up" problem of drugs control. If one high level dealer is detained, another will step in to take his or her place. Ironically, this substitute may even have been the person or organisation providing the information leading to the detention of the original supplier. If we are referring to a seizure of drugs rather than people it can readily be seen that replacements will become available fairly rapidly unless we have also successfully curbed the production of drugs, an aim which, as seen in the last section, is in itself not unproblematic.

The final method of customs control we consider - monitoring drugs related profits exiting from the country - is not one which is presently engaged in to any very significant degree. However, it has been suggested as a potentially more viable proposition than more direct methods of curbing drug supplies (Neville 1993). A belief in its potential effectiveness rests on two points. First that it is, broadly speaking, less reliant on international consensus than other methods of control.

Second that it reduces the profits of drug dealing at source and hence provides a primary deterrent to drug dealers. The function of monitoring the movement of profits is similarly twofold. It both allows drugs related profits to be seized and provides information on the destination of those profits and hence on the identity of higher level drug dealers.

Whilst in principle having these advantages, this method is in practice likely to be outweighed by as many disadvantages as the more traditional methods. The major disadvantage in this case being the rather fluid nature of the 'profits' concerned. When a seizure of illicit drugs is made, no-one is in any doubt about its identity. The link between assumed 'profits' and the illicit activity itself is less direct and hence easier to conceal or deny. The tracking and seizure of any profits is also in itself problematic whether or not their identity is in dispute. The profits considered by the majority of proponents of this form of control are naturally monetary rather than profits 'in kind'. Although for lower level transactions any money exchanged will be in the form of physical currency, transport of money, in contrast to transport of goods, need not be accomplished as a physical exchange. Particularly across international boundaries, it may instead be achieved by computer aided transfer. Seizure of profits at this level would require an extremely swift and well-justified response. Any mistakes would be potentially costly both in legal terms and in terms of international relations.

Finally, it is important to note that even *successful* customs efforts are not without their drawbacks. Other aspects of this issue are discussed later in this chapter. Here we consider only the *economic* necessity of balancing effective control against the necessary expenditure of resources. In strictly economic terms the cost of drugs control must be less than the cost of failing to control. Whilst the 'cost of failure' is difficult to measure in purely financial terms, the likely cost of success can be readily illustrated. At the height of the 'war on drugs', for example, when customs control measures were placed at a premium, annual expenditure on customs control was estimated to be around £23 million (Wagstaff and Maynard 1988). At roughly the same time, estimates suggested that the most successful of customs efforts intercepted no more than 10% of all drugs imported into any given country (Lawrence 1986). Whilst both figures are now somewhat out of date, their accuracy was not disputed at the time and they provide considerable insight into the likely cost/benefit ratio of any determined customs control efforts. Even making the generous and almost certainly unrealistic assumption that customs efforts have improved by as much as 500% in the intervening six years, with very little increase in expenditure, we would be looking at spending a fairly substantial sum without fully solving the drugs problem.

Since Lawrence's work, little empirical research has been directed at assessing the actual effectiveness of customs control measures. In part, this is because it is now recognised that the task may be an unrealistically complex one. Instead, a number of econometric models have been used to judge the *potential* effectiveness of customs control measures. One very detailed model is given in the Wagstaff and Maynard report referred to above. This model used data on the heroin market to argue that a doubling of the interception rate achieved by Customs and Excise would result in an increase in street price, taken as a proxy for availability, of only one quarter. The point being that increased expenditure is unlikely to be matched by comparable returns in supply reduction. The link between increased expenditure on control and decreased availability of drugs is not a direct one.

The type of cost/benefit calculations outlined above are not uncontroversial. In the first place, the tacit assumption behind such models is that economic considerations are paramount. Secondly, they assume the validity of particular methods of measuring the effectiveness of customs control. The measures used are necessarily simplistic. Lawrence's estimates, for example, were based on the quantity of drugs seized, Wagstaff and Maynard's estimates on a presumed link between street price and availability. Both types of estimate may be flawed. More importantly, a quantitative analysis of the effectiveness of customs control may simply be a logically untenable goal. Customs control measures are not independent of the efforts of other agencies and consequently their success may be 'invisible'. Similarly, aims such as information gathering are designed to have a long term rather than an immediate impact and consequently their effectiveness may be concealed by models considering only the the short term picture.

Notwithstanding all of this, the acid test of any measure oriented towards the control of supply must be the ease of access anyone wishing to use a drug has to the drug of their choice. Whatever the likely success of future customs control measures, our data suggest on this basis that the success of past measures has been somewhat limited. Britain is not at present a large domestic producer of controlled drugs, yet the vast majority of our drug users reported little or no problem of availability. Where any consistent shortage of supply was reported, the casualties seemed to be minor drugs and in particular cannabis. This is a common finding (cf. Unell 1991). Cannabis is a fairly easy drug to seize, being bulky and consequently difficult to conceal. Unfortunately, it is a rather low priority drug both in terms of its street value and in terms of the levels of harm it is likely to inflict.

In summary, the potential response of Customs and Excise to supply control has a broad base, ranging from seizures of both illicit drugs and the couriers of these drugs, through information gathering to the sequestration of any profits derived from drug dealing. Unfortunately, the extent and sophistication of efforts to deter the importation of illicit drugs is beset with an equally broad range of potential problems. Amongst the most salient of these problems are the level of international co-operation required for the success of most supply control ventures and the ready replaceability of both the dealers and the drugs themselves. Assessing the effectiveness of customs control is difficult. It is particularly difficult if we wish to assess the effect of customs control in isolation from other methods of supply reduction. With this caveat in mind, available estimates (e.g Wagstaff and Maynard 1988) suggest that in cost/benefit terms past efforts towards customs control may not have been an optimum form of supply control in economic terms. Our own estimates of availability would support this picture in terms which are less closely associated with economic considerations. The likely effectiveness of future efforts towards customs control remains, of course, a matter for debate.

Controlling distribution

Once illicit drugs have entered the country, supply control becomes a matter of controlling their distribution to the end user. This aspect of drugs control is one which is most prominently the responsibility of the police rather than other control oriented agencies such as Customs and Excise. In making this distinction we are not implying that the division of labour is absolute. Police officers are frequently seconded to help customs control ventures and similarly customs control may provide information to help the policing of drugs distribution. Nevertheless, the domains covered by the two agencies are broadly separate.

In the past, the distinction between the two forms of supply control could be adequately summarised by noting that whilst the primary focus of customs control lay in seizing the drugs themselves, the primary focus of police efforts lay in seizing the distributors. This distinction is becoming increasingly less clear-cut as drugs prevention develops, as is the precise role of the police in more general terms. In line with other developments in policing, Kleiman and Smith (1990) note that the range of drugs related police activity now covers a broad array of methods, not all of which are even strictly oriented towards controlling drugs distribution. To give some flavour of the diversity of these methods we list below those activities which apply now to British policing as well as to the US pattern of policing Kleiman and Smith were more specifically concerned with:

- Observation based arrests
- Undercover operations
- Collation of forensic evidence
- Electronic surveillance
- Development of design oriented responses
- Community based information gathering and support
- Drugs education

For the purposes of the following discussion, we will categorise methods such as the above under the following headings:

- direct intervention
- information gathering
- mobilising the community
- provision of drugs prevention advice

Since only the first three of these are closely associated with supply control, we will deal with these in the greatest detail here. Police responses to demand reduction and the provision of drugs education are dealt with in later sections of this chapter.

Historically, direct intervention has been the most prominent response of the police to supply side drugs control. Such interventions have also tended to concentrate largely on retail level operations, since these are the most accessible, at least in terms of community based policing. As such, they are clearly unlikely to be responsible for seizing any very large absolute quantities of drugs. However, they are of importance in disrupting local supply chains and, at least temporarily, removing dealers from the market and addicts from the street. Although valuable in both these respects, retail level policing runs into the same problem of replaceability noted for customs control measures. Removing either addicts or dealers from the streets is a task of sorcerer's apprentice type proportions. As dealers and addicts are removed from the street new dealers and addicts step in to take their place with remarkable speed and regularity. If policing is particularly successful the courts are consequently faced with increasing demands on their time and prisons or community programmes become overloaded, whilst in all probability the number of dealers and hence the availability of drugs remains in the long term quite static.

A further difficulty is noted by Dorn and South (1986), who suggest that successful police work may alienate a population which is becoming increasingly involved in this form of alternative economy. As our own survey attests, many members of the public have an acquaintanceship with drug users. A number of these may also have indirect contact with at least low-level drug dealers. Any heavily interventionist approach towards policing may therefore serve only to give a sizeable minority of the public a rather negative view of police action. In addition, the demographic profile of drug distribution may result in a targeting of police action which itself may be disapproved of by the general public. Those areas with a particularly prominent drugs market tend to be those which are economically the most deprived. As a consequence they are often also those areas with a substantial proportion of ethnic minorities. Even well intentioned retail level policing is as a result likely to come under attack for racism or for differentially targeting poor areas. Since the police are quite heavily reliant on the support of the community any loss of public support would be a very unfortunate side effect of policing drug networks.

Rather than aiming at strictly interventionist measures, the police could direct their efforts instead at containing or directing the drugs market. 'Inconvenience policing' can be a very effective method of shaping the market, preventing the development of more organised drugs networks and drawing boundaries for smaller scale drugs operations. However, to the public such inherently practical approaches are likely to smack of 'giving in' to the dealers. Any resulting public relations problem is likely to be particularly acute in those areas where drug dealing is common. People living in such areas may, quite justifiably, want to know why *their* area has been chosen to become a 'no go area' for drugs policing.

In contrast to the low level forms of policing outlined above, the larger scale initiatives which tend to be the consequence of information gathering exercises *are* likely to gain substantial public support. A relatively large haul of cocaine, seized as the consequence of perhaps a year's painstaking work, generally hits the local if not national headlines. Whilst good for public relations, however, it is less clear that such hauls are a viable response in practice. Information gathering is a very time consuming and consequently a very expensive task. It is also a fairly specialist task and, until the recent introduction of suitable computer facilities, one which most police forces were inadequately equipped to deal with. As the sophistication of drugs networks increases, the need for drugs related police work to become equally sophisticated implies a very heavy financial investment in terms of both the type and size of workforce required and the equipment needed for the police to stay one step ahead of large scale drugs suppliers.

It can readily be seen that information-gathering by the police faces all the problems outlined above for similar customs control measures. In addition it presents particular problems of its own. Although little research has been done in this area, recent studies suggest (e.g. Bean 1993) that in the case of drugs work police are peculiarly dependent on informers who are themselves engaged in the illicit activity in question. Although we would question whether this in practice differentiates drug distribution from any other sort of illicit activity, there *is* a fairly acute 'amnesty problem' attached to using drug users or dealers as informants.

The amnesty problem we refer to derives from the fact that any dependence on informers is likely to imply a provision of some sort of immunity. Clearly, such immunity will only be justified if the information given leads to seizures or arrests of greater value than the alternative action of removing the informants themselves from circulation. In this equation we need to balance not only the likelihood of misinformation and similarly unintentionally inaccurate information but also the possibility that drugs may be channelled through 'immune' dealers. Even assuming that these very specific problems can be countered however, past experience suggests that the use of informants is unlikely to be a popular tactic in the public's eyes, notably where it involves any bartering with a perceived 'criminal'. So the police are again caught in a cleft stick, attempting to balance successful policing with good public relations.

Mobilising the community to engage in its own 'policing' of drugs distribution is a relatively new approach and mimics that recently taken by the police towards low level crime in general. As such it is also subject to the same central problem of public relations. Many communities and individuals are very happy to engage in 'policing' themselves, at least by adopting crime reduction measures, but there is always the potential for people to respond to such suggestions by accusing the police of ducking their responsibilities. Perhaps more disturbingly there is the converse possibility that the community may become too enthusiastic about their role and engage in vigilante action.

Community based police action also faces a problem which is rather more specific to the drugs issue. Both drug usage and drug dealing are 'invisible' forms of activity in comparison to other types of crime. They pose an internal rather than an external threat in the sense that the individual's own actions, whether or not directed or encouraged by the actions of others, tend to put themselves or close associates 'at risk' rather than threatening the community at large. If a neighbourhood is susceptible to burglary, local members of the community may be eager to support police in reducing further burglaries threatening their own property, but what relevant aim will they see in reducing the effects of drug usage and dealing? Many of the people in a position to help will be engaged in the drugs trade themselves. As our data suggest, those local residents who are *not* themselves involved will tend to regard low-level dealing as more of a nuisance than a threat. Where dealing becomes more serious the dangers of becoming involved at any level are quite severe and obviously the public should not be encouraged to put themselves at risk.

Even assuming that a community is willing to address the problem and runs no risk in doing so, how should they go about it? Again unlike the case for other types of crime, there are no obvious 'crime reduction' techniques in the case of drug usage or dealing. If the police were in any position to give the public convincing advice on how to avoid the problems associated with usage or dealing at this level, we would presumably be in a rather more promising position with regard to drugs prevention as a whole than in fact we are. At the wider level, drug related problems are not ones which are likely to be amenable to community action. To take one example, a community is unlikely to be in a position to make itself less deprived and hence less prone to drug related problems.

The police therefore face two major problems in mobilising communities to address their own drug problem. In the first place they need to persuade communities that either drug usage or dealing is a behaviour posing a relevant and pertinent threat to their own lives. Thereafter, the problem lies in determining what concrete advice the police *can* actually give people on how to avoid or solve a problem the nature of which and the cures for which are themselves still matters of considerable debate. This is not to say that the police have *no* useful role to play in taking the problem of drug usage to the community. Indeed, they may have a very valuable role in providing community based drugs education. The point we wish to make here, is simply that the problem of drug usage or dealing within a community *cannot* be equated with more distinct and in essence more straightforward problems such as burglary.

As with customs control, it is difficult to assess the *actual* effectiveness of police work in relation to drugs. Nevertheless, as noted earlier, econometric work has been carried out with the aim of providing some ballpark figures of cost and benefit. Again, we take Lawrence's (1986) estimates, which were based on seizure rates and calculated at a time when control was at a premium. Using these estimates we find that although police work shows a higher relative seizure *rate* than customs work, it is in terms of absolute *quantities* of drugs an even less successful method. Overall, Lawrence found police work in general to be responsible for netting only 1-2% of estimated total drug imports. For the same year, expenditure on drugs related police work was around the £22 million mark. Whilst again, such figures are speculative, the econometric models of Wagstaff and Maynard *(op cit.)* suggest that however we manipulate police enforcement of drug dealing, the link between expenditure and effectiveness is unlikely to be direct.

If we move away from financial considerations and examine broader issues, such as levels of harm, the picture appears, superficially, to be more positive. That a lower quantity of drugs would be seized by police than by customs control is only to be expected and the fairly high rate of seizures therefore seems quite encouraging, despite any likely cost. However, even this high seizure rate has recently been put into perspective by Unell (1991), using data which cannot be said to be speculative. Unell points out that across all British police forces, 86% of drugs seizures in 1990 were for cannabis. Taking convictions as an alternative source of information, 90% were for cannabis. Clearly the apparently high success rate, as indeed we find with customs measures, rests largely on the seizure of low priority drugs.

Police efforts to tackle the distribution of drugs in general and high priority drugs in particular clearly face quite substantial problems. Although the effectiveness of policing methods could to an extent be enhanced by further injections of capital, it is worth noting here Hough and Mayhew's (1983) general conclusion that "a substantial body of research indicates that it is difficult to enhance the police effect on crime". There are inherent difficulties in drugs-related police work. It represents a heavy demand in terms of both direct financial commitment and resources such as workforce hours.

The need for specialist units or at least specialist training implies a further cost and the tendency of such work to catch users rather than dealers and to disrupt small localised distribution networks rather than large, possibly international, ones suggests that such investment might be uneconomic. In addition there remains a problem which is more acute for the police than for Customs and Excise, namely ensuring the support of the community.

In summary, although low level policing of retail drugs distribution can be effective as a short term measure, it is not clear that it can have any broader impact. In addition to the replaceability problem faced by customs, locally based police work suffers from the problem of maintaining community support. Higher level police operations, on the other hand, may more readily gain public support, but in purely quantitative terms are unlikely to have any very substantial impact on the availability of drugs. As with customs control efforts, research suggests that those drugs most likely to be intercepted by the police are those which hold the lowest priority in terms of both street value and potential levels of harm.

Controlling supply *and* demand

Whilst, as suggested earlier, the division between supply control and the control of demand is not in any case clear cut, there are certain measures for which this is particularly true. We present two quite distinct examples of this type of drugs prevention measure below. In addition to being measures which address both the supply and demand aspects of the drugs problem, they are also measures for which the division of responsibility is less clear cut. No single agency being self-evidently the one most responsible for their promotion. As a function of this, they are also measures which face a considerable degree of external pressure, however likely they are in themselves to be effective.

Strengthening deterrence

The role of deterrence is central to many of the measures we consider in the course of this discussion, whether these are primarily directed at the control of supply or at controlling demand. It is therefore of some importance that we consider both its nature and its viability. When deterrence is mentioned, it is often thought to be primarily the domain of the police. However, whilst a number of potential deterrents *do* directly and solely involve the work of the police, others are more likely to be either supported or mediated by agencies such as Customs and Excise. Any form of legal deterrent must of course also rest on the work of the courts. The potential nature of any deterrent is also broader than is often assumed, since deterrence can be aimed at either people *or* environments and, as suggested above, can be aimed at either supply or demand reduction.

This diversity notwithstanding, two assumptions lie behind all forms of deterrence-based measure. The first is that deterrence works at the psychological level to make individuals less likely to carry out a given behaviour on future occasions. The second is that deterrence can be directed effectively at selected targets. In the case of drug usage, both assumptions are questionable. To illustrate this, we consider two deterrence methods which can be aimed at either individuals or organisations. These are:

- the introduction of high maximum penalties for drug usage or dealing
- depriving dealers of the 'fruits of their labour'.

The problem with the first of these options is that little evidence exists to support the notion that even maximum penalties - for example, the life sentence and death penalty options employed in Malaysia and Thailand - actually reduce *either* drug dealing or usage to any very considerable degree. Dealing is particularly difficult to reduce using such threats because large scale dealers are unlikely to be directly affected by any penalties and smaller dealers or couriers may be driven by fear of their employers or even simply by poverty to continue their trade in the face of such risks.

With regard to demand oriented deterrence a particularly acute problem lies in ensuring that individuals *internalise* the risks of capture and penalty. The chemical nature of at least some drug usage is such that a physical craving is established which may well override any fear of legal penalties relating to the acquisition of drugs. This suggests that deterrence based options, whilst perhaps being effective for casual users, are unlikely to affect established addicts. Even should present users be effectively deterred, however, drug usage is unlikely to cease as a consequence, since new users will be found to replace those prevented from using drugs.

Deterrence measures extreme enough to deter a majority of potential users are likely, as suggested earlier, to risk alienating the public. A significant minority of our respondents had experienced drug usage themselves and had at least some contact with drug users. This may account for the fact that support for methods aimed at drug users was rather lower than support for methods targeting suppliers. It also suggests that any aggressive deterrence of drug users, however successful in the short term, might in the long term prove counterproductive, by removing public support. Similar problems are less likely to apply in the case of drug dealers, but here there is also a need to balance deterrence against community support.

Polich et al. (1984) have carried out one of the very few empirical studies relevant to the likely effects of deterrence based responses. Using data on both cocaine and marijuana markets they concluded that increased expenditure on law enforcement responses in general and deterrence based responses in particular - at any level of the drugs market - would leave drugs consumption largely unchanged. Since this study was based in the US, it would be desirable to have similar data from Britain before drawing any broad conclusions, but there is no reason for assuming *a priori* that the outcome would be any different.

Depriving dealers of the fruits of their drug dealing is equally problematic, as we suggested earlier. At the level of small local dealers it may be a viable strategy, but new dealers will step forward to replace any who are deterred. If dealing stems from a broader more international base, the replacement factor *may* be less of an immediate problem, at least in the short term, but other problems still exist. Depriving invisible and potentially very powerful individuals or organisations of their resources is an expensive and politically risky strategy requiring a great deal of co-operation between nations.

As an illustration of the latter type of resource deprivation approach, we can take the recommendations of the UN Commission on Narcotic Drugs (1984). A central recommendation of this commision was the sequestration of assets at an international level where individuals or organisations are thought to be engaged in drug dealing. The Commission acknowledged that this move requires not only international co-operation but also a very different and potentially more costly type of personnel from that generally used to pursue drug dealers. In particular, it requires the services of trained international lawyers.

Securing international co-operation is, as we suggested earlier, in itself a problematic task in relation to the drugs issue. The need to train and fund international lawyers is not only a costly move but also serves as an illustration of the sort of logistical problems caused by a need for international co-operation. If each country independently trains and funds its own lawyers they may simply end up acting in opposition to each other. If, on the other hand, this type of resource is centrally funded and controlled there remains the question of which countries can and should pay for and hence, in practice, control the resource. A more fundamental problem of this nature and one not dealt with by the Commission is the fact that the laundering of money without regard to its source is routinely carried out by many legitimate and indeed sometimes state controlled business concerns. This is a distinctly intractable problem at the present time and is one which could severely reduce the effectiveness of asset sequestration.

Returning to lower level forms of deterrence, it is worth considering briefly the possibility of secondary, or indirect, deterrents. One example of this form of deterrent, now being widely used as a response to other forms of illicit activity, is the design, or re-design of local environments. Those features of the environment found to associate with an illicit activity are simply removed or replaced with alternative features. Although such measures have met with some success, they tend to rely on crime occurring in public spaces, susceptible to such alteration. Given the nature of drug dealing and drug usage any effective design measures would be more likely to displace than to deter this type of illicit activity. Again we are faced with the problem that the drugs market is both less specifically victim oriented and less 'opportunistic' than the broad range of other illicit activities.

In summary, low level deterrence measures are unlikely to be effective both because of the 'replaceability factor' and because addicted users and highly motivated dealers are not prone to internalise any overt threat. Higher level forms of deterrence such as the sequestration of assets appear at face value to be more promising, but they are also very costly and involve strategies which may not be viable given the present state of international politics. Secondary forms of deterrence, involving strategies such as redesigning the local environment have been used with some success in controlling other illicit activities. They have not, in the main, been tried in relation to drugs prevention. However, they are also less likely to be effective in this case since drug dealing at least is not in any immediate sense an 'opportunistic' type of crime.

Controlling medically supplied drugs

In the foregoing discussions, we have been concerned with forms of supply and demand reduction based on controlling individuals who are, notably with regard to dealers, *intentionally* engaged in the drugs business. However, both addiction *per se* and the entry of addictive drugs into the illicit market may be a function also of *un*intentional actions. By way of illustration, the most common assumption behind stringent controls on *medically* supplied drugs is that such drugs seep into the illicit market if insufficient care is taken. Similarly one common claim made against maintenance prescribing is that it is likely to contribute to the release of drugs onto the resale market.

Considerations such as these do not present a convincing argument against any form of medical practice taken individually. The absolute amount of drugs introduced in this way is unlikely to be significant in any single case and any resulting problems can be controlled by careful monitoring of the medical practice in question. However, the quantities of drugs inadvertently or inappropriately released via the *sum* of medical and pharmaceutical practices across the country may comprise a quite significant absolute volume of drugs.

The unintentional release of medical drugs onto the market can occur as a consequence of two types of practice. On the one hand medical professionals may themselves be responsible, either by over-prescribing, and hence encouraging re-sale, or by prescribing inappropriately, encouraging inadvertent addiction. The latter form of prescribing practice contributes *directly* to the problem of drug usage. For example, medical practitioners may prescribe chemical forms of treatment for conditions which could suitably have been dealt with by referral to a counsellor or behaviour therapist. Similarly they may also prescribe a drug which, although appropriate for the condition in question, is addictive. On the other hand, clinics or surgeries may be the 'victims' of either planned or opportunistic burglaries, or of more subtle manipulations by drug dealing or using clients.

As with the other drugs prevention options outlined earlier, the controls most likely to be effective in terms of the medical supply of drugs tend also to be in practical terms the most expensive and the least viable. Persuading doctors to change their prescribing habits would entail not only an extensive campaign of re-education, but would also entail the provision of alternative services, which are in very limited supply at the present time. An increase in the level of monitoring and spot checking carried out on stores of drugs would be relatively easy to achieve but given the likely effect on the drugs market would produce only negligible results. Stopping or reducing the number of burglaries relating to such stores would be more effective, but again much less achievable.

Although this particular drugs prevention measure, like others we have considered, suffers from a range of problems, it may on the whole be a more promising avenue to explore. We say this because focusing drugs control on medically supplied drugs would remove an *unnecessary* additional problem for drugs prevention. It is also rather more likely to have the support of the 'dealer' - the medical profession being an inadvertent rather than a deliberate contributor to the *illicit* drugs market - and hence is more likely to succeed. This is certainly not the case for other contributors to the drugs market. On the more negative side, removing this problem may in itself only have marginal effects on the illicit drugs market.

> **In summary,** although the control of medically supplied drugs is subject to a variety of problems, it provides a *relatively* hopeful avenue of drugs control to explore further since those individuals primarily responsible for releasing drugs onto the market via this route tend to be doing so *in*advertently. It may also be worth exploring for the sole reason that it presents an unnecessary addition to the drugs problem. From a more pragmatic viewpoint, it should be noted that whilst such control represents a more readily attainable long term goal than other options, it is equally likely to involve considerable expense and may only result in a marginal decrease in the illicit drugs market.

The elasticity of the drugs market

Before moving on to consider those prevention measures which are aimed specifically at demand rather than supply, we will address one final issue which relates to the viability of control oriented drugs prevention. A recurring theme in the above discussions has been the *replaceability* of drug supplies, drug dealers and drug users. This aspect of the drugs market is just one instance of a more general hallmark of the drugs trade, namely its elasticity. In addition to the simple fact of replaceability, the elasticity of the drugs market can be illustrated by:

- the link between controls and profits
- the changing profile of favoured drugs

Of some importance in the present context is the fact that both of the above features of the 'drugs problem' help to determine the actual effects of *successful* supply side control. In the foregoing discussion, our main focus was largely on possible *constraints* on supply control. Here, we would like to consider further the likely outcome of *successful* controls on supply and in particular the links between the impact of supply side control and the elasticity of the drugs market. This issue is a valuable one to address for two distinct reasons. In the first place, it helps us to judge whether supply side efficiency is *in itself* likely to be a worthwhile goal. Since the success of supply side measures is difficult to judge accurately it is of some importance to determine whether their aim is in any case a coherent one. In the second place, the issue of elasticity *within* the drugs market provides some insight into a further and potentially quite powerful mechanism for drugs prevention.

The elasticity of the drugs market and its interaction with supply side control is most readily demonstrated by considering prices and profits. The drugs market is an adept mimic of legal consumer markets. Not only are profits introduced at all levels of the supply chain, but supply - and perhaps also demand - is inversely related to retail prices. The consequence of which is that effective supply control measures are prone to operate in conflict with deterrence oriented measures by increasing profit margins. To elaborate on this, if the *availability* of drugs is reduced, exporters will increase prices to compensate and the profit margin on each unit sold will increase relative to the cost of supplying that unit to the 'consumer'. If on the other hand supply control is effective in reducing the number of *dealers* - an effect most likely to occur at lower levels of the dealing hierarchy - the profit margin on each unit sold will be increased to cover heightened risks to the dealer and again the unit profit margin will be increased.

Alongside rising profit margins for the dealer, there is a danger that increased prices will also serve to amplify those drug-related problems more closely associated with the user. A possible example being the need for users to begin to commit crimes or to commit increasingly serious crime to support their by now expensive habit. In short, basic economic forecasting suggests that as long as the demand for drugs exists and profits are likely to be made, supply side controls will in some sense fail to solve the drugs problem even when they succeed in countering availability and distribution.

It is important to note that there is one crucial caveat to the rather bleak scenario presented above. The link between supply side control and profit margins depends on whether the drugs market can maintain its elasticity. Anything which renders the market *in*elastic will weaken the link. To date the most common arguments for the weakening of this link involve features of the drugs market oblique to supply control measures themselves. Specifically, it has been suggested that:

- as prices rise *non*-addicted users will cease to take drugs
- increases in 'collateral damage' will be matched by increased arrest or referral for treatment
- as prices rise addicted users will switch from one drug to another

Whilst we agree with the logic of all three arguments, we would suggest that in practice the third is most likely to reduce the elasticity of pricing, although the first two may in themselves have other beneficial effects. The effect of non-addicted users dropping out of the market is strongly dependent on precisely what the 'replaceability quotient' of drug users is. It is similarly dependent on what price threshold provides an effective deterrent. Perhaps more importantly than either of these, its impact depends also on the extent to which drug dealers can make a profit out of addicts alone. Whilst none of these factors completely undermines the viability of this threat to the elasticity of pricing, they do suggest that any effect on the link between supply side control and profit margins will be to weaken rather than break it.

The rationale behind increases in drugs related damage being associated with improved arrest and treatment rates is particularly pertinent to crime which is committed to *fund* drug usage. The argument being that as drug users are forced to commit more serious crimes they will open themselves up to a greater likelihood of apprehension, both as a consequence of their own lack of experience and as a consequence of the higher overall clear-up rates for more serious crimes. The assumption is that, as prices rise, more drug users and in particular addicted users will be removed from the streets and diverted to either prisons or treatment centres.

Although the logic of the above argument is valid, its effect on the elasticity of drug prices again relies rather heavily on both the replaceability of drug users and the level of increase of profit margins. It is consequently also likely to have a partial rather than a complete effect on weakening the link between profit margins and supply side controls. In addition to which it of course implies the associated problems of overcrowded prisons and overburdened treatment and rehabilitation services.

Finally, we turn to the likelihood that as prices rise users will switch from expensive drugs to those with more acceptable prices. There is considerable evidence that such 'cross-over' usage or even, more significantly, 'cross-over' *addiction* is precisely what *does* happen when drug prices rise (cf. Silverman and Spurill 1977,

Young 1982). This movement across drug types is more likely to snap the link between supply and profit margins - at least for individual drugs - than the effects noted above because it is less dependent on other considerations such as the replaceability of users and the likelihood that serious addicts will drop out of the market entirely. Instead it is based simply on consumer economics. If an alternative and acceptable drug is available and cheaper than the first drug of choice, users are likely to switch to it.

Cross-over usage will, of course, serve to change rather than totally undermine the drugs market. There is also a further problem with any reliance on consumer economics in this context. Not *all* drugs are price elastic or *necessarily* elastic over all price structures. This can be illustrated quite simply by the fact that addicts will tolerate higher prices for their drug of choice and that different drugs vary both in how addictive they are and in how readily their effects can be substituted for by another drug, whether addictive or not (White and Luksetich 1983). So, whilst for some drugs the market can be readily shifted by price rises, for other drugs and at some price thresholds we are back to the question of how readily dealers can make profits solely from addicts as opposed to occasional or leisure users.

The above is a very simplified version of an economic analysis of the drugs market, models of which can become extremely convoluted, taking into account a large and eclectic range of factors (cf. Levin et al. 1975). Nevertheless, even this limited account does bring out the main problems associated with the link between supply side control and the drugs market itself. Increasing the effectiveness of our controls on drug supplies will not necessarily *either* decrease the net total of drug users *or* decrease the profits of the dealer. In addition it may even result in an increase in the collateral damage associated with drug usage.

On a more optimistic note, we would like to highlight the implications which the above discussion has for *improving* the effectiveness of supply side approaches to the 'drugs problem'. It is standard practice in the licit consumer market for the habits of the consumer to be manipulated by the 'supply side' pressures of manufacturers. Frequently, this process is a 'mutual' one with consumers providing the information which allows the manufacturer to manipulate. Since the drugs market very closely mimics any other consumer market, there is no *a priori* reason why it should not be manipulated in the same way. To an extent, 'inconvenience policing' and customs drives against particular drugs are already aimed at precisely this type of tactic. Specifically, such activities aim to divert drug usage and drug dealing into channels which are either less harmful to the individual or easier to control. This is an extremely valuable approach to the drugs market and it has the added advantage of being also a realistic one.

Although manipulating the drugs market into less harmful avenues is a promising approach to the problem, it must also be a well-informed approach if it is to be effective. Very little econometric or systems-analytic work has been done in relation to the drugs market in general and in particular with regard to determining the most appropriate supply side tactics. This is unfortunate given the potential such forms of modelling may have. It is also understandable. There are two problems with this type of approach. Firstly, it is information-intensive. Secondly, it is an approach which, like containment of the drugs market at the retail end, is *assumed* not to appeal to the general public. We feel that both problems can in principle be resolved. As indicated by our survey, consumer-based information on drug usage is *not* impossible to collect. Furthermore, even the general, non-drug taking, public appear to be quite open and willing to consider a broad variety of issues raised by the 'drugs problem' and equally a range of distinct measures for drugs prevention. This area of research may well be worth developing in an attempt to avoid organisations such as the police and Customs and Excise being forced to wage a largely *symbolic* war on drugs.

In summary, one very hopeful avenue of exploration in supply side control is the possibility of using economic models of the drugs market to reduce levels of harm and contain the problem within controllable boundaries. Both the police and Customs and Excise are to some extent already using the implied tactics for precisely these purposes. However, they are often operating with inadequate information and are perhaps also constrained in such activities by the perception that the public prefers an 'all out' war on drugs. Our data suggest in contrast that people are fairly open to considering the drugs issue at a range of levels and also suggest that even at the population level the collection of data on personal drug usage is not as problematic as has previously been thought to be the case.

Controlling demand

The discussions above concerning the actual and potential effectiveness of supply side controls are an indication of how crucial the development of controls on *demand* are to solving the drugs problem. In addition to broad issues such as the problems facing supply side control, a number of very specific considerations can also be used to highlight this need. One issue which has received very widespread attention is the link between drug usage and the spread of HIV. This problem alone makes it imperative that we control or at least direct the demand for drugs.

A number of factors militate against the likelihood that demand will decrease of its own accord. Our own data suggest, for example, that the level of experimental or 'one off' usage of drugs within the population as a whole is by no means trivial. In particular sections of the population such usage is in fact extremely common. This despite a determined 'war on drugs' spanning nearly twenty years. Figures for availability and more specific 'environmental' factors - such as recent proposals to develop the domestic growth of hemp and the recent phenomenon of 'popper shops' where young adults can openly buy mood changing but presently licit drugs such as amyl nitrite - suggest that any demand is also likely to be satisfied.

If we are to reduce demand, we have essentially two options. We can prevent people entering the drugs market in the first place and/or we can remove them from the market once they have entered it. Both can in principle be effected by legal deterrents on drug usage, as discussed earlier. Here, we will consider less interventionist measures, namely drugs education and treatment and rehabilitation.

Drugs education

As noted in previous chapters, the public's response to drugs education is in general an extremely positive one. This is perhaps a reflection of the fact that educational measures are seen as being a response with no inherent drawbacks. The provision of accurate and helpful information is, almost by definition, unlikely to be *counter-productive*. The level of positive response may also be a function of the public's perception that drugs education is, or should be aimed primarily at prevention *per se*, rather than, for example, at harm reduction or the removal of addicts from the drugs market. In practice, neither view entirely reflects the reality of drugs education. Although drugs education is unlikely in itself to be counter-productive, *particular methods* of drugs education may well be. Nor is drugs education by any means a unitary phenomenon. It is aimed not only at preventing the initial use of drugs but also at a variety of other compatible but distinct goals and equally at a range of potential targets. By necessity it also encompasses a very broad range of methods.

The diverse nature of drugs education make it an area which is both difficult to investigate and difficult to *evaluate*. Dorn and Murji (1992) in an attempt to rationalise this position discuss five basic *formats* which drugs education - broadly defined - can adopt. These are:

- School or institution based education programmes
- Media campaigns
- Deficit based programmes
- Resistance training
- Substitution programmes

Unlike the case for supply-side forms of control, a substantial amount of research has been devoted to assessing the *effectiveness* of each of these drugs education measures. We will give a brief overview of this research here, but a more in-depth analysis can be found in Dorn and Murji *(op cit.)* and in O'Connor and Sanders (1992).

Taking school-based drugs education programmes first, there appears to be little consensus about the overall effect achieved. Success rates - defined either as a decrease in the proportion of students turning to drugs or an increased resistance to drugs on the part of present users - seem to depend on a variety of factors including who gives the training and how intensive or long term it is. A number of authors have found drugs education in this context to have minimal effect (e.g. Goodstadt 1978, Bukoski 1986), others have found it to be counter-productive, serving to encourage rather than discourage experimentation with drugs (e.g. Stuart 1974, Kinder et al. 1980) and others have found it valuable in terms of increased knowledge *but* ineffective in changing attitudes or behaviours (Schaps et al. 1981).

Media campaigns have been less fully researched, but the available information suggests that they are very potent educators, at least when warning messages are presented to the public in a moderate and balanced way (Williams et al 1985). Our own data would go some way towards supporting their power given the exaggerated levels of harm ascribed by the public to such media-hyped drugs as heroin. Although the potential *problems* of such campaigns have not been looked at specifically in the context of drugs education, data from the recent AIDS campaign (cf. Power 1989) provide us with some insight into potential pitfalls. One possible difficulty is that some of the target groups at greatest risk are likely to be ahead of the media in the level of their specific knowledge of any dangers. As a consequence, campaigns have to be very realistic and detailed if they are going to help this group. In which case they risk either confusing or alienating the broader sweep of the population. On the other hand, some sections of the general population and in particular some target groups already engaged in very risky behaviour may simply be beyond the reach of the media, either because they have no access to it for whatever reason or because they fail to internalise the messages being given, seeing them perhaps as irrelevant to their own lives.

Deficit programmes are based on the premise that drug usage is a by-product of other social, attitudinal or general life-skills problems. The aim being to reduce drug usage by first resolving these problems. The broad consensus of research on such programmes suggests that, regardless of the problem being targeted, there is an improvement in the behaviour *focused* on by the programme but no concomitant change in drug using behaviour in the long term (cf. Moskowitz et al. 1982, Coggans et al. 1989). Since the majority of studies on this issue consider only those individuals who are already engaged in drug usage, it may be that such programmes could be more effective if used as a preventive rather than as a *post hoc* response. Equally, although long term change may not be secured by deficit programmes, short term gains are clearly of value and improving an individual's life skills must in itself be regarded as a positive outcome.

The profile of resistance training in the literature looks rather more hopeful. The majority of studies conducted on this type of drugs education suggest a positive outcome, notably when such training is peer-led rather than institution-led (Botvin and Dusenbury 1989). There are some caveats to this encouraging picture, however. In the first place, Glynn (1983) argues that the programmes work by providing those partaking with negative rather than flexible attitudes. This is problematic for two reasons. Firstly, it suggests that any drug related responses will be very specific rather than generalisable to new situations involving, for example, new drugs, different pressures or further conflicting information. Secondly, the negative attitudes are achieved by socialisation to quite strong and frequently heavily disapproving peer pressure. This raises issues about both the desirability and the likely effects of such social coercion. Other authors (cf. Resnick and Gibbs 1988) suggest in addition that it is largely the *trainers* rather than the participants who benefit in the long term. Although this is of course also of benefit, it appears to be a function of cognitive dissonance (Jaspars 1983) and hence might be more economically achieved by means other than the very resource intensive and heavily supervised structure of resistance training groups.

Education, or more accurately, *diversion* programmes based around the provision of alternative 'occupations' also show a fairly positive consensus of success in the literature, but again with very specific caveats. The premise behind these programmes is that the need for drugs can be satisfied not only with the drugs themselves, but with other displacement activities such as sport, friendship groups etc. Whilst such programmes do work, the effects again seem to be largely short term. They are also strongly dependent on a continuation of the activity concerned, which may be terminated either through the participants' lack of interest or through a lack of resources (Ventura and Dundon 1974). A more specific problem with diversion programmes is that the particular activities found to be effective may not be universally favoured. Jessor and Jessor (1977) noted for example that an interest in religion seemed to be the single most effective substitution for drugs. A finding which our own lifestyle analysis of drug usage, outlined in Chapter 3, would support. In terms of future research, it is worth adding here that this specificity entails the need for a very close matching of control groups to 'experimental' groups. Previous research has tended to assume that matching groups on broad demographic variables is a sufficiently stringent method, but this is clearly not the case if the effects we are looking at can be so precise in their operation.

In addition to the rather programme-specific problems noted above, drugs education is likely to face a range of more generalised and pragmatic problems. Some drug users may withdraw from mainstream society and this in itself could prevent education campaigns reaching a prime target group. Even assuming that we can reach the relevant targets, with effective educational programmes, the fiscal costs are likely to be great. Education is very much a long term and *continuous* form of drugs prevention and its scope alone gives some indication of the costs involved. Dorn and Murji *(op cit.)* point to two further problems, namely the need for multi-agency work and the need to achieve the level of community involvement which will support such multi-agency work.

Both of these latter issues are ones which are beginning to be addressed. As we noted in earlier chapters, the general public strongly approves of some forms of multi-agency work, measured specifically in our survey by their approval of the police co-operating with drugs related agencies. Fortunately, this type of multi-agency response is very much on the policy agenda as well. Again using the police as a pertinent example, it is apparent that drugs education is no longer seen as something which should either be contained within institutions or remain the domain only of educators as strictly defined. The police now fairly commonly engage in education based programmes and a priority in their work is seen as involving the community and more importantly going out to meet the community within its own environs. Community involvement in more general terms is also very clearly on the political agenda.

Whilst such recent developments should in themselves be encouraging, any positive effects may be offset by pragmatic or policy considerations which, whilst stimulated by rather different issues, indirectly affect the type of 'multi-agency' community oriented response to drugs outlined above. By way of illustration we can consider here the recent move towards a reduction in the number of community workers and equally the re-organisation of their role in the community. Similarly, we can look at the move towards the privatisation of prisons. Both measures, although carried out for reasons oblique to the drugs issue have potentially quite profound implications for drugs related work. The effect of the former, for example, is likely to be a reduction in community outreach work much of which, directly or indirectly, provides support and diversionary activities for drug users. A possible effect of the privatisation of prisons on the other hand is an increase in the problems of inter-agency co-ordination already apparent in prison-centred drugs education programmes. These are only two recent developments, but they provide a good case in point for the likely problems which may be engendered by a tension between policy in principle and policy in practice.

As the public has perhaps already realised, none of the problems cited above are *inherent* to drugs education. This is a fact which highlights a crucial distinction between drugs education measures and more control oriented responses such as the supply-side measures discussed earlier. Many, although not all, of the problems and potential problems we noted for control oriented measures were a *necessary* function or by-product of the operation of the control measures themselves. There is, for example, necessarily an escalating conflict between Customs and Excise and large scale drug exporters. Similarly there is a necessary link, assuming demand to continue, between the police effectively cracking down on drug dealing in one area and such dealing moving to another area or dispersing across a range of areas. Given the economic motivations of drug dealing it is hard to imagine any form of control measure which would *not* encounter such difficulties.

Drugs education on the other hand does not have any such intrinsic problems, although as noted above the *particular methods* adopted may well do so. More importantly, it addresses the question of demand which in itself provides the spur leading to the problems experienced by the more control oriented responses. Drugs education is therefore in principle a very hopeful avenue of drugs prevention to explore, both in its own right and as a necessary adjunct to other forms of drugs prevention. The main focus of further research in this area should clearly be to develop and monitor educational programmes in an attempt to avoid the particular problems outlined above.

As a footnote to the very positive picture presented above, it is worth pointing out that although drugs education does not suffer from any intrinsic problems, its goal may be somewhat ephemeral. To put it bluntly, we are assuming that if people are given a greater insight into either their drug usage or their behaviour more generally, they will be deterred from using drugs. A recent study by Collison (1993) illustrates the obvious flaw in this reasoning quite effectively. Collison interviewed twenty drug-using inmates of a young offenders institution about their drug usage and found that the majority had a fairly realistic grasp of the risks of drug usage. Furthermore, their knowledge seemed to stem from some form of local cultural transmission rather than from any more 'official' source. The end result achieved by this very cheap and apparently effective form of education was to allow them to weigh *which* risks they were willing to take rather than to deter them from taking *any*. Whilst it can be argued that they were not *really* well informed about drug usage, or had not *internalised* the dangers, this type of scenario does illustrate quite sharply the fact that lack of knowledge is not the only problem in drug usage. Young people may quite simply like *taking* risks, or at least be willing to do so on a limited basis to achieve some other desired goal.

This does not completely undermine the likely effectiveness of drugs education. Giving people the opportunity to make an informed choice about the risks they take is, after all, a desirable end in itself. What it *does* tell us, however, is that, as is the case with other forms of drugs prevention including supply-side control, we may need to delineate our aims fairly carefully and be willing to accept realistic rather than optimal targets. A case in point is given by a number of studies into the effectiveness of school based education programmes. Many studies viewed drugs education as a 'failure' because the target group of children had - in spite of the programme - engaged in *experimental* drug usage. Obviously experimental usage is a more negative outcome than *no* drug usage, but in many cases such usage did not continue to develop into a longer term or more serious drug habit. So on the basis of other, perhaps more realistic, criteria, the programmes could have been regarded as a success!

In addition to aiming for realistic targets, we may also need to make drugs education programmes more specific to the issue they are trying to address. A substantial body of research exists to indicate the precise nature of the chemical and psychological appeal of drugs. This can be usefully exploited in a number of ways. For example, education based programmes can be used to give people more precise insights into the reasons behind their own behaviour. Similarly, deficit or substitution type programmes can be more finely tuned to allow them to adequately resolve or replace the problems or needs associated with drug usage. Drugs education, like drugs prevention in general, is a subject still in its infancy. There is much which remains to be learned about this potentially very fruitful field.

In summary, The concept of drugs education as a method of drugs prevention does not carry with it the inherent disadvantages entailed by other more control oriented measures. The provision of accurate and helpful information is, for example, almost by definition unlikely to be counter-productive. This suggests that the most pertinent question regarding the use of drugs education as a prevention method centres not on the viability of education as such, but rather on the viability of particular methods of drugs education. Further research into the most effective methods of drugs education would be of value.

Treatment and rehabilitation

As noted earlier, the treatment and rehabilitation of drug users provides a common current through otherwise diverse forms of drugs policy. Only in the most extreme examples of the penal or legalisation approaches are these aims viewed as dispensable. Although moral considerations no doubt underlie this fact to a significant degree, purely practical considerations also provide support. If peer group encouragement is one path to drug usage, it is important to rehabilitate users before they can 'convert' other non-users to their own behaviour pattern. Furthermore, if present users are at no point rehabilitated then - unless drug use even at the most extreme levels is simply a phase through which the majority of users pass - the expected regular addition of new users may cause absolute numbers of individuals using drugs to rise to proportions incommensurate with society's ability to cope with them.

Although by their nature, treatment and rehabilitation are devoid of intrinsic problems, since neither is likely *in itself* to have negative effects, they are responses which, like drugs education, are subject to a variety of practical difficulties. One of the primary problems, of course, being cost. Effective treatment and rehabilitation schemes tend not to be substantially less expensive than the supply side methods of drugs prevention considered earlier. King (1993) has discussed in some detail the very acute problem already faced by drugs rehabilitation units in securing funding and recent debates regarding health-related public spending serve to indicate that future resources are if anything likely to be somewhat more restricted.

As with drugs education, both the appropriateness and effectiveness of *particular* treatment and rehabilitation techniques may also be a matter for concern. Should treatment and rehabilitation take place in the community or in a 'secure' residential setting? Should it be biased towards harm reduction or prevention *per se*? Should it be exclusively targeted at drug users themselves, or also at their families or associates? These are only some of the questions remaining unanswered in this particular field of drugs prevention. Whilst most research on the issue to date suggests that almost all treatment programmes show *some* level of success (cf. Ghodse 1989) it is clearly of importance to ensure that the most effective methods are those most generally used. To date, the monitoring of treatment and rehabilitation programmes has been rather less than systematic.

Even if careful monitoring is carried out, there is no guarantee that even the most successful programmes will meet with enthusiastic support from either the public in general or the client group themselves. Our own research suggests, for instance, that the public is *not* overwhelmingly supportive of harm reduction as a primary goal of drugs prevention. Similarly, needle exchange schemes frequently meet with resistance when an attempt is made to establish them in the local community. The proposed client group may also be reluctant to take up the options provided. Collison's *(op cit.)* drug users for example felt that treatment and rehabilitation were issues rather oblique to their own needs. They saw their drug usage as a rational form of leisure pursuit and felt that any problems they had were not directly linked with such usage. In a similar vein, options for treatment and rehabilitation can also be subject to very real ethical dilemmas, the use of compulsory treatment orders with probation being a case in point.

The combined problems of tailoring treatment and rehabilitation to the needs of a target group and ensuring that this target group is able and willing to take up the options available to it, are perhaps the most salient difficulties faced by this mode of drugs prevention. Even assuming that we can determine which aims and methods are the most appropriate, the further difficulties of deciding who to target and where to place resources remain. Should we respond to the shortage of funds by targeting only 'problem users', however defined? Or should we concentrate instead on users of particular drug types? Should we, as presently, site treatment and rehabilitation units only in those areas felt to be most in need of or least resistant to their establishment, or should they be a more widely spread resource? As with the nature of the most appropriate treatment and rehabilitation methods, these and similar questions remain unanswered.

The above concerns are in practice exacerbated by the conceptual difficulty of how we define drug usage. The aims and effectiveness of both treatment and rehabilitation are peculiarly susceptible to the tension between the differing views of drug usage outlined early on in this chapter. The attitudes of Collison's drug users provide one example of the difficulties arising from varying definitions of drug usage. If drug usage is perceived to be a legitimate leisure pursuit, then treatment and rehabilitation options are unlikely to be taken full advantage of by drug users, however carefully they are developed and targeted.

It is important to realise that the attitudes of drug users are not the only bar to successful treatment and rehabilitation. The conceptual models of drug usage adopted by those aiming to prevent drug usage or to reduce drug related harm can be equally as problematic in this context. Referring back to the three models of drug usage outlined at the beginning of this chapter, it can be seen, for example, that in all models other than that legitimating *both* drug usage and dealing, there is some tension relating to how we should deal with drug users within the criminal justice system. A pertinent example of this type of problem at the present time is provided by the conflicting goals which appear to be present in the most recent Criminal Justice Act (Wasik and Taylor 1991).

As Lee (1993) has argued, the emphasis in the Criminal Justice Act on community care and treatment for drug users balances rather awkwardly with the equal emphasis the Act gives to the link between drugs and crime and the need for carceral punishment. A likely consequence of this type of inconsistent attitude towards drug users, as Lee's research implies, is that the treatment options available for arrested drug users will depend on the vagaries of individual magistrates and of other local authorities involved with the judicial system. Whether from the point of view of drug users themselves or from that of the authorities with whom they come into contact, the concept of a 'drug user' is likely to have as direct an effect on the process of treatment and rehabilitation as the siting or targeting of treatment and rehabilitation resources.

As with drugs education, none of the above problems are intrinsic to the nature of treatment and rehabilitation. Indeed, all the points discussed may, with some degree of effort, be resolvable. Nevertheless, they serve to illustrate that even the most straightforward response to the 'drugs problem' is beset with both conceptual and practical difficulties. We are not dealing with a simple issue.

In summary, as with drugs education, drugs prevention methods based on harm reduction carry with them few *intrinsic* problems. They are taken in direct response to the presentation of a problem and consequently are likely to have either a positive effect on drug usage or to be oblique to the issue altogether. The only practical problem intrinsic to treatment and rehabilitation, again as with drugs education, is the fiscal commitment entailed. This said, a variety of problems *extrinsic* to the treatment and rehabilitation of drugs users may impinge upon their success. Specific examples are provided by the public's reluctance to accept harm reduction as a primary goal of drugs prevention; the reluctance of some drug users to come forward for treatment and the equivocal status of drug users within the criminal justice system.

Alternatives to control

To a greater or lesser extent, all of the options outlined in the foregoing discussion, with the exception of treatment and rehabilitation, have tacitly assumed that the primary aim of any drugs prevention policy is to substantially reduce the level of drug usage. The supply-side control options discussed have further assumed that drug usage, or at least drug dealing, should remain an illegal activity. In terms of the models of drug usage outlined at the beginning of this chapter, the majority of policies discussed therefore conceptualise the drug user as either a victim or a criminal. Approaches exist, however, which seek to undercut this view and which present available control and prevention policies as being oblique to the real drugs issue. These alternative approaches to the 'drugs problem' are outlined below.

Legalisation

Proponents of legalisation adopt the view that a drug user is exercising a legitimate choice of leisure pursuit. This view has been argued for from a number of perspectives ranging in their political and philosophical emphases from liberal to libertarian. At the more extreme end of the pro-legalisation debate are claims such as those made by Scheerer (1992), who argues that since drug usage cannot be legitimately defined as criminal - having no visible victim other than the self - the use of legal sanctions relating to this behaviour represents an illegitimate attempt to marginalise those elements in society which are disapproved of by controlling individuals or groups. Put in less emotive terms - why are we willing to accept cultural, social, or individual variation in, for example, food choice but *not* willing to accept similar variation in preferred forms of drug usage?

Less extreme proponents of legalisation have argued for the removal of legal sanctions on the basis that the true harm of drug usage lies in the secondary problems *caused* by these sanctions, rather than in the drug usage itself. This is a form of the legalisation argument which can coherently claim to bring such a response to the drugs issue within the domain of prevention policies. Problems which have been laid at the door of legal sanctions against drug usage include:

- the likelihood that an individual will have to engage in crime to support their drug habit
- the reluctance of drug users to come forward for treatment where penal or social sanctions are likely to result
- the unintentional but inevitable marginalisation of drug users
- the high risk forms of drug usage associated with alternative drug economies

The type of legalisation argument centring around these aspects of the drugs issue mimics the medico-centric model of drugs control in assuming that the legitimate distribution of drugs stands in a functional relationship to the illicit drugs market. Putting the case in more strictly economic terms, the basic assumption is that legal intervention is not 'pareto-relevant' (Wagstaff and Maynard *op cit.*). That is, the costs of keeping drugs illegal are viewed as higher than the costs of allowing legal consumption of drugs. Note here that whilst the definition of 'cost' is always to some extent dependent on one's value system, this is particularly the case in the drugs debate. It depends, for example, on whether one assumes that individuals are taking risks of which they are personally unaware, on what level of drug usage one terms 'addiction' and on whether one accepts that the physical effects of drug usage are more or less damaging than the effects of other activities in which individuals engage.

A further, more mercenary, argument in favour of legalisation rests on the increased revenue which would be made available to governments as a consequence of the ability to tax sales of drugs, in the same way many have traditionally taxed sales of tobacco and alcohol. To put this argument in a more favourable light it can be expressed in terms of allowing developing countries to make a profit out of one of the few crops they can viably grow and market. Similarly it can be couched in 'harm reduction' terms, with taxes on drug usage and dealing being ringfenced to fund treatment and rehabilitation.

In addition to the legalisation arguments outlined above, there are also a range of 'semi-legalisation' arguments which suggest the possibility of using legalisation as a form of control policy, for example, by combining selective legalisation of drugs with control methods such as crop substitution. The drugs selected for legalisation are either chosen on the basis of attributions regarding medical or social harm, or are chosen on the more utilitarian grounds of which are most open to control by other methods. The assumption behind such semi-legalisation approaches is that targeting the more dangerous and/or the more readily controlled drugs will increase the effectiveness of control measures.

At the least radical end of the legalisation continuum lies the plaintive argument that since we can do nothing about the 'problem' of drug usage we might as well let it continue legally. This is an argument which would seem to have some at least tacit if not explicit support within the rather beleaguered police force. The latter point is important, since it demonstrates that not all proponents of legalisation are 'woolly liberals' or for that matter libertarians. To illustrate this point, Manning (1985) has discussed a number of interviews she carried out with high standing drug squad officials. Many of these officials felt the 'drugs problem' to be intractable and viewed legalisation as being in practice the only viable approach to drug usage.

The diverse arguments in favour of legalisation are matched by an equally diverse set of arguments against this option. The arguments *against* legalisation are well summarised by Inciardi and McBride (1991). These authors have disputed the validity of the legalisation arguments on the grounds that:

- drug related activities *are* criminal
- legalisation will increase drug usage and/or the number of drug users

- the regulation of legal drug usage would be problematic
- legalisation will impose unnecessary burdens on society
- legalisation will not solve the fundamental social or psychological problems of drug users

The first type of argument outlined by Inciardi and McBride is a common one in the literature and tends to be supported either on moral grounds (often on an *a priori* basis), or from the viewpoint that self-harm (or activities which will tend to injure health) is to be deplored on social, pragmatic or aesthetic grounds. When presented in moral or aesthetic terms the argument is not open to logical debate, being more closely aligned to matters of taste than to intellectual considerations. Inciardi and McBride argue for it instead on the pragmatic basis that the voting public disapprove of legalisation and in a democracy must have their views taken as paramount. This formulation of the argument is of particular interest to us, since one of the main aims of the present survey was to assess just what the attitudes of the public *are* to drug usage and drugs prevention. We will therefore leave this argument aside for the present and discuss it in greater depth in a later section of the chapter.

Leaving aside also any purely moral or aesthetic viewpoints on legalisation, it can be seen that all of the arguments listed above, to a greater or lesser extent, demand empirical assessment. Such assessment would obviously be of value, but as yet no systematic empirical research has been carried out on these issues. Even the Amsterdam experience of semi-legalisation has to date been addressed in the main anecdotally rather than in any more rigorous fashion. Although given recent work such as that of Sandwijk et al (1991) there is some hope that this position will improve in the near future, we will of necessity here confine our discussion to the logical content of the arguments against legalisation rather than attempting to consider their basis in fact. At the same time, we would like to emphasise that no real conclusion to the debate can be reached until we *do* have access to adequate empirical data.

Turning first to the issue of possible increases in drug usage following legalisation, we would argue that in fact this is a more complex problem than Inciardi and McBride suggest. An 'increase' can be measured by either prevalence *per se* or by increases in particular modes of usage. An increase in prevalence need not imply a commensurate increase in any given mode of usage. A proponent of legalisation could therefore respond that whilst prevalence *may* increase, following legalisation, levels of problematic usage would in the event either remain constant or perhaps even decrease. This type of response throws the argument back onto definitions of what constitutes an acceptable level of drug usage or of drugs related harm. At which point the issue becomes, on the one hand, whether we are willing to retain the concept of the drug user as a criminal regardless of potential side-effects and, on the other hand, whether we are willing to accept any increase in drug usage even if it turns out to be largely experimental or in the main unproblematic.

To approach the problem from a different angle, it is in any case not clear that any increase in the usage of previously illicit drugs following legalisation would represent an increase in *absolute* levels of drug usage. Individuals presently using either alcohol or tobacco might simply swap to a different form of drug whilst non-drug users remained non-drug users, resulting in a zero or marginal increase in the total consumption of drugs. Inciardi and McBride point out, quite rightly, that our entrepreneurial market economic system could readily serve to create, expand and maintain high levels of demand for 'new' drugs. Although this is a valid point, it leaves the issue of whether drug usage would increase *purely* in response to legalisation untouched. The desirability of a market system which is able to stimulate such demand and yet remain untouched by any form of regulation is an issue at least logically if not practically distinct from the question of whether present levels of demand could be affected by legalisation as such.

A further difficulty in considering the possible degree to which drug use might increase following legalisation is implicit in this last point. It relates to the extent and nature of the regulatory climate which would develop following legalisation. The position if there were to be unrestricted availability is clearly quite different from that pertaining if the supply or the place of consumption were to be regulated (as currently occurs with alcohol and tobacco). Inciardi and McBride acknowledge this, but respond by stating that regulation is a further *problem* with legalisation rather than a potential rein on any possible negative effects. In support of this they cite difficulties such as determining who should be allowed to buy the new legal drugs, how to determine which strengths are allowable and where drugs should be sold. This argument is open to challenge in that it fails to consider the fact that these are issues which we have already had to come to terms with in respect of presently legal drugs such as alcohol and tobacco. Whether regulation as such is enforceable is a moot point, but again, it is not one which can be used to *distinguish* between presently licit and presently illicit drugs.

Even if accepted, the claim that the more readily available drugs are, the more likely people are to try them and thereafter to continue using or misusing them, does not answer those arguments for legalisation which rest on the right of the individual to self determination. It cannot logically do so because it takes as its base point the idea that our main aim must be to reduce the level of drug usage, *regardless* of the wishes of the individual. As noted above, proponents of legalisation who do not view the rights of the individual as paramount can on the other hand dispute with it on practical grounds claiming that one or both of its predictions are incorrect. In the absence of empirical data supporting or refuting this claim, further discussion is difficult. It is important to note in this context that both sides are able to claim that the burden of proof lies with their opponent, since both sides claim that some level of harm attaches directly to the alternative policy.

The argument that legalisation will impose unnecessary burdens on society is similarly open to debate at both the theoretical and the practical level. At the theoretical level it can be countered by citing the equivalent burdens imposed by legal practices such as alcohol or tobacco consumption. At the practical level it can be countered by the libertarian suggestion of a reliance on insurance and mandatory charges, whether these are to cover self-inflicted problems or forms of direct or indirect injury inflicted on others as a consequence of drug usage.

Inciardi and McBride's response to arguments such as those outlined above is couched in somewhat emotive terms. They state for example that "the legalisation of drugs would be an elitist and racist policy supporting the neo-colonialist views of underclass population control". Restating their argument in less value-laden terms, the point being made is that any increase in the level of drug related problems consequent on legalisation is seen as likely to *disproportionately* affect an already over-burdened section of society. Specifically, these authors point to the tendency of companies presently marketing legal drugs to boost their consumption amongst lower socioeconomic groups. Similarly they argue that women in the 'underclass' are more susceptible to drug addiction than women in other sections of society and that people from minority ethnic groups are more likely to be found in the types of socially disadvantaged environment which are seen as engendering drug usage.

Interestingly, Inciardi and McBride do *not* go on to suggest the removal of present inequalities as a solution to the drugs problem. This is possibly because the logical structure of their argument does not allow them to do so. For the argument to remain intact the evils noted above must be *intrinsic* to the use of presently illicit drugs. In fact they are logically, although again perhaps not in practice, distinct from drug usage. Legalisation in itself does not entail any particular practice by companies marketing drugs, nor indeed does it determine the approach we take to regulating these companies. It certainly does not imply that people from minority ethnic groups should be forced to remain in poverty or that any form of vulnerability should be localised in particular sections of the population. These issues are clearly not irrelevant to the issue of legalisation, but they are *oblique* to the issue and cannot logically be used to undermine the type of legalisation argument outlined above. Rather, they are problems which must be addressed in their own right.

The final argument cited by Inciardi and McBride, namely that legalisation will not solve the problems associated with drug usage, is logically coherent. However, it is an argument which has also been used by proponents of legalisation. The form it adopts in this context is that drug usage is just one consequence of an undesirable set of social or psychological conditions which in themselves cannot be countered simply by countering drug usage. Those in favour of legalisation argue that if these adverse conditions are resolved or their necessary consequences diverted, there will be no need to use legal sanctions to reduce the demand for drugs.

In summary, none of the central arguments used against legalisation have fully succeeded in countering *all* of the disparate claims made by proponents of legalisation, although they clearly point up the potential problems of an entirely unregulated move to legalisation. The claim that drug related activities are criminal is difficult to support philosophically in a society where alcohol and tobacco are freely available, unless it is a claim defined circularly or purely by *recent* historical precedent. It is particularly difficult to support in the case of drug *users*, since upholding such a claim would logically entail the acceptance that other activities producing self inflicted harm were similarly criminal. Other theoretical arguments against legalisation suffer from similar departures from logic, notably in suggesting as a bar to legalisation the existence of problems which are in fact only contingently rather than necessarily linked with this option. Unfortunately, the need for empirical evidence - which could perhaps provide the most forceful argument either for or against legalisation - has not yet been addressed. It is worth noting, finally, that although opposition to legalisation is difficult to justify logically and little evidence exists to justify it empirically, it can be and frequently is, defended simply by accepting the illegality of drugs related activities or the need for a reduction in drug usage as valid *a priori*.

Decriminalisation

Ethan Nadelmann (1992) has, justifiably, complained that the legalisation debate has been simplified to the point where any support for legalisation is seen as a license to sell drugs "like candy" rather than being viewed as a considered response more closely linked with drugs prevention and harm reduction. He argues that the idea of a completely drug free society is more of a moral crusade than a practical proposition and suggests that a realistic and desirable goal would be to minimise the usage of all drugs - including presently legal drugs - whilst simultaneously aiming to minimise the 'collateral damage' associated with drug usage. This type of response to the legalisation issue has stimulated the development of a 'middle ground' in the debate centring around the prospect of decriminalisation.

Although the theoretical issues involved are more convoluted, in practice the distinction between legalisation and decriminalisation is essentially that the former defines both usage and dealing as legitimate activities, whilst the latter interprets usage as legitimate but dealing as *ill*egitimate. The rationale for this distinction is generally that drug dealing encourages individuals to inflict harm on themselves.

Proponents of decriminalisation have argued for this limited form of legalisation on the following grounds:

- it is a way station for legalisation
- it is a form of harm reduction
- it is a practical response to the problems of drugs control

Two approaches are taken by those supporting decriminalisation as a way station for legalisation. The first approach takes this option to be a means of testing the likely reaction of the general public to legalisation. The second, perhaps more considered, approach takes decriminalisation to be a means of testing the likely *effects* of legalisation on drug usage. It provides, for example, a means of establishing whether informal social controls on drug usage take over once legal controls are removed. The remaining two arguments mimic those for legalisation as such and will not be discussed in detail here. The 'harm reduction' argument for decriminalisation is based on the idea that the illegality of drug usage itself has disadvantages, such as preventing drug users from coming forward for help. In this way, illegality can again be seen as inadvertently promoting secondary forms of harm associated with drug usage. The final approach to decriminalisation is self explanatory and again matches similar arguments in support of legalisation.

As with *support* for decriminalisation, any *opposition* to decriminalisation centres largely around similar arguments to those made against legalisation and again these will not be further considered here. What is worth noting however, is that empirical evidence relating to decriminalisation may be more readily accessible than similar information relating to legalisation. Any concentration of control policies on dealers rather than users represents, for example, *de facto* decriminalisation. Since the present climate would seem to favour such a polarity of response, we may well be in a position to gather pertinent empirical data in the near future.

In summary, decriminalisation represents a theoretical and practical 'middle ground' between legalisation and maintaining present legal sanctions against drug usage. Although it is both supported and opposed using similar arguments to those used in the debate surrounding legalisation it has the advantage that its effects can be made amenable to empirical assessment without the need for any very extreme shift in present drugs control policies.

Public views regarding legalisation and decriminalisation

As noted earlier, one common argument against legalisation or decriminalisation is that drug usage simply *is* illegal. The more coherent forms of this argument rely on the fact that within a democracy the views of the general population must be taken into account and these views are assumed to hold legalisation in disfavour. Interestingly the American data cited by Inciardi and McBride in support of this position, whilst admittedly showing two recent decreases in the popularity of legalisation, also show a more long term trend *in favour* of such measures. As they correctly point out, however, those supporting legalisation nevertheless remain for the present in the minority.

One item in our interview schedule allowed us to address the present views of the British public on

177

legalisation and decriminalisation. This item presented a composite of the two views to respondents by asking them to indicate which, if any, of the following statements matched their own views on legalisation:

- all drugs should be legal, without any restrictions
- all drugs should be legal, but with *some* restrictions
- some drugs should be legal, without any restrictions
- some drugs should be legal but *with* restrictions
- all drugs currently prohibited should remain illegal

The five options were mutually exclusive. A detailed outline of the responses obtained to this item is given in Tables 9.1 to 9.6 in Appendix 1. A brief summary, averaged across locations is given in Figure 9.1 below.

Not surprisingly, the vast majority of our respondents were not in favour of the most extreme option of legalising all drugs without any restrictions. Only 1% or less of respondents in the main samples supported this option and only 2% to 3% of respondents in the booster samples did so. However, support *was* substantially higher for all options in which a *limited* form of legalisation was presented. Between 4% and 7% of respondents in the main samples were in favour of making some drugs (e.g. cannabis) legal with *no* controls and between 9% and 15% of respondents in the booster samples were in favour of this option. Equivalent levels of support were noted for the option of making some drugs legal but with *restrictions* and again the booster samples showed a higher level of support for this option than the main samples.

Interestingly, the option of making *all* drugs legal with some restrictions found greater favour amongst the *main* samples than amongst the booster samples. It is possible that this unanticipated disparity results from a tendency for the more 'knowledgeable' respondents to distinguish to a greater extent than main sample respondents between the levels of harm associated with different drugs. That is, booster sample respondents may have been more inclined to feel that some drugs needed no restriction whilst other drugs should under no circumstances be introduced to a legal market. This being a more polarised response than that shown by the main samples who felt perhaps that all drugs require some control but that no distinction need be drawn between drug types.

The above summary presents our findings for each individual statement separately. However, in the context of our earlier discussion regarding the legalisation issue, it in fact makes more sense to approach this item

Figure 9.1
Respondents' views regarding legalisation and decriminalisation

Main sample

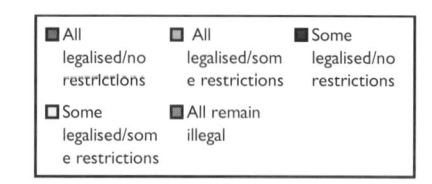

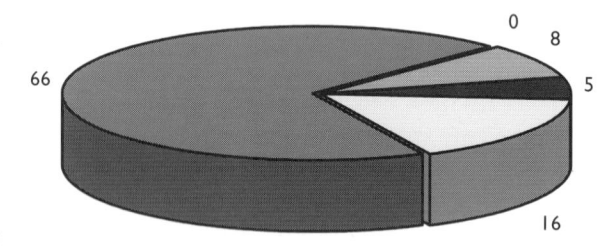

Booster sample

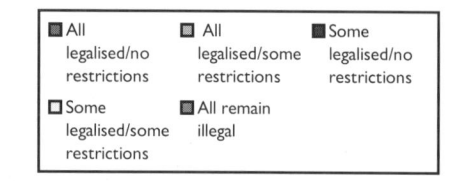

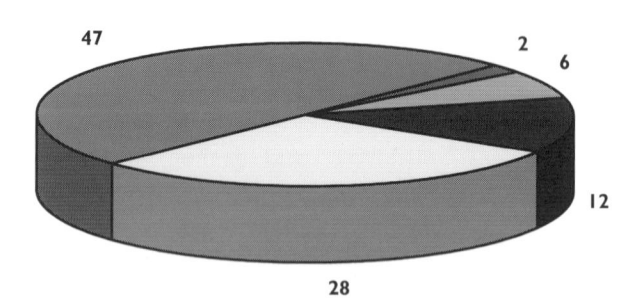

Percentage of respondents stating that all drugs should be legalised with no restrictions/Percentage of respondents stating that all drugs should be legalised but with some restrictions/Percentage of respondents stating that some drugs should be legalised with no restrictions/Percentage of respondents stating that some drugs should be legalised but with some restrictions/Percentage of respondents stating that all drugs presently illegal should remain illegal

in the questionnaire *as* a composite. The five statements shown to respondents were broadly representative of the range of legalisation/decriminalisation options presently available. Since the options were presented to our respondents as mutually exclusive, responses to similar options can be pooled. This allows us to estimate general levels of support for the loosening of present legal controls on drug usage. Taking this approach, it can be seen from the combined data given in Figure 9.2 that around 30% of main sample respondents and around 50% of booster sample respondents were in favour of *some* form of legalisation or decriminalisation. Given that neither the legalisation debate nor the problems of supply-side control have yet been addressed to any noticeable extent in the public forum and that the public *has* had considerable exposure to messages regarding the harmfulness of drugs, these can be regarded as fairly substantial percentages in favour of legalising or at least decriminalising a presently illegal practice.

Figure 9.2
Proportion of respondents in favour of some form of legalisation or decriminalisation

Main sample

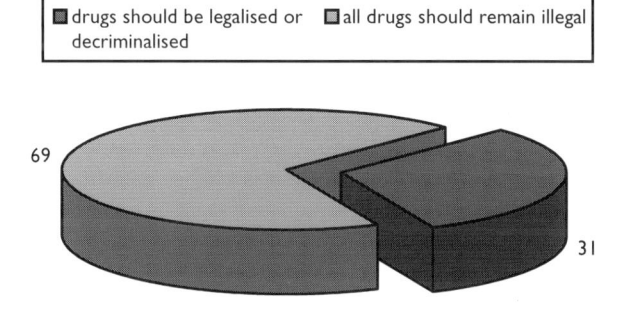

- drugs should be legalised or decriminalised: 31
- all drugs should remain illegal: 69

Booster sample

- drugs should be legalised or decriminalised: 50
- all drugs should remain illegal: 50

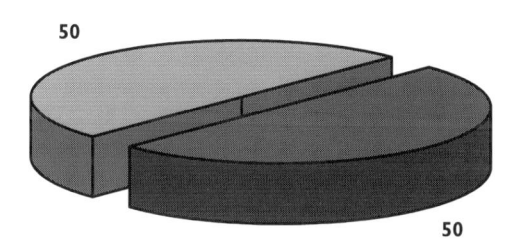

Percentage of respondents in favour of some form of legalisation or decriminalisation/Percentage of respondents feeling that all drugs should remain illegal

Clearly, some distinction between main and booster samples existed, with the booster samples generally regarding legalisation more favourably than the main samples. There was also some evidence of locational variation, with Bradford showing the lowest level of support for legalisation in both main and booster samples. However, locational variation was consistently *less* important than sample type. In the main samples, for example, Glasgow showed the greatest percentage of respondents in favour of some form of legalisation, but in the booster samples it showed the least. Similarly, the identity of the location showing the greatest preference for any *one* legalisation option differed across sample types. Notwithstanding such variation, the levels of support shown by our samples for a reduction in present legal controls on drug usage can only be described as surprisingly high in the circumstances.

In summary, a fairly sizeable minority of our respondents were willing to endorse some form of legalisation or decriminalisation for at least a restricted range of drugs. Support for this option reached a slight majority when a target sample of individuals 'at risk' of drug usage was considered.

Demographic variation in support for legalisation

Whilst a considerable minority of our sample appeared to favour some form of legalisation or decriminalisation, it was of course entirely possible that this minority represented only a very specific subset of the population, for example, drug users or the young. Such demographic factors, for example, almost certainly account for a number of broad disparities noted between the main samples and their booster sample counterparts. If demographic factors had also fully accounted for the distinction between those favouring legalisation/decriminalisation and those retaining a preference for legal controls, the results would have been less surprising than in fact they were. Sub-groups can be found in the population who are in favour of most things, but they do not represent the views even of a minority of the *general* population. In fact, the demographic profile of responses to our legalisation item proved to be much less polarised than this, suggesting at the very least that support for reducing present legal controls on drug usage is *not* restricted to young drug users.

Tables 9.2 to 9.4 in Appendix 1 summarise our respondents' views on legalisation, taking into account a respondent's demographic profile and their experience of drug usage. For the purposes of these tables, those in favour of 'legalisation' are regarded as individuals who favoured legalisation of some or all drugs with *no* restrictions, whilst those in favour of 'decriminalisation' are those who supported a more restricted form of legalisation with some imposed constraints.

Before moving on to consider the issue further, we would like to emphasise that the data do *not* suggest that demographic variation is *irrelevant* to the legalisation issue. Far from it. Respondents aged under 35 *were* more likely to favour legalisation than older respondents. Drug users *were* more likely to favour the loosening of present legal controls than non-drug users. Other forms of demographic variation were also apparent and we will discuss these in detail before going on to put the results in a broader context. The point we *are* making with regard to demographic variation is rather that our data do *not* support simple stereotypes of legalisation which view the loosening of legal controls as being an option favoured only by 'hippies, drug users and middle class intellectuals'.

So what types of people *were* in favour of legalisation? As noted above, the under 35 age group were more likely to favour legalisation than their older counterparts. Male respondents were also slightly more likely to favour legalisation than female respondents. Similarly, respondents from ethnic minorities were more likely to favour legalisation than white respondents. The gender and ethnic profile was common to both main and booster samples. The age bias, not surprisingly, was present only in the main sample. In contrast to many other attitudinal issues, support for legalisation showed no clear effect for socioeconomic status in either main or booster sample, with any apparent trend being largely location dependent.

The profile of those respondents wishing to keep all drugs *illegal* was for the most part the mirror image of this demographic distribution, as one might expect. One exception to this being that no clear pattern emerged for the effect of ethnicity. Taking the data as a whole it appeared that whilst white respondents tended to spread their responses across all three options (legalisation, decriminalisation and keeping all drugs illegal), respondents from ethnic minorities tended rather to polarise their responses around the legal/illegal dimension.

Looking at the demographic profile of those favouring *decriminalisation*, a broad socioeconomic split did emerge, with respondents from groups AB and C1 being more likely to be in favour of decriminalisation than respondents from the C2 or DE groups. The split between males and females was also more extreme than that noted for legalisation, with again a higher percentage of males than females in favour of decriminalisation in both main and booster samples. The ethnic profile was as indicated above.

If we separate those respondents in favour of some form of legalisation or decriminalisation from those respondents in favour of maintaining present legal controls, the most noticeable distinction is, rather predictably, that between drug users and non-drug users - with the former group being significantly more likely to favour both legalisation and decriminalisation than the latter. Although this is a predictable pattern to emerge, there are a number of interesting points to be made alongside this broad observation. Firstly, drug users were more likely to favour decriminalisation than the more extreme option of legalisation. Secondly, the distinction between drug users and non-users was not restricted to that between respondents *presently* using drugs and those not using drugs. Those who had in the past used drugs but who had chosen to stop doing so were still more likely to be in favour of some form of legalisation than non-drug users. A final point to note is that users of opiates were more likely to favour *both* legalisation and decriminalisation than users of either non-opiates or cannabis.

The above points are important in that they stand in contrast to a number of common assumptions regarding legalisation. In the first place, drug users would not seem, on the whole, to favour all-out legalisation. The fact that users of the more heavily controlled drugs *are* more likely to favour extreme forms of legalisation is not unexpected, since they are the group most likely to face severe penalties as the law stands at present. However, this point in itself undermines any suggestion that cannabis or other 'soft' drug users are the main proponents of legalisation within the drug using community. In line with this latter point, it would seem also that those who *do* have some experience of using drugs, but who may have a more balanced or long-term perspective than *present* users by virtue of the fact that they have stopped using drugs, still feel disposed towards legalisation, or at least decriminalisation. Taken as a whole these features of the data present a more balanced picture of the type of support given by the drug using community to legalisation than that which is often presented by, for example, the media.

This notwithstanding, it becomes apparent, comparing across the demographic profiles outlined above, that the distinctions noted in attitudes towards legalisation broadly match those noted for drug *usage*. Again, this is not unexpected, but how much of the variation can we actually explain on this basis? If we removed drug users and perhaps also the young from the debate would the public be 100% against legalisation? To answer this type of question and more generally to establish the actual importance of demographic variables in explaining attitudes towards legalisation, we ran a regression model for both main and booster samples, using the extent of support for legalisation (in favour of legalisation *per se,* in favour of restricted legalisation/decriminalisation, or in favour of keeping drugs illegal) as a target variable.

The variables we put into the regression equation as possible mediators of the variance observed were location, age group, gender, socioeconomic status, ethnicity, whether the respondent had *ever* taken an unprescribed drug and their present frequencies of using cannabis, non-opiates and opiates. The latter being measured on a scale ranging from 'not at all' to 'daily'. The results of our regression models are outlined in detail in Tables 9.5 and 9.6 in Appendix 1 and summarised below in Figure 9.3.

Figure 9.3
Summary of regression model for views on legalisation: Main sample

Response	Variables in final model	Direction of effect	% of variance explained
Main Sample			
extent of agreement with legalisation or decriminalisation	ever taken illicit drugs	user>non-user	11
	frequency of taking cannabis	user>non-user	
	age group	younger>older	
	gender	males>females	
Booster Sample			
extent of agreement with legalisation or decriminalisation	ever taken illicit drugs	user>non-user	14
	frequency of taking cannabis	user>non-user	

variables in equation: *location, whether ever taken any illicit drug, frequency of taking cannabis, frequency of taking non-opiate, frequency of taking opiates, age group, socioeconomic status, gender, ethnicity (white, black, asian)*

The regression models tell us two things. First, although in the booster sample demographic variance did not have any effect independent of drug usage, in the main sample two of the demographic variables *were* of independent value. Older respondents and females, independently of their experience of drug usage, appeared to be less likely to favour legalisation than their demographic counterparts. So, as our earlier summary of the data suggested both personal experience of drug usage and some aspects of demography can have an independent link with one's views on legalisation. Having said which, it is important to note from these multivariate analyses that any effects of ethnicity or socioeconomic status appeared to be an artifact of the more salient effects of age, gender and personal drug usage. The second and, in the present context, more important aspect of the models was that, taking both drug usage and demography into account, we were able to explain less than 15% of the variance observed in support for legalisation in both main and booster samples.

Whilst certainly not a negligible proportion of the variance, this is clearly insufficient to justify any claim that views regarding legalisation polarise solely around the dimensions formed by demography and drug usage. Evidently, other factors are involved. It may be, for example, that those supporting legalisation were *either* the most well informed, or the least well informed of our respondents on the drugs issue. Whatever reason an individual respondent had for favouring legalisation or decriminalisation, the point here is that the significant minority of our sample who supported legalisation or decriminalisation were *not* culled solely from a particular demographic group or from a sub-section of the population who themselves used drugs. Rather, they derived from a range of demographic groups and were equally diverse in terms of their personal experience of drug usage. In short, the 'young drug user' stereotype does not come close to explaining the levels of support we found for relaxing present legal controls on drug usage.

In summary, responses to an item in our questionnaire dealing with the issue of legalisation suggest that around 30% of the general population and around 50% of individuals in groups at risk of drug usage may be in favour or some limited form of legalisation or decriminalisation. Whilst in the case of the general population such figures suggest that this option remains a minority preference, the numbers favouring legalisation are still surprisingly high given that neither legalisation nor the problems faced by supply side control are issues which have as yet been addressed in the public domain. Multivariate analyses suggested further that demographic profiles and personal experience of drug usage were not the sole motivators behind any support for legalisation.

Altering social or economic structures

Legalisation and decriminalisation are not the only options which have been suggested as alternatives to the traditional approach of drugs control policies. There is an alternative to drugs control which argues for an even more fundamental restructuring of existing practices. This approach relies on the assumption, noted earlier, that drug usage and, in particular, problematic drug usage is a function of problems outside of the behaviour itself. Popular candidates for this type of causal account of drug usage are represented by the concepts of psychological, economic and social alienation.

Proponents of 'causal' models of drug usage naturally see the solution to the drugs problem as lying in our ability to change the social, economic or psychological structures seen as resulting in drug usage. Such approaches are epitomised, for example, by the statements of Ferman and Ferman (1973) who note that "drug pushing is part of the irregular economy. This economy is known to expand in periods of economic restructuring, recession and unemployment". The implication being that, since drug usage is a function of such factors as the polarisation of wealth and the decay of the urban infrastructure, it can only effectively be dealt with by broad changes in a country's social and economic structure.

As is the nature of causal models, none of the links are put forward as absolutes. Not all depressed or otherwise alienated people take drugs, not everyone in a poverty stricken ghetto takes drugs. The argument is rather that certain conditions promote drug dealing and usage. Urban ghettos are, for example, a natural market place for illicit activities. In terms of drug usage it is difficult to 'just say no' if there are no alternative options to say 'yes' to. Similarly, with regard to drug dealing, deprived areas provide a large labour pool available to work at the most exposed level of distribution. As Maccoun and Reuter (1992) rather ironically phrase it, the wages of sin may be $30 an hour. Since the links between alienation or inequality and drug usage are not seen to be absolute, proponents of the causal models do not suggest that any solutions would be absolutes. Their position is perhaps best summarised by Segal (1972) who notes that "even if a utopia could be established .... people would probably still use drugs, but the extent of use might be much different from that in today's society".

A recent more specific application of the general thesis of alienation or inequality is that drug usage has over time moved to a section of society for which it has different and perhaps more problematic meanings. A good summary of this type of approach is given in Collison *(op cit.)*. Essentially the rationale is that two forms of societal change are acting in opposition to one another. At the same time as we develop consumerism and stimulate expectations of increased leisure and the enjoyment of material goods across a broader section of society, we are in fact engaged in polarising access to these resources. The presumed consequence being that individuals will strive to satisfy the needs and desires which have been created without regard to the sanctions imposed by society on their attempt to do so. The 'drugs problem' enters this picture at two points. Firstly it enters as a part of the leisure/luxury culture. In this context drugs are a motivator to crime or other misadventure. Secondly it enters as a further form of social division. Drug usage is a behaviour which is more readily resolvable and less likely to lead to secondary problems in conditions where the individual has access to support, whether social, emotional or financial. Such support, it is argued, matches other societal trends in becoming increasingly polarised. So those who are perhaps most strongly motivated to use drugs are in fact those least able to cope with doing so at a variety of levels.

Whilst both the above forms of causal approach to the drugs problem have a great deal of theoretical and intellectual appeal, Dorn and South (1986) have argued that practical problems militate against the objective value of any such 'deeper structure' approach to drugs prevention. In particular, they note "the high fiscal cost of success and the high political cost of failure". This pragmatic argument can be strengthened further by noting that even a 'success' in social terms may be definable as a moral or political failure. An inherent irony of this argument is, of course, that such factors could themselves readily be incorporated into the 'alienation' model. Nevertheless, the broad nature of the claims being made in the more 'causal' models of drug usage is unfortunately a real problem. Although strong theoretical arguments are presented supporting the links suggested, these remain in essence an empirical issue and the data required to substantiate such models are sufficiently extensive *and* eclectic to render validation untenable unless we adopt a long term perspective. Perhaps, in the short term, the main value of the causal or social structure view of drugs prevention lies in simply raising the question of *why* a substantial proportion of our urban, low socioeconomic status, young adults do appear to feel the need to indulge in the use of psychoactive drugs.

In summary, a range of causal models have been offered which suggest a 'deeper structure' approach to drugs prevention. Specifically, these models take the 'drugs problem' to be one aspect of a more fundamental problem linked to psychological, economic or social alienation. Whilst promising at the theoretical level, such models are unlikely in practice to provide a short term solution to the immediate problems of drug usage or dealing. Nevertheless, they do serve to highlight those aspects of the 'drugs problem' which associate with present societal structures.

Summary of Chapter 9

The data we outlined in earlier sections of this report suggested that the public regard drug usage and drugs control as being in a largely unidirectional causal relationship. Some form of positive intervention in drug usage is preferred, a variety of quite distinct methods of control are approved of, and all are seen as likely to be at least partially effective in significantly reducing the misuse of drugs.

The real picture, as outlined in the present chapter, suggests that the nature of the drug usage/drugs prevention relationship is rather more convoluted. Control methods *may* reduce drug misuse to some extent, but they are equally likely to show a more symbiotic relationship with both dealing and usage and may even be completely *oblique* to the issue. Given which, the high fiscal cost associated with putting control into practice could be difficult to justify. On the other hand, a reduction in, or complete withdrawal of, control on drug usage may conflict with firmly held moral or philosophical views on the nature of drug usage. A substantial minority of our respondents appeared to be in favour of some restricted form of legalisation, but the general attitude towards drug usage nevertheless placed drug users in the category of victims or criminals rather than legitimate consumers. This leaves the very pertinent dilemma that, whilst control measures have a high fiscal cost, any removal of control may have an equivalently high political cost.

To avoid both pitfalls, it might be possible to *redirect* rather than reduce or remove drugs control, for example, by shifting the emphasis from less effective to more effective methods, or from supply reduction to the reduction of demand. Although providing a potential political and financial solution to the drugs issue, this option is also problematic. It entails an ability to monitor and compare the outcome of methods which are not only qualitatively distinct in terms of their operation, but which also presuppose a range of different end points in the ascription of 'success'. In addition to such immediate problems we are also left with the more long term difficulty of establishing what the deeper causal structure of the 'drugs problem' actually is. Clearly, there is no easy or short term solution to the problem of drug usage - however this is defined.

Chapter 10

THE VIEWS AND HABITS OF THE GENERAL PUBLIC: MESSAGES FROM THE HOUSEHOLD DRUGS SURVEY

The aim of the Household Drugs Survey was to inform policy on drugs prevention and, indeed, drugs policy generally, by undertaking the first large scale public survey in Great Britain of illicit drug usage and attitudes towards drugs usage, drugs prevention and drugs control. It is not a national survey and it is not possible to derive national statistics directly from our findings. The survey does, however, provide a relatively detailed picture of four towns and our results suggest that the profile of drug usage and attitudes towards drugs prevention will be similar in any areas with an equivalent demographic profile to our chosen locations.

The locations used for the survey - Bradford, Glasgow, Nottingham and the London Borough of Lewisham - were selected on the basis of two distinct criteria. Firstly they had to be areas in which Drugs Prevention Initiative teams were already working. Secondly, they needed to represent quite distinct areas in Britain. For each of the four locations, we surveyed two different samples. One sample was taken from the general population. This allowed us to gain an idea of the overall prevalence of drug usage and differences in attitudes across the whole spread of demographic groups in the population. The size of this sample in each town was about 1,000 people. The second sample was taken from a target group of the population seen as being at high 'risk' of drug usage and involved about 250 people in each location. Since we had no information on which to draw to construct the best profile for this 'at risk' sample, we based the sample around housing areas defined through ACORN variables as likely to be those of greater *relative* deprivation. Within these areas, we sampled only those aged between 16 and 25, to try to maximise the likelihood of finding those who might have experience of recent drugs usage and who would constitute a relatively informed population in terms of the availability of drugs and other drugs-related issues. Although we kept quite closely to this sample design, some respondents in our booster sample inevitably turned out to be slightly older than we had intended or to come from areas which could not in all honesty be described as deprived. Nevertheless, the vast majority of our booster sample do fit this general profile of an 'at risk' group.

The range of data available to us from these two samples enabled us not only to consider the target issues of drug usage and perceptions of drugs usage and drugs control, but also to look at a broader variety of issues relating to the drugs problem. Amongst these were the locational clustering of drug usage, the profile of drugs related problems in local areas in comparison to other crimes and problems in the same areas, and the controversial issue of the legalisation or decriminalisation of presently illicit drugs.

Self-reported drug usage

The patterns of self-report drug usage obtained from the survey suggested that a significant minority of the general population had direct personal experience of drug usage and that a slightly higher proportion had indirect knowledge of usage obtained via an acquaintanceship with users. As we had predicted, levels of both direct and indirect knowledge of drugs were substantially higher amongst the target group of low socioeconomic status young adults living in areas of urban deprivation than amongst the general population sample.

Although drug usage was clearly not negligible in our samples, the data gave little indication of any high risk patterns of usage. Cannabis was the drug of which the greatest proportion of respondents had direct experience and the number of respondents presently using or having in the past tried opiate based drugs such as heroin or cocaine was minimal. Similarly, figures for injecting usage were very low indeed. These aspects of our data and other aspects relating to the comparatively low levels of drug usage amongst minority ethnic groups set the present survey apart from a range of high risk drug usage studies conducted over the last few years. We suggest in the report that this disparity is a function of the methodologies used in high risk studies and argue that the general population picture of drug usage is in fact far less disturbing than such studies might suggest.

Knowledge about drugs and the extent of drug usage

As might be expected given the numbers of respondents with some experience of drugs, the public's general awareness of drug usage as an issue was quite high.

However, it was also quite targeted. Apart from cannabis, the drugs most likely to be named by respondents as being used illicitly were largely those for which there has been a degree of media attention, for example, heroin and ecstasy. This was true for both the general population sample and the at risk sample. A particularly noticeable and perhaps disturbing gap in the public's knowledge base was the illicit use of medically relevant drugs such as tranquillisers. Very few respondents chose to name these drugs as subject to illicit usage.

Although the general population sample and the 'at risk' sample differed in their levels of drug usage they did *not* differ substantially in their views regarding either the nature of the drugs 'problem' or the options available for controlling drug usage. Both samples regarded drug usage as a very big problem nationally. Views relating to the causes of drug usage suggest that the population perceives drug usage as a reaction to environmental stresses, within the normal range of behaviour. They see the first experimentation with drugs as largely accidental, or dependent on circumstance, in the sense that introduction to drugs occurs via peers who are taking drugs or via social events at which drugs are being taken. Interestingly, the views of drug users and non-drug users showed no broad distinctions on this issue of causality.

Although our respondents were clearly aware of drug usage as a problem, they were apt to think of the problem as primarily a national one - or as a local one for someone else! Furthermore, even respondents living within areas which we knew to be quite heavily populated with drug users were likely to say that their area was experiencing a much *lower* level of the drugs problem than other areas. Similar findings, however, pertain for other social problems, such as general crime levels, where people are loathe to ascribe problematic status to their own neighbourhood. A comparison between those with direct experience of drug usage and those without such experience did, however, suggest that exposure to the drugs issue as a concrete rather than an abstract problem led to higher estimates of the actual level of the problem.

The types of drug problem which appeared to be of greatest concern, both to those with and those without direct experience of drug usage, were the existence of drug users as such and the association between drug usage and crime, in particular crimes such as theft. Comparing our respondents' concerns regarding such problems with other fears and worries regarding crime and other problems in their neighbourhood suggested, however, that drug usage had a fairly low profile in the general hierarchy of local problems. Certainly it did not appear greatly to influence either the levels of satisfaction individuals displayed with their neighbourhoods or their fear of walking around alone in that neighbourhood or otherwise being unprotected.

Locational variation in patterns of drug usage

The fairly rosy picture drawn by at least some individuals in certain high drug usage areas was in sharp contrast to the actual picture we obtained of locational variation in drug usage. Our data supports the work of a number of researchers in suggesting that drug usage clusters in fairly distinct neighbourhoods. Furthermore, the 'drug using' neighbourhoods we managed to partition out from our samples showed distinct demographic profiles. They were virtually all characterised by high levels of inner city or council owned housing (as defined by ACORN, the housing classification system on which our selection of the booster sample was also based) and equally high levels of individuals in socioeconomic groups D and E. Both measures are of course associated with greater levels of poverty and deprivation.

ACORN is not an ideal social indicator, but other measures, such as direct Census variables, were not available for recent years at the time of writing this report. The particular deficiencies of ACORN in the present context included the fact that the profiling we used to allocate housing types to these neighbourhoods may not be able to be directly equated with poverty or deprivation in the case of our Scottish city. A more general point is that ACORN ratings are a rather complex mixture of categorisations of housing type, relative wealth, and type of residents. With these caveats in mind and considering also the distinction between our booster sample and our main sample in terms of patterns of drug usage, we have reached the tentative conclusion that drug usage *does* cluster along the lines drawn by urban deprivation and that as a function of this larger pattern, particular local neighbourhoods will be subject to higher than average levels of drug usage. The extent of this local variation makes it important to conduct further *localised* surveys of drug usage and attitudes rather than relying solely upon national figures.

Drugs prevention and drugs control

Turning finally to the issue of drugs prevention, both of our types of sample appeared to feel that some form of positive intervention to reduce drugs misuse would be desirable. A variety of quite distinct control measures were favoured and all were thought to be likely to succeed in controlling drugs misuse to some extent.

We obtained quite extensive data on one particular method of drugs prevention, namely education. This method met with almost unanimous approval amongst our respondents, with 12 to 18 year olds being seen as the most appropriate targets of drugs education. Parents in particular expressed a strong desire for such education to be instituted where it was *not* available and almost complete approval of drugs education where it *was* available. This was in itself interesting given that parents appeared quite reluctant either to admit to drug usage amongst their children's peer groups or to admit of the possibility that their children might themselves one day take drugs (although it is worth noting here that drug users did have a rather more realistic view on this latter point). Respondents also held strong views on *who* should provide drugs education, with schools or the government being seen as much the most appropriate organisations to hold such responsibility by a broad cross-section of demographic groups. With regard to the aims of drugs education, the most appropriate form of education was seen to be education aimed at prevention rather than harm reduction, although a substantial proportion of respondents, notably in the high risk sample, would support a combination of these approaches. Understandably, drug users were more likely to favour harm reduction forms of education than were non-drug users, although on the whole even drug users felt that aiming education both at harm reduction and prevention would be an appropriate goal.

Rather sadly, given the obvious interest in drugs prevention, spontaneous awareness of agencies able to provide drugs-related help and information was minimal in both the general population and high risk samples. Most respondents and, in particular, the sub-group of respondents who were parents, felt that very little provision existed in their local area for drugs-related advice. The first likely point of contact was judged by most people to be their local GP or clinic. However, a description given to respondents of the Drugs Prevention Teams established a clear expectation that statutory organisations such as these should be responsible for giving drugs related advice. The description also seemed to convince respondents that the potential effectiveness of these Teams in reducing drugs misuse was quite high (although the visibility of the Teams was clearly very low at the time of the survey).

Actual estimates of effectiveness by individuals with some direct or indirect contact with a variety of drugs related agencies suggested that, although overall levels of satisfaction with the advice given by agencies were quite high, they were also very variable, depending on a variety of factors including the type of agency, its location and the demographic characteristics of the respondent. Specialist local and voluntary drugs agencies were seen as the most satisfactory of the agencies mentioned, with national agencies such as Social Services proving less popular. Although understandable, given the different briefs of these two forms of agency, this finding sits uncomfortably with the general consensus that government agencies of some sort should be responsible for service provision. The most popular option for this responsibility proved to be the Drugs Prevention Teams, however, which perhaps provide a useful compromise here, being in essence a *government funded* form of local agency providing some support for drugs prevention together with information and advice.

Finally, it is of interest to note that public expectations regarding drugs control methods were in distinct contrast to the potential scope of such methods in leading to considerable decreases in drugs usage. The public expressed some satisfaction with the idea of customs control and police enforcement (with both customs control and multi-agency police action being more strongly supported than street level police enforcement against users), yet neither method is likely to reduce drug usage substantially below its current level. There was also a surprisingly high degree of public support for a response to the drugs issue which has not yet been tried in practice, namely limited legalisation or decriminalisation of illicit drugs. A substantial minority of respondents in both the general population sample and the high risk sample were in favour of such an approach. Although certain demographic biases were noted - for example the predictable bias that younger respondents and drug users were more likely to be in favour of legalisation or decriminalisation than older respondents or non-drug users - this minority was, in general, drawn from a broad demographic spread of the population. This is a notable finding, given that the issue of legalisation has not yet been firmly confronted in the public arena. Perhaps the central point to pull out from this aspect of the survey is that the public feels that *something* positive should be done about the misuse of drugs and it is willing to entertain a range of options to this end.

Messages from the study

This survey is the first general population study to be published in Great Britain. It covered a very wide remit, with, necessarily, only sketchy coverage of many areas, particularly the different forms of drugs control policy. Our conclusions must be tentative - and they are constrained very much by the questions we were able to cram into just one interview with each person. It may be helpful, however, for us to give our own conclusions as to the major messages which arise from the study, so that they can help to formulate the further research and development which is obviously vital in this area.

From the evidence of our data, we feel it is not possible to conclude that the general population is ignorant of the likelihood of drugs being available in their town or their area. A substantial minority will have taken illegal drugs themselves at some time in their lives, athough only a few will currently be doing so. Moreover, they are very aware that people they know may be offered drugs, and that their children may be exposed to drugs. People seemed to find no difficulty in talking about the possibility of drug usage in their local area. They wanted more information, more possibilities for advice, more action of a sensible and sensitive kind. They were not rejecting the thought of drugs usage, or refusing to contemplate the necessity for a drugs prevention policy. In fact, we gained the impression that the general public is less worried about discussing an integrated drugs policy including prevention, treatment and control than are people in government or in statutory and voluntary drugs agencies. Certainly they are less worried about discussing controversial issues such as legalisation.

The patterns of usage we uncovered showed a clear separation between the frequency of usage of, on the one hand, cannabis and a group of relatively common drugs based largely on non-opiate derivatives and, on the other hand, opiate based drugs such as heroin, cocaine and crack. The prevalence of usage and the perceived availability of cannabis and the 'non-opiate' drugs (amphetamines, LSD, magic mushrooms etc.) means that young people in all our towns were likely to come into contact with such drugs, or with people who take them. In our view, this implies that there is a need to make sure that young people's reactions to such contact are *informed* reactions. They should know what these substances are (so that they cannot all be passed off as being entirely innocuous), what effects they may have and, in particular, the very substantial dangers of taking cocktails of drugs, or mixing other drugs with alcohol. We are not minimising the work already being done in relation to specific drugs such as heroin and equally in relation to particular prevention measures such as needle exchange schemes, AIDS education etc. rather, we would like to emphasise that drugs prevention needs to be extended to cover the particular profiles of a broader range of drugs and equally it needs to move further away from a medical perspective into a broader social definition of health care.

The strong support from all sections of the population for drugs education, especially from parents, means, we feel, that work needs urgently to be undertaken to develop such education with at least 12-18 year olds. We suspect that this means not only the development of packages and teaching aids, but also the provision of training and support for teachers, including the development of referral possibilities in this context. Clearly, there is a need for far more research and evaluation in this area, especially if we are to work out the most effective messages, and to keep up to date with fashions in drug taking and drug availability.

It is with regard to the work of different agencies and drugs control in general that the study's results are most tantalising, but also most incomplete. Quite clearly, the public has views about both supply and demand oriented methods of social control, which we were only skating over within the confines of this study. As it becomes more important that we develop adequate methods for discussing priorities in social control within local areas, so we hope that local surveys (as well as nationally organised ones) will include broad questions on drugs control policies, as well as dealing with more specific issues such as reaction times for police incident response etc. As we develop national, European and regional agencies for drugs control, establishing public views and hence the acceptability of the processes we are adopting becomes even more important.

The importance of this type of research is highlighted by our own respondents' views on the relative merits of different harm reduction and primary prevention strategies within the very new field of drugs prevention. Although we were not able properly to tap the public's views on such issues, quite clear preferences emerged. Whilst we suspect that with further information the public would support both types of strategy, their first priority at this moment is clearly based on a preference for primary prevention. Interestingly, we were unable to compare our findings with those from other countries, simply because there is no other European public survey on drugs *prevention*.

If there is to be more drugs education, more primary preventive action and more public discussion of drugs issues, then clearly, the pressure on advice agencies and drugs agencies generally is going to increase. The survey showed that people do not know necessarily where to turn at this moment. Their first thought was to turn to GPs, a reflection perhaps of the medicalisation of drugs issues in the past. They were not aware of voluntary advice agencies, even though these seemed to be what people were seeking. The history of the development of structures to cope with other needs for support and advice from the public (such as Victim Support and Citizens Advice Bureaux) indicates that specialist voluntary agencies or local, governmentally supported agencies are the most effective means of delivering services to the general public. Statutory agencies (such as social services) of necessity have to concentrate on priority areas of greatest need (such as child abuse). The existence of coercive legal powers of intervention also tends to put people off applying to such statutory agencies for help and support, certainly in relation to illicit behaviours. The history of other fields also indicates, however, that voluntary agencies need to have a local presence and to have guaranteed funding for core expenses (so that they do not have to spend all their time fund-raising).

This comparison with other services renders the lack of current visibility, but the considerable degree of approval, for Drugs Prevention Initiative activities less anomalous. It also implies that as they become more visible, the demand for their services is likely to increase substantially. It would be extremely unfortunate if a surge in the awareness of drugs prevention, stimulated for example by drugs education, were to coincide with a decrease in the availability of the agencies seen by the public as being most likely to meet their needs for advice and support. The concern we have is that the current pattern of agencies is very diverse, stemming from different disciplines, different models of how drug users are perceived, and different kinds of funding. It is not clear that there is any integrated pattern of drugs prevention in local areas, nor are there always open and fruitful paths of communication between agencies providing different services and playing different roles. We suspect strongly that the public considers that there *should* be and that drugs prevention needs to match this growing awareness in developing beyond its infancy.

REFERENCES

Advisory Council on the Misuse of Drugs (1984) *Prevention.* **London: HMSO.**

Auld, J. N., Dorn, N, and South, N. (1986) Irregular work, irregular pleasures: Heroin in the 1980s, in R. Matthews and J. Young (1986) (eds.) *Confronting Crime* **London: Sage.**

Awiah, J., Butt, S. and Dorn, N. (1990) The last place I would go: Black people and drug services in Britain *Druglink* 5: 5 pgs. 14-15

Baldwin, J. and Bottoms, A.E. (1976) *The Urban Criminal.* **London: Tavistock.**

Bean, P. (1993) *'Police informers and drug use'* Paper presented to the **British Criminology Conference** 28-31 July 1993, Cardiff.

Bean, P. T. and Pearson, Y. (1992) 'Cocaine and crack in Nottingham 1989/90 and 1991/1992'. in J. Mott (ed.) (1992) *Crack and Cocaine in England and Wales.* **Home Office: Research and Planning Unit Paper 70.**

Bell, C. and Battjes, R. (1985) 'Overview of drugs prevention research'. in C. Bell and R. Battjes (1985) (eds.) *Prevention Research: Deterring Drug Abuse Amongst Children and Adolescents.* **NIDA Research Monograph 63 Rockville, Md.: NIDA.**

Berridge, V. (ed.) (1990) *Drug Research and Policy in Britain.* **Aldershot: Avebury.**

Bottoms, A.E. , Claytor, A. and Wiles, P. (1989) *'Housing and Crime in Sheffield: A Report to the Home Office'.* **Sheffield: Centre for Criminological and Socio-Legal Studies.**

Bottoms, A.E. and Wiles, P. (1986a) *Crime and Housing Policy: A Framework for Crime Prevention Analysis.* **London: HMSO.**

Bottoms, A.E. and Wiles, P (1992a) 'Explanations of crime and place', in D.J. Evans, N.R. Fyfe and D.T. Herbert (eds.): *Crime, Policing and Place.* **London: Routledge.**

Bottoms, A.E. and Wiles, P. (1986b) 'Housing Tenure and Community Crime Careers in Britain', in A.J. Reiss and M. Tonry (eds): *Communities and Crime.* **Chicago: University of Chicago Press.**

Bottoms, A.E., Claytor, A. and Wiles, P. (1992b) 'Housing markets and residential community crime careers', in D.J. Evans, N.R. Fyfe and D.T. Herbert (eds.): *Crime, Policing and Place.* **London: Routledge.**

Bottoms, A.E., Claytor, A and Wiles, P. (1990) *Housing Crime in Sheffield: A Research Report.* **Sheffield: Centre for Criminological & Socio-Legal Studies.**

Botvin, G. and Dusenbury, L. (1989) 'Substance abuse prevention and the promotion of competence', in L. Bond and B. Compas (eds.): *Primary Prevention in the Schools.* **London: Sage.**

Bukoski, W. (1986) 'School based substance abuse prevention: a review of program research', in S. Griswold-Ezekoye, K. Kumpfer, and W. Bukoski (eds.): *Childhood and Chemical Abuse: Prevention and Intervention.* **New York: Haworth Press.**

Burr, A. (1987) 'Chasing the Dragon'. *'British Journal of Criminology'* 27: (4) pgs. 333-357.

Coggans, N., Shewan, D., Henderson, M., Davies, J. and O'Hagan, F. (1989) *National Evaluation of Drug Education in Scotland.* **University of Strathclyde.**

Cohen, A. P. (ed.) (1982) *Belonging: Identity and Social Organisation in British Rural Cultures* **Manchester: Manchester University Press**

Collins, J.J., Hubbard, R. L. and Rachal, J. V. (1985) 'Expensive drug use and illegal income: a test of explanatory hypotheses' *Criminology,* 23: pgs. 743-763.

Collison, M. (1993) *'Drug Offenders and Criminal Justice: Careers, Compulsion, Commitment and Penalty.'* Paper presented to the **British Criminology Conference** 28-31 July 1993, Cardiff.

Dembo, R. , Blount, W.R. , Schmeidler, J. and Burgos, W. (1986) 'Perceived environmental drug use risk and the correlates of early drug use or non-use among inner-city youths: The motivated actor' *International Journal of the Addictions,* 21: 9-10 pgs. 977-1000.

Dembo, R. and Burgos, W. (1976) 'A framework for developing drug abuse prevention strategies for young people in ghetto areas'. *Journal of Drug Education,* 6 (4): pgs. 313-325.

Ditton, J. and Speirits, K. (1984) *The Rapid Increase of Heroin Addiction in Glasgow during 1981* **University of Glasgow: Department of Sociology**

Dorn, N. , Murji, K. and South, N. (1991) *Traffickers: Drug Markets and Law Enforcement.* **London: Routledge.**

Dorn, N. and Murji, K. (1992) *Drug prevention: A Review of the English language literature.* **ISDD Research Monograph 5 London: ISDD.**

Dorn, N. and South, N. (1986) 'Criminology and economics of drug distribution in Britain; Options for control'. *Journal of Drug Issues.* 16 pgs.523-35.

Dorn, N. and South, N. (1987) *A Land Fit for Heroin? Drug Policies, Prevention and Practice.* **London: MacMillan.**

Duster, T. (1970) *The Legislation of Morality.* **London: MacMillan.**

Edwards, G. (1981) The home office index as a basic monitoring system. In G.Edwards and C. Busch (eds.) *Drug problems in Britain: A Review of Ten Years.* **London: Academic Press.**

Elliot, D. (1993) *A Developmental Perspective on Social Integration: Explaining Individual Patterns of Violent Crime over the Life-span.* Paper presented to the **British Criminology Conference** 28-31 July 1993, Cardiff.

Eysenck, H. J. (1976) *Sex and Personality.* **London: Open Books.**

Eysenck, H. J. (1964) (ed) *Experiments with Drugs.* **New York: Pergamon Press.**

Ferman, L. and Ferman, P. (1973) 'The structural underpinnings of the irregular economy'. *Poverty and Human Resources Abstracts*, 8, pgs.13-17.

Forster, B. and Salloway, J. (1990) (eds.) *The Socio-Cultural Matrix of Alcohol and Drug Use: A Source Book of Patterns and Factors.* **Lampeter: Metheun.**

Forsyth, A. J. M. , Hammersley, R. H. , Lavelle, T. L. and Murray, K. J. (1992) *Geographical aspects of scoring illegal drugs (in press).*

Frischer, M. (1992) 'Estimated prevalence of injecting drug use in Glasgow' *British Journal of Addiction.* 87 pgs. 235-243.

Gabe, J. (1988) Race and tranquilliser use in N. Dorn, L. Lucas, N. South (eds): *Drug Questions: An Annual Research Register Issue 4.* **London: Institute for the Study of Drug Dependence.**

Ghodse, A. H and Rawson, N. S. (1978) 'Distribution of drug related problems among London casualty departments' *British Journal of Psychiatry* 132: pgs. 467-472.

Ghodse, H. (1989) *Drugs and Addictive Behaviour: a Guide to Treatment.* **Oxford: Blackwell.**

Glynn, T. (ed.) (1983) *Drug Abuse Prevention Research Research Issues Series 33.* **Rockville: Md.: NIDA.**

Goodstadt, M. (1978) *Alcohol and Drug Education: Models and Outcomes.* **Health Education Monographs** 6, (3); pgs 263-79

Haw, S. (1985) *Drug problems in greater Glasgow* **Glasgow: SCODA.**

Headley, B. (1989) 'War Ina' Babylon: Dynamics of the Jamaican informal drug economy' *Social Justice,* 15 3-4: pgs. 61-86.

Herbert, D. T. (1982) *The Geography of Urban Crime.* **London: Longman.**

Home Office (1985) *Tackling Drug Misuse: A Summary of the Government's Strategy.* **London: Home Office.**

Hough, M. and Mayhew, P. (1983) *The British Crime Survey.* **Home Office Research Study 76. London: HMSO.**

Hough, M. and Mayhew, P. (1985) *Taking account of crime: Key findings from the second British Crime Survey.* **London: HMSO.**

Inciardi, J. and McBride, D. (1991) 'The case against legalisation' in J. A. Inciardi (ed.) *The Legalization Debate, Studies in Crime, Law and Justice Volume 7.* **London: Sage.**

Jaspars, J. M. F. (1983) 'The process of causal attribution in common sense' in M. Hewstone (ed.) *Attribution Theory: Social and Functional Extensions* **Oxford: Blackwell.**

Jessor, R. and Jessor, S. (1977) *Problem Behaviour and Psycho-social Development: A Longitudinal Study of Youth.* **New York: Academic Press.**

Jones, T., MacClean, B., and Young, J. (1986) *The Islington Crime Survey: Crime, Victimisation and Policing in Inner-city.* **London Aldershot: Gower.**

Kinder, B., Pape, N. and Walfish, S. (1980) 'Drug and alcohol education programmes: a review of outcome studies'. *International Journal of the Addictions,* 15 (7): pgs. 1035-1054.

King, J. (1993) 'Survival stakes'. *Community Care,* 22 July.

Kinsey, R. (1984) *Merseyside Crime Survey: First Report.* **Liverpool: Police Commitee Support Unit.**

Kleiman, M. A. R. and Smith, K. D. 1990). 'State and local drug enforcement', in M. Tonry and J. Q. Wilson (eds.) *Drugs and Crime.* **Chicago and London: University of Chicago Press.**

REFERENCES

Knol, F. A. and Soetenhorst, J. (1979) 'Multi-level Analysis: Dimensions in the Relation Between Community Variables Standing for the Social Climate and Variability of Behaviour Concerning going out in the Evening'. Paper given to the **Workshop Meeting of the Research Committee for the Sociology of Deviance and Social Control**, 30-31 August, 1979 The Hague.

Kury and H-J. Albrecht (eds): *Victims and Criminal Justice* **Frieburg: Max -Planck-Institut fr auslṣndisches und internationaales Strafrecht.**

Lavelle, T. Hammersley, R. And Forsyth, A. (1992) *Working paper on drug usage in Glasgow.* **Glasgow University: Behavioural Sciences Group.**

Lavrakas, P. J. (1985) 'Citizen self-help and neighbourhood crime prevention policy', in L. Curtis (ed.) *American Violence and Public Policy.* **New Haven, CT: Yale University Press.**

Lawrence, J. (1986) cited in Lawrence, J. (1988) 'Shooting up the desperate (Great Britain)' *New Statesman and Society,* 1: pgs.8-9 September 23rd.

Lee, M. (1993) *Criminal Justice Act in Practice: Three Perspectives on Multi-agency Work with Drug-using Offenders.* Paper presented to the **British Criminology Conference** 28-31 July 1993, Cardiff.

Leek, M. M. and Smith, P. K. S. (1989) *Trait Clustering in the Human Population as a Function of K Selection* **University of Sheffield: Department of Psychology.**

Leitner, M. Shapland, J. and Wiles, P. (1992) *Self-report drug usage: Proposed validation study.* Unpublished report to the Central Drugs Prevention Unit.

Levin, G., Roberts, E. B. and Hirsch, G. B. (1975) *The Persistent Poppy: a Computer-Aided Search for Heroin Policy.* **Cambridge Mass.: Ballinger.**

MacCoun, R. and Reuter, P. Are the wages of sin $30 an hour? **Crime and delinquency** 38: (4).

MacGregor, S. and Ettorre, B. (1987) from treatment to rehabilitation: aspects of the evaluation of British policy on the care of drug-takers in Dorn, N. and South, N. *A Land Fit for Heroin? Drug Policies, Prevention and Practice.* **London: MacMillan.**

Malyon, T. (1985) 'Love seeds and cash crops - the cannabis commodity market' cited in Malyon, T. (1987) Visions of addiction (symposium) *Journal of Drug Issues,* 17: pgs. 1-215.

Manning, M. (1985) *The Drugs Menace.* **London: Columbus.**

Marks, P. (1973) *Public attitudes to drug taking.* An unpublished report to the Home Office.

Maxfield, M. (1984) *Fear of Crime in England and Wales* **Home Office Research Study 78 London: HMSO.**

Mayhew, P and Hough, M. (1991) 'The British Crime Survey: The First Ten Years' in Kaiser, H. Mayhew, P., Elliott, D. and Dowds, L. (1989) *The 1988 British Crime Survey.* **Home Office Research Study no. 111 London: HMSO.**

Mayhew, P. and Aye Maung, N. (1992) *Surveying crime: Findings for the 1992 British Crime Survey* **Home Office Research and Statistics Department Research Findings no. 2 London: HMSO.**

McKegany, N., Barnard, M., Bloor, M. and Leyland, A. (1990) 'Injecting drug use and female streetworking prostitution in Glasgow'. *AIDS,* 4: pgs. 1153-1155.

Mensch, B. and Kandel, D. (1988) 'Do job conditions influence the use of drugs?'. *Journal of Health and Social Behaviour,* 29: pgs. 169-184.

Mirza, H. Pearson, G. and Phillips, S. (1991) *Drugs, People and Services in Lewisham.* **University of London: Goldsmiths' College.**

Moskowitz, J., Schaps, E. and Malvin, J. (1982) 'Process and outcome evaluation in primary prevention: the magic circle programme' *Evaluation Review,* 6: pgs. 775-78.

Nadelmann, E. (1992) 'Legalisation: Or the debate' *International Journal on Drug Policy,* 3 (2): pgs. 76-79.

Neville, J. (1993) *Drug Dealing and the Impact of Policing.* Paper presented to the **British Criminology Conference** 28-31 July 1993, Cardiff.

NIDA (National Institute on Drug Abuse) (1988) *National Household Survey on Drug Abuse.* **Rockville Md.: US Department of Health and Human Services.**

NOP Market Research Ltd. (1982) *Survey of Drug Use in the 15-21 Age Group undertaken for the Daily Mail.* **London: NOP.**

Directorate General for Employment, Industrial and Social Affairs (1993) *Euro-Barometer 37.* **Commission of the European Communities.**

Nurco, D. N., Shaffer, J. W. and Cisin, I. H. (1984) 'An ecological analysis of the interrelationships among drug abuse and other indices of social pathology' *International Journal of the Addictions,* 19 4: pgs. 441-451.

O'Connor, J. and Sanders. B (1992) 'Drug education - An appraisal of a popular preventive'. *The International Journal of the Addictions*, 27(2): pgs. 165-185.

Office of Population Censuses and Surveys (1980) *Classification of Occupations 1980*; London: Government Statistical Services.

Parker, H. , Newcombe, R. and Bakx, K. (1988) *Living with Heroin. the Impact of a Drugs 'Epidemic' on an English Community.* Milton Keynes/Philadelphia: Open University Press.

Pearson, G. (1991) 'Drug-control Policies in Britain' in M. Tonry (ed.) *Crime and Justice: a Review of Research.* Chicago: Univeresity of Chicago Press.

Peck, D. F. and Plant, M.A. (1986) 'Unemployment and illegal drug use: Concordant evidence from a prospective study and national trends' *British Medical Journal,* 293: pgs. 929-932.

Pettiway, L. (1987) 'Participation in crime: Partnerships by female drug users - the effects of domestic arrangements, drug use and criminal involvement' *Criminology* 25: pgs. 741-766.

Polich, J. M., Ellickson, P. L., Reuter, P. and Kalion, J. P. (1984) *Strategies for Controlling Adolescent Drug Use.* Santa Monica: Rand Corporation R-3076-CHF.

Power, R. (1989) 'Drugs and the media: prevention campaigns and television', in MacGregor, S. (ed) *Drugs and British Society.* London: Routledge.

Public Attitude Surveys Ltd. (1992) *Technical Report on the Drugs Prevention Initiative Survey.* Unpublished report to the Central Drugs Prevention Unit.

Raj, D. (1972) *The Design of Sample Surveys,* New York: McGraw-Hill.

Research Surveys of Great Britain (1992) *Drugs Information Line Interim Report.* Unpublished report to the Home Office Central Drugs Prevention Unit.

Resnik, H. and Gibbs, J. (1988) 'Types of peer program approaches', in NIDA (1988) *Adolescent Peer Pressure: Theory, Correlates and Program Implications for Drug Abuse Prevention.* Rockville: Md.: US Department of Health and Human Services.

Sandwijk, J. P., Cohen, P. D. A. and Musterd, S. (1991) *Licit and illicit drug use in Amsterdam.* Universiteit van Amsterdam: Instituut voor Sociale Geografie.

Schaps, E., DiBartolo, R., Moskowitz, J., Palley, C. and Churgin, S. (1981) 'A review of 127 drug abuse prevention program evaluations'. *Journal of Drug Issues:* 11 (1): pgs. 17-42.

Scheerer, S. (1991) *Political Ideologies and Drug Policy.* Paper presented to the Third European Colloquium on Crime and Public Policy in Europe 5-8th July 1991, Noordwijkerhout.

Segal, M. (1972) 'Drug education: Toward a rational approach'. *International Journal of the Addictions:* 7: pgs. 97-107.

Shapland, J. , Wiles, P. and Leek, M. (1990) *Policing in Sussex: A Report of a Survey.* Sheffield: Centre for Criminological and Socio-legal studies.

Shapland, J. , Wiles, P. and Wilcox, P. *(in press) Targeted Crime Reduction in Local Areas.* Home Office Crime Prevention Unit paper London: Home Office.

Shapland, J. and Vagg, J. (1988) *Policing by the Public.* London/New York: Routledge.

Silverman, L. P. and Spurill, N. L. (1977) 'Urban crime and the price of heroin'. *Journal of Urban Economics,* 4: pgs. 80-103.

Skogan, W. G. (1990) *Disorder and decline: Crime and the Spiral of Decay in American cities.* New York: Free Press.

Skogan, W. G. and Maxfield, M. G. (1981) *Coping with Crime.* Beverly Hills: Sage.

Smart, C. (1985) 'Drug dependence units in England and Wales - the results of a national survey'. *Drug and Alcohol Dependence,* 15 1-2: pgs. 131-144.

Smart, R. and Adlef, E. (1986) 'Patterns of drug use among adolescents: The past decade'. *Social Science and Medicine,* 23 7: pgs. 717-719.

Smith, D. E. and Gay, G. R. (eds.) (1971) *I'ts so good, don't even try it once.* Englewood Cliffs NJ: Prentice Hall.

Sokal, M., Stark, C. and Sykes, R. (1989) 'Buprenorphine and temazepam abuse by drug takers in Glasgow - an increase'. *British Journal of Addiction,* 84: pgs. 439-441.

Stanko, E. (1987) 'Hidden violence against women', in M. Maguire and J, Pointing (eds) *Victims of Crime: A New Deal?* Milton Keynes: Open University Press.

Strang, J. Griffiths, P. and Gossop, M. (1990) 'Crack and Cocaine use in South London drug addicts: 1987-1989'. *British Journal of Addiction* 85 (2): pgs. 193-196.

REFERENCES

Stuart, R. (1974) 'Teaching facts about drugs: pushing or preventing?' *Journal of Educational Psychology* 66: pgs. 189-201.

Tonry, M. and Morris, N. (1988) *Crime and Justice*. Chicago: University of Chicago Press.

Tonry, M. and Wilson, J. Q. (1990) (eds.) *Drugs and Crime*. Chicago and London: University of Chicago Press.

UN Commission on Narcotic Drugs (1985) *Situation and Trends in Drug Abuse and the Illicit Traffic Including Reports of Subsidiary Bodies Concerned with the Traffic in Drugs: Review of the Illicit Traffic.* New York: United Nations

Unell, J. (1991) *Drug use in Nottingham: A report to the Central Drugs Prevention Initiative.* Unpublished report to the Home Office

van Dijk J. J. M. and Mayhew, P. (1992) *Criminal Victimisation in the Industrialised World: Key Findings of the 1989 and 1992 International Crime Surveys* The Hague: Ministry of Justice, Directorate of Crime Prevention and UNICRI.

van Dijk J.J.M. (1990) *Future perspectives regarding crime and criminal justice* Report to the **Fourth Conference on Crime Policy.** Council of Europe 9-11th May 1990 Strasbourg.

van Dijk, J.J.M. (1978) *The Extent of Public Information and the Nature of Public Attitudes Towards Crime* The Hague: Research and Documentation Centre, Ministry of Justice.

Ventura, M. and Dundon, M. (1974) 'A challenging experience in canoeing and camping as a tool in approaching the drug problem'. *Journal of Drug Education*, 4 (1): pgs. 123-27.

Wagstaff, A. and Maynard, A. (1988) *Economic aspects of the illicit drug market and drug enforcement policies in the United Kingdom.* **Home Office Research Study 95 London: HMSO.**

Walmsley, R. (1986) *Personal Violence.* **Home Office Research Study no. 89 London: HMSO.**

Wasik, M. and Taylor, R. D. (1991) *Criminal Justice Act.* **London: Blackstone.**

Whitaker, C. (1986) *Crime Prevention Measures.* **Washington DC: U.S Department of Justice, Bureau of Justice Statistics.**

White, M. D. and Luksetich, W. A. (1983) 'Heroin, price elasticity and enforcement strategies'. *Economic Inquiry*, 21: pgs. 557-564.

Whitehead, M. (1987) *The Health Divide, Inequalities in Health in the 1980s* **London: Health Education Council.**

Whynes, D. K. and Bean, P. (1991) (eds.) *Policing and Prescribing* **Basingstoke: Macmillan.**

Wikstrm P-O.H. (1990) *Crime and Measures Against Crime in the City.* **Stockholm: National Council for Crime Prevention.**

Wiles, P. (1992) 'Ghettoization in Europe?' *European Journal of Criminal Policy and Research*, 1(1):.

Williams, R. (1976) *Keywords.* **Glasgow: Fontana/Croom Helm**

Williams, R., Ward, D. and Gray, L. (1985) 'The persistence of experimentally induced cognitive change: a neglected dimension of drug prevention programs'. *Journal of Drug Education*, 15 (1): pgs. 33-42.

Willmott, P. (ed.) *Policing and the community. PSI Discussion Paper 16.* **London: Policy Studies Institute.**

Winkel, F. W. (1987) 'Response generalisation in prevention campaigns'. *British Journal of Criminology* 27: pgs. 155-73

Young, T. (1982) 'Addiction asymmetry and the demand for coffee'. *Scottish Journal of Political Economy*, 29 (1): pgs. 89-98.

APPENDIX I

TABLES IN APPENDIX I (CHAPTER 2)

Note that in all tables in this appendix the symbol ' – ' indicates 'less than one percent'.

Table 2.1
Self report usage by location : Percentage of respondents who have ever taken a drug

N = Percent of Valid   *N* = Valid N   (N) = Actual N

Drug	Nott. Main		Glas. Main		Lew. Main		Brad. Main		Nott. Boost.		Glas. Boost.		Lew. Boost.		Brad. Boost.	
	992		959		1107		993		236		256		233		225	
cannabis	13	(138)	17	(168)	21	(241)	10	(99)	34	(84)	49	(126)	42	(97)	27	(63)
heroin	–	(7)	–	(7)	1	(15)	–	(1)	2	(5)	3	(8)	3	(7)	–	(0)
amphetamines	2	(28)	5	(51)	5	(65)	2	(20)	9	(22)	17	(45)	8	(19)	6	(15)
LSD	2	(22)	5	(49)	5	(58)	3	(27)	11	(28)	9	(54)	13	(31)	9	(21)
cocaine	–	(9)	1	(16)	4	(51)	–	(4)	3	(7)	3	(9)	6	(14)	2	(5)
ecstasy	1	(11)	2	(24)	1	(22)	1	(11)	5	(13)	12	(31)	12	(28)	4	(9)
crack	–	(1)	–	(1)	–	(1)	–	(0)	2	(4)	–	(2)	3	(7)	–	(1)
psilocybin	3	(36)	3	(36)	4	(55)	3	(30)	11	(28)	16	(42)	8	(18)	9	(21)
methadone	–	(1)	–	(3)	–	(5)	–	(0)	1	(3)	2	(5)	–	(2)	–	(1)
diconal	–	(0)	–	(2)	–	(0)	–	(0)	–	(1)	2	(4)	–	(0)	–	(0)
amyl nitrite	3	(37)	2	(19)	4	(46)	1	(13)	12	(29)	10	(26)	10	(24)	4	(10)
temazepam	–	(3)	1	(17)	–	(4)	–	(4)	2	(4)	11	(28)	2	(5)	3	(6)
temgesic	–	(1)	–	(4)	–	(3)	–	(0)	–	(1)	3	(7)	–	(1)	–	(0)
semeron	–	(0)	–	(0)	–	(0)	–	(0)	–	(1)	–	(1)	–	(1)	–	(0)
barbiturates	–	(4)	–	(7)	1	(12)	–	(3)	1	(3)	3	(7)	2	(4)	–	(2)
DF118s	–	(4)	1	(12)	–	(7)	–	(0)	–	(2)	6	(16)	1	(3)	–	(1)
triazelam	–	(0)	–	(6)	–	(0)	–	(0)	–	(1)	4	(10)	–	(0)	–	(1)
pills	2	(20)	2	(24)	2	(30)	1	(12)	2	(6)	7	(18)	3	(8)	4	(10)
tranquillisers	1	(11)	1	(16)	2	(24)	–	(7)	1	(3)	4	(11)	3	(6)	1	(3)
glue sniffing	–	(7)	1	(14)	1	(11)	2	(18)	6	(16)	–	(2)	5	(11)	5	(11)
no drugs	83		80		76		86		60		48		54		67	

Percentage of respondents who claim to have taken a named drug at least once

DRUG USAGE AND DRUGS PREVENTION: THE VIEWS AND HABITS OF THE GENERAL PUBLIC

Table 2.2
Self–report usage by location: Percentage of respondents who have taken a drug recently

N = Percent of Valid   N = Valid N   (N) = Actual N

Drug	Nott. Main		Glas. Main		Lew. Main		Brad. Main		Nott. Boost.		Glas. Boost.		Lew. Boost.		Brad. Boost.	
	992		960		1106		993		236		256		233		225	
cannabis	6	(59)	8	(80)	8	(87)	4	(39)	25	(62)	33	(85)	25	(59)	16	(36)
heroin	–	(1)	–	(0)	–	(1)	–	(0)	–	(1)	1	(3)	–	(2)	–	(0)
amphetamines	1	(13)	3	(27)	1	(12)	–	(8)	4	(11)	11	(28)	3	(7)	4	(9)
LSD	–	(9)	2	(20)	–	(7)	1	(11)	7	(17)	9	(24)	6	(13)	5	(12)
cocaine	–	(2)	–	(6)	1	(15)	–	(1)	–	(2)	–	(2)	2	(5)	–	(1)
ecstasy	1	(10)	1	(15)	1	(14)	–	(8)	4	(10)	9	(24)	6	(14)	3	(7)
crack	–	(1)	–	(0)	–	(0)	–	(0)	1	(3)	–	(0)	1	(3)	–	(1)
psilocybin	–	(6)	1	(11)	–	(7)	–	(7)	4	(11)	4	(10)	2	(5)	2	(5)
methadone	–	(0)	–	(0)	–	(1)	–	(0)	–	(1)	–	(1)	–	(1)	–	(0)
diconal	–	(0)	–	(1)	–	(0)	–	(0)	–	(0)	–	(2)	–	(0)	–	(0)
amyl nitrite	1	(10)	1	(10)	–	(5)	–	(2)	6	(14)	3	(9)	3	(6)	2	(4)
temazepam	–	(2)	–	(7)	–	(1)	–	(1)	1	(3)	5	(12)	–	(2)	1	(3)
temgesic	–	(0)	–	(0)	–	(1)	–	(0)	–	(0)	2	(4)	–	(0)	–	(0)
semeron	–	(0)	–	(0)	–	(0)	–	(0)	–	(0)	–	(0)	–	(0)	–	(0)
barbiturates	–	(1)	–	(2)	–	(0)	–	(1)	–	(1)	–	(0)	–	(1)	–	(1)
DF118s	–	(1)	–	(2)	–	(1)	–	(0)	–	(0)	3	(7)	–	(1)	–	(0)
triazelam	–	(0)	–	(1)	–	(0)	–	(0)	–	(0)	2	(6)	–	(0)	–	(0)
pills	–	(6)	–	(8)	–	(7)	–	(6)	–	(1)	–	(1)	1	(3)	–	(1)
tranquilizers	–	(2)	–	(3)	–	(4)	–	(1)	–	(1)	–	(2)	–	(0)	–	(1)
glue sniffing	–	(1)	–	(1)	–	(0)	–	(1)	–	(2)	–	(1)	–	(1)	–	(2)
no drugs	93		91		91		95		71		65		72		83	

Percentage of respondents who claim to have taken a named drug within the last year

Table 2.3
Self–report usage by location: Percentage of respondents who are taking a drug regularly

N = Percent of Valid   N = Valid N   (N) = Actual N

Drug	Nott. Main			Glas. Main			Lew. Main			Brad. Main			Nott. Boost.			Glas. Boost.			Lew. Boost.			Brad. Boost.		
cannabis	30	(18)	54	54	(43)	74	46	(40)	86	28	(11)	35	48	(30)	60	52	(44)	81	58	(34)	57	61	(22)	31
heroin	–	(0)	0	–	(0)	0	–	(0)	1	–	(0)	0	100	(1)	1	33	(1)	3	100	(2)	2	–	(0)	0
amphetamines	38	(5)	13	30	(8)	23	33	(4)	12	62	(1)	8	27	(3)	11	29	(8)	27	29	(2)	7	44	(4)	9
LSD	22	(3)	9	10	(2)	20	14	(1)	6	27	(3)	10	18	(3)	16	29	(7)	24	15	(2)	13	50	(6)	12
cocaine	–	(0)	1	17	(1)	4	7	(1)	11	–	(0)	1	–	(0)	2	50	(1)	2	20	(1)	4	100	(1)	1
ecstasy	40	(4)	10	53	(8)	13	21	(3)	14	37	(3)	7	40	(4)	9	46	(11)	23	29	(4)	14	71	(5)	7
crack	–	(0)	0	–	(0)	0	–	(0)	0	–	(0)	0	–	(0)	3	–	(0)	0	33	(1)	2	100	(1)	1
psilocybin	17	(1)	5	9	(1)	11	14	(1)	7	–	(0)	7	9	(1)	10	–	(0)	10	60	(3)	5	40	(2)	5
methadone	–	(0)	0	–	(0)	0	–	(0)	0	–	(0)	0	–	(0)	0	–	(0)	2	–	(0)	0	–	(0)	0
amyl nitrite	20	(2)	9	–	(0)	9	20	(1)	5	50	(1)	2	29	(4)	14	44	(4)	8	–	(0)	6	–	(0)	3
temazepam	–	(0)	1	14	(2)	6	100	(1)	1	–	(0)	1	–	(0)	3	67	(8)	11	50	(1)	2	67	(2)	3
temgesic	–	(0)	0	–	(0)	0	–	(0)	0	–	(0)	0	–	(0)	0	25	(1)	3	–	(0)	0	–	(0)	0
semeron	–	(0)	0	–	(0)	0	–	(0)	0	–	(0)	0	–	(0)	0	–	(0)	0	–	(0)	0	–	(0)	0
barbiturates	–	(0)	0	–	(0)	0	–	(0)	0	–	(0)	0	–	(0)	1	–	(0)	0	–	(0)	1	100	(1)	1
DF118s	–	(0)	0	50	(1)	2	100	(1)	1	–	(0)	0	–	(0)	0	43	(3)	7	100	(1)	1	–	(0)	0
triazelam	–	(0)	0	–	(0)	0	–	(0)	0	–	(0)	0	–	(0)	0	17	(1)	6	–	(0)	0	–	(0)	0
pills	–	(1)	5	12	(4)	5	12	(2)	8	33	(2)	5	100	(1)	1	–	(0)	1	67	(2)	3	–	(0)	1
tranquillizers	–	(0)	2	–	(0)	2	25	(1)	4	100	(1)	1	–	(0)	1	–	(0)	2	–	(0)	0	100	(1)	1
glue sniffing	–	(0)	0	–	(0)	0	–	(0)	0	–	(0)	0	–	(0)	2	–	(0)	1	–	(0)	1	50	(1)	2

Percentage of recent drug users claiming to use a named drug with a regularity greater than or equal to once per month

APPENDIX 1

Table 2.4
Self–report usage by location: Percentage of respondents who have injected a drug

N = Percent of Valid   *N* = Valid N   (N) = Actual N

Drug	Nott. Main	Glas. Main	Lew. Main	Brad. Main	Nott. Boost.	Glas. Boost.	Lew. Boost.	Brad. Boost.
cannabis	– (0) 48	– (0) 63	– (0) 70	– (0) 30	– (0) 58	– (0) 70	2 (1) 50	– (0) 29
heroin	– (0) 0	– (0) 0	100 (1) 1	– (0) 0	– (0) 1	67 (2) 3	– (0) 2	– (0) 0
amphetamines	15 (2) 10	4 (1) 20	– (0) 10	– (0) 6	– (0) 11	– (0) 25	– (0) 6	– (0) 7
LSD	11 (1) 8	5 (1) 17	14 (1) 7	– (0) 8	– (0) 15	– (0) 23	– (0) 11	– (0) 9
cocaine	– (0) 1	– (0) 4	13 (2) 15	– (0) 1	– (0) 2	– (0) 2	– (0) 4	– (0) 0
ecstasy	10 (1) 9	7 (1) 11	– (0) 10	– (0) 5	– (0) 9	– (0) 20	– (0) 12	– (0) 6
crack	– (0) 0	– (0) 0	– (0) 0	– (0) 0	– (0) 3	– (0) 0	– (0) 3	– (0) 1
psilocybin	– (0) 5	9 (1) 8	– (0) 5	– (0) 6	– (0) 10	– (0) 8	– (0) 4	– (0) 5
methadone	– (0) 0	– (0) 0	– (0) 0	– (0) 0	– (0) 0	– (0) 0	– (0) 1	– (0) 0
diconal	– (0) 0	– (0) 0	– (0) 0	– (0) 1	– (0) 0	100 (2) 2	– (0) 0	– (0) 0
amyl nitrite	– (0) 9	10 (1) 10	– (0) 4	– (0) 0	– (0) 14	– (0) 6	– (0) 6	– (0) 3
temazepam	– (0) 0	14 (1) 7	– (0) 0	– (0) 0	– (0) 2	8 (1) 11	– (0) 2	– (0) 3
temgesic	– (0) 0	– (0) 0	– (0) 0	– (0) 1	– (0) 0	25 (1) 4	– (0) 0	– (0) 0
semeron	– (0) 0	– (0) 0	– (0) 0	– (0) 0	– (0) 0	– (0) 0	– (0) 0	– (0) 0
barbiturates	– (0) 0	– (0) 0	– (0) 0	– (0) 0	– (0) 1	– (0) 0	– (0) 1	– (0) 1
DF118s	– (0) 0	– (0) 0	– (0) 1	– (0) 0	– (0) 0	– (0) 5	– (0) 1	– (0) 0
triazelam	– (0) 0	– (0) 0	– (0) 0	– (0) 0	– (0) 0	17 (1) 6	– (0) 0	– (0) 0
pills	– (0) 6	– (0) 7	– (0) 8	– (0) 5	– (0) 1	– (0) 1	– (0) 3	– (0) 1
tranquillizers	– (0) 2	– (0) 2	– (0) 4	100 (1) 1	– (0) 1	– (0) 2	– (0) 0	– (0) 1

Percentage of recent users of a named drug claiming to have injected that drug

Table 2.5
Self–report usage by location: Availability of drugs

N = Percent of Valid   *N* = Valid N   (N) = Actual N

Drug	Nott. Main	Glas. Main	Lew. Main	Brad. Main	Nott. Boost.	Glas. Boost.	Lew. Boost.	Brad. Boost.
cannabis	88 (52) 59	81 (65) 80	90 (78) 87	79 (31) 39	97 (60) 62	88 (75) 85	91 (54) 59	81 (29) 31
heroin	100 (1) 1	– (0) 0	100 (1) 1	– (0) 0	100 (1) 1	100 (3) 3	100 (2) 2	– (0) 0
amphetamines	92 (12) 13	85 (23) 27	100 (12) 12	87 (7) 8	91 (7) 11	89 (10) 28	100 (7) 7	89 (7) 9
LSD	89 (8) 9	95 (19) 20	71 (5) 7	81 (9) 11	94 (16) 17	87 (21) 24	92 (12) 13	92 (11) 12
cocaine	100 (2) 2	33 (2) 6	80 (12) 15	100 (1) 1	100 (2) 2	50 (1) 2	100 (5) 5	100 (1) 1
ecstasy	100 (10) 10	80 (12) 15	86 (12) 14	75 (6) 8	90 (9) 10	87 (21) 24	93 (13) 14	100 (7) 7
crack	100 (1) 1	– (0) 0	– (0) 0	– (0) 0	100 (3) 3	– (0) 0	100 (3) 3	– (1) 1
psilocybin	83 (5) 6	63 (7) 11	57 (4) 7	71 (5) 7	54 (6) 11	70 (7) 10	60 (3) 5	100 (5) 5
methadone	– (0) 0	– (0) 0	100 (1) 1	– (0) 0	– (0) 1	100 (1) 1	100 (1) 1	– (0) 0
diconal	– (0) 0	– (0) 0	– (0) 0	– (0) 0	– (0) 0	100 (2) 2	– (0) 0	– (0) 0
amyl nitrite	100 (10) 10	60 (6) 10	80 (4) 5	100 (2) 2	100 (14) 14	67 (6) 9	83 (5) 6	75 (3) 4
temazepam	100 (2) 2	71 (5) 7	100 (1) 1	100 (1) 1	67 (2) 3	100 (12) 12	50 (1) 2	100 (3) 3
temgesic	– (0) 0	– (0) 0	100 (1) 1	– (0) 0	– (0) 0	100 (4) 4	– (0) 0	– (0) 0
semeron	– (0) 0	– (0) 0	– (0) 0	– (0) 0	– (0) 0	– (0) 0	– (0) 0	– (0) 0
barbiturates	100 (1) 1	50 (1) 2	– (0) 12	100 (1) 1	– (1) 1	– (0) 0	100 (1) 1	100 (1) 1
DF118s	100 (1) 1	100 (2) 2	100 (1) 1	– (0) 0	– (0) 0	100 (7) 7	100 (1) 1	– (0) 0
triazelam	– (0) 0	– (0) 6	– (0) 0	– (0) 0	– (0) 0	100 (6) 6	– (0) 0	– (0) 0
pills	67 (4) 6	62 (5) 8	62 (5) 7	67 (4) 6	100 (1) 1	100 (1) 1	33 (1) 3	100 (1) 1
tranquilizers	100 (2) 2	67 (2) 3	62 (3) 4	100 (1) 1	100 (1) 1	100 (2) 2	– (0) 0	100 (1) 1

Percentage of recent users of a drug claiming that the drug is readily available within their city or borough

Table 2.6
Summary values for self–report drug usage by location

N = Percent of Valid	N = Valid N	(N)= Actual N						
	Nott. Main	Glas. Main	Lew. Main	Brad. Main	Nott. Boost.	Glas. Boost	Lew. Boost.	Brad. Boost.
Self ever	998 / 17	970 / 19	1130 / 23	1002 / 13	244 / 40	258 / 52	231 / 45	230 / 32
Self recently	1003 / 7	971 / 9	1133 / 8	1002 / 5	244 / 28	258 / 35	233 / 28	231 / 16
Self frequency	68 / 2	88 / 5	98 / 4	48 / 1	69 / 13	90 / 18	66 / 15	38 / 9
Injecting usage	68 / 3	88 / 1	98 / 3	48 / 2	69 / –(0)	90 / 2	66 / 1	38 / –(0)
Availability	68 / 84	88 / 78	98 / 86	48 / 75	69 / 96	90 / 89	66 / 89	38 / 81

Percentage of respondents who answered positively to the five self report items for at least one named drug / Note that frequency of usage, injecting usage and availability were all items applying only to individuals using a drug within the last year.

Table 2.7
Summary statistics for variations in self–report drug usage: differences between and within samples

Item	Significance of chi squared main samples	Significance of chi squared booster samples	Significance of chi squared main versus booster
Self ever	.000001	.0007	.000001
Self recently	.009	.0004	.000001
Regularity	.0002	NS	.000001
Injecting	NS	NS	NS

Significance levels achieved by chi squared statistics for the four self-report drug usage items: variation within samples (across location) and between samples (booster sample profile versus main sample profile)

APPENDIX I

Table 2.8
Polydrug usage of a range of drug types: Main sample

N = Percent of Valid   *N* = Valid N   (N)= Actual N

drug category	other drugs used	Nottingham	Glasgow	Lewisham	Bradford
		8	*11*	*11*	*7*
takes pills or tranquillizers	cannabis	25	67	27	28
	heroin	– (0)	– (0)	– (0)	– (0)
	LSD	12	37	12	– (0)
	cocaine	75	82	54	86
	ecstasy	12	27	9	– (0)
	amphetamines	25	27	18	– (0)
		59	*80*	*87*	*39*
takes cannabis	pills/tranquillizers	3	7	4	5
	heroin	2	– (0)	1	– (0)
	LSD	14	23	7	26
	cocaine	3	6	17	2
	ecstasy	17	16	17	18
	amphetamines	21	30	12	18
		1		*1*	
takes heroin	pills or tranquillizers	– (0)	no users	– (0)	no users
	cannabis	100		100	
	LSD	100		100	
	cocaine	100		– (0)	
	ecstasy	100		100	
	amphetamines	100		100	
		9	*20*	*7*	*11*
takes LSD	pills or tranquillizers	11	16	17	– (0)
	cannabis	89	95	100	91
	heroin	11	– (0)	17	– (0)
	cocaine	22	5	33	– (0)
	ecstasy	67	42	83	54
	amphetamines	78	74	50	36
		2	*6*	*15*	*1*
takes cocaine	pills or tranquillizers	– (0)	– (0)	– (0)	– (0)
	cannabis	100	83	100	100
	heroin	50	– (0)	– (0)	– (0)
	LSD	100	17	14	– (0)
	ecstasy	100	67	36	– (0)
	amphetamines	100	33	14	– (0)
		10	*15*	*14*	*8*
takes ecstasy	pills tranquillizers	10	20	7	– (0)
	cannabis	100	87	100	87
	heroin	10	– (0)	7	– (0)
	LSD	60	53	36	75
	cocaine	20	27	36	– (0)
	amphetamines	80	67	57	50
		13	*27*	*12*	*8*
takes amphetamines	pills tranquillizers	15	11	18	– (0)
	cannabis	92	92	91	87
	heroin	8	– (0)	9	– (0)
	LSD	54	54	27	50
	cocaine	15	8	18	– (0)
	ecstasy	61	38	73	50

Percentage of recent users of named drugs who have also taken other types of drug

Table 2.9
Polydrug usage of a range of drug types: Booster sample

N = Percent of Valid   N = Valid N   (N)= Actual N

drug category	other drugs used	Nottingham	Glasgow	Lewisham	Bradford
		2	3	3	2
takes pills or tranquillizers	cannabis	100	50	33	50
	heroin	– (0)	– (0)	33	– (0)
	LSD	100	50	– (0)	– (0)
	cocaine	– (0)	– (0)	33	– (0)
	ecstasy	– (0)	100	– (0)	– (0)
	amphetamines	– (0)	50	33	50
		62	85	59	36
takes cannabis	pills/tranquillizers	2	2	2	1
	heroin	– (0)	3	3	– (0)
	LSD	21	27	20	33
	cocaine	3	2	7	3
	ecstasy	14	27	20	17
	amphetamines	16	29	12	25
		1	3	2	
takes heroin	pills or tranquillizers	– (0)	– (0)	50	no users
	cannabis	– (0)	100	100	
	LSD	100	33	50	
	cocaine	– (0)	33	100	
	ecstasy	100	67	50	
	amphetamines	– (0)	67	50	– (0)
		17	24	14	7
takes LSD	pills or tranquillizers	6	1	– (0)	– (0)
	cannabis	76	96	92	100
	heroin	6	4	8	– (0)
	cocaine	6	8	8	8
	ecstasy	41	58	54	42
	amphetamines	23	62	31	50
		2	2	5	1
takes cocaine	pills or tranquillizers	– (0)	– (0)	20	– (0)
	cannabis	100	100	80	100
	heroin	– (0)	50	40	– (0)
	LSD	50	100	20	100
	ecstasy	50	100	40	– (0)
	amphetamines	– (0)	100	20	100
		10	24	14	7
takes ecstasy	pills tranquillizers	– (0)	2	– (0)	– (0)
	cannabis	90	96	86	86
	heroin	10	8	7	– (0)
	LSD	70	58	50	71
	cocaine	10	8	14	– (0)
	amphetamines	40	58	21	57
		11	28	7	9
takes amphetamines	pills tranquillizers	– (0)	2	14	1
	cannabis	91	89	100	100
	heroin	– (0)	7	14	– (0)
	LSD	36	54	57	67
	cocaine	– (0)	7	14	11
	ecstasy	36	50	43	44

Percentage of recent users of named drugs who have also taken other types of drug

APPENDIX I

Table 2.10
Polydrug usage by location: Lifetime usage of unprescribed drugs

N = Percent of Valid   N = Valid N   (N)= Actual N

	Nott. Main	Glas. Main	Lew. Main	Brad. Main	Nott. Boost.	Glas. Boost.	Lew. Boost.	Brad. Boost.
	172	188	261	134	98	135	106	74
Used one drug only	56	57	54	60	41	34	40	40
Used two drugs	19	16	18	21	21	23	32	24
Used three-five drugs	16	15	18	16	25	25	17	32
Used six-nine drugs	3	7	8	4	10	12	10	9
Used ten + drugs	2	4	2	- (0)	2	5	1	1

Percentage of drug users who had used only one or more than one type of drug during their lifetime

Table 2.11
Polydrug usage by location: Usage of unprescribed drugs within the last year

N = Percent of Valid   N = Valid N   (N)= Actual N

	Nott. Main	Glas. Main	Lew. Main	Brad. Main	Nott. Boost.	Glas. Boost.	Lew. Boost.	Brad. Boost.
	70	88	92	47	68	90	64	38
Used one drug only	68	51	70	57	49	51	54	47
Used two drugs	12	24	11	21	22	11	27	24
Used three-five drugs	12	17	17	21	27	29	15	29
Used six-nine drugs	6	8	- (0)	- (0)	1	8	2	3
Used ten + drugs	1	- (0)	1	- (0)	- (0)	- (0)	2	- (0)

Percentage of recent drug users who had used one or more than one type of drug within the last year

Table 2.12
Association between usage of different drug types: Main sample

N = Percent of Valid   N = Valid N   (N)= Actual N

	% used cannabis within last year		% used non-opiates within last year		% used opiates within last year	
Used cannabis within last year		/	36	265	7	265
Had not used cannabis within last year		/	1	3856	- (1)	3856
Used non-opiates within last year	72	128		/	11	128
Had not used non-opiates within last year	43	3993		/	2	3993
Used opiates within last year	96	25	56	25		/
Had not used opiates within last year	6	4096	2	4096		/

Percentage of recent users of each drug type who had also used at least one other drug type, averaged across location

203

Table 2.13
Association between usage of different drug types: Booster sample

N = Percent of Valid   *N* = Valid N   (N)= Actual N

	% used cannabis within last year		% used non-opiates within last year		% used opiates within last year	
Used cannabis within last year		/	47	725	3	725
Had not used cannabis within last year		/	1	242	– (5)	242
Used non–opiates within last year	86	131		/	11	131
Had not used non–opiates within last year	15	836		/	– (3)	836
Used opiates within last year	78	17	86	17		/
Had not used opiates within last year	24	950	12	950		/

Percentage of recent drug users of each drug type who had also used at least one other drug type, averaged across location

TABLES IN APPENDIX 1 (CHAPTER 3)

Table 3.1
Summary of self-report drug usage by age group: Main sample

N = Percent of Valid   *N* = Valid N   (N)= Actual N

	% 16-19	%20-24	%25-29	%30-34	%35-44	%45-59	%60+
	183	344	520	511	739	751	1065
Ever used any drug	36	41	34	25	21	8	1
Recently used any drug	26	21	14	9	5	2	– (2)
Frequency of use GE monthly	14	8	6	4	1	– (0)	– (0)
Ever injected	– (0)	– (2)	– (2)	– (2)	– (2)	– (1)	– (0)
Readily available	89	84	74	81	79	56	50
Recently used cannabis	25	20	12	8	4	1	– (0)
Recently used non–opiate	12	10	5	4	2	– (2)	– (0)
Recently used opiate	– (1)	1	2	– (1)	– (1)	– (0)	– (0)

*Percentage of respondents in each age group showing the stated self-report responses, averaged across location. Note that frequency of usage, injecting usage, cannabis, non–opiate and opiate usage are all items applying only to individuals using a drug **within the last year.***

Table 3.2
Summary of self–report drug usage by age group: Booster sample

N = Percent of Valid   *N* = Valid N   (N)= Actual N

	% 16–19	%20–24	%25–29
	392	486	89
Ever used any drug	42	44	32
Recently used any drug	30	26	21
Frequency of use GE monthly	15	13	13
Ever injected	– (1)	– (3)	– (0)
Readily available	89	88	77
Recently used cannabis	26	24	21
Recently used non–opiate	17	12	6
Recently used opiate	2	1	1

*Percentage of respondents in each category showing the stated self-report responses, averaged across location. Note that frequency of usage, injecting usage, cannabis, non-opiate and opiate usage are all items applying only to individuals using a drug **within the last year.***

APPENDIX I

Table 3.3
Summary of self–report drug usage by gender

N = Percent of Valid   N = Valid N   (N)= Actual N

	Main sample		Booster sample	
	% males	% females	%males	% females
	1760	2361	467	500
Ever used any drug	23	13	45	37
Recently used any drug	10	5	37	32
Frequency of use GE monthly	4	2	38	32
Ever injected	– (8)	– (1)	– (4)	– (0)
Readily available	84	81	83	74
Recently used cannabis	9	4	31	19
Recently used non–opiate	5	1	18	9
Recently used opiate	1	– (6)	3	1

*Percentage of male and female respondents showing the stated self-report responses, averaged across location. Note that frequency of usage, injecting usage, cannabis, non-opiate and opiate usage are all items applying only to individuals using a drug **within the last year.***

Table 3.4
Summary of self–report drug usage by socioeconomic status

N = Percent of Valid   N = Valid N   (N)= Actual N

	Main sample				Booster sample			
	%AB	%C1	%C2	%DE	%AB	%C1	%C2	%DE
	490	1072	996	1552	43	216	211	491
Ever used any drug	28	23	14	14	37	44	34	42
Recently used any drug	10	9	5	6	23	33	22	27
Frequency of use GE monthly	3	3	2	3	12	13	9	17
Ever injected	– (2)	– (4)	– (1)	– (2)	– (0)	– (0)	– (0)	– (4)
Readily available	76	84	87	79	75	70	91	93
Recently used cannabis	9	8	4	5	31	31	18	25
Recently used non–opiate	3	3	2	3	19	14	15	12
Recently used opiate	1	1	– (5)	– (3)	1	– (1)	1	3

*Percentage of respondents in each socioeconomic group showing the stated self-report responses, averaged across location. Note that frequency of usage, injecting usage, cannabis, non-opiate and opiate usage are all items applying only to individuals using a drug **within the last year.***

Table 3.5
Summary of self-report drug usage by ethnicity

N = Percent of Valid   N = Valid N   (N)= Actual N   * no relevant respondents

	Main sample				Booster sample			
	%White	%Black	%Asian	%Other	%White	%Black	%Asian	%Other
	3666	213	123	49	766	83	89	12
Ever used any drug	18	17	7	1	46	61	11	39
Recently used any drug	7	6	2	– (0)	30	40	1	10
Frequency of use GE monthly	3	3	2	– *	15	19	1	3
Ever injected	– (8)	– (1)	– (0)	– *	– (4)	– (0)	– (0)	– (0)
Readily available	83	49	33	– *	87	97	100	50
Recently used cannabis	6	5	2	– (0)	27	39	1	10
Recently used non–opiate	3	1	2	– (0)	15	4	1	5
Recently used opiate	1	– (1)	– (0)	– (0)	2	– (0)	1	– (0)

*Percentage of respondents in each ethnic group showing the stated self-report responses, averaged across location. Note that frequency of usage, injecting usage, cannabis, non-opiate and opiate usage are all items applying only to individuals using a drug **within the last year**.*

Table 3.6
Summary of respondents' drug usage by present and long term employment status: Main sample

N = Percent of Valid   N = Valid N   (N)= Actual N

	% Presently in employment	% Not employed at present	% Have been employed	% Never been employed
	3700	419	1013	235
Ever used any drug	17	24	21	20
Recently used any drug	6	11	9	13
Frequency of use GE monthly	3	6	4	8
Ever injected	– (7)	5	2	– (0)
Readily available	84	72	77	91
Recently used cannabis	6	9	8	12
Recently used non–opiate	3	6	4	6
Recently used opiate	– (2)	– (1)	– (5)	– (1)

*Percentage of respondents in each employment category showing the stated self-report responses, averaged across location. Note that frequency of usage, injecting usage, cannabis, non-opiate and opiate usage are all items applying only to individuals using a drug **within the last year**.*

APPENDIX I

Table 3.7
Summary of respondents' drug usage by present and long term employment status: Booster sample

N = Percent of Valid   *N* = Valid N   (N)= Actual N

	% Presently in employment	% Not employed at present	% Have been employed	% Never been employed
	726	239	422	243
Ever used any drug	38	54	46	42
Recently used any drug	24	36	30	31
Frequency of use GE monthly	11	22	16	15
Ever injected	1	1	1	– (0)
Readily available	87	89	81	82
Recently used cannabis	22	33	28	28
Recently used non–opiate	11	20	14	15
Recently used opiate	1	3	1	2

*Percentage of respondents in each employment category showing the stated self-report responses, averaged across location. Note that frequency of usage, injecting usage, cannabis, non-opiate and opiate usage are all items applying only to individuals using a drug **within the last year**.*

Table 3.8
Summary statistics for variations in self-report drug usage: demographic differences in lifetime drug usage

Location	Age	Gender	Socioeconomic status	Ethnicity	Lifetime employment	Present employment
Nottingham Main	.00000	.00001	.001	NS	NS	NS
Glasgow Main	.00000	.008	.03	NS	NS	.04
Lewisham Main	.00000	.00000	.00000	NS	NS	NS
Bradford Main	.00000	.003	NS	NS	NS	NS
Nottingham Booster	NS	.001	NS	NS	NS	NS
Glasgow Booster	NS	.01	NS	.05	NS	NS
Lewisham Booster	NS	.05	NS	NS	NS	.01
Bradford Booster	NS	NS	NS	.0002	.02	.003

Significance levels achieved by chi squared statistics : variations in lifetime drug usage across demographic groups

Table 3.9
Summary statistics for variations in self-report drug usage: demographic differences in recent drug usage

Location	Age	Gender	Socioeconomic status	Ethnicity	Lifetime employment	Present employment
Nottingham Main	.00000	.004	.001	NS	NS	NS
Glasgow Main	.00000	NS	NS	NS	.008	NS
Lewisham Main	.00000	.00000	.0007	NS	NS	.001
Bradford Main	.00000	.05	NS	NS	NS	.004
Nottingham Booster	NS	.01	NS	NS	NS	.03
Glasgow Booster	NS	.004	NS	.04	NS	NS
Lewisham Booster	NS	NS	NS	.05	NS	.04
Bradford Booster	NS	.04	NS	.009	NS	.01

Significance levels achieved by chi squared statistics for variations in drug usage within the last year across demographic groups

Table 3.10
Summary statistics for variations in self-report drug usage: demographic differences in frequency of drug usage

Location	Age	Gender	Socioeconomic status	Ethnicity	Lifetime employment	Present employment
Nottingham Main	.0002	.0005	NS	.001	NS	NS
Glasgow Main	.00000	NS	NS	NS	.001	NS
Lewisham Main	.00000	.00005	NS	NS	NS	NS
Bradford Main	.00000	NS	NS	NS	NS	.00000
Nottingham Booster	NS	NS	NS	NS	NS	.03
Glasgow Booster	NS	.009	NS	.04	NS	NS
Lewisham Booster	NS	NS	.05	NS	NS	.0005
Bradford Booster	NS	.008	NS	NS	NS	.003

Significance levels achieved by chi squared statistics : variations in frequency of drug usage across demographic groups

Table 3.11
Summary statistics for variations in self-report drug usage: demographic differences in injecting usage

Location	Age	Gender	Socioeconomic status	Ethnicity	Lifetime employment	Present employment
Nottingham Main	NS	NS	NS	NS	NS	.04
Glasgow Main	NS	NS	NS	NS	NS	.02
Lewisham Main	NS	.05	NS	NS	NS	NS
Bradford Main	NS	NS	NS	NS	NS	NS
Nottingham Booster	NS	NS	NS	NS	NS	NS
Glasgow Booster	NS	NS	NS	NS	NS	NS
Lewisham Booster	NS	NS	NS	NS	NS	NS
Bradford Booster	NS	NS	NS	NS	NS	NS

Significance levels achieved by chi squared statistics : variations in injecting drug usage across demographic groups

Table 3.12
Summary statistics for variations in self-report drug usage: demographic differences in recent cannabis usage

Location	Age	Gender	Socioeconomic status	Ethnicity	Lifetime employment	Present employment
Nottingham Main	.00000	.0007	.008	NS	NS	NS
Glasgow Main	.00000	NS	NS	NS	.001	NS
Lewisham Main	.00000	.00000	.00000	NS	NS	NS
Bradford Main	.00000	.004	NS	NS	NS	.0002
Nottingham Booster	NS	.04	NS	NS	NS	.05
Glasgow Booster	NS	.003	NS	.04	NS	NS
Lewisham Booster	NS	NS	NS	NS	NS	.02
Bradford Booster	NS	.01	NS	.005	NS	.02

Significance levels achieved by chi squared statistics : variations in cannabis usage across demographic groups

APPENDIX I

Table 3.13
Summary statistics for variations in self-report drug usage: demographic differences in recent non-opiate usage

Location	Age	Gender	Socioeconomic status	Ethnicity	Lifetime employment	Present employment
Nottingham Main	.00000	.006	.07	NS	NS	NS
Glasgow Main	.00000	.05	NS	NS	.007	NS
Lewisham Main	.00002	.00001	NS	NS	NS	.007
Bradford Main	.00000	.01	NS	NS	NS	.0004
Nottingham Booster	NS	.01	NS	NS	NS	NS
Glasgow Booster	NS	.03	NS	NS	NS	NS
Lewisham Booster	NS	NS	NS	NS	NS	NS
Bradford Booster	.03	.01	NS	NS	NS	.001

Significance levels achieved by chi squared statistics : variations in non-opiate usage across demographic groups

Table 3.14
Summary statistics for variations in self-report drug usage: demographic differences in recent opiate usage

Location	Age	Gender	Socioeconomic status	Ethnicity	Lifetime employment	Present employment
Nottingham Main	NS	NS	NS	NS	NS	.04
Glasgow Main	.006	NS	NS	NS	NS	NS
Lewisham Main	.0006	.0005	.04	NS	NS	NS
Bradford Main	.002	NS	NS	NS	NS	NS
Nottingham Booster	.07	NS	NS	NS	NS	NS
Glasgow Booster	NS	NS	NS	NS	NS	NS
Lewisham Booster	NS	NS	NS	NS	NS	NS
Bradford Booster	NS	NS	NS	NS	NS	NS

Significance levels achieved by chi squared statistics : variations in opiate usage across demographic groups

Table 3.15
Summary statistics for variations in self-report drug usage: demographic differences in availability

Location	Age	Gender	Socioeconomic status	Ethnicity	Lifetime employment	Present employment
Nottingham Main	.00000	.004	.005	NS	NS	NS
Glasgow Main	.00000	.05	NS	NS	NS	.01
Lewisham Main	.00000	.00000	.0005	NS	NS	NS
Bradford Main	.00000	NS	NS	NS	.01	NS
Nottingham Booster	NS	.04	NS	NS	.03	NS
Glasgow Booster	NS	.0008	NS	.04	NS	NS
Lewisham Booster	NS	NS	NS	NS	.04	NS
Bradford Booster	NS	NS	NS	NS	.03	NS

Significance levels achieved by chi squared statistics: variations in the availability of unprescribed drugs across demographic groups

Table 3.16
Summary of demographic regression models for drug usage: Main sample

Response	final model	beta	t	sig.t	Adj. R squared
lifetime usage	age	.34	23.06	.0000	.14
(N = 1221)	gender	.12	8.01	.0000	
	ethnicity	.09	6.34	.0000	
	socioeconomic status	.08	5.69	.0000	
usage within last year	age	.25	16.16	.0000	.07
(N =1221)	gender	.09	6.00	.0000	
	ethnicity	.08	5.25	.0000	
	socioeconomic status	.03	2.04	.04	
frequency of usage	age	−.14	−8.74	.0000	.02
(N =1221)	gender	−.07	−4.34	.0000	
	ethnicity	−.05	−3.26	.001	
injecting usage	gender	−.04	−2.76	.006	.002
(N =1221)	age	−.03	−2.03	.04	
drugs readily	age	−.26	−9.44	.0000	.09
available	gender	−.12	−4.46	.0000	
(N =1221)	ethnicity	−.11	−4.10	.0000	
	socioeconomic status	−.08	−2.85	.004	

variables in equation: location, age, gender, ethnicity (white, black, asian, other), socioeconomic status, presently employed, ever employed

Table 3.17
Summary of demographic regression models by drug type: Main sample

Response	final model	beta	t	sig.t	Adj. R squared
cannabis usage	age	.22	7.72	.0000	.07
(N = 1219)	gender	.10	3.72	.0002	
	ethnicity	.11	3.88	.0001	
	ever employed	−.09	−3.15	.002	
non-opiate usage	age	.14	4.87	.0000	.03
(N = 1218)	gender	.10	3.65	.0003	
	race	.08	2.69	.007	
opiate usage	no variables reached criterion				

variables in equation: location, age, gender, ethnicity (white, black, asian, other), socioeconomic status, presently employed, ever employed

Table 3.18
Summary of demographic regression models for drug usage: Booster sample

Response	final model	beta	t	sig.t	Adj. R squared
lifetime usage	ethnicity	.19	6.05	.0000	.06
(N =647)	gender	.17	5.30	.0000	
usage within last year	ethnicity	.17	5.35	.0000	.05
(N =647)	gender	.14	4.50	.0000	
	age	.09	2.80	.005	
frequency of usage	gender	−.13	−4.02	.0001	.02
(N =647)	ethnicity	−.10	−3.22	.001	
injecting usage	gender	−.07	−2.06	.04	.003
(N =647)					
drugs readily available	gender	−.17	−4.31	.0000	.04
	ethnicity	−.15	−3.95	.0001	

(N =647)

variables in equation: location, age, gender, ethnicity (white, black, asian, other), socioeconomic status, presently employed, ever employed

Table 3.19
Summary of demographic regression models by drug type: Booster sample

Response	final model	beta	t	sig.t	Adj. R squared
cannabis usage	gender	.13	3.35	.0008	.04
(N = 647)	ethnicity	.10	2.66	.008	
	presently employed	.09	2.32	.02	
non–opiate usage	presently employed	.13	3.43	.0006	.02
(N = 640)					
opiate usage	ever employed	−.11	−2.74	.006	.01
(N = 647)	presently employed	.10	2.53	.01	

variables in equation: location, age, gender, ethnicity (white, black, asian, other), socioeconomic status, presently employed, ever employed

Table 3.20
Summary statistics for variation in drug usage between main and booster sample for respondents aged 29 or under

	Nottingham	Glasgow	Lewisham	Bradford
Self report ever	NS	NS	NS	NS
Self report recently	.03	.03	.01	NS
Frequency GE monthly	.02	NS	.05	NS
Inject	NS	NS	NS	NS

Significance levels achieved by chi-squared statistics: drug usage in main samples versus drug usage in booster samples

Table 3.21
Summary of demographic regression models for drug usage: Full sample

Response	final model	beta	t	sig.t	Adj. R squared
lifetime usage	age	.29	11.32	.0000	.15
(N=1867)	ethnicity	.16	7.30	.0000	
	gender	.11	4.25	.0000	
	sample type	−.08	−3.41	.001	
	presently in employment	.07	2.66	.01	
	socioeconomic status	.05	2.53	.01	
usage within last year	age	.22	8.51	.0000	.13
(N=1867)	gender	.13	8.51	.0000	
	ethnicity	.15	6.65	.0000	
	sample type	−.12	−4.82	.0000	
	socioeconomic status	.05	2.17	.03	
	ever employed	−.05	−2.11	.03	
frequency of usage	age	.14	5.27	.0000	.06
(N=1869)	gender	.09	4.11	.0000	
	sample type	−.08	−2.98	.003	
	ethnicity	.08	3.59	.0003	
	ever employed	−.05	−2.23	.02	
injecting usage	gender	−0.05	−1.99	.05	.001
(N=1869)					
drugs readily available	age	−.22	−8.13	.0000	.12
(N=1869)	gender	−.13	−6.11	.0000	
	ethnicity	−.13	−5.95	.0000	
	sample type	.09	3.21	.001	
	socioeconomic status	−.06	−2.72	.006	

variables in equation: location, whether booster or main sample, ethnicity (white, black, asian), gender, age, socioeconomic status, whether presently in employment, whether ever employed

Table 3.22
Summary of demographic regression models by drug type: Full sample

Response	final model	beta	t	sig.t	Adj. R squared
cannabis usage	age	−.22	−14.2	.0000	.11
(N=1869)	sample type	.15	9.82	.0000	
	ethnicity	−.10	−7.65	.0000	
	gender	−.10	−7.55	.0000	
non-opiate usage	age	−.15	−9.55	.0000	.06
(N=1869)	sample type	.12	7.70	.0000	
	gender	−.09	−6.61	.0000	
	ethnicity	−.07	−5.47	.0000	
opiate usage	age	−.07	−4.99	.0000	.005
(N=1869)					

variables in equation: location, whether booster or main sample, age, gender, ethnicity (white, black, asian, other), socioeconomic status, presently employed, ever employed, sample type

Table 3.23
Summary of personal contact with drug users and drug usage by sample and location

N = Percent of Valid   N = Valid N

	Nott. Main	Glas. Main	Lew. Main	Brad. Main	Nott. Boost.	Glas. Boost.	Lew. Boost.	Brad. Boost.
	954	942	1095	939	239	253	229	219
% Know offered	31	35	35	28	70	76	73	52
	964	794	1076	945	238	252	232	231
% Know taken	33	37	38	30	69	80	74	53
	969	926	1105	963	240	249	220	223
% Know regular taker	18	26	24	17	48	63	53	42
	941	918	1085	807	229	249	219	221
% At social event	16	22	29	13	51	64	62	34

Percentage of respondents in each sample and location who knew someone who had been offered an unprescribed drug / Percentage of respondents in each sample and location who knew someone who had once taken an unprescribed drug / Percentage of respondents in each sample and location who knew a regular taker of unprescribed drugs / Percentage of respondents in each sample and location who had attended a social event at which drugs were taken.

Table 3.24
Summary statistics for variations in contact with drug users and drug usage: differences between and within samples

Item	Significance of chi squared main samples	Significance of chi squared booster samples	Significance of chi squared main versus booster
Know offered	.006	.00000	.00000
Know taken	.0008	.00000	.00000
Know regular taker	.00000	.00005	.00000
At social event	.00000	.00000	.00000

Significance levels achieved by chi squared statistics for the four exposure to drug usage items : variation within samples (across location) and between samples (booster sample profile versus main sample profile)

Table 3.25
Contact with drug users and personal drug usage: Main sample

N = Percent of Valid   N = Valid N   (N) = Actual N

	Know offered Y	Know offered N	Know taken Y	Know taken N	Know regular taker Y	Know regular taker N	At social event Y	At social event N
	1319	2793	1410	2699	878	3239	822	3294
% Have taken unprescribed drug	44	5	44	4	52	9	59	8
% Taken drug within last year	19	1	19	–(17)	26	2	30	1
% Take drug GE monthly	8	–(12)	8	–(5)	11	–(17)	13	–(16)
% Taken cannabis	18	1	18	–(8)	23	1	27	1
% Taken non-opiates	8	1	8	–(12)	11	1	13	1
% Taken opiates	2	–(1)	2	–(0)	3	–(1)	3	–(0)

Percentage of respondents with and without contact with drug users or drug usage who had themselves used drugs, averaged across location

DRUG USAGE AND DRUGS PREVENTION: THE VIEWS AND HABITS OF THE GENERAL PUBLIC

Table 3.26
Contact with drug users and personal drug usage: Booster sample

N = Percent of Valid   N = Valid N   (N) = Actual N

	Know offered Y	N	Know taken Y	N	Know regular taker Y	N	At social event Y	N
	651	309	663	298	499	464	509	454
% Have taken unprescribed drug	56	12	56	9	64	19	66	16
% Taken drug within last year	37	4	37	3	44	8	45	6
% Take drug GE monthly	19	2	19	1	24	2	24	3
% Taken cannabis	34	4	34	3	41	7	42	7
% Taken non-opiates	19	2	19	2	23	3	23	2
% Taken opiates	2	–(1)	2	–(1)	2	–(4)	3	–(2)

Percentage of respondents with and without contact with drug users or drug usage who had themselves used drugs, averaged across location

Table 3.27
Summary of association with drug use models of drug usage (Main sample)

Response	final model	beta	t	sig.t	Adj. R squared
frequency of taking cannabis (N = 4120)	drugs at social event	–0.26	–15.3	.000	0.16
	know regular user	–0.20	–11.4	.000	
frequency of taking non-opiates (N = 4117)	drugs at social event	–0.17	–8.69	.000	0.07
	know regular user	–0.12	–5.35	.000	
	know someone offered drugs	–0.06	–2.81	.005	
	know occasional taker		0.05	1.99	.05
frequency of taking opiates	no variables reached criterion				

variables in equation: location, whether know anyone who has been offered the named type of drug, whether know anyone who has taken the named type of drug, whether know anyone who is a regular taker of the named type of drug, whether have been at social event where the named type of drug was taken

Table 3.28
Summary of association with drug use models of drug usage : Booster sample

Response	final model	beta	t	sig.t	Adj. R squared
frequency of taking cannabis (N = 966)	know regular user	–0.23	–6.66	.000	0.14
	drugs at social event	–0.21	–6.00	.000	
frequency of taking non-opiates (N = 958)	know regular user	–0.15	–4.02	0.000	0.06
	drugs at social event	–0.14	–3.99	0.000	
frequency of taking opiates	no variables reached criterion				

variables in equation: location, whether know anyone who has been offered the named type of drug, whether know anyone who has taken the named type of drug, whether know anyone who is a regular taker of the named type of drug, whether have been at social event where the named type of drug was taken

APPENDIX I

Table 3.29
Choice of entertainment by sample type and location

N = Percent of Valid   N = Valid N

	Nott. Main	Glas. Main	Lew. Main	Brad. Main	Nott. Boost.	Glas. Boost.	Lew. Boost.	Brad. Boost.
	1004	968	1136	1002	245	258	232	231
Visit friends	90	89	90	92	94	95	97	96
Public house	71	59	51	63	80	72	60	61
Cafe	71	54	68	66	52	55	66	60
Dance	39	44	42	37	70	64	74	60
Church	24	36	28	29	11	12	23	16
Evening class	12	5	11	10	5	3	13	3
Play sport	35	26	31	33	47	39	49	41
Watch sport	24	20	20	23	25	20	27	18
Cinema	55	46	54	43	70	64	78	45
Bingo	6	12	5	9	5	7	5	8
Other	3	1	2	1	1	3	3	1

Percentage of respondents who stated that they take part in particular forms of entertainment

Table 3.30
Choice of entertainment and drug usage: Main sample

N = Percent of Valid   N = Valid N   (N) = Actual N

	% use alcohol daily or several times per week	% use cigarettes daily or several times per week	% used cannabis within last eyar	% used non-opiates within last year	% used opiates within last year
	1530	1488	265	128	25
Visit friends	37	28	7	3	– (0)
Public House	45	40	10	4	1
Cafe	41	33	9	4	1
Dance	47	39	12	7	1
Church	34	25	3	2	– (0)
Evening class	42	23	12	3	1
Play sports	49	30	10	4	1
Watch sports	51	58	9	4	1
Cinema	44	33	9	4	1
Bingo	30	56	3	2	– (0)
Other	38	50	7	1	1

Percentage of respondents taking part in each form of entertainment who use drugs, averaged across location

Table 3.31
Choice of entertainment and drug usage: Booster sample

N = Percent of Valid   *N* = Valid N   (N) = Actual N

	% use alcohol daily or several times per week	% use cigarettes daily or several times per week	% used cannabis within last year	% used non-opiates within last year	% used opiates within last year
	315	*443*	*242*	*131*	*17*
Visit friends	32	42	25	3	1
Public House	45	52	31	5	2
Cafe	37	43	28	2	2
Dance	41	48	32	8	2
Church	28	36	17	1	1
Evening class	29	40	16	2	– (0)
Play sports	39	38	28	5	2
Watch sports	42	23	31	4	3
Cinema	36	39	26	4	2
Bingo	22	69	13	2	4
Other	35	47	57	1	– (0)

Percentage of respondents taking part in each form of entertainment who use drugs, averaged across location

Table 3.32
Summary of choice of entertainment regression models for unprescribed drug usage: Main sample

Response	final model	beta	t	sig.t	Adj. R squared
frequency of	dance	0.14	8.53	.000	0.04
using cannabis	pub	0.08	4.72	.000	
(N = 4120)	church	–0.07	–4.47	.000	
	cinema	0.06	3.50	.000	
	cafe	–0.06	–3.45	.000	
frequency of	dance	.10	6.04	.000	.01
using non-opiates	pub	.04	2.59	.01	
(N = 4117)	cafe	–.04	–2.48	.01	
	sports	0.03	2.03	.04	
frequency of	dance	0.03	2.20	0.03	.003
using opiates	pub	0.03	2.10	0.03	
(N = 4120)					

variables in equation: *location, whether visit friends, whether go to pub, whether go to restaurant or cafe, whether go to dances or discos, whether go to church, whether go to evening classes, whether play sports, whether watch sports, whether go to cinema, whether go to bingo, whether choose other form of entertainment*

APPENDIX I

Table 3.33
Summary of choice of entertainment regression models for unprescribed drug usage: Booster sample

Response	final model	beta	t	sig.t	Adj. r squared
frequency of	dance	0.20	6.30	.000	0.07
using cannabis	pub	0.11	3.40	.001	
(N = 966)	bingo	−0.07	−2.27	0.02	
frequency of	dance	0.17	5.20	.000	0.05
using non-opiates	church	−0.08	−2.58	0.01	
(N = 958)	pub	0.07	1.20	0.05	
frequency of using opiates	no variables reached criterion				

variables in equation: location, whether visit friends, whether go to pub, whether go to restaurant or cafe, whether go to dances or discos, whether go to church, whether go to evening classes, whether play sports, whether watch sports, whether go to cinema, whether go to bingo, whether choose other form of entertainment

Table 3.34
Frequent usage of alcohol and tobacco by location

N = Percent of Valid   N = Valid N

	Nott. Main	Glas. Main	Lew. Main	Brad. Main	Nott. Boost.	Glas. Boost	Lew. Boost.	Brad. Boost.
	1000	968	1133	998	245	258	233	230
Alcohol	46	29	52	38	43	29	30	28
	1000	969	1130	996	245	257	231	230
Tobacco	32	45	34	35	49	49	44	43

Percentage of respondents in each location using alcohol or tobacco daily or several times per week

Table 3.35
Summary of frequent alcohol and tobacco usage by age group: Main sample

N = Percent of Valid   N = Valid N

	% 16–19	%20–24	%25–29	%30–34	%35–44	%45–59	%60+
	183	344	520	511	739	751	1065
Alcohol	25	42	38	37	44	40	29
Tobacco	30	42	42	38	37	39	29

Percentage of respondents, averaged across location, who used alcohol or tobacco daily or several times per week

Table 3.36
Summary of frequent alcohol and tobacco usage by age group: Booster sample

N = Percent of Valid   N = Valid N

	% 16–19	%20–24	%25–29
	392	486	89
Alcohol	28	37	26
Tobacco	39	49	53

Percentage of respondents, averaged across location, who used alcohol or tobacco daily or several times per week

Table 3.37
Summary of frequent alcohol and tobacco usage by gender

N = Percent of Valid   N = Valid N

	Main sample % males	% females	Booster sample %males	% females
	1760	2361	467	500
Alcohol	52	26	42	23
Tobacco	42	33	45	46

Percentage of respondents, averaged across location, who used alcohol or tobacco daily or several times per week

217

DRUG USAGE AND DRUGS PREVENTION: THE VIEWS AND HABITS OF THE GENERAL PUBLIC

Table 3.38
Summary of frequent alcohol and tobacco usage by socioeconomic status

N = Percent of Valid   N = Valid N

	Main sample				Booster sample			
	AB	C1	C2	DE	AB	C1	C2	DE
	490	1072	996	1552	43	216	211	491
Alcohol	56	45	37	25	41	47	35	25
Tobacco	18	28	36	46	32	35	42	52

Percentage of respondents, averaged across location, who used alcohol or tobacco daily or several times per week

Table 3.39
Summary of frequent alcohol and tobacco usage by ethnicity

N = Percent of Valid   N = Valid N

	Main sample				Booster sample			
	White	Black	Asian	Other	White	Black	Asian	Other
	3666	213	123	49	766	83	89	12
Alcohol	40	29	11	21	37	49	7	13
Tobacco	38	33	18	27	51	45	18	31

Percentage of respondents, averaged across location, who used alcohol or tobacco daily or several times per week

Table 3.40
Summary of respondents' alcohol and tobacco usage by present and long term employment status: Main sample

N = Percent of Valid   N = Valid N

	Presently in employment	Not employed at present	Have been employed	Have never been employed
	3700	419	1013	235
Alcohol	45	39	29	16
Tobacco	34	56	47	25

Percentage of respondents, averaged across location, who used alcohol or tobacco daily or several times per week

Table 3.41
Summary of respondents' alcohol and tobacco usage by present and long term employment status: Booster sample

N = Percent of Valid   N = Valid N

	Presently in employment	Not employed at present	Have been employed	Have never been employed
	726	239	422	243
Alcohol	33	32	31	24
Tobacco	41	63	56	36

Percentage of respondents, averaged across location, who used alcohol or tobacco daily or several times per week

APPENDIX I

Table 3.42
Summary statistics for variations in alcohol and tobacco usage: demographic differences

Alcohol

Location	Age	Gender	Socioeconomic status	Ethnicity	Lifetime employment	Present employment
Nottingham Main	.01	.00000	.00000	.006	NS	.007
Glasgow Main	.003	.00000	.02	.009	NS	.05
Lewisham Main	NS	.00000	.00000	.00000	.03	NS
Bradford Main	.00000	.00000	.00000	.00000	.00000	.02
Nottingham Booster	NS	NS	NS	.00005	NS	NS
Glasgow Booster	.03	.005	NS	NS	NS	NS
Lewisham Booster	NS	.001	NS	.00000	NS	NS
Bradford Booster	.04	NS	NS	.00000	NS	.04

Tobacco

Location	Age	Gender	Socioeconomic status	Ethnicity	Lifetime employment	Present employment
Nottingham Main	NS	.05	.002	NS	.01	.0001
Glasgow Main	NS	.05	.00002	.0005	.05	.00005
Lewisham Main	NS	.003	.0008	.01	.007	.006
Bradford Main	NS	NS	.00000	.05	.0006	.00002
Nottingham Booster	NS	NS	NS	NS	NS	.03
Glasgow Booster	NS	NS	NS	.00000	NS	.001
Lewisham Booster	NS	NS	NS	.002	.01	NS
Bradford Booster	NS	NS	NS	.00000	.008	NS

Significance levels achieved by chi squared statistics: variations in alcohol and tobacco usage across demographic groups

Table 3.43
Summary of demographic regression model for alcohol and tobacco usage: Main sample

Response	final model	beta	t	sig.t	Adj. R squared
alcohol usage	gender	.23	7.12	.0000	.20
(N = 1213)	ethnicity	.26	9.83	.0000	
	socioeconomic status	.17	6.44	.0000	
	ever employed	.09	3.39	.0007	
	age	.11	4.15	.0000	
	presently employed	.08	2.49	.01	
tobacco usage	socioeconomic status	−.21	−7.79	.0000	.13
(N = 1212)	ever employed	.13	4.48	.0000	
	presently employed	.16	5.58	.0000	
	ethnicity	.12	4.28	.0000	
	age	.11	3.84	.0001	

variables in equation: *location, age, gender, socioeconomic status, ethnicity (white/black/asian), presently employed, ever employed*

Table 3.44
Summary of demographic regression model for alcohol and tobacco usage : Booster sample

Response	final model	beta	t	sig.t	Adj. R squared
alcohol usage	ethnicity	.34	9.22	.0000	.19
(N = 647)	gender	.16	4.49	.0000	
	socioeconomic status	.14	3.92	.0001	
	age	−.09	−2.38	.02	
	ever employed	.09	2.38	.02	
tobacco usage	ethnicity	.16	4.34	.0000	.13
(N = 644)	socioeconomic status	−.14	−3.56	.0004	
	ever employed	.11	2.76	.006	
	presently employed	.14	3.67	.0003	
	age	−.09	−2.25	.02	

variables in equation: location, age, gender, socioeconomic status, ethnicity (white, black, asian), presently employed, ever employed

Table 3.45
Summary of choice of entertainment regression models for alcohol and tobacco usage: Main sample

Response	final model	beta	t	sig.t	Adj. R squared
frequency of	pub	0.43	29.46	.000	0.26
using alcohol	dance	0.07	5.09	.000	
(N=4098)	plays sports	0.04	2.93	.000	
	bingo	−0.05	−4.07	.000	
	church	−0.06	−4.30	.000	
	watches sports	0.05	3.65	.000	
	cafe	0.05	3.65	.000	
frequency of	church	−0.11	−7.28	.000	0.07
using tobacco	bingo	0.11	7.36	.000	
(N=4094)	cinema	−0.12	−7.43	.000	
	pub	0.11	6.83	.000	
	plays sports	−0.07	−4.60	.000	
	dance	0.07	4.39	.000	
	evening class	−0.05	−3.27	.001	
	other entertainment	0.03	2.19	.03	

variables in equation: location, whether visit friends, whether go to pub, whether go to restaurant or cafe, whether go to dances or discos, whether go to church, whether go to evening classes, whether play sports, whether watch sports, whether go to cinema, whether go to bingo, whether choose other form of entertainment

Table 3.46
Summary of choice of entertainment regression models for alcohol and tobacco usage: Booster sample

Response	final model	beta	t	sig.t	Adj. R squared
frequency of	pub	0.53	20.2	.000	0.39
using alcohol	dance	0.19	7.37	.000	
(N= 965)	visit friends	−0.05	−2.02	.04	
frequency of	pub	0.20	6.61	.000	0.08
using tobacco	cinema	−0.16	−5.12	.000	
(N=962)	plays sports	−0.12	−3.87	.000	

variables in equation: location, whether visit friends, whether go to pub, whether go to restaurant or cafe, whether go to dances or discos, whether go to church, whether go to evening classes, whether play sports, whether watch sports, whether go to cinema, whether go to bingo, whether choose other form of entertainment

APPENDIX I

Table 3.47
Summary of drug usage regression model for opiate usage: Main sample

Response	final model	beta	t	sig.t	Adj. R squared
opiate usage	non-opiate usage	.18	10.1	.000	.06
(N = 4081)	cannabis usage	.11	6.40	.000	

variables in equation: *location, cannabis usage, usage of other non-opiates (pills, tranquillisers, amphetamines, LSD, ecstasy, psilocybin, amyl nitrite), alcohol usage, tobacco usage*

Table 3.48
Summary of drug usage regression model for opiate usage: Booster sample

Response	final model	beta	t	sig.t	Adj. R squared
opiate usage	non-opiate usage	.28	7.45	.000	.12
(N = 954)	cannabis usage	.10	2.53	.01	

variables in equation: *location, cannabis usage, usage of other non-opiates (pills, tranquillisers, amphetamines, LSD, ecstasy, psilocybin, amyl nitrate), alcohol usage, tobacco usage*

Table 3.49
Summary of drug usage regression model for non-opiate usage: Main sample

Response	final model	beta	t	sig.t	Adj. R squared
non-opiate usage	cannabis usage	0.51	37.83	.000	0.26
(N = 4084)					

variables in equation: *cannabis usage, alcohol usage, tobacco usage, location*

Table 3.50
Summary of drug usage regression model for non–opiate usage : Booster sample

Response	final model	beta	t	sig.t	Adj. R squared
non-opiate usage	cannabis usage	0.60	23.0	.000	0.37
(N = 962)					

variables in equation: *cannabis usage, alcohol usage, tobacco usage, location*

Table 3.51
Summary of drug usage regression model for cannabis usage : Main sample

Response	final model	beta	t	sig.t	Adj. R squared
cannabis usage	tobacco usage	.14	9.34	.0000	.03
(N=4084)	alcohol usage	.11	7.16	.0000	

variables in equation: *alcohol usage, tobacco usage, location*

Table 3.52
Summary of drug usage regression model for cannabis usage : Booster sample

Response	final model	beta	t	sig.t	Adj. R squared
cannabis usage	tobacco usage	.22	6.93	.0000	.08
(N=962)	alcohol usage	.16	5.13	.0000	

variables in equation: *alcohol usage, tobacco usage, location*

DRUG USAGE AND DRUGS PREVENTION: THE VIEWS AND HABITS OF THE GENERAL PUBLIC

TABLES IN APPENDIX 1 (CHAPTER 4)

Table 4.1
Distribution of drug users across postal districts: Drug usage within the last year

Location	% of districts with cannabis users	Sig. Chi-sq.	% of districts with non-opiate users	Sig. Chi-sq.	% of districts with opiate users	Sig. Chi-sq.
Nottingham Main	92	.00000	61	.00000	15	NS
Glasgow Main	96	NS	78	NS	25	NS
Lewisham Main	77	.008	88	NS	22	NS
Bradford Main	83	NS	61	NS	5	NS
Nottingham Booster	69	.001	61	NS	38	NS
Glasgow Booster	88	.05	75	.05	17	NS
Lewisham Booster	88	NS	88	NS	33	NS
Bradford Booster	55	NS	39	.005	11	NS

Percentage of sampled postal districts which had drug users - based on drug usage within the last year

Table 4.2
Distribution of drug users across postal districts: Frequency of usage greater than or equal to monthly

Location	% of districts with cannabis users	Sig. Chi-sq.	% of districts with non-opiate users	Sig. Chi-sq.	% of districts with opiate users	Sig. Chi-sq.
Nottingham Main	38	.00000	23	.05	Too few regular users	
Glasgow Main	79	NS	25	NS	1	NS
Lewisham Main	78	.02	55	NS	22	NS
Bradford Main	39	NS	11	.05	Too few regular users	
Nottingham Booster	46	.0001	15	.02	8	NS
Glasgow Booster	83	NS	12	.004	8	NS
Lewisham Booster	88	NS	44	NS	11	NS
Bradford Booster	50	.04	33	NS	17	NS

Percentage of sampled postal districts which had respondents using a drug at least once per month

Table 4.3
Distribution of drug users across enumeration districts: Drug usage within the last year

Location	Mean % EDs with cannabis users	Sig. Chi-sq.	Mean % EDs with non-opiate users	Sig. Chi-sq.	Mean % EDs with opiate users	Sig. Chi-sq.
Nottingham Main	36	.00000	17	.00005	4	NS
Glasgow Main	65	NS	30	.008	8	NS
Lewisham Main	57	NS	24	.05	12	NS
Bradford Main	26	NS	22	NS	5	.04
Nottingham Booster	21	.004	22	NS	5	NS
Glasgow Booster	56	NS	33	NS	3	NS
Lewisham Booster	33	NS	21	NS	2	NS
Bradford Booster	15	NS	9	NS	1	NS

Percentage of sampled enumeration districts which had drug users - based on drug usage within the last year and averaged across all postal districts sampled in a location

APPENDIX I

Table 4.4
Distribution of drug users across postal districts: Frequency of usage greater than or equal to monthly

Location	% of districts with cannabis users	Sig. Chi-sq.	% of districts with non-opiate users	Sig. Chi-sq.	% of districts with opiate users	Sig. Chi-sq.
Nottingham Main	10	.00000	6	NS	Too few regular users	
Glasgow Main	34	NS	6	.0008	1	NS
Lewisham Main	28	NS	7	NS	2	NS
Bradford Main	8	NS	3	.003	Too few regular users	
Nottingham Booster	13	.00009	2	NS	1	NS
Glasgow Booster	36	NS	3	.002	2	NS
Lewisham Booster	26	NS	5	NS	1	NS
Bradford Booster	11	NS	5	NS	2	NS

Percentage of sampled enumeration districts which had respondents using a drug at least once per month, averaged across all postal districts sampled in a location

Table 4.5
Distribution of drug users within postal districts

Location	Usage within last year				Regular usage			
	<30% of EDs	30-50% of EDs	50-70% of EDs	70-100% of EDs	<30% of EDs	30-50% of EDs	50-70% of EDs	70-100% of EDs
Lewisham Main	0	3	3	3	6	2	1	0
Bradford Main	9	7	2	0	18	0	0	0
Glasgow Main	1	9	7	7	12	6	5	1
Nottingham Main	5	5	2	1	12	0	1	0
Lewisham Booster	3	5	1	0	4	5	0	0
Bradford Booster	7	4	2	0	9	4	0	0
Glasgow Booster	3	0	0	4	4	0	1	2
Nottingham Booster	4	3	2	0	6	3	0	0

Number of postal districts in each location with the specified proportion of enumeration districts containing drug users

Table 4.6
Comparison of 'drug areas' and 'non-drug areas' by socioeconomic status: Main sample

	%AB	%C1	%C2	%DE	Sig. Chi Squared
Nottingham (Recent usage)					
Non-drug areas	7	26	29	37	.001
Drug areas	17	27	24	32	
Nottingham (Regular usage)					
Non-drug areas	19	22	28	31	.002
Drug areas	10	49	14	37	
Glasgow (Recent usage)					
Non-drug areas	22	22	8	47	.00000
Drug areas	3	14	21	61	
Glasgow (Regular usage)					
Non-drug areas	19	27	16	37	.00000
Drug areas	4	16	22	58	
Lewisham (Recent usage)					
Non-drug areas	9	32	25	34	.009
Drug areas	11	42	20	27	
Lewisham (Regular usage)					
Non-drug areas	8	31	26	35	.003
Drug areas	8	46	23	22	
Bradford (Recent usage)					
Non-drug areas	10	19	27	44	NS
Drug areas	10	20	24	45	
Bradford (Regular usage)					
Non-drug areas			Too few regular users		
Drug areas					

Percentage of respondents in each socioeconomic group in those postal districts with a particularly high and a particularly low proportion of drug users as measured by recent or frequent usage

Table 4.7
Comparison of 'drug areas' and 'non-drug areas' by socioeconomic status: Booster sample

	%AB	%C1	%C2	%DE	Sig. Chi Squared
Nottingham (Recent usage)					
Non-drug areas	1	25	62	12	.0008
Drug areas	16	32	7	45	
Nottingham (Regular usage)					
Non-drug areas	3	19	30	46	.002
Drug areas	8	26	13	53	
Glasgow (Recent usage)					
Non-drug areas	33	33	33	1	.00000
Drug areas	25	13	60	2	
Glasgow (Regular usage)					
Non-drug areas	33	17	16	50	.00000
Drug areas	1	30	12	57	
Lewisham (Recent usage)					
Non-drug areas	1	33	30	37	.009
Drug areas	11	32	17	40	
Lewisham (Regular usage)					
Non-drug areas	12	32	32	24	.003
Drug areas	15	33	17	35	
Bradford (Recent usage)					
Non-drug areas	4	1	41	54	NS
Drug areas	1	4	27	68	NS
Bradford (Regular usage)					
Non-drug areas		Too few regular users			
Drug areas					

Percentage of respondents in each socioeconomic group in those postal districts with a particularly high and a particularly low proportion of drug users as measured by recent or frequent usage

Table 4.8
Comparison of 'drug areas' and 'non-drug areas' by gender: Main sample

	% Male	% Female	Sig. Chi-Squared
Nottingham (Recent usage)			
Non-drug areas	45	55	NS
Drug areas	47	52	
Nottingham (Regular usage)			
Non-drug areas	43	56	.03
Drug areas	56	44	
Glasgow (Recent usage)			
Non-drug areas	45	55	NS
Drug areas	38	62	
Glasgow (Regular usage)			
Non-drug areas	41	59	NS
Drug areas	37	65	
Lewisham (Recent usage)			
Non-drug areas	43	57	NS
Drug areas	46	54	
Lewisham (Regular usage)			
Non-drug areas	42	58	NS
Drug areas	47	53	
Bradford (Recent usage)			
Non-drug areas	41	59	NS
Drug areas	42	58	
Bradford (Regular usage)			
Non-drug areas		Too few regular users	
Drug areas			

Percentage of respondents of each gender in those postal districts with a particularly high and a particularly low proportion of drug users as measured by recent or frequent usage

Table 4.9
Comparison of 'drug areas' and 'non-drug areas' by gender: Booster sample

	% Male	% Female	Sig. Chi-Squared
Nottingham (Recent usage)			
Non-drug areas	37	62	NS
Drug areas	54	45	
Nottingham (Regular usage)			
Non-drug areas	47	53	NS
Drug areas	55	45	
Glasgow (Recent usage)			
Non-drug areas	33	67	NS
Drug areas	38	62	
Glasgow (Regular usage)			
Non-drug areas	67	33	NS
Drug areas	42	57	
Lewisham (Recent usage)			
Non-drug areas	48	52	NS
Drug areas	50	50	
Lewisham (Regular usage)			
Non-drug areas	56	44	NS
Drug areas	42	58	
Bradford (Recent usage)			
Non-drug areas	50	50	NS
Drug areas	46	54	
Bradford (Regular usage)			
Non-drug areas		Too few regular users	
Drug areas			

Percentage of respondents of each gender in those postal districts with a particularly high and a particularly low proportion of drug users as measured by recent or frequent usage

APPENDIX 1

Table 4.10
Comparison of 'drug areas' and 'non-drug areas' by age group: Main sample

	%16-19	%20-24	%25-29	%30-34	%35-44	%45-59	%60+	Sig. Chi-Sq.
Nottingham (Recent usage)								
Non-drug areas	6	8	11	11	18	24	23	NS
Drug areas	4	13	12	13	16	16	25	
Nottingham (Regular usage)								
Non-drug areas	4	8	9	11	19	22	27	.0003
Drug areas	4	16	21	16	11	7	24	
Glasgow (Recent usage)								
Non-drug areas	4	7	16	16	19	17	21	NS
Drug areas	6	12	17	11	16	15	23	
Glasgow (Regular usage)								
Non-drug areas	2	10	15	14	16	19	22	NS
Drug areas	5	13	16	12	15	14	25	
Lewisham (Recent usage)								
Non-drug areas	4	8	13	12	16	17	30	.002
Drug areas	2	9	19	16	20	11	23	
Lewisham (Regular usage)								
Non-drug areas	4	6	9	11	14	20	35	.00002
Drug areas	2	9	20	16	18	14	19	
Bradford (Recent usage)								
Non-drug areas	6	7	15	12	16	18	26	NS
Drug areas	5	6	12	13	20	19	25	
Bradford (Regular usage)								
Non-drug areas		Too few regular users						
Drug areas								

Percentage of respondents in each age group in those postal districts with a particularly high and a particularly low proportion of drug users as measured by recent or frequent usage

Table 4.11
Comparison of 'drug areas' and 'non-drug areas' by age group: Booster sample

	%16-19	%20-24	%25-29	Sig. Chi-squared
Nottingham (Recent usage)				
Non-drug areas	12	87	1	NS
Drug areas	45	48	7	
Nottingham (Regular usage)				
Non-drug areas	40	54	5	NS
Drug areas	43	52	6	
Glasgow (Recent usage)				
Non-drug areas	98	1	1	.04
Drug areas	30	64	6	
Glasgow (Regular usage)				
Non-drug areas	50	49	1	NS
Drug areas	30	62	7	
Lewisham (Recent usage)				
Non-drug areas	52	41	7	NS
Drug areas	50	44	6	
Lewisham (Regular usage)				
Non-drug areas	40	44	16	NS
Drug areas	35	56	10	
Bradford (Recent usage)				
Non-drug areas	41	45	14	NS
Drug areas	39	45	16	
Bradford (Regular usage)				
Non-drug areas	Too few regular users			
Drug areas				

Percentage of respondents in each age group in those postal districts with a particularly high and a particularly low proportion of drug users as measured by recent or frequent usage

Table 4.12
Comparison of 'drug areas' and 'non-drug areas' by ethnicity: Main sample

	%White	%Black	%Asian	%Other	Sig. Chi-squared
Nottingham (Recent usage)					
Non-drug areas	98	2	0	0	.002
Drug areas	92	6	2	0	
Nottingham (Regular usage)					
Non-drug areas	96	2	1	1	.008
Drug areas	88	7	4	1	
Glasgow (Recent usage)					
Non-drug areas	97	1	1	1	NS
Drug areas	98	0	2	0	
Glasgow (Regular usage)					
Non-drug areas	95	0	5	0	NS
Drug areas	98	0	2	0	
Lewisham (Recent usage)					
Non-drug areas	80	17	1	2	NS
Drug areas	80	14	2	4	
Lewisham (Regular usage)					
Non-drug areas	85	12	1	2	.008
Drug areas	74	21	1	4	
Bradford (Recent usage)					
Non-drug areas	73	2	24	1	.00000
Drug areas	97	1	2	0	
Bradford (Regular usage)					
Non-drug areas		Too few regular users			
Drug areas					

Percentage of respondents in each ethnic group in those postal districts with a particularly high and a particularly low proportion of drug users as measured by recent or frequent usage

Table 4.13
Comparison of 'drug areas' and 'non-drug areas' by ethnicity: Booster sample

	%White	%Black	%Asian	%Other	Sig. Chi-squared
Nottingham (Recent usage)					
Non-drug areas	100	0	0	0	NS
Drug areas	72	15	8	5	
Nottingham (Regular usage)					
Non-drug areas	100	0	0	0	.002
Drug areas	82	12	5	2	
Glasgow (Recent usage)					
Non-drug areas	100	0	0	0	NS
Drug areas	94	4	2	0	
Glasgow (Regular usage)					
Non-drug areas	100	0	0	0	NS
Drug areas	92	5	2	1	
Lewisham (Recent usage)					
Non-drug areas	67	30	4	0	NS
Drug areas	73	19	5	3	
Lewisham (Regular usage)					
Non-drug areas	76	16	0	8	NS
Drug areas	71	21	4	4	
Bradford (Recent usage)					
Non-drug areas	38	0	57	0	.01
Drug areas	71	1	28	0	
Bradford (Regular usage)					
Non-drug areas			Too few regular users		
Drug areas					

Percentage of respondents in each ethnic group in those postal districts with a particularly high and a particularly low proportion of drug users as measured by recent or frequent usage

Table 4.14
Comparison of 'drug areas' and 'non-drug areas' by employment status: Main sample

	% presently employed	% not employed presently	Sig. Chi-sq.	% have been employed	% never employed	Sig. Chi-sq.
Nottingham (Recent usage)						
Non-drug areas	90	10	NS	78	22	NS
Drug areas	89	11		75	25	
Nottingham (Regular usage)						
Non-drug areas	92	8	.01	86	14	.02
Drug areas	84	16		69	31	
Glasgow (Recent usage)						
Non-drug areas	88	12	.002	83	17	NS
Drug areas	75	25		81	19	
Glasgow (Regular usage)						
Non-drug areas	95	5	.00000	83	17	NS
Drug areas	73	26		79	21	
Lewisham (Recent usage)						
Non-drug areas	92	8	NS	76	24	NS
Drug areas	92	8		85	15	
Lewisham (Regular usage)						
Non-drug areas	93	7	NS	76	24	NS
Drug areas	90	10		86	14	
Bradford (Recent usage)						
Non-drug areas	89	11	NS	72	28	.004
Drug areas	89	11		91	9	
Bradford (Regular usage)						
Non-drug areas			Too few regular users			
Drug areas						

Percentage of respondents in each employment category in those postal districts with a particularly high and a particularly low proportion of drug users as measured by recent or frequent usage

Table 4.15
Comparison of 'drug areas' and 'non-drug areas' by employment status: Booster sample

	% presently employed	% not employed presently	Sig. Chi-sq.	% have been employed	% never employed	Sig. Chi-sq.
Nottingham (Recent usage)						
Non-drug areas	75	25	NS	100	0	.03
Drug areas	77	23		44	56	
Nottingham (Regular usage)						
Non-drug areas	73	27	NS	75	24	NS
Drug areas	78	22		65	35	
Glasgow (Recent usage)						
Non-drug areas	33	67	.05	67	33	NS
Drug areas	81	19		70	30	
Glasgow (Regular usage)						
Non-drug areas	83	17	NS	80	20	NS
Drug areas	85	15		67	33	
Lewisham (Recent usage)						
Non-drug areas	67	33	NS	59	41	NS
Drug areas	80	20		57	42	
Lewisham (Regular usage)						
Non-drug areas	64	36	NS	75	25	NS
Drug areas	9	21		64	36	
Bradford (Recent usage)						
Non-drug areas	77	23	NS	50	50	NS
Drug areas	77	23		54	46	
Bradford (Regular usage)						
Non-drug areas		Too few regular users				
Drug areas						

Percentage of respondents in each employment category in those postal districts with a particularly high and a particularly low proportion of drug users as measured by recent or frequent usage

APPENDIX I

Table 4.16
Comparison of 'drug areas' and 'non-drug areas' by ACORN category: Main sample

	% Affluent Housing	% Retirement Housing	% Other Housing	% Council or Inner City Housing	Sig. Chi-sq.
Nottingham (Recent usage)					
Non-drug areas	32	0	44	24	.00000
Drug areas	35	0	22	42	
Nottingham (Regular usage)					
Non-drug areas	44	2	27	27	.00000
Drug areas	26	0	27	46	
Glasgow (Recent usage)					
Non-drug areas	40	7	0	54	.00000
Drug areas	3	7	4	86	
Glasgow (Regular usage)					
Non-drug areas	37	8	0	54	.00000
Drug areas	4	9	5	82	
Lewisham (Recent usage)					
Non-drug areas	32	1	3	64	.00000
Drug areas	17	4	5	73	
Lewisham (Regular usage)					
Non-drug areas	36	0	4	61	.00000
Drug areas	9	2	4	84	
Bradford (Recent usage)					
Non-drug areas	41	0	10	49	NS
Drug areas	33	0	13	54	
Bradford (Regular usage)					
Non-drug areas			Too few regular users		
Drug areas					

Percentage of respondents living in accomodation with the stated ACORN category in those postal districts with a particularly high and a particularly low proportion of drug users as measured by recent or frequent usage

Table 4.17
Respondents' views of their own neighbourhood as a 'drug area'

Sample	Valid N	% of EDs in which a majority feel their area is high in drug users	% of EDs in which a majority feel their area is low in drug users
Bradford Main	724	4	66
Nottingham Main	757	6	78
Glasgow Main	808	11	45
Lewisham Main	793	2	38
Bradford Booster	184	8	28
Nottingham Booster	214	12	50
Glasgow Booster	230	27	20
Lewisham Booster	203	10	22

Percentage of total number of enumeration districts in a location in which a majority of respondents felt their local area to have a lower or a higher number of drug users than the city/borough generally

Table 4.18
Association between assumed and actual prevalence of drug use in an area: Main sample

N = valid N

Association between:	Lewisham	Bradford	Glasgow	Nottingham
	793	724	808	757
Areas perceived as high in drug usage/actual proportion regular drug users	0.10	0.08	0.11	0.30
Areas perceived as high in drug usage/actual proportion recent drug users	0.01	0.14	0.33	0.55
Areas perceived as low in drug usage/actual proportion regular drug users	−0.01	−0.05	−0.10	−0.11
Areas perceived as low in drug usage/actual proportion recent drug users	−0.10	−0.17	−0.33	−0.32

*Pearson's correlation coefficients showing the association between the **majority view** of an area as an area high or low in drug usage and the **actual** proportion of recent and frequent drug users within that area.*

Table 4.19
Association between assumed and actual prevalence of drug use in an area: Booster sample

N = valid N

Association between:	Lewisham	Bradford	Glasgow	Nottingham
	203	184	230	224
Areas perceived as high in drug usage/actual proportion regular drug users	0.20	0.10	0.24	0.25
Areas perceived as high in drug usage/actual proportion recent drug users	0.14	0.24	0.09	0.14
Areas perceived as low in drug usage/actual proportion regular drug users	−0.30	−0.28	−0.004	−0.14
Areas perceived as low in drug usage/actual proportion recent drug users	−0.07	−0.32	−0.04	−0.02

*Pearson's correlation coefficients showing the association between the **majority view** of an area as an area high or low in drug usage and the **actual** proportion of recent and frequent drug users within that area.*

Table 4.20
Personal knowledge of drug use or drug users and the belief that drug dealing is associated with specific areas: Main sample

'Y' = respondents **with experience** of drugs or drug users
'N' = respondents with **no experience** of drugs or drug users
N = Percent of Valid
N = Valid N

	Lewisham		Bradford		Glasgow		Nottingham	
	Y	N	Y	N	Y	N	Y	N
	215	547	120	184	641	143	143	549
specific areas	84	82	86	85	90	87	91	90
no specific areas	16	17	14	14	10	13	9	9

*Percentage of respondents who feel that drug dealing **is** associated with specific areas in their city or borough / Percentage of respondents who feel that drug dealing is not associated with specific areas in their city or borough*

Table 4.21
Personal knowledge of drug use or drug users and the belief that drug dealing is associated

'Y' = respondents **with experience** of drugs or drug users
'N' = respondents with **no experience** of drugs or drug users
N = Percent of Valid
N = Valid N

	Lewisham		Bradford		Glasgow		Nottingham	
	Y	N	Y	N	Y	N	Y	N
	94	93	59	107	125	107	94	117
specific areas	79	71	76	64	88	84	85	83
no specific areas	21	29	24	36	12	16	15	17

Percentage of respondents who feel that drug dealing is associated with specific areas in their city or borough / Percentage of respondents who feel that drug dealing is not associated with specific areas in their city or borough

APPENDIX 1

Table 4.22
Personal knowledge of drug use or drug users and the ability to name a place where drugs are obtained

'Y' = respondents **with experience** of drugs or drug users
'N' = respondents with **no experience** of drugs or drug users
N = Percent of Valid
N = Valid N

	Lewisham Y	Lewisham N	Bradford Y	Bradford N	Glasgow Y	Glasgow N	Nottingham Y	Nottingham N
	184	455	105	503	174	565	136	494
Main sample	73	51	79	57	94	70	83	59
	77	71	56	70	106	98	79	101
Booster sample	73	51	76	39	83	71	81	67

Percentage of respondents able to name a particular area as associated with drug dealing

Table 4.23
Types of areas labelled as 'drug dealing' areas : Main sample

'Y' = respondents **with experience** of drugs or drug users
'N' = respondents with **no experience** of drugs or drug users
N = Percent of Valid
N = Valid N   (N) = Actual N

	Lewisham Y	Lewisham N	Bradford Y	Bradford N	Glasgow Y	Glasgow N	Nottingham Y	Nottingham N
	134	232	83	287	163	395	113	291
City centre	4	2	3	2	2	3	7	6
Pubs or clubs	– (0)	– (0)	2	3	– (0)	– (1)	1	1
Council estates	– (0)	1	1	1	2	– (0)	1	– (2)
Deprived areas	– (1)	– (1)	– (0)	1	1	– (1)	2	1
Named district	64	80	57	67	85	88	79	83
Specific place (named pub, road etc)	12	14	15	16	2	1	4	8
Other	– (0)	– (1)	– (0)	2	– (0)	– (1)	– (0)	– (1)

Percentage of respondents stating that a particular area or type of area was associated with drug dealing / In Lewisham 'city centre' refers to either Lewisham town centre or the general phrase 'London'

Table 4.24
Types of areas labelled as being associated with drug dealing: Booster sample

'Y' = respondents **with experience** of drugs or drug users
'N' = respondents with **no experience** of drugs or drug users
N = Percent of Valid
N = Valid N   (N) = Actual N

	Lewisham Y	Lewisham N	Bradford Y	Bradford N	Glasgow Y	Glasgow N	Nottingham Y	Nottingham N
	56	36	42	27	88	69	64	68
City centre	1	– (0)	5	4	2	2	1	– (0)
Pubs or clubs	1	– (0)	2	8	2	2	3	– (0)
Council estates	1	– (0)	– (0)	– (0)	– (0)	– (0)	– (0)	– (0)
Deprived areas	– (0)	– (0)	– (0)	– (0)	– (0)	– (0)	1	4
Named district	78	76	83	82	50	67	92	92
Specific place (named pub, road etc)	– (0)	12	12	4	– (0)	– (0)	3	4
Other	4	3	– (0)	– (0)	– (0)	6	1	– (0)

Percentage of respondents stating that a particular area or type of area was associated with drug dealing / In Lewisham 'city centre' refers to either Lewisham town centre or the general phrase 'London'

Table 4.25
Number of districts assumed to be and actually associated with drugs

Location	Number of districts named as 'drug areas'	Number of areas actually high in drug usage
Nottingham	46	10
Glasgow	80	11
Lewisham	37	10
Bradford	38	11

Absolute numbers of districts named as being 'drug areas' / Absolute numbers of districts in which more than 50% of the enumeration districts had recent drug users / Taken across main and booster samples

Table 4.26
Personal knowledge of drugs or drug users and the ability to label correctly a 'drug area'

N = Percent of Valid   N = Valid N

Sample	Respondent has knowledge of drug use or users	Respondent has no knowledge of drugs
Nottingham Main	21 113	15 291
Glasgow Main	7 163	7 395
Lewisham Main	12 134	9 232
Bradford Main	12 83	14 287
Nottingham Booster	23 64	14 68
Glasgow Booster	18 88	13 69
Lewisham Booster	13 56	15 36
Bradford Booster	3 42	11 27

Percentage of respondents naming an area which from our data actually had a high proportion of drug users as a 'drug area'

Table 4.27
Sources of knowledge regarding 'drug areas': Main sample

'Y' = respondents **with experience** of drugs or drug users   N = Percent of Valid
'N' = respondents with **no experience** of drugs or drug users   N = Valid N   (N) = Actual N

	Lewisham Y	Lewisham N	Bradford Y	Bradford N	Glasgow Y	Glasgow N	Nottingham Y	Nottingham N
	196	447	135	473	241	500	149	485
Direct knowledge	38	13	33	9	38	18	38	12
Family or friends	13	8	16	7	24	14	18	5
Neighbours	8	4	13	5	16	9	10	3
Rumour	30	15	39	22	55	32	41	26
Local press	22	21	19	30	25	24	21	26
National press	7	5	2	1	11	11	1	1
Local radio	2	2	2	3	3	3	5	4
National radio	1	– (0)	– (0)	– (2)	1	1	– (0)	– (2)
Local TV	7	6	3	6	19	16	9	10
National TV	3	4	– (0)	– (0)	5	5	1	– (0)
Other	– (1)	– (2)	– (0)	– (0)	– (2)	– (3)	– (0)	– (2)

Percentage of those respondents who named an area associated with drug dealing citing a particular source of knowledge as their major source of information on 'drug areas'

Table 4.28
Sources of knowledge regarding 'drug areas': Booster sample

'Y' = respondents **with experience** of drugs or drug users N = Percent of Valid
'N' = respondents with **no experience** of drugs or drug users N = Valid N (N) = Actual N

	Lewisham Y	Lewisham N	Bradford Y	Bradford N	Glasgow Y	Glasgow N	Nottingham Y	Nottingham N
	107	126	75	156	135	123	97	147
Direct knowledge	31	15	31	7	31	24	37	13
Family or friends	18	9	13	12	24	15	11	4
Neighbours	11	6	14	3	15	12	10	4
Rumour	42	22	50	20	64	42	44	42
Local press	17	12	9	10	10	14	4	12
National press	3	3	– (0)	1	12	6	– (0)	– (0)
Local radio	– (1)	– (1)	1	– (1)	2	1	2	3
National radio	– (1)	– (0)	– (0)	– (1)	– (0)	1	– (0)	– (0)
Local TV	13	3	3	4	9	16	– (0)	7
National TV	4	3	– (0)	– (0)	1	2	– (0)	– (1)
Other	– (0)	3	1	1	1	– (1)	– (0)	2

Percentage of those respondents who named an area associated with drug dealing citing a particular source of knowledge as their major source of information on 'drug areas'

TABLES IN APPENDIX 1 (CHAPTER 5)

Table 5.1
Integration into the local area and satisfaction with the local area by sample

N = Percent of valid   N = Valid N

Sample	Lived	Help	Own way	Mix	Satis
Nottingham Main	76 1002	27 976	53 976	17 976	88 1004
Bradford Main	75 1000	27 961	48 961	20 961	88 999
Lewisham Main	72 1137	25 1092	50 1092	20 1092	84 1133
Glasgow Main	79 969	32 940	49 940	16 940	80 972
Nottingham Booster	51 244	19 239	61 239	20 239	77 245
Bradford Booster	35 231	30 222	50 222	20 222	70 230
Lewisham Booster	59 232	15 226	65 226	21 226	79 231
Glasgow Booster	62 258	27 248	57 248	16 248	79 258

Percentage of respondents having lived in the area for five years or more (Lived) / Percentage of respondents who felt that the neighbourhood was one in which people tended to do things together (Help) /Percentage of respondents who felt that the neighbourhood was one in which everyone went their own way (Own Way) / Percentage of respondents who felt that the neighbourhood was a mixture of people doing things together and people going their own way (Mix) /Percentage of respondents very or fairly satisfied with the area (Satis)

Table 5.2
Problems in the area by sample

N = Percent of valid   N = Valid N

Problem	Nott Main	Brad Main	Lew Main	Glas Main	Nott Boost	Brad Boost	Lew Boost	Glas Boost
noisy neighbours	11 1003	12 997	16 1132	11 970	19 245	28 231	18 231	17 257
teenagers	29 1002	32 995	24 1121	40 963	42 245	48 230	30 233	51 257
drunks	7 993	8 974	14 1115	21 956	24 242	20 225	24 231	35 257
dogs	31 1002	38 999	29 1132	42 960	42 245	52 230	27 233	46 255
abandoned cars	8 993	10 980	15 1106	10 949	21 240	22 224	16 231	17 252
litter	30 1001	43 1001	28 1133	43 962	48 245	74 231	46 233	61 257
racially motivated attacks	4 956	6 949	8 991	6 893	10 234	20 224	26 209	8 247
glue sniffing	10 846	15 839	12 883	24 830	24 210	32 201	28 195	31 234
drug users	10 994	16 788	21 894	43 818	37 217	42 194	50 210	64 244
drugs offered	7 784	12 745	16 763	34 750	31 214	35 187	44 201	58 237
drug illness	4 759	5 723	11 730	26 730	16 201	18 176	30 176	42 231
theft for drugs	12 766	15 743	22 797	45 794	37 205	43 188	49 186	63 240
crime under influence of drugs	10 747	14 731	20 792	42 673	31 215	39 181	43 186	52 233

Percentage of respondents regarding the following as 'very big' or 'fairly big' problems in their area

Table 5.3
Worries about becoming a victim of crime by sample

N = Percent of valid   N = Valid N

Sample	burglary	mugging	theft from car	theft of car	rape
Nottingham Main	62 1004	39 1002	44 695	41 698	37 558
Bradford Main	68 999	39 990	43 991	43 693	32 554
Lewisham Main	66 1133	48 1130	33 1128	35 676	48 606
Glasgow Main	67 970	48 960	27 968	27 403	40 551
Nottingham Booster	64 245	46 245	26 75	24 75	55 121
Bradford Booster	69 230	42 231	37 109	39 110	54 118
Lewisham Booster	64 232	55 233	30 84	29 87	53 117
Glasgow Booster	66 258	51 257	17 59	18 56	53 138

Percentage of respondents very worried or fairly worried about being a victim of burglary (burglary) / Percentage of respondents very worried or fairly worried about being mugged (mugging) / Percentage of car owning respondents very worried or fairly worried about having their car stolen (theft of car) / Percentage of car owning respondents very worried or fairly worried about things being stolen from their car (theft from car) / Percentage of female respondents very worried or fairly worried about being victims of rape

APPENDIX I

Table 5.4
A comparison between national and local pictures of crimes and problems by sample

N = Percent of valid   N = Valid N

Problem	Nott Main	Brad Main	Lew Main	Glas Main	Nott Boost	Brad Boost	Lew Boost	Glas Boost
burglary	10 992	13 966	21 1118	16 952	17 243	18 227	19 233	27 250
drunks	4 965	4 916	11 1083	14 924	16 244	7 219	17 229	20 253
car theft	15 964	12 959	16 1077	15 918	23 240	19 224	15 229	25 244
litter	10 988	18 975	15 1107	19 948	18 243	30 229	27 231	33 257
vandalism	9 987	12 972	14 1099	15 949	15 240	19 226	20 228	30 256
racially motivated attacks	2 956	10 931	9 1002	3 885	7 239	9 214	12 221	4 247
theft for drugs	2 907	5 873	11 994	15 874	7 229	10 202	12 220	27 246
crime under influence of drugs	2 900	4 865	9 994	13 862	6 223	4 199	9 220	26 244
drug illness	1 895	2 853	5 985	11 838	2 229	3 195	7 218	21 232
drugs offered	4 895	3 855	9 1012	13 852	9 233	7 205	15 224	29 248
glue sniffing	3 901	5 857	6 982	9 823	7 233	8 200	8 214	20 224

*Percentage of respondents feeling that the following are more of a problem **locally** than nationally*

Table 5.5
Comparison between national and local pictures of crimes and problems by sample

N = Percent of valid   N = Valid N

Problem	Nott Main	Brad Main	Lew Main	Glas Main	Nott Boost	Brad Boost	Lew Boost	Glas Boost
burglary	37 992	37 952	39 1118	27 966	24 243	24 250	30 233	17 227
drunks	62 965	65 924	54 1083	41 916	38 244	41 253	35 229	26 219
car theft	36 964	41 918	46 1077	37 959	23 240	30 244	34 229	32 224
litter	45 988	40 948	47 1107	31 975	26 243	19 257	36 231	24 229
vandalism	50 987	50 949	49 1099	37 972	30 240	26 256	39 228	23 226
racially motivated attacks	77 956	70 885	61 1002	82 931	52 239	55 247	56 221	76 214
theft for drugs	67 907	65 874	57 994	40 873	41 229	44 246	44 220	27 202
crime under influence of drugs	69 900	69 862	59 994	42 865	43 223	49 244	47 220	29 199
drug illness	74 895	76 838	65 985	50 853	55 229	59 232	49 218	36 195
drugs offered	69 895	70 852	59 1012	44 855	43 233	44 248	38 224	23 205
glue sniffing	60 901	59 823	61 982	46 857	41 233	37 224	49 214	32 200

*Percentage of respondents feeling that the following are more of a problem **nationally** than locally*

DRUG USAGE AND DRUGS PREVENTION: THE VIEWS AND HABITS OF THE GENERAL PUBLIC

Table 5.6
Comparison of the views of drug users and non-drug users on drug related problems: Main sample

'Y' = have used drugs   N = Percent of valid
'N' = have not used drugs   N = Valid N

	Nottingham Y	Nottingham N	Glasgow Y	Glasgow N	Lewisham Y	Lewisham N	Bradford Y	Bradford N
Problem								
glue sniffing	15 149	12 690	34 157	27 671	20 193	14 686	27 119	17 719
drug users	23 146	10 638	66 174	47 642	35 207	25 680	32 115	18 672
drugs offered	18 146	8 620	57 166	41 583	28 201	19 649	25 112	14 632
drug illness	9 142	4 610	47 156	32 573	22 178	14 601	9 108	8 615
theft for drugs	25 143	14 616	70 167	51 625	39 191	28 627	36 113	17 629
crime under influence of drugs	18 134	13 606	68 161	49 610	33 188	26 616	29 113	16 617

Percentage of respondents feeling each problem to be a 'very big' or 'fairly big' problem in their neighbourhood

Table 5.7
Comparison of the views of drug users and non-drug users on drug related problems: Booster sample

'Y' = have used drugs   N = Percent of valid
'N' = have not used drugs   N = Valid N

	Nottingham Y	Nottingham N	Glasgow Y	Glasgow N	Lewisham Y	Lewisham N	Bradford Y	Bradford N
Problem								
glue sniffing	24 82	23 127	32 123	30 111	27 85	30 108	33 64	31 136
drug users	40 85	35 131	63 130	65 114	57 99	45 109	48 66	38 127
drugs offered	33 89	30 124	55 130	63 107	48 96	40 103	40 67	32 119
drug illness	11 82	20 118	42 127	41 104	30 77	30 97	22 64	16 111
theft for drugs	39 85	37 119	59 128	67 112	55 87	46 97	48 65	40 122
crime under influence of drugs	28 87	33 126	58 125	67 108	43 88	45 96	42 62	37 119

Percentage of respondents feeling each problem to be a 'very big' or 'fairly big' problem in their neighbourhood

Table 5.8
Changing patterns of crime and drug use by sample

N=Percent of Valid   N=Valid N   (N)=Actual N

	More crime	Less crime	More drugs	Less drugs
Nottingham Main	58 843	3 853	22 504	3 504
Bradford Main	62 845	3 845	27 473	2 473
Lewisham Main	45 848	7 848	27 647	4 647
Glasgow Main	55 840	6 840	48 695	3 695
Nottingham Booster	45 166	7 166	47 137	5 137
Bradford Booster	56 196	8 196	69 160	4 160
Lewisham Booster	46 174	9 174	52 149	7 149
Glasgow Booster	54 199	5 199	70 182	– (1) 182

Percentage of respondents stating that there is a lot more or a little more crime in their area now in comparison to two years ago (More Crime) / Percentage of respondents stating that there is a lot less or a little less crime in their area now in comparison to two years ago (Less Crime) / Percentage of respondents stating that a lot more people or slightly more people in their area are using drugs now in comparison to two years ago (More drugs) / Percentage of respondents stating that a lot less or slightly less people in their area are using drugs now in comparison to two years ago (Less drugs)

Table 5.9
Likelihood of staying alone at home at night or walking alone after dark by sample

	Valid N	Alone	Walking
Nottingham Main	1006	68	53
Bradford Main	1004	66	51
Lewisham Main	1139	67	54
Glasgow Main	972	73	52
Nottingham Booster	245	66	75
Bradford Booster	231	58	68
Lewisham Booster	233	69	74
Glasgow Booster	258	65	72

Percentage of respondents who sometimes stay alone at home at night (Alone) / Percentage of respondents who sometimes walk alone after dark (Walking)

Table 5.10
Fear of being alone after dark at home or outside by sample

N=Percent of Valid / N=Valid N

Sample	Actual fear walking	Perceived fear walking	Actual fear at home	Perceived fear at home
Nottingham Main	17 527	53 453	11 663	15 314
Bradford Main	15 508	51 476	13 651	16 333
Lewisham Main	25 608	63 507	8 755	14 359
Glasgow Main	21 506	59 442	12 703	22 250
Nottingham Booster	20 183	61 57	12 160	17 81
Bradford Booster	18 157	64 73	10 135	21 95
Lewisham Booster	21 173	60 60	9 160	11 71
Glasgow Booster	28 187	75 69	13 168	22 90

Percentage of respondents who do go out alone at night who feel a bit unsafe or very unsafe (Actual fear walking) / Percentage of respondents who do not go out alone at night who think that they would feel a bit unsafe or very unsafe if they did (Perceived fear walking) / Percentage of respondents who do stay at home alone who feel a bit unsafe or very unsafe doing so (Actual fear at home) /

Percentage of respondents who do not stay at home alone who think that they would feel a bit unsafe or very unsafe if they did (Perceived fear at home)

Table 5.11
Summary of regression equations for crime model: Main sample

Response	final model	beta	t	sig.t	Adj. R squared
actual fear of walking alone at night (N=1951)	mugging	−0.38	−18.5	.000	0.17
	racist attacks	−0.11	−5.5	.000	
perceived fear of walking alone at night (N=1693)	mugging	−0.36	−16.0	.000	0.15
	theft of car	0.14	6.2	.000	
	racist attacks	−0.05	−2.05	.04	
satisfaction with area (N=3717)	burglary	−0.12	−6.43	.000	0.04
	racist attacks	−0.10	−5.99	.000	
	theft of car	0.07	4.35	.000	
	mugging	−0.06	−3.42	.000	
	length of time in area	−0.05	−2.94	.003	

variables in equation: *location, length of time in area, worried about burglary, worried about mugging, worried about theft of car, worried about theft from car, worried about racist attacks*

Table 5.12
Summary of regression equations for drugs model: Main sample

Response	final model	beta	t	sig.t	Adj. R squared
actual fear of walking alone at night (N=1951)	drug users	−0.13	−3.60	.000	0.03
	glue sniffing	−0.07	−2.07	.04	
perceived fear of walking alone at night (N = 1109)	drug users	−0.17	−5.86	.000	0.03
	length of time in area	0.07	2.44	.01	
satisfaction with area (N = 2577)	drug related crime	−0.17	−4.80	.000	0.09
	drug users	−0.14	−4.12	.000	
	length of time in area	−0.06	−3.36	.001	

variables in equation: location, length of time in area, problem of glue sniffing, problem of drug users, problem of people being offered drugs, problem of drug related illness, problem of theft for drugs, problem of drug related crime

Table 5.13
Summary of regression equations for comparative crime model: Main sample

Response	final model	beta	t	sig.t	Adj. R squared
actual fear of walking alone at night (N = 1942)	burglary	−0.10	−4.50	.000	.01
	racist attacks	−0.05	−2.31	.02	
perceived fear of walking alone at night (N = 1855)	burglary	−0.14	−6.10	.000	.02
satisfaction with area (N = 3717)	burglary	−0.12	−6.32	.000	.02
	racist attacks	−0.04	−2.19	.03	
	car theft	−0.04	−1.98	.04	

variables in equation: location, length of time in area, national versus local problem of burglary, national versus local problem of car theft, national versus local problem of racist attacks

APPENDIX I

Table 5.14
Summary of regression equations for comparative drugs model: Main sample

Response	final model	beta	t	sig.t	Adj. R squared
actual fear of walking alone at night (N = 1456)	drug users	−0.12	−4.51	.000	0.03
	drug illness	−0.08	−3.15	.002	
perceived fear of walking alone at night (N = 1085)	drug users	−0.21	−7.04	.000	0.04
satisfaction with area (N=3228)	drug users	−0.21	−10.18	.000	.07
	drug theft	−0.11	−5.59	.000	
	length of time in area	−0.04	−2.41	.016	
	location	0.04	1.97	.05	

variables in equation: location, length of time in area, drug users locally versus nationally, theft for drugs locally versus nationally, drug related crime locally versus nationally, glue sniffers locally versus nationally, drug related illness locally versus nationally, drugs offered for sale locally versus nationally

Table 5.15
Summary of regression equation for problems model: Main sample

Response	final model	beta	t	sig.t	Adj. R squared
satisfaction with area (N = 3896)	litter	−.14	−7.81	.000	0.14
	noisy neighbours	−.13	−8.09	.000	
	teenagers	−.11	−6.14	.000	
	drunks	−.08	−4.72	.000	
	abandoned cars	−.05	−2.94	.003	
	dogs	−.03	−2.02	.04	

variables in equation: location, length of time in area, noisy neighbours, teenagers, drunks, dogs, abandoned cars, litter

Table 5.16
Summary of regression equations for crime model: Booster sample

Response	final model	beta	t	sig.t	Adj. R squared
actual fear of walking alone at night (N = 658)	mugging	−0.35	−9.70	.000	0.12
perceived fear of walking alone at night (N = 242)	mugging	−0.21	−2.91	.004	0.10
	burglary	−0.16	−2.26	.02	
satisfaction with area (N = 904)	mugging	−0.10	−3.00	.003	0.02
	racist attacks	−0.10	−2.89	.004	

variables in equation: location, length of time in area, worried about burglary, worried about mugging, worried about theft of car, worried about theft from car, worried about racially motivated attacks

Table 5.17
Summary of regression equations for drugs model: Booster sample

Response	final model	beta	t	sig.t	Adj. R squared
actual fear of walking alone at night (N = 496)	theft for drugs	−0.15	−3.79	.001	0.02
perceived fear of walking alone at night	no variables reached criterion				
satisfaction with area (N = 668)	theft for drugs	−0.25	−6.59	.000	0.06

variables in equation: location, length of time in area, glue sniffing, drug users, people being offered drugs, drug related illness, theft for drugs, drug related crime

Table 5.18
Summary of regression equations for comparative crime model: Booster sample

Response	final model	beta	t	sig.t	Adj. R squared
actual fear of walking alone at night (N = 630)	burglary	−0.11	−2.83	.005	0.01
perceived fear of walking alone at night (N = 238)	burglary	−0.19	−3.09	.002	0.03
satisfaction with area	no variables reached criterion				

variables in equation: location, length of time in area, national versus local problem of burglary, national versus local problem of car theft, national versus local problem of racially motivated attacks

Table 5.19
Summary of regression equations for comparative drugs model: Booster sample

Response	final model	beta	t	sig.t	Adj. R squared
actual fear of walking alone at night	no variables reached criterion				
perceived fear of walking alone at night (N = 221)	drug related illness	−0.14	−2.13	.03	0.01
satisfaction with area (N = 809)	drug related crime	−0.13	−3.71	.000	0.01

variables in equation: location, length of time in area, drug users locally versus nationally, theft for drugs locally versus nationally, drug related crime locally versus nationally, glue sniffers locally versus nationally, drug related illness locally versus nationally, drugs offered for sale locally versus nationally

APPENDIX I

Table 5.20
Summary of regression equation for problems model: Booster sample

Response	final model	beta	t	sig.t	Adj. R squared
satisfaction with area	litter	−0.18	−5.32	.000	0.08
(N = 230)	teenagers	−.16	−4.82	.000	

variables in equation: noisy neighbours, teenagers, drunks, dogs, abandoned cars, litter

TABLES IN APPENDIX I (CHAPTER 6)

Table 6.1
Summary data for awareness of drugs in the main samples

N = Valid N   N = Percent of valid

	Glasgow Main	Lewisham Main	Nottingham Main	Bradford Main	Chi squared between locations
	959	1120	988	986	
% Spontaneously aware	80	86	81	82	.008
	971	1134	1004	1003	
% Known offered	35	34	31	28	.006
	972	1134	1001	1002	
% Known taken	37	38	32	29	.0008
	972	1139	1004	1002	
% Know regular taker	26	24	18	17	.000001
	971	1137	1005	1003	
% At social event	22	28	16	12	.000001

Percentage of respondents spontaneously aware of one or more illicit drugs / Percentage of respondents who knew someone who had been offered an illicit drug / Percentage of respondents who knew someone who had taken an illicit drug / Percentage of respondents who knew someone who regularly took illicit drugs / Percentage of respondents who had attended a social event where drugs had been taken.

Table 6.2
Summary data for awareness of drugs in the booster samples

N = Percent of valid   N = Valid N

	Glasgow Booster	Lewisham Booster	Nottingham Booster	Bradford Booster	Chi squared between locations
	251	221	239	226	
% Spontaneously aware	95	94	94	87	.000001
	258	229	242	231	
% Known offered	76	71	69	52	.000001
	258	229	243	231	
% Known taken	79	72	68	53	.000001
	258	230	244	231	
% Know regular taker	63	52	48	42	.00005
	258	231	243	231	
% At social event	64	61	50	34	.000001

Percentage of respondents spontaneously aware of one or more illicit drugs / Percentage of respondents who knew someone who had been offered an illicit drug / Percentage of respondents who knew someone who had taken an illicit drug / Percentage of respondents who knew someone who regularly took illicit drugs /Percentage of respondents who had attended a social event where drugs had been taken.

Table 6.3
Spontaneous awareness of drugs

N = Percent of valid   N = Valid N   (N) = Actual N

Drug	Nott. Main	Glas. Main	Lew. Main	Brad. Main	Nott. Boost.	Glas. Boost.	Lew. Boost.	Brad. Boost.
	1006	972	1139	1004	218	237	202	218
cannabis	45	51	60	53	68	83	80	67
heroin	54	49	58	56	64	57	74	63
amphetamines	23	22	22	24	31	53	35	24
LSD	30	25	26	34	48	50	50	46
cocaine	48	33	58	47	54	41	81	46
ecstasy	23	36	29	28	40	61	51	34
crack	35	12	44	28	24	15	41	18
psilocybin	1	3	1	5	4	5	5	9
methadone	1	1	2	2	-(1)	3	-(2)	3
diconal	-(1)	-(6)	-(4)	-(4)	-(0)	2	-(0)	-(2)
amyl nitrite	2	1	2	2	5	5	4	5
temazepam	-(4)	22	-(7)	1	1	35	-(2)	2
temgesic	-(1)	9	-(3)	-(7)	-(0)	21	-(0)	-(1)
semeron	-(0)	-(1)	-(1)	-(3)	-(0)	-(1)	-(0)	-(2)
barbiturates	6	4	6	5	3	4	5	3
DF118s	-(1)	1	-(4)	-(4)	-(1)	5	-(2)	1
triazelam	-(1)	1	-(8)	-(8)	2	3	-(1)	-(1)
pills	5	4	4	5	3	6	6	2
tranquilizers	10	9	7	9	7	6	9	4
glue sniffing	10	7	12	13	8	6	12	17
no drugs	17	18	12	15	4	2	1	11

Percentage of respondents showing spontaneous awareness of named drugs

Table 6.4
Prompted awareness of drugs

N = Percent of valid   N = Valid N   (N) = Actual N

Drug	Nott. Main		Glas. Main		Lew. Main		Brad. Main		Nott. Boost.		Glas. Boost.		Lew. Boost.		Brad. Boost.	
cannabis	50	554	44	476	33	456	37	472	29	70	17	37	18	40	29	72
heroin	41	463	43	496	35	408	36	442	31	78	38	102	23	52	32	81
amphetamines	53	775	46	758	48	888	41	763	49	150	36	111	37	131	33	166
LSD	61	704	61	729	58	843	49	662	46	91	44	118	38	101	35	120
cocaine	46	523	55	651	34	478	40	431	43	100	53	140	17	38	44	96
ecstasy	56	775	45	719	47	809	45	723	46	131	38	92	41	99	45	144
crack	55	654	61	855	44	638	53	723	68	166	70	201	51	119	61	179
psilocybin	59	996	55	943	42	1128	56	954	83	209	84	225	65	192	67	198
methadone	44	996	40	962	39	1116	32	984	34	217	40	230	35	200	20	211
diconal	6	1005	6	966	5	1135	4	1000	3	218	5	232	3	202	2	216
amyl nitrite	31	986	22	962	29	1116	24	984	49	207	41	225	39	194	28	207
temazepam	16	1002	43	758	13	1132	16	994	16	216	45	154	12	200	14	214
temgesic	8	1005	30	884	5	1136	6	993	7	218	33	187	5	202	6	217
semeron	2	1006	3	971	1	1138	2	1001	3	218	3	236	2	202	3	216
barbiturates	69	946	51	933	59	1071	58	954	50	211	47	227	43	192	29	211
DF118s	6	1005	16	962	5	1137	5	1000	4	217	26	225	7	200	3	216
triazelam	9	1005	20	962	5	1136	8	996	9	214	34	230	8	201	6	217
pills	57	956	48	933	50	1093	44	954	62	211	61	223	50	190	39	214
tranquillizers	58	905	52	884	52	1009	48	914	65	203	66	223	52	184	36	209
glue sniffing	82	905	78	904	76	1002	75	874	88	200	85	223	80	178	72	181
no drugs	1	1006	2	972	3	1139	6	1004	-(1)	218	3	237	-(2)	202	4	218

Percentage of respondents who failed to spontaneously cite a named drug but who were able to recognise the drug following prompting / Percentage of respondents remaining unaware of any drugs following prompting

Table 6.5
Acquaintance with someone who has been offered a drug

N = Percent of valid Drug	Nott. Main	Glas. Main	Lew. Main	Brad. Main	Nott. Boost.	Glas. Boost.	Lew. Boost.	Brad. Boost.
	954	*942*	*1095*	*939*	*239*	*253*	*229*	*219*
cannabis	23	26	30	20	51	68	65	43
heroin	6	10	9	5	16	23	23	12
amphetamines	10	14	12	8	25	44	25	21
LSD	12	14	13	10	42	43	42	27
cocaine	7	9	13	4	18	17	33	14
ecstasy	12	17	14	10	45	52	54	32
crack	5	4	6	4	15	11	18	9
psilocybin	10	11	9	11	38	41	24	25
methadone	1	2	3	-(8)	2	6	3	4
diconal	-(5)	-(4)	1	-(3)	1	2	-(1)	-(0)
amyl nitrite	7	5	7	4	26	19	21	14
temazepam	1	11	1	2	4	35	3	6
temgesic	-(8)	7	-(8)	-(3)	2	24	-(2)	-(1)
semeron	-(0)	-(1)	-(5)	-(1)	-(1)	-(1)	-(1)	-(0)
barbiturates	3	5	5	3	9	11	9	3
DF118s	-(6)	4	1	-(4)	1	15	1	2
triazelam	-(4)	3	-(10)	-(5)	-(2)	14	1	-(2)
pills	3	6	3	2	7	19	7	3
tranquillizers	3	7	4	2	8	20	9	4
glue sniffing	7	10	7	8	25	21	23	16
no drugs	69	65	65	72	30	24	27	48

Percentage of respondents claiming to know someone who had been offered a named drug

Appendix 1

Table 6.6
Acquaintance with someone who has taken a drug

N = Percent of valid   N = Valid N   (N) = Actual N

Drug	Nott. Main	Glas. Main	Lew. Main	Brad. Main	Nott. Boost.	Glas. Boost.	Lew. Boost.	Brad. Boost.
	964	794	1076	945	238	252	232	231
cannabis	23	29	33	20	54	70	63	43
heroin	5	10	8	5	13	22	23	12
amphetamines	8	13	11	6	24	43	24	22
LSD	10	13	11	9	38	45	40	24
cocaine	6	7	12	3	17	15	31	12
ecstasy	11	17	13	10	43	53	49	28
crack	3	3	5	4	14	7	15	7
psilocybin	10	12	8	10	35	37	23	22
methadone	1	2	2	-(7)	3	6	3	4
diconal	-(3)	-(3)	-(7)	-(1)	1	2	-(0)	-(0)
amyl nitrite	6	4	5	4	24	19	19	12
temazepam	1	12	2	1	4	33	3	5
temgesic	-(6)	8	-(4)	-(4)	2	21	-(1)	-(1)
semeron	-(0)	-(0)	-(3)	-(1)	-(1)	-(0)	-(0)	-(0)
barbiturates	2	4	4	2	8	10	7	4
DF118s	1	4	1	-(3)	-(2)	15	2	1
triazelam	-(3)	4	-(7)	-(5)	-(2)	13	-(2)	1
pills	3	6	2	2	6	16	8	3
tranquilizers	3	6	3	2	8	19	7	5
glue sniffing	8	10	6	10	26	23	24	17
no drugs	67	63	62	70	31	20	26	47

Percentage of respondents claiming to know someone who had taken a named drug

Table 6.7
Acquaintance with a regular drug taker

N = Percent of valid   N = Valid N   (N) = Actual N

Drug	Nott. Main	Glas. Main	Lew. Main	Brad. Main	Nott. Boost.	Glas. Boost.	Lew. Boost.	Brad. Boost.
	969	926	1105	963	240	249	220	223
cannabis	13	22	20	13	40	56	45	35
heroin	1	6	4	2	3	10	9	8
amphetamines	3	8	3	4	11	27	8	13
LSD	3	6	3	5	18	26	11	17
cocaine	1	3	4	1	4	8	13	6
ecstasy	6	9	5	6	24	35	24	18
crack	-(7)	2	1	2	5	3	7	3
psilocybin	2	4	1	2	12	16	8	9
methadone	-(4)	1	1	-(3)	-(2)	5	1	2
diconal	-(0)	-(1)	-(2)	-(0)	-(0)	2	-(0)	-(0)
amyl nitrite	2	2	2	1	9	10	6	6
temazepam	-(5)	7	-(8)	-(4)	1	21	2	2
temgesic	-(1)	5	-(1)	-(1)	-(2)	15	-(0)	-(0)
semeron	-(0)	-(0)	-(0)	-(0)	-(0)	-(0)	-(0)	-(0)
barbiturates	-(7)	2	1	-(4)	1	5	2	2
DF118s	-(1)	2	-(1)	-(1)	-(0)	10	1	-(1)
triazelam	-(0)	2	-(3)	-(1)	-(0)	6	-(2)	-(2)
pills	1	3	1	-(8)	-(2)	10	2	2
tranquillizers	1	3	1	-(8)	-(2)	12	-(2)	2
glue sniffing	2	4	2	3	6	7	4	7
no drugs	82	74	76	83	52	37	47	58

Percentage of respondents claiming to know a regular taker of a named drug

DRUG USAGE AND DRUGS PREVENTION: THE VIEWS AND HABITS OF THE GENERAL PUBLIC

Table 6.8
Attendance at a social event where drugs are being taken

N = Percent of valid N = Valid N (N) = Actual N

Drug	Nott. Main	Glas. Main	Lew. Main	Brad. Main	Nott. Boost.	Glas. Boost.	Lew. Boost.	Brad. Boost.
	941	918	1085	807	229	249	219	221
cannabis	14	19	27	11	42	55	54	30
heroin	1	1	1	1	2	6	8	4
amphetamines	3	6	4	2	11	30	13	13
LSD	3	5	5	3	23	31	21	14
cocaine	1	2	5	–(8)	5	7	14	4
ecstasy	5	8	7	4	26	37	34	17
crack	–(7)	–(9)	1	–(8)	5	3	8	3
psilocybin	3	3	3	2	12	14	9	8
methadone	–(2)	–(2)	–(5)	–(1)	–(1)	3	–(2)	2
diconal	–(1)	–(2)	–(0)	–(0)	–(1)	–(2)	–(0)	–(0)
amyl nitrite	3	2	2	1	15	10	12	8
temazepam	–(3)	3	–(4)	–(3)	1	17	–(2)	2
temgesic	–(2)	2	–(0)	–(0)	–(1)	9	–(0)	–(0)
semeron	–(0)	–(1)	–(1)	–(0)	–(0)	–(0)	–(0)	–(0)
barbiturates	–(4)	1	–(6)	–(2)	3	3	2	2
DF118s	–(1)	–(8)	–(2)	–(0)	–(1)	7	–(2)	–(2)
triazelam	–(1)	–(9)	–(0)	–(0)	–(2)	6	–(0)	–(2)
pills	–(4)	1	–(6)	–(3)	3	8	–(2)	1
tranquillizers	–(4)	1	–(3)	–(3)	2	7	–(2)	2
glue sniffing	–(3)	1	1	–(8)	9	5	4	3
no drugs	84	78	71	87	49	36	38	66

Percentage of respondents claiming to have been at a social event where a named drug was taken

Table 6.9
Perceptions of prevalence and the extent of the 'drugs problem'

N = Percent of valid N = Valid N

	Nott. Main	Glas. Main	Lew. Main	Brad. Main	Nott. Boost.	Glas. Boost.	Lew. Boost.	Brad. Boost.
	914	936	1036	895	237	254	231	213
How many take drugs	70	89	74	74	87	96	87	87
	959	951	1073	930	242	251	229	215
How big a problem	88	95	87	87	93	95	91	89

Percentage of respondents who feel that 'a lot' or 'quite a lot' of people take drugs / Percentage of respondents who feel that drugs are a 'very big' or 'fairly big' problem nationally

Table 6.10
Summary of regression model for perceived prevalence and the extent of the 'drugs problem': Main sample

Response	final model	beta	t	sig.t	Adj. R squared
How many take drugs	socioeconomic status	−0.19	−13.6	.000	0.06
(N = 4622)	location	−0.09	−6.00	.000	
	gender	−0.09	−6.34	.000	
	frequency of taking cannabis	0.08	5.38	.000	
How big a problem	socioeconomic status	−0.21	−13.03	.000	0.06
(N = 3712)	gender	−0.09	−5.40	.000	
	frequency of taking cannabis	0.07	4.59	.000	

variables in equation: location, age group, gender, socioeconomic status, ethnicity (black, white, asian), frequency of taking cannabis, frequency of taking non-opiates, frequency of taking opiates

Table 6.11
Summary of regression models for perceived prevalence and the extent of the 'drugs problem': Booster sample

Response	final model	beta	t	sig.t	Adj. R squared
How many take drugs	socioeconomic status	−0.11	−3.38	.001	0.04
(N = 909)	gender	−0.12	−3.58	.000	
	frequency of taking cannabis	0.10	3.08	.002	
	location	−0.10	−3.01	.003	
How big a problem	frequency of taking cannabis	−0.15	−4.63	.000	0.05
(N = 911)	socioeconomic status	−0.14	−4.41	.000	
	gender	−0.07	−2.04	.04	

variables in equation: location, age group, gender, socioeconomic status, ethnicity (white, black, asian), frequency of taking cannabis, frequency of taking non-opiates, frequency of taking opiates

Table 6.12
Perceived harmfulness of drugs

N = Percent of valid *N* = Valid N

Drug	Nott. Main		Glas. Main		Lew. Main		Brad. Main		Nott. Boost.		Glas. Boost.		Lew. Boost.		Brad. Boost.	
cannabis	45	982	45	928	30	1094	38	966	35	241	28	252	17	229	31	219
heroin	87	985	88	949	81	1111	82	971	82	234	88	255	81	228	83	225
amphetamines	48	982	56	946	42	1096	44	959	41	243	47	254	38	221	42	224
LSD	69	729	72	685	62	609	62	666	59	69	59	171	51	139	56	140
cocaine	77	542	82	601	72	291	73	745	75	161	80	171	71	170	70	164
ecstasy	62	917	72	643	58	884	58	606	53	147	59	180	42	143	56	137
crack	80	712	79	638	81	615	72	664	81	165	83	177	79	144	76	146
psilocybin	33	598	54	548	30	485	33	544	25	182	44	201	17	135	28	153
methadone	42	448	49	395	35	458	42	335	34	75	51	99	33	72	34	49
diconal	50	61	57	64	37	61	38	44	50	65	47	17	14	61	66	49
amyl nitrite	38	326	41	222	35	347	42	256	24	112	39	104	23	84	24	69
temazepam	38	164	57	550	27	154	32	169	35	36	47	163	26	26	35	34
temgesic	40	81	56	273	28	60	36	605	44	15	50	112	41	10	50	14
semeron	57	20	58	30	100	12	45	203	71	65	33	8	25	40	87	67
barbiturates	44	713	55	515	41	700	45	603	36	112	45	116	33	92	42	68
DF118s	46	61	55	164	40	59	44	54	45	88	53	70	42	16	60	67
triazelam	38	91	45	202	43	59	40	88	43	197	40	85	31	17	35	14
pills	35	595	53	587	39	575	46	470	33	137	51	150	37	107	39	87
tranquillizers	38	126	56	468	43	631	46	529	34	146	52	161	41	104	41	84
glue sniffing	82	843	84	773	80	798	82	786	74	194	81	203	72	166	76	167

Percentage of those respondents who had heard of a drug stating that it was 'very harmful'

APPENDIX I

Table 6.13
Summary of regression models for perceived harmfulness of a range of drugs: Main sample

Response	final model	beta	t	sig.t	Adj. R squared
harmfulness of cannabis (N=3896)	tried cannabis	−0.20	−11.2	0.000	0.07
	ethnicity	−0.12	−7.80	0.000	
	location	−0.08	−5.43	0.000	
	know regular user	−0.07	−4.12	0.000	
	age group	−0.04	−2.27	0.02	
harmfulness of heroin (N=4865)	age group	−0.18	−10.85	0.000	0.04
	ethnicity	−1.10	−7.40	0.000	
	socioeconomic status	−0.10	−6.95	0.000	
	location	−0.07	−4.18	0.000	
	know regular user	0.03	2.46	0.01	
harmfulness of ecstasy (N=4810)	age group	−0.24	−14.9	0.000	0.11
	ethnicity	−0.17	−7.07	0.000	
	socioeconomic status	−0.12	−8.93	0.000	
	location	−0.05	−3.51	0.000	
	know regular user	0.05	3.41	0.001	
	gender	−0.04	−2.82	0.005	
	tried ecstasy	−0.04	−2.49	0.01	
harmfulness of tranquillizers (N=4933)	socioeconomic status	−0.16	−11.4	0.000	0.07
	ethnicity	−0.14	−10.10	0.000	
	age group	−0.16	−10.10	0.000	
	location	−0.11	−6.87	0.000	
	know regular user	0.08	5.71	0.000	
harmfulness of amphetamines (N=4833)	ethnicity	−0.14	−6.11	0.000	0.11
	socioeconomic status	−0.18	−13.0	0.000	
	age group	−0.20	−12.4	0.000	
	location	−0.10	−6.35	0.000	
	know regular user	0.08	5.83	0.000	
	gender	−0.05	−4.00	0.000	

variables in the equations: *whether tried the relevant drug, whether know someone who is a regular user of the relevant drug, age group, gender, ethnicity (white, black, asian), location, soicoeconomic status*

Table 6.14
Summary of regression models for perceived harmfulness of a range of drugs: Booster sample

Response	final model	beta	t	sig.t	Adj. R squared
harmfulness of cannabis (N=922)	tried cannabis	-0.27	-7.78	0.000	0.14
	know regular user	-0.14	-3.93	0.000	
	gender	0.07	2.43	0.01	
harmfulness of heroin (N=924)	age group	-0.18	-10.8	0.000	0.04
	ethnicity	-0.10	-7.32	0.000	
	socioeconomic status	-0.10	-6.97	0.000	
	location	-0.07	-4.24	0.000	
	know regular user	0.03	2.46	0.01	
harmfulness of ecstasy (N=915)	age group	-0.24	-14.9	0.000	0.11
	ethnicity	-0.17	-7.07	0.000	
	socioeconomic status	-0.12	-8.93	0.000	
	location	-0.05	-3.51	0.000	
	know regular user	0.05	3.41	0.007	
	gender	-0.04	-2.82	0.005	
	tried ecstasy	-0.04	-2.49	0.01	
harmfulness of tranquillizers (N=938)	socioeconomic status	-0.16	-11.4	0.000	0.07
	ethnicity	-0.14	-10.04	0.000	
	age group	-0.16	-10.10	0.000	
	location	-0.11	-6.87	0.000	
	know regular user	0.08	5.71	0.000	
harmfulness of amphetamines (N=923)	ethnicity	-0.14	-6.11	0.000	0.11
	socioeconomic status	-0.18	-13.01	0.000	
	age group	-0.20	-12.4	0.000	
	location	-0.10	-6.35	0.000	
	know regular user	0.08	5.83	0.000	
	gender	-0.05	-4.00	0.000	

variables in the equations: *whether tried the relevant drug, whether know someone who is a regular user of the relevant drug, age group, gender, ethnicity (white, black, asian), location, soicoeconomic status*

Table 6.15
Comparison between consumption of cannabis and alcohol or tobacco consumption

N = Percent of valid	N = Valid N							
	Nott. Main	Glas. Main	Lew. Main	Brad. Main	Nott. Boost.	Glas. Boost.	Lew. Boost.	Brad. Boost.
	912	856	1029	877	232	251	223	218
	36	35	38	34	52	49	56	47

Percentage of respondents who 'agree strongly' or 'agree slightly' with the statement that "there is little difference in health terms between smoking cannabis and smoking tobacco or drinking alcohol"

Table 6.16
Summary of regression models for comparative views on cannabis: Main sample

Response	final model	beta	t	sig.t	Adj.R squared
there is little difference	age group	0.17	9.98	0.000	0.07
between alcohol or tobacco	frequency of cannabis usage	0.10	6.29	0.000	
and cannabis	socioeconomic status	0.07	4.24	0.000	
(N = 3584)	gender	0.07	4.02	0.000	
	ethnicity	0.10	3.72	0.000	
	frequency of alcohol usage	0.04	2.40	0.02	

variables in the equation: location, age group, gender, socioeconomic status, ethnicity (white, black, asian), whether taken any illicit drug, frequency of taking cannabis, frequency of taking non-opiates, frequency of taking opiates, frequency of using alcohol, frequency of using tobacco

Table 6.17
Summary of regression models for comparative views on cannabis: Booster sample

Response	final model	beta	t	sig.t	Adj.R squared
there is little difference	frequency of cannabis usage	0.22	6.71	0.000	0.05
between alcohol or tobacco	socioeconomic group	0.07	2.06	0.04	
and cannabis					
(N = 894)					

variables in the equation: frequency of using alcohol, frequency of using tobacco, frequency of using cannabis, frequency of using non-opiates, frequency of using opiates, location, gender, age group, socioeconomic status, ethnicity (white, black, asian)

Table 6.18
Perceived causes of drug usage

N = Percent of valid N = Valid N

Cause	Nott. Main		Glas. Main		Lew. Main		Brad. Main		Nott. Boost.		Glas. Boost.		Lew. Boost.		Brad. Boost.	
boredom	68	952	69	937	66	1088	67	919	64	241	72	253	60	232	64	225
stress	44	947	36	917	49	1075	43	916	48	240	50	247	54	232	46	224
excitement	83	950	80	945	83	1098	86	947	83	243	79	257	81	231	89	227
bad parenting	81	968	76	942	76	1100	74	939	65	238	60	252	71	231	62	224
clubs	91	968	90	948	89	1108	89	945	90	242	91	256	90	233	92	227
unemployment	64	959	79	953	71	1100	71	938	64	242	76	253	71	232	59	224
unhappy home	68	961	72	917	74	1094	67	933	71	243	74	250	74	233	65	222
mental illness	41	893	35	858	40	985	34	865	37	231	35	224	37	208	32	212
fun	70	947	74	916	73	1057	74	916	61	236	69	247	70	228	75	219
peer pressure	87	972	91	949	89	1101	87	955	84	243	87	256	87	233	93	228
moral decline	64	934	70	907	64	1068	65	915	47	225	46	233	58	224	54	212
coping strategy	71	948	73	913	68	1064	68	925	62	239	72	250	67	227	65	223

Percentage of respondents endorsing a suggested cause of drug use as an actual cause of drug use

Table 6.19
Perceived causes of drug usage by respondent's personal experience of drug usage: Main sample

'Y' = have taken illicit drugs   N = Percent of valid
'N' = have not taken illicit drugs   N = Valid N

Cause	Nottingham Y			N		Glasgow Y			N		Lewisham Y			N		Bradford Y			N	
boredom	72	166	72	778	76	188	70	747	69	257	68	822	79	132	72	785
stress	43	165	48	774	38	187	38	728	53	257	51	809	43	132	48	782
excitement	90	166	88	776	85	189	81	754	89	257	86	832	88	135	91	810
bad parenting	76	164	86	796	68	190	81	750	68	255	82	836	61	131	82	806
clubs	90	166	95	794	92	190	91	756	85	257	94	842	92	133	95	810
unemployment	63	165	68	786	84	190	80	761	73	256	74	836	63	133	68	803
unhappy home	68	166	73	787	82	187	75	728	73	255	76	830	69	133	72	799
mental illness	41	157	48	728	34	174	41	682	37	232	49	745	24	127	43	736
fun	70	166	76	773	77	187	79	728	77	251	81	797	84	126	81	788
peer pressure	92	165	89	799	91	189	93	759	91	256	92	836	86	135	92	818
moral decline	49	162	73	765	58	181	79	725	44	250	76	809	56	126	74	787
coping strategy	73	166	76	774	79	187	78	725	71	255	74	800	71	130	74	793

Percentage of respondents who cited a particular cause as a 'very important' or 'fairly important' cause of drug usage

Table 6.20
Perceived causes of drug usage by respondent's personal experience of drug usage: Booster sample

'Y' = have taken illicit drugs   N = Percent of valid
'N' = have not taken illicit drugs   N = Valid N

Cause	Nottingham Y			N		Glasgow Y			N		Lewisham Y			N		Bradford Y			N	
boredom	69	96	62	144	82	133	66	120	65	105	57	125	68	72	64	152
stress	48	95	50	144	55	130	49	117	64	104	47	126	53	72	46	151
excitement	87	97	82	145	87	135	71	122	83	103	82	126	89	73	91	153
bad parenting	60	94	72	143	56	131	67	121	70	105	73	124	50	74	72	149
clubs	93	97	91	144	92	135	92	121	89	105	81	126	90	73	95	153
unemployment	69	97	62	144	81	131	73	118	67	105	66	125	53	73	65	150
unhappy home	76	96	69	146	83	135	70	120	80	105	72	126	66	71	69	150
mental illness	32	89	44	141	41	135	39	105	44	95	40	111	37	68	35	143
fun	73	97	57	138	75	130	70	117	69	103	73	123	84	70	76	148
peer pressure	82	97	88	145	91	119	85	122	90	105	86	126	91	73	96	154
moral decline	46	92	55	132	50	130	53	113	62	102	61	120	52	68	63	143
coping strategy	67	97	61	141	79	134	70	117	65	101	72	124	67	72	67	150

Percentage of respondents who cited a particular item as a 'very important' or 'fairly important' cause of drug usage

Table 6.21
Summary of regression model for views on the progression from 'soft drugs' to 'hard drugs': Main sample

Response	final model	beta	t	sig.t	Adj.R squared
soft drugs lead to hard drugs (N—3711)	ever used illicit drug	-0.30	-18.21	.000	0.24
	frequency of using cannabis	-0.17	-10.65	.000	
	age group	-0.13	-8.43	.000	
	socioeconomic status	-0.09	-6.15	.000	
	ethnicity	0.10	4.54	.000	

variables in the equation: *frequency of using alcohol, frequency of using tobacco, frequency of using cannabis, frequency of using non-opiates, frequency of using opiates, location, gender, age group, socioeconomic status, ethnicity (white, black, asian)*

Table 6.22
Booster sample

Response	final model	beta	t	sig.t	Adj.R squared
soft drugs lead to hard drugs (N = 908)	frequency of using cannabis	-0.27	-7.79	0.000	0.23
	ever used illicit drug	-0.25	-7.12	0.000	
	age group	0.07	2.27	0.02	
	socioeconomic status	-0.06	-2.04	0.04	
	ethnicity	-0.16	-2.81	0.005	

variables in the equation: location, age group, gender, socioeconomic status, race, whether taken any illicit drug, frequency of taking cannabis, frequency of taking non-opiates, frequency of taking opiates

Table 6.23
How well informed respondents feel about drugs

N = Percent of valid	N = Valid N							
	Nott. Main	Glas. Main	Lew. Main	Brad. Main	Nott. Boost.	Glas. Boost.	Lew. Boost.	Brad. Boost.
	997	959	1108	985	243	258	233	231
Well informed	40	42	47	39	65	63	72	70

Percentage of respondents who regard themselves as 'well informed' or 'fairly well informed'

Table 6.24
Summary of regression model for how well informed a respondent feels on the drugs issue: Main sample

Response	final model	beta	t	sig.t	Adj.R squared
Well informed (N = 3970)	age group	0.25	16.0	.000	0.12
	frequency of taking cannabis	0.10	5.45	.000	
	gender	0.10	6.91	.000	
	socioeconomic status	0.10	6.83	.000	
	ethnicity	0.15	6.31	.000	
	frequency of taking 'soft' drugs	0.04	2.20	.03	

variables in equation: location, age group, gender, socioeconomic status, ethnicity (black, white, asian), frequency of taking cannabis, frequency of taking non-opiates, frequency of taking opiates

Table 6.25
Summary of regression models for how well informed a respondent feels on the drugs issue: Booster sample

Response	final model	beta	t	sig.t	Adj.R squared
Well informed (N = 938)	frequency of taking cannabis	0.22	6.98	.000	0.08
	gender	0.11	3.59	.000	
	location	-0.08	-2.63	.000	
	age group	0.08	2.42	0.01	

variables in equation: location, age group, gender, socioeconomic status, ethnicity (white, black, asian), frequency of taking cannabis, frequency of taking non-opiates, frequency of taking opiates

TABLES IN APPENDIX (CHAPTER 7)

Table 7.1
The importance and likely effectiveness of drugs education

N = Percent of Valid   N = Valid N

Statement	Nott. Main	Glas. Main	Lew. Main	Brad. Main	Nott. Boost.	Glas. Boost.	Lew. Boost.	Brad. Boost.
	978	952	1104	959	242	250	226	225
Education a disincentive	72	75	71	71	66	65	70	73
	971	913	1097	948	245	251	230	224
Education effective	91	90	92	92	94	88	94	93
	995	968	1133	993	245	258	233	228
Education important	98	98	98	97	99	98	99	95

Percentage of respondents stating that they 'agree strongly' or 'agree slightly' with the statement: "if people were better educated about the risks of taking drugs, many would not take them" / Percentage of respondents stating that drugs education would be 'very effective' or 'fairly effective' / Percentage of respondents stating that educating people about drugs is 'very important' or 'fairly important'

Table 7.2
Summary of regression models for respondents' views on education: Main sample

Response	final model	beta	t	sig. t	Adj. R Squared
Education a disincentive	ethnicity	-0.10	2.60	.000	0.01
(N = 3918)	frequency of taking cannabis	-0.09	-4.08	.000	
	socioeconomic status	-0.06	-3.61	.000	
	age group	-0.04	-2.73	.006	
Education effective	socioeconomic status	-0.11	-6.70	.000	0.02
(N = 3853)	ethnicity	-0.08	-5.10	.000	
	frequency of taking cannabis	-0.06	-3.67	.000	
Education important	no variables reached criterion				

variables in equation: *location, gender, age group, socioeconomic status, ethnicity (white, black, asian), frequency of taking cannabis, frequency of taking non-opiates, frequency of taking opiates*

Table 7.3
Summary of regression models for respondents' views on education: Booster sample

Response	final model	beta	t	sig. t	Adj. R Squared
Education a disincentive	ethnicity	-0.17	-5.14	.000	0.04
(N = 923)	frequency of taking cannabis	-0.09	-2.79	.005	
Education effective	frequency of taking cannabis	-0.15	-4.70	.000	0.03
(N = 912)	socioeconomic status	-0.07	-2.23	.03	
	ethnicity	-0.07	-2.16	.03	
Education important	no variables reached criterion				

variables in equation: *location, gender, age group, socioeconomic status, ethnicity (white, black, asian), frequency of taking cannabis, frequency of taking non-opiates, frequency of taking opiates*

APPENDIX I

Table 7.4
Appropriate categories for education

N = Percent of Valid   N = Valid N   (N) = Actual N

Category	Nott. Main	Glas. Main	Lew. Main	Brad. Main	Nott. Boost.	Glas. Boost.	Lew. Boost.	Brad. Boost.
	945	881	1052	937	236	251	219	212
9 to 11	36	47	36	37	26	34	37	38
12 to 18	58	54	54	58	56	56	62	64
19 to 25	33	31	35	33	23	28	35	35
parents	42	36	36	40	30	34	44	35
teachers	35	29	29	35	20	28	32	32
all adults	25	22	22	21	16	19	30	14
everyone	29	30	33	30	35	37	28	28
other category	- (0)	1	1	1	- (0)	- (0)	3	- (2)

Percentage of respondents endorsing particular categories as suitable targets for drugs education

Table 7.5
Parents' views on drugs education for their own children

N = Percent of Valid   N = Valid N

Statement	Nott. Main	Glas. Main	Lew. Main	Brad. Main	Nott. Boost.	Glas. Boost.	Lew. Boost.	Brad. Boost.
Child 1 receives education	22 185	30 188	37 185	24 211	- 2	100 3	- 2	- 3
Child 2 receives education	29 79	39 66	44 79	40 108		100 3		
Child 3 receives education	21 14	50 14	50 14	30 23		100 2		
Child 4 receives education	60 5	- 1	67 3	- 5				
Approve child 1 education	97 39	100 57	99 68	92 47		100 3		
Approve child 2 education	96 22	100 26	94 34	100 43		100 3		
Approve child 3 education	100 3	100 7	100 7	100 7		100 2		
Approve child 4 education	100 3	100 1	100 2	100 1				
Like education for child 1	84 141	92 129	90 112	89 159	100 2		100 2	100 3
Like education for child 2	82 55	92 39	95 44	88 64				
Like education for child 3	91 11	86 6	100 7	94 16				
Like education for child 4	100 2	100 1	100 1	100 5				

Percentage of parents stating that their children receive drugs education / Percentage of parents whose children are receiving drugs education who state that they approve of such education /Percentage of parents whose children are not receiving drugs education who state that they would like them to receive such education

Table 7.6
Parents' views on the likelihood of their children taking drugs

N = Percent of Valid   N = Valid N   (N) = Actual N

Category	Nott. Main	Glas. Main	Lew. Main	Brad. Main	Nott. Boost.	Glas. Boost.	Lew. Boost.	Brad. Boost.
	181	170	176	193	2	3	2	3
Children likely to take drugs	14	12	17	11	- (0)	33	50	- (0)

Percentage of parents stating that their children were 'very likely' or 'fairly likely' to take drugs in the future / Note that in the booster samples there were very few people with children so the percentages cannot be taken as being representative of the views of this sub-section of the population

Table 7.7
Perception of the likelihood that respondents' children will take drugs by own experience of drug usage: Main sample only

N = Percent of Valid   N = Valid N

Own experience:	Nottingham Tried	Nottingham Not Tried	Glasgow Tried	Glasgow Not Tried	Lewisham Tried	Lewisham Not Tried	Bradford Tried	Bradford Not Tried
	35	144	33	137	35	139	22	171
Very likely	3	2	12	3	8	1	14	2
Fairly likely	17	10	27	5	28	11	18	9
Not very likely	48	46	45	43	46	33	50	55
Not at all likely	31	31	15	49	17	54	18	34

Percentage of respondents in each category who believed that their children were 'very likely' or 'fairly likely' to take drugs in the future

Table 7.8
Perception of the likelihood that respondents' children will take drugs by type of personal drug experience

N = Percent of Valid   N = Valid N   (N)=Actual N

Own experience	Nottingham	Glasgow	Lewisham	Bradford
Taken cannabis	11	28	55	100
Not taken cannabis	14	11	15	11
Taken non-opiates	25	-( )	50	40
Not taken non-opiates	14	13	17	11
Taken opiates	no children	-( )	50	no children
Not taken opiates	14	13	17	12

Percentage of respondents in each category who believed that their children were 'very likely' or 'fairly likely' to take drugs partitioned by personal experience of drug usage

Table 7.9
Public's views on government provision of drugs education

N = Percent of Valid   N = Valid N

Statement	Nott. Main	Glas. Main	Lew. Main	Brad. Main	Nott. Boost.	Glas. Boost.	Lew. Boost.	Brad. Boost.
	994	960	1127	972	245	255	230	226
Education is the responsibility of the government	86	89	89	84	93	90	92	88

Percentage of respondents stating that they 'agree strongly' or 'agree slightly' with the statement that "it is the responsibility of the government to provide education about the risks of taking drugs"

APPENDIX I

Table 7.10
Public's views on the agencies responsible for providing drugs education

N = Percent of Valid   N = Valid N

Agency	Nott. Main	Glas. Main	Lew. Main	Brad. Main	Nott. Boost.	Glas. Boost.	Lew. Boost.	Brad. Boost.
	891	885	1034	893	230	250	221	219
government	53	52	58	53	58	46	63	48
local council	24	25	33	25	2	18	39	25
schools	64	62	68	64	68	64	74	65
doctors	35	32	33	33	26	31	39	31
social services	18	22	23	17	13	23	31	16
police	28	27	22	30	33	29	33	29
all agencies	11	14	11	11	11	23	12	16
other agency	7	5	6	6	3	4	3	2

Percentage of respondents stating that each of the listed agencies should be responsible for drugs education

Table 7.11
Agencies perceived as most directly responsible for drugs education partitioned by respondent's personal experience of drug usage: Main sample

'Y' = have used illicit drugs   N = Percent of Valid
'N' = have not used illicit drugs   N = Valid N   (N) = Actual N

Agency	Nottingham Y	Nottingham N	Lewisham Y	Lewisham N	Glasgow Y	Glasgow N	Bradford Y	Bradford N
	157	734	233	801	182	703	126	767
government	43	43	45	43	43	42	40	36
local council	10	4	6	6	7	5	6	5
schools	38	37	36	38	40	38	46	43
doctors	6	7	7	6	7	7	4	8
social services	1	2	- (1)	3	- (0)	3	1	1
police	4	6	1	3	3	5	2	6
other agency	- (0)	- (2)	- (1)	- (2)	- (0)	- (0)	- (0)	- (4)

Percentage of respondents who feel that a particular agency is 'most responsible' for providing drugs education

Table 7.12
Agencies perceived as most directly responsible for drugs education partitioned by respondent's personal experience of drug usage: Booster sample

'Y' = have used illicit drugs   N = Percent of Valid
'N' = have not used illicit drugs   N = Valid N   (N) = Actual N

Agency	Nottingham Y	Nottingham N	Lewisham Y	Lewisham N	Glasgow Y	Glasgow N	Bradford Y	Bradford N
	91	139	100	121	131	119	70	149
government	47	42	47	45	34	30	21	32
local council	4	6	5	3	4	1	3	9
schools	41	34	34	45	46	55	56	46
doctors	4	9	9	2	5	7	12	7
social services	2	1	2	2	4	2	1	1
police	1	7	3	2	7	4	6	5
other agency	- (0)	- (0)	- (0)	- (0)	1	- (0)	- (0)	- (0)

Percentage of respondents who feel that a particular agency is 'most responsible' for providing drugs education

Table 7.13
Summary of regression model for respondents' perception that the government is responsible for providing drugs education: Main sample

Response for	final model	beta	t	sig. t	Adj. R Squared
government should educate (N = 3976)	age group	0.06	3.59	.000	.006
	ethnicity	-0.05	-3.12	.002	

variables in equation: location, age group, gender, socioeconomic status, ethnicity (white, black, asian), frequency of taking cannabis, frequency of taking non-opiates, frequency of taking opiates

Table 7.14
Summary of regression model for respondents' perception that the government is responsible for providing drugs education: Booster sample

Response for	final model	beta	t	sig. t	Adj. R Squared
government should educate (N = 930)	socioeconomic status	0.07	2.09	.04	.06

variables in equation: location, age group, gender, socioeconomic status, ethnicity (white, black, asian), frequency of taking cannabis, frequency of taking non-opiates, frequency of taking opiates

Table 7.15
Views on police methods of drugs control

N = Percent of Valid   N = Valid N

Statement	Nott. Main	Glas. Main	Lew. Main	Brad. Main	Nott. Boost.	Glas. Boost.	Lew. Boost.	Brad. Boost.
	973	936	1112	968	243	253	232	229
Searching on suspicion	58	65	40	61	49	45	36	50
	966	926	1089	964	243	253	229	227
Cautioning not prosecuting	41	37	54	54	42	44	53	40
	690	813	695	599	204	234	189	168
Effectiveness of local police	50	43	41	41	42	28	34	34

Percentage of respondents stating that police searching on suspicion would be a 'very useful' or 'fairly useful' method of controlling drug usage / Percentage of respondents stating that police cautioning but not prosecuting drug users would be a 'very useful' or 'fairly useful' method of controlling drug usage / Percentage of respondents stating that their local police dealt 'very well' or 'fairly well' with drugs control

APPENDIX I

Table 7.16
Summary of regression models on views on policing: Main sample

Response	final model	beta	t	sig.t	Adj. R squared
police should search on suspicion (N=3912)	ever tried illicit drugs	-0.14	-7.63	.000	0.09
	ethnicity	0.26	10.33	.000	
	age group	-0.08	-4.74	.000	
	socioeconomic status	-0.07	-4.82	.000	
	frequency of using cannabis	-0.07	-3.86	.000	
	location	0.04	2.69	.007	
	frequency of using opiates	-0.03	-1.99	.05	
police should caution not prosecute (N=3872)	location	-0.06	-4.10	.000	0.01
	ever tried illicit drug	0.06	3.43	.001	
	age group	-0.07	-4.19	.000	
	socioeconomic status	0.05	3.15	.002	
	frequency of taking cannabis	0.05	3.15	.002	
how well local police deal with drug usage (N = 2753)	age group	-0.18	-9.43	.000	0.09
	ever used illicit drug	-0.17	-8.68	.000	
	socioeconomic status	0.07	3.74	.000	
police should catch suppliers not users (N=3937)	age group	-0.08	-4.96	.000	0.009
	ever tried illicit drug	0.07	4.16	.000	
	ethnicity	-0.04	-2.76	.006	
	socioeconomic status	-0.04	-2.41	.01	
police should bust suppliers (N=3965)	frequency of using cannabis	-0.16	-8.31	.000	0.05
	ethnicity	0.17	6.76	.000	
	ever used illicit drug	-0.07	-3.84	.000	
	socioeconomic status	-0.05	-3.53	.000	
	frequency of using non-opiates	0.05	2.84	.004	
	age group	-0.04	-2.67	.008	
police should bust users (N=3950)	ever used illicit drug	-0.18	-10.32	.000	0.15
	age group	-0.15	-9.11	.000	
	frequency of using cannabis	-0.12	-7.35	.000	
	socioeconomic status	-0.10	-6.85	.000	
	ethnicity	0.14	5.92	.000	
	gender	-0.05	-3.43	.001	
	location	0.04	2.84	.005	

variables in equation: *location, age group, gender, socioeconomic status, ethnicity (white, black, asian), whether ever tried an illicit drug, frequency of taking cannabis, frequency of taking non-opiates, frequency of taking opiates*

Table 7.17
Summary of regression models on views on policing: Booster sample

Response	final model	beta	t	sig.t	Adj. R squared
police should search on suspicion (N = 930)	ever taken illicit drug	-0.18	-5.18	.000	0.05
	frequency of taking non-opiates	-0.10	-2.54	.01	
	age group	0.07	2.14	.03	
police should caution not prosecute (N = 925)	ever taken illicit drug	0.13	3.90	.000	0.03
	frequency of taking non-opiates	0.10	2.52	.01	
how well local police deal with drug usage (N = 774)	whether ever used illicit drug	-0.17	-4.72	.000	0.03
	socioeconomic status	0.10	2.84	.005	
police should catch suppliers not users	no variables reached criterion				
police should bust suppliers (N = 934)	frequency of using cannabis	-0.18	-5.48	.000	0.03
police should bust users (N = 929)	ever taken illicit drug	-0.17	-4.63	.000	0.10
	frequency of taking cannabis	-0.15	-4.00	.000	
	gender	-0.10	-3.09	.002	
	age group	0.07	2.11	.03	

variables in equation: *location, age group, gender, socioeconomic status, ethnicity (white, black, asian), whether ever tried an illicit drug, frequency of taking cannabis, frequency of taking non-opiates, frequency of taking opiates*

Table 7.18
Comparison between police efforts targeting users and targeting suppliers

N = Percent of Valid   N = Valid N

Statement	Nott. Main	Glas. Main	Lew. Main	Brad. Main	Nott. Boost.	Glas. Boost.	Lew. Boost.	Brad. Boost.
	981	955	1111	967	243	257	231	229
catch suppliers not users	85	87	86	86	85	89	90	89
	985	955	1114	973	245	254	231	226
bust users	79	79	65	78	64	55	52	65
	982	962	1121	977	244	256	233	228
bust suppliers	92	94	88	93	90	89	88	86

Percentage of respondents stating that they 'agree strongly' or 'agree slightly' with the statement "police time would be better spent catching drug suppliers rather than clamping down on users" / Percentage of respondents stating that police busting or raiding the houses of users would be a 'very useful' or 'fairly useful' measure in reducing drug usage / Percentage of respondents stating that police busting or raiding the houses of suppliers would be a 'very useful' or 'fairly useful' measure in reducing drug usage

APPENDIX I

Table 7.19
Views regarding customs control

N = Percent of Valid   N = Valid N

Statement	Nott. Main	Glas. Main	Lew. Main	Brad. Main	Nott. Boost.	Glas. Boost.	Lew. Boost.	Brad. Boost.
	978	952	1104	959	245	251	230	224
Money better spent on education	34	39	35	37	40	42	43	57
	987	959	1114	975	242	253	233	227
Major police or customs efforts	96	95	94	94	93	89	95	93
	1006	972	1139	1004	245	258	233	231
Increase security at ports and airports	84	87	81	81	81	77	75	84

Percentage of respondents stating that they 'agree strongly' or 'agree slightly' with the statement that "money would be better spent on education and TV campaigns rather than on trying to stop drugs being brought into the country" / Percentage of respondents stating that major efforts by police or customs targeting sources of supply would be 'very useful' or 'fairly useful' in reducing drug usage / Percentage of respondents stating that they 'agree strongly' or 'agree slightly' with the statement that "the way to decrease the number of people using drugs is to increase security at ports and airports'

Table 7.20
Summary regression models for views regarding supply control

Response	final model	beta	t	sig.t	Adj. R squared
Main sample					
police and customs	frequency of using cannabis	−0.15	−9.00	.000	0.07
target supply	ever used illicit drug	−0.10	−5.80	.000	
sources	age group	−0.82	−5.01	.000	
(N=3958)					
Booster sample					
police and customs	frequency of using cannabis	−0.20	−6.24	.000	0.04
target supply					
sources					
(N=928)					

variables in equations: *location, age group, gender, socioeconomic status, ethnicity (white, black, asian), whether ever tried an illicit drug, frequency of taking cannabis, frequency of taking non–opiates, frequency of taking opiates*

Table 7.21
Views on the appropriate aims of drugs education and on the provision of medical help for drug users

N=Percent of Valid   N=Valid N

Statement	Nott. Main	Glas. Main	Lew. Main	Brad. Main	Nott. Boost.	Glas. Boost.	Lew. Boost.	Brad. Boost.
	1006	972	1139	1004	245	258	233	231
Prevention	74	63	56	63	56	45	50	43
Harm reduction	6	5	3	5	12	8	8	6
Both	17	29	39	28	31	45	42	48
	967	943	1097	949	241	254	231	225
Medical help	67	71	74	66	67	73	81	75

Percentage of respondents stating that education should be aimed at prevention / Percentage of respondents stating that education should be aimed at harm reduction / Percentage of respondents stating that both aims are appropriate / Percentage of respondents in favour of spending more money on medical help for drug users

Table 7.22
Percentage of respondents in favour of drugs prevention as the main aim of drugs education, partitioned by demographic profile and drug usage

N=Percent of Valid   N=Valid N   (N)=Actual N

	Nott. Main	Glas. Main	Lew. Main	Brad. Main	Nott. Boost	Glas. Boost	Lew. Boost	Brad. Boost
Present cannabis user	52 58	50 79	39 85	44 37	55 62	43 81	41 59	36 35
Present non-opiate user	65 26	54 44	35 33	46 24	50 36	42 41	37 30	40 19
Present opiate user	50 2	33 6	62 16	100 1	67 6	75 4	20 5	100 2
Used drugs in past	69 166	54 189	46 257	52 130	54 97	43 131	46 105	38 72
Never used drugs	76 807	65 757	59 849	65 828	58 145	47 121	53 125	45 152
Age 16–19	67 51	54 46	40 42	43 38	62 92	46 98	48 104	50 90
Age 20–24	72 86	52 87	49 88	55 79	55 137	44 134	50 103	34 107
Age 25–29	68 111	56 124	45 162	62 113	36 14	45 20	56 25	53 28
Age 30–34	67 108	62 117	50 156	62 116				
Age 35–44	75 175	60 159	55 199	65 194				
Age 45–59	80 215	70 172	62 168	66 184				
Age 60+	77 235	69 240	65 297	66 233				
Male	78 425	63 387	56 499	63 410	56 123	47 116	51 114	47 107
Female	72 566	63 561	55 616	63 550	57 120	43 136	48 118	39 118
SES AB	69 137	64 76	54 116	67 152	54 11	50 6	57 21	40 5
SES C1	76 251	66 176	53 403	69 227	50 50	43 64	55 71	47 29
SES C2	78 278	64 204	56 255	65 237	61 53	39 37	46 65	41 53
SES DE	72 312	61 491	59 338	56 340	57 126	47 144	46 73	43 138
White	75 931	64 919	57 866	66 865	56 213	46 240	50 156	44 144
Black	45 22	–2 (0)	63 178	54 11	64 14	50 2	49 65	–2 (0)
Asian	73 11	36 14	60 12	34 69	60 5	40 5	33 6	42 73
Other	50 4	67 3	38 34	37 8	100 2	–3 (0)	60 5	50 2

Percentage of respondents in each demographic category regarding drugs prevention as the most appropriate aim of drugs education

Table 7.23
Percentage of respondents in favour of helping drug users as the main aim of drugs education, partitioned by demographic profile and drug usage

N=Percent of Valid	N=Valid N as Table 7.22		(N)=Actual N					
	Nott. Main	Glas. Main	Lew. Main	Brad. Main	Nott. Boost	Glas. Boost	Lew. Boost	Brad. Boost
Present cannabis user	22	11	10	20	14	9	15	11
Present non–opiate user	15	11	9	17	22	9	20	10
Present opiate user	50	–(0)	6	–(0)	–(0)	–(0)	20	–(0)
Used drugs in past	12	8	5	9	9	10	10	11
Never used drugs	4	4	3	4	14	6	6	4
Age 16–19	18	4	7	9	11	8	9	10
Age 20–24	10	8	6	13	9	8	8	4
Age 25–29	10	10	4	4	50	5	4	–(0)
Age 30–34	6	2	7	1				
Age 35–44	5	4	3	3				
Age 45–59	4	3	–(0)	5				
Age 60+	1	5	2	4				
Male	5	6	5	4	13	5	10	5
Female	6	4	2	5	11	10	6	7
SES AB	69	64	54	67	9	–(0)	5	–(0)
SES C1	5	5	4	3	6	8	7	–(0)
SES C2	5	3	4	6	11	10	6	6
SES DE	7	6	2	6	14	7	12	8
White	5	5	4	5	12	8	7	8
Black	10	–(0)	2	–(0)	14	–(0)	11	–(0)
Asian	–(0)	7	10	3	–(0)	–(0)	–(0)	3
Other	25	–(0)	6	12	–(0)	33	–(0)	–(0)

Percentage of respondents in each demographic category regarding helping drug users as the most appropriate aim of drugs education

Table 7.24
Percentage of respondents in favour of both prevention and helping drug users as appropriate aims for education, partitioned by demographic profile and drug usage

N=Percent of Valid   N=Valid N as Table 7.22   (N)=Actual N

	Nott. Main	Glas. Main	Lew. Main	Brad. Main	Nott. Boost	Glas. Boost	Lew. Boost	Brad. Boost
Present cannabis user	24	37	48	31	31	42	44	50
Present non-opiate user	19	34	53	37	28	40	43	45
Present opiate user	–(0)	67	31	–(0)	33	25	60	–(0)
Used drugs in past	19	37	47	36	37	44	44	49
Never used drugs	17	28	36	27	27	45	40	48
Age 16–19	16	37	52	38	25	42	42	38
Age 20–24	17	40	43	28	36	46	42	59
Age 25–29	21	32	48	32	14	50	40	40
Age 30–34	24	33	41	31				
Age 35–44	19	36	41	28				
Age 45–59	15	24	37	26				
Age 60+	1	5	2	4				
Male	15	29	37	30	31	46	37	44
Female	20	30	40	27	31	44	46	52
SES AB	26	28	37	29	36	50	38	60
SES C1	18	27	43	25	44	48	38	50
SES C2	15	30	38	25	26	47	48	52
SES DE	16	30	36	31	28	43	40	46
White	17	29	37	27	31	44	41	45
Black	45	100	47	27	28	50	40	100
Asian	27	57	50	43	20	60	67	53
Other	25	33	26	37	–(0)	67	40	50

Percentage of respondents in each demographic category regarding drugs prevention and helping drug users as equally important aims for drugs education

Table 7.25
Summary of regression models for the provision of medical treatment for drug users

Response	final model	beta	t	sig.t	Adj. R squared
Main sample					
there should	age group	0.07	4.41	.000	0.02
be more	socioeconomic status	0.06	3.65	.000	
medical help	frequency of cannabis usage	0.06	3.46	.000	
for drug users	ethnicity	–0.05	–3.09	.002	
(N=3881)	gender	–0.04	–2.74	.006	
Booster sample					
there should be more medical help for drug users (N=924)	socioeconomic status	0.09	2.91	.004	0.008

variables in equations: *location, age group, gender, socioeconomic status, ethnicity (white, black, asian), whether ever tried an illicit drug, frequency of taking cannabis, frequency of taking non–opiates, frequency of taking opiates*

APPENDIX I

TABLES IN APPENDIX I (CHAPTER 8)

Table 8.1
Spontaneous awareness of drugs related agencies

N = Percent of Valid   *N* = Valid N   (N)=Actual N

Agency	Nott. Main	Glas. Main	Lew. Main	Brad. Main	Nott. Boost.	Glas. Boost.	Lew. Boost.	Brad. Boost.
	1003	970	1115	993	245	258	231	231
DPT (no prompt)	–(3)	–(2)	2	1	–(0)	–(0)	–(2)	–(0)
DPT (single prompt)	14	21	9	12	13	20	9	10
DPT (dual prompt)	–(0)	3	2	1	2	3	2	3
Brockley			4				3	
Dual Team			–(3)				–(0)	
Phoenix			3				4	
DDA	2				2			
Health shop	–(3)				1			
Bridge Project				4				6
Project Six				1				1
Local Agency		10				8		
Other Agency	1	3	2	–(8)	–(0)	–(2)	4	–(1)

Percentage of respondents stating that they had heard of listed agencies / Blank indicates not applicable

Table 8.2
Awareness of drug agencies by demographic variables and drug usage: Lewisham Main

N = Percent of Valid   *N* = Valid N   (N) = Actual N

	DPT (no prompt)		DPT (single prompt)		DPT (dual prompt)		Brock	Phoenix	Dual Team	Other
									(Valid N as for DPT no prompt)	
Present cannabis user	1	87	7	86	3	80	7	5	–(0)	3
Present non-opiate user	–(0)	34	3	32	9	31	3	9	–(0)	3
Present opiate user	–(0)	16	6	16	6	15	6	12	–(0)	12
Used drugs in past	3	261	10	253	1	228	21	5	–(0)	3
Never used drugs	2	869	9	851	2	775	2	2	–(3)	2
Age 16–19	–(0)	42	7	41	2	38	–(0)	5	–(0)	2
Age 20–24	1	89	6	83	–(0)	78	2	1	–(0)	1
Age 25–29	2	167	8	163	1	150	7	3	–(0)	3
Age 30–34	1	157	8	152	2	140	5	6	–(0)	2
Age 35–44	3	201	15	199	3	169	5	3	–(1)	3
Age 45–59	3	170	10	168	2	151	3	3	–(0)	1
Age 60+	2	309	7	303	2	283	1	1	1	1
Male	2	508	8	496	2	456	3	3	–(0)	2
Female	2	631	10	617	2	555	4	3	–(3)	2
SES AB	2	120	13	117	2	102	5	4	–(0)	6
SES C1	2	405	12	395	2	348	6	4	–(2)	3
SES C2	2	260	7	258	1	240	1	2	–(0)	–(0)
SES DE	2	351	6	340	2	20	1	2	–(1)	1
White	2	882	9	862	2	77	3	3	–(2)	3
Black	7	178	35	174	4	61	9	4	–(0)	–(1)
Asian	–(0)	12	81	12	–(0)	2	–(0)	–(0)	–(0)	–(0)
Other	–(0)	34	–(0)	21	5	21	5	–(0)	–(0)	–(1)

Percentage of each category of respondent who had heard of the listed agencies

Table 8.3
Awareness of drug agencies by demographic variables and drug usage: Lewisham Booster

N = Percent of Valid   N = Valid N   (N) = Actual N

	DPT (no prompt)		DPT (single prompt)		DPT (dual prompt)		Brock	Phoenix	Dual Team	Other
									(Valid N as for DPT no prompt)	
Present cannabis user	–(0)	59	5	59	–(0)	56	3	5	–(0)	3
Present non-opiate user	–(1)	30	10	29	–(0)	7	7	7	–(0)	7
Present opiate user	–(0)	5	–(0)	5	–(0)	5	–(0)	20	–(0)	–(0)
Used drugs in past	–(1)	105	9	102	–(0)	93	4	5	–(0)	3
Never used drugs	6	126	8	124	–(0)	114	2	3	–(0)	3
Age 16–19	–(1)	105	14	103	–(0)	89	1	3	–(0)	1
Age 20–24	2	103	3	100	–(0)	97	5	5	–(0)	5
Age 25–29	–(0)	25	8	25	–(0)	23	–(0)	4	–(0)	4
Male	2	115	10	113	–(0)	102	3	4	–(0)	3
Female	–(0)	118	7	118	–(0)	110	2	3	–(0)	2
SES AB	–(0)	21	9	21	–(0)	19	5	9	–(0)	–(0)
SES C1	1	71	3	68	–(0)	66	3	6	–(0)	1
SES C2	1	65	11	64	–(0)	57	5	3	–(0)	5
SES DE	–(0)	74	12	74	–(0)	65	–(0)	1	–(0)	4
White	1	157	8	154	–(0)	142	4	4	–(0)	3
Black	–(1)	65	28	63	–(0)	45	–(0)	11	–(0)	6
Asian	–(0)	6	50	6	–(0)	3	–(0)	–(0)	–(0)	50
Other	–(0)	5	–(0)	5	–(0)	5	–(0)	–(0)	–(0)	–(0)

Percentage of each category of respondent who had heard of the listed agencies

APPENDIX I

Table 8.4
Awareness of drug agencies by demographic variables and drug usage: Nottingham Main

N = Percent of Valid   N = Valid N   (N) = Actual N

	DPT (no prompt)		DPT (single prompt)		DPT (dual prompt)		DDA	Health Shop	Other
							(Valid N as for DPT no prompt)		
Present cannabis user	–(0)	59	17	59	–(0)	49	7	2	2
Present non-opiate user	–(0)	26	15	26	–(0)	22	4	4	–(0)
Present opiate user	–(0)	2	–(0)	2	–(0)	2	–(0)	–(0)	–(0)
Used drugs in past	–(1)	167	30	163	–(0)	114	5	1	3
Never used drugs	–(3)	831	14	809	1	696	2	–(1)	1
Age 16–19	–(0)	51	16	50	2	42	2	–(0)	2
Age 20–24	1	86	13	85	1	74	3	–(0)	2
Age 25–29	–(1)	112	12	109	–(0)	96	5	1	1
Age 30–34	–(0)	110	11	107	–(0)	102	4	–(0)	2
Age 35–44	1	177	19	172	–(0)	139	3	1	1
Age 45–59	–(0)	217	19	209	1	169	1	–(0)	–(1)
Age 60+	–(0)	253	9	248	1	226	–(1)	–(0)	1
Male	–(1)	434	12	423	–(2)	372	2	–(2)	1
Female	–(2)	572	16	557	1	468	2	–(1)	1
SES AB	1	138	16	133	–(0)	111	2	1	1
SES C1	–(0)	255	16	247	–(1)	208	4	1	2
SES C2	–(1)	283	13	276	1	240	1	–(0)	2
SES DE	–(1)	327	13	321	1	281	1	–(0)	–(1)
White	–(3)	955	14	931	1	801	2	–(3)	1
Black	–(0)	22	31	22	–(0)	15	25	–(0)	–(0)
Asian	–(0)	11	33	11	–(0)	7	–(0)	–(0)	–(0)
Other	–(0)	4	25	4	–(0)	3	–(0)	–(0)	–(0)

Percentage of each category of respondent who had heard of the listed agencies

Table 8.5
Awareness of drug agencies by demographic variables and drug usage: Nottingham Main

N = Percent of Valid   N = Valid N   (N) = Actual N

	DPT (no prompt)		DPT (single prompt)		DPT (dual prompt)		DDA	Health Shop	Other
							(Valid N as for DPT no prompt)		
Present cannabis user	–(0)	62	10	61	3	55	8	2	21
Present non-opiate user	–(0)	36	6	36	6	34	11	3	28
Present opiate user	–(0)	6	–(0)	6	9	6	33	–(0)	67
Used drugs in past	–(1)	97	13	96	3	84	5	3	22
Never used drugs	–(1)	147	12	144	1	127	1	–(0)	12
Age 16–19	–(1)	94	14	93	2	80	3	2	18
Age 20–24	–(1)	137	11	134	1	119	1	1	15
Age 25–29	–(0)	14	21	14	7	11	7	–(0)	7
Male	–(1)	123	11	121	2	108	2	2	12
Female	–(1)	122	15	120	2	102	2	1	20
SES AB	–(0)	11	18	11	–(0)	9	9	9	36
SES C1	–(0)	50	10	50	6	45	2	2	24
SES C2	–(0)	54	11	54	–(0)	48	4	–(0)	15
SES DE	–(0)	127	14	127	2	109	2	1	11
White	–(1)	215	12	211	2	186	2	1	14
Black	–(0)	14	14	7	–(0)	6	–(0)	–(0)	57
Asian	–(0)	5	80	5	–(0)	1	–(0)	100	100
Other	–(0)	2	50	2	–(0)	1	–(0)	–(0)	–(0)

Percentage of each category of respondent who had heard of the listed agencies

DRUG USAGE AND DRUGS PREVENTION: THE VIEWS AND HABITS OF THE GENERAL PUBLIC

Table 8.6
Awareness of drug agencies by demographic variables and drug usage: Glasgow Main

N = Percent of Valid   N = Valid N   (N) = Actual N

	DPT (no prompt)		DPT (single prompt)		DPT (dual prompt)		Other Local agency	Other
							(Valid N as for DPT no prompt)	
Present cannabis user	–(0)	80	21	80	–(0)	63	14	4
Present non-opiate user	–(0)	44	34	44	–(0)	29	18	2
Present opiate user	–(0)	6	17	6	–(0)	5	17	–(0)
Used drugs in past	–(1)	190	23	184	1	142	16	3
Never used drugs	–(1)	780	20	757	2	603	8	2
Age 16–19	–(0)	48	12	48	–(0)	42	12	4
Age 20–24	–(0)	87	16	83	1	70	13	2
Age 25–29	–(0)	126	21	123	1	97	10	2
Age 30–34	1	120	20	117	1	94	10	1
Age 35–44	–(0)	159	23	153	3	35	9	4
Age 45–59	1	176	26	170	3	126	12	3
Age 60+	–(0)	256	20	249	3	199	7	2
Male	–(1)	395	22	381	1	297	11	3
Female	–(1)	577	20	562	3	450	9	2
SES AB	–(0)	78	26	77	–(0)	57	13	3
SES C1	1	178	24	175	2	133	7	4
SES C2	–(1)	208	20	201	4	740	9	2
SES DE	–(0)	507	19	489	2	396	11	2
White	–(2)	941	21	912	2	819	10	3
Black	–(0)	2	14	2	–(0)	2	–(0)	–(0)
Asian	–(0)	14	33	14	–(0)	9	11	–(0)
Other	–(0)	3	50	2	–(0)	1	–(0)	–(0)

Percentage of each category of respondent who had heard of the listed agencies

Table 8.7
Awareness of drug agencies by demographic variables and drug usage: Glasgow Booster

N = Percent of Valid   *N* = Valid N   (N) = Actual N

	DPT (no prompt)		DPT (single prompt)		DPT (dual prompt)		Other Local agency (Valid N as for DPT no prompt)	Other
Present cannabis user	–(0)	85	18	80	5	66	11	2
Present non-opiate user	–(0)	45	11	43	9	38	13	–(0)
Present opiate user	–(0)	4	25	4	–(0)	3	25	–(0)
Used drugs in past	–(0)	135	19	128	4	104	11	1
Never used drugs	–(0)	123	22	117	1	94	4	–(0)
Age 16–19	–(0)	102	16	97	3	82	6	2
Age 20–24	–(0)	136	21	128	3	101	9	–(0)
Age 25–29	–(0)	20	45	20	–(0)	21	10	–(0)
Male	–(0)	118	15	108	3	92	9	1
Female	–(0)	140	25	137	2	103	6	1
SES AB	–(0)	6	18	6	–(0)	4	33	–(0)
SES C1	–(0)	65	10	60	3	54	6	1
SES C2	–(0)	38	11	36	3	32	3	–(0)
SES DE	–(0)	148	14	142	3	122	9	1
White	–(0)	234	20	234	3	227	7	1
Black	–(0)	3	67	3	–(0)	1	–(0)	–(0)
Asian	–(0)	4	25	4	–(0)	3	–(0)	–(0)
Other	–(0)	3	2	3	–(0)	1	–(0)	–(0)

Percentage of each category of respondent who had heard of the listed agencies

Table 8.8
Awareness of drug agencies by demographic variables and drug usage: Bradford Main

N = Percent of Valid	N = Valid N		(N) = Actual N					
	DPT (no prompt)		DPT (single prompt)		DPT (dual prompt)		Bridge	Proj. 6	Other
							(Valid N as for DPT no prompt)		
Present cannabis user	8	39	15	36	–(0)	31	13	3	–(0)
Present non-opiate user	8	24	8	22	–(0)	20	17	4	–(0)
Present opiate user	–(0)	1	100	1		–0	–(0)	–(0)	–(0)
Used drugs in past	3	135	13	134	–(0)	117	10	1	–(0)
Never used drugs	–(7)	867	12	837	1	737	3	1	1
Age 16–19	5	42	16	40	–(0)	34	7	–(0)	–(0
Age 20–24	1	82	13	80	1	70	7	1	–(0)
Age 25–29	2	115	12	114	1	101	3	2	1
Age 30–34	–(1)	124	11	119	1	106	4	2	1
Age 35–44	–(1)	202	19	193	1	156	5	1	–(0)
Age 45–59	1	188	19	183	1	148	5	1	2
Age 60+	1	247	9	238	1	217	2	1	1
Male	1	423	12	411	–(0)	49	5	1	1
Female	1	581	13	562	1	489	3	1	1
SES AB	1	154	17	151	1	125	8	3	1
SES C1	3	234	15	231	–(0)	196	8	1	1
SES C2	1	245	10	239	1	203	2	1	–(1)
SES DE	–(1)	367	11	348	2	310	1	1	–(2)
White	1	888	13	868	1	155	4	1	1
Black	–(0)	11	12	11	–(0)	10	–(0)	–(0)	–(0)
Asian	–(0)	86	17	86	2	71	9	–(0)	–(0)
Other	–(0)	8	–(0)	8	–(0)	8	–(0)	–(0)	–(0)

Percentage of each category of respondent who had heard of the listed agencies

APPENDIX I

Table 8.9
Awareness of drug agencies by demographic variables and drug usage: Bradford Booster

N = Percent of Valid   N = Valid N   (N) = Actual N

	DPT (no prompt)		DPT (single prompt)		DPT (dual prompt)		Bridge	Proj. 6	Other
							(Valid N as for DPT no prompt)		
Present cannabis user	–(0)	36	11	36	3	32	22	–(0)	–(0)
Present non-opiate user	–(0)	20	10	20	–(0)	8	15	–(0)	–(0)
Present opiate user	–(0)	2	50	2	–(0)	1	–(0)	–(0)	–(0)
Used drugs in past	–(0)	74	13	74	3	64	15	1	–(0)
Never used drugs	–(0)	156	8	154	3	140	1	1	1
Age 16–19	–(0)	91	10	91	3	80	7	1	–(0)
Age 20–24	–(0)	110	12	108	4	95	5	1	–(0)
Age 25–29	–(0)	30	3	30	–(0)	21	3	3	3
Male	–(0)	111	12	110	4	97	8	1	–(0)
Female	–(0)	120	8	119	2	110	3	2	1
SES AB	–(0)	5	–(0)	5	–(0)	5	–(0)	–(0)	–(0)
SES C1	–(0)	29	13	29	7	25	3	–(0)	–(0)
SES C2	–(0)	54	7	54	4	50	9	2	–(0)
SES DE	–(0)	11	11	141	2	126	5	1	1
White	–(0)	12	12	148	1	130	7	2	1
Black	–(0)	2	–(0)	2	–(0)	2	–(0)	–(0)	–(0)
Asian	–(0)	6	6	73	14	68	2	–(0)	–(0)
Other	–(0)	2	–(0)	2	–(0)	2	50	–(0)	–(0)

Percentage of each category of respondent who had heard of the listed agencies

Table 8.10
Views on the availability of agencies giving drugs related advice

N = Percent of Valid   N = Valid N

Agency	Nott. Main	Glas. Main	Lew. Main	Brad. Main	Nott. Boost.	Glas. Boost.	Lew. Boost.	Brad. Boost.
	1006	972	1139	1004	245	258	233	231
DPT	10	10	18	16	12	8	18	9
GP	29	39	37	35	33	39	39	21
clinic	11	25	19	17	12	21	20	17
named agency	3		3	5	4		3	7
other agency	5	9	8	5	4	13	9	9
CAB	5	4	8	5	4	4	10	3
social services	9	14	14	8	12	12	16	10
other	28	31	22	25	30	31	44	8
none	13	11	14	11	16	11	19	26

Percentage of respondents stating that each agency was available to give advice in their town / Blank indicates not applicable

DRUG USAGE AND DRUGS PREVENTION: THE VIEWS AND HABITS OF THE GENERAL PUBLIC

Table 8.11
Which agencies parents would turn to for advice if their children used drugs

N = Percent of Valid   N = Valid N   (N) = Actual N

Agency	Nott. Main	Glas. Main	Lew. Main	Brad. Main	Nott. Boost.	Glas. Boost.	Lew. Boost.	Brad. Boost.
	185	188	185	211	2	3	2	3
GP	11	11	8	9	– (0)	67	– (0)	– (0)
school	4	3	3	4	– (0)	– (0)	– (0)	– (0)
social services	2	3	2	2	– (0)	– (0)	– (0)	– (0)
police	4	5	3	5	– (0)	– (0)	– (0)	– (0)
friend or family	2	3	3	3	– (0)	– (0)	50	33
other	78	71	75	74	50	– (0)	– (0)	– (0)
no one	14	17	24	26	50	– (0)	– (0)	– (0)

Percentage of respondents stating that their first recourse would be to the listed agencies

Table 8.12
Contact with users of advice agencies

N = Percent of Valid   N = Valid N   (N) = Actual N

Agency	Nott. Main	Glas. Main	Lew. Main	Brad. Main	Nott. Boost.	Glas. Boost.	Lew. Boost.	Brad. Boost.
DPT	1 103	12 94	4 200	4 162	3 30	14 22	2 42	– (0) 20
GP	9 292	11 376	9 425	4 352	7 82	20 103	12 91	12 49
clinic	17 111	17 243	14 214	7 167	7 30	22 55	11 47	20 40
named agency	40 33		27 31	33 154	57 13		25 8	20 10
other agency	16 49	36 92	17 86	16 55	16 9	18 33	20 20	14 21
CAB	8 52	5 40	10 95	13 53	13 10	– (0) 9	– (0) 24	– (0) 6
social services	12 89	23 135	14 155	16 76	16 29	25 32	16 37	9 23
other	18 139	15 188	18 129	15 148	15 45	21 38	27 51	17 12

Percentage of respondents stating that they were aware of someone who had attended an advice agency / Blank indicates not applicable

Table 8.13
Views on the actual effectiveness of agencies

N = Percent of Valid   N = Valid N   (N) = Actual N

Agency	Nott. Main	Glas. Main	Lew. Main	Brad. Main	Nott. Boost.	Glas. Boost.	Lew. Boost.	Brad. Boost.
DPT	– (0) 1	36 11	55 9	100 6	– (0) 1	67 3	– (0) 1	
named agency	89 11		62 8	54 15	100 6		50 2	– (0) 3
GP	52 27	52 42	72 39	56 16	50 6	52 21	73 11	67 6
clinic	74 19	56 41	67 30	64 11	50 2	50 12	40 5	50 8
CAB	25 4	– (0) 2	70 10	43 7	– (0) 1			
social services	18 11	52 31	43 23	67 12	– (0) 5	62 8	33 6	50 2
other agency	75 8	64 83	80 15	56 9	– (0) 1	50 6	75 4	33 3
other	52 25	68 28	35 23	56 23	75 4	87 8	50 14	100 2

Percentage of respondents stating that individuals attending the agencies had found their advice 'very helpful' or 'fairly helpful' / Blank indicates not applicable

APPENDIX I

Table 8.14
Views on the potential effectiveness of DPTs

N = Percent of Valid N = Valid N

Statement	Nott. Main	Glas. Main	Lew. Main	Brad. Main	Nott. Boost.	Glas. Boost.	Lew. Boost.	Brad. Boost.
	1006	972	1139	1004	245	258	233	231
DPTs could be effective	85	84	80	80	84	84	80	74

Percentage of respondents stating that the drug prevention teams could be 'very effective' or 'fairly effective' in their area

Table 8.15
Views on which agencies should be responsible for giving advice

N = Percent of Valid N = Valid N (N) = Actual N

Agency	Nott. Main	Glas. Main	Lew. Main	Brad. Main	Nott. Boost.	Glas. Boost.	Lew. Boost.	Brad. Boost.
DPT	77	70	77	77	76	76	81	70
GP	61	63	59	64	66	65	62	54
clinic	59	61	60	57	57	66	69	61
voluntary advice agency	44	42	44	37	38	57	46	29
social services	41	47	44	37	41	49	54	31
other	93	93	93	91	96	95	94	85

Percentage of respondents stating that each of the listed agencies should be responsible for giving help and advice

Table 8.16
Views on cooperation between the police and drugs related agencies

N = Percent of Valid N = Valid N

Statement	Nott. Main	Glas. Main	Lew. Main	Brad. Main	Nott. Boost.	Glas. Boost.	Lew. Boost.	Brad. Boost.
	979	956	1109	960	240	251	232	227
Useful for police to work with agencies	91	92	94	91	92	89	93	82

Percentage of respondents stating that it would be 'very useful' or 'fairly useful' for police to work with advice agencies

DRUG USAGE AND DRUGS PREVENTION: THE VIEWS AND HABITS OF THE GENERAL PUBLIC

TABLES IN APPENDIX I (CHAPTER 9)

Table 9.1
Views on legalisation and decriminalisation

N = Percent of Valid   N = Valid N   (N) = Actual N

Statement	Nott. Main	Glas. Main	Lew. Main	Brad. Main	Nott. Boost.	Glas. Boost.	Lew. Boost.	Brad. Boost.
	984	934	1112	958	240	250	231	219
All/no	– (9)	– (9)	1	1	2	2	3	3
All/some	10	7	8	7	6	6	8	4
Some/no	4	6	7	5	11	14	15	9
Some/some	16	15	20	14	26	34	31	22
All illegal	67	67	62	68	53	41	41	56

Percentage of respondents stating that all drugs should be legalised with no restrictions / Percentage of respondents stating that all drugs should be legalised but with some restrictions / Percentage of respondents stating that some drugs should be legalised with no restrictions / Percentage of respondents stating that some drugs should be legalised but with some restrictions / Percentage of respondents stating that all drugs should remain illegal

Table 9.2
Percentage of respondents who favour legalisation by demographic and drug usage profile

N = Percent of Valid   N = Valid N   (N) = Actual N

	Nott. Main	Glas. Main	Lew. Main	Brad. Main	Nott. Boost.	Glas. Boost.	Lew. Boost.	Brad. Boost.
Present cannabis user	31 58	33 79	43 86	33 39	32 60	29 83	42 59	42 36
Present non-opiate user	35 26	38 42	41 34	43 23	37 35	38 45	47 30	45 20
Present opiate user	50 2	20 5	44 16	– (0) 1	67 6	50 4	20 5	100 2
Used drugs in past	20 166	23 186	27 258	24 131	27 94	28 132	34 104	28 72
Never used drugs	14 810	13 746	12 854	13 825	15 145	14 118	21 125	12 146
Age 16–19	12 50	8 47	21 42	32 41	17 92	25 97	29 105	19 85
Age 20–24	20 86	26 83	25 87	21 81	20 135	21 134	27 101	14 105
Age 25–29	19 112	15 123	16 165	16 111	31 13	10 19	20 25	21 29
Age 30–34	22 110	14 118	17 155	10 117				
Age 35–44	12 176	12 154	16 195	11 195				
Age 45–59	11 212	13 168	10 167	12 179				
Age 60+	15 238	15 241	16 297	14 231				
Male	16 426	18 383	18 499	14 413	22 121	25 116	27 114	19 103
Female	15 558	12 551	14 613	14 545	17 119	19 134	26 117	15 116
SES AB	10 137	21 76	11 119	13 149	30 10	– (0) 6	19 21	– (0) 5
SES C1	19 249	13 172	18 397	16 225	16 49	11 65	22 69	10 29
SES C2	10 278	16 207	14 256	12 234	19 53	27 37	31 65	15 52
SES DE	19 317	14 479	16 337	15 346	21 125	25 141	31 74	19 133
White	15 935	15 904	16 863	14 857	18 211	22 238	26 156	22 144
Black	32 21	– (0) 2	16 172	18 9	57 14	50 2	26 64	– (0) 1
Asian	27 11	7 14	30 12	7 75	– (0) 5	– (0) 5	33 6	7 66
Other	– (0) 4	50 2	14 32	37 9	– (0) 2	33 3	60 5	– (0) 2

Percentage of respondents in each demographic and drug usage category who stated that all drugs should be legalised with no restrictions

APPENDIX I

Table 9.3
Percentage of respondents who favour decriminalisation by demographic and drug usage profile

N = Percent of Valid   Valid N as for Table 9.2   (N) = Actual N

	Nott. Main	Glas. Main	Lew. Main	Brad. Main	Nott. Boost.	Glas. Boost.	Lew. Boost.	Brad. Boost.
Present cannabis user	47	57	48	49	52	55	51	42
Present non-opiate user	31	43	44	35	54	44	40	40
Present opiate user	50	60	50	100	– (0)	50	80	– (0)
Used drugs in past	44	45	45	40	44	52	51	40
Never used drugs	10	8	13	10	16	17	16	16
Age 16–19	22	36	29	24	33	32	30	21
Age 20–24	31	26	24	21	22	37	35	27
Age 25–29	27	28	33	17	31	42	24	21
Age 30–34	18	20	33	14				
Age 35–44	12	12	16	11				
Age 45–59	14	6	10	12				
Age 60+	3	4	6	6				
Male	21	17	26	18	31	36	37	28
Female	15	12	14	14	22	35	26	20
SES AB	28	17	39	21	40	33	43	40
SES C1	20	23	25	14	37	48	32	28
SES C2	11	11	16	14	19	43	35	23
SES DE	12	14	11	12	24	28	24	23
White	16	16	21	15	27	37	38	28
Black	18	– (0)	22	9	36	50	20	– (0)
Asian	27	7	20	8	20	20	17	11
Other	– (0)	50	15	– (0)	– (0)	– (0)	– (0)	50

Percentage of respondents in each demographic and drug usage category who stated either that all drugs should be legalised but with some restrictions or that some drugs should be legalised with no restrictions or that some drugs should be legalised but with some restrictions

Table 9.4
Percentage of respondents who favour keeping drugs illegal by demographic and drug usage profile

N = Percent of Valid   Valid N as for Table 9.2   (N) = Actual N

	Nott. Main	Glas. Main	Lew. Main	Brad. Main	Nott. Boost.	Glas. Boost.	Lew. Boost.	Brad. Boost.
Present cannabis user	22	10	9	18	17	16	7	17
Present non-opiate user	35	19	15	22	9	18	13	15
Present opiate user	– (0)	20	6	– (0)	33	– (0)	– (0)	– (0)
Used drugs in past	36	32	29	37	30	20	15	32
Never used drugs	75	79	75	77	69	69	63	73
Age 16–19	66	55	50	44	50	43	41	60
Age 20–24	49	47	51	58	58	42	39	59
Age 25–29	54	56	51	67	38	47	56	59
Age 30–34	60	65	50	75				
Age 35–44	69	71	56	69				
Age 45–59	74	80	80	76				
Age 60+	81	81	78	80				
Male	63	64	56	68	46	39	36	52
Female	73	73	70	74	61	46	47	65
SES AB	62	62	50	66	30	67	38	60
SES C1	61	63	56	70	47	41	46	62
SES C2	79	72	69	74	62	30	34	61
SES DE	69	72	73	73	55	46	45	58
White	69	69	63	71	55	42	36	49
Black	45	100	71	54	14	– (0)	52	50
Asian	45	93	70	72	80	80	50	73
Other	80	– (0)	65	50	100	67	40	50

Percentage of respondents in each demographic and drug usage category who stated that all drugs should remain illegal

APPENDIX I

Table 9.5
Summary of regression model for legalisation question: Main sample

Response	final model	beta	t	sig.t	Adj. R squared
to what extent agree with legalisation - based on the distinction between legalisation, decriminalisation and all drugs remaining illegal (N = 3911)	ever taken illicit drug	0.20	11.1	.000	0.11
	frequency of taking cannabis	0.14	8.53	.000	
	age group	0.06	3.49	.000	
	gender	0.05	3.39	.000	

variables in equation: location, whether ever taken any illicit drug, frequency of taking cannabis, frequency of taking non-opiates, frequency of taking opiates, age group, socioeconomic status, gender, ethnicity (white, black, asian)

Table 9.6
Summary of regression model for legalisation question: booster sample

Response	final model	beta	t	sig.t	Adj. R squared
to what extent agree with legalisation - based on the distinction between legalisation, decriminalisation and all drugs remaining illegal (N = 914)	ever taken illicit drug	0.26	7.18	.000	0.14
	frequency of taking cannabis	0.21	5.69	.000	

variables in equation: location, whether ever taken any illicit drug, frequency of taking cannabis, frequency of taking non-opiates, frequency of taking opiates, age group, socioeconomic status, gender, ethnicity (white, black, asian)

APPENDIX 2

APPENDIX 2

Public Attitude Surveys Ltd

Market Research   Social Research

Rye Park House London Road High Wycombe Bucks HP11 1EF
Telephone: 0494-532771 Fax: 0494-521404

Dear Householder,

Public attitudes to crime, fear of crime, and drugs : survey in four major cities

Your household is one of 1500 selected in each of four cities, for a major survey of public perceptions of crime, fear of crime, and drugs. The four cities are Glasgow, Bradford, Nottingham and London (the Borough of Lewisham). In each location we have chosen a cross-section of households at random to take part in our survey and yours is one of them.

The interviews are being carried out by Public Attitude Surveys Limited (PAS), one of the country's leading social research companies. The results from the survey will be written up by the University of Sheffield, in a report likely to be published towards the end of the year, or early in 1993. The report is intended to provide a better basis for public discussion and policy making. The University has been funded by a government department to carry out this work independently.

An interviewer from PAS will be calling on your household in the next week or so. All interviewers carry a Market Research Society Identity Card with a picture of themselves. You should ask to see this when the interviewer calls on you.

Within each household, we need to interview one adult aged 16 years or over. It is important that we obtain a good cross section of all adults so the interviewer will ask you for the names of all adults in your household. They will then select one adult at random to be interviewed. If that person is not available at the time then the interviewer will seek to make an appointment for a later date. Likewise, if there is a need for a different language other than English then we will do our best to make alternative arrangements. The interview should last no longer than half an hour for most people.

The questionnaire itself covers a variety of topics, some more sensitive than others. **We promise that your answers will be treated as wholly confidential**. The findings from this survey will not be analysed or presented in any way which relates to individual replies.

Should you have any questions about the survey which our interviewer cannot answer, you can get further information by ringing PAS. Their telephone number is 0494-532771 and you should ask to speak to Caroline Wright. PAS can even put you in touch with the relevant part of the University of Sheffield (the Centre for Criminology and Legal Research) should you so wish.

We do hope that you will agree to help us in this survey. It is important that we get the views of as wide a cross section of the public as possible - we thank you in advance for your help and co-operation.

Yours faithfully

Nick Smith
Research Director, PAS

Registered in England (No. 1407911)
Directors: Barry Lee (Managing) Tom Costley Chris Eynon Kevin Mulcahey
Stuart Robinson Nick Smith Christopher Smith (Non-executive)

Member of AMSO IQCS

APPENDIX 2

PAS 12834	CRIME, FEAR OF CRIME AND DRUGS SURVEY - INITIAL CONTACT SHEET

NAME(S) AND ADDRESS

SURVEY NO
12834
(1 - 5)

Q'AIRE NUMBER
(6 - 9)

CARD NO.
(10)   (1)

ED NO.
(11 - 12)

SERIAL NO:
(13 - 16)

CALL RECORD:

	TIME	DATE	OUTCOME
FIRST	....	....	....
SECOND	....	....	....
THIRD	....	....	....
FOURTH	....	....	....
FIFTH	....	....	....
SIXTH	....	....	....

TOTAL NUMBER OF CALLS ---->   (17)

FINAL OUTCOME:

WRITE IN FULL DETAILS ABOUT REFUSAL:

	(18)
SUCCESSFUL INTERVIEW	1
<-------- REFUSED TO BE INTERVIEWED	2
HOUSEHOLD NO CONTACT AFTER 6+ CALLS	3
INDIVIDUAL NON CONTACT AFTER 6+ CALLS	4
ON HOLIDAY/AWAY	5
EMPTY/BOARDED UP	6
LANGUAGE DIFFICULTY	7
OTHER REASON FOR NON INTERVIEW:	8

(19)

DECLARATION OF CONTACT RECORD:

I certify that this is a true record of an interview for this survey with a person unknown to me and has been condcuted within the code of conduct.

(20 - 23)

SIGNATURE ....   DATE: ....   NUMBER: [ ][ ][ ]

DRUG USAGE AND DRUGS PREVENTION: THE VIEWS AND HABITS OF THE GENERAL PUBLIC

PAS 12834/CLW   **SELECTION PROCEDURE**   FEBRUARY/MARCH 1992

INTRODUCTION
Good morning/afternoon/evening, I am .... (SHOW ID CARD) from Public Attitude Surveys, and we are doing a survey on the opinions of local people about the area, and, in particular, crime and drug use. The survey involves talking to a random sample of people, and to select this sample I need to find out who lives at each chosen address.

Q.A   What are the names of the people aged 16 years or over living in this household, starting with the eldest? ENTER NAMES IN DESCENDING ORDER OF AGE WITHIN HOUSEHOLD, GRID BELOW

	WRITE IN NAMES OF 16+ YEARS	SELECTED PERSON (TICK ONE ONLY)
1st		
2nd		
3rd		
4th		
5th		
6th		
7th		
8th		
9th		
10th		

TOTAL NO. OF 16+ IN HOUSEHOLD (THIS IS THE "NO. OF ELIGIBLE PEOPLE LISTED FOR FINAL KISH SELECTION"). ———> [ ]

- IF NUMBER OF ELIGIBLE PEOPLE IS 01 GO TO Q.B
- IF NUMBER IS 02 OR MORE, DECIDE WHETHER TO SELECT THE FIRST, SECOND, THIRD ETC PERSON, USING THE KISH GRID BELOW, AND TICK THE SELECTED PERSON ABOVE.

		TOTAL NUMBER OF ELIGIBLE PEOPLE (AGED 16+) LISTED ABOVE									
		1	2	3	4	5	6	7	8	9	10
LAST DIGIT OF ADDRESS NUMBER	1	1st	1st	2nd	3rd	1st	4th	2nd	7th	1st	1st
	2	1st	2nd	3rd	4th	2nd	5th	3rd	8th	2nd	2nd
	3	1st	1st	1st	1st	3rd	6th	4th	1st	3rd	3rd
	4	1st	2nd	2nd	2nd	4th	1st	5th	2nd	4th	4th
	5	1st	1st	3rd	3rd	5th	2nd	6th	3rd	5th	5th
	6	1st	2nd	1st	4th	1st	3rd	7th	4th	6th	6th
	7	1st	1st	2nd	1st	2nd	4th	1st	5th	7th	7th
	8	1st	2nd	3rd	2nd	3rd	5th	2nd	6th	8th	8th
	9	1st	1st	1st	3rd	4th	6th	3rd	7th	9th	9th
	0	1st	2nd	2nd	4th	5th	1st	4th	8th	1st	10th

Q.B   The person I need to talk to is ..... READ OUT NAME

- IF YOU HAVE SELECTED THE PERSON YOU ARE TALKING TO, GO TO MAIN QUESTIONNAIRE.
- IF OTHER PERSON IS SELECTED, ASK TO SPEAK TO THEM AND GO TO MAIN QUESTIONNAIRE, AFTER EXPLAINING SURVEY. IF NOT AVAILABLE MAKE AN APPOINTMENT TO RETURN.

WRITE IN DETAILS OF APPOINTMENT:

DATE ....   TIME ....

THIS FORM IS THE PROPERTY OF PUBLIC ATTITUDE SURVEYS LIMITED, RYE PARK HOUSE, LONDON ROAD, HIGH WYCOMBE, BUCKS HP11 1EF.

APPENDIX 2

RESPONDENT NAME: _____ **SERIAL NO.** _____

START CARD 2

A. GENERAL VIEWS OF THE LOCAL AREA

ASK ALL

Q.1 How many years have you lived in this area? [i.e. within 15 minutes walk]

(11)
LESS THAN ONE YEAR	1
1 BUT LESS THAN 2 YEARS	2
2 BUT LESS THAN 5 YEARS	3
5 BUT LESS THAN 10 YEARS	4
10 YEARS OR MORE	5
(DON'T KNOW)	8

Q.2 SHOW CARD A Overall, how satisfied or otherwise are you with living in this area? Please choose your answer from this card.

(12)
VERY SATISFIED	1
FAIRLY SATISFIED	2
NEITHER NOR	3
FAIRLY DISSATISFIED	4
VERY DISSATISFIED	5
(DON'T KNOW)	8

Q.3 Would you say this is a neighbourhood in which people tend to do things together and try to help each other or one in which people mostly go their own way? ONE CODE ONLY

(13)
HELP EACH OTHER	1
GO OWN WAY	2
MIXTURE	3
(DON'T KNOW)	8

Q.4 Do you ever walk around in this area after dark on your own?

(14)
YES	1 - ASK Q.5
NO	2 - SKIP TO Q.6

Q.5 SHOW CARD B How safe do you feel walking alone in this area after dark?

(15)
VERY SAFE	1	
FAIRLY SAFE	2	SKIP
A BIT UNSAFE	3	TO Q.7
VERY UNSAFE	4	
(DON'T KNOW)	8	

ASK ALL WHO DO NOT WALK OUT ALONE AT NIGHT

Q.6 SHOW CARD B How safe do you think you would feel walking alone in this area after dark?

(16)
VERY SAFE	1
FAIRLY SAFE	2
A BIT UNSAFE	3
VERY UNSAFE	4
(DON'T KNOW)	8

DRUG USAGE AND DRUGS PREVENTION: THE VIEWS AND HABITS OF THE GENERAL PUBLIC

ASK ALL
Q.7 Are you <u>ever</u> alone in your home at night?

	(17)
YES	1 - ASK Q.8
NO	2 - SKIP TO Q.9

Q.8 <u>SHOW CARD B AGAIN</u> How safe do you feel when you are alone in your home at night?

	(18)	
VERY SAFE	1	
FAIRLY SAFE	2	
A BIT UNSAFE	3	NOW SKIP
VERY UNSAFE	4	TO Q.10
(DON'T KNOW)	8	

ASK ALL NEVER ALONE AT HOME AT NIGHT
Q.9 <u>SHOW CARD B AGAIN</u> How safe do you think you would feel if you were alone in your home at night?

	(19)
VERY SAFE	1
FAIRLY SAFE	2
A BIT UNSAFE	3
VERY UNSAFE	4
(DON'T KNOW)	8

ASK ALL
Q.10 <u>SHOW CARD C</u> Most of us *worry* at some time or other about being the victim of crime. Using one of the phrases on this card, could you tell me how worried you are about .... READ OUT EACH STATEMENT IN TURN

	VERY WORRIED	FAIRLY WORRIED	NOT VERY WORRIED	NOT AT ALL WORRIED	NOT APPLI-CABLE	(DON'T KNOW) (DON'T	
having your home broken into and something stolen?	1	2	3	4	////// //////	8	(20)
being mugged and robbed in this area?	1	2	3	4	////// //////	8	(21)
having your car stolen in this area	1	2	3	4	5	8	(22)
having things stolen from your car in this area?	1	2	3	4	5	8	(23)
ASK FEMALE RESPONDENTS:							
being raped in this area?	1	2	3	4	5	8	(24)

Q.11 How much would you say the crime rate in this area has changed since two years ago? (ie. within 15 minutes walk). In this area, would you say there is more crime or less crime? PROMPT: Is that a lot or a little more/less? <u>ONE</u> CODE ONLY.

	(25)
A LOT MORE CRIME	1
A LITTLE MORE CRIME	2
ABOUT THE SAME	3
A LITTLE LESS CRIME	4
A LOT LESS CRIME	5
(NOT ANY CRIME)	6
(NOT LIVED IN AREA FOR TWO YEARS)	7
(DON'T KNOW)	8

APPENDIX 2

ASK ALL
Q.12 SHOW CARD D For the following things I read out, can you tell me how much of problem you think they are in your area. READ OUT EACH IN TURN AND CODE BELOW.

	VERY BIG PROBLEM	FAIRLY BIG PROBLEM	NOT A VERY BIG PROBLEM	NOT A PROBLEM AT ALL	(DON'T KNOW)
Noisy neighbours or loud parties	1	2	3	4	8 (26)
Teenagers hanging around on the streets	1	2	3	4	8 (27)
Drunks on the streets	1	2	3	4	8 (28)
Dogs	1	2	3	4	8 (29)
Abandoned cars	1	2	3	4	8 (30)
Rubbish and litter lying about	1	2	3	4	8 (31)
Racially motivated attacks	1	2	3	4	8 (32)
Children and young people sniffing glue, gas or aerosols	1	2	3	4	8 (33)
People using drugs	1	2	3	4	8 (34)
People being offered drugs for sale?	1	2	3	4	8 (35)
People becoming ill or dying due to the use of drugs?	1	2	3	4	8 (36)
People thieving in order to get money to buy drugs?	1	2	3	4	8 (37)
People committing crimes because they are acting under the influence of drugs?	1	2	3	4	8 (38)

ASK ALL
Q.13 How much would you say the number of people using drugs in this area has changed since two years ago? (ie. within 15 minutes walk). Would you say there are more people using drugs or less? PROMPT: Is that a lot or slightly more/less? ONE CODE ONLY.

```
                                                    (39)
                               A LOT MORE PEOPLE     1
                          SLIGHTLY MORE PEOPLE       2
                                 ABOUT THE SAME      3
                          SLIGHTLY LESS PEOPLE       4
                               A LOT LESS PEOPLE     5
                           (NO ONE USING DRUGS)      6
               (NOT LIVED IN AREA FOR TWO YEARS)     7
                                    (DON'T KNOW)     8
```

DRUG USAGE AND DRUGS PREVENTION: THE VIEWS AND HABITS OF THE GENERAL PUBLIC

ASK ALL

Q.14 Thinking about this area (ie. within 15 minutes walk) do you think the number of people <u>using</u> drugs here is higher, lower or about the same compared to the rest of .... (TOWN/'South London' IN WHICH RESPONDENT LIVES)?

	(40)
HIGHER	1
THE SAME	2
LOWER	3
(DON'T KNOW)	8

Q.15 Do you think that there are particular areas in this town/South London where people take drugs? [INTERVIEWER: STRESS CONFIDENTIALITY]

	(41)	
YES	1	- ASK Q.16
NO	2 ⎤	SKIP TO
(DON'T KNOW)	8 ⎦	SECTION B

Q.16 In which areas in particular? PROMPT: 'Which others?' WRITE IN ALL AREAS MENTIONED [INTERVIEWER: STRESS CONFIDENTIALITY]

(42)	(43)
(44)	(45)
(46)	(47)
(48)	(49)

ASK ALL AWARE OF ANY AREAS. REST, SKIP TO SECTION B

Q.17 People hear about these things in different ways. How are <u>you</u> aware of people taking drugs in this/these areas? PROMPT: How else?
[INTERVIEWER: STRESS CONFIDENTIALITY]

DIRECT KNOWLEDGE/EXPERIENCE	1	(50)
FROM FAMILY/FRIENDS	1	(51)
FROM NEIGHBOURS/FRIEND	1	(52)
GENERAL WORD OF MOUTH	1	(53)
LOCAL PRESS	1	(54)
NATIONAL PRESS	1	(55)
LOCAL RADIO	1	(56)
NATIONAL RADIO	1	(57)
LOCAL TV NEWS	1	(58)
NATIONAL TV	1	(59)
OTHER (CODE AND WRITE IN)	1	(60)
(DON'T KNOW)	8	(61)

(62)	(63)

APPENDIX 2

B. **COMPARISON OF LOCAL AND NATIONAL PICTURE**

We have been discussing your views of your area, and the problems of crime and drugs within the area. I would now like to ask you to compare the area in which you live to what is happening nationally/elsewhere in Great Britain.

ASK ALL

Q.18 <u>SHOW CARD E</u> For the following things I read out, can you tell if you think it is more of a problem <u>locally</u>, more of a problem <u>nationally</u> or about the same everywhere? READ OUT EACH IN TURN AND CODE BELOW.

	MORE OF A PROBLEM LOCALLY	SAME	MORE OF A PROBLEM NATIONALLY	(DON'T KNOW)
Burglary	1	2	3	8 (64)
Drunks on the streets	1	2	3	8 (65)
Car theft	1	2	3	8 (66)
Rubbish and litter lying about	1	2	3	8 (67)
Vandalism, graffiti and deliberate damage to property	1	2	3	8 (68)
Racially motivated attacks	1	2	3	8 (69)
People thieving in order to get money to buy drugs	1	2	3	8 (70)
People committing crimes because they are under the influence of drugs	1	2	3	8 (71)
People becoming ill or dying as a result of taking drugs	1	2	3	8 (72)
People selling drugs	1	2	3	8 (73)
Children and young people sniffing glue, gases or aerosols	1	2	3	8 (74)

COLS (75-80) BLANK

DRUG USAGE AND DRUGS PREVENTION: THE VIEWS AND HABITS OF THE GENERAL PUBLIC

C. NATIONAL DRUGS SCENE

ASK ALL

Q.19 How many people do you think take drugs nationally/in Great Britain? Is it .... (READ OUT AND CODE <u>ONE</u> ONLY)

(11)
- ... a lot of people — 1
- ... quite a lot of people — 2
- ... a few people — 3
- ... very few people — 4
- (DON'T KNOW) — 8

Q.20 <u>SHOW CARD D</u> So how much of a problem would you say drug usage is <u>nationally</u>?

(12)
- VERY BIG PROBLEM — 1
- FAIRLY BIG PROBLEM — 2
- NOT A VERY BIG PROBLEM — 3
- NOT A PROBLEM AT ALL — 4
- (DON'T KNOW) — 8

NO Q.21

ASK ALL

Q.22 <u>SHOW CARD F</u> I'd now like you to consider different influences that people have suggested for taking drugs. Using one of the phrases on this card, I would like you to tell me how important or otherwise you think each influence is. So, firstly .... READ OUT EACH STATEMENT IN TURN AND CODE

	VERY IMPORTANT INFLUENCE	FAIRLY IMPORTANT INFLUENCE	NOT VERY IMPORTANT INFLUENCE	NOT AN IMPORTANT INFLUENCE	(DON'T KNOW)	
Being bored	1	2	3	4	8	(13)
Stress at work	1	2	3	4	8	(14)
Need for excitement/ something new	1	2	3	4	8	(15)
Lack of parental guidance	1	2	3	4	8	(16)
Going to clubs and parties where drugs available	1	2	3	4	8	(17)
Unemployment	1	2	3	4	8	(18)
Unhappiness at home	1	2	3	4	8	(19)
Mental illness	1	2	3	4	8	(20)
Because taking drugs is fun	1	2	3	4	8	(21)
Fitting in with friends	1	2	3	4	8	(22)
Declining moral standards	1	2	3	4	8	(23)
Because taking drugs can be a way of coping with life	1	2	3	4	8	(24)

APPENDIX 2

D. **KNOWLEDGE OF SPECIFIC DRUGS**

Having talked about drugs in general, I would now like to look at particular drugs and their effects. Note that when we are talking about specific drugs, we are not just referring to *illegal* drugs, but also to drugs *available* over a chemist's counter or on a doctor's prescription, but *not* being used as *prescribed*. Please remember that we are interested in everyone's views, regardless of how much or little they feel they know about particular drugs.

COL 25 BLANK

NB NO Q.23

ASK ALL
Q.24 When you think about drugs, what names come to mind for drugs that people use other than on prescription? CODE ALL MENTIONS IN GRID

ASK ALL
Q.25 SHOW SORT CARDS (Beyond those that you have just mentioned), which, if any, of these drugs have you heard of (as used without a doctor's prescription)? PROMPT: Which others? CODE IN GRID AND PUT ALL 'AWARE' DRUGS TOGETHER (SPONTANEOUS AND PROMPTED)

IF NO DRUGS MENTIONED AT Q.24/25 SKIP TO Q.27. REST:
Q.26 SHOW SORT BOARD In your opinion how beneficial or harmful are these drugs - POINT TO THOSE AWARE OF. Please use this board to position the different drugs according to your opinion. ALLOW RESPONDENT TIME TO SORT CARDS AND THEN RECORD ANSWERS IN GRID.

DRUG USAGE AND DRUGS PREVENTION: THE VIEWS AND HABITS OF THE GENERAL PUBLIC

	CARD 3		CARD 4					
	Q.24	Q.25	Q.26					
	SPONT AWARE NESS	PROMPT AWARE NESS	VERY BENEFI CIAL	BENEFI CIAL	NEITH ER/NOR	HARM FUL	VERY HARM FUL	(DON'T KNOW)
1. **CANNABIS** (also called MARIJUANA, GRASS, HASH, DRAW, GANJA, WEED)	1 (26)	1 (49)	1	2	3	4	5	8(11)
2. **HEROIN** (also called SMACK, TACKLE, GEAR, H)	1 (27)	1 (50)	1	2	3	4	5	8(12)
3. **AMPHETAMINES** (also called SPEED, WHIZZ, UPPERS, SULPH, BILLY, BUZZ)	1 (28)	1 (51)	1	2	3	4	5	8(13)
4. **LSD** (also called ACID, TABS, TRIPS)	1 (29)	1 (52)	1	2	3	4	5	8(14)
5. **COCAINE** (also called COKE, ICE, ROCKS, SNOW)	1 (30)	1 (53)	1	2	3	4	5	8(15)
6. **ECSTASY** (also called E)	1 (31)	1 (54)	1	2	3	4	5	8(16)
7. **CRACK** (also called ROCK, ICE)	1 (32)	1 (55)	1	2	3	4	5	8(17)
8. **MAGIC MUSHROOMS**	1 (33)	1 (56)	1	2	3	4	5	8(18)
9. **METHADONE** (also called MST, PHYSEPTONE)	1 (34)	1 (57)	1	2	3	4	5	8(19)
10. **DICONAL**	1 (35)	1 (58)	1	2	3	4	5	8(20)
11. **AMYL NITRATE** (alo called POPPERS, LIQUID GOLD, RUSH)	1 (36)	1 (59)	1	2	3	4	5	8(21)
12. **TEMAZEPAM** (also called JELLIES, EGGS, BEANS)	1 (37)	1 (60)	1	2	3	4	5	8(22)
13. **TEMGESIC** (also called TEMS, MIDGET GEMS)	1 (38)	1 (61)	1	2	3	4	5	8(23)
14. **SEMERON**	1 (39)	1 (62)	1	2	3	4	5	8(24)
15. **BARBITURATES** (also called DOWNERS, BARBIES)	1 (40)	1 (63)	1	2	3	4	5	8(25)
16. **DF118s** (also called DFs, HYDRA, SCRATCHERS)	1 (41)	1 (64)	1	2	3	4	5	8(26)
17. **TRIAZELAM** (also called UPJOHNS)	1 (42)	1 (65)	1	2	3	4	5	8(27)
18. UNPRESCRIBED USE OF **SLEEPING PILLS**	1 (43)	1 (66)	1	2	3	4	5	8(28)
19. UNPRESCRIBED USE OF **TRANQUI- LISERS** (eg VALIUM, LIBRIUM, ATIVAN)	1 (44)	1 (67)	1	2	3	4	5	8(29)
20. **SNIFFING GLUE, GAS, AEROSOL**	1 (45)	1 (68)	1	2	3	4	5	8(30)
OTHER (CODE AND WRITE IN) 1 _____	1 (46)	1 (69)	1	2	3	4	5	8(31)
2 _____	1 (47)	1 (70)	1	2	3	4	5	8(32)
NONE OF THE ABOVE/NONE	1 (48)	1 (71)	///////	///////	///////	///////	///////	///////

COLS (72-80) BLANK

APPENDIX 2

	CARD 4		CARD 5	
	Q.27	Q.28	Q.29	Q.30
	KNOW BEEN DEFERRED	KNOWN TAKEN	REGULARLY TAKES	SOCIAL GATHERINGS
1 CANNABIS	1(33)	1(57)	1(11)	1(35)
2 HEROIN	1(34)	1(58)	1(12)	1(36)
3 AMPHETAMINES	1(35)	1(59)	1(13)	1(37)
4 LSD	1(36)	1(60)	1(14)	1(38)
5 COCAINE	1(37)	1(61)	1(15)	1(39)
6 ECSTASY	1(38)	1(62)	1(16)	1(40)
7 CRACK	1(39)	1(63)	1(17)	1(41)
8 MAGIC MUSHROOMS	1(40)	1(64)	1(18)	1(42)
9 METHADONE	1(41)	1(65)	1(19)	1(43)
10 DICONAL	1(42)	1(66)	1(20)	1(44)
11 AMYL NITRATE	1(43)	1(67)	1(21)	1(45)
12 TEMAZEPAM	1(44)	1(68)	1(22)	1(46)
13 TEMGESIC	1(45)	1(69)	1(23)	1(47)
14 SEMERON	1(46)	1(70)	1(24)	1(48)
15 BARBITURATES	1(47)	1(71)	1(25)	1(49)
16 DF118s	1(48)	1(72)	1(26)	1(50)
17 TRIAZELAM	1(49)	1(73)	1(27)	1(51)
18 UNPRESCRIBED USE OF SLEEPING PILLS	1(50)	1(74)	1(28)	1(52)
19 UNPRESCRIBED USE OF TRANQUILISERS	1(51)	1(75)	1(29)	1(53)
20 SNIFFING GLUE, GAS, AEROSOL	1(52)	1(76)	1(30)	1(54)
OTHER (CODE AND WRITE IN)				
1 _ _ _ _ _ _ _ _ _ _	1(53)	1(77)	1(31)	1(55)
2 _ _ _ _ _ _ _ _ _	1(54)	1(78)	1(32)	1(56)
YES, BUT DON'T KNOW WHICH DRUGS	8(55)	8(79)	8(33)	8(57)
NONE OF THE ABOVE/NONE	1(56)	1(80)	1(34)	1(58)

E.   **USAGE OF DRUGS**

REASSURE ABOUT CONFIDENTIALITY AND THAT WE ARE INTERESTED IN THE DRUGS, AND **NOT** INDIVIDUALS

ASK ALL

Q.27   SHOW CARD G   Are you aware of anyone who has been offered any of these drugs (apart from on a doctor's prescription)? PROMPT: Which drugs?   PROMPT: Which others?   CODE ALL DRUGS MENTIONED

Q.28   STILL SHOWING CARD G   Are you aware of anyone who taken any of these drugs (in the last five years) (apart from on a doctor's prescription)? PROMPT: Which drugs? PROMPT: Which others? CODE ALL DRUGS MENTIONED

ASK ALL WHO KNOW SOMEONE WHO HAS TAKEN ANY DRUGS AT Q.28 REST SKIP TO Q.30

Q.29   STILL SHOWING CARD G   And are you aware of anyone who regularly takes any of these drugs (apart from on a doctor's prescription)? PROMPT: Which drugs? PROMPT: Which others? CODE ALL DRUGS MENTIONED

ASK ALL

Q.30   STILL SHOWING CARD G   Have you been at any social gathering (in the past five years) where others have been taking drugs? CODE ALL DRUGS MENTIONED.

```
ALL:
HAND RESPONDENT SELF COMPLETION BOOKLET - ALLOW TIME
READ INTRODUCTION AND ASK QUESTIONS - YOU MAY OFFER TO
HELP THEM COMPLETE IT IF THEY SO REQUEST
```

APPENDIX 2

SELF COMPLETION BOOKLET

CONFIDENTIAL

- We promise that your answers are **totally confidential** and will not be seen by the interviewer if you hand back this booklet sealed in the envelope provided.

- The person who opens the envelope (and thousands are being collected) will never know who you are and all the answers will be added together by computer. No names or addresses will be entered on the computer.

- **Please answer honestly.** It is important that we should have a complete picture of the way people behave.

- Please ignore the numbers next to the boxes. These are for office use.

> To answer these questions, just tick the answers in the boxes which apply to you.
> If there's anything that's unclear, please ask the interviewer.

DRUG USAGE AND DRUGS PREVENTION: THE VIEWS AND HABITS OF THE GENERAL PUBLIC

These questions are about drugs which people are not supposed to take unless they have a doctor's prescription. Just tick the answers which apply in the boxes at each question.

	UNPRESCRIBED USE OF SLEEPING PILLS	UNPRESCRIBED USE OF TRANQUILISERS (eg. VALIUM, LIBRIUM, ATIVAN)	CANNABIS (also called MARIJUANA, GRASS, HASH, DRAW, GANJA, WEED)	HEROIN (also called SMACK, TACKLE, GEAR, H)	AMPHETAMINES (also called SPEED, WHIZZ, UPPERS, SULPH, BILLY, BUZZ)	LSD (also called ACID, TABS, TRIPS)	COCAINE (also called COKE, ICE, ROCKS, SNOW)	ECSTASY (also called E)	CRACK (also called ROCK, ICE)
Q1. Which, if any, of these have you <u>ever tried</u>, even if it was a long time ago (except on a doctor's prescription)?	☐ 1	☐ 1	☐ 1	☐ 1	☐ 1	☐ 1	☐ 1	☐ 1	☐ 1
Q2. Which, if any, have you tried in the <u>last 12 months</u> (except on a doctor's perscription)?	☐ 1	☐ 1	☐ 1	☐ 1	☐ 1	☐ 1	☐ 1	☐ 1	☐ 1

Please answer Q's 3, 4 and 5 about each of the

Q3. On average, how often do you take this drug?									
Daily	☐ 1	☐ 1	☐ 1	☐ 1	☐ 1	☐ 1	☐ 1	☐ 1	☐ 1
Several times a week	☐ 2	☐ 2	☐ 2	☐ 2	☐ 2	☐ 2	☐ 2	☐ 2	☐ 2
Once a week	☐ 3	☐ 3	☐ 3	☐ 3	☐ 3	☐ 3	☐ 3	☐ 3	☐ 3
Once a fortnight	☐ 4	☐ 4	☐ 4	☐ 4	☐ 4	☐ 4	☐ 4	☐ 4	☐ 4
Once a month	☐ 5	☐ 5	☐ 5	☐ 5	☐ 5	☐ 5	☐ 5	☐ 5	☐ 5
Less often	☐ 6	☐ 6	☐ 6	☐ 6	☐ 6	☐ 6	☐ 6	☐ 6	☐ 6
Only tried once	☐ 7	☐ 7	☐ 7	☐ 7	☐ 7	☐ 7	☐ 7	☐ 7	☐ 7

Q4. Have you <u>ever</u> injected this drug?									
Yes	☐ 1	☐ 1	☐ 1	☐ 1	☐ 1	☐ 1	☐ 1	☐ 1	☐ 1
No	☐ 2	☐ 2	☐ 2	☐ 2	☐ 2	☐ 2	☐ 2	☐ 2	☐ 2

Q5. Is this drug usually available in your City?									
Yes	☐ 1	☐ 1	☐ 1	☐ 1	☐ 1	☐ 1	☐ 1	☐ 1	☐ 1
No	☐ 2	☐ 2	☐ 2	☐ 2	☐ 2	☐ 2	☐ 2	☐ 2	☐ 2
Don't know	☐ 8	☐ 8	☐ 8	☐ 8	☐ 8	☐ 8	☐ 8	☐ 8	☐ 8

Thank you for answering these questions. Now please seal the b

APPENDIX 2

nswer them honestly. Remember that the answers you give are completely confidential.
pply, please tick "NONE OF THESE".

DICONAL	AMYL NITRATE (also called POPPERS, LIQUID GOLD, RUSH)	TEMAZEPAM (also called JELLIES, EGGS, BEANS)	TEMGESIC (also called TEMS, MIDGET GEMS)	SEMERON	BARBITURATES (also called DOWNERS, BARBIES)	DF118s (also called DFs, HYDRA, SCRATCHERS)	TRIAZELAM (also called UPJOHNS)	SNIFFING GLUE, GAS, AEROSOLS	OTHER DRUG (PLEASE WRITE IN)	NONE/NONE OF THE DRUGS LISTED
☐ 1	☐ 1	☐ 1	☐ 1	☐ 1	☐ 1	☐ 1	☐ 1	☐ 1	☐ 1	☐ 1
☐ 1	☐ 1	☐ 1	☐ 1	☐ 1	☐ 1	☐ 1	☐ 1	☐ 1	☐ 1	☐ 1

tried in the last 12 months:

☐ 1	☐ 1	☐ 1	☐ 1	☐ 1	☐ 1	☐ 1	☐ 1	☐ 1	☐ 1	**↓** IF YOU HAVE NOT TRIED ANY IN THE LAST 12 MONTHS, THEN PLEASE PUT THIS QUESTION- NAIRE IN THE ENVELOPE
☐ 2	☐ 2	☐ 2	☐ 2	☐ 2	☐ 2	☐ 2	☐ 2	☐ 2	☐ 2	
☐ 3	☐ 3	☐ 3	☐ 3	☐ 3	☐ 3	☐ 3	☐ 3	☐ 3	☐ 3	
☐ 4	☐ 4	☐ 4	☐ 4	☐ 4	☐ 4	☐ 4	☐ 4	☐ 4	☐ 4	
☐ 5	☐ 5	☐ 5	☐ 5	☐ 5	☐ 5	☐ 5	☐ 5	☐ 5	☐ 5	
☐ 6	☐ 6	☐ 6	☐ 6	☐ 6	☐ 6	☐ 6	☐ 6	☐ 6	☐ 6	
☐ 7	☐ 7	☐ 7	☐ 7	☐ 7	☐ 7	☐ 7	☐ 7	☐ 7	☐ 7	
☐ 1	☐ 1	☐ 1	☐ 1	☐ 1	☐ 1	☐ 1	☐ 1			☐ 1
☐ 2	☐ 2	☐ 2	☐ 2	☐ 2	☐ 2	☐ 2	☐ 2			☐ 2
☐ 1	☐ 1	☐ 1	☐ 1	☐ 1	☐ 1	☐ 1	☐ 1			☐ 1
☐ 2	☐ 2	☐ 2	☐ 2	☐ 2	☐ 2	☐ 2	☐ 2			☐ 2
☐ 8	☐ 8	☐ 8	☐ 8	☐ 8	☐ 8	☐ 8	☐ 8			☐ 8

elope provided and return it to the interviewer.

ⓐ c,
ⓑ supp d, f
e, g laissez-faire

APPENDIX 2

F. ATTITUDES TO DRUGS AND HOW THEY SHOULD BE DEALT WITH IN THE COMMUNITY

People have differing views about the use of drugs and what the community should do about it.

ASK ALL

Q.31 SHOW CARD H I am going to read out a list of statements that people have made about taking drugs, and I would like you to tell me how much you agree or disagree with each of the statements.
ROTATE START POINT BETWEEN RESPONDENTS, TICK POINT STARTED

TICK START POINT	AGREE STRONGLY	AGREE SLIGHTLY	NEITHER NOR	DISAGREE SLIGHTLY	DISAGREE STRONGLY	DON'T KNOW	
☐ It is the responsibility of the government to provide education about the risks of taking drugs.	1	2	3	4	5	8	(59)
The way to decrease the number of people using drugs is to increase security at the ports and airports.	1	2	3	4	5	8	(60)
☐ There is little difference in health terms between smoking cannabis and smoking tobacco or drinking alcohol	1	2	3	4	5	8	(61)
Police time would be better spent catching drug suppliers rather than clamping down on users.	1	2	3	4	5	8	(62)
Money would be better spent on education and TV campaigns rather than on trying to stop drugs being smuggled into the country.	1	2	3	4	5	8	(63)
People who use cannabis (and other 'softer' drugs) are likely to progress onto 'harder' drugs such as cocaine and heroin.	1	2	3	4	5	8	(64)
☐ If people were better educated about the risks of taking drugs, many would not take them.	1	2	3	4	5	8	(65)
More money needs to be spent on helping drug users and giving them medical treatment	1	2	3	4	5	8	(66)

DRUG USAGE AND DRUGS PREVENTION: THE VIEWS AND HABITS OF THE GENERAL PUBLIC

ASK ALL

Q.32 There has been talk about whether certain drugs should be made legal, perhaps with restrictions on their availability. <u>SHOW CARD J</u> Using one of the phrases on this card, please tell me your opinion of this idea? <u>ONE</u> CODE ONLY.

	(67)
ALL DRUGS SHOULD BE LEGAL, WITHOUT ANY RESTRICTIONS	1
ALL DRUGS SHOULD BE LEGAL, BUT WITH SOME RESTRICTIONS (EG ONLY ON DOCTOR'S PRESCRIPTION)	2
SOME DRUGS (EG CANNABIS) SHOULD BE LEGAL, WITHOUT ANY RESTRICTIONS	3
SOME DRUGS (EG CANNABIS) SHOULD BE LEGAL BUT WITH RESTRICTIONS, EG LICENSING OF A FEW SHOPS/BARS ONLY	4
ALL DRUGS CURRENTLY PROHIBITED SHOULD REMAIN ILLEGAL	5
(DON'T KNOW)	8

Q.33 <u>SHOW CARD K</u> The police have different methods of trying to deal with the use of illegal drugs, aimed at either the user or supplier. I am going to read out a list of different ways, and I would like you to tell me how useful or otherwise you think each would be in helping to reduce the number of people using drugs. INTERVIEWER: REASSURE CONFIDENTIALITY IF NEEDED

	VERY USEFUL	FAIRLY USEFUL	NOT VERY USEFUL	NOT AT ALL USEFUL	(DON'T KNOW)	
Stopping and searching people on suspicion in the street or in public places	1	2	3	4	8	(68)
'Busting' or raiding houses where they believe there to be <u>suppliers</u>	1	2	3	4	8	(69)
'Busting' or raiding houses where they believe there to be <u>users</u>	1	2	3	4	8	(70)
Police warning or cautioning users about the risks but <u>not</u> prosecuting them	1	2	3	4	8	(71)
Major efforts by customs and police (such as at airport, ports) targeting sources of **supply**	1	2	3	4	8	(72)
Working with help and advice agencies against drug usage	1	2	3	4	8	(73)

ASK ALL

Q.34 <u>SHOW CARD L</u> How well do you think the police deal with drugs in .... (NAME TOWN/'South London')?

	(74)
VERY WELL	1
FAIRLY WELL	2
NOT VERY WELL	3
NOT AT ALL WELL	4
(DON'T KNOW)	8

COLS (75-80) BLANK

APPENDIX 2

ASK ALL

Q.35 SHOW CARD M How important do you think it is to *educate* people about the effects and risks of taking drugs?

	(11)	
VERY IMPORTANT	1	
FAIRLY IMPORTANT	2	ASK Q.36
NOT VERY IMPORTANT	3	
NOT AT ALL IMPORTANT	4	SKIP TO Q.39
(DON'T KNOW)	8	

Q.36 SHOW CARD N Who do you think should be given this education? PROMPT 'Who else?' IF MORE THAN ONE ASK: For whom is it <u>most</u> important to receive this education?

	ALL MENTIONS	MOST IMPORTANT (ONE ONLY)
		(21)
CHILDREN AGED 9 TO 11	1 (12)	1
CHILDREN AGED 12 TO 18	1 (13)	2
YOUNG ADULTS (19-25)	1 (14)	3
PARENTS	1 (15)	4
TEACHERS	1 (16)	5
ALL ADULTS	1 (17)	6
OTHER (CODE AND WRITE IN)	1 (18)	7
		(22)
(EVERYONE)	1 (19)	1
(DON'T KNOW)	8 (20)	8

Q.37 SHOW CARD P And how effective or otherwise do you think such education would be in reducing the number of people using drugs?

	(23)
VERY EFFECTIVE	1
FAIRLY EFFECTIVE	2
NOT VERY EFFECTIVE	3
NOT AT ALL EFFECTIVE	4
(DON'T KNOW)	8

Q.38 SHOW CARD Q Which organisations do you think should be responsible for providing such education? PROMPT: Who else? IF MORE THAN ONE ASK: Who should be <u>mostly</u> responsible?

	ALL MENTIONS	MOST RESPONSIBLE (ONE ONLY)
		(33)
THE GOVERNMENT	1 (24)	1
LOCAL COUNCIL	1 (25)	2
SCHOOLS/COLLEGES	1 (26)	3
DOCTORS; MEDICAL PROFESSION	1 (27)	4
SOCIAL SERVICES	1 (28)	5
POLICE	1 (29)	6
OTHER (CODE AND WRITE IN)	1 (30)	7
		(34)
(EVERYONE)	1 (31)	1
(DON'T KNOW)	8 (32)	8

DRUG USAGE AND DRUGS PREVENTION: THE VIEWS AND HABITS OF THE GENERAL PUBLIC

ASK ALL
Q.39 Do you think that education should aim mainly at trying to prevent people <u>starting</u> to take drugs or at drug <u>users</u> on how to avoid some of the worst effects of drugs, such as overdoses and the danger of catching AIDS? CODE <u>ONE</u> ONLY

	(35)
EDUCATION SHOULD MAINLY BE PREVENTION FROM STARTING DRUGS	1
EDUCATION SHOULD MAINLY HELP THOSE ALREADY TAKING DRUGS	2
BOTH	3
(DON'T KNOW)	8

Q.40 <u>SHOW CARD R</u> At present, how well informed do you think that <i>you</i> are about the different drugs around and the effects and risks of taking them?

	(36)
VERY WELL INFORMED	1
FAIRLY WELL INFORMED	2
NOT VERY WELL INFORMED	3
NOT AT ALL WELL INFORMED	4
(DON'T KNOW)	8

Q.41 What organisations are you aware of locally working to increase people's awareness about drugs or to provide advice, information or help? PROMPT: What others?

<u>ALL TOWNS</u>: DRUGS PREVENTION TEAM	1	(37)
<u>LONDON</u>: BROCKLEY DRUGLINE	1	(38)
THE DUAL TEAM	1	(39)
PHOENIX HOUSE	1	(40)
<u>NOTTINGHAM</u>: DRUGS DEPENDENTS ANONYMOUS (DDA)	1	(41)
THE HEALTH SHOP	1	(42)
<u>BRADFORD</u>: THE BRIDGE PROJECT	1	(43)
PROJECT 6	1	(44)
<u>GLASGOW</u>: LOCAL ADVICE AGENCY	1	(45)
(CODE AND WRITE IN)		

	(46)	(47)	(48)	(49)	(50)
OTHER CODE AND WRITE IN)	1				
NONE	7				
(DON'T KNOW)	8				

ASK ALL WHO DO NOT MENTION DRUGS PREVENTION TEAM AT Q.41. REST SKIP TO INSTRUCTION ABOVE Q.43
Q.42 Can I just check, have you heard of the Drugs Prevention Team based in .... (NAME TOWN)?

	(51)
YES	1
NO	2
DON'T KNOW	8

READ : The (QUOTE TOWN) Drugs Prevention Team has just started to work with local people to identify possible drugs misuse problems in their neighbourhoods and looking at what they can do about them with the advice and financial help of the team. HAND DESCRIPTIVE CARD AND ALLOW TIME TO READ.

ASK ALL WHO HAVE NOT HEARD OF THE DRUGS PREVENTION TEAM AT Q.41 OR Q.42. REST SKIP TO Q.44
Q.43 Have you heard anything about this team in .... (NAME TOWN)?

	(52)
YES	1
NO	2
DON'T KNOW	8

APPENDIX 2

ASK ALL

Q.44 <u>SHOW CARD P</u> How effective do you think the work of this team could be in .... (NAME TOWN)?

	(53)
VERY EFFECTIVE	1
FAIRLY EFFECTIVE	2
NOT VERY EFFECTIVE	3
NOT AT ALL EFFECTIVE	4
(DON'T KNOW)	8

Q.45 Can I just check, do you have any children aged 9-18 in full time education?

	(54)	
YES	1	- ASK Q.46
NO	2	- SKIP TO Q.52

Q.46 What ages are they? WRITE IN AGES OF UP TO FOUR CHILDREN, STARTING WITH THE YOUNGEST

CHILD 1 ---> _____ (55-56)

CHILD 2 ---> _____ (57-58)

CHILD 3 ---> _____ (59-60)

CHILD 4 ---> _____ (61-62)

NOW ASK Q.47 FOR EACH CHILD:

Q.47 Are you aware of your children receiving any education at school (college) on the effects and risks of drugs?

	CHILD 1	CHILD 2	CHILD 3	CHILD 4	
	(63)	(64)	(65)	(66)	
YES	1	1	1	1	- ASK Q.48
NO	2	2	2	2	ASK
(DON'T KNOW)	8	8	8	8	Q.49

ASK ALL WITH CHILDREN RECEIVING EDUCATION AT Q.47.
REST (IE CHILDREN NOT RECEIVING EDUCATION) SKIP TO Q.49

Q.48 Do you approve of your children receiving such education at their school/college?

	CHILD 1	CHILD 2	CHILD 3	CHILD 4
	(67)	(68)	(69)	(70)
YES	1	1	1	1
NO	2	2	2	2
(DON'T KNOW)	8	8	8	8

ASK ALL WITH CHILDREN NOT RECEIVING EDUCATION AT Q.47

Q.49 Would you like your children to receive such education at their school (college)?

	CHILD 1	CHILD 2	CHILD 3	CHILD 4
	(71)	(72)	(73)	(74)
YES	1	1	1	1
NO	2	2	2	2
(DON'T KNOW)	8	8	8	8

COL 75=BLANK

DRUG USAGE AND DRUGS PREVENTION: THE VIEWS AND HABITS OF THE GENERAL PUBLIC

ASK ALL WITH CHILDREN AGED 9 TO 18 AT Q.45. REST, SKIP TO Q.52

Q.50 <u>SHOW CARD G</u> Are you aware of any of your children's friends or classmates taking any of these drugs or drugs being passed around? PROMPT FOR ALL DRUGS BEING TAKEN

	CHILD 1	CHILD 2	CHILD 3	CHILD 4
CANNABIS	1 (76)	1 (28)	1 (50)	1 (72)
HEROIN	1 (77)	1 (29)	1 (51)	1 (73)
AMPHETAMINES	1 (78)	1 (30)	1 (52)	1 (74)
LSD	1 (79)	1 (31)	1 (53)	1 (75)
COCAINE [START CARD 7]	1 (80)	1 (32)	1 (54)	1 (76)
ECSTASY	1 (11)	1 (33)	1 (55)	1 (77)
CRACK	1 (12)	1 (34)	1 (56)	1 (78)
MAGIC MUSHROOMS	1 (13)	1 (35)	1 (57)	1 (79)
METHADONE	1 (14)	1 (36)	1 (58)	1 (80)
DICONAL	1 (15)	1 (37)	1 (59)	1 (11) START CARD 8
AMYL NITRATE	1 (16)	1 (38)	1 (60)	1 (12)
TEMAZEPAM	1 (17)	1 (39)	1 (61)	1 (13)
TEMGESIC	1 (18)	1 (40)	1 (62)	1 (14)
SEMERON	1 (19)	1 (41)	1 (63)	1 (15)
BARBITURATES	1 (20)	1 (42)	1 (64)	1 (16)
DF118s	1 (21)	1 (43)	1 (65)	1 (17)
TRIAZELAM	1 (22)	1 (44)	1 (66)	1 (18)
UNPRESCRIBED SLEEPING PILLS	1 (23)	1 (45)	1 (67)	1 (19)
UNPRESCRIBED TRANQUILISERS	1 (24)	1 (46)	1 (68)	1 (20)
SNIFFING GLUE, GAS, AEROSOLS	1 (25)	1 (47)	1 (69)	1 (21)
OTHER (CODE AND WRITE IN)	1 (26)	1 (48)	1 (70)	1 (22)
	(27)	(49)	(71)	(23)
YES, BUT DON'T KNOW WHICH DRUGS	1	1	1	1
NONE/NONE OF ABOVE	7	7	7	7
(DON'T KNOW)	8	8	8	8

Q.51a <u>SHOW CARD S</u> So how likely do you think it is that your children <u>may</u> become involved in taking illegal drugs?

	(24)
VERY LIKELY	1
FAIRLY LIKELY	2
NOT VERY LIKELY	3
NOT AT ALL LIKELY	4
(DON'T KNOW)	8

Q.51b If you found or thought that your child/children was/were taking illegal drugs, who would you turn to for help and advice? PROMPT: 'Who else'? CODE ALL MENTIONS

GP	1	(25)
TEACHER/SCHOOL	1	(26)
SOCIAL WORKER/SOCIAL SERVICES	1	(27)
FRIEND/RELATIVE	1	(28)
POLICE	1	(29)
OTHER (CODE AND WRITE IN)	1	(30)
	1	(31)
(DON'T KNOW)	8	(32)

308

APPENDIX 2

ASK ALL
Q.52 Where can people go for advice and help about drugs in (QUOTE TOWN)? PROMPT 'Where else?'

FOR EACH SERVICE AWARE OF AT Q.52, ASK Q.53. IF NONE KNOWN, SKIP TO Q.55

Q.53 Do you know anyone who has ever approached ... (NAME PLACE) for help?

ASK FOR EACH MENTION AT Q.53. IF NONE, SKIP TO Q.55

Q.54 SHOW CARD T How helpful or otherwise did they find the advice or information?

Q.52 SERVICES AVAILABLE		Q.53 YES	Q.53 NO	Q.54 VERY HELPFUL	Q.54 FAIRLY HELPFUL	Q.54 NOT VERY HELPFUL	Q.54 NOT AT ALL HELPFUL	Q.54 (DON'T KNOW)
GP	1 (33)	1	2 (42)	1	2	3	4	8 (51)
CLINIC/HOSPITAL	1 (34)	1	2 (43)	1	2	3	4	8 (52)
DRUGS PREVENTION TEAM	1 (35)	1	2 (44)	1	2	3	4	8 (53)
NOTT'M: DRUGS DEPENDANT ANONYMOUS (DDA)	1 (36)	1	2 (45)	1	2	3	4	8 (54)
BRADFORD: THE BRIDGE PROJECT	2							
LONDON: BROCKLEY DRUGS LINE	3							
NOTT'M: THE HEALTH SHOP	1 (37)	1	2 (46)	1	2	3	4	8 (55)
BRADFORD: PROJECT 6	2							
LONDON: THE DUAL TEAM	3							
OTHER VOLUNTARY ADVICE AGENCY	1 (38)	1	2 (47)	1	2	3	4	8 (56)
CAB	1 (39)	1	2 (48)	1	2	3	4	8 (57)
SOCIAL SERVICES	1 (40)	1	2 (49)	1	2	3	4	8 (58)
OTHER (CODE AND WRITE IN)	1 (41)	1	2 (50)	1	2	3	4	8 (59)
NONE	2							
(DON'T KNOW)	8							

ASK ALL
Q.55 SHOW CARD U Which organisations do you think *should* be helping people who wish to stop taking drugs? PROMPT: Who else? IF MORE THAN ONE ASK: Who should be mostly responsible?

	ALL MENTIONS	MOST RESPONSIBLE (ONE ONLY)
		(66)
DRUG PREVENTION TEAM	1 (60)	1
GP	1 (61)	2
CLINIC/HOSPITAL	1 (62)	3
SOCIAL SERVICES	1 (63)	4
VOLUNTARY ADVICE AGENCY	1 (64)	5
OTHER (CODE AND WRITE IN)	1 (65)	6
		(67)
(DON'T KNOW)	8	8

H. DEMOGRAPHICS

Finally, it will be useful for us to look at people's replies in the light of the type of people they are and the things that they do.

ASK ALL

Q.56 SHOW CARD W Which of these places do you ever go to?
PROMPT: 'Which others?'

ASK Q.57 FOR ALL MENTIONS AT Q.56. IF NONE, SKIP TO Q.58

Q.57 SHOW CARD X How often, on average, do you go to ...?

	Q.56 EVER DO	Q.57 - FREQUENCEY							
		DAILY	2/3 TIMES A WEEK	SEVERAL TIMES /WEEK	ONCE WEEK	SEVERAL TIMES MONTH	ONCE A MONTH	LESS OFTEN	(DON'T KNOW)
FRIENDS'/RELATIVES' HOMES	1 (68)	1	2	3	4	5	6	7	8 (79
PUB	1 (69)	1	2	3	4	5	6	7	8 (80
CAFE/RESTAURANT	1 (70)	1	2	3	4	5	6	7	8 (11
DANCE/DISCO/PARTY/CLUB	1 (71)	1	2	3	4	5	6	7	8 (12
CHURCH/PLACE OF WORSHIP	1 (72)	1	2	3	4	5	6	7	8 (13
EVENING CLASS	1 (73)	1	2	3	4	5	6	7	8 (14
SPORTS CENTRE/PARTICIPATION IN SPORTS EVENT	1 (74)	1	2	3	4	5	6	7	8 (15
WATCHED SPORTS EVENT	1 (75)	1	2	3	4	5	6	7	8 (16
CINEMA/THEATRE	1 (76)	1	2	3	4	5	6	7	8 (17
BINGO	1 (77)	1	2	3	4	5	6	7	8 (18
OTHER (CODE AND WRITE IN)	1 (78)	1	2	3	4	5	6	7	8 (19
NONE OF THE ABOVE	2 - SKIP TO Q.58	///////	///////	///////	///////	///////	///////	///////	///////

START CARD 9

ASK ALL

Q.58 SHOW CARD X AGAIN How often do you have an alcoholic drink (NB. ANYWHERE)? CODE IN GRID BELOW

Q.59 SHOW CARD X AGAIN How often do you smoke cigarettes, cigars or a pipe? CODE IN GRID BELOW

	Q.58 ALCOHOL	Q.59. CIGARETTES, ETC
	(20)	(22)
DAILY	1	1
2/3 TIMES A WEEK	2	2
SEVERAL TIMES A WEEK	3	3
WEEK	3	3
ONCE A WEEK	4	4
SEVERAL TIMES A MONTH	5	5
ONCE A MONTH	6	6
LESS OFTEN	7	7
NEVER	8	8
(DON'T KNOW)	(21) 8	(23) 8

APPENDIX 2

Q.60 Which local papers, if any, do you read? PROMPT: Which others?

LONDON: LONDON EVENING STANDARD	1 (24)
NOTTINGHAM: NOTTINGHAM EVENING POST	1 (25)
BRADFORD: TELEGRAPH/ARGUS	1 (26)
GLASGOW: EVENING TIMES	1 (27)
GLASGOW HERALD	1 (28)
OTHER (CODE AND WRITE IN)	(29) (30) (31) (32) (33)
NONE	7
(DON'T KNOW)	8

Q.61 Which local radio stations, if any do you listen to? PROMPT: Which others?

LONDON: CAPITAL/CAPITAL GOLD	1 (34)
LBC/LBC NEWSTALK/LONDON TALKBACK	1 (35)
KISS FM	1 (36)
JAZZ FM	1 (37)
MELODY RADIO	1 (38)
SPECTRUM RADIO	1 (39)
BBC-GREATER LONDON RADIO	1 (40)
NOTTINGHAM: RADIO TRENT	1 (41)
TRENT FM/GEM AM	1 (42)
BBC-RADIO NOTTINGHAM	1 (43)
BRADFORD: RADIO AIRE/MAGIC 828	1 (44)
PENNINE FM/CLASSIC GOLD	1 (45)
BRADFORD CITY RADIO	1 (46)
GLASGOW: RADIO CLYDE/CLYDE FM	1 (47)
EASTEND RADIO	1 (48)
BBC-RADIO TWEED	1 (49)
OTHER (CODE AND WRITE IN)	(50) (51) (52) (53) (54)
NONE	7
(DON'T KNOW)	8

Q.62 SHOW CARD Y Which of these phrases best describes your current situation?

(55)
EMPLOYED 24+ HOURS/WEEK	1
EMPLOYED, 16-23 HOURS	2
EMPLOYED 1-15 HOURS/WEEK	3 } SKIP TO Q.64a)
SELF-EMPLOYED	4
GOVERNMENT TRAINEE	5
STUDENT	6
SEEKING WORK	7 } ASK Q.63
UNABLE TO WORK - DISABILITY	8
HOUSEWIFE/MOTHER	9
FULLY RETIRED	0 - SKIP TO Q.64a

Q.63 Can I just check have you (ever) had <u>permanent</u> full or part time work?

(56)
YES	1 - ASK Q.64a
NO	2 - SKIP TO CLASS.

DRUG USAGE AND DRUGS PREVENTION: THE VIEWS AND HABITS OF THE GENERAL PUBLIC

ASK ALL WHO ARE, OR HAVE EVER WORKED AT Q.62/63. REST, SKIP TO CLASSIFICATION

Q.64 a) What is your current/was your last job title? (WRITE IN)

   b) Please describe briefly to me the type of work you do/did most of the time in your job? (WRITE IN) IF NECESSARY, ASK: What materials or machinery do you use?

   c) What training or qualification is needed for the job? (WRITE IN)

   d) What does the firm/organisation you work/worked for actually make/do? (WRITE IN)

	SOC		
a.	(57)	(58)	(59)
b.			
	SEG		
c.	(60)	(61)	
d.			

Q.65 Are/were you directly responsible for organising other people's work?

	(62)
YES	1 – ASK Q.66
NO (DON'T KNOW)	2 ┐ SKIP 8 ┘ TO CLASSIFICATION

Q.66 How many people?

WRITE IN (USING LEADING ZERO(S)) -> [ ][ ][ ]   (63 - 65)

- NOW COLLECT CLASSIFICATION DETAILS
- THANK RESPONDENT AND CLOSE, HANDING LETTER WITH TELEPHONE NUMBERS IF ASKED

APPENDIX 2

J. CLASSIFICATION

```
NAME: MR/MRS/MISS/MS: ................
........................................
TELEPHONE NO: ........................
OCCUPATION OF HEAD OF HOUSEHOLD
........................................
OCCUPATION OF CWE (IF APPLICABLE)
........................................
SKILL/QUALIFICATION
........................................
RELATIONSHIP OF HOH/CWE TO RESPONDENT
........................................
```

SEX
                                 (66)
                     MALE   1
                 FEMALE   2

AGE (WRITE IN AND CODE)

   _____ (67) (68)   (69)
                       16-19   1
                       20-24   2
                       25-29   3
                       30-34   4
                       35-44   5
                       45-59   6
                         60+   7

ETHNIC IDENTITY (SHOW CARD Z)
Q. To which of the groups on this card do you consider you belong?
                            (70)
                      WHITE   1
          BLACK-CARIBBEAN   2
            BLACK-AFRICAN   3
              BLACK-OTHER   4
       (WRITE IN AND CODE 4)

                     INDIAN   5
                 PAKISTANI   6
             BANGLADESHI   7
                 CHINESE   8
  ANY OTHER ETHNIC GROUP
    (WRITE IN AND CODE 9)   9

OCCUPATION GROUP:
                 (71)
      AB   1
      C1   2
      C2   3
      DE   4

RELATIONSHIP TO HOH:
                 (72)
   RESPONDENT IS HOH   1

  HUSBAND/WIFE/PARTNER   2 ⎤
       SON/DAUGHTER   3 ⎬ CODE
     OTHER RELATIVE   4 ⎬ AGE
      NON RELATIVE   5 ⎦

AGE OF HOH
                 (73)
     16-19   1
     20-24   2
     25-29   3
     30-34   4
     45-59   5
     60+   6

HOUSEHOLD SIZE: (74) (75)

    WRITE IN NUMBER -->   ☐ ☐

PRIVACY DURING INTERVIEW?
                 (76)
        ADEQUATE   1
   FAIRLY ADEQUATE   2
  FAIRLY INADEQUATE   3
  TOTALLY INADEQUATE   4

                 (77)
   NO ONE ELSE IN ROOM   1
 ONE OTHER PERSON IN ROOM   2
TWO OR MORE PEOPLE IN ROOM   3

                (78) (79)

LENGTH: (OUO)   ☐ ☐

I certify that this is a true record of an interview for this survey with a person unknown to me and has been conducted within the code of conduct.

Signature .... NO. ☐☐☐☐ Date ....

This form is the property of Public Attitude Surveys Limited, Rye Park House, London Road, High Wycombe, Bucks HP11 1EF.

APPENDIX 3
SAMPLING METHODS AND SAMPLE STRUCTURE

As discussed in Chapter 1, the structure of the survey was such that respondents were drawn from two types of sample each of which covered the same four distinct geographic locations. The rationale for both types of sample, the selection methods used in obtaining the samples and the potential biases which may have been introduced in each are discussed below.

Main sample 'random' selection of respondents

The rationale behind our decision to use as our main sample a group of respondents representative of the general population is fairly transparent. We wished to establish the views and habits of 'ordinary' people in relation to drug usage. The methods used in obtaining such a representative sample are rather less self-evident. They were also subject to the usual constraints of time and finance.

As a function of these constraints we chose not to spread the 1,000 main sample interviews conducted in each of the four locations across the full extent of the area but instead to achieve a pseudo-random spread of interviews across each area by basing selection on a primary sampling unit represented by Enumeration Districts. Enumeration Districts are essentially arbitrary geographic units defined for the purposes of delivery and collection of census forms. In effect, an Enumeration District comprises the number of addresses which a census enumerator can cover in a single day. On average, this is taken to be around 150 addresses. The salient benefit of these arbitrary units in the present instance, is that they *are* fairly small and yet have attached to them a range of demographic information which can be readily accessed.

One aspect of such demographic information is ACORN coding. ACORN codes are based on housing type and by inference refer to the socioeconomic structure of the populations to which they attach. There are 11 broad ACORN categories - listed below - which are subdivided into a total of 39 housing types. These are attached to an address on the basis of its detailed postal code, the assumption being that all houses within a span of about 15 addresses are likely to be of a similar type.

A Agricultural areas
B Modern family housing, higher incomes
C Older housing of intermediate status
D Older terraced housing
E Council Estates - category I (e.g. recent/relatively affluent)
F Council Estates - category II (e.g. low rise/inter-war)
G Council Estates - category III (e.g. overspill estates/ overcrowded estates)
H Mixed inner metropolitan area
I High status non–family areas
J Affluent suburban housing
K Better off retirement areas

Although ACORN codes are by no means a perfect geo–demographic measure, they do provide a broad indication of the likely structure of very small local areas. They are also one of the few measures available for the whole of Great Britain, based on relatively recently compiled data. Doing this survey in 1992, when the most recent national Census results available were from 1981, precluded us choosing any other measure. The use of ACORN codes also, of course, provided some further comparability with the British Crime Survey which also uses this system of housing classification.

We used the ACORN information to stratify those Enumeration Districts which fell completely within each of the four districts we had chosen – the boundaries for which are given in Chapter 1. That is, we listed the EDs within each location in order of their attached *broad level* ACORN code. Within each ACORN code we listed each ED in order of its estimated adult population size. Both ACORN codes and population size being provided by CACI, a company specialising in such data.

The total number of adults in each location *as a whole* was then divided by the number of EDs to be sampled in total (100 in each district), this defined the sampling interval. Using a random start point, with a value less than the sampling interval, EDs were then picked from the list on the basis of the *cumulative* total of the adult population assigned to them by virtue of their position in the list. The outcome of the above selection methods being that the probability of selection for any given ED was a function both of its ACORN categorisation and of the adult population count. So, in effect, we maintained a broad socioeconomic spread of EDs whilst ensuring that the number of adults available for interview was maximised.

Within each ED we drew addresses from the Postcode Address File (PAF). PAF is a record, collated and updated by the Post Office, of all addresses to which mail is delivered. Each address is flagged as domestic or commercial and a tally is kept of the quantity of mail delivered. The section of PAF used for present purposes being the 'small domestic user' file. PAF was selected in preference to the Electoral Register because of the known under–representation of ethnic minorities and the poorer economic groups on this register which has resulted from the introduction of the community charge. In each area addresses were sampled at random, selecting every nth address within a given ED. A larger number of addresses was sampled at this stage than would in the event be required, to ensure that we were able to cover any shortfall resulting from refusals, non–contacts etc. Bradford and Lewisham proved to be the most problematic locations in this latter respect, as will be discussed later.

Since PAF is a list of addresses rather than individuals it was necessary to include one further step in the selection of respondents for the main sample. Upon making contact with someone at a selected address, interviewers selected a random respondent to target for the interview using the familiar Kish Grid technique. This involves listing all members (aged over 16 in this instance) of a household in decreasing order of age. From this list, the number of the person to be interviewed was selected by taking the last digit of the address serial number on the contact sheet as the label for selection.

In summary, the selection of respondents for the main sample followed a fixed hierarchical decision process. Whilst as far as possible the sampling methods used resulted in a random sample of individuals from a broad geo–demographic range, biases may have crept into the data. These potential biases are discussed in greater detail later.

Booster sample 'quota' selection of respondents

Whilst the rationale behind the selection of respondents for the main sample was to obtain a sample broadly representative of the population, the rationale behind our selection of booster sample respondents was to obtain responses from a very specific section of the population. In particular, we wanted the responses of those individuals felt to be at some significant risk of drug usage. To this end the booster sample was selected from young individuals living largely in the less affluent sections of the four locations being studied.

As with the main sample, the booster sample was chosen on the basis of ACORN values for EDs. However, the specification here was that the sample should be drawn *only* from areas in which the predominant housing type fell into categories D, G, H and I. These categories being respectively, 'older terraced housing' 'council estates' 'inner metropolitan areas' and 'non–family housing'. The rationale was to provide a sample drawn from areas of urban deprivation which *also* matched the BCS description of 'deprivation'. Following the BCS description of deprivation introduced the problem that the last category on this list is *not* in fact an adequate representation of relative deprivation. Fortunately, it was also in the event the least evident in our booster sample. Nevertheless for the purposes of those calculations in Chapter 4 for which an ascription of deprived living conditions was crucial, we removed from our analysis any respondents living in housing corresponding to this ACORN category. It should be noted also that due to the over–sampling we carried out in order to accommodate refusals and non–contacts, a small minority of respondents in the booster sample stem from housing classified by ACORN as C, E and F. This is not a severe problem, since in England at least such classifications are, broadly speaking, also a measure of *relative* deprivation.

The 250 interviews to be achieved for the booster sample in each location were divided equally amongst all EDs which fell into the above ACORN codes. Age and gender quotas were then set to ensure an even spread of these salient demographic categories across the areas sampled. Gender quotas were based on the population structure of each of the four locations – this data again being provided for us by CACI. Age quotas were less precisely structured, since the available data did not distinguish between those individuals in age bands under the 25 year old cut off mark. Instead interviewers were instructed to obtain roughly half of their interviews in each ED from under 20 year olds and the remainder from 21–25 year olds. In the event, although the vast majority of respondents in the booster sample were aged under 25, a not insubstantial minority were in the age bracket 25–29. The labelling of age groups in the report has been chosen both to reflect this fact and to enable closer comparisons to be drawn between the booster and main samples in respect of age.

Two further constraints were also set on the booster sample. Firstly, respondents were to be selected only from addresses *not* used for the main sample. Secondly, only one person could be interviewed at any given address. Although, as a quota sample, no call–backs were stipulated for interviewers, they were asked to make a later appointment to talk to young people where a suitable address had been found but the young person was not at home at the time they called.

In summary, the selection methods chosen for the booster sample resulted in a sample which were largely aged under 25 and largely from areas of relative deprivation. These specifications clearly preclude the sample from being representative of the general population. They do however allow the sample to be representative of individuals 'at risk' of drug usage.

Response rates

Main sample

The effective response rate stipulated by the CDPU for our main sample in the first instance was 70% in Lewisham and 75% in those areas outside of London. The calculation of such response rates is to an extent a matter of taste, since a variety of potential interview outcomes can be included or excluded from the calculation as desired (cf. Table A3.1). Here, effective (i.e. not gross) response rates have been calculated on the

Table A3.1
Response profile by location: main sample

Response outcome	Nottingham	Glasgow	Lewisham	Bradford
Successful	1006	972	1139	1004
Refusal	276	192	476	495
No contact (household)	43	55	205	127
No contact (individual)	30	32	45	50
On holiday/away	10	22	23	29
Empty/boarded up	36	67	114	117
Language difficulty	5	11	20	15
Other (e.g. business)	94	149	188	113

Call outcome following up to six repeat calls on a household or individual—absolute numbers

basis that business and empty properties are excluded but other outcomes are included in the sum total of responses. This represents a fairly stringent method of calculating response rate. On this basis, effective response rates of 71% were achieved in Glasgow and Nottingham. In Lewisham and Bradford a rather lower effective response rate of 57% was achieved. Table A3.1 provides a breakdown of interview responses for each main sample location. Note that although these are based on a stipulation that interviewers call at an address on six separate occasions, the average number of calls made prior to obtaining a successful interview was about three.

Booster sample

Since the booster sample was derived on the basis of a set quota which interviewers had to fulfil, it is not meaningful to discuss outcomes or response rates. However, it *is* worth looking at the range of contacts experienced by interviewers to determine whether the booster sample was subject to the same types of problem as the main sample. Interviewers had been instructed by PAS to complete a pro forma for every address at which they made contact but failed to obtain an interview. The data from these pro forma suggest that in the booster sample the most common reason for non-interview (96%) was that there was no–one in the chosen household within the stipulated age band. In contrast to the main sample, only 1% of recorded failures stemmed from a refusal by the potential respondent.

Table A3.2
Sample size and number of enumeration districts

values cited are absolute numbers

Sample	Total interviews completed	Number of EDs
Nottingham Main	1006	99
Bradford Main	1004	100
Lewisham Main	1139	99
Glasgow Main	972	100
Nottingham Booster	245	32
Bradford Booster	231	39
Lewisham Booster	233	60
Glasgow Booster	258	56

Refusal rates in the main sample

A detailed account of the causes for failure to obtain an interview can be obtained from the technical report provided by PAS (PAS 1992). It is apparent from table A3.1 however that refusals formed the single most prominent cause of failure. It is important to note here that refusal rates differed between the four locations, the distinction between locations accounting for the lower response rates achieved in Lewisham and Bradford. 14% of effective contacts in Glasgow were refusals, as were 19% of such contacts in Nottingham. In Lewisham and Bradford, however, these figures were 24% and 28% respectively.

The second point to be made here, is that the *pattern* of calls needed to obtain a successful interview also varied, albeit slightly, across demographic groups. Younger males of higher socio–economic status were, for example, the group requiring the greatest number of calls prior to a successful interview. On the other hand, the majority of *successful* interviews with individuals from a minority ethnic group were obtained within the first few calls. An analysis of response rates by ED further suggests that both refusal rates and non–contacts differed between local populations. None of these biases appeared to stem solely from an interviewer effect, although there were of course differences between the success rates of different interviewers.

> **In summary**, distinct biases in response rates both between and within the four locations emerged. A comparison of refusal rates with call outcome profiles for the different demographic groups suggests that whilst any age, gender and socio–economic biases within our main sample may be the consequence of failure to contact the relevant individuals, any ethnic bias is more likely to stem from higher refusal rates in these groups. Refusal rates did not appear to be a major problem in the booster sample.

Structure of the sample

Since the above discussion suggests that certain biases may have crept into our sample, it is worth discussing sample structure in some detail. It is also worth bearing in mind, however, that in this type of survey such biases are not unexpected. As noted earlier, there is in research no such thing as a truly random sample. The salient point here, is therefore to determine how substantive any potential biases are – particularly in the main sample – and to allow this discussion to inform future methodologies for drugs research.

Geographic structure of the sample

Final sample numbers of respondents and enumeration districts are given for each location in Table A3.2 above. Within sample type, it can be seen that the numbers of respondents are roughly equivalent for the four cities. The numbers of enumeration districts sampled within each city are also roughly similar for the main samples, but vary quite widely in the case of the booster samples. Note that the number of enumeration districts is of greatest importance in the case of the main samples, since these need to cover a wide enough range of areas to allow them to be representative of the general population in each city.

Table A3.3
Association between actual and obtained demographic composition of the main sample

values cited are Pearson's correlation coefficients for the association between actual and obtained proportions of individuals in the named demographic categories across the four locations

	Nottingham	Glasgow	Lewisham	Bradford
% Asians	0.32	0.39	0.20	0.90
% 16–25	0.05	0.09	0.10	0.05
% men 16–25	0.003	0.10	0.04	0.08
% women 16–25	0.06	0.22	0.10	0.05
% over 65	0.30	0.42	0.14	0.32

Although the large number of enumeration districts used for the main sample in each city has ensured that no extreme geographic bias exists within the sample drawn from each city, it is worth noting that the methods used for selecting *which* enumeration districts were sampled by PAS may have resulted in some clustering of the data by geographic area. As noted earlier, a criterion for the selection of enumeration districts was that they should be chosen in such a manner that respondents would represent a broad spread of socioeconomic groups. Enumeration districts were also, for more practical purposes, ordered by the number of adults living within them.

This two–tiered ordering of the EDs for the main sample resulted in certain EDs having in practice a greater probability of selection than other EDs, although technically the selection made was random. It should be noted that the selection of EDs *has* resulted in some geographic clustering, most noticeably in Glasgow and Bradford. Precisely what difference this has made to the responses obtained is difficult to judge in the absence of recent further information regarding the population structure of each area within the two cities (pending the availability of the 1991 Census data). However, it is useful to note this slight clustering by area in the event that our data should be used for later comparisons with other drugs data relevant to the cities used here.

Demographic structure of the sample

Table A3.3 provides a summary of the associations

between actual and obtained demographic values for the enumeration districts used in each city in which the survey was carried out. Correlations were obtained using each enumeration district as a unit of measurement. PAS provided the data used to draw the comparisons and it should be noted that this derives from post–community charge electoral roll data. It should be borne in mind, therefore, that values for the 'actual' composition of areas provide only base level data. Although no specific measures of the accuracy of the present electoral roll in our four areas are available, it is reasonable to assume that, as appears to be the general case, the electoral roll in these areas now under–represents the poorer and more mobile sections of society, for example the young, those individuals in lower socioeconomic groups, and those from ethnic minorities.

The electoral roll data provided by PAS was also fairly restricted. It provided information regarding only the extreme ends of the age spectrum and data on gender and ethnicity were limited to a small range of categories, with a gender split being available only for individuals aged 16 to 25 and the collective term 'Asian' being the only label for ethnicity. Although the correlations noted between actual and obtained populations should, therefore, be considered only as guidelines to our sample structure, they are nonetheless of substantial value in assessing sample structure. Tables A3.4 to A3.7 provide more detailed information regarding the age, gender, socioeconomic structure and ethnic composition of the obtained sample.

Table A3.4
Gender distribution of sample

values cited are percentages of individuals in each of the named demographic categories across the four locations

Sample	Valid N	% male	% female
Nottingham Main	1006	43	57
Bradford Main	1004	42	58
Lewisham Main	1139	45	55
Glasgow Main	972	41	59
Nottingham Booster	245	50	50
Bradford Booster	231	48	52
Lewisham Booster	233	49	51
Glasgow Booster	258	46	54

Age structure of the sample

The samples were selected in such a way that inherent statistical biases exist in age. The main samples were selected from members of the population aged over 16, since collecting data on drug usage from a younger age group entailed ethical and practical problems which were held to outweigh the likely value of such additional data. The booster samples were deliberately selected from young individuals. Having said which, although the skew towards a younger age group was to an extent intentional, there is also an *un*intentional skew towards mid–range and younger individuals in all four of our booster samples. All four main samples showed an unintentional skew in the *opposite* direction, tending towards older age groups, as a consequence of the data collection methods used.

This latter age trend is quite pronounced and is a common problem with data collected using market research methods, occurring because older individuals are more likely to be found at home when interviewers call. Although the Kish grid method does to an extent overcome this problem, it rarely succeeds in excluding all bias (cf. Raj 1972). In particular, it fails to exclude biases towards the elderly. As a function of the Kish Grid method, those living alone have a greater probability of being interviewed than individuals living in communal circumstances. Generally speaking those individuals living alone are more likely to be the elderly and young adults. Since young adults tend to be less readily contactable, the elderly therefore have a disproportionate chance of being selected for interview using this sampling method.

Table A3.5
Socioeconomic distribution of sample

values cited are percentages of individuals in each of the named demographic categories across the four locations

Sample	Valid N	%AB	%C1	%C2	%DE
Nottingham Main	1006	14	25	28	32
Bradford Main	1004	15	23	24	36
Lewisham Main	1139	10	35	23	31
Glasgow Main	972	8	18	21	52
Nottingham Booster	245	4	20	22	52
Bradford Booster	231	2	13	23	61
Lewisham Booster	233	9	30	28	32
Glasgow Booster	258	2	25	15	57

The extent of the age skew in our data was equivalent for all four main samples and has resulted in a greater overall weighting of the 50+ age groups in the main sample. Although there is a similar age skew in the general population, the data summarised in Table A3.4 suggest that our main samples are not in fact well matched to the *actual* age structure of the areas from which they were chosen, *as far as we could tell given the antiquity of the Census data available to us*. The alternative explanation, which may well be the dominant one, is that the areas we sampled had changed considerably in the age of their population since 1981. We will not be able to test whether it is our sampling, or the inadequacy of the area comparison information, which is at fault until we can test the data against the 1991 Census returns.

Taking the 1981 data as comparison (with all its faults), the closest association between actual and obtained percentages of individuals in the 16 to 25 age category is for example the correlation of 0.10 noted in Lewisham. The association between actual and obtained percentages of individuals in the over 65 category for which we also have data is necessarily rather better, with correlations of between 0.14 and 0.42. These remain rather low values, however and consequently we cannot feel confident that the age structure of the sample is representative of that of the general population from the relevant areas. Furthermore, the observed statistical biases in age mean that the booster and main samples show a polarity of age groups greater than that initially intended.

Gender structure of the sample

All four main samples were also skewed towards female respondents (Table A3.4), although in this case the bias was *not* consistent across samples. Note that the age of the comparison sample (the 1981 Census) also pertains to these comparisons. Glasgow's main sample shows a slightly greater preponderance of females than the other three main samples. The distribution of males and females in the booster samples is rather more balanced, probably as a consequence of the quota selection method used, although Glasgow's booster sample again stands out from the other three samples as having a slight skew towards females. Note again that to the extent the statistical gender bias in the main samples matches their age bias, they might be taken to reflect similar differences in the general population. At least in the case of the younger age groups (16–25) however, there is little support for the idea that the gender bias noted is representative of the populations from which the sample was drawn. The highest correlation noted between the actual and obtained percentage of men in this age group was 0.10 and for women in this age group it was 0.22. Both values pertaining to the Glasgow data. Clearly, in this age group at least, the main sample data is not an accurate reflection of the gender structure of the local population, *if the comparison data is accurate*.

Socioeconomic structure of the sample

All four main samples are also skewed towards lower status socioeconomic groups (Table A3.5). Again, the main Glasgow sample stands out as having a slightly greater preponderance of individuals in social groups D and E than the three other samples. In the booster samples, the skew towards individuals in lower status socioeconomic groups is pronounced. This is an expected consequence of the deliberate selection of individuals from within deprived urban areas. Bradford shows a slightly greater skew in this direction than the other three. The statistical bias in socioeconomic status noted in the main samples *cannot* be said to reflect a similar trend in the general population, where the distribution of socioeconomic status, almost by definition, follows a normal curve. Unfortunately we do not have any data which would allow us to judge whether or not the socioeconomic structure of our sample allows it to be representative of the populations from which it was drawn.

Table A3.6
Age distribution of sample

values cited are percentages of individuals in the named demographic categories across the four locations

Sample	Valid N	% 16–19	% 20–24	% 25–29	% 30–34	%35–44	%45–59	%60+
Nottingham Main	1006	5	8	11	11	17	21	25
Bradford Main	1004	4	8	11	12	20	19	25
Lewisham Main	1139	4	8	15	14	18	15	27
Glasgow Main	972	5	9	13	12	16	18	26
Nottingham Booster	245	38	56	6				
Bradford Booster	231	39	48	13				
Lewisham Booster	233	45	44	11				
Glasgow Booster	258	39	53	8				

APPENDIX 3 SAMPLING METHODS AND SAMPLE STRUCTURE

Table A3.7
Structure of the sample by ethnicity

values cited are percentages of individuals in the named demographic categories across the four locations

Sample	Valid N	%White	%Black Caribbean	%Black African	%Black other	%Asian	%Chinese	%other ethnic
Nottingham Main	1006	96	2	– (1)	– (4)	1	– (0)	– (4)
Bradford Main	1004	89	– (8)	– (2)	– (1)	9	– (2)	– (6)
Lewisham Main	1139	78	11	3	2	1	1	2
Glasgow Main	972	98	– (1)	– (1)	– (0)	1	– (1)	– (2)
Nottingham Booster	245	91	3	– (0)	3	2	– (0)	– (2)
Bradford Booster	231	66	– (2)	– (0)	– (0)	32	– (0)	– (2)
Lewisham Booster	233	66	15	6	8	3	– (0)	2
Glasgow Booster	258	96	– (0)	– (1)	– (1)	2	– (2)	– (1)

Ethnic structure of the sample

Table A3.7 provides a summary of the ethnic structure of the main and booster samples. Note that the distinction between the fairly negligible numbers of individuals from ethnic minorities within the main sample and the much larger ethnic minority group in the booster samples is to be expected, since ethnic minorities have a greater chance of being in the areas targeted for the booster samples. As noted earlier, we have *actual* population data from only one minority ethnic group. In the absence of more detailed information regarding local population structures from the chosen areas, we cannot make any conclusive statements regarding the match between the actual and obtained racial mix in our target areas.

Although we do have more detailed self–report data on ethnicity, we also cannot judge the extent to which our sample matches the population as a whole, since data from the most recent Census (the first to contain such information) is not yet available. Using the very limited data we do have, however, it appears that the match between actual and obtained percentages of minority ethnic groups is rather better in most cases than the match noted for other demographic variables (probably because this is more recently gathered data). In Bradford for example, the association between actual and obtained percentages of individuals of Asian origin reaches 0.90. For the other three samples, the values are rather lower, ranging between 0.20 in Lewisham and 0.39 in Glasgow. Note that any failure of the obtained values to match the actual values stems from an under–representation of Asians within the samples rather than an over–representation.

Table A3.8
Respondents' present employment status by sample and location

N = Percent of Valid   N = Valid N   (N) = Actual N

	Nott. Main	Glas. Main	Lew. Main	Brad. Main	Nott. Boost.	Glas. Boost	Lew. Boost.	Brad. Boost.
	1005	971	1139	1004	245	257	232	231
Retired	20	21	23	19	– (0)	– (0)	– (0)	– (0)
Works 24+ hours	38	30	40	36	22	24	29	23
Works 16–23 hours	5	4	4	6	2	2	3	3
Works 1–15 hours	5	3	2	5	4	1	2	2
Self–employed	4	2	5	4	2	– (0)	3	– (1)
Government trainee	– (3)	1	– (3)	1	– (0)	5	1	1
Student	5	3	5	2	24	25	33	28
Unemployed	5	9	6	6	25	27	22	20
Disabled	4	6	2	2	1	1	1	1
Housekeeper	13	20	13	17	18	15	6	21

Percentage of respondents in each employment category by sample and location

Employment structure of the sample

The distribution of long–term and present employment within our samples is necessarily a function of the demographic structure of the samples *per se*. Having said which, it also gave a fairly close match to expected patterns within the population as a whole. The majority of our main sample had experienced employment in their lives and indeed were employed at present, whilst the pattern for our booster sample was more equivocal. Since employment is very much dependent on other aspects of demography, we will not discuss employment structure in further detail here. For the interested reader Tables A3.8 to A3.10 provide further details.

Table A3.9
Whether respondent has ever worked by sample and location

N=Percent of Valid   Valid N as for previous table

	Nott. Main	Glas. Main	Lew. Main	Brad. Main	Nott. Boost.	Glas. Boost.	Lew. Boost.	Brad. Boost.
% Have been employed in a full time occupation	79	83	80	81	72	67	58	56

Percentage of respondents who have been employed in a full time job at some point in their lifetime, by sample and location

Table A3.10
Summary statistics for employment: variations between and within samples

	Main sample variation	Booster sample variation	Main versus Booster sample
Presently in work	.00000	NS	.00000
Ever worked	NS	.005	.00000

Are our samples representative of the towns?

Our conclusion from the discussion of age, gender, socioeconomic and ethnic biases of the sample above must be that although certain demographic biases *were* apparent we do not currently know whether our main samples were representative of the general population in those towns. The sampling methods we used have some (slight) known biases in producing a more aged and lower socio–economic group than the general population. Yet until we have more recently compiled comparison data to use (in particular, the 1991 Census), we cannot really say how well the sampling was carried out. There have been major economic changes for young people, in particular, in recent years, which are likely to have resulted in significant social changes in where young people are living. The proportions of young people living in certain enumeration districts in 1981 are likely to be very different to the numbers living there now (particularly since an enumeration district is so small that a difference of say 30 young people will be a major effect). We look forward to being able to specify more closely the nature of our sample when the 1991 Census data are available to us.

In summary, a comparison of the structure of the eight samples as outlined in the Tables suggests that *within* main and booster groups the samples are fairly well matched. Although the comparative data available to us are rather limited, there is some suggestion that the slight under–representation of at least one minority ethnic group may be due to higher refusal rates in this population group than in the dominant white population group. Finally, it seems that in two of the samples (Glasgow and Lewisham) the range of areas from which our sample derives is rather limited. Statistical biases within the booster sample are of less importance, since this sample makes no claims to be representative of the general population. However it should be noted that there is some statistical bias towards the younger age groups in the booster sample which results in a greater *polarity* of general population and booster sample age groups than was originally intended.

Note that although statistical biases in the data could have been counteracted by weighting the data, we have chosen not to take this approach. In the absence of detailed population data, the only appropriate weighting to apply would have been to counteract the selection effect introduced by the number of residents in a house. Controlling for this factor, which may account for a proportion of the age and gender bias in the sample, would unfortunately also have exaggerated the statistical bias in socioeconomic status already present in the sample. Consequently, the data presented in this report are raw data.

As a final comment regarding sample structure, it should be noted that although in the report the views of both main and booster samples are presented, a case could be made for rating the importance of one type of sample as greater than the other in the case of certain topics. For example, in a discussion of what the type, structure and approach of agencies should be, perhaps the views of those 'at risk' of being drug users are the more appropriate ones to consider. Conversely, in a discussion of legalisation the main population samples might present the most appropriate base point.